12th Simulation Workshop (SW25)

Exeter, United Kingdom
31 March – 2 April 2025

Editors:

Alison Harper
Martino Luis
Thomas Monks
Navonil Mustafee

ISBN: 979-8-3313-1507-8

Printed from e-media with permission by:

Curran Associates, Inc.
57 Morehouse Lane
Red Hook, NY 12571

Some format issues inherent in the e-media version may also appear in this print version.

The Operational Research Society
Seymour House
12 Edward Street
Birmingham
B1 2RX
United Kingdom

Phone: +44 (0)121 233 9300

www.theorsociety.com

Additional copies of this publication are available from:

Curran Associates, Inc.
57 Morehouse Lane
Red Hook, NY 12571 USA
Phone: 845-758-0400
Fax: 845-758-2633
Email: curran@proceedings.com
Web: www.proceedings.com

TABLE OF CONTENTS

PAPERS

PANEL ABSTRACT

POSTER ABSTRACTS

Welcome from the Co-Chairs of the Simulation Workshop 2025

On behalf of the organisation committee of The OR Society's 12th biennial Simulation Workshop 2025 (SW25), we welcome you to the international workshop on computer modelling and simulation at Exeter! At the very outset, we thank the authors whose contribution of scholarly work and in-person presence at SW25 made the conference possible; we thank the members of the SW25 International Technical Program Committee, which consists of over 35 academics and practitioners, for their time in peer-reviewing papers, posters and tutorials; we thank Decision Lab, Smith Institute and the University of Exeter (Business School and Engineering) for sponsoring SW25.

There are many firsts with SW25! This is the first time in SW's 25-year history that the workshop is organised *"in cooperation"* with both INFORMS I-SIM and ACM SIGSIM. This is the first time that SW will have three parallel sessions to accommodate close to 50 technical presentations. This is the first SW where the vast majority of the organisation committee are from the University of Exeter, namely, the *Centre of Simulation Analytics and Modelling (CSAM)* at the Business School, the *Exeter Digital Enterprise Systems (ExDES)* Centre in the Engineering Department and the Exeter Medical School. A couple of members have since moved to other universities, however, a committee made up of different Exeter faculties and schools (including several PhD students and early career researchers) brings to focus the relevance of our field to multiple disciplines and shows the breadth of simulation research here in the University of Exeter! This is the first time that SW has included hybrid sessions for the Africa Focus tracks (three tracks with a total of eight presentations) with complimentary registrations provided by The OR Society (as part of the *Journal of Simulation Africa Focus initiative*). Also, for the first time, ACM SIGSIM awarded the workshop two travel grants to encourage the attendance of delegates from underrepresented countries.

We have two keynote speakers, with both plenary talks on digital twins. Professor Mamadou K. Traoré from the University of Bordeaux (France) keynote address is on multi-scale and multi-perspective digital twins and experiences with an urban digital twin living lab being developed by the University of Bordeaux, Bordeaux Metropolis and partners. Our second keynote is Professor Christine Currie from the University of Southampton (UK). Her talk is on digital twin simulation for operational decision-making. The talk will cover some of the key concepts that enable digital twins to support real-time decision-making, including metamodeling, multi-fidelity simulation optimisation and simulation analytics.

The program includes a special session from the EU-funded project ARSINOE project (2nd April). The project will be introduced by Albert Chen and includes three papers on the use of simulation for climate resilience. Other program highlights include advance tutorials, lightening poster talks, a drinks reception and a gala dinner. The Editorial Board meeting of the Journal of Simulation and the meeting of the OR Society's Special Interest Group on Simulation (SIG Simulation) will also take place during the workshop.

As per SW tradition, the closing plenary will be a panel session. This year's panel is on the practice of M&S research and the challenges and opportunities for international collaboration. The panel will be chaired by a co-chair of SW25 (Nav Mustafee). Again, perhaps for the first time in SW's history, the panellists are mainly drawn from our international delegates attending the conference, from Algeria (Mehdi Souier), France (Mamadou Traoré), Germany (Oliver Rose), India (Varun Ramamohan and Jayendran Venkateswaran) and the US (John Fowler). UK will be represented by Masoud Fakhimi and Anastasia Anagnostou, who are the Chair and the Secretary of SIG simulation, and Tillal Eldabi.

We would like to thank the SW25 organisation committee for their hard work which has made the workshop possible. In particular, we would like to thank Alison Harper and Martino Luis whose diligent work enabled timely peer-review and the preparation of the proceedings. We thank Okechukwu Okorie and Ahmed Attar for leading the poster submissions. We thank Fatemeh Alidoost, Yanyan Tian, Esmaeil Khedmati Morasae, Marta Staff, Shuang Dai and Voicu Ion Sucala for contributing to social media, publicity, social media and local organisation of the workshop. We thank Stewart Robinson and Simon Taylor for accepting our invitation to serve on the awards committee, and Caitlin Griffin, Elli Michael, Sophie Rouse, Carol Mclaughlin, Sarah Davies and colleagues at OR Society for the numerous operational activities associated with organising an international workshop of this scale.

The workshop ends on 2nd April 2025; however, the work also continues. As in previous years, the Journal of Simulation will have a special issue dedicated to the workshop. Authors presenting at SW25 are invited to submit extended versions of their work for the special issue – the deadline is 15th September. Please visit the Journal of Simulation web pages for further information.

Nav Mustafee and Tom Monks

Co-Chairs, Simulation Workshop 2025

Proceedings of the Operational Research Society Simulation Workshop 2025 (SW25)
M. Luis, A. Harper, T. Monks, N. Mustafee, eds.
https://doi.org/10.36819/SW25.001

MULTI-SCALE AND MULTI-PERSPECTIVE DIGITAL TWIN: EXPERIENCE WITH AN URBAN LIVING LAB

Dr. Mamadou K. Traoré

University of Bordeaux
351 Cours de la Libération, 33405 Talence Cedex, France
Mamadou-kaba.traore@u-bordeaux.fr

ABSTRACT

As global urbanization accelerates, urban areas face significant pressure on service systems. This pressure is compounded by the need to address climate change and mitigate urban vulnerabilities to crises such as pandemics or geopolitical conflicts. To enhance urban resilience and sustainability, Urban Digital Twins (UDTs) have emerged as a promising tool. UDTs, virtual replicas of territories, can integrate complex data from multiple sectors and simulate scenarios to optimize urban and periurban planning decisions. However, their widespread adoption is hindered by some challenges. This paper explores these challenges in the context of a project developing UDT-based predictive and prescriptive services. It discusses the UDT framework being developed and highlights key elements to address the limitations of current model-based approaches, offering insights toward advancing UDTs for improved urban resilience and sustainability.

Keywords: Urban Digital Twin, Multi-scale, Multi-perspective, Urban resilience, Urban sustainability

1 INTRODUCTION

It is now well-established that nearly 70% of the global population is expected to reside in urban areas by 2050 (UN-Habitat, 2022). This urbanization surge exerts substantial pressure on urban service systems, marking a defining trend of the 21st century. This encompasses the expansion of public transport networks, energy grids, waste management circuits, and measures to combat the spread of disease and preserve air quality. This is particularly crucial considering the context of the escalating climate change challenge, which demands a drastic reduction of carbon footprint in major urban activities like mobility, logistics, and energy. Furthermore, recurring events, such as energy crises following geopolitical conflicts or disruptions to public transport networks after pandemics (Allam et al., 2022) highlight the vulnerability of urban territories as they face increasing challenges leading to cascading disasters, impacting economic strength but also jeopardizing the well-being of citizens. It becomes imperative for urban and periurban areas to proactively mitigate the associated risks, highlighting the urgent need for increased resilience and sustainability of cities and communities.

The Urban Digital Twin (UDT), used as a model-based approach for urban policy development and governance, is currently one of the most prominent research topics in the scientific debate of the urban planning discipline. A model-based approach is a methodology that leverages digital models and simulations to support the entire life-cycle of a system (Zeigler et al., 2018). Adopting model-based approaches to analyze and anticipate geopolitical, natural, and health crises is necessary for increased resilience. Also, model-based approaches enable the exploration of "what-if" scenarios, in search of the optimal conditions of low carbon emission for greater sustainability. However, existing model-based approaches to analyzing and evaluating urban development planning decisions to address long-standing urban issues are insufficient (Raimbault et al., 2020). While these tools sometimes provide accurate diagnoses, they often remain sectoral (while urban systems have several interwoven sectors), overlook multi-scale systemic interactions (a characteristic of urban systems), and above all do not fully exploit the wealth of data that has become available thanks to smart technologies. UDTs, which are virtual replica of smart cities and smart territories, have the potential to overcome these limitations.

The concept of smart cities (Eremia et al., 2017) has recently evolved into that of smart territories (Navio-Marco et al., 2020). A smart territory seeks to solve public problems through digital technology and in partnership with multiple stakeholders, with the aim of generating more sustainable economic development and a better quality of life. In line with this goal, the concept of UDT offers a promising solution to navigate system complexity, providing rapid analysis of multidisciplinary data and delivering easily understood outputs. The main scientific obstacles to UDT wide adoption are the following: (i) The lack of standards and interoperability between UDT technological fragments at multiple scales from building to city levels; It has recently been reported that "*the main challenge is an integration challenge of technology bricks*" (Kung et al., 2023); (ii) The low level of integration of social community dynamics into UDTs; it is well-acknowledged by scientists that current urban decision-making approaches are often uninformed by the collective behavior of communities across time and in different locations, traditional digital tools being limited in their ability to locate and capture the collective interactions of different communities (Mavrokapnidis et al., 2021). It is equally admitted that the combination of immersive solutions with appropriate social dynamics modeling methods has the potential to overcome such limitations, contributing to proactive and collaborative urban and periurban management (Bers and Chau, 2006); and (iii) The lack of reusable evidence-based UDT-driven urban development practices; some of the well-known UDT applications include the smart city platform of Helsinki (Ruohomäki et al., 2018) and the 3D city model of ETH Zurich (Schrotter and Hürzeler, 2020). However, the scarcity of reusable packages implementing tools as well as associated strategies showing how a UDT is deployed to improve community resilience and sustainability in various specific domains (such as Net-Zero or disaster planning and resilience), is a delaying factor to the wide adoption of UDTs despite their promises.

This paper highlights some key aspects of developing a multi-scale and multi-perspective UDT, in the context of an on-going project aiming at offering the public domain with UDT-based predictive and prescriptive services and immersive solutions. A multi-scale UDT is a UDT which models span from an individual level to building, district and city levels. A multi-perspective UDT is a UDT that integrates different phenomenon of the built, natural, and social environment, encompassing not only the mobility and transportation, but one or more other urban concerns, including energy use and production, water distribution, waste management, urban asset maintenance, etc. We do not give here a complete solution to the three challeges previously mentioned, we only present major elements that can provide additional insights to fully address them.

The remainder of the paper is organized as follows. Section 2 introduces the contextual project driving our research efforts. Section 3 presents the UDT framework being developed to achieve the goals of the project. Section 4 presents and discusses some key elements of this solution. Section 5 concludes the paper.

2 LIVING LAB APPROACH AND CHALLENGES

The Living Lab approach is a design and research methodology for developing and testing approaches to co-creation with project participants, which take place in real-life settings, involving further cooperation with public, non-profit and private stakeholders.

The University of Bordeaux (France) and its partners (including the Bordeaux Metropolis and various private operators) are engaged in the ACT (Augmented university for Campus and world Transition) project, the objectives of which are as follows: (i) to make the University of Bordeaux a Living Lab and an incubator to develop, test, validate and disseminate new ways of addressing the major challenges of energy, environmental and digital transitions; (ii) to mobilize the multidisciplinary expertise and diversity of its community, external stakeholders and citizens in general; and (iii) to pilot a complex process of transformation and transition towards an experimental campus, by continuously testing solutions for a new socially inclusive and ecologically sustainable paradigm. In this context, the project aims to develop and deploy a UDT (called ACT UDT), i.e., a set of data-rich digital models of the university campuses, capturing in real time the processes related to energy, mobility, and infrastructures and activities qualified as urban. These models, used for monitoring, diagnostic, prediction, control and optimization purposes, are intended to provide assistance to public decision-making, but also to mobilize and serve citizens and private stakeholders, on issues of sustainability, but also resilience (in the face of growing climatic, geopolitical and health uncertainties), in the general context of reducing the carbon footprint.

The ACT UDT is intended to be of great strategic importance, as an experimental laboratory for the metropolitan urban area in which the campuses of interest are located, which is facing new sustainable development challenges. Examples include the extension of public transport networks due to the pressure of ever-growing students batches, measures to promote green mobility on campus, measures to preserve air quality and their impact on public health, and infrastructures promoting the energy transition. Since there is no simple answer to such important issues (such as simply closing a traffic to cope with a peak in air pollution), current tools for analyzing and evaluating decision performance are insufficient. Indeed, although they sometimes provide fairly accurate diagnoses, these tools remain sectoral and ignore multi-scale systemic interactions (such as the link between urban transport, weather and population dynamics). Moreover, these models become obsolete as the system they represent evolves. Consequently, new analysis models require functionalities to integrate heterogeneous levels of explanation of the same system, as well as an automatic update capacity.

3 UDT FRAMEWORK

Figure 1 illustrates the UDT value chain. From a scientific perspective, smart territories operate on large, time-varying, and heterogeneous data, utilizing sensors and actuators connected via the Internet of Things (IOT). These data are stored in data lakes, mixing data sources managed at various computational levels (Farshad et al., 2022), from centralized cloud level (i.e., repositories publicly shared via Internet, such as open data) to decentralized fog level (i.e., repositories shared privately inside an organization, such as an institutional intranet) and distributed edge levels (i.e., data collected directly from user's personal devices, such as cell phones and individual sensors). This enables the design of data-rich digital models capturing real-time processes related to energy, mobility, water, etc., using Artificial Intelligence (AI) techniques, Operations Research (OR) techniques, or more possibly hybrid modelling approaches that combine various modelling formalisms and various quantitative methods (Brailsford et al., 2020). These models enable monitoring (i.e., continuous 2D/3D visualization of key indicators), prediction (i.e., simulation and forecasting of key indicators), diagnosis (i.e., evaluation of current key indicators, and detection of abnormalities), optimization (i.e., exploration of "what-if" scenarios and determination of the best option) and control services (i.e., feed-back commands to automatically manage the system of interest). Such a set up often requires High Performance Computation (HPC).

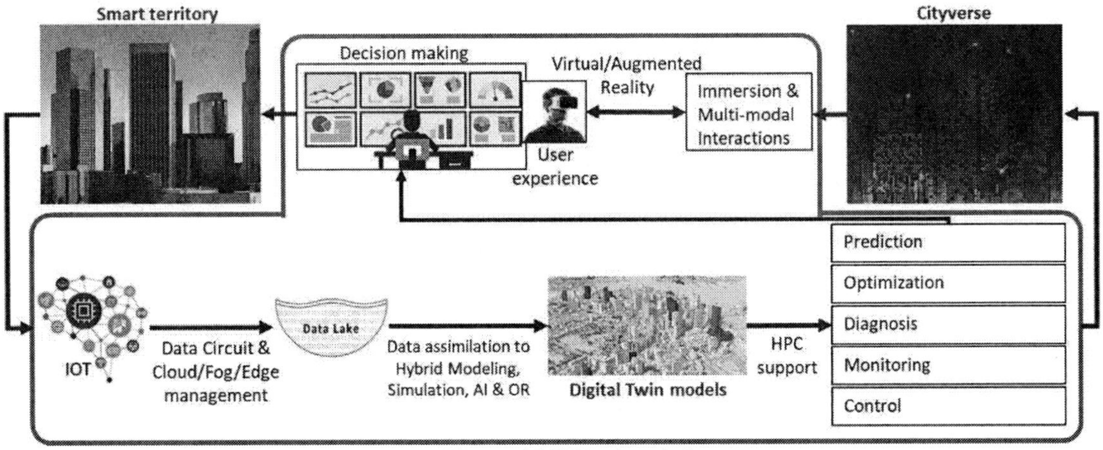

Figure 1 UDT value chain

A growing interest is in the use of a Metaverse, i.e., a 3D virtual space in which users are represented by avatars (Ning et al., 2023) and can experience immersive interactions through Virtual/Augmented Reality devices. This will enhance citizen engagement. We have termed this approach Cityverse (for

"Smart city" and "Metaverse"). It considers the multi-sectoral effects of events and policies, guiding decision-making and transition to resilient and sustainable areas. It not only focuses on technologies but on human aspects too, by (i) modeling smart territories' infrastructures, processes, and stakeholders; (ii) implementing them both in web, mobile and immersive environments; and (iii) demonstrating how they enable policy and decision-makers to tackle pressing challenges related to the transformation of urban modernization through technological innovation.

3.1 Conceptual UDT framework

Our conceptual UDT framework is displayed in Figure 2. It provides a general overview of the value chain of a UDT, which focuses on the following three interdependent stakeholders: (i) the Smart territory to be managed, (ii) the core of the UDT, and (iii) the Human.

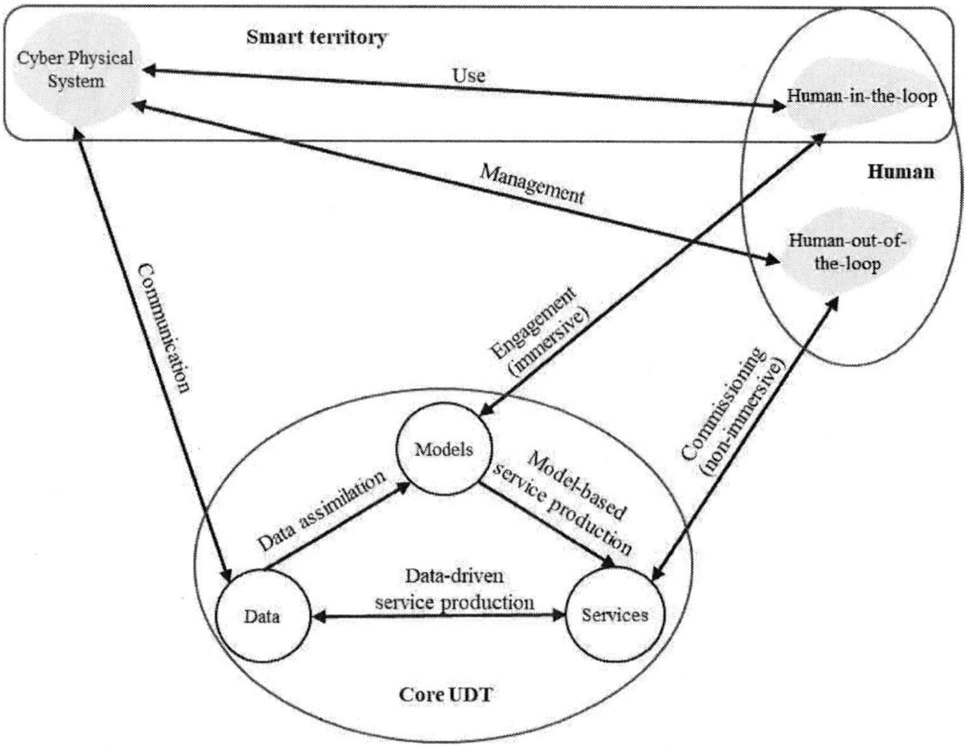

Figure 2 UDT conceptual framework

Human appears mainly in two different roles: either as a decision maker (such as urban planners and managers) who explores use cases and alternative scenarios and consequently develop urban strategies for the smart territory, or as users/consumers of urban and periurban services (such as citizens) who can be engaged in the UDT through their avatars. We refer to the latter as Human-in-the-loop and to the former as Human-out-of-the-loop.

The smart territory is the world of interest, which mixes physical and cyber entities (i.e., infrastructures, processes, sensors, actuators…) and involve human using them as well. That's why the Smart territory node overlaps with the Human node.

The core UDT is defined as a symbiotic association of data, models and services nodes (Traoré, 2023). The Data node relates to data from various sources, including real-time collection from sensors on ground, legacy data sources (e.g. smartphones, embedded cameras), open data and Internet APIs (e.g. Google map). The Models node is a set of abstractions of reality, each designed to answer specific questions related to mobility, energy, etc. (e.g. how will the city evolve under given circumstances? What is the impact of modifying some facilities?). The Services node includes predictive maintenance (i.e., continuous diagnostic of assets and anticipation of failures), safety control (i.e., risk assessment, crisis detection, disaster forecasting, and automated alerts), and optimization (e.g., remote control of urban facilities' operations, optimized setup of streets/buildings assets, etc.). The Data-Models link addresses how data can be assimilated for detecting changes in the real system and real-time updating models accordingly. The Models-Services link addresses how models are used/combined to provide the expected services. The Data-Services link focuses on services that can be provided directly from data (e.g. monitoring of historical data).

The Data node is the communication gate for the Physical-Digital interactions (i.e., between the cyber physical system of the smart territory and the UDT); the Models and Services nodes are gateways for Digital-Human interactions, respectively enabling UDT commissioning by urban decision-makers (i.e., Human-out-of-the-loop sollicitating UDT services through a web-based/standalone interface), and citizen engagement via avatars in the models (i.e., Human-in-the-loop participating to UDT models through a virtual/augmented reality device).

3.2 Formal UDT framework

To formally specify a UDT, we adopt a system-theoretic approach (Zeigler, 1976; Traoré and Muzy, 2006), where the structure of a model is defined as a black box with inputs and outputs interfacing the model with its environment (in the case of a UDT, the interface is realized with sensors and actuators).

As shown at the left-hand side of Figure 3, basic entities are the source system (i.e., the system under study), the context, the model, and the experimental frame (EF) – a last entity, the simulator, is not represented here. The system under study acts as a source of behavioral data. The context is the set of conditions under which the system is being observed. The model is a set of rules or mathematical equations that give an abstract representation of the system, which is used to replicate its behavior. Equally, the EF, which gives an abstract representation of the context, is a model component to be coupled with the system model to produce the data of interest under specified conditions. The simulator (not represented) is the automaton that is able to execute the instructions of the resulting coupled model.

In contrast, a UDT model (right-hand side of Figure 3) once built is regularly updated with data collected from the source system. Hence, an inference mechanism is needed to allow such a regular update of the model, in order to preserve its validity within the same EF. We then formally specify our UDT framework, which we call the DMSμ framework, the following way:

$$Sys_{UDT} = \langle D, M, S, \mu \rangle \text{ where:}$$

- D is the set of collected data
- $M \in \mathcal{M}$ is the UDT model of the smart territory
- $S \in \mathcal{M}$ is the UDT service, parameterized by M and D
- $\mu : \Omega_D \times \mathcal{M} \rightarrow \mathcal{M}$ is the data assimilation function,
  where Ω_D is the set of admissible data segments
  and $\mathcal{M}$ is the set of all possible models

We also formally capture each element of D as a data segment composed of a value and stamped by a date; hence, for each $\omega \in \Omega_D$, we have:

$$\omega : T_U \rightarrow D, \text{ where}$$

- T_U represents universal time, and $Dom(\omega) \subset TU$, and $Im(\omega) \subset D$
- The internal composition law $\oplus$ is defined on Ω_D such that if $dom(\omega 1) \cap dom(\omega 2) = \varnothing$, then $\omega 1 \oplus \omega 2 = \omega 1$ over $dom(\omega 1)$ and $\omega 2$ over $dom(\omega 2)$.

Finally, we formally specify all dynamic models (including services, which are specified as dynamic models as well) as the following 7-tuple:

$$M = \langle \Lambda, X, Y, \Phi, \Sigma, \Delta, \Delta^* \rangle, \text{ where:}$$

- Λ is the parameter set; it models all assumptions made on the context in which the DT model is used. $\forall \lambda \in \Lambda$, $dom(\lambda)$ is the set of all admissible values for λ. Λ is defined by variables which values can be updated by the sensors pairing the UDT with the smart territory.
- X is the input set; it models the influences received from the UDT environment ($\forall x \in X$, $dom(x)$ is the set of all admissible values for x).
- Y is the output set; it models the UDT influences on the environment ($\forall y \in Y$, $dom(y)$ is the set of all admissible values for y). X and Y are defined by variables which values can be updated by the sensors pairing the UDT with the smart territory.

- Φ is the phase set; it models the stable discrete/continuous steps of the UDT model. Each phase is defined by its properties, as well as the amount of time that expires before it changes to another phase (via an internal transition), and the activities performed during the phase.
- $\forall\ \varphi \in \Phi$, $\Phi_\varphi = \langle \pi_\varphi, \theta_\varphi, \tau_\varphi \rangle$ is the phase's definition, with:
  → π_φ is the phase properties, a predicate on Σ (noted $\pi_\varphi \in \wp(\Sigma) \cup \{NIL\}$) giving the semantics of π in Σ
  → θ_φ is the phase activity, a predicate on Σ modeling the computations performed during φ
  → τ_φ is the phase's time advance, a delay (i.e., expected lifetime of φ; $\tau_\varphi \in \mathbb{R}_+$) before the model changes from φ to another phase.
- Σ is the semantic domain; this is the set of variables, which the phases are mapped onto ($\forall\ \sigma \in \Sigma$, dom($\sigma$) is the set of all admissible values for σ). Σ is defined by variables which values can be updated by the sensors pairing the UDT with the smart territory.
- $\Delta = \{\Delta_{i?}^{j}, \Delta_{i}^{j!}, \Delta_{i?}^{j!}, i \in \Phi, j \in \Phi\}$ is the phase-to-phase transition set. $\Delta_{i?}^{j}$, $\Delta_{i}^{j!}$, and $\Delta_{i?}^{j!}$ are respectively external, internal, and confluent transitions, from phase to phase (an internal transition occurs when the delay of the current phase elapses; an external transition is triggered by the receipt of an input; a confluent transition occurs when both internal and external transition conditions occur simultaneously), with:
  → $\Delta_{i?}^{j} = \langle \omega_{i?,j}, \varepsilon_{i?,j}, \theta_{i?,j} \rangle$ where $\omega_{i?,j} \in \wp(X)$ is the condition of input receipt,
  $\varepsilon_{i?,j} \in \wp(\Sigma) \cup \{NIL\}$ is the condition of transition, and
  $\theta_{i?,j} \in \wp(\Sigma) \cup \{NIL\}$ is the action performed in transition.
  → $\Delta_{i}^{j!} = \langle \varepsilon_{i,j!}, \rho_{i,j!}, \theta_{i,j!} \rangle$ where $\varepsilon_{i,j!} \in \wp(\Sigma) \cup \{NIL\}$ is the condition of transition,
  $\rho_{i,j!} \in \wp(Y) \cup \{NIL\}$ is the output sending predicate, and
  $\theta_{i,j!} \in \wp(\Sigma) \cup \{NIL\}$ is the action performed in transition.
  → $\Delta_{i?}^{j!} = \langle \omega_{i?,j!}, \varepsilon_{i?,j!}, \rho_{i?,j!}, \theta_{i?,j!} \rangle$ where $\omega_{i?,j!} \in \wp(X)$ is the condition of input receipt,
  $\varepsilon_{i?,j!} \in \wp(\Sigma) \cup \{NIL\}$ is the condition of transition,
  $\rho_{i?,j!} \in \wp(Y) \cup \{NIL\}$ is the output predicate, and
  $\theta_{i?,j!} \in \wp(\Sigma) \cup \{NIL\}$ is the action done.
- $\Delta^* = \langle i^*, \theta^*, \tau^* \rangle$ is the initialization, giving the phase and action prior to the DT execution, where:
  → i^* is the initial phase
  → θ^* is the activity performed in initializing the model
  → τ^* is the time already elapsed in the initial phase.

This formal approach enables the identification of different levels of self-updating capabilities, i.e., the ability of the μ function to detect and respond to changes, either in values (low level of knowledge) or in structure (high level of knowledge) of specific elements within the formal specification of M (Diakité and Traoré, 2024), using statistical inference estimation techniques (such as Data fitting, Bayesian Inference, Kalman Filter, etc.). The identified self-updating capabilities include self-initializing (where Δ^* is updated) , self-coding (where Σ is updated) , self-aligning (where Φ is updated, self-interfacing (where X/Y are updated), self-regulating (where Δ is updated) and self-calibrating UDTs (where Λ is updated).

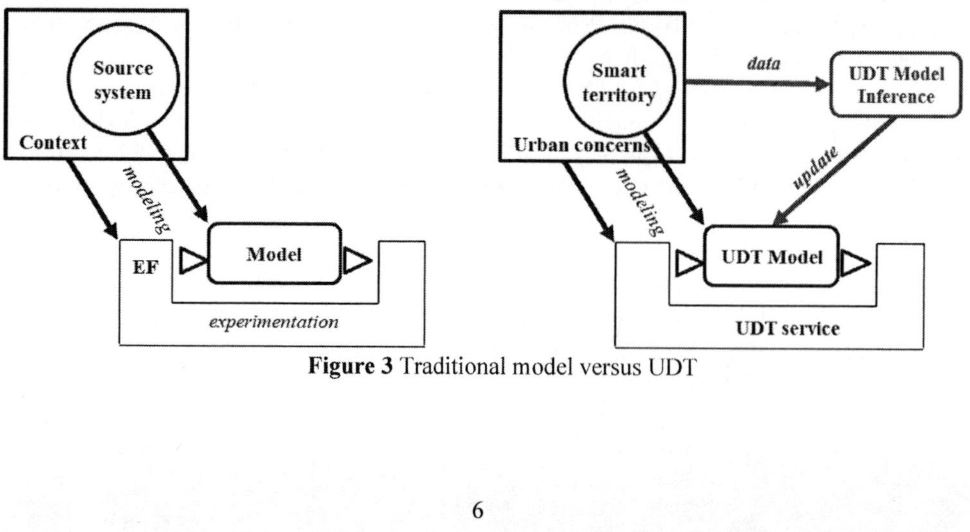

Figure 3 Traditional model versus UDT

4 MULTI-SCALE AND MULTI-PERSPECTIVE UDT

Our proposed architectural framework starts from the smart territory's physical ecosystem by incorporating the processes, events, or activities within urban spaces. It then subsequently incorporates the Data, Models and Services core components of the UDT, as well as the human elements of stakeholders involvement, as shown in figure 4.

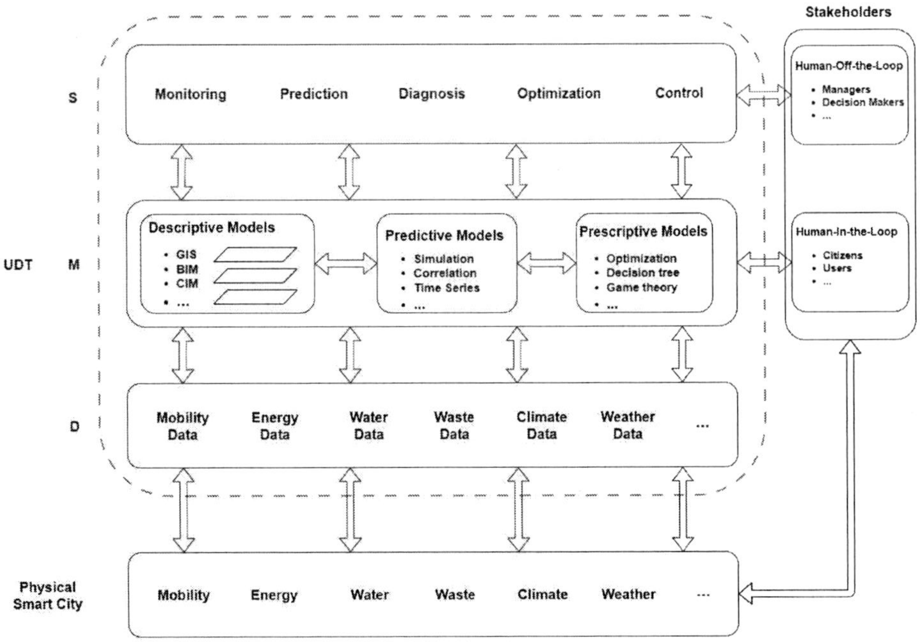

Figure 4 Multi-scale and multi-perspective UDT framework

This multi-scale and multi-perspective architecture originates by leveraging the smart city's physical ecosystem, encompassing the urban infrastructure as well as dynamic processes, events, and activities occurring within urban spaces. The urban environment is a complex system composed of various phenomena. A UDT should address the urban phenomenon for which it is intended. Several urban phenomena are interdependent and could evolve mutually. The complexity of effective UDT implementation lies in addressing the exact phenomena and their interplay.

Urban phenomena can provide information and data through the integration of sensors, IoT, embedded devices, and other smart systems. These systems facilitate capturing the data from the smart territory and enable communication between the physical and cyber part, by leveraging the smart territory's data to the data layer of the UDT architectural framework with the advantage of IoT systems. The data layer plays a pivotal role in data handling and management. This layer consists of data series and is responsible not only for handling the data originating from the physical city through embedded systems as well as incorporating data from diverse sources, such as databases, APIs, etc. Upon processing the data operations, the data layer transfers the refined data to the model layer, which constitutes the framework's heart.

In our architectural framework, the model layer could consist of a single model or series of interoperable models depending on the UDT application and functionalities targeted. A single UDT may contain several kinds of models of an urban ecosystem, such as descriptive, predictive, and/or prescriptive models. Descriptive models provide a detailed description of city phenomena as they exist or occurred in the past. GIS (Geographical Information System), BIM (Building Information Model), and CIM (City Information Model) are the existing mature descriptive data models of the urban ecosystem that provide information about the city phenomena and are important foundations for creating a 3D territory model/platform. However, the utilization of these models is not necessary for building a UDT. Predictive models make forecasts and predictions about future territory events and outcomes. Prescriptive models go beyond the prediction and offer the recommended actions or strategies to achieve the desired outcome in a territory such as diagnosis and optimization. Predictive models can couple with optimization techniques to provide prescriptive solutions for optimization and diagnosis. Furthermore, UDT models may or not be data-driven and, hence may or not require continuous data for updating, refining, and depicting the exact UDT state.

Next to the model layer is the service layer. UDT services could be data-driven or model-driven services. Indeed, the UDT can provide information about the current state of the physical system using only the input data, or leverage descriptive, predictive, perspective, AI, ML, etc. models for the provision of prediction, diagnosis, and optimization services.

The architectural framework recognizes the crucial role of humans, the way they are identified in the conceptual framework, i.e., Human-in-the-loop profiles (who are engaged with the UDT model), and Human-out-of-the-loop profiles (who commission the UDT services).

4.1 Mobility model

In the ACT UDT, a flow model was initially designed (as shown on top of Figure 5, right hand side), using the Anylogic Modeling and Simulation environment, and covering a pilot campus chosen among all the five university campuses (top of Figure 6, left hand side). This agent-based model captures public transport movements (tram and bus), but also vehicle and pedestrian movements in the area. It was then extended to cover the other campuses of the University (bottom of Figure 6, left hand side, with the pilot campus indicated in a red ellipse). The corresponding road network was fully modeled, and all buildings of interest in this parameter were identified in the CIM of the platform (bottom of Figure 6, right hand side).

The approach used to create this model is based on the basic principle that every individual in the smart territory has a function and an objective that define his/her mobility scheme, i.e., the schedule and movement pattern of that individual. In a university environment, the types of objectives that can be achieved by different people profiles is definite as it is dependent on the objectives that can be achieved using the university's infrastructure (which is also definite). Objectives considered include: To Learn, To Teach, To Research, To Manage, To Maintain, To Visit, etc. Modularity being a key element incorporated into the construction of this model, it is however extensible and other objectives can be incorporated in the future.

Having established that each individual must have one or more objectives to accomplish within the university's premises, these objectives must be accomplished using a resource in the university. Resources include: buildings, parkings, restaurants, laboratories, entrances, etc. Since the individual has to move to the location of these resources in order to use them, mobility is established and the resources can be called Destinations. Individual speed and time spent on each objective need to be mapped as well. All together, individuals constitute moving agents flowing from one resource agent to another one, hence producing the flow model shown at the top right hand side of Figure 6.

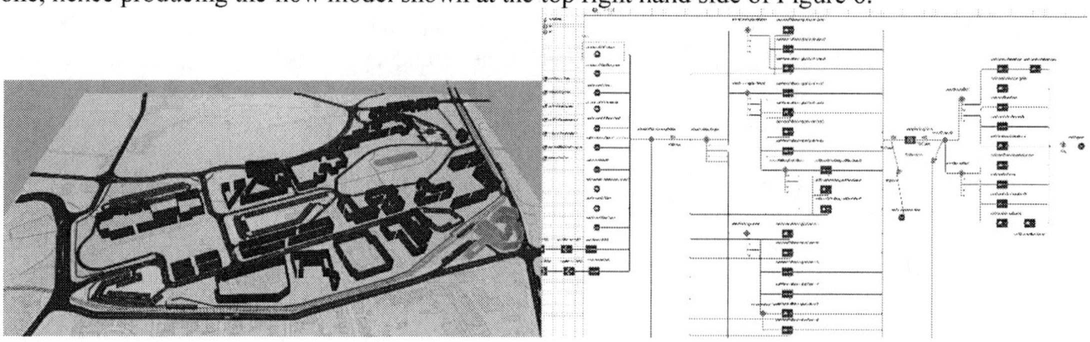

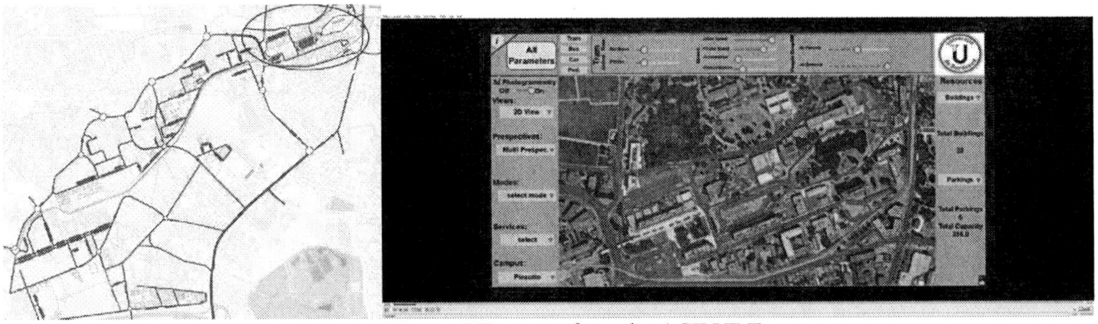

Figure 5 Excerpts from the ACT UDT

4.2 Integrative building model

The interplay of mobility and energy is captured through building modeling and the movement of pedestrians within buildings. By incorporating detailed pedestrian dynamics (as visualized in Figure 6), such as movement between floors, room selection, time spent in different areas, and the use of electrical equipment, each building model enables the estimation of energy consumption (i.e., energy used by the building regardless of occupants, such as security and networks consumption), based on both passive energy consumption and active enrgy consumption (i.e., energy consumed by building occupants when using elements like lighting, elevators, computers, etc.).

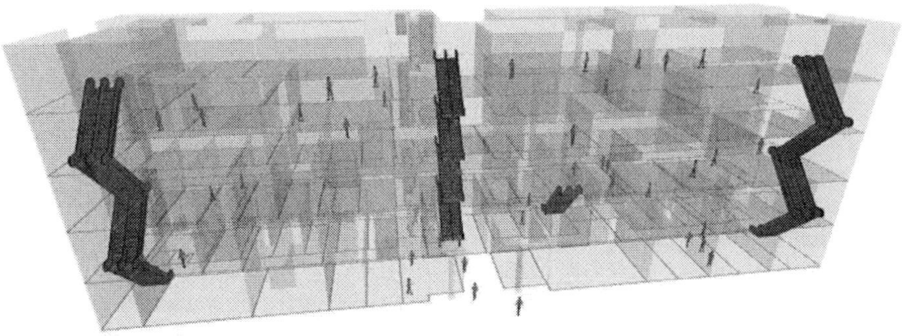

Figure 6 Agent movement in building defining the level of energy consumption

4.3 Data synchronization

As previously explained, models withion the UDT are permanently enriched with data collected from the university campuses. Such an enrichment requires a data synchronization infrastructure be deployed, connecting the UDT models with data sources.

The data synchronization considered in the ACT UDT is shown by Figure 7. From sensors deployed across the campuses, data are regularly sent into a central information system (fog computing approach). The current values of models structural elements are regularly updated with new values computed by a data fitting module (Label 3 in Figure 6), which consistently fetches data from the information system to that purpose (Label 2 in Figure 6). To this purpose, we have distinguished three types of synchronization data: (i) System data, associated with variables in the semantic domain (Σ) and indicating a phase change; (ii) Context data, related to parameters (Λ) and indicating a contextual change in the smart territory; and (iii) Interface data, related to the UDT's inputs and outputs (X/Y). A 3-month rolling time window is used to continuously select data from the information system and feed the fitting module.

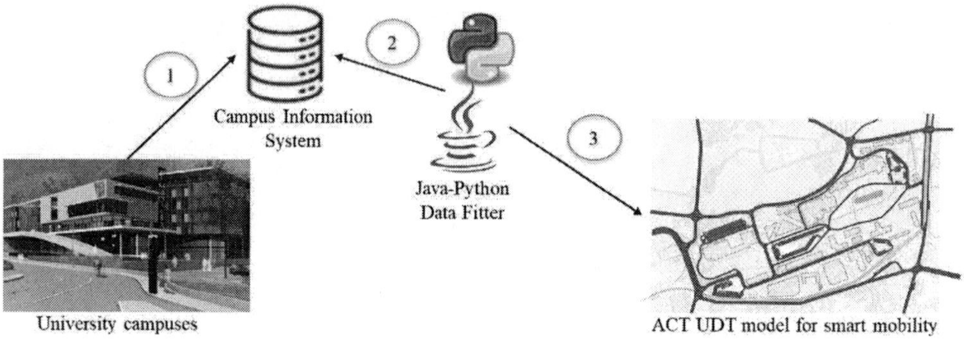

Figure 7 Data synchronization infrastructure

5 CONCLUSION

The ACT UDT is an on-going project, but some key advantages can already be derived based on current insights gained from our experience. Our holistic approach to UDT integrates heterogeneous levels of system explanation (i.e., multi-scale, multi-data, and multi-objective models, to serve mobility and energy management services) and possesses self-updating features (i.e., data assimilation to dynamically update models). This ensures a more comprehensive and adaptable representation of urban dynamics, addressing the shortcomings of current models and offering decision-makers an unprecedented level of insight into complex urban systems. Moreover, the integration of social behaviors and immersive capabilities enhance the engagement of citizens, decision-makers, and private operators. The Living Lab approach adopted allows for the definition of scalable strategies that address current knowledge gaps, build the evidence, and inform current and future policies to get as close as possible to Net-Zero urban emission, and thus combat the effects of climate change in cities.

Much remains to be achieved. This includes the synergistic coupling of detailed-level simulation models with strategic high-level urban planning models, as well as a very fine-grain understanding of the interplay of mobility and energy, among others. Finally, there is very little insight into two major concerns, that are acceptability and behavior change. It is of key importance to understand the technical and cognitive barriers to UDT adoption, and enablers to overcome it. It is equally important to identify the impact of the UDT adoption on individual behavior increase, as regards to urban activities (such as energy use and mobility strategies).

REFERENCES

Allam Z, Bibri S E and Sharpe S A (2022). The Rising Impacts of the COVID-19 Pandemic and the Russia–Ukraine War: Energy Transition, Climate Justice, Global Inequality, and Supply Chain Disruption. *Resources* 11(11): 99.

Bers M U and Chau C (2006). Fostering Civic Engagement by Building a Virtual City. *Journal of Computer-Mediated Communication* 11(3): 748-770.

Brailsford S C, Eldabi T, Kunc M, Mustafee N and Osorio A F (2019). Hybrid simulation modelling in operational research: A state-of-the-art review. *European Journal of Op. Res.* 278(3): 721-737.

Diakité M and Traoré M K (2024). Formalizing a Framework of Inference Capabilities for Digital Twin Engineering. *Simulation*: 00375497241228281.

Eremia M, Toma L and Sanduleac M (2017). The Smart City Concept in the 21st Century. *Procedia Engineering* 181: 12-19.

Farshad F, Farahani B and Marinšek A (2022). The Convergence and Interplay of Edge, Fog, and Cloud in the AI-driven Internet of Things (IoT). *Information Systems* 107: 101840.

Kung A, Myers J and Lahrin T (2023). Report of TWG CitiVerse: Standardisation Landscape for CitiVerse. *Zenodo*, https://doi.org/10.5281/zenodo.10262579.

Mavrokapnidis D, Mohammadi N and Taylor J (2021). Community Dynamics in Smart City Digital Twins: A Computer Vision-based Approach for Monitoring and Forecasting Collective Urban Hazard Exposure. *Proceedings of the Annual Hawaii International Conference on System Sciences*.

Navío-Marco J, Rodrigo-Moya B and Gerli P (2020). The Rising Importance of the Smart Territory Concept: Definition and Implications. *Land Use Policy* 99: 105003.

Ning H, Wang H, Lin Y, Wang W, Dhelim S, Farha F, Ding J and Daneshmand M (2023). A Survey on the Metaverse: The State-of-the-Art, Technologies, Applications, and Challenges. *IEEE Internet of Things Journal.*

Raimbault J, Denis E and Pumain D (2020). Empowering Urban Governance through Urban Science: Multi-scale Dynamics of Urban Systems Worldwide. *Sustainability* 12(15): 5954.

Ruohomäki T, Airaksinen E, Huuska P, Kesäniemi O, Martikka M and Suomisto J (2018). Smart City Platform Enabling Digital Twin. *IEEE Internl Conference on Intelligent Systems*, pp. 155-161).

Schrotter G and Hürzeler C (2020). The Digital Twin of the City of Zurich for Urban Planning. *Journal of Photogrammetry, Remote Sensing and Geoinformation Science* 88(1): 99-112.

Traoré M K (2023). High-Level Architecture for Interoperable Digital Twins. *Preprint posted on October 11. DOI: 10.20944/preprints202310.0659.v1.*

Traoré M K and Muzy A (2006). Capturing the Dual Relationship Between Simulation Models and their Context. *Simulation Modelling Practice and Theory* 14(2): 126-142.

UN-Habitat (2022). World Cities Report Envisaging the Future of Cities. *ISBN 978-92-1-132894-3.*

Zeigler B P (1976) Theory of Modeling and Simulation. *Wiley-Interscience*, New York (NY, USA).

Zeigler B, Mittal S and Traoré M K (2018). MBSE with/out Simulation: State of the Art and Way Forward. *Systems* 6(40).

AUTHOR BIOGRAPHY

Mamadou Kaba TRAORE is full Professor at the University of Bordeaux, France, where he is the Deputy Director of the Integration from Material to System lab (IMS), specifically in charge of international research. He got his MSc in Mathematical Engineering in 1989 and his PhD in Computer Science in 1992, both at the Blaise Pascal University (France). His research interests are in Hybrid Modeling & Simulation, with focus on combining DEVS (Discrete Event Systems Specification), and Digital Twins Engineering, with application to cyber physical systems in Industry, smart cities, and connected healthcare. He received the international DEVS award in 2011 (Boston, MA, USA). Overall, he has published and co-published 10 books, a dozen book chapters, and 150+ papers in international peer reviewed journals and conferences. He has various editorial responsibilities, including being associate editor of Journal of Simulation, and Simulation: Transactions of THE SCS, and the organization of several SCS conferences, as General Chair or Program Chair. He has been rewarded by the Outstanding DEVS Symposium Program Chair award in 2010 (Orlando, FL, USA). He is member of the review committee of a dozens of international journals, and has given several invited talks in prestigious institutions, such as the National Institute for Standards and Technologies (NIST, Gaithersburg, MD, USA). He also served in the World Bank-led scientific advisory board that created the African University of Science and Technology (AUST) in Nigeria, which he became the President from 2012 to 2014. He coordinated several EU-funded research and industrial projects, and developed collaboration with many universities in Africa, Europe, Canada and USA.

Proceedings of the Operational Research Society Simulation Workshop 2025 (SW25)
M. Luis, A. Harper, T. Monks and N. Mustafee, eds.
https://doi.org/10.36819/SW25.002

DIGITAL TWIN SIMULATION FOR OPERATIONAL DECISION MAKING

Christine S.M. Currie

University of Southampton
Highfield, Southampton
SO17 1BJ
christine.currie@soton.ac.uk

ABSTRACT

Simulation models are commonly used as part of system design or management projects and are only now beginning to appear as part of operational control systems. When used to solve problems in real time, simulation models are typically described as being, or forming part of, a digital twin. Using a simulation model as part of a digital twin enables testing of different strategies or system settings based on the current state of the system. For this to be effective, results need to be returned quickly, requiring efficient algorithms for simulation optimization and effective use of data analytics and machine learning methods to complement the simulation modelling. Beginning with a discussion of digital twin models in the context of process simulation, we cover some of the key concepts that enable digital twins to support real-time decision-making, including metamodelling, multi-fidelity simulation optimization and simulation analytics.

Keywords:

Digital twin, simulation analytics, simulation optimization, metamodelling.

1 INTRODUCTION

Simulation has traditionally been used as a testbed for trying out different ways of running a system as a means of improving system design and management. Data are collected from the real system and used to fit input distributions and set up the logical processes within the simulation model in advance of running experiments. Experimental results are then presented to management in order to make decisions on the appropriate action to take. This works very successfully and the application of simulation modelling to solve such problems is relatively mature, as described in well-known textbooks on the topic (e.g., Banks et al. (2010), Law (2024), Robinson (2014)).

The use of a simulation model as part of a digital twin allows testing of different options conditional on the current state of the system. New methodology that draws on simulation optimization, metamodelling and simulation analytics can speed this up, enabling results to be returned in close to real time. Advances in the methodology used to support digital twins have benefits across the simulation area, leading to faster convergence of simulation optimization, improvements in generalisable simulation models and methods for improving the understanding of dynamic behaviour. We consider in turn digital twins and how data from the real system can be integrated into the simulation model, simulation optimization with a focus on returning results in close to real time and simulation analytics. There are still challenges to using simulation in a real-time environment and we discuss these alongside suggestions for future work in the conclusion.

2 DIGITAL TWINS

The term *digital twin* was originally used to describe a digital model of a physical object, but the concept has expanded to include process models of systems. The type of digital twin that we describe here incorporates a computer simulation model that is used to mimic a real-world process and a two-way interaction between the simulation and the real system. It is worth emphasizing the fact that information is flowing in both directions between the simulation and the real system.

An alternative term for this variety of digital twins is *symbiotic simulation*, introduced by Fujimoto et al. (2020) at the Dagstuhl seminar on Grand Challenges for Modelling and Simulation in 2002. A more detailed discussion and definition is given in Aydt et al. (2008) and, while the term symbiotic simulation seems to have been superceded by the more general digital twin, much of the discussion in Aydt et al. (2008) applies to the methodologies we describe here. Table 1 in Aydt et al. (2008) provides a list of different classes of symbiotic system and we focus on the first three classes: control of a physical system, support of an external decision maker and forecasting of a physical system.

While not specifically mentioned in Xu et al. (2016), the vision the authors give for the use of simulation optimization as part of *operational control* of a system matches the definitions given above for a digital twin. They place the use of simulation optimization as part of the concept of Industry 4.0, the so-called fourth industrial revolution, in which the widespread use of the internet enables much easier communications between machines, humans and complex control systems. We come back to their discussion of the use of simulation optimization in the next section but their justification for the use of simulation is worth noting. Unlike other approaches, using a simulation enables the complexity of the system and its dynamics to be accounted for when testing different options.

Building a simulation model for a digital twin project has different challenges compared with building a simulation model to be used outside of an operational control system. In recent work, Onggo and Currie (2024) describe how standard simulation methodology should be adapted when building a digital twin simulation, focusing on conceptual modelling, input modelling, model development, validation and output analysis. The work suggests that there are additional challenges that need to be overcome when feeding a model with data in real time and that there are still many open research questions. Here, we focus on methodology that is particularly important when using digital twins for operational decision making, typically via implementing simulation optimization methods.

3 INTEGRATING DATA INTO A DIGITAL TWIN

There are different levels of data integration in a digital twin simulation.

1. Real-time data are used to set the initial conditions of the simulation model to ensure that it runs from the current system state.
2. Real-time data are used for parameterization of the simulation model, updating input parameters as system behaviour changes.
3. Real-time data are used to set the logic of the simulation model, accounting for changes in the processes followed in the real system.

Many digital twins will only reach the first of this levels, but even this can be more difficult than it sounds. The simulation model needs to be designed in a way that it can be started from a given state, a so called *hot start*. Getting the right level of detail in translating the current system state into a simulation state is a balancing act. Too much detail will make the process unwieldy within the physical system, requiring a considerable amount of data to be transferred, and increase the complexity of the simulation model. Conversely, when too little detail is used to describe the system state, the results can be too generic, losing the benefits of knowing the current state. There is some discussion of this trade off in Cao (2024), which describes the use of a digital twin and multi-fidelity simulation optimization methods to find the appropriate repair strategy to follow when a number of machines are broken on a production line. The line is complex, with a large number of machines, each having a buffer before it in the form of a conveyor. As a result, deciding on the best description of the system and simulation states requires some careful thought. Goodwin et al. (2024) use the concept of a *context* in their work rather than a system state, but the principle still holds of determining the best strategy based on characteristics of the state of the physical system.

As discussed in Onggo and Currie (2024), it is hard to find research describing methods to support real-time parameterization of simulation models, despite its importance. As data availability and quality increases, the principle of using empirical distribution functions drawn from real system data has become more prevalent. As part of a digital twin, this removes the need to update parametric statistical input distributions. Methods for detecting when the simulation model no longer matches the real system can be used to trigger a recalibration. While this can be done by comparing static statistics such as means and variances, recent work examining the representation of the system trajectory in the frequency domain, obtained by a Fourier transform, allows the dynamic behaviour to be compared (Morgan and Barton 2022).

Automated updating of model logic, the third level of data integration, typically makes use of process mining techniques, as described by van der Aalst (2016). Heib et al. (2023) describes how process mining can be used to determine and update processes in a hospital emergency department using timestamp data on hospital records. Similar work has been carried out by Lugaresi and Matta (2021) but for a manufacturing line. Process mining can produce overly complex models, or spaghetti models to use the technical term, and automating a process to guard against spaghettification is an interesting area of research. Following process mining, the results then need to be incorporated into the simulation model, effectively automating the programming of the logical processes within the simulation.

The design of algorithms for reparameterisation and automatic updating of model logic have applications outside of digital twins. They can help to speed up model design but, perhaps more importantly, they can be useful tools in the design of generalisable models. Boyle et al. (2022) define generalisable models to be models that can represent multiple similar systems (e.g., hospital emergency departments) and through customisation using real system data can be used to investigate site-specific problems. By embedding algorithms that update both inputs and logic from real system data, a simulation model becomes generalisable to other systems with similar data structures. This is a valuable by-product of digital twin methods.

4 SIMULATION OPTIMIZATION

Simulation optimization, also known as optimization via simulation, aims to solve an optimization problem where the objective function value is returned by a stochastic simulation model. Typically the simulation model is treated as a black box, and each objective function value it returns is subject to random noise. Simulation optimization can be a very powerful method for optimizing complex stochastic systems, and by its nature, those systems do not need to comply to any restrictions on their structure or assumptions.

Hong and Nelson (2009) provide a useful classification for simulation optimization problems, dividing them into three main groups:

1. **Ranking and Selection:** the feasible region for x has a small number of solutions; sufficiently small that it is possible to test all of them in the simulation model and select the solution with the best result.
2. **Continuous Simulation Optimization:** the vector of decision variables, x, is continuous.
3. **Discrete Simulation Optimization:** the vector of decision variables, x, is discrete and integer ordered.

Fu (2015) provides an introduction to these problems and methods for solving them, while Currie and Monks (2021), presented at the Simulation Workshop in 2021, gives a tutorial on solving ranking and selection problems.

Somewhat orthogonal to the list are multi-objective optimization problems, which can fit into any of the above three categories but require different treatment to allow for trade-offs between the multiple objectives. Hunter et al. (2019) provides a review of multi-objective simulation optimization. A more recent category, partly resulting from increased computing power, are large-scale simulation optimization problems. A recent review (Fan et al. 2024), defines these as problems with a large number of feasible solutions, higher-dimensional decision variables, or both, where the number of decision variables is in the thousands or hundreds of thousands. In such cases parallelization is essential, but the authors argue that the approach is different from that used for moderate-sized problems. The optimization problems encountered in a digital twin project are unlikely to be of a very high dimensionality given the restricted time available to solve them, although some of the methods developed for parallelisation may be beneficial for improving computation times.

When used as part of a decision support tool for operational decision making, simulation optimization needs to be computationally efficient. Cloud computing and parallel processing can increase the processing speed significantly but often not sufficiently for real-time decision-making. In this case, building a metamodel or surrogate model of the simulation can be used either to reduce the number of simulation replications that are needed, e.g., via multi-fidelity simulation optimization, introduced by Xu et al. (2016); or to avoid the need to run the simulation model at all during the operational phase.

Barton (2023) describes the use of metamodels as a "computationally inexpensive proxy" for the more complex simulation model that they are being used to approximate. The tutorial suggests several different forms for metamodels including linear regression, Gaussian process models and artificial neural networks. Building a metamodel of the simulation effectively enables work to be done in advance of an operational decision, reducing the computational work needed in real-time. There are links between metamodelling and simulation analytics, as discussed in Section 5.

Among the first methods for multi-fidelity simulation optimization was MO^2TOS, Multi-fidelity Optimisation with Ordinal Transformation & Optimal Sampling, introduced by Xu et al. (2016). In MO^2TOS, the low-fidelity model is used to group possible solutions according to their likely performance. OCBA (Chen et al. 2000) is then used to choose which group of solutions to sample from and the high-fidelity model is run for a randomly chosen solution from that group. Cao et al. (2021) adapts MO^2TOS by altering the sizes of the groups dependent on the ranking of the solutions within them: this increases the chances of sampling solutions found to perform well on the low-fidelity model. An alternative approach, SAMPLE, combines results from machine learning models with simulation outputs generated as part of the real-time process in order to return a recommended solution (Goodwin et al. 2024).

5 SIMULATION ANALYTICS

Although first introduced in a grand challenges paper at Winter Simulaion Conference in 2013 (Taylor et al. 2013), the more commonly cited definition of simulation analytics comes from a paper looking at tactical problems for simulation from 2016 (Nelson 2016). In essence, simulation analytics describes the application of data analytics methods to the analysis of transactional data generated within simulation models. The aim is to provide more insights into how the system will behave under different conditions, which could be the current state of the system, the simulation time and/or the choice of input parameters. The narrative suggests a change of mindset in terms of how simulation models are viewed, seeing them as generators of dynamic sample paths used to feed data analytics and machine learning methods. In the context of using digital twin simulation models for operational decision-making, the idea of building models to describe the conditional behaviour of outputs has some value in reducing the need to run the full simulation model in real-time, instead relying on data analytics models that describe the likely future behaviour of the system. The ideas have some similarities to the multi-fidelity simulation optimization methods described previously.

As discussed by Nelson (2016), there are some specific challenges associated with simulation analytics that are not observed in typical data analytics problems. Some of these are demonstrated in Lin et al. (2019), who use a k nearest neighours algorithm to estimate *virtual statistics* for simulation models. Virtual statistics are estimators of performance measures conditional on an event occurring, e.g., the expected waiting time of an individual entering the system at a time τ_0. They discuss how the mix of correlated and independent data in the inputs to the prediction models mean that some care needs to be taken when carrying out cross-validation and estimating variance. Laidler et al. (2020) also use a k nearest neigbour algorithm to provide real-time predictions of stochastic performance of a simulation model, specifically binary classification of outcomes. Their model uses the state of the system as its input rather than simply the simulation time. An important component of a k nearest neighbour model is a way of measuring the distance between neighbours in order to identify which are close and they use *metric learning* to evaluate similarity in system states. Jiang et al. (2019) carry out a similar problem in financial risk management that uses logistic regression to predict a binary outcome using a simulation.

As seen above, much of the early work in this area has focused on classification, while Cao et al. (2021) and Cao (2024) instead solve a regression problem. An artificial neural network (ANN) is used to describe the simulation output based on the current state of the simulation model. Instead of using similar data points to dictate the output as is done in Laidler et al. (2020) and Jiang et al. (2019), the dimensionality of the state space is reduced, decreasing the computational time needed to fit the ANN. Although fitting of the ANN takes place offline, there are practical limits on how long the fitting process should take and potential issues with overfitting if the dimensionality is too high.

6 CONCLUSIONS AND FUTURE DIRECTIONS

The conclusion of Onggo and Currie (2024) provides a relatively comprehensive list of research directions for digital twin simulation modelling methodology and these tend to reflect the key differences between a static simulation project and one in which there are two-way interactions between the simulation model and the real system. Several of the identified research directions concern the automation of model building, fitting and validation to enable the evolution of the digital twin simulation as the system changes, but there is also a clear need to ensure that simulation optimization can return sensible responses in a short period of time.

Much of the previous work on simulation optimization as part of a digital twin has focused on ranking and selection problems, ignoring continuous and discrete simulation optimization, where there is some ordering in the decision variables. Osorio and Bierlaire (2014) considers a problem of this type in which the optimization is used for a fixed time signal control problem in a traffic management setting. They combine a simulation model, an analytical queueing model and a quadratic metamodel, within a trust region algorithm and relatively tight computational constraints. Placing such optimization methods within the context of a digital twin could increase their use in real time decision-making, expanding to all three groups of simulation optimization problems described in Section 4.

As data analytics and machine learning methods develop, so too will the field of simulation analytics. The evolution of tools such as SimPy (SimPy 2020) and Simmer (Ucar et al. 2019) and their increased use makes it easier for developers to build adaptive algorithms that work with transactional data from discrete event simulation models, generating the dynamic sample paths needed for simulation analytics procedures. While transactional data can be obtained from commercial packages, there is some computational and programming cost in transferring the data from the simulation package to the program carrying out the analysis.

There is a great deal of promise in the use of simulation within digital twins to solve operational control problems. Nonetheless, there are still open research challenges in the area that will help to improve the efficiency and effectiveness of digital twin simulations.

References

Aydt, H., S. J. Turner, W. Cai, and M. Y. H. Low. 2008. "Symbiotic Simulation Systems: An Extended Definition Motivated by Symbiosis in Biology". In *Proceedings of the 22nd Workshop on Principles of Advanced and Distributed Simulation (PADS)*, 109–116. July 3rd-6th, Rome, Italy: IEEE.

Banks, J., J. Carson, B. Nelson, and D. Nicol. 2010. *Discrete-Event System Simulation 5th Edition*. Pearson Education.

Barton, R. R. 2023. "Metamodelling: power, pitfalls, and model-free interpretation". In *Proceedings of the Operational Research Society Simulation Workshop*, edited by C. S. Currie and L. Rhodes-Leader. ORS.

Boyle, L. M., A. H. Marshall, and M. Mackay. 2022. "A framework for developing generalisable discrete event simulation models of hospital emergency departments". *European Journal of Operational Research* 302 (1): 337–347.

Cao, Y. 2024. *The Use of Multi-Fidelity Simulation Optimisation for Real-Time Management of a Manufacturing Line*. Ph. D. thesis, University of Southampton.

Cao, Y., C. Currie, B. S. Onggo, and M. Higgins. 2021. "Simulation Optimization for a Digital Twin Using a Multi-Fidelity Framework". In *2021 Winter Simulation Conference (WSC)*, 1–12.

Chen, C. H., J. Lin, E. Yücesan, and S. E. Chick. 2000. "Simulation budget allocation for further enhancing the efficiency of ordinal optimization". *Discrete Event Dynamic Systems: Theory and Applications* 10 (3): 251–270.

Currie, C. S., and T. Monks. 2021. "Tutorial on optimisation via simulation: how to choose the best set up for a system". In *Proceedings of the Operational Research Society Simulation Workshop*, edited by M. Fakhimi, D. Robertson, and T. Boness. ORS.

Fan, W., L. J. Hong, G. Jiang, and J. Luo. 2024. "Review of Large-Scale Simulation Optimization". *arXiv*. https://arxiv.org/abs/2403.15669.

Fu, M. C. 2015. *Handbook of Simulation Optimization*. 1st ed. New York, USA: Springer.

Fujimoto, R., W. H. Lunceford Jr, E. Page, and A. M. Uhrmacher. 2020. "Grand Challenges for Modelling and Simulation". In *Dagstuhl Seminar Report 350*, 1–75. Leibniz-Zentrum für Informatik: Schloss Dagstuhl.

Goodwin, T., J. Xu, N. Celik, and C.-H. Chen. 2024. "Real-Time Digital Twin-Based Optimization with Predictive Simulation Learning". *Journal of Simulation* 18:47–64.

Heib, A. R., C. S. Currie, B. S. Onggo, H. K. Smith, and J. Kerr. 2023. "A Generalized Symbiotic Simulation Model of an Emergency Department for Real-Time Operational Decision-Making". In *2023 Winter Simulation Conference (WSC)*, 1042—-1053.

Hong, L. J., and B. L. Nelson. 2009. "A brief introduction to optimization via simulation". In *Proceedings of the 2009 Winter Simulation Conference*, edited by M. D. Rossetti, R. R. Hill, B. Johansson, A. Dunkin, and R. G. Ingalls, 75–85. Piscataway, New Jersey: IEEE.

Hunter, S. R., E. A. Applegate, V. Arora, B. Chong, K. Cooper, O. Rincón-Guevara, and C. Vivas-Valencia. 2019. "An Introduction to Multiobjective Simulation Optimization". *ACM Trans. Model. Comput. Simul.* 29 (1).

Jiang, G., H. L.J., and B. Nelson. 2019. "Online Risk Monitoring Using Offline Simulation". *INFORMS Journal on Computing* 32:356–375.

Laidler, G., L. Morgan, B. Nelson, and N. Pavlidis. 2020. "Metric Learning for Simulation Analytics". In *2020 Winter Simulation Conference (WSC)*, 349–360.

Law, A. M. 2024. *Simulation Modeling & Analysis*. 6th ed. New York: McGraw-Hill, Inc.

Lin, Y., B. Nelson, and L. Pei. 2019. "Virtual Statistics in Simulation via k Nearest Neighbors". *INFORMS Journal on Computing* 31:576–592.

Lugaresi, G., and A. Matta. 2021. "Automated Manufacturing System Discovery and Digital Twin Generation". *Journal of Manufacturing Systems* 59:51–66.

Morgan, L. E., and R. R. Barton. 2022. "Fourier Trajectory Analysis for System Discrimination". *European Journal of Operational Research* 296 (1): 203–217.

Nelson, B. L. 2016. "Some tactical problems in digital simulation' for the next 10 years". *Journal of Simulation* 10:2–11.

Onggo, B. S., and C. S. Currie. 2024. "Extending simulation modeling methodology for digital twin applications". In *2024 Winter Simulation Conference*. In press.

Osorio, C., and M. Bierlaire. 2014. "A Simulation-Based Optimization Framework for Urban Transportation Problems". *Operations Research* 21:1333—1345.

Robinson, S. 2014. *Simulation: The Practice of Model Development and Use*. 2nd ed. Hoboken, NJ, USA: John Wiley & Sons, Inc.

SimPy 2020. "SimPy". https://simpy.readthedocs.io.

Taylor, S. J. E., S. E. Chick, C. M. Macal, S. Brailsford, P. L'Ecuyer, and B. L. Nelson. 2013. "Modeling and simulation grand challenges: An OR/MS perspective". In *2013 Winter Simulations Conference (WSC)*, 1269–1282.

Ucar, I., B. Smeets, and A. Azcorra. 2019. "simmer: Discrete-Event Simulation for R". *Journal of Statistical Software* 90 (2): 1–30.

van der Aalst, W. 2016. *Process Mining: Data Science in Action*. 2 ed. Berlin: Springer.

Xu, J., E. Huang, L. Hsieh, L. H. Lee, Q. S. Jia, and C. H. Chen. 2016. "Simulation optimization in the era of Industrial 4.0 and the Industrial Internet". *Journal of Simulation* 10 (4): 310–320.

Xu, J., S. Zhang, E. Huang, C. H. Chen, L. H. Lee, and N. Celik. 2016. "MO2TOS: Multi-fidelity optimization with ordinal transformation and optimal sampling". *Asia-Pacific Journal of Operational Research* 33 (3): 1–26.

AUTHOR BIOGRAPHIES

CHRISTINE CURRIE is a Professor of Operational Research in Mathematical Sciences at the University of Southampton and a member of the Centre for Operational Research, Management Sciences and Information Systems (CORMSIS). She was Editor-in-Chief for the Journal of Simulation from 2015 - 2024. Her research interests include simulation optimization, digital twins, applications of simulation, and optimal pricing for transportation. Her email address is christine.currie@soton.ac.uk and her homepage is https://www.southampton.ac.uk/people/5wzzxf/professor-christine-currie.

Proceedings of the Operational Research Society Simulation Workshop 2025 (SW25)
M. Luis, A. Harper, T. Monks and N. Mustafee, eds.
https://doi.org/10.36819/SW25.003

A TUTORIAL ON KRIGING-BASED STOCHASTIC SIMULATION OPTIMIZATION

Sasan Amini

Hasselt University
Agoralaan, 3590 Diepenbeek, Belgium
sasan.amini@uhasselt.be

Inneke Van Nieuwenhuyse

Hasselt University
Agoralaan, 3590 Diepenbeek, Belgium
inneke.vannieuwenhuyse@uhasselt.be

ABSTRACT

This tutorial focuses on kriging-based simulation optimization, emphasizing the importance of data efficiency in optimization problems involving expensive simulation models. It discusses how kriging models contribute to developing algorithms that minimize the number of required simulations, particularly in the presence of noisy evaluations. The tutorial compares the performance of kriging-based algorithms against traditional polynomial-based optimization methods using an illustrative example. Additionally, it discusses key extensions of kriging-based algorithms, including multi-objective and constrained optimization, providing insights into their application in complex, real-world settings.

Keywords: Simulation Optimization, Metamodel, Kriging, Data Efficient Global Optimization

1 INTRODUCTION

Simulation optimization refers to the process of finding optimal decisions in complex systems where analytical methods are not applicable, and outcomes can only be evaluated through (often stochastic) simulation models (Fu et al. 2015, Amaran et al. 2016, Nelson et al. 2021). Classical stochastic simulation optimization methods, such as the genetic algorithms used in Ding et al. (2005) and Pasandideh and Niaki (2006), are computationally intensive as they require the evaluation of a large number of potential solutions. Additionally, multiple replications at each solution are needed to improve the accuracy of performance estimates, further increasing the computational burden. In this tutorial, our focus is on problems for which the simulation model is expensive to evaluate, such that the analyst can only afford a limited number of evaluations. Furthermore, the simulation model is a black box where only input/output (I/O) information is available (we have no access to, for instance, derivative information that might guide the optimization).

To solve such challenging problems, researchers have increasingly relied on metamodels (Barton 2023b) as a way to approximate the behavior of simulation models. Metamodels, also known as surrogate models (Gramacy 2020, Hong and Zhang 2021), act as simplified representations of the underlying simulation model, enabling efficient exploration of the solution space without the need for excessive computational resources. The use of metamodels has been widely studied in the literature, particularly for problems where simulation costs are high, making them invaluable in industrial settings, see, e.g., Stavropoulos et al. (2023), Pietrusewicz (2019), and Hassannayebi et al. (2019). For a systematic literature review of metamodeling-based simulation optimization, we refer to Hong and Zhang (2021) and do Amaral et al. (2022).

Traditional metamodeling approaches often rely on linear or quadratic regression models (Kleijnen 2018). While these models are computationally inexpensive and simple to implement, they often lack the flexibility required to accurately capture the complex, nonlinear I/O relationships that are common in many real-world systems (Barton 2023a). This reduces their effectiveness, particularly when the simulation response surface exhibits significant curvature or interactions among variables that cannot be captured by simple polynomial terms. In more recent years, *kriging* metamodels have emerged as a powerful and versatile tool in simulation optimization (do Amaral et al. 2024). Kriging models, also known as Gaussian process regression (GPR) models in the field of machine learning and statistics (Shahriari et al. 2015, Gramacy 2020), do not only provide accurate predictions of system performance but also estimate the uncertainty related to these predictions, referred to as the kriging variance. This is a key advantage, which has proven useful in *data-efficient global optimization*, particularly since the seminal work of Jones et al. (1998). In engineering and machine learning, this area of research is often referred to as Bayesian optimization (Garnett 2023).

2 Kriging models

This method, originally developed for approximating I/O relationships in mining geology and named after South African engineer Danie G. Krige (Krige 1951), has later been extended to computer simulation experiments by Sacks et al. (1989). Kriging is a spatial interpolation method used to obtain predictions at unsampled locations based on observed data (Kleijnen 2009). It assumes that the distance between sample points reflects a spatial correlation that can be used to explain variation in the surface, i.e., the underlying unknown function (Chilès and Desassis 2018).

2.1 Kriging for deterministic responses

Kriging models can approximate the input-output (I/O) relationships of deterministic simulation models, i.e. models for which it can be assumed that the evaluation of the system for a given set of input values results in an *exact* (i.e., non-noisy) observation of the corresponding output. In other words, if you were to repeat the evaluation at the same point, you would always get the same result; there is no randomness or variability on the output for a given input.

Ordinary kriging models the output of the unknown response function at a given input vector $\mathbf{x}$ as the sum of a constant term, and an observation from a zero-mean covariance-stationary Gaussian random field:

$$f(\mathbf{x}) = \beta_0 + M(\mathbf{x}) \tag{1}$$

where β_0 then represents the overall surface mean. In its most general form, this first term may also consist of a combination of prespecified functions at $\mathbf{x}$; this is referred to as *universal kriging* (Palar and Shimoyama 2017). Yet, the modeling assumption with the constant term is most common in the literature.

Given the modeling assumption, the resulting kriging model yields a probability distribution over functions, such that for any finite set of input points, the corresponding function values are jointly Gaussian distributed (Gramacy 2020, Rasmussen and Williams 2006). The Gaussian random field is uniquely characterized by its mean $m(.)$, which is assumed to be zero, and its covariance function $k(.)$, also referred to as *kernel*. This covariance function models the pairwise covariances between function values (outputs) at different input locations. The basic assumption here is that the output values of two distinct points in the solution space are spatially correlated (Rasmussen and Williams 2006); i.e., the correlation between the output values depends on the distance between the input locations. Data points that are close to each other (in the solution space) are more likely to have similar output values, so they tend to have high correlation. As the spatial separation between data points increases, the correlation decreases. Many different types of covariance functions can be used; the choice of covariance function directly impacts the model's ability to capture the underlying function (Archetti and Candelieri 2019, Garnett 2023, Wang et al. 2023). Commonly used kernel functions in the literature are the squared exponential (Equation 2), Matérn$_{3/2}$ (Equation 3), and Matérn$_{5/2}$ (Equation 4).

In Equations (2), (3), and (4), d is the Euclidean distance between the two input locations, σ^2 is the variance of the kriging model, and l is a hyperparameter known as the *length-scale*, which controls how quickly the correlation between the output of two input points decreases as they move further away in the solution space. Figure (1) illustrates the concept of spatial correlation using the squared exponential kernel. The x-axis represents the distance from a reference point x_0, while the y-axis shows the resulting covariance between the output values (for ease of interpretation, the plot assumes $\sigma^2 = 1$; hence, the covariance values are equal to the correlation values). Clearly, a smaller length-scale implies that the correlation drops more rapidly with distance, which may cause function values to change quickly over short distances. By contrast, a larger length-scale implies that the correlation decreases more gradually, implying smoother variations in the data (Rasmussen and Williams 2006).

$$k_{SE}(.,.) = \sigma^2 exp(-\frac{d^2}{2l^2}) \tag{2}$$

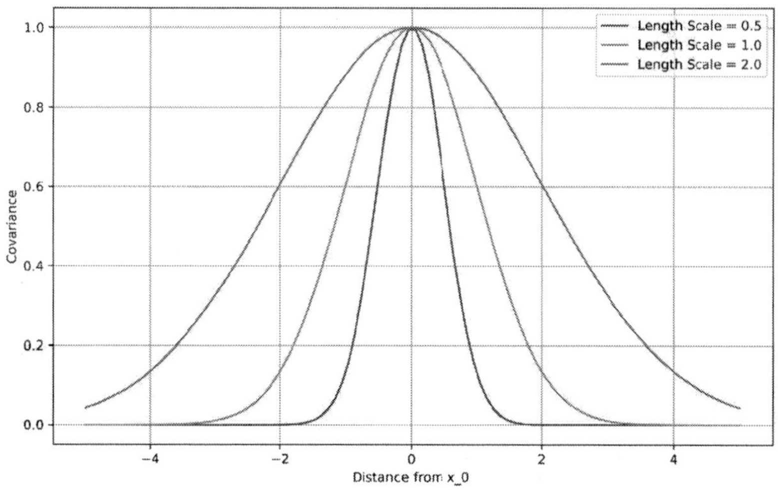

Figure 1: Effect of distance and length-scale on spatial correlation using a squared exponential covariance function, assuming $\sigma^2 = 1$

$$k_{M_{3/2}}(.,.) = \sigma^2(1+\frac{\sqrt{3}d}{l})exp(-\frac{\sqrt{3}d}{l}) \tag{3}$$

$$k_{M_{5/2}}(.,.) = \sigma^2(1+\frac{\sqrt{5}d}{l}+\frac{5d^2}{3l^2})exp(-\frac{\sqrt{5}d}{l}) \tag{4}$$

Ideally, the properties of the chosen covariance function, such as smoothness assumptions and the ability to capture specific patterns, should align with the characteristics of the function under study (Archetti and Candelieri 2019). This, however, requires an understanding of the problem domain and prior knowledge about the underlying function. Often, this information is not available. In such cases, kernel choice relies on expert knowledge and involves hyperparameter tuning techniques such as maximum likelihood estimation or cross-validation (Duvenaud 2014, Duvenaud et al. 2013). Some authors (Roman et al. 2014, Roman et al. 2019) also study the dynamic change of kernel functions during the optimization process using their proposed kernel selection criteria.

For a chosen covariance function $k(.)$ and a set of p observed points, $\mathbf{x}_1,...,\mathbf{x}_p$, we can calculate the $p \times p$ covariance matrix:

$$K = \begin{pmatrix} k(\mathbf{x}_1,\mathbf{x}_1) & \cdots & k(\mathbf{x}_1,\mathbf{x}_p) \\ \vdots & \ddots & \vdots \\ k(\mathbf{x}_p,\mathbf{x}_1) & \cdots & k(\mathbf{x}_p,\mathbf{x}_p) \end{pmatrix} \tag{5}$$

The predictor value of the unknown function $f(\mathbf{x})$ at an arbitrary point $\mathbf{x}_{p+1}$ is given by

$$\mu(\mathbf{x}_{p+1}) = \hat{\beta}_0 + \mathbf{k}^T K^{-1}(f_{1:p} - \mathbf{1}\hat{\beta}_0) \tag{6}$$

and the variance (also referred to as mean squared error, MSE) of this predictor by

$$s^2(\mathbf{x}_{p+1}) = k(\mathbf{x}_{p+1},\mathbf{x}_{p+1}) - \mathbf{k}^T K^{-1}\mathbf{k} + \frac{(1-\mathbf{1}^T K^{-1}\mathbf{k})^2}{\mathbf{1}^T K^{-1}\mathbf{1}} \tag{7}$$

where $\mathbf{k} = \left[k(\mathbf{x}_{p+1},\mathbf{x}_1), k(\mathbf{x}_{p+1},\mathbf{x}_2), \ldots, k(\mathbf{x}_{p+1},\mathbf{x}_p)\right]$, and $f_{1:p}$ is the matrix of the observed output values so far. In Equations (6) and (7), $\hat{\beta}_0$ is an estimation of β_0, the overall surface mean and can be calculated by:

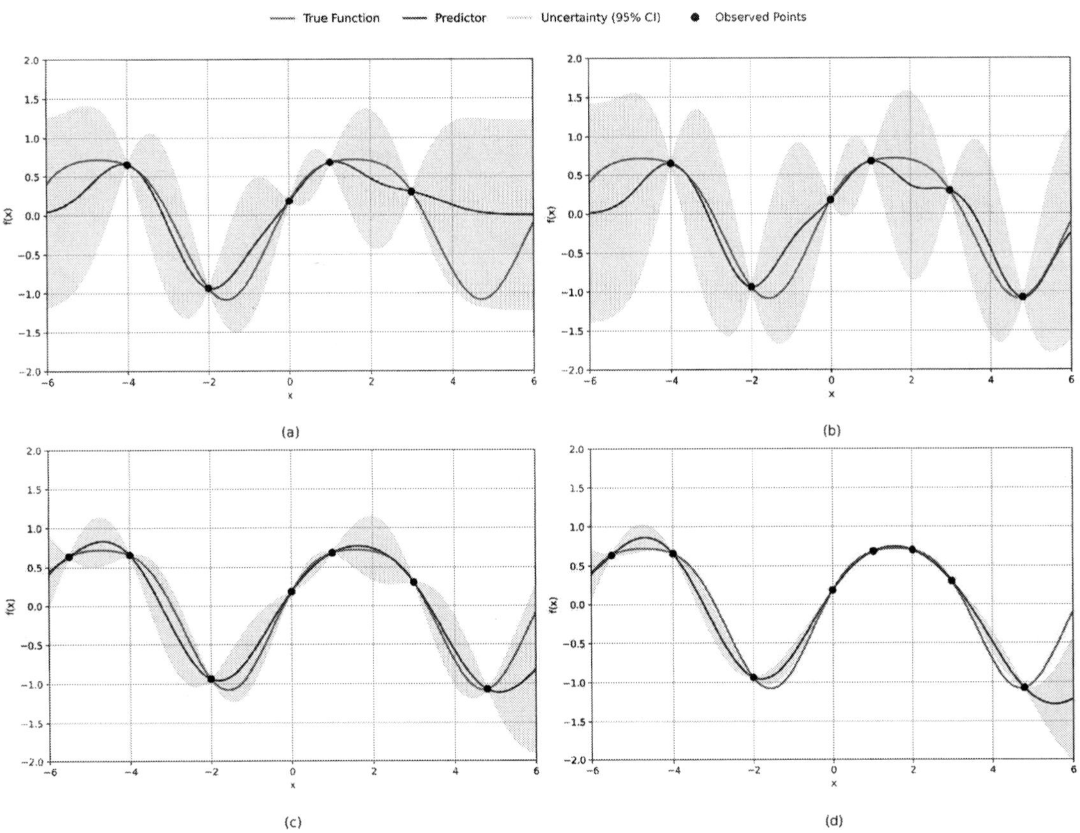

Figure 2: Progressive improvement of kriging model predictions as additional data points are added

$$\hat{\beta}_0 = \frac{\mathbf{1}^T k^{-1} f_{1:p}}{\mathbf{1}^T K^{-1} \mathbf{1}} \tag{8}$$

The last term in Equation (7) which adjusts the uncertainty to account for the estimation of the constant mean, β_0, drops when β_0 will be considered as a given parameter and known.

The key modeling assumption implies that the joint distribution of the observed outputs and the unknown output at a new input location ($\mathbf{x}_{p+1}$) is a multivariate normal distribution. The predictive distribution of the unknown output at the individual location $\mathbf{x}_{p+1}$ is thus normally distributed, with mean equal to the predictor value, and variance given by the MSE. As will be shown in section 3, this distribution information significantly aids the exploration-exploitation balance within the context of efficient global optimization (Garnett 2023). As the output observations are treated as *deterministic*, the kriging model interpolates between these observations: at simulated input/output locations, the predictor value coincides with the simulated outputs, and the MSE of the predictor is zero.

Figure (2) demonstrates how the kriging model progressively improves its predictions as additional data points are incorporated. In the top-left plot, the model starts with only five observed points, showing relatively high uncertainty in regions without data. In the top-right plot, an additional point is added, reducing uncertainty around the corresponding region and improving prediction accuracy. The plots in the bottom row show how observing more points further refines the model's predictions.

Note also that the model's uncertainty (represented by the blue-shaded regions) drops to zero at the observed points, as the observed outputs are treated as deterministic.

2.2 Kriging for stochastic responses: stochastic kriging

In real-world simulations, we often deal with stochastic systems: evaluating the system at the same point multiple times yields different results, as the system's behavior is influenced by inherent randomness. Consequently, the output observations are noisy, and multiple independent evaluations (referred to as

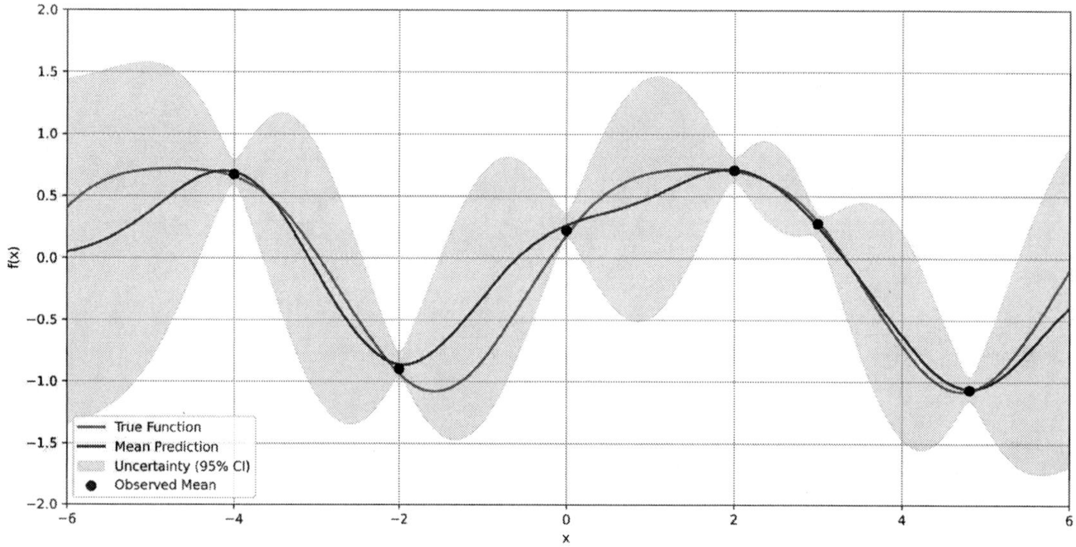

Figure 3: Non-zero uncertainty at observed points in stochastic kriging

replications) are typically required to estimate system performance reliably. In real-life systems, this noise is often *heteroscedastic*, meaning that it differs depending on the input location.

One way to account for this uncertainty in the outputs is the use of Stochastic Kriging (Ankenman et al. 2010). For other methods and more details, we refer to Binois et al. (2018). Stochastic kriging assumes that, at an arbitrary design point $\mathbf{x}$, the function value obtained in the rth replication can be modelled as:

$$f_r(\mathbf{x}) = \beta_0 + M(\mathbf{x}) + \varepsilon_r(\mathbf{x}) \tag{9}$$

The first two terms of this equation are the same as for deterministic responses. The term $\varepsilon_r(\mathbf{x})$ is referred to as *intrinsic uncertainty*, as it is the uncertainty inherent in stochastic simulation. The intrinsic uncertainty is (naturally) independent and identically distributed across replications, having mean 0 and variance $\tau^2(\mathbf{x})$ at any arbitrary point x_i. Note that the model allows for heteroscedastic noise, implying $\tau^2(\mathbf{x})$ need *not* to be constant throughout the design space. The stochastic kriging prediction at an arbitrary location $\mathbf{x}$ (whether observed or not) is given by:

$$\mu_{sk}(\mathbf{x}) = \hat{\beta}_0 + \mathbf{k}^T[K+K_\varepsilon]^{-1}(\overline{f}_{1:p} - \mathbf{1}\hat{\beta}_0) \tag{10}$$

where $\overline{f}$ is the $p \times 1$ vector containing the sample means obtained at the p observed design points. K_ε is a diagonal matrix of size $p \times p$, showing the variance of the sample means on the main diagonal. K_ε thus reflects the intrinsic uncertainty of the system, as it is caused by the (heteroscedastic) noise in the output observations. The mean squared error (MSE) of this predictor is given by:

$$s^2_{sk}(\mathbf{x}) = k(\mathbf{x},\mathbf{x}) - \mathbf{k}^T[K+K_\varepsilon]^{-1}\mathbf{k} + \frac{\Gamma^T\Gamma}{1_p{}^T[K+K_\varepsilon]^{-1}1_p} \tag{11}$$

where $\Gamma = 1 - 1_p{}^T[K+K_\varepsilon]^{-1}\mathbf{k}$. The essential difference between stochastic kriging and ordinary kriging is the presence of K_ε in the expressions for the predictor and the MSE. In the absence of noise, K_ε disappears from the equations, and the stochastic kriging predictor and MSE expressions boil down to the expressions of the ordinary kriging model.

Figure (3) illustrates the behavior of stochastic kriging in a setting with noisy observations. Contrary to ordinary kriging, which interpolates between observed points, the stochastic kriging predictor does not coincide with the sample means at the observed locations, and the corresponding MSE reflects the intrinsic uncertainty.

3 Data-efficient simulation optimization with kriging models

Kriging-based simulation optimization is a sequential optimization method that is particularly well suited for problems involving expensive, potentially nonconvex black box functions and a limited computational budget (Garnett 2023, Wang et al. 2023, Frazier 2018, Candelieri 2021). Various algorithms have been developed, yet they all share the same key steps, shown in Figure 4. In what follows, we discuss these steps in more detail.

- **Initial sample:** The first step is the generation of an initial sample. It has been shown that the success of metamodel-based optimization algorithms in achieving fast convergence to the optimal solution largely depends on the quality of the initial data used to train the metamodels (Vu et al. 2017). The purpose of this step is to create a space-filling set of design points, i.e. a set of points that effectively covers the entire space without leaving significant gaps or underrepresented regions (Greenhill et al. 2020). Various mathematical techniques and algorithms, such as Latin hypercube sampling (Jones et al. 1998) and Sobol sequences (Picheny et al. 2013), have been employed in the literature to generate space-filling designs.
  When repeatedly solving similar optimization problems, the analyst may learn how to set the initial design for the optimization algorithm from experience. Some authors have proposed sophisticated *warm start* initialization procedures for hyperparameter tuning; see (Feurer et al. 2015) for more details. In general, the Latin Hypercube Sampling (LHS) design (Park 1994) is the most often used method in the Bayesian Optimization (BO) literature, given its space-filling and non-collapsing features. For more details on initial sampling techniques for surrogate models, we refer to Vu et al. (2017).
- **Evaluation:** Information about the unknown function(s) is acquired by running the expensive simulator at the selected points. In stochastic simulations, variability is inherent in the simulation(Nelson et al. 2021). Increasing the number of replications improves the accuracy of the sample means in such settings, yet, as the total number of evaluations is limited, there is a trade-off between the number of simulations spent to replicating already observed points, and those spent to evaluate new points in the design space.
- **Build/Update Metamodel:** In this step, the kriging metamodel is fit to the available I/O observations, such that the belief about the unknown function is updated (Frazier 2018).
- **Search:** Kriging-based simulation optimization is a sequential process, so after evaluating a new design point, the collected data is incorporated into the existing data, and the metamodel is updated. In this step, an *acquisition function* (also referred to as *infill criterion* (Rojas-Gonzalez and Van Nieuwenhuyse 2020)) is used to determine the next solution to evaluate. This criterion quantifies the desirability of simulating a new solution (Frazier 2018, Archetti and Candelieri 2019) based on the metamodel information.
  The uncertainty measure is crucial for guiding the search for optimal solutions, helping the optimization algorithm identify areas of the solution space that require further exploration. By combining the kriging predictions and the kriging variance, the acquisition function enhances the efficiency of simulation optimization, particularly in data-scarce environments where simulation runs are costly (Kleijnen 2018). It typically trades off exploitation of the search space (i.e., sampling in areas with promising predictor values) versus exploration (sampling in areas with high predictor uncertainty). During the early stages of optimization, exploration is often prioritized to gather diverse samples and gain a better understanding of the search space. This allows the algorithm to build an initial surrogate model that estimates the overall behavior of the function. As the optimization progresses, the surrogate model becomes more accurate, and the algorithm shifts towards exploitation (Gupta et al. 2006, Gan et al. 2021). This allows for a more targeted search, potentially leading to a more accurate surrogate model in the neighborhood of the optimal solution and, as a result, faster convergence. This iterative process of model updating and acquisition function maximization continues until the stopping criterion is met.
  The choice of acquisition function depends on the specific problem characteristics, and is further discussed in Section 4. While some of these may outperform others in specific settings, to the best of our knowledge, there is no evidence that any of them consistently outperform others.

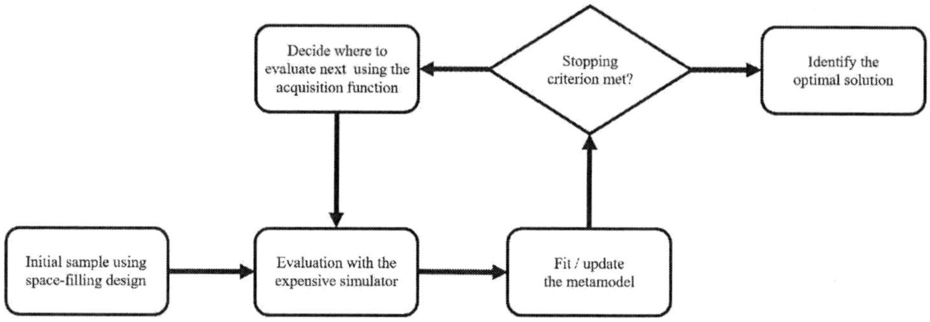

Figure 4: General steps in a kriging-based simulation optimization algorithm

- **Termination:** At some moment, the optimization algorithm has to stop. Usually, this happens when it has reached a satisfactory solution (Nguyen 2023), when it has depleted the available budget (Garnett 2023), or when the expected gain from the optimal observation is no longer worth the cost of the evaluation (Archetti and Candelieri 2019).
- **Identification:** When the stopping criterion is met, the algorithm needs to identify the optimal solution(s). In the current literature, the main focus is on finding a solution that maximizes the expected performance of the objective function of interest, and it is common to identify the solution with the best-observed performance (i.e., the best function outcome in case of deterministic simulation, and the best sample mean in case of stochastic simulation) as the optimum (Carpio et al. 2018).

4 Acquisition functions

The acquisition function, combined with the metamodel, forms the "heart" of every kriging-based optimization algorithm (Garnett 2023). As mentioned above, it determines the next point to evaluate, given the current probabilistic belief about the function behaviour (i.e., the kriging model). In deterministic settings, Probability of Improvement (PI) and Expected Improvement (EI) are undoubtedly among the most popular functions. PI (Kushner 1964) is evaluated as:

$$PI(\mathbf{x}) = Pr\big(f(\mathbf{x}) \leq f_{min})\big) = \Phi\Big(\frac{f_{min} - \mu(\mathbf{x})}{s(\mathbf{x})}\Big) \tag{12}$$

where f_{min} represents the best objective function value observed so far, and Φ denotes the normal cumulative distribution. Expected Improvement (EI), first proposed by Jones et al. (1998), has been widely used in the literature and has triggered the development of many variants. EI estimates the *magnitude* of the improvement over the current best observed value, and is given by:

$$EI(\mathbf{x}) = [f_{min} - \mu(\mathbf{x})]\,\Phi\left(\frac{f_{min}-\mu(\mathbf{x})}{s(\mathbf{x})}\right) + s(\mathbf{x})\phi\left(\frac{f_{min}-\mu(\mathbf{x})}{s(\mathbf{x})}\right) \tag{13}$$

where ϕ denotes the normal probability density function. Other popular acquisition functions in deterministic settings are confidence bounds, where upper and lower are used, respectively, for maximization and minimization problems.

The acquisition functions discussed so far are myopic, in the sense that they focus on immediate improvements without considering the long-term impact of a sampling decision. In contrast, the Knowledge Gradient (KG) acquisition function evaluates the expected value of information that a new sample will provide (Garnett 2023). It focuses on maximizing the expected improvement in the decision-making process by considering how much each new observation will reduce uncertainty about the objective function, not just the immediate improvement.

Another form of *look-ahead* acquisition function is *Entropy Search*, which aims to reduce the uncertainty (quantified as the entropy) in the *location* of the estimated optimum. The next point to be evaluated is the one that leads to the biggest decrease in the entropy of the estimated optimum location(Villemonteix et al. 2009, Hennig and Schuler 2012):

$$ES(\mathbf{x}) = \mathrm{H}\left[\mathbf{x}^*|\mathscr{D}\right] - \mathbb{E}\left[\mathrm{H}\left[\mathbf{x}^*|\mathscr{D}\cup\{(\mathbf{x},\mathbf{y})\}\right]\right] \tag{14}$$

In this expression, H is the entropy function, $\mathbf{x}^*$ is the optimal solution of the problem, and $\mathscr{D}$ is the set of solutions observed so far. *ES* provides a measure of the information gained on x^* after observing the functions at point $\mathbf{x}$, resulting in the set of outputs $\mathbf{y}$.

Different authors have made attempts to extend EI to handle noisy settings (Ament et al. 2023, Zhou et al. 2024). Most of these approaches, e.g., Letham et al. (2019), rely on Monte Carlo methods, which sample from the posterior distribution to approximate the true expected improvement in the presence of noise. Quan et al. (2013) proposed a modified version of the EI criterion, referred to as the *modified expected improvement*:

$$MEI(\mathbf{x}) = [\mu_{sk}(x_{min}) - \mu_{sk}(\mathbf{x})]\,\Phi\left(\frac{\mu_{sk}(x_{min}) - \mu_{sk}(\mathbf{x})}{s(\mathbf{x})}\right) + s(\mathbf{x})\,\phi\left(\frac{\mu_{sk}(x_{min}) - \mu_{sk}(\mathbf{x})}{s(\mathbf{x})}\right) \tag{15}$$

In stochastic settings, this criterion improves the efficiency and effectiveness of the search compared with the traditional EI acquisition function. The MEI criterion is analogous to the *EI* criterion, except for the use of $\mu_{sk}(x_{min})$ (the stochastic kriging predictor) instead of f_{min} (the best-simulated value so far). This is a straightforward choice, as it provides an unbiased prediction given the heteroscedastic nature of the noise (Quan et al. 2013, Ankenman et al. 2010).

The *Augmented Expected Improvement (AEI)*, proposed by (Huang et al. 2006), incorporates a noise-adjustment term:

$$AEI(x) = \mathbb{E}\left[\max\left(\mu(x_{min}) - \mu(x), 0\right)\right] \times \left(1 - \frac{\tau}{\sqrt{\tau^2 + s^2(x)}}\right) \tag{16}$$

where τ^2 represents the variance of the noise. The goal is to avoid oversampling in very noisy regions. Note, however, that *AEI* assumes homogeneous noise (some authors, e.g., Jalali et al. (2017), replace τ^2 with $\tau^2(x)$ to reflect the presence of heteroscedastic noise). AEI performs best when the noise variance is known; in real-life applications, however, this is usually not the case. Researchers then often employ an additional Kriging model to estimate this variance (Wang and Ierapetritou 2018).

Correlated Knowledge Gradient acquisition function in Frazier et al. (2009) is developed to handle heteroscedastic noise. Empirical studies in Jalali et al. (2017) and Picheny et al. (2013) show that Knowledge Gradient acquisition functions can be effective in noisy environments.

Maximizing acquisition functions is nontrivial, as they tend to be highly nonlinear and multi-modal (Nguyen 2023). Heuristic algorithms such as adaptive random search (Zabinsky 2003, Zhigljavsky 2012) or evolutionary methods (Tzanetos et al. 2020, Scott et al. 2011) can be used, as well as local optimization approaches with multi-start (e.g., Loka et al. (2024)). Multi-start methods enhance search efficiency by repeatedly restarting from new initial solutions, combining exploration of diverse regions with local search refinement. This approach helps avoid local optima and improves the chances of finding high-quality solutions. All of these are heuristic methods, which may require many function evaluations. Fortunately, this is usually not an issue as most acquisition functions are cheap to evaluate (exceptions are knowledge gradient and entropy search). The optimality of a heuristic approach cannot be guaranteed, though, and its performance typically depends on a number of user-defined parameters. To avoid these issues, some authors (Gonzalez et al. 2020, Jalali et al. 2017, Angun and Kleijnen 2023) discretize the search space into a finite (but potentially large) space-filling set of so-called *candidate points*. The acquisition function value is then evaluated for all unvisited alternatives, and the one with the highest value is chosen as the next infill point. This approach helps to ensure that differences in observed performance across algorithms are not caused by the heuristic at hand, but by differences in algorithmic approach. In high-dimensional problems, the use of candidate sets may become impractical, as the number of required points increases sharply with the number of dimensions.

While discretization is beneficial in studying and comparing different algorithms' performance, it has its downside. The optimization of a continuous problem by discretizing the solution space can sometimes lead to suboptimal solutions, regardless of the quality of the optimization algorithm. This arises from the fact that, no matter how extensive the discrete set is or how it is sampled, there is no assurance that this resulting set encompasses the global optimum of the problem. Consequently, it becomes impossible for any algorithm to discover this global optimum during the optimization process.

5 Kriging vs. polynomial models: an illustrative example

This section compares the performance of kriging and polynomial regression models in simulation optimization, using a simple (R,s,S) inventory management system as an illustrative example.

Simulation Model. We adapted the (R,s,S) inventory system described in Law (2015) to develop our simulation model. In this system, the inventory position (I) is monitored at the start of each month. When it falls to or below a specified reorder point (s), a replenishment order is placed such that the inventory position reaches the order-up-to level (S). Customer demands are met immediately if there are enough items in stock. If not, the excess demand is backlogged and is met as soon as there are enough units in inventory. The time between demands is IID exponentially distributed with a mean of 0.1 months. The demand sizes are IID integer random variables; they follow a discrete distribution with values between 1 and 4 (occurring with probability $\frac{1}{6}$, $\frac{1}{3}$, $\frac{1}{3}$, and $\frac{1}{6}$ respectively). Once a replenishment order has been placed, the time required for it to arrive (called the delivery lead time (Durán-Micco et al. 2023)) is random, following a uniform distribution between 0.5 and 1 month.

There is a fixed cost associated with placing an order ($32). Holding costs are incurred for each unit in stock at the end of each month ($1 per item per month). Backlog costs arise when demand exceeds available stock, costing $5 per unit per month. The system is evaluated over 120 months of operation. Further detail on the simulation model can be found in Law (2015). The goal of the optimization is to determine the values s and S such that the expected total cost (consisting of holding, shortage, and order costs) is minimized. Each (R,s,S) solution that needs to be evaluated is replicated 5 times in the simulation.

Optimization algorithms: Three different optimization algorithms are compared. The first algorithm, SK/MEI, is a kriging-based optimization algorithm using stochastic kriging (with a squared exponential kernel (Equation 2)) to fit the observed costs, and applying the MEI acquisition function (Equation 15) to select the next point to evaluate. The second algorithm, OK/EI, fits an ordinary kriging model (using the same kernel) to the observed sample means (thereby neglecting the noise on these sample means), and uses the EI acquisition function (Equation 13). The third algorithm, Polynomial Regression, fits a second-order polynomial to the sample means, with the next point chosen based solely on the predicted output. While SK/MEI and OK/EI use acquisition functions that account for metamodel uncertainty, Polynomial Regression selects points based on predicted values alone.

We evaluate each algorithm on 25 macro-replications of the (s,S) system, where each macroreplication starts from a different lhs design (consisting each time of 10 points).All three algorithms use the same initial design per macroreplication, to ensure a fair comparison. The candidate set of solutions consists of a two-dimensional grid of (s,S) locations, with s and S integer values between 1 and 100; evidently, $s < S$ such that the grid consists of 4950 values in total. Each macroreplication ends after 100 infill points have been added. The observed solution with the smallest sample mean is then returned as the estimated optimal solution.

Discussion: Figure (5) shows the evolution in the best expected total cost obtained, over the 100 sequential iterations, for each of the three algorithms. The lines show the average over the 25 macroreplications, and the shaded areas reflect the 95% t-confidence intervals on this average. SK/MEI, leveraging stochastic kriging and MEI to effectively balance exploration and exploitation, clearly outperforms OK/EI by focusing quickly on promising regions of the solution space. This is not surprising, as OK/EI treats the noisy sample means as deterministic information, which may mislead the search. The solution quality obtained after 100 iterations by OK/EI is reached by SK/MEI within approx. $1/2$ of this budget. The noise handling within SK/MEI is key in improving data efficiency. Polynomial Regression shows the slowest convergence, and hence performs worst in terms of solution quality for this limited simulation budget.

6 Extensions of kriging-based simulation optimization

Thus far, we have focused exclusively on single-objective problems without constraints. However, many real-world optimization scenarios are more complex, involving multiple objectives simultaneously and/or

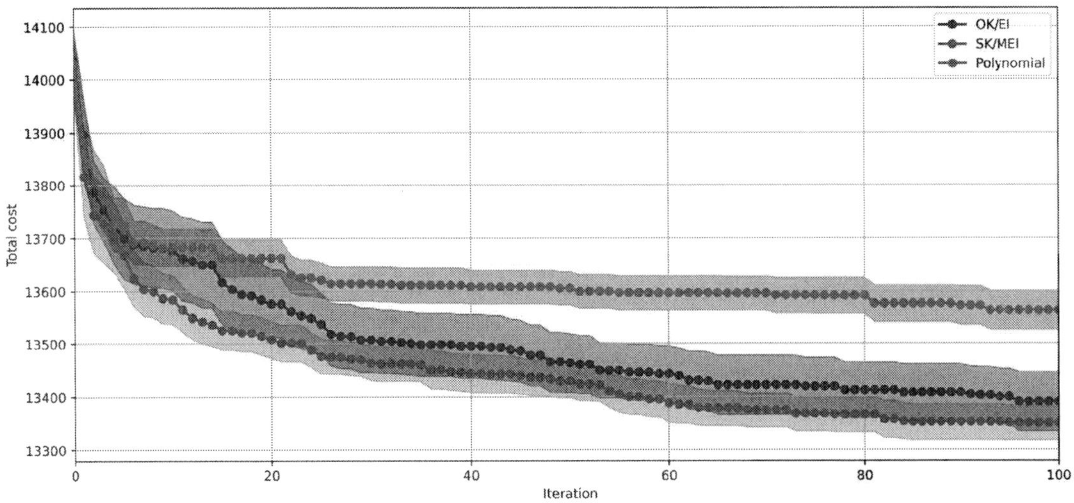

Figure 5: Convergence comparison of three optimization Algorithms: SK/MEI, OK/EI, and Polynomial regression over 100 iterations, results of 25 macro-replications

constraints that limit the feasible solution space. These challenges have resulted in extensions of the basic framework described above; in this section, we briefly explore these extensions.

6.1 Multi-objective optimization

In multi-objective optimization, the aim is to find solutions that simultaneously optimize multiple conflicting objectives. Without any preference information from the decision maker, the outcome is a set of Pareto-optimal solutions, where improving one objective means compromising at least one other objective (Hunter et al. 2019). A common method for approximating the Pareto frontier is by means of scalarization functions, which combine multiple objectives into a single value by assigning weights. The algorithm then attempts to obtain a high-quality approximation of the Pareto front by varying these weights. The Augmented Tchebycheff function is often preferred over other scalarization methods, such as the Weighted Sum, because it better maintains diversity along the Pareto front and ensures that points on nonconvex regions of the front can be detected (Miettinen 1999).

Multi-objective optimization in settings with noisy evaluations is challenging. Simply relying on noisy sample means to detect the front may lead to misclassification (truly Pareto-optimal solutions may be identified as dominated, while dominated solutions are considered Pareto-optimal). These errors prevent the correct identification of the truePareto-optimal solutions, especially when the replication budget is limited.

According to Rojas-Gonzalez and Van Nieuwenhuyse (2020), acquisition functions in kriging-based multi-objective simulation optimization fall into two categories. The first type consists of single-objective acquisition functions, originally designed for single-objective problems but adapted to multi-objective contexts by assessing improvement for each objective individually or through a scalarized version. The second type includes multi-objective acquisition functions, which measure the contribution of new points to the Pareto front using metrics such as hypervolume improvement, see, e.g., Yang et al. (2019).

6.2 Constrained optimization

The key challenge in constrained kriging-based simulation optimization is ensuring that the algorithm accurately identifies feasible regions defined by (possibly stochastic) constraints. Failing to do so introduces a significant risk of returning infeasible or suboptimal solutions as the final outcome (Amini 2024). In these problems, the selection of infill points is not only driven by how promising points are for improving the objective function, but also by how they may contribute to the estimation of the feasible region.

Despite its importance, constrained kriging-based stochastic simulation optimization remains relatively underexplored (Amini et al. 2025). Wang and Ierapetritou (2018) developed an algorithm to address stochastic simulation optimization problems with only one constraint. Their acquisition function balances two factors: the point's potential for improving the objective function and its likelihood of satisfying the constraint. This balance helps the algorithm in finding better solutions while learning the boundaries of the feasible region, reducing the risk of selecting infeasible solutions. Amini and Van Nieuwenhuyse (2023) extended this framework to handle problems with multiple constraints, incorporating stochastic kriging and a barrier function approach, which penalizes infeasible points and guides the search towards the optimal solution within the feasible region. Meanwhile, Angun and Kleijnen (2023) integrates the Karush-Kuhn-Tucker (KKT) conditions into kriging-based simulation optimization. Their acquisition function multiplies the expected improvement by a cosine function, which measures how well a point satisfies the KKT conditions.

In constrained optimization, it is crucial to focus on enhancing feasibility estimations in areas where the objective function is estimated to have small values (in the case of minimization). This allows the algorithm to prioritize regions likely to contain the optimal solution, rather than spending resources in less relevant areas, making the algorithm more data-efficient. Both Wang and Ierapetritou (2018) and Amini and Van Nieuwenhuyse (2023) emphasize this approach, underscoring its importance for efficiency. In contrast, Angun and Kleijnen (2023) take a different approach, aiming to enhance accuracy across the entire feasible region. While this improves overall precision, it requires a larger computational budget, making the algorithm less data-efficient.

7 Conclusion

In this tutorial, we explored the basics of kriging-based simulation optimization, emphasizing its data efficiency, particularly when handling stochastic problems with heteroscedastic noise. By comparing kriging-based methods to traditional polynomial approaches, we highlighted that kriging models are more flexible and better capture complex, non-linear relationships in I/O data. Furthermore, better uncertainty modeling in stochastic kriging leads to faster and more reliable convergence.

In industrial settings, data-efficient simulation optimization is essential for addressing complex, resource-intensive problems. Kriging-based methods provide a powerful framework for optimizing process or product designs within fewer simulation runs, reducing costs, and accelerating decision-making. This efficiency, coupled with the ability to handle noisy data, makes kriging-based optimization a vital tool for companies seeking to enhance competitiveness. As industries become increasingly reliant on simulation models and digital twins for product development and operational improvements, the use of data-efficient methods like kriging will continue to play a key role in driving innovation and sustaining growth.

ACKNOWLEDGMENTS

The authors are grateful to the anonymous reviewers for their thoughtful feedback, which has enhanced the clarity of this work. This work was supported by the Flanders Artificial Intelligence Research Program (FAIR2) and the Research Foundation Flanders (FWO), grant number: G0A4624N.

REFERENCES

Amaran, S., N. V. Sahinidis, B. Sharda, and S. J. Bury. 2016. "Simulation optimization: a review of algorithms and applications". *Annals of Operations Research* 240:351–380.

Ament, S., S. Daulton, D. Eriksson, M. Balandat, and E. Bakshy. 2023. "Unexpected improvements to expected improvement for bayesian optimization". *Advances in Neural Information Processing Systems* 36:20577–20612.

Amini, S. 2024. *Constrained Bayesian Optimization with Barrier Functions; Impact of heteroscedastic noise on the search and identification phases*. Ph. D. thesis, Hasselt University.

Amini, S., and I. Van Nieuwenhuyse. 2023. "A Bayesian Optimization Algorithm for Constrained Simulation Optimization Problems with Heteroscedastic Noise". In *International Conference on Learning and Intelligent Optimization*, 78–91. Springer.

Amini, S., I. Vannieuwenhuyse, and A. Morales-Hernández. 2025. "Constrained Bayesian Optimization: A Review". *IEEE Access* 13:1581–1593.

Angun, E., and J. Kleijnen. 2023. "Constrained optimization in Random Simulation: Efficient Global Optimization and Karush-Kuhn-Tucker Conditions (Revision of CentER DP 2022-022)". 2023-010. CentER Discussion Paper Nr. 2023-010.

Ankenman, B., B. L. Nelson, and J. Staum. 2010. "Stochastic Kriging for Simulation Metamodeling". *Operations Research* 58 (2): 371–382.

Archetti, F., and A. Candelieri. 2019. *Bayesian optimization and data science*, Volume 849. Springer.

Barton, R. R. 2023a. "Metamodelling: Power, pitfalls, and model-free interpretation". In *11th Operational Research Society Simulation Workshop, SW 2023*, 48–62. Operational Research Society.

Barton, R. R. 2023b. "Tutorial: Basics of Metamodeling". In *2023 Winter Simulation Conference (WSC)*, 1516–1530. IEEE.

Binois, M., R. B. Gramacy, and M. Ludkovski. 2018. "Practical heteroscedastic Gaussian process modeling for large simulation experiments". *Journal of Computational and Graphical Statistics* 27 (4): 808–821.

Candelieri, A. 2021. "A gentle introduction to Bayesian optimization". In *2021 Winter Simulation Conference (WSC)*, 1–16. IEEE.

Carpio, R. R., R. C. Giordano, and A. R. Secchi. 2018. "Enhanced surrogate assisted framework for constrained global optimization of expensive black-box functions". *Computers & Chemical Engineering* 118:91–102.

Chilès, J.-P., and N. Desassis. 2018. "Fifty years of kriging". *Handbook of mathematical geosciences: Fifty years of IAMG*:589–612.

Ding, H., L. Benyoucef, and X. Xie. 2005. "A simulation optimization methodology for supplier selection problem". *International Journal of Computer Integrated Manufacturing* 18 (2-3): 210–224.

do Amaral, J. V. S., J. A. B. Montevechi, R. de Carvalho Miranda, and W. T. de Sousa Junior. 2022. "Metamodel-based simulation optimization: A systematic literature review". *Simulation Modelling Practice and Theory* 114:102403.

do Amaral, J. V. S., J. A. B. Montevechi, R. de Carvalho Miranda, and C. H. dos Santos. 2024. "Adaptive Metamodeling Simulation Optimization: Insights, Challenges, and Perspectives". *Applied Soft Computing*:112067.

Durán-Micco, J., S. A. Jordehi, and C. Macharis. 2023. "Evaluating synchromodal transport with agent-based simulation". *Transportation Research Procedia* 72:619–626.

Duvenaud, D. 2014. "The kernel cookbook: Advice on covariance functions". *URL https://www. cs. toronto. edu/duvenaud/cookbook*.

Duvenaud, D., J. Lloyd, R. Grosse, J. Tenenbaum, and G. Zoubin. 2013. "Structure discovery in nonparametric regression through compositional kernel search". In *International Conference on Machine Learning*, 1166–1174. PMLR.

Feurer, M., J. Springenberg, and F. Hutter. 2015. "Initializing Bayesian hyperparameter optimization via meta-learning". In *Proceedings of the AAAI Conference on Artificial Intelligence*, Volume 29/1.

Frazier, P., W. Powell, and S. Dayanik. 2009. "The knowledge-gradient policy for correlated normal beliefs". *INFORMS journal on Computing* 21 (4): 599–613.

Frazier, P. I. 2018. "Bayesian optimization". In *Recent advances in optimization and modeling of contemporary problems*, 255–278. Informs.

Fu, M. C. et al. 2015. *Handbook of simulation optimization*, Volume 216. Springer.

Gan, W., Z. Ji, and Y. Liang. 2021. "Acquisition functions in Bayesian optimization". In *2021 2nd International Conference on Big Data & Artificial Intelligence & Software Engineering (ICBASE)*, 129–135. IEEE.

Garnett, R. 2023. *Bayesian optimization*. Cambridge University Press.

Gonzalez, S. R., H. Jalali, and I. Van Nieuwenhuyse. 2020. "A multiobjective stochastic simulation optimization algorithm". *European Journal of Operational Research* 284 (1): 212–226.

Gramacy, R. B. 2020. *Surrogates: Gaussian process modeling, design, and optimization for the applied sciences*. Chapman and Hall/CRC.

Greenhill, S., S. Rana, S. Gupta, P. Vellanki, and S. Venkatesh. 2020. "Bayesian optimization for adaptive experimental design: A review". *IEEE access* 8:13937–13948.

Gupta, A. K., K. G. Smith, and C. E. Shalley. 2006. "The interplay between exploration and exploitation". *Academy of Management journal* 49 (4): 693–706.

Hassannayebi, E., M. Boroun, S. A. Jordehi, and H. Kor. 2019. "Train schedule optimization in a high-speed railway system using a hybrid simulation and meta-model approach". *Computers & Industrial Engineering* 138:106110.

Hennig, P., and C. J. Schuler. 2012. "Entropy Search for Information-Efficient Global Optimization.". *Journal of Machine Learning Research* 13 (6).

Hong, L. J., and X. Zhang. 2021. "Surrogate-based simulation optimization". In *Tutorials in Operations Research: Emerging Optimization Methods and Modeling Techniques with Applications*, 287–311. INFORMS.

Huang, D., T. T. Allen, W. I. Notz, and N. Zeng. 2006. "Global optimization of stochastic black-box systems via sequential kriging meta-models". *Journal of global optimization* 34:441–466.

Hunter, S. R., E. A. Applegate, V. Arora, B. Chong, K. Cooper, O. Rincón-Guevara, and C. Vivas-Valencia. 2019. "An introduction to multiobjective simulation optimization". *ACM Transactions on Modeling and Computer Simulation (TOMACS)* 29 (1): 1–36.

Jalali, H., I. Van Nieuwenhuyse, and V. Picheny. 2017. "Comparison of kriging-based algorithms for simulation optimization with heterogeneous noise". *European Journal of Operational Research* 261 (1): 279–301.

Jones, D. R., M. Schonlau, and W. J. Welch. 1998. "Efficient global optimization of expensive black-box functions". *Journal of Global optimization* 13:455–492.

Kleijnen, J. P. 2009. "Kriging metamodeling in simulation: A review". *European journal of operational research* 192 (3): 707–716.

Kleijnen, J. P. 2018. *Design and analysis of simulation experiments*. Springer.

Krige, D. G. 1951. "A statistical approach to some basic mine valuation problems on the Witwatersrand". *Journal of the Southern African Institute of Mining and Metallurgy* 52 (6): 119–139.

Kushner, H. J. 1964. "A new method of locating the maximum point of an arbitrary multipeak curve in the presence of noise". *Journl of fluids engineering*.

Law, A. M. 2015. *Simulation modeling and analysis*. 5 ed. Mcgraw-hill New York.

Letham, B., B. Karrer, G. Ottoni, and E. Bakshy. 2019. "Constrained Bayesian Optimization with Noisy Experiments". *Bayesian Analysis* 14 (2): 495 – 519.

Loka, N., M. Ibrahim, I. Couckuyt, I. Van Nieuwenhuyse, and T. Dhaene. 2024. "Cheap-expensive multi-objective Bayesian optimization for permanent magnet synchronous motor design". *Engineering with Computers* 40 (4): 2143–2159.

Miettinen, K. 1999. *Nonlinear multiobjective optimization*, Volume 12. Springer Science & Business Media.

Nelson, B. et al. 2021. *Foundations and methods of stochastic simulation*. Springer.

Nguyen, Q. 2023. *Bayesian Optimization in Action*. MANNING.

Palar, P. S., and K. Shimoyama. 2017. "On multi-objective efficient global optimization via universal Kriging surrogate model". In *2017 IEEE Congress on Evolutionary Computation (CEC)*, 621–628. IEEE.

Park, J.-S. 1994. "Optimal Latin-hypercube designs for computer experiments". *Journal of statistical planning and inference* 39 (1): 95–111.

Pasandideh, S. H. R., and S. T. A. Niaki. 2006. "Multi-response simulation optimization using genetic algorithm within desirability function framework". *Applied mathematics and computation* 175 (1): 366–382.

Picheny, V., T. Wagner, and D. Ginsbourger. 2013. "A benchmark of kriging-based infill criteria for noisy optimization". *Structural and multidisciplinary optimization* 48:607–626.

Pietrusewicz, K. 2019. "Metamodelling for design of mechatronic and cyber-physical systems". *Applied Sciences* 9 (3): 376.

Quan, N., J. Yin, S. H. Ng, and L. H. Lee. 2013. "Simulation optimization via kriging: a sequential search using expected improvement with computing budget constraints". *Iie Transactions* 45 (7): 763–780.

Rasmussen, C. E., and C. K. Williams. 2006. *Gaussian processes for machine learning*, Volume 2. MIT press Cambridge, MA.

Rojas-Gonzalez, S., and I. Van Nieuwenhuyse. 2020. "A survey on kriging-based infill algorithms for multiobjective simulation optimization". *Computers & Operations Research* 116:104869.

Roman, I., R. Santana, A. Mendiburu, and J. A. Lozano. 2014. "Dynamic kernel selection criteria for Bayesian optimization". In *BayesOpt 2014: NIPS Workshop on Bayesian Optimization*.

Roman, I., R. Santana, A. Mendiburu, and J. A. Lozano. 2019. "An experimental study in adaptive kernel selection for Bayesian optimization". *IEEE Access* 7:184294–184302.

Sacks, J., W. J. Welch, T. J. Mitchell, and H. P. Wynn. 1989. "Design and Analysis of Computer Experiments". *Statistical Science* 4 (4): 409 – 423.

Scott, W., P. Frazier, and W. Powell. 2011. "The correlated knowledge gradient for simulation optimization of continuous parameters using Gaussian process regression". *SIAM Journal on Optimization* 21 (3): 996–1026.

Shahriari, B., K. Swersky, Z. Wang, R. P. Adams, and N. De Freitas. 2015. "Taking the human out of the loop: A review of Bayesian optimization". *Proceedings of the IEEE* 104 (1): 148–175.

Stavropoulos, P., A. Papacharalampopoulos, K. Sabatakakis, and D. Mourtzis. 2023. "Metamodelling of manufacturing processes and automation workflows towards designing and operating digital twins". *Applied Sciences* 13 (3): 1945.

Tzanetos, A., I. Fister Jr, and G. Dounias. 2020. "A comprehensive database of Nature-Inspired Algorithms". *Data in Brief* 31:105792.

Villemonteix, J., E. Vazquez, and E. Walter. 2009. "An informational approach to the global optimization of expensive-to-evaluate functions". *Journal of Global Optimization* 44:509–534.

Vu, K. K., C. d'Ambrosio, Y. Hamadi, and L. Liberti. 2017. "Surrogate-based methods for black-box optimization". *International Transactions in Operational Research* 24 (3): 393–424.

Wang, X., Y. Jin, S. Schmitt, and M. Olhofer. 2023. "Recent advances in Bayesian optimization". *ACM Computing Surveys* 55 (13s): 1–36.

Wang, Z., and M. Ierapetritou. 2018. "Constrained optimization of black-box stochastic systems using a novel feasibility enhanced Kriging-based method". *Computers & Chemical Engineering* 118:210–223.

Yang, K., M. Emmerich, A. Deutz, and T. Bäck. 2019. "Multi-objective Bayesian global optimization using expected hypervolume improvement gradient". *Swarm and evolutionary computation* 44:945–956.

Zabinsky, Z. B. 2003. *Stochastic adaptive search for global optimization*, Volume 72. Springer Science & Business Media.

Zhigljavsky, A. A. 2012. *Theory of global random search*, Volume 65. Springer Science & Business Media.

Zhou, H., X. Ma, and M. B. Blaschko. 2024. "A corrected expected improvement acquisition function under noisy observations". In *Asian Conference on Machine Learning*, 1747–1762. PMLR.

AUTHOR BIOGRAPHIES

Sasan Amini is a postdoctoral researcher in the Computational Mathematics research group at Hasselt University, Belgium. He holds a Ph.D. in Business Economics, and his research primarily focuses on constraint handling methods in black-box optimization problems, with a particular emphasis on stochastic settings and problems involving expensive-to-evaluate functions.

Inneke Van Nieuwenhuyse is a Professor at Hasselt University and KU Leuven, Belgium. Her research interests focus on (multi-objective) optimization of stochastic systems, especially in settings that are expensive to evaluate. To that end, she combines operations research techniques with machine learning approaches.

Proceedings of the Operational Research Society Simulation Workshop 2025 (SW25)
M. Luis, A. Harper, T. Monks and N. Mustafee, eds.
https://doi.org/10.36819/SW25.004

BUILDING HEALTHCARE DISCRETE-EVENT SIMULATION MODELS IN FREE AND OPEN SOURCE SOFTWARE: AN INTRODUCTORY TUTORIAL

Thomas Monks

University of Exeter Medical School
University of Exeter
t.m.w.monks@exeter.ac.uk

Alison Harper

University of Exeter Business School
University of Exeter
a.l.harper@exeter.ac.uk

Amy Heather

University of Exeter Medical School
University of Exeter
a.heather2@exeter.ac.uk

Andrew Mayne

Somerset NHS Foundation Trust
Taunton
andrew.mayne@somersetft.nhs.uk

Navonil Mustafee

University of Exeter Business School
University of Exeter
n.mustafee@exeter.ac.uk

ABSTRACT

This tutorial aims to support modellers working in healthcare research or practice to build Discrete-Event Simulation models using the Free and Open Source Software *SimPy* and Python. We provide a step-by-step guide to building a stylised urgent care telephone call centre model. Open materials that accompany the tutorial, including models and exercises, are available online and can be run without installing Python. As the materials are introductory, we also provide a "next steps" section that describes simple, intermediate and advanced extensions to the work.

1 INTRODUCTION

Computer simulation has long been used as a tool for decision support in healthcare process design and optimisation, particularly in supporting healthcare decision makers to ask 'what-if' we delivered care differently. Within the academic literature, Discrete-Event Simulation (DES) has become the predominant approach in healthcare modelling (Salleh et al. 2017). Recent reviews of the field demonstrate the wide-ranging applications of DES in health service delivery, for example, evaluating operational performance, improving patient flow, and optimizing service scheduling (Vázquez-Serrano et al. 2021, Forbus and Berleant 2022, Roy et al. 2021). DES models are valuable for decision making and are also valuable research artefacts in and of themselves: models are time-consuming to code and document in natural language; require significant clinical, methods, and informatics expertise; and depend on specialized software and logic. Given the cost that goes into a developing a coded model we argue that Free and Open Source Software (FOSS) and its value to Open Science (Monks et al. 2024) has a substantive role to play in increasing the ability for models to be shared and reused across health services.

This paper provides an introduction to building DES models in FOSS. By the end of the tutorial readers will have the skills to code and extend a simple queuing model in Python and *SimPy*. Before providing a step-by-step coding of a DES model in health, we introduce the concept of FOSS and what this means for computer simulation studies. We then briefly review the availability of FOSS

DES packages; the barriers associated with using them for research compared to modern Commercial Off-The-Shelf (COTS) simulation packages; and the other initiatives available that aim to increase FOSS uptake in research.

2 FREE AND OPEN SOURCE SOFTWARE

In data science, it is typical to use FOSS. For example, a data scientist working in Machine Learning is likely to use one of the popular Python libraries such as *Scikit-Learn*, *TensorFlow* or *PyTorch*. The benefit of FOSS tools like these libraries are that they are openly licensed, and grant users four key freedoms:

0. The freedom to run the program as you wish, for any purpose.
1. The freedom to study how the program works and modify it to suit your needs.
2. The freedom to redistribute copies to help your neighbours.
3. The freedom to distribute copies of your modified versions to others, allowing the whole community to benefit from your changes.

Importantly, FOSS involves more than just open source code; it grants users the right to freely adapt and distribute copies of code. FOSS repositories often include a *permissive* license like MIT or BSD-2 licenses. These grant users the four freedoms (within commercial or non-commercial work), waive liability, and require crediting (citation) of the authors and their software in subsequent work.

FOSS is increasingly used for computer simulation, such as DES (Monks and Harper 2023a). This tutorial will focus on DES in Python, as it is the language we use in our practical health care simulation studies (e.g. Harper et al. (2023)).

2.1 Python simulation tools

Dagkakis and Heavey (2016) reviewed open source software for DES. They identified three FOSS Python packages: *SimPy* (Team SimPy 2020), *PySimulator* (Pfeiffer et al. 2012) and *ScipySim* (McInnes and Thorne 2011). *PySimulator* and *ScipySim* were last updated in 2014 and 2010 respectively. *SimPy* continues to be maintained (last updated November 2023) and has been used in several publications relevant to Operations Research (Bovim et al. 2021, Allen et al. 2020).

An updated list of Python DES packages now includes *Salabim* (van der Ham 2018, MIT licensed, last updated September 2024), *Ciw* (Palmer et al. 2019, MIT licensed; last updated July 2024), and *DE-Sim* (Goldberg and Karr 2020, MIT licensed, last updated November 2020). *Salabim* is a fork of SimPy and includes many simulation tools including automatic results collection and animation. *Ciw* (the Welsh word for queue) was developed at Cardiff University and allows users to very quickly build complex multi-class queuing networks. An advanced feature of *Ciw* is network deadlock detection (when the DES model enters a state where their is circular blocking of activities). Palmer and Tian (2021b) provide two reproducible, open source implementations of Ciw for hybrid modelling (DES and System Dynamics), archived here (Palmer and Tian 2021a). *DE-Sim* is an object-orientated (OO) framework for developing complex interacting DES models. The *DE-Sim* authors argue that their OO framework is an advancement over *SimPy*'s process-based worldview; although we note that *SimPy* itself is highly flexible and can easily be used within an OO framework; for example see (Allen et al. 2020).

2.2 FOSS: Barriers and initiatives in DES

For modellers used to working with COTS simulation tools, the switch to FOSS and code based DES models can be daunting, costly, and challenging (Monks and Harper 2023a). In other data science disciplines, such as machine learning, there is extensive community support, package documentation, applied examples, and dedicated code repositories available. A critical mass of equivalent materials that lowers the cost of entry to FOSS DES is not yet available; although there are positive signs that support is beginning to build in simulation. One example that supports FOSS for Agent Based Simulation is CoMSES.net[1]. The initiative includes a model library linking to a large number of ABS models

[1]https://www.comses.net

typically developed in NetLogo (and in October 2024, there were 1162 models: 61% NetLogo and 7% Python, etc). Taking a different approach, the Sharing Tools and Artefacts for Reusable Simulations (STARS) framework for healthcare aims to support simulation researchers to share a version of their FOSS computer simulation model that is accessible and reusable by others (Monks et al. 2024). STARS provides details of both architecture to share models, and also published applied examples of Python models for others to adapt and reuse. A software-specific initiative to highlight is the extensive and growing documentation to *Ciw*[2] that now contains over 40 topics of support (as of October 2024). Another software-specific intiative provides a tutorial to use *Streamlit* to build a browser based user-interface to Python models (Monks and Harper 2023b). Lastly, in the UK, the NIHR Applied Research Collaboration South West Peninsula funds the Health Service Modelling Associates Programme[3] that has developed the "Little Book of DES" (https://des.hsma.co.uk/). The book teaches simulation methods to the NHS using Python and *Simpy*.

3 TUTORIAL OVERVIEW AND SETUP

3.1 Aims

Given the relatively low use of FOSS in healthcare DES relative to COTS (Monks and Harper 2023a) and the documented barriers to entry for new users, we provide introductory tutorial materials to using Python for DES. Our materials are a starting place for modellers looking to use Python in their DES studies. The materials are most suitable for individuals familiar with DES and coding. Although we use Python, the introductory nature of the material should make them accessible to individuals with experience in different coding languages such as R, Julia, Java, C etc. We also aim to make the example simulation code included in our tutorial simple for others to run and not require direct installation on their machine. Given the introductory level of the tutorial, we make several simplifications to the code that would need to be addressed in real studies. We discuss these limitations in the final section and provide more advanced supplementary material illustrating how code could be improved.

3.2 Case study model

This case study uses a simple model of an urgent care telephone call centre, similar to the NHS 111 service in the UK (NHS 2024). In this model, calls to the centre arrive randomly and operators handle them on a first-in-first-out basis. It does not include features like reneging, time dependency, shift work, or referrals and callbacks from medical or nursing practitioners. The simulation time units are in minutes. On average there are 100 new callers per hour (an inter-arrival time of 60.0 / 100 per minute). There are 13 caller operators available. Table 1 lists the statistical distributions and their parameters for the two activities in the model.

Table 1: Case study distributions.

Activity	**Distribution**
Inter-arrival time of callers	Exponential(mean = 60.0 / 100)
Call triage by operator	Triangular(low = 5.0, mode = 7.0, high = 10.0)

3.3 Simulation software

This tutorial uses *SimPy*: a popular FOSS DES package in Python with a process-based simulation worldview. To build a DES model in SimPy, users define Python generator functions (described in Section 5.3) and implement logic to request and release resources. Although *SimPy* provides a full DES engine, it does not contain some of the additional features offered by COTS packages - for example, the user interfaces available with *Arena* or *Simul8*. However, *SimPy* is a lightweight, flexible tool that can be integrated with the rest of the Python data science ecosystem.

It has been used to model a wide variety of health condition pathways and healthcare operations. For example, COVID-19 (Anagnostou et al. 2022, Bovim et al. 2023), renal services (Allen et al. 2020), stroke (Ren et al. 2021, Ren et al. 2020), heart failure (Wise et al. 2021), cancer care (Richardson

[2]https://ciw.readthedocs.io

[3]https://sites.google.com/nihr.ac.uk/hsma/hsma-resources

and Cohn 2018), end-of-life care (Chalk et al. 2021), and operating theatre management (Hassanzadeh et al. 2023, Harper et al. 2023).

3.4 Availability of code and materials

In following sections, we provide step-by-step code to build the case study model, which is explained in detail. Whilst code listings are included in this paper, we strongly recommend using the interactive online materials, if you are interested in building the model. These materials are shared as notebooks using JupyterLite (v0.4) with the Xeus-Python kernel[4]. The notebooks run in a pre-built Python environment in Jupyter-Lab, a popular notebook integrated development environment (IDE). JupyterLite is powered by WebAssembly, that allows readers to run and modify our Python code examples in their browser without having to install Python or *SimPy* locally. Our interactive materials are available at this URL: https://pythonhealthdatascience.github.io/intro-open-sim/. Alternatively the Jupyter notebooks can be downloaded directly from our GitHub repository https://github.com/pythonhealthdatascience/intro-open-sim. The version of the code used in this tutorial is archived at Zenodo (Monks et al. 2025). All code was developed in Python 3.11 and *SimPy* 4.1.1 (Team SimPy 2020).

3.5 Structure of tutorial

The tutorial is organised into the following sections:

- **Section 4**: Introduces the basic tools to model variability in Python via the *NumPy* library.
- **Section 5**: Creates a basic *SimPy* model to simulate the arrival process.
- **Section 6**: Adds queuing and service components to the model.
- **Section 7**: Adds basic result collection logic to the model.
- **Section 8**: Discusses where a reader should look next in their studies as well as highlighting some additional resources available in our online supplementary material.

4 MODELLING VARIABILITY IN PYTHON

In our call centre model, there is variation in (a) the time spent waiting for an operator, (b) the duration of the call, and (c) the time interval between successive callers. We model this using standard statistical distributions such as the uniform and exponential distributions. In Python, the *NumPy* packages provide an efficient and user-friendly implementation of many statistical distributions. For example, in Listing 1, we draw one million samples from a **uniform** distribution.

- **Line 1**: Imports the *NumPy* package and aliases it as *np*.
- **Line 3**: Creates a Pseudo-Random Number Generator (PRNG; using the seed 42). This is a standard approach in *NumPy* and makes use of the Permuted Congruential Generator 64-bit (PCG64; period = 2^{128}; maximum number of streams = 2^{127}).
- **Line 4**: Uses the PRNG object to create one million samples and stores the results in a *NumPy* array called samples.

Here we used the **uniform** method of the PRNG object, but we could have **similarly** used the exponential method.

```
1 import numpy as np
2
3 rng = np.random.default_rng(42) # define arrivals PRNG
4 samples = rng.uniform(low=10, high=40, size=1_000_000)
```

Listing 1: Efficient sampling using the *NumPy* package

[4]https://xeus-python.readthedocs.io/en/latest

5 MODELLING AN ARRIVAL PROCESS

In our initial *SimPy* model, we have only included the arrivals of new callers (and excluded all queuing and service, which we add in Section 6). The model code is provided in Listing 2 and explained in Sections 5.1 to 5.4.

```
1 import numpy as np
2 import simpy
3
4
5 def arrivals_generator(env):
6     """Model caller arrival process."""
7     arrival_rng = np.random.default_rng()
8
9     while True:
10         inter_arrival_time = arrival_rng.exponential(60.0 / 100.0)
11         yield env.timeout(inter_arrival_time)
12         print(f"Call arrives at: {env.now}")
13
14
15 # model parameters
16 RUN_LENGTH = 100
17
18 # create the simpy environment object
19 env = simpy.Environment()
20
21 # tell simpy that the 'arrival_generator' is a process to model
22 env.process(arrivals_generator(env))
23
24 # run the simulation model
25 env.run(until=RUN_LENGTH)
26 print(f"end of run. simulation clock time = {env.now}")
```

Listing 2: Modelling caller arrivals

5.1 The environment

SimPy processes execute in an **environment**. In *SimPy* models, the environment is the DES engine. Once an environment is created, users can access its attributes (such as the current simulation time) and methods (for example, creating a new process or running the model). In Listing 2, Line 2 imports the *SimPy* package. Using *SimPy*, Line 19 creates an instance of an environment that is assigned to a variable called `env`.

5.2 Delays

We can include **delays** or **activities** within a *SimPy* process model. For example, these might be the duration of a patient's stay on a ward or the duration of an operation. In this case, we introduce a time between arrival events (inter-arrival time). In Listing 2, an inter-arrival time is sampled on Line 10. This is used on Line 11 to create a delay via the `timeout` method of the environment object `env`. Model logic can access the simulation time before and after delays using `env.now` (e.g. line 12).

5.3 Processes

In *SimPy*, the event-process mechanism is implemented using Python **generators**. A generator is a Python object that can return a sequence of values; for example, a sequence of times between patient arrivals. A simple way to visualise the arrival processes in *SimPy* is as an infinite loop of delays, where each delay represents the time until the next arrival. Unlike a standard Python loop, a generator can be paused and resumed at later time, making it ideal for event-scheduling in *SimPy*.

For each arrival process in our model, we create a new generator process. In Listing 2, we have created a single arrival process (for callers) modelled by the generator function `arrivals_generator` (Lines 5 to 12). The generator function contains an infinite loop (here implemented as a **while** loop). On each iteration, a new inter-arrival time is sampled from the Exponential distribution and an environment timeout (delay) of the same duration is yielded. The keyword **yield** before the timeout is essential in Listing 2 Line 11: it is needed to tell the Python interpreter that the function is a Python generator. On line 11 `yield` is combined with `env.timeout()` to schedule the end of the event (the next caller arrival).

5.4 The setup script

In Listing 2, Lines 16 to 26 setup and run the DES model. Two new concepts are introduced here. Line 22 configures *SimPy* to execute `arrivals_generator` as a **process**. Line 25 run the model until the simulation clock reaches time 100 (i.e. generate arrivals until that time).

6 MODELLING A SERVICE PROCESS

We now expand the model to include a resource-bound service process: speaking with an operator. To do this we will:

1. Add a Python generator called `service` which contains the queuing and call activity logic (Listing 3).
2. Create a *SimPy* resource called `operator` (Listing 4)
3. Modify `arrivals_generator` to create and schedule the `service` process, which uses `operator`, as each caller arrives to the model (Listing 4).

6.1 A service generator

Listing 3 implements a simple *SimPy* process model of calls queuing for service with one of a set of call operator resources. We have implemented the following logic in the `service` process:

1. A caller service process requests a call operator resource. If none are available, the caller process waits in a queue.
2. Once an operator resource becomes available, the call process is assigned and undergoes a phone triage (represented as a delay). The duration of this delay is sampled from a triangular distribution.
3. After the call process is completed, the operator resource is released, and the caller process exits the model.

```
def service(identifier, operators, env, service_rng):
    """Simulates the service process for a call operator"""

    # record the time that call entered the queue
    start_wait = env.now

    # request an operator
    with operators.request() as req:
        yield req

        # record the waiting time for call to be answered
        waiting_time = env.now - start_wait
        print(f"operator answered call {identifier} at " + f"{env.now:.3f}")

        # sample call duration.
        call_duration = service_rng.triangular(left=5.0, mode=7.0, right=10.0)

        # schedule process to begin again after call_duration
        yield env.timeout(call_duration)

        # print out information for patient.
        print(
            f"call {identifier} ended {env.now:.3f}; "
```

```
24             + f"waiting time was {waiting_time:.3f}"
25         )
```

Listing 3: Modelling caller queuing and service time

6.1.1 Parameters

The `service` generator accepts four parameters (as in Line 1 of Listing 3):

- `identifier`: a unique caller ID.
- `operators`: the *SimPy* resource representing the call operators.
- `env`: the simulation environment object.
- `service_rng`: the PRNG for service processes. It provides the stream of random numbers used to sample service times.

6.1.2 Requesting, seizing, and releasing a resource

The pattern of seizing and releasing a resource in `service_process` in Listing 3 is typical of how simple queue and service mechanism is implemented in *SimPy* models.

Line 8 uses Python's **with** statement to open a context manager, which managers the request queuing, seizing and releasing of a *SimPy* resource. It calls the **request** method of the `operator` resource and assigns it to a variable called `req`. The subsequent lines are then indented by four spaces, which tells the Python interpreter that all of the code within the **with** block executes **while holding on to the seized resource**.

Line 9 **yields** the request - this simulates the queuing in the process. The process will pause at Line 9 until an operator resource becomes available (for example, when another call completes). When an operator becomes available Line 12 to 19 are executed. Line 19 simulates the delay to the caller while being triaged by an operator. The *SimPy* simulation engine will pause the process at Line 19. *SimPy* will check if there are any other processes due to complete before this time i.e. new caller arrivals or completion of other calls and resume those first. Once these are complete the service process for this caller will resume.

6.2 Starting a service process after an arrival

Before modifying the arrival process (in Listing 2), it is important to understand the relationship between the arrival and service process in the *SimPy* model. The arrival process spawns multiple instances of the service process - one for each new arrival - and so this can be thought of as **a one-to-many relationship**. To simulate queuing, the multiple service processes share a common resource (the operators). *SimPy* manages all of these processes for you. It pauses and resumes them depending on if operators are available or if a delay is scheduled.

Listing 4 illustrates a modified arrivals process. The following modifications have been made:

1. A *SimPy* resource called `operator` is passed to the `arrivals_generator` (Line 6).
2. A second pseudo-random number stream called `service_rng` is created (Line 12).
3. The arrivals loop is modified to count the number of callers that have arrived (`caller_count`)(Line 15).
4. After a call has arrived, a service process is created and scheduled (Line 21).

```
1 import numpy as np
2 import itertools
3 import simpy
4
5
6 def arrivals_generator(env, operators):
7
8     # create the arrival process rng
9     arrival_rng = np.random.default_rng()
10
```

```
11     # create the service rng that we pass to each service process created
12     service_rng = np.random.default_rng()
13
14     # with a counter variable that we can use for unique Ids
15     for caller_count in itertools.count(start=1):
16         inter_arrival_time = arrival_rng.exponential(60.0 / 100.0)
17         yield env.timeout(inter_arrival_time)
18         print(f"call arrives at: {env.now:.3f}")
19
20         # create a new simpy process for serving this caller.
21         env.process(service(caller_count, operators, env, service_rng))
22
23
24 # model parameters
25 RUN_LENGTH = 100
26 N_OPERATORS = 13
27
28 # create simpy environment and operator resources
29 env = simpy.Environment()
30 operators = simpy.Resource(env, capacity=N_OPERATORS)
31
32 env.process(arrivals_generator(env, operators))
33 env.run(until=RUN_LENGTH)
34 print(f"end of run. simulation clock time = {env.now}")
```

Listing 4: A modified arrival process and run script used to created service processes

6.2.1 A second pseudo-random number stream

For each sampling process in the model, it is good practice to include a unique PRNG. Although it is out of scope for this introductory tutorial, this practice is particularly useful if we later want to implement Common Random Numbers across experiments with the model (as described in Section 8.3.1).

In Listing 4, Line 12 creates a second PRNG `service_rng` to use with service processes. This is created *before* the main arrivals loop as we only need to create one PRNG that is shared across all service processes.

6.2.2 Counting callers

We use the built-in Python library *itertools* (imported on Line 2) to count the number of callers. This is implemented inside the **for** loop on Line 15, with the variable `caller_count` referring to arrival number of the next caller.

6.2.3 Scheduling a service process for each arrival

Line 21 schedules a new service process for each arrival. This is done using the `env.process` method, and its argument is a new instance of a `service` process. The call to create the process includes the current unique caller number (`caller_count`), the shared *SimPy* resource for call operators (`operators`), the simulation environment (`env`), and the PRNG for sampling (`service_rng`). The line is indented within the arrivals loop, ensuring that a new service process is created for every arrival.

6.3 Creating a *SimPy* resource

In Listing 4, Lines 25 to 34 represent a modified script to run the model. In Line 30, we create an instance of *SimPy*'s Resource class called `operators` and set its capacity to 13. This object represents the call operators used across all service processes in the model. In Line 32, we schedule the arrival process and pass the `operators` resource as a parameter.

7 BASIC RESULTS COLLECTION

As *SimPy* models are just Python code, there are many ways to implement results collection. Three possible ways include:

1. **Code an auditor/observer process**. This process will periodically observe the state of the system. We can use this to collect information on the current state at time t. For example, how many callers are queuing and how many have a call in progress, at certain timepoints throughout the day.
2. **Store process metrics during a run and perform calculations at the end of a run**. For example, if you want to calculate mean patient waiting time then store each caller waiting time in a list and calculate the mean at the end of the run.
3. **Monitor resources to calculate time weighted statistics**. Resource utilisation and mean queue length can be tracked as resources are requested and released. This is more a advanced approach to results collection that requires both knowledge of theory and Object Orientated Programming to implement. The method is beyond the scope of our tutorial, but we provide an example implementation in our online supplementary material.

In this tutorial, we will calculate the mean waiting time for a single replication of the model using method 2. To do this we will make the following modifications to the code:

- Replace all calls to Python's print function with a custom `trace` function that can be used to toggle the display of model output on or off.
- Create a Python **dictionary** called `results` that will store all waiting times for service. For simplicity, we will give this global variable scope.
- Modify `service` to calculate caller waiting times and store these in `results`.
- Create a function called `single_run` that will run the model once and return the mean waiting time as a result.

7.1 Modifying the service process

Listing 5 contains the modifications to the `service` generator for recording wait times:

- **Line 17**: Computes the waiting time (current simulation time minus the arrival time, which we already recorded on Line 10).
- **Line 18**: Stores this time in `results` (the global dictionary) by appending to a list stored under the key `waiting_times`.

Lines 20 and 25 are also modified to call the function `trace`, defined in Lines 1 to 4. This simple function prints output messages depending on whether a constant called `TRACE` is set to true or false.

```
1  def trace(msg):
2      """Wrap print function to toggle simulation printed output on/off"""
3      if TRACE:
4          print(msg)
5
6
7  def service(identifier, operators, env, service_rng):
8      """Simulates the service process for a call operator"""
9      # record the time that call entered the queue
10     start_wait = env.now
11
12     # request an operator
13     with operators.request() as req:
14         yield req
15
16         # record the waiting time for call to be answered
17         waiting_time = env.now - start_wait
18         results["waiting_times"].append(waiting_time)
```

```

        trace(f"operator answered call {identifier} at " + f"{env.now:.3f}")

        call_duration = service_rng.triangular(left=5.0, mode=7.0, right=10.0)
        yield env.timeout(call_duration)

        trace(
            f"call {identifier} ended {env.now:.3f}; "
            + f"waiting time was {waiting_time:.3f}"
        )
```

Listing 5: Setup of results collection mode

7.2 A run function and global variables

In Listing 6, our original code to create the simulation environment and run the model has been encapsulated into the function `single_run` (Lines 1 to 13). It also has some additional end-of-replication result processing; in this case, finding the mean of all the recorded waiting times.

The advantage of encapsulating a single replication of the model in a function is that we can now easily run multiple independent replications: by creating a loop repeatedly calling `single_run`, and storing the results of each replication as it iterates. In this instance we only run a single replication of the model. We do so by modifying the run script (Lines 17 to 26). We provide example code to run and analyse multiple replications in our supplementary material (see `07_experiments.ipynb`).

We also create the `results` dictionary on Lines 17 and 18, with the key `waiting_times` pointing to an empty Python List. This is the results global variable that is referenced in `service`.

```
1  def single_run(run_length, n_operators):
2      """Perform a single replication of the simulation model and
3      return the mean waiting time as a result"""
4      env = simpy.Environment()
5      operators = simpy.Resource(env, capacity=n_operators)
6
7      env.process(arrivals_generator(env, operators))
8      env.run(until=run_length)
9      print(f"end of run. simulation clock time = {env.now}")
10
11     # Calculate results on notebook level variables.
12     mean_waiting_time = np.mean(results["waiting_times"])
13     return mean_waiting_time
14
15
16 # script to run the model
17 results = {}
18 results["waiting_times"] = []
19
20 # toggle event logging to "off"
21 TRACE = False
22
23 # model parameters
24 RUN_LENGTH = 1000
25 N_OPERATORS = 13
26
27 mean_waiting_time = single_run(RUN_LENGTH, N_OPERATORS)
28 print("Simulation Complete")
29 print(f"Waiting time for call operators: {mean_waiting_time:.2f} minutes")
```

Listing 6: Modifications to collect basic waiting time results

8 DISCUSSION AND NEXT STEPS

This paper provides an introductory tutorial for building healthcare DES models in Python and *SimPy*. It aims to provide modellers familiar with DES and coding the basic materials to begin building their own *SimPy* FOSS models.

The model introduced is only elementary and does not fully reflect the complexities seen in real health systems, or the requirements of rigorous reproducible simulation research. For some aspects of DES modelling, the extensions are trivial and our materials can be adapted. We provide several simple, intermediate and advanced extensions below.

8.1 Simple Extensions

8.1.1 Multiple arrival processes

In some healthcare problems, there will be multiple patient types with differing arrival rates. For example, Griffiths et al. (2010) develop a DES model of a Critical Care Unit. In their model, patients arrive from six sources at differing rates: emergency department, x-ray, emergency surgery, inter-hospital transfers, and elective operations. To model this in *SimPy*, we can create six arrival processes each with their own PRNG and sampling distribution. We would also modify `single_run` to schedule these six generators to run in the *SimPy* DES engine.

8.1.2 Service processes dependent on patient class

Some health systems may share a common patient arrival process, but then have multiple patient classes, each with different treatment processes. A common way to model this problem is to include probabilities that each type of arrival is a different class of patient that follows a specific process. For example, in an urgent care centre, there might be a 10% chance a new patient has trauma injuries and a 90% chance that a patient has a medical emergency. The processes that each class of urgent care patient follows will be very different (for example, trauma patients may need urgent stabilisation/resuscitation and medical patients may just need to follow a less urgent triage and medical consultation process). Our example can be extended by creating two service generator functions encapsulating each process. We would then modify the arrivals generator to (a) sample the class of patient arriving and (b) include conditional logic (a Python if statement) to schedule the appropriate service process. We provide an example of an extended version of the call centre model in our online supplementary material (see the `08_full_model.ipynb` notebook).

8.1.3 Introducing a warm-up period

To remove initialisation bias from the output of a non-terminating system, a model should include a warm-up period. At the end of a warm-up period, all result collection processes should be reset. Implementing a warm-up in *SimPy* requires a modeller to i.) partition the run length parameter of the model into durations for warm-up and data collection; and ii.) create a new *SimPy* process that is scheduled to execute when the simulation time equals the warm-up time. We provide an example of implementing a warm-up period in our online supplementary material (see the `08_full_model.ipynb` notebook).

8.2 Intermediate Extensions

8.2.1 Separating parameters from model logic

In our simple tutorial, we passed parameters and simulation objects (e.g. number of operators, simulation environment, PRNGs) as individual arguments to the functions and generators we code. We also limited the number of parameters we needed to pass by hard coding parameters for distributions (e.g. the parameters for the triangular distribution in Listing 3). In a real simulation study, there may be tens or hundreds of parameters (including data files) that a modeller wishes to vary for experimentation, sensitivity analysis or optimisation. It is impractical to pass these individually to each function and generator used in the modelling.

Several options in Python exist for separating parameters from model logic including dictionaries, dataclasses and classes. Our recommendation is to create an `Experiment` class that we pass to the `single_run` (or multiple replications) function. This class should contain default values and a way to quickly set all of the parameters. By using a class, the number of parameters passed to each function within a model is minimal (as low as one: the `Experiment` object). When using this approach, we would also recommend eliminating all global variables (which have only been included in our tutorial for simplicity). Monks and Harper (2023b) provide an advanced tutorial describing this object-oriented approach using classes, and apply it to both *SimPy* and *Ciw* models. We provide an applied example using an `Experiment` class in our supplementary online material (see the `07_experiments.ipynb` notebook).

8.2.2 Time dependent arrival rates

It is common to encounter time dependency in the arrival of patients to healthcare systems; for example, following a Non-Stationary Poisson Process (NSPP). Unlike COTS packages, tools like *SimPy* do not include built-in algorithms for sampling from a NSPP such as thinning or from a piece-wise linear function. A modeller is therefore required to implement these algorithms themselves. To help, we direct users to applied example 2 in Monks et al. (2024), which includes an implementation of NSPP via thinning.

8.3 Advanced Extensions

8.3.1 Common Random Numbers

Common Random Numbers (CRN) - also known as streaming - is a variance reduction approach: a method to reduce the variation (sampling noise) between experiments conducted with a simulation model. We note that CRN are not essential for simulation research but, on a practical level, CRN reduce both the number of replications that need to be run to compare experiments, and help support repeatable results for each replication of a model. In this tutorial, we have taken some steps to implement CRN by introducing a PRNG for each sampling process included (arrivals and service). To fully implement CRN, a method is needed to create non-overlapping streams of PRNs for each replication. In Python, *NumPy's* PRNG tools can be used to spawn non-overlapping streams for each replication with only a small amount of code. For an example implementation of this approach, we again refer readers to Applied Example 2 in Monks et al. (2024). We also provide an applied example using CRN in our supplementary online material (see the `07_experiments.ipynb` notebook).

8.3.2 Reproducible pipelines and experiments

Reproducible analytical pipelines (RAPs), in the context of model experimentation, are automated processes for the parameterisation, execution, output analysis, and reporting of simulation models. For example, imagine a journal article that reports the results of two experiments with our urgent care call centre. Each experiment produces a formatted table of performance measures. A RAP here would reproduce the exact figures reported in the table (including potentially LaTeX formatting). The RAP would parameterise the model, run it in an identical software environment, use the same random number streams, analyse the results, and report tables identical to those found in the journal article. Code-based models such as those built in *SimPy* lend themselves to a RAP approach (which is good science), but require more time to develop as code will need to be structured appropriately.

9 SUMMARY

Our aim in this tutorial is to support modellers in their journey to build and share FOSS DES models. When compared to DES models built using COTS packages, FOSS models are still relatively rare. We hope this tutorial will be part of the solution to increase the FOSS DES prevalence in the literature. This is because we feel that - in order for the modelling and simulation community to learn and adopt the skills needed to build FOSS models - we need to build a critical mass of open models. As discussed, the tutorial we provide is only introductory, but it is relatively simple to extend our work to health systems with more detailed processes and patient pathways. We hope that the intermediate and advanced next steps we outline also open readers to new ideas, such as RAPs, and an understanding of how their DES models work and could be organised.

ACKNOWLEDGMENTS

TM is supported by the NIHR Applied Research Collaboration South West Peninsula. The views expressed in this publication are those of the author(s) and not necessarily those of the NIHR or the Department of Health and Social Care.

FUNDING

This work was supported by the Medical Research Council [MR/Z503915/1].

REFERENCES

Allen, M., A. Bhanji, J. Willemsen, S. Dudfield, S. Logan, and T. Monks. 2020. "A simulation modelling toolkit for organising outpatient dialysis services during the COVID-19 pandemic". *PLoS One* 15 (8): e0237628.

Anagnostou, A., D. Groen, S. J. Taylor, D. Suleimenova, N. Abubakar, A. Saha, K. Mintram, M. Ghorbani, H. Daroge, T. Islam, Y. Xue, E. Okine, and N. Anokye. 2022. "FACS-CHARM: A Hybrid Agent-Based and Discrete-Event Simulation Approach for Covid-19 Management at Regional Level". In *2022 Winter Simulation Conference (WSC)*, 1223–1234.

Bovim, T. R., A. N. Gullhav, H. Andersson, J. Dale, and K. Karlsen. 2021, December. "Simulating emergency patient flow during the COVID-19 pandemic". *Journal of Simulation* 0 (0): 1–15. Publisher: Taylor & Francis _eprint: https://doi.org/10.1080/17477778.2021.2015259.

Bovim, T. R., A. N. Gullhav, H. Andersson, J. Dale, and K. Karlsen. 2023. "Simulating emergency patient flow during the COVID-19 pandemic". *Journal of Simulation* 17 (4): 407–421.

Chalk, D., S. Robbins, R. Kandasamy, K. Rush, A. Aggarwal, R. Sullivan, and C. Chamberlain. 2021. "Modelling palliative and end-of-life resource requirements during COVID-19: implications for quality care". *BMJ open* 11 (5): e043795.

Dagkakis, G., and C. Heavey. 2016. "A review of open source discrete event simulation software for operations research". *Journal of Simulation* 10 (3): 193–206.

Forbus, J. J., and D. Berleant. 2022. "Discrete-Event Simulation in Healthcare Settings: A Review". *Modelling* 3 (4): 417–433.

Goldberg, A. P., and J. R. Karr. 2020. "DE-Sim: an object-oriented, discrete-event simulation tool for data-intensive modeling of complex systems in Python". *Journal of Open Source Software* 5 (55): 2685.

Griffiths, J. D., M. Jones, M. Read, and J. E. Williams. 2010. "A simulation model of bed-occupancy in a critical care unit". *Journal of Simulation* 4 (1): 52–59.

Harper, A., T. Monks, R. Wilson, M. T. Redaniel, E. Eyles, T. Jones, C. Penfold, A. Elliott, T. Keen, M. Pitt et al. 2023. "Development and application of simulation modelling for orthopaedic elective resource planning in England". *BMJ open* 13 (12): e076221.

Hassanzadeh, H., J. Boyle, S. Khanna, B. Biki, F. Syed, L. Sweeney, and E. Borkwood. 2023. "A discrete event simulation for improving operating theatre efficiency". *The International Journal of Health Planning and Management* 38 (2): 360–379.

McInnes, A. I., and B. R. Thorne. 2011. "ScipySim: Towards Distributed Heterogeneous System Simulation for the SciPy Platform".

Monks, T., and A. Harper. 2023a. "Computer model and code sharing practices in healthcare discrete-event simulation: a systematic scoping review". *Journal of Simulation* 0 (0): 1–16. Publisher: Taylor & Francis _eprint: https://doi.org/10.1080/17477778.2023.2260772.

Monks, T., and A. Harper. 2023b. "Improving the usability of open health service delivery simulation models using Python and web apps". *NIHR Open Research* 3:48.

Monks, Thomas and Harper, Alison and Heather, Amy 2025, February. "An introduction to Discrete-Event Simulation using Free and Open Source Software".

Monks, T., A. Harper, and N. Mustafee. 2024. "Towards sharing tools and artefacts for reusable simulations in healthcare". *Journal of Simulation* 0 (0): 1–20.

NHS 2024. "NHS 111 Online Service". https://111.nhs.uk/. Accessed: 2024-10-10.

Palmer, Geraint and Tian, Yawen 2021a, March. "Source code for Ciw hybrid simulations.".
Palmer, G. I. et al. 2019. "Ciw: An open-source discrete event simulation library". *Journal of Simulation* 13 (1): 68–82.
Palmer, G. I., and Y. Tian. 2021b. "Implementing hybrid simulations that integrate DES+ SD in Python". *Journal of Simulation*:1–17.
Pfeiffer, A. et al. 2012. "PySimulator–A simulation and analysis environment in Python with plugin infrastructure".
Ren, Y., M. Phan, P. Luong, J. Wu, D. Shell, C. D. Barras, S. Chryssidis, H. K. Kok, M. Burney, B. Tahayori, J. Maingard, A. Jhamb, V. Thijs, D. M. Brooks, and H. Asadi. 2021. "Application of a computational model in simulating an endovascular clot retrieval service system within regional Australia". *Journal of Medical Imaging and Radiation Oncology* 65 (7): 850–857.
Ren, Y., M. Phan, P. Luong, J. Wu, D. Shell, C. D. Barras, H. K. Kok, M. Burney, B. Tahayori, H. M. Seah, J. Maingard, K. Zhou, A. Lamanna, A. Jhamb, V. Thijs, D. M. Brooks, and H. Asadi. 2020. "Geographic Service Delivery for Endovascular Clot Retrieval: Using Discrete Event Simulation to Optimize Resources". *World Neurosurgery* 141:e400–e413.
Richardson, D. B., and A. E. M. Cohn. 2018. "MODELING THE IMPACT OF MAKE-AHEAD CHEMOTHERAPY DRUG POLICIES THROUGH DISCRETE-EVENT SIMULATION". In *2018 Winter Simulation Conference (WSC)*, 2690–2700.
Roy, S., S. P. Venkatesan, and M. Goh. 2021. "Healthcare services: A systematic review of patient-centric logistics issues using simulation". *Journal of the Operational Research Society* 72 (10): 2342–2364.
Salleh, S., P. Thokala, A. Brennan, R. Hughes, and A. Booth. 2017. "Simulation Modelling in Healthcare: An Umbrella Review of Systematic Literature Reviews". *PharmacoEconomics* 35 (9): 937–949.
Team SimPy 2020. "SimPy 3.0.11". https://simpy.readthedocs.io/en/latest/index.html.
van der Ham, R. 2018. "Salabim: open source discrete event simulation and animation in python". In *Proceedings of the 2018 Winter Simulation Conference*, 4186–4187.
Vázquez-Serrano, J. I., R. E. Peimbert-García, and L. E. Cárdenas-Barrón. 2021. "Discrete-Event Simulation Modeling in Healthcare: A Comprehensive Review". *International Journal of Environmental Research and Public Health* 18 (22): 12262.
Wise, A. F., L. E. Morgan, A. Heib, C. S. Currie, A. Champneys, R. Nadarajah, C. Gale, and M. Mamas. 2021. "Modeling Of Waiting Lists For Chronic Heart Failure In The Wake Of The COVID-19 Pandemic". In *2021 Winter Simulation Conference (WSC)*, 1–11.

AUTHOR BIOGRAPHIES

THOMAS MONKS is an Associate Professor of Health Data Science at University of Exeter Medical School. His research interests include open science for computer simulation, urgent and emergency care, and real-time discrete-event simulation. His email address is t.m.w.monks@exeter.ac.uk

ALISON HARPER is a lecturer in operations and analytics at the Centre for Simulation, Analytics and Modelling, University of Exeter. Her research interests include applied health and social care modelling and simulation, real-time simulation, and reusable modelling in healthcare. Her email address is a.l.harper@exeter.ac.uk

AMY HEATHER is a Postdoctoral Research Associate the Peninsula Collaboration for Health Operational Research and Data Science (PenCHORD) at the University of Exeter. Her research interests include health data science and open science. Her email address is a.heather2@exeter.ac.uk

ANDREW MAYNE is Chief Scientist for Data, Operational Research and Artificial Intelligence at Somerset NHS Foundation Trust. He is also Chief Technology Officer for the South West Secure Data Environment. His interests are in admission prediction and simulation modelling of patient pathways in the NHS. His email address is andrew.mayne@somersetft.nhs.uk

NAVONIL MUSTAFEE is Professor of Analytics and Operations Management at the University of Exeter Business School, UK. His research focuses on modelling and simulation methodologies, including hybrid modelling and real-time simulation, and their application in healthcare, supply chain management, circular economy and climate change adaptation and resilience. He is a Joint Editor-in-Chief of the Journal of Simulation (UK OR Society journal). His email address is n.mustafee@exeter.ac.uk

Proceedings of the Operational Research Society Simulation Workshop 2025 (SW25)
M. Luis, A. Harper, T. Monks and, N. Mustafee, eds.
https://doi.org/10.36819/SW25.005

WANT TO BUILD A MOONBASE? THE SIMULATION EXPLORATION EXPERIENCE (SEE)

Maziar Ghorbani
Simon J. E. Taylor
Nura T. Abubakar
Hridyanshu Aatreya
Anastasia Anagnostou

Brunel University London
Modeling & Simulation Group
Department of Computer Science
Uxbridge, UB8 3PH, UK
maziar.ghorbani@brunel.ac.uk

Damon Curry

Pitch Technologies US
37 North Orange Avenue
Suite 545
Orlando, Florida FL, 32801 USA
damon.curry@pitchtechologies.com

ABSTRACT

The Simulation Exploration Experience (SEE) is an annual international initiative that brings together teams of students, researchers, and professionals to collaboratively design and implement distributed simulations for space exploration. The project allows student teams from universities worldwide to develop and integrate simulations of critical systems such as transportation, communication, and resource management. This paper outlines how students design and contribute to different aspects of the moonbase simulation, utilizing High-Level Architecture (HLA) for simulation interoperability and integrating 3D visualizations. Additionally, it highlights the educational benefits of the SEE, offering students hands-on experience in distributed simulation technologies, space mission planning, and collaborative problem-solving, with support from NASA volunteers, the Simulation Interoperability Standards Organization (SISO), and other industry partners.

1 INTRODUCTION

For over a decade, the Simulation Exploration Experience (SEE) (SEE, 2019, 2024) has run annually, enabling teams of researchers, graduates, and undergraduate students to collaborate in building a distributed simulation of a moonbase and its associated elements, such as drones, robots, spaceships, and satellite networks. SEE is supported by volunteers from NASA, the Simulation Interoperability Standards Organization (SISO) (Möller et al., 2020), universities, and industry partners. Student teams from around the world gain hands-on experience with distributed simulation technologies and develop expertise in the High-Level Architecture (HLA) for simulation interoperability (Taylor, 2019).

Distributed simulation (Okan Topçu, 2017) is a method of simulating complex systems by integrating multiple independent components across different locations. These simulations rely on a networked framework, where each component (or federate) interacts in real-time while being managed by a central simulation infrastructure. Distributed simulation is widely used in defence, aerospace, and space exploration, where large-scale, interconnected systems must operate cohesively (Dahmann, Fujimoto, and Weatherly, 1997). SEE provides students with practical exposure to these concepts, allowing them to experiment with HLA, a key standard for enabling simulation interoperability.

This paper provides an overview for educators and students about the SEE and the process of creating a distributed simulation of a lunar habitat using HLA. Section 1 introduces the SEE program and its goals. Section 2 provides background information on HLA exploring the technologies used in the SEE project. Section 4 discusses the Baseball Card and Interaction Matrix as tools for federate conceptualization and communication. Section 5 guides readers on getting started with SEE and running a federate locally. Section 6 provides more details on transitioning from local to remote communications. Finally, Section 7 concludes the paper with key takeaways.

2 BACKGROUND

The High-Level Architecture (HLA) was developed to simplify and standardise the creation of distributed and interoperable simulations. It defines a set of standards that ensure different simulation components can communicate effectively. These include integration rules, a Runtime Infrastructure (RTI) for managing data exchange (IEEE, 2010b), an Object Model Template (OMT) for structuring shared data, and a development process to guide implementation (IEEE, 2010a).

The Simulation Interoperability Standards Organization (SISO) (Möller et al., 2020) serves as the primary community supporting and advancing HLA. Like many industry standards, HLA benefits from an active community that drives its evolution. SISO plays a key role in maintaining and refining the standard, with a new version currently in development (Crues et al., 2022), while also contributing to the creation of domain-specific standards to enhance simulation interoperability across different fields.

Figure 1 illustrates the key components of an HLA-based distributed simulation, including the federates and their interactions. One crucial element shown is the RTI Ambassador, which serves as the interface between a federate and the RTI. The RTI Ambassador allows federates to send and receive simulation data, interact with other federates, and synchronize execution according to HLA rules.

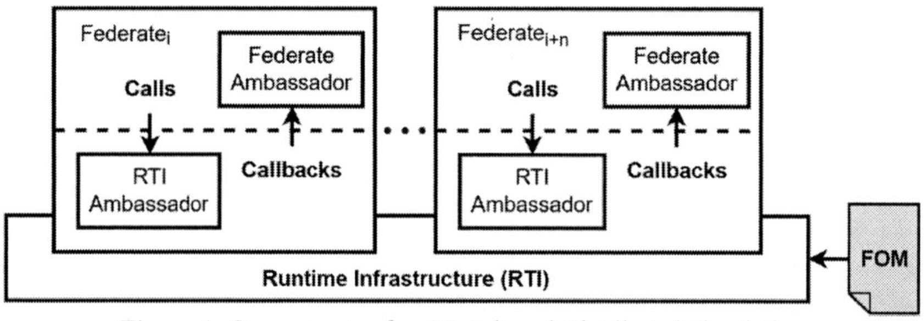

Figure 1: Components of an HLA-based Distributed Simulation

Interaction between the federates is via communicated data exchange (e.g., messages) which are defined in each Federate Object Model (FOM) based on the general OMT. Federates interact through the HLA RTI middleware and the RTI is responsible for the overall synchronization and control of the federation. For example, there could be an HLA-based distributed simulation of several drones exploring the moon's surface. Each federate simulates its own drone and reacts to the positions of the others. Before performing its simulation for the next period, a federate will "ask" the RTI if there are any updates of the position of the drones from the other federates (as defined by the FOM). If there are updates, the RTI passes these to the federate and then that federate updates its simulation (e.g., the new positions of the other drones). The federate will then perform its simulation and then inform the RTI of the new position of its own drone. The other federates will do this in parallel at the same time. Federates can be on the same or different geographically dispersed computers (SEE has federates running in several different countries).

Despite the benefits of HLA, developing a distributed simulation remains a complex task. The HLA shares some conceptual similarities with Service-Oriented Architecture (SOA) (Laskey & Laskey, 2009), particularly in how distributed components interact. However, while SOA is commonly taught in undergraduate and master's computer science programs, HLA is less frequently included in standard curricula, as its primary focus is on simulation interoperability rather than general software architecture.

Unlike topics such as networking or SOA, HLA is not widely covered in traditional degree programs, and dedicated courses on HLA tend to appear at the postgraduate level. Some universities offer specialized MSc courses that include HLA as part of their distributed simulation or modelling and simulation programs. Examples include the MSc in Modelling & Simulation at the Naval Postgraduate School (USA) and the MSc in Computational Science and Engineering at Cranfield University (UK), both of which include elements of HLA-based distributed simulation in their coursework.

There are very few opportunities to study HLA in traditional Operational Research (OR) degree programs, as OR primarily focuses on optimisation, decision-making models, and analytical methods rather than distributed simulation frameworks. However, some OR applications, such as military logistics, supply chain optimisation, and emergency response planning, have started integrating simulation-based approaches, including HLA-driven distributed simulations, to model complex systems more effectively.

Recognizing this gap, SEE was established in 2011 (originally as the Simulation Smackdown) to provide both postgraduate and undergraduate students with hands-on experience in HLA-based distributed simulation. Beyond technical training, the program was also designed to foster a uniquely international collaboration, enabling students from diverse backgrounds to work together on the future of space exploration.

SEE has had scenarios on the Moon, Cislunar Space, and Mars. Cislunar space refers to the region of space between Earth and the Moon, including the Moon's orbit and areas where future space operations, such as lunar gateways and orbital refuelling stations, may be established.

As space exploration evolves, SEE has aligned its objectives with NASA's Artemis plan, marking a shift towards future-oriented technologies, systems, and capabilities expected to emerge by the mid-2050s. This transition is reflected in SEE 2024's scenario, which focuses on establishing lunar infrastructure while laying the groundwork for future Martian expeditions, in alignment with NASA's Moon to Mars Campaign Strategy.

To support these simulations, SEE teams have access to a wide range of distributed simulation technologies and software solutions. These tools, which include both open-source and commercial software, enable teams to build, test, and refine their simulations effectively. Many commercial providers generously donate software licenses for the duration of SEE, allowing participants to explore innovative simulation environments. The following section provides an overview of the key technologies available to SEE teams.

Various RTI implementations exist, including both open-source and commercial options. For example, Pitch Technologies provides Pitch pRTI, a licensed HLA RTI that is fully compliant with the HLA standard. SEE teams benefit from Pitch's support, which includes access to Pitch pRTI and additional productivity tools such as Pitch Visual OMT and Pitch Commander (Pitch Technologies, 2024).

HLA RTI (Open Source and Commercial): Various RTI implementations exist, including both open-source and commercial options. For example, Pitch Technologies provides Pitch pRTI, a licensed HLA RTI that is fully compliant with the HLA standard. SEE teams benefit from Pitch's support, which includes access to Pitch pRTI and additional productivity tools such as Pitch Visual OMT and Pitch Commander (Pitch Technologies, 2024). While commercial RTI solutions like Pitch pRTI are widely used in industry and supported in SEE, open-source alternatives are also available. Teams that learn the fundamental concepts of HLA using licensed tools can later transition to open-source RTI implementations, such as TrickHLA or other freely available HLA-compliant solutions. This flexibility allows teams to continue developing HLA-based simulations beyond their participation in SEE.

HLA Starter Kit (Open Source): The SEE HLA Starter Kit was designed to streamline the development of HLA federates within the SEE project. This kit includes the Starter Kit framework (SKF) for Java-based federate development, along with comprehensive technical documentation, user guides, and reference examples (Falcone et al., 2017).

TrickHLA (Open Source): TrickHLA, a middleware solution supporting the IEEE 1516 HLA simulation interoperability standard within the Trick Simulation Environment. TrickHLA simplifies the integration of HLA into simulations by abstracting away the complexities of distributed simulation, allowing users to focus on simulation development without requiring extensive HLA expertise (NASA, 2024c).

Trick Simulation Environment (Open Source): The Trick Simulation Environment, originating from NASA's Johnson Space Center, stands as a robust framework for simulation development, offering a versatile platform for constructing applications across various stages of space vehicle development. With Trick, users can efficiently generate simulations for diverse purposes, including initial vehicle design, performance assessment, flight software development, dynamic load analysis of flight vehicles, and training in virtual or hardware-in-the-loop environments (NASA, 2024b).

JSC Engineering Orbital Dynamics (Open Source): JSC Engineering Orbital Dynamics (JEOD) is a sophisticated simulation tool tailored to integrate with the NASA Trick Simulation Environment. It specializes in generating vehicle trajectories through the solution of complex numerical dynamical models, segmented into four key categories. Environment models encapsulate the vehicle's surrounding conditions, while Dynamics models focus on integrating equations of motion. Interaction models represent the vehicle's interactions with the environment, complemented by a suite of mathematical and orbital dynamics Utility models (NASA, 2024a).

Distributed Observer Network (DON): DON is a data presentation tool developed by NASA to visualize and showcase simulation outcomes. By leveraging modern gaming technology, DON provides an interactive 3D environment where users can observe the evolution and interactions of graphical models within a simulated scenario (NASA, 2024a). DON is available through a license request from NASA, allowing SEE teams to access and integrate it into their simulations. However, other data streaming and visualization tools can also be used to achieve similar functionality. Open-source alternatives and commercial solutions exist for streaming simulation data and creating real-time 3D visualizations, providing flexibility for teams that may not have access to DON.

3 PARTICIPATING IN THE SIMULATION EXPLORATION EXPERIENCE

The SEE term runs from January to March/April with weekly 2–3-hour sessions. A live virtual event (takes place at the end of SEEE, where the teams join to run their distributed simulations. Onboarding begins in September, during which teams can get advice about the requirements and the technologies involved in SEE. Teams interested in participating in SEE first look at the documents and videos available at Simulation Exploration Experience Website (SEE, 2024), where they can see examples and details of the scenario and details on how to apply. Brunel's How-to Guide (Taylor et al., 2023) also provides further explanation.

Brunel began developing its SEE simulation in 2022 with a conceptual design, followed by the creation of a simple Lunar Rover Federate in 2023. Building on this foundation, the team expanded the simulation to include four federates in 2024, representing key on-site lunar base facilities: a Communications Hub, Storage Depot, Launch Complex, and Habitation Quarters. The HLA federate codebase and 3D models can be found at (Ghorbani, 2024).

In terms of project management, the SEE program utilizes Businessmap (Kanbanize, 2024), a software platform designed to streamline workflows through Kanban-based task management. Formerly known as Kanbanize, Businessmap enables teams to visualize their progress, automate workflows, and track key performance metrics, helping them maintain efficiency throughout the project lifecycle. By using customizable boards, task dependencies, and automated notifications, SEE participants can coordinate tasks, manage resources effectively, and ensure adherence to project milestones and deadlines.

Active teams participating in SEE follow a structured process to develop, test, and integrate their federates within the distributed simulation environment. The journey begins with the conceptualization phase, where each team defines the key functionalities, data elements, and interactions of their federates. This is documented using a Baseball Card, a summary format that outlines the role and behavior of each federate in the simulation.

Once the conceptual groundwork is established, teams proceed to set up the necessary software infrastructure. They first request and install NASA's DON software, which allows them to monitor and interact with simulations across the SEE network. Following this, an Interaction Matrix is developed to map out the relationships between federates, ensuring clear communication and synchronization within the simulation. The RTI software is then installed, enabling federates to exchange data efficiently within the HLA framework.

With the software environment in place, teams move on to initial testing and connectivity setup. They begin by running a simple federate system, locally, verifying its basic functionality and ensuring that it can operate within the intended simulation parameters. Once this is confirmed, they connect to the SEE Virtual Private Network (VPN), which provides a secure connection for federates to access the SEE networks, ensuring reliable remote communications to the federation infrastructure.

The next phase involves collaborative testing and integration. Teams conduct interoperability tests using RTI, ensuring their federates function correctly within the larger simulation. To prevent any technical issues, a comprehensive dry run is organized before the final event. During this phase, teams refine their federates, resolve potential integration challenges, and make necessary adjustments based on peer feedback. This is followed by 3D model integration, where the federates' functionality is validated in conjunction with visual representations, ensuring seamless interaction between the simulation components.

The SEE experience culminates in the final event, where all teams deploy their federates in a live, distributed simulation. This event serves as a showcase of their technical achievements, collaboration, and problem-solving efforts throughout the SEE program. By following this structured approach, teams gain hands-on experience with distributed simulation technologies, enhancing their understanding of HLA-based interoperability while contributing to the broader simulation ecosystem.

During the early stages of SEE, teams define objectives, coordinate with others, and engage in active learning through discussions and problem-solving. Weekly meetings facilitate peer-to-peer feedback, helping students refine their skills while fostering collaboration and knowledge-sharing. A key aspect of SEE's pedagogy is its mentorship model, where experienced teams guide newcomers, supported by volunteers from NASA, SISO, and industry partners. This structured yet flexible learning environment bridges the gap between theory and practice, while guest speakers introduce students to advanced topics in Modeling & Simulation, enriching their exposure to real-world applications.

4 BASEBALL CARD AND INTERACTION MATRIX

The "Baseball Card" has become a key part of a team's activities as it serves as a tool for federate conceptualization, documentation, and presentation. Usually, there is one Baseball Card per federate as shown in Figure 2:

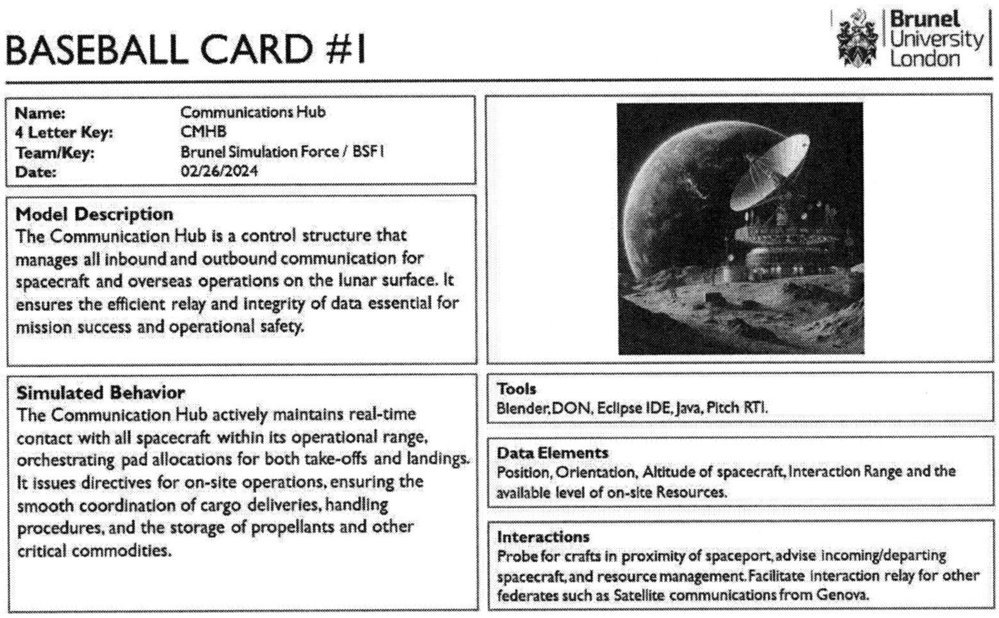

Figure 2: Brunel University Baseball Card for a Communications Hub

The Baseball Card serves as both a documentation and communication tool for teams participating in SEE. It provides a structured way to conceptualize and present each federate, ensuring clarity in design, functionality, and interactions. Each Baseball Card captures key aspects of a federate, allowing teams to quickly understand the role and behaviour of different simulation components.

At its core, the Baseball Card introduces the team and federate details, offering a snapshot of the federates identity and its intended function within the SEE simulation. It then provides a model description, explaining the federates primary objectives, operational scope, and the rationale behind its development. This is complemented by an overview of the simulated behaviour, which details how the federate interacts within the distributed simulation environment, including its responses to external inputs and its engagement with other federates.

To enhance clarity and engagement, the Baseball Card incorporates visual elements, such as diagrams or images, that illustrate the federates design and functionality. Additionally, it outlines the software tools and technologies used in the federates development, ensuring transparency in the simulation's technical foundation. The data elements section specifies the inputs and outputs that the federate processes, highlighting how it exchanges information within the simulation framework. Finally, the interactions section maps out the federates connections with other teams and federates, providing insight into its collaborative role in the broader SEE ecosystem. SEE employs an Interaction Matrix to map the interaction between simulations. Structured in a tabular format, it outlines the potential communications and dependencies across federates and helps to ensure a coherent and synchronized federation as well as giving a clear picture of what interacts with what. The first row and column of the matrix list the names of the federates involved, with the intersecting cells designated to detail the specific interactions between these entities.

The Interaction Matrix plays a crucial role in defining the relationships between federates within the SEE simulation, ensuring smooth communication and coordination. A prime example of this is the Brunel team's Communication Hub, which serves as a central node for coordinating interactions among various simulation components of the moonbase.

One key interaction involves the University of Genova, which has developed a lunar satellite designed to relay critical data such as altitude, longitude, orbital periods, and regular status updates. This satellite acts as a communication bridge between rockets and landers, transmitting essential information through the Communication Hub. Similarly, FACENS has focused on developing a Cable Car system, which facilitates passenger transport between the Spaceport and the Habitation Quarters. To ensure seamless transit operations, the Cable Car team relies on the Communication Hub to transmit schedule updates and arrival times, enabling real-time coordination within the lunar environment. Additionally, the University of Central Florida (UCF) has contributed to the development of a lunar rover. The lunar rover enables exploration and logistics support within the simulation. This system integrates with the Communication Hub, allowing for data exchange and improved operational efficiency.

Beyond these specific examples, multiple teams working on various lunar vehicles also integrate with the Communication Hub. These vehicles depend on the hub to facilitate essential data exchanges, ensuring consistent and reliable communication across the simulation. By mapping these interactions, the Interaction Matrix provides a structured framework for managing interoperability between federates, ultimately enhancing the realism and functionality of the SEE simulation. The interaction matrix has evolved to encapsulate the internal dynamics of our federates and incorporate external interactions with federates from other teams.

5 GETTING STARTED

Participating in SEE is a continuous learning process, where teams develop expertise in distributed simulation through hands-on experience. Mastering the SEE Starter Kit Framework (SKF) is a crucial step for teams choosing to use it, as it simplifies HLA-based space simulations by providing structured tools and functionalities (Falcone et al., 2017; Falcone & Garro, 2016). SKF accelerates development, reduces technical barriers, and enables seamless federate integration.

However, SEE teams have flexibility in selecting their simulation tools. While our team has chosen to explore SKF, other teams may opt for alternatives such as TrickHLA, which also supports HLA-based simulation development. The choice of tools depends on team objectives, experience, and technical requirements. This section focuses on SKF, but similar principles apply to other frameworks used within the SEE ecosystem.

A fundamental component of SKF is its Reference Frames module, which manages the International Celestial Reference Frame (ICRF), a fixed coordinate system based on distant quasars. This ensures precise orbital mechanics and spacecraft trajectory simulations. The Celestial Bodies module supports space object representation, allowing teams to create planetary models, while the Space Time Manager synchronizes epochs across time standards (e.g., TT, UTC, J2000). SKF also includes Mathematical Utilities to assist in spatial and temporal calculations, ensuring accuracy in federate behaviour.

SKF's application layer simplifies development through core classes such as *SEEAbstractFederate* and *SEEAbstractAmbassador*, allowing teams to focus on federate behaviour rather than low-level RTI management. Federate operations are divided into proactive lifecycle management and reactive RTI interactions, ensuring smoother execution and interoperability.

Understanding RTI is essential for simulation coordination. The Central RTI Component (CRC) orchestrates federation operations, offering both graphical and command-line interfaces for monitoring. RTI APIs support multiple languages (C++, Java, or wrappers for other languages), providing flexibility in federate development. Teams can also integrate the SISO Space Reference Federation Object Model (Space FOM) (Möller et al., 2020) for standardized federate interactions.

SEE participants receive access to SKF tutorials and a presentation from SKF developers on best practices. Using Eclipse IDE, teams set up federates, integrating essential libraries (booster1516.jar, prti.jar), configuration files, and logging tools. The *LunarRoverFederate* class, part of the SKF Starter Kit, allows teams to drive a simple lunar rover and share its coordinates.

Federate Configuration & Execution

To join the SEE Federation, federates:

1. Configure the SKF environment and apply settings for HLA integration.
2. Connect to the RTI, specifying the CRC host and port (e.g., MAK, Pitch Technologies).
3. Join the SEE Federation execution, subscribing to required updates.
4. Synchronize with the federation timeline and confirm readiness.
5. Manage execution control, updating configurations and publishing mode transitions.
6. Handle object and interaction management, ensuring seamless data exchange.
7. Set up HLA Time Management, aligning simulation timing and synchronization points.
8. Launch simulation execution, integrating federates into the SEE distributed environment.

To visualize 3D objects, the simulation interoperates with the Distributed Observer Network (DON) using *SpaceMaster*, *SpaceReferenceFramePublisher*, and *HLA2DON*. *SpaceMaster* ensures synchronization across federates, while *SpaceReferenceFramePublisher* maps spatial interactions to DON, allowing for real-time visualization. *HLA2DON* further facilitates the integration of HLA simulation data into the DON environment, ensuring seamless data translation and rendering.

All these tools are provided by SEE as part of its GitHub repository, giving teams access to essential software components for integrating their federates with DON and enhancing the visual representation of simulation interactions. This structured process ensures federates are accurately integrated, synchronized, and effectively visualized within the SEE environment.

Our team is actively working on developing additional federates to expand the scope of our SEE participation. While these efforts go beyond the scope of this edition, we plan to document our experiences, techniques, and lessons learned in future editions. This will provide deeper insights into the challenges, methodologies, and best practices we have explored in advancing HLA-based simulations within SEE.

6 RUNNING A FEDERATE REMOTELY

To operate a federate remotely within the SEE Federation, teams must configure their system to establish a secure network connection while ensuring seamless integration into the distributed simulation environment. This process begins with VPN activation, which provides a secure communication channel, allowing teams to access the SEE network. However, HLA remains responsible for managing the actual interactions between federates, ensuring synchronisation and data exchange within the simulation.

Once the secure network connection is established, teams must configure their federate settings to ensure proper integration into the SEE Federation. This involves updating the local settings designator, which previously referenced local or intranet CRC addresses, to the designated IP address or hostname provided by the SEE Network Admin. This adjustment allows the federate to access the SEE network infrastructure and establish communication.

With these configurations in place, the federate is ready to join the SEE Federation's distributed simulation. This step follows the same setup as the local configuration but now operates within the federation's broader network. Connecting to the federation enables teams to participate in scheduled dry run tests, which help identify and resolve potential issues while ensuring interoperability before the final event. Once testing is complete, the federate is fully prepared to integrate into the live distributed simulation, contributing to the SEE program's collaborative efforts.

A properly configured federate ensures a seamless transition from local development to full-scale remote operation. Aligning the federate settings with the remote CRC requirements and participating in dry run tests allows teams to validate functionality and troubleshoot early. This structured approach ensures readiness for both the dry runs and the final event, where teams fully integrate into the SEE real-time distributed simulations event.

7 CONCLUSION

This tutorial has provided an overview of the Simulation Exploration Experience (SEE), offering insights into its scope and the challenges new teams may encounter. SEE presents a unique opportunity for students to engage with distributed simulation technologies, develop HLA-based interoperability skills, and collaborate on an international scale. While the learning curve can be steep, the enthusiastic support from volunteers, experienced teams, and industry professionals ensures that newcomers can quickly adapt and contribute meaningfully to the project.

Beyond technical skill development, SEE serves as a valuable educational model for simulation pedagogy. It fosters an environment of experiential learning, where students acquire not only technical expertise but also teamwork, problem-solving, and project management skills. The mentorship model within SEE, where experienced teams assist new participants, reinforces the importance of peer learning and knowledge-sharing. Furthermore, by working in a distributed, real-world simulation setting, students gain exposure to collaborative software development practices and the challenges of synchronization, debugging, and integration in complex systems.

Reflecting on our participation in SEE, several key lessons have emerged that can benefit future teams. Early preparation is critical, securing software licenses, installing tools, and troubleshooting technical issues early prevents delays later in the project. Team structure also plays a crucial role in efficiency; assigning roles based on individual skills and interests (e.g., software development, 3D modeling, and simulation design) enhances productivity. Regular communication, both internally and with other SEE teams, is essential for successful HLA interactions, as early coordination ensures a clear roadmap for collaboration. Additionally, providing structured support for new members, such as software templates and introductory tasks, helps them integrate more effectively. Finally, continuous testing and validation are vital to ensure that the simulation performs as expected during the final event.

Brunel University's participation in SEE illustrates these principles in action. A team of second-year computer science students successfully completed most of their objectives while collaborating with 10-15 teams from various countries. While many SEE participants are postgraduate students, the program remains an invaluable learning experience for students at all levels, providing hands-on exposure to innovative simulation technologies and an opportunity to engage with a global community of researchers and engineers.

We encourage you to watch the latest SEE final event video (SEE Event, 2024) to witness the creativity and achievements of SEE teams.

ACKNOWLEDGMENTS

We thank the SEE team volunteers for providing technology, expertise and technical support. We also acknowledge the excellent work done by all teams from all SEE "years"!

REFERENCES

Ghorbani, M. (2024). SEE-GitHub. https://github.com/mzrghorbani/SEE2024

Crues, E. Z., Dexter, D. E., Möller, B., Falcone, A., & Garro, A. (2022). SpaceFOM: An Interoperability Standard for Space Systems Simulations. 2022 IEEE Aerospace Conference (AERO), 1–10. https://doi.org/10.1109/AERO53065.2022.9843262

Dahmann, J. S., Fujimoto, R. M., & Weatherly, R. M. (1997). The Department of Defense High Level Architecture. Proceedings of the Winter Simulation Conference (WSC), 142–149. https://doi.org/10.1145/268437.268465

Falcone, A., Garro, A., Taylor, S. J. E., Anagnostou, A., Chaudhry, N. R., & Salah, O. (2017). Experiences in Simplifying Distributed Simulation: The HLA Development Kit Framework. Journal of Simulation, 11(3), 208–227. https://doi.org/10.1057/s41273-016-0039-4

IEEE. (2010a). IEEE Standard for Modeling and Simulation (M&S) High Level Architecture (HLA)–Federate Interface Specification.

IEEE. (2010b). IEEE Standard for Modeling and Simulation (M&S) High Level Architecture (HLA)–Framework and Rules.

Kanbanize. (2024). Businessmap. https://businessmap.io/

Laskey, K. B., & Laskey, K. (2009). Service oriented architecture. WIREs Computational Statistics, 1(1), 101–105. https://doi.org/10.1002/wics.8

Möller, B., Rydell, A., Crues, E. Z., Dexter, D., Falcone, A., & Garro, A. (2020). SISO Space Reference FOM-Tools and Testing. SISO 2020 Simulation Innovation Workshop, JSC-E-DAA-TN76473.

NASA. (2024a). Trick Simulation Environment. https://github.com/nasa/trick

NASA. (2024b). TrickHLA. https://github.com/nasa/TrickHLA

NASA. (2024c). DON. https://public.ksc.nasa.gov/don/

NASA. (2024d). JEOD. https://github.com/nasa/jeod/

Okan Topçu, H. O. (2017). Guide to Distributed Simulation with HLA (H. O. Okan Topçu, Ed.). Springer.

Pitch Technologies. (2024). Pitch2024. https://pitchtechnologies.com/products/

SEE. (2019). SEE 2019. https://www.liophant.org/conferences/2022/see/

SEE. (2024). SEE 2024. https://simulationexplorationexperience.org/

Taylor, S. J., Anagnostou, A., Abubakar, N., Saha, A., & Ghorbani, M. (2023). Simulation Exploration Experience: How-to Guide. Available at: https://brunel.figshare.com/articles/conference_contribution/Simulation_Exploration_Experience_How-to_Guide/26293426?file=47659741

Taylor, S. J. (2019). Distributed Simulation: State-of-the-Art and Potential for Operational Research. European Journal of Operational Research, 273(1), 1–19. https://doi.org/10.1016/j.ejor.2018.04.032

SEE Event 2024. Simulation Exploration Experience. https://www.youtube.com/live/7Bcr8zwpZVY?si=Si0JZtekbNpj34dc

AUTHOR BIOGRAPHIES

MAZIAR GHORBANI is an Associate Lecturer in Computer Science at Brunel University London, holding a PhD in Experimental Physics (2022). His research spans mathematics, engineering, computer science, and physics, contributed to High-Luminosity LHC Upgrade, STAMINA, SEAVEA, and ITFLOWS projects. He co-leads the SEE team, applying his expertise in simulation technologies. His email is maziar.ghorbani@brunel.ac.uk.

SIMON J. E. TAYLOR is a Full Professor and Co-Director of the Modeling & Simulation Group at Brunel University London. His research has impacted millions of students and hundreds of universities, as well as SMEs and large enterprises, Ford and Sellafield. He co-founded the Journal of Simulation, the UK Simulation Workshop series, and serves as Executive Chair of SEE. He is a former ACM SIGSIM Chair and Program Chair for WSC 2025. His email is simon.taylor@brunel.ac.uk.

NURA TIJJANI ABUBAKAR is an Associate Lecturer in Computer Science at Brunel University London. His research focuses on inter-cloud distributed simulation, and he has co-led SEE for several years. He previously served as Head of the Department of Innovation Technology at Jigawa State Institute of Information Technology, Nigeria. He has contributed to STAMINA, HORIZON2020, and Science Gateways Africa. His ORCID ID is https://orcid.org/0000-0002-4216-3057, and his email is nura.abubakar2@brunel.ac.uk.

HRIDYANSHU AATREYA is a student and Associate Teaching Assistant at Brunel University London. His research interests include operating systems, computer networks, and distributed simulation. In SEE 2024, he was the project architect for the Brunel team, focusing on HLA frameworks and gaming technology integration. His email is 2200096@brunel.ac.uk.

DAMON CURRY has 30 years of experience in distributed simulation, 3D visualization, terrain, and simulated radio. He is President of Simulation Exploration Experience Inc., North America Business Development Manager at Pitch Technologies, and President of SISO. He holds two patents in real-time image processing for VR. A former US Air Force engineer, he worked on cruise missiles, F-16 avionics, and radio systems. He holds a BSc in Electrical Engineering from The Ohio State University. His email is damon.curry@simexplore.org.

ANASTASIA ANAGNOSTOU is a Senior Lecturer at Brunel University London and Co-Lead of the Modeling & Simulation Group. Her research spans Advanced Computing for M&S, Open Science, and Healthcare Simulation. She has held leadership roles at WSC and serves as ACM SIGSIM Vice Chair and Associate Editor for the Journal of Simulation. She is Program Chair for WSC 2025. Her email is anastasia.anagnostou@brunel.ac.uk.

Proceedings of the Operational Research Society Simulation Workshop 2025 (SW25)
M. Luis, A. Harper, T. Monks, N. Mustafee, eds.

https://doi.org/10.36819/SW25.006

SYSTEM DYNAMICS POLICY IMPACT ASSESSMENT OF THE WATER-ENERGY-FOOD-ECOSYSTEM NEXUS IN THE INKOMATI-USUTHU WATER MANAGEMENT AREA, SOUTH AFRICA

Janez Sušnik

IHE Delft Institute for Water Education
Delft, The Netherlands
j.susnik@un-ihe.org

Blaine Haupt, Daniella Kristensen, Gareth Simpson

Jones & Wagener
PO Box 1434 Rivonia, 2128, South Africa
haupt@jaws.co.za

Antonio Trabucco
IAFES Division, CMCC Foundation—Euro-Mediterranean Centre on Climate Change
Sassari, Italy
antonio.trabucco@cmcc.it

Roberto Roson
CF Applied Economics, Fondazione Università Ca'Foscari
Venice, Italy
roson@unive.it

ABSTRACT

Water, energy, food, and ecosystems are linked in a complex system known as the WEFE nexus. Implementing policies in this system affects all other sectors, often in unanticipated ways. Integrated modelling and assessment of the system is necessary to start to understand these complex linkages. In this paper, a system dynamics model of the WEFE nexus in the Inkomati-Usuthu Water Management Area, South Africa, is presented that models the nexus as a complete, coherent system and assesses the impact of policy actions against reference scenarios. Results show that enacting individual policies tend sto have relatively minor impacts confined to one or two WEFE sectors. Implementing many policies in parallel has mich larger system wide impacts, often being detrimental (e.g. negatively affecting the water balance). Such modelling can help policy makers understand this complexity, and can start discussions on to design policies to avoid negative impacts and leverage synergies.

Keywords: policy impact assessment; System dynamics; water-energy-food-ecosystems nexus.

1 INTRODUCTION

The water-energy-food (WEF) nexus has emerged since the 2011 Bonn Nexus Conference (Hoff, 2011) as a concept promoting imtegrated natural resources management. The WEF nexus has been expanded to include ecosystems (forming the WEFE nexus) as foundational to providing the WEF services (Lucca et al., 2023). WEFE nexus sectors provide outputs which are products and amenities demanded, exploited, and used by society. Exploitation of resources threatens their security. The WEFE nexus sectors are tied to each other through socio-economic connections, for example as the food sector depends on energy and water generation, acquisition, and supply for the generation of food products. WEFE sectors are governed through governance systems and policies. These are largely developed in distinct silos that overlook the connections between sectors. Better understanding of these trade-offs and highlighting opportunities for improved policy and governance design could lead to more effective and efficient management of resources (John et al., 2023; Suda et al., 2024).

Due to the interconnectedness between WEFE sectors, a comprehensive systems approach is critical to better understand and analyse system-wide impacts. The nexus concept attempts to improve on sectoral resources management paradigms such as IWRM (Lalawmpuii, 2023) as it intends to be holistically integrative (Roidt and Avellán, 2019). However, a major shortfall is the urgent need to move from 'nexus thinking' to 'nexus doing' (Simpson and Jewitt, 2019). Despite this, the nexus concept is gaining traction as a way of thinking more broadly and coherently about efficient and sustainable integrated resources management.

In this regard, this paper presents the development of a holistic quantitative system dynamics WEFE nexus model in the Inkomati-Usuthu Water Management Area (IUCMA), South Africa. The model captures key interactions between the WEFE sectors as well as policy implementation. It assesses system trajectories to 2050 under climate and socio-economic pathways. The model integrates important policies linked to each of the WEFE sectors to assess their impact across sectors under different future pathways. This work aims to: i) contribute to the better understanding of multi-sectoral response to policy implementation in the IUCMA region; ii) provide updated and comprehensive information to policy and decision makers regarding the WEFE nexus and its long-term response to policy actions; iii) promote a more holistic, integrated way of thinking about natural resources management and policy development in the region. The study showcases a number of novel aspects including integrating ecosystems explicitly into WEFE nexus models, quantification of uncertainty in WEFE nexus models, and the potential implication of implementing policies on the whole WEFE system in the IUCMA, where such an analysis has yet to be carried out.

2 CASE STUDY AND METHODS

The Inkomati-Usuthu Water Management Area (IUWMA) is a transboundary river basin shared between Eswatini, South Africa, and Mozambique covering approximately 46 800 km^2 in total. In this study, only the South African part of the IAWMA, in Mpumalanga Province, was modelled. The dominant economic activities are agriculture, ecotourism, forestry and mining, which are critical for ensuring energy security, food security, and livelihoods. Several of these pose a threat to water quality and water availability, as well as to land quality. The IUWMA contains critical conservation areas including part of the Kruger National Park. Irrigated agriculture and forestry provide about 60% of jobs and use most of the water, with 31% and 21% being utilised for irrigation and forestry, respectively (www.iucma.co.za). While irrigated sugarcane is a significant water and land user, the sugarcane and sugar industry are also major employers. Surface water makes up the most important water supply source. Negative impacts on water quality stem from poorly managed wastewater infrastructure, informal settlements and illegal connections, mining effluents, land conversion and diffuse pollution. Based on data associated with the 2011 Census (www.statssa.gov.za) together with 2021 mid-year population estimates (www.statssa.gov.za), the population in the IUWMA was estimated to be 2.3 million in 2021. In 2012 it was estimated that the Gross Geographic Product (GGP) of the IUWMA contributed 0.3% of South Africa's Gross Domestic Product (GDP) (DWAF, 2012). The manufacturing and mining sectors were the most significant contributors. Coal mining and agriculture are critical for ensuring to ensure energy and food security but impact on water quality and water availability. Climate change is expected to exacerbate resource sector challenges and threatens economic development. In the study area, water, energy, food, ecosystems, climate, and socio-economic considerations all converge, posing development challenges in the near to mid term future.

In this paper conceptual mapping of the case study (Sokolowski and Banks, 2010) was used for qualitative understanding of the links between nexus sectors and to support system dynamics modelling (SDM; Sterman, 2000) for quantitative assessment. Such a system dynamics modelling approach has been adopted in similar studies (e.g. Kotir et al., 2017; Purwanto et al., 2021; Sušnik et al. 2021; Wang et al. 2023; Mirindi et al., 2024). Both approaches underwent many iterations until final versions were validated by local partners in stakeholder workshops. The SDM was implemented in STELLA Professional (www.iseesystems.com), a dedicated SDM modelling software. All modelling languages, notations, and formulas are based on the STELLA system. The model covers the period 2015-2050, and runs at a monthly timestep (420 months).

There are three primary domains for which data were sourced in this work: (i) biophysical domain (e.g. climate, hydrology, land); (ii) socio-economic domain (e.g. GDP, population) and; (iii) local domain (e.g. local statistics, policy documents). Biophysical and climate data come from the Inter-Sectoral Impact Model Intercomparison Project (ISIMIP). ISIMIP modelling outcomes, at 0.5 degrees spatial resolution, are based on climate drivers based on the Coupled Model Intercomparison Project

(CMIP) projections. The data cover sectors including: water, ecosystem biomes, agriculture and food production, forests, terrestrial biodiversity, and climate variables and cover the period 1971-2070 under two Representative Concentration Pathways (RCPs; van Vuuren et al., 2011): RCP 2.6, and RCP 8.5. For agricultural water use and production data, the SIMETAW_GIS (Simulation of Evapotranspiration of Applied Water; Mancosu et al., 2015) model is used. Data from SIMETAW are available at monthly scale for the entire modelling period. For socio-economic data, the primary data source is the GTAP global Social Accounting Matrix (Aguiar et al., 2019). Underlying the database are several data sources, including among others: national input-output tables, trade, macroeconomic, energy and protection data. These data are complemented by sources such as regional statistics provided by Eurostat, allowing a disaggregation of some macroeconomic data at NUTS2 regional level. The GTAP database is employed to calibrate structural parameters in the dynamic, general equilibrium model of the world economy, G-RDEM (Roson and Britz, 2021). G-RDEM is itself steered by a limited set of aggregate macroeconomic indicators, obtained from the OECD Env-Growth model (Dellink et al., 2017), which in turn provide a quantification of the IPCC Shared Socio-economic Pathways (SSP; O'Neill et al., 2015). In this work, two SSPs are considered: SSP2, and SSP4. SSP2 (middle of the road) represents a world that follows a path in which social, economic, and technological trends do not shift markedly from historical patterns. SSP4 (inequality) describes highly unequal investments in human capital, combined with increasing disparities in economic opportunity and political power, lead to increasing inequalities and stratification. Because data from the biophysical and socioeconomic domains contain uncertainties (e.g. multi-model ensembles), it was essential to capture this uncertainty in the SDM to reflect the fact that future projections are uncertain. To do this, uniform distributions between the minimum and maximum values in input data were stochastically sampled at every timestep in the SD modelling and fed through to the results. In this way, outputs also contain uncertainty, which can be used in communicaiton with end users to highlight the fact that future trajectories are not deterministic. This aims to help develop more robust policies that are flexible under uncertain conditions. The local data used as model input were land use data. Data for 2015 were used as the base year. Local data also provided information on transboundary water obligations. A number of policy scenarios (12) were simulated in the SDM. These policy scenarios were simulated under each RCP-SSP combination to assess their relative impact to WEFE nexus resource trajectories under different climatic and socio-economic futures. The policy scenarios are based on actual policy ambitions in South Africa/the IUWMA, and cover all WEFE nexus sectors.

3 RESULTS

The conceptual map details the main connections between the WEFE nexus sectors and gives an impression of the complexity of this system. In the water sector, both quantity and quality are emphasised. Water is sourced from groundwater and surface water resources. Water is consumed by a wide range of sectors, with irrigated agriculture and mining activities featuring prominently. Food production and mining alter land use and ecosystems, with impacts on water quality. Food is produced in rainfed and irrigated agriculture. Water quantity and quality affect food production. The amount of local food demand is driven by population. Changes in food production affect the energy consumed in the agricultural sector, and emissions from livestock. Many larger farmers are energy-independent through the development of small-scale solar power. Nutrient and pesticide applications, energy demand, and changes in land use characteristics impact on ecosystems. In the energy sector, most energy is sourced from thermal power stations outside the study area. Population changes drive energy demand. Challenges relate to boosting renewable sources, and creating energy storage solutions for more reliable supply. Ecosystems are impacted by, and impact upon, several nexus sectors. Biodiversity, biomass, wetland water storage, forestry, and food production all impact ecosystems, either directly, or indirectly by altering land use patterns and patterns of nutrient and pollutant loads. Ecosystems are impacted by climate change, but can also meditate climate impacts by sequestering GHGs.

The SDM consists of eight interacting modules (Figure 1). The pink arrows indicate a computational connection between modules, showing that if changes are made in one sector, this has impacts in many other sectors. For example, the water module consists of water resources and demand,

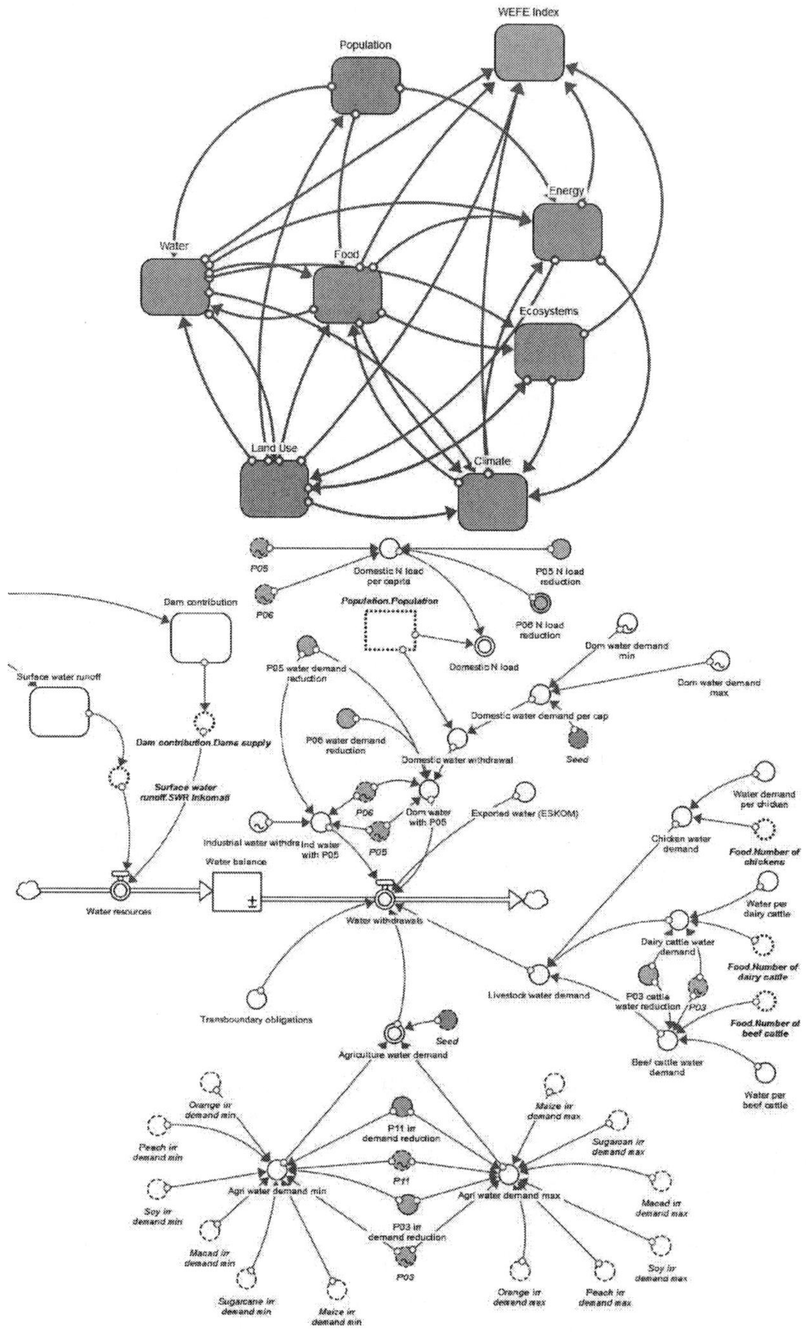

Figure 1 *top - the modular structure of the SDM for the IUWMA. Pink lines indicate dynamic connections between resources sectors in the model. Bottom – detail showing part of the water module*

with the water balance computed as the difference between the two. Water resources consist of surface water runoff and contribution from dams. Water demand consists of: transboundary obligations; water exported to other regions in South Africa; industrial demand; domestic demand; livestock demand; and agricultural water demand. The demand from agriculture considers only irrigated crops, with the crops considered being oranges, peaches, soy, macadamia, sugarcane, and maize. The land covered by each crop is specified in the land use module, which itself can be impacted by policy decisions.

In the reference scenarios, water balance (Figure 2a) shows a positive trend, implying that less water is demanded/abstracted than available. Results mask potential seasonal water stress periods when supply may limit demand that can be supplied. Crop production shows significant differences between RCPs 2.6 and 8.5, with RCP2.6 results showing lower overall totals. Nitrogen leaching trends are similar between the scenarios, although the RCP8.5 simulations show greater uncertainty than those for RCP2.6. Above ground biomass trends are similar between all simulations. Greenhouse gas emissions trends (Figure 2b) are comparable in all simulations, as are the carbon sequestration trends (Figure 2c).

(a)

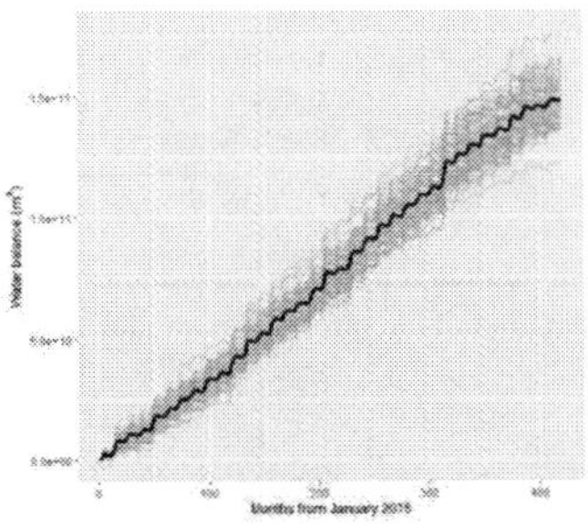

(b)

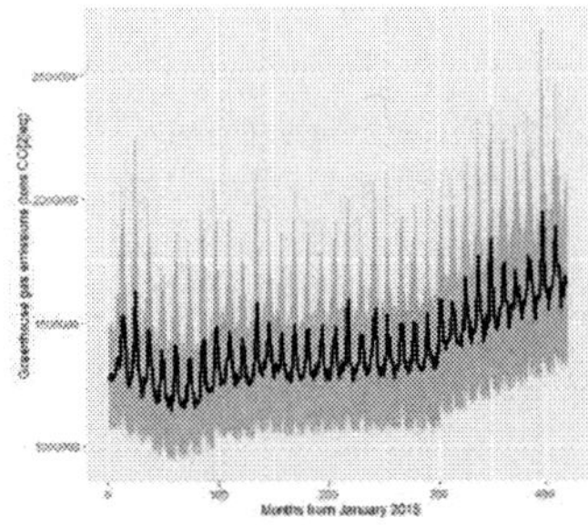

(c)

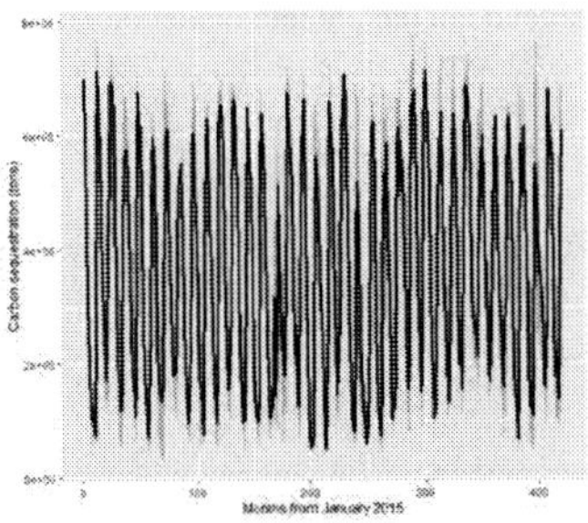

Figure 2 *reference scenario results showing trends in: (a) the water balance; (b) greenhouse gas (GHG) emissions; and (c) carbon sequestration, under the reference scenarios. Light grey lines are the results of 100 Monte-Carlo simulations. Black line is the mean of all simulations.*

When policies are implemented individually, the impacts are assessed relative to the RCP2.6-SSP4 and RCP8.5-SSP4 reference scenarios. Implementing policies one-at-a-time has negligible impacts to the water balance and carbon sequestration. Crop production is impacted to different degrees depending on the policy implemented. Nitrogen leakage is only significantly impacted by one policy, as is above ground biomass. Greenhouse gas emissions are affected to different degrees depending on the policy, though all seem to indicate a reduction in emissions when individually implemented. When every policy is implemented simultaneously, the impacts across sectors are significantly different to when implemented individually. Under all RCP-SSP combinations, the water balance significantly deteriorates compared to the reference scenarios (Figure 3a). Crop production increases significantly over the reference, but so does nitrogen leaching. Above ground biomass is increased significantly. A notable detrimental impact is that results indicate that greenhouse gas emissions increase significantly (Figure 3b) while carbon sequestration appears relatively unaffected (Figure 3c).

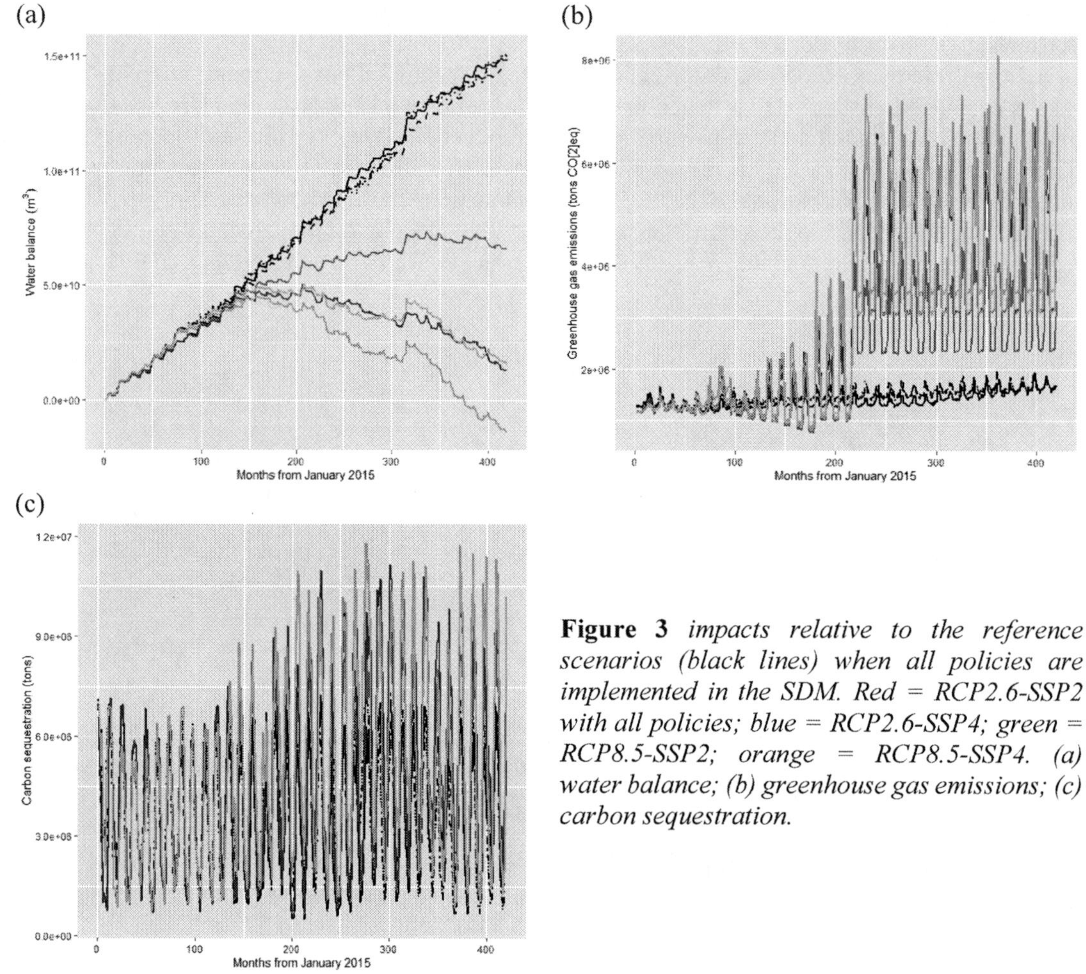

Figure 3 *impacts relative to the reference scenarios (black lines) when all policies are implemented in the SDM. Red = RCP2.6-SSP2 with all policies; blue = RCP2.6-SSP4; green = RCP8.5-SSP2; orange = RCP8.5-SSP4. (a) water balance; (b) greenhouse gas emissions; (c) carbon sequestration.*

4 DISCUSSION

Individual policies do not impact significantly the water balance in the basin or carbon sequestration estimations for example. However, certain policies show large impacts on other sectors. All individually-applied policies appear to marginally reduce greenhouse gas emissions whether this is due to changes in land-use makeup, energy use reductions and/or clean energy initiatives, or changes to energy demand across sectors.

When all policies are implemented together, the resultant impacts compared to individually-applied policies change significantly. The overall dynamics are of compounding benefits or losses, or of cancelling effects between policies. For example, the water balance (Figure 3a) shows significant detrimental trends when all policies are combined, resulting from increases to irrigated agriculture, expansion of agricultural land, and demand increases. This is particularly important in the region as several studies have suggested that water resources may become increasingly stressed due to supply-side decreases and demand-side increases (Matondo, 2020; Nkosi et al., 2021). Under some scenarios, crop production is simulated to grow to unreasonably high levels, likely reflecting assumptions in the model about the reality of compounding individual policy actions on ever-larger tracts of land. Actual production would be unlikely to reach the levels simulated here, particularly as it is suggested that much of South Africa's cropping systems are degraded (van der Laan et al., 2017), and because it is suggested that crop yields will drop for a number of staple crops (Olabanji et al., 2021). Nitrogen leaching is simulated to rise dramatically, which is also due to the assumption of different policies all trying to act on 'their own' rather that working together on existing agricultural areas/smaller expansion areas. While there may be increases in N leaching it is unlikely that such dramatic increases will be realised, especially as it is suggested that the intensity of nitrogen applications in South Africa is decreasing (Tongwane et al., 2020). Greenhouse gas emissions show significantly different trends from the individual policy application cases. Agricultural emissions spike as increasingly large areas of land are converted to agriculture. The use of fossil fuels increases as the irrigated area expands and more water needs to be supplied to this new irrigated land. Less dominant is the increase in domestic water and energy demand due to population increases. These add up to lead to the increase observed in greenhouse gas emissions. In reality, it would be very unlikely that it would happen as suddenly as simulated, but monitoring fossil fuel use and corresponding emissions is still prudent. Such a dramatic increase is unexpected partly because studies suggest that emissions from certain sectors, especially transport, in South Africa may decline in the near future (Oladunni et al., 2022). Conversely, other analyses suggest emissions growth in South Africa of up to four-fold by mid-century (Winkler et al., 2011), reinforcing the need to monitor and mitigate emissions across sectors.

In reality, the reference scenarios and the single-scenario simulations are unlikely to be realised. Multiple policies tend to be enacted concurrently yet consideration of their joint impact is rarely considered from a systems perspective. Individually-applied policies often showed relatively minor impacts that tended to be constrained to the sector in which they were applied. It is when all policies in were implemented that reference scenario results were significantly altered. The general conclusion is that implementing all policies together leads to a general worsening of reference scenario trends. Measures to expand irrigated agricultural land seem to more than offset concurrent policies aiming to reduce water demand or energy use. The land sector is a key node, with subsequent impacts on the water, food, energy, climate, and ecosystems sectors. Recognising sectoral interconnectedness will be critical to holistic, integrated policy development. Much work is ongoing in the wider Southern African Development Community (SADC) region towards WEFE nexus approach implementation in policy and governance, especially when attempting to achieve multiple Sustainable Development Goals important in the region (Senzanje et al., 2022). Some of the messages from this analysis could contribute to these ongoing initiatives, especially in highlighting sectoral interconnections, critical policy actions that impact most sectors, and showing the fact that multiple policies enacted in parallel can have often unanticipated, effects. This aims to lead to more optimal policy formulation across sectors that work together to minimize trade-offs and that are robust under future uncertainties regarding climate and socioeconomic change.

ACKNOWLEDGMENTS

This project has received funding from the European Union's Horizon 2020 research and innovation programme under Grant Agreement No. 101003881 NEXOGENESIS. This article and the content included in it do not represent the opinion of the European Union, and the European Union is not responsible for any use that might be made of its content.

REFERENCES

Aguiar A., Chepeliev M., Corong EL., McDougall R., van der Mensbrugghe D. 2019 The GTAP Data Base: Version 10. Journal of Global Economic Analysis. 4: 1–27. DOI: 10.21642/JGEA.040101AF

Dellink R., Chateau J., Lanzi E., Magné B. 2017. Long-term economic growth projections in the Shared Socioeconomic Pathways. Global Environmental Change. 42: 200-214.

DWAF. 2012. Draft Business Case for the establishment of the Inkomati-Usuthu Catchment Management Agency.

Hoff H. 2011. Understanding the Nexus: Background Paper for the Bonn 2011 Nexus Conference. 51pp. Available at www.sei-international.org/publications?pid=1977

John T.W., Sušnik J., Masia S., Jewitt G. 2023. Towards realization of nexus-doing at the grassroots level: Water-energy-food governance assessment in the Songwe River Basin (Tanzania and Malawi). Environmental Science and Policy. 150: 103596. DOI: 10.1016/j.envsci.2023.103596

Kotir, J.H., Brown, G., Marshall, N., Johnstone, R., 2017. Systemic feedback modelling for sustainable water resources management and agricultural development: an application of participatory modelling approach in the Volta River Basin. Environmental Modelling and Software. 88: 106–118. https://doi.org/10.1016/j.envsoft.2016.11.015.

Lalawmpuii PKR. 2023. Role of water-energy-food nexus in environmental management and climate action. Energy Nexus. 11: 100230. DOI: 10.1016/j.nexus.2023.100230

Lucca E., El Jeitany J., Castelli G., Pacetti T., Bresci E., Nardi F., Caporali E. 2023. A review of water-energy-food-ecosystems Nexus research in the Mediterranean: evolution, gaps and applications. Environmental Research Letters. 18: 083001. DOI: 10.1088/1748-9326/ace375

Mancosu N., Spano D., Orang M., Sarreshteh S., Snyder RL. 2015. SIMETAW# - a model for agricultural water demand planning. Water Resources Management. 30: 541-557. DOI: 10.1007/s11269-015-1176-7

Matondo JI. 2020. Assessing runoff changes in major catchments in Swaziland due to climate change. In: Matondo JI., Alemaw BF., Sandwidi WJP. (eds). Climate Variability and Change in South Africa: Perspectives, experiences, sustainability. Spinger Nature Sustainable Development Goals Series. 208pp. DOI: 10.1007/978-3-030-31543-6

Mirindi D., Sušnik J., Masia S., Jewitt G. 2024. A system dynamics modelling assessment of water-energy-food resource demand futures at the city scale: Goma, Democratic Republic of Congo. World Development Sustainability. 5: 100159. DOI: 10.1016/j.wds.2024.100159

Nkosi M., Mathivha FI., Odiyo JO. 2021. Impact of Land Management on Water Resources, a South African Context. Sustainability. 13: 701. DOI: 10.3390/su13020701

O'Neill, B.C., Kriegler, E., Ebi, K.L., Kemp-Benedict, E., Riahi, K., Rothman, D.S., van Ruijven, B.J., van Vuuren, D.P., Birkmann, J., Kok, K., Levy, M., Solecki, W. 2015. The roads ahead: Narratives for shared socioeconomic pathways describing world futures in the 21st century. Global Environmental Change. DOI: 10.1016/j.gloenvcha.2015.01.004

Olabanji MF., Ndarana T., Davis N. 2021. Impact of Climate Change on Crop Production and Potential Adaptive Measures in the Olifants Catchment, South Africa. Climate. 9: 6. DOI: 10.3390/cli9010006

Oladunni OJ., Mpofu K., Olanrewaju OA. 2022. Greenhouse gas emissions and its driving forces in the transport sector of South Africa. Energy Reports. 8: 2052-2061. DOI: 10.1016/j.egyr.2022.01.123

Purwanto, A., Sušnik, J., Suryadi, F.X., de Fraiture, C., 2021. Quantitative simulation of the water-energy-food (WEF) security nexus in a local planning context in Indonesia. Sustainable Production and Consumption. 25, 198–216. https://doi.org/10.1016/j.spc.2020.08.009.

Roidt M., Avellán T. 2019. Learning from Integrated Management Approaches to Implement the Nexus. Journal of Environmental Management. 237: 609–616. DOI: 10.1016/j.jenvman.2019.02.106

Roson R., Britz W. 2021. Simulating long run structural change with a dynamic general equilibrium model. International Journal of Computational Economics and Econometrics. 11: 368–405.

Senzanje A., Mudhara M., Tirivamwe L. 2022. The water-energy-food nexus as an approach for achieving sustainable development goals 2 (food), 6 (water), and 7 (energy). In: Madhaudi T., Senzanje A., Modi A., Jewitt G., Massawe F. (eds.). Water-energy-food nexus narratives and resource securities. A Global South perspective. pp 181-197. ISBN: 978-0-323-91223-5

Simpson GB., Jewitt GPW. 2019. The water-energy-food nexus in the anthropocene: moving from 'nexus thinking' to 'nexus action'. Current Opinion in Environmental Sustainability. 40: 117-123. DOI: 10.1016/j.cosust.2019.10.007

Sokolowski, JA., Banks, CM. 2010. Modeling and Simulation Fundamentals: Theoretical underpinnings and Practical Domains. John Wiley and Sons. 437pp. DOI: https://doi.org/10.1002/9780470590621.

Sterman, J.D., 2000. Business Dynamics: Systems Thinking and Modeling for a Complex World. 6th edn. Mc Graw Hill India, New Delhi.

Suda AO., Sušnik J., Masia S., Jewitt G. 2024. Policy coherence assessment of water, energy, and food resources policies in the Tana River Basin, Kenya. Environmental Science and Policy. 159: 103816. DOI: 10.1016/j.envsci.2024.103816.

Sušnik J., Masia S., Indriksone D., Brēmere I., Vamvakeridou-Lyroudia L.S. 2021. System dynamics modelling to explore the impacts of policies on the water-energy-food-land-climate nexus in Latvia. Science of the Total Environment. 775: 145827. DOI: 10.1016/j.scitotenv.2021.145827

Tongwane MI., Moeletsi ME., Tsubo M. 2020. Trends of carbon emissions form applications of nitrogen fertiliser and crop residues to agricultural soils in South Africa. Journal of Environmental Management. 272: 111056. DOI: 10.1016/j.jenvman.2020.111056

van Vuuren DP., Edmonds JA., Kainuma M., Riahi K., Weyant J. A special issue on the RCPs. Climatic Change. 109: 1. DOI: 10.1007/s10584-011-0157-y

van der Laan M., Bristow KL., Stirzaker RJ., Annandale JG. 2017. Towards ecologically sustainable crop production: A South African perspective. Agriculture, Ecosystems & Environment. 236: 108-119. DOI: 10.1016/j.agee.2016.11.014

Wang X., Dong Z., Sušnik J. 2023. System dynamics modelling to simulate regional water-energy-food nexus combined with the society-economy-environment system in Hunan Province, China. Science of the Total Environment. 863: 160993. DOI: 10.1016/j.scitotenv.2022.160993.

Winkler H., Hughes A., Marquard A., Haw M., Merven B. 2011. South Africa's greenhouse gas emissions under business-as-usual: The technical basis of 'Growth without Constraints' in the Long-Term Mitigation Scenarios. Energy Policy. 39: 5818-5828. DOI: 10.1016/j.enpol.2011.06.009

Proceedings of the Operational Research Society Simulation Workshop 2025 (SW25)
M. Luis, A. Harper, T. Monks and N. Mustafee, eds.
https://doi.org/10.36819/SW25.007

SOLVING A REAL COMPLEX SCHEDULING PROBLEM WITH A SIMULATION-BASED OPTIMIZATION METHOD

Mr. Chakib Medjkane

University of Science and Technology
USTHB University, BP32
Bab-Ezzouar, 16111, Algiers, Algeria
chakibmedjkane@gmail.com

Ms. Yasmine Rihane

University of Science of Technology
USTHB University, BP32
Bab-Ezzouar, 16111, Algiers, Algeria
yasminerih2h2@gmail.com

Dr. Nacira Chikhi

University of Science and Technology USTHB
Department of Operation Research, USTHB University,
BP32, Bab-Ezzouar, 16111, Algiers, Algeria
nchikhi@usthb.dz

ABSTRACT

In this paper, we have studied a complex industrial production problem in the algerian engineering service company - General Electric oil and gaz. The objective of our work is to schedule the most critical part of the ALGESCO workshop by integrating an industrial system simulation with an optimization algorithm. This new method consists in determining the optimal order of passage of the jobs to be treated in the queue of each machine of the workshop given the large size of the data and the flexibility of the model. Two proposed simulation models treat the problem were designed. The first model minimises the completion time of all jobs (Makespan) while the second minimizes the sum of the delays. A simulation based optimisation algorithm is proposed to solve this problem. It is a combination of the simulation software Flexim and a genetic algorithm. The effectiveness of the approach has been illustrated by numerical experiments on real company data. The results show the efficiency of the proposed method.

1 Introduction

The integration of Genetic Algorithms (GAs) with simulation techniques has been extensively explored to address the complexities inherent in Job Shop Scheduling Problems (JSSPs). This approach leverages the strengths of GAs in exploring large solution spaces and the capabilities of simulation in evaluating dynamic and stochastic system behaviors. The study in (Phanden, Jain, and Verma 2012) presents a simulation-based GA approach for optimizing JSSPs, focusing on minimizing mean tardiness and makespan. The authors introduced a restart scheme within the GA to prevent premature convergence, demonstrating improved performance in job shop environments. The authors in (Luo and El Baz 2018) examined parallel GAs for shop scheduling problems, discussing various parallelization strategies to enhance computational efficiency and solution quality in complex scheduling scenarios. The research proposed in (Wang, van Stein, Emmerich, and Bäck 2020) is a tailored NSGA-III algorithm for flexible JSSPs, integrating smart initialization and diverse crossover operators. The study highlighted the effectiveness of combining GAs with advanced initialization and local search strategies to solve multi-objective scheduling problems. The authors in (Vaghefinezhad and Wong 2012) developed a GA approach for flexible JSSPs, focusing on maximizing total profit while adhering to constraints. Their model considered dynamic factors such as time-varying raw material costs and demand fluctuations, showcasing the adaptability of GA-simulation coupling in realistic manufacturing settings.

In this paper, we studied a complex industrial production problem in the Algerian engineering service company - General Electric oil and gaz. The objective of our work is to schedule the most important part of the workshop of Algesco by proposing a coupling between a simulation of the industrial system and an algorithm of optimization. The coupling of Genetic Algorithms with simulation presents a powerful methodology for tackling the complexities of Job Shop Scheduling Problems, offering a balance between exploration and practical evaluation to derive effective and adaptable scheduling solutions.

The industrial revolution has led to the discovery of many sources of energy, such as oil and natural gas, which are so much in demand by both developed and developing countries. A large part of the Algerian economy is based on the revenues from drilling and exports of oil and gas, and production of electricity that supplies a large part of the electricity grid in Algeria is covered by gas turbines. With the evolution of production systems, scheduling has become a very important and interesting area to study. There are several methods and techniques to solve real-time scheduling problems, among these approaches we mention the management of queues by priority rules, which allows to act effectively and in real time. This approach consists of determining the best queue management rules combination ; these rules are used to define the order or the sequence of jobs to be processed at each step. In th following, we will first try to describe the current situation and then define the problem and try to match the theoretical side to the practical situation.

2 Problem statement and contribution

As the only workshop specialized in turbo-machinery technology in Algeria, ALGESCO is in charge of the inspection, maintenance and repair of more than 440 GE technologies in Algeria, and despite the human resources composed of more than a hundred engineers, technicians and managers qualified in different fields and material resources represented by very sophisticated machines and advanced technologies, the workshop has a difficult time to meet the demands of its customers in time which is causing problems at the workshop level because of the overload of parts accumulated in the shop. In the majority of cases this is due to the type of parts to be repaired when it comes to essential components in oil and gas fields. In our work we will focus on the repair of the *(low and high pressure)* blades of the different ranges and different stages of gas turbines

There are two types of repair at the work shop a light repair (if the number of badly damaged parts of the same job is not very big) or a full repair (if this number exceeds a certain threshold), this decision is made after the inspection phase made by qualified and experienced engineers.

A job represents a batch of parts of the same stage of the same turbine. These parts will undergo the same treatment during the repair. The choice of considering a job as being the set of parts constituting the same batch and not a single part is due to several reasons related to the regulations of the workshop. It is not advisable to treat two different batches on the same machine simultaneously, for reasons of internal organization and also to avoid the dispersion of parts of the same batch in the workshop. In addition, some treatments such as heat treatment or mounting on the rotor disc require that all parts of the same batch be grouped at the same time. All the pieces of the same lot have the same date of availability, processing time on each machine, and the same due date. The processing time on each machine is considered as the time of passage of all the parts that make up the same batch (job), whatever the type of the machine (simple machine or batch machine). Each job has an identifier assigned at the shop floor (job number) and each piece has serial number.

Our main contribution consists in studying a complex industrial production problem in the Algerian engineering service company - General Electric oil. The objective of our work is to schedule the most critical part of the ALGESCO workshop by integrating an industrial system simulation with an optimization algorithm (Goldberg and Corruble 1994) to manage the order of the jobs at the queues of each machine given the large size of the data and the flexibility of the model. To do this, we used on the one hand a genetic algorithm (Holland 1975) that will generate a set of scenarios in the form of a combination of priority rules (Lopez and Roubellat 2001) that vary each time will cover the set of solutions to find a good solution. Then, we modeled the workshop using FLEXSIM simulation software that will test each rule set on each machine simulating the repair of the jobs already programmed in the system. We implemented 7 heuristics used the diferent rules (FIFO, EDD, LRPT, SRPT, LIFO, STIS,

LTIS). Communication between Java and Flexsim is done through sockets for sending and receiving values for both programs.

3 Design and Implementation

In the following, we explain the application of a genetic algorithm coupled with a workshop simulation model to solve the problem posed above, which is to determine the best set of rules to manage the flow circulating in the studied part of the workshop. The management is done at the level of the queues placed in front of each machine. Flexsim not only allows to model the workshop but also to program algorithms that determine the pull strategy *Pull strategy* thanks to its development environment. The optimization is done using a genetic algorithm programmed in the JAVA language.

Coding a solution is the first step to take when designing a genetic algorithm. The GA generates a solution in the form of a chromosome of size *m*, which represents the number of machines available in the workshop ordered from 1 to *m*. each bit of this chromosome contains an integer between 1 and 7 and (each number represents a heuristic). Individuals are randomly generated, which promotes a very useful concept in GAs which is diversity.

The communication between the GA and Flexsim is done through sockets connecting the two programs. A solution is transmitted from netbeans to Flexsim to calculate its fitness. For example, if the first bit of the chromosome contains the number 3 and the second bit contains the number 4, this will activate heuristic number 3 in the first machine and heuristic number 4 in the second machine and so on until the heuristics are assigned to the machines. During the communication between the optimization algorithm and Flexsim, the GA is waiting for a return message from Flexsim; the latter will return the makespan calculated after the launch of the simulation by applying the combination of rules coded in the chromosome. This response will guide the GA in its future choices. We note that we use the hstring method The principle of this method is to convert an individual that is represented by a vector of integers, into a string of characters, and this by concatenating each gene of the individual with a letter. The goal of this step is to facilitate the reading of the solution by the Flexsim simulator when decoding it for the evaluation of this solution.

3.1 Modeling by FLEXSIM

Two simulation models were designed to address the problem, the first model minimizes the completion time of all jobs while the second minimizes the sum of the delays. We describe the model created using the Flexsim software which illustrates the operation of the workshop. The components of the model are the input and output of the system, the machines, queues.

3.1.1 Input and output of the system:

We define at the beginning an *arrival style* which represents the mode of arrival of the batches to be repaired, We chose the mode *arrival schedule* in the form of a calendar where each batch will have a *arrival time* arrival time at the system defined at the start.
Number of arrivals represents the number of batches to be repaired. A color will be assigned to each product range, the range will be identified by the *ItemType*, in our case we have 12 ranges.
Number of labels represents the number of Labels specific to each batch and which will help later in programming the resolution method. The output of the system is done through a queue *End.* As soon as a job reaches the end of repair, we check if this job has had a delay or not by checking its *EDD* with the difference between its (*Arrival time*) its creation date and its (*Entry time*) the date of arrival at this queue, In this case this delay will be sent, plus the delays of all the other jobs to java thanks to the sockets programmed in *Sink*, the output of the system.

3.1.2 Machines:

We have 8 machines which are: Welding, CD, Sandblast, heat treatment furnace, FPI , Coating, Shot peening and Coordinate measuring machine-CMM. Each machine has a processing time which is the time required for processing of a batch of a defined turbine At the end of each processing step the machine-specific labels will be updated due to triggers at the end of processing (triggers at the end of the process).

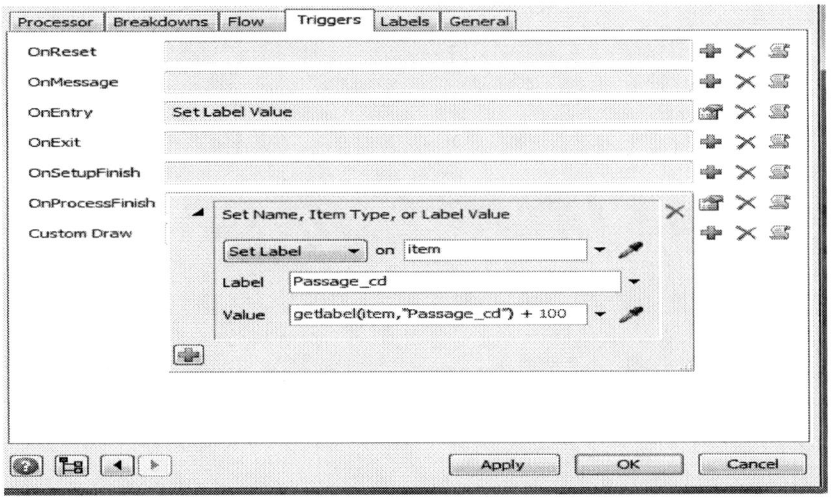

Figure 1: Triggers at the end of processing

To define the path that must take each range we intervene in the part Flow of each machine, the input allows to manage the entry of the batch to the machine. The rules(heuristics) are programmed in flexcode (programming language of Flexsim). input is from a machine-specific waiting connected directly to this last. The output is the output of the machine it differs from one machine to another according to the range of the batch and the next step of repair. A strategy has been put in place to differentiate each range which is to condition the output.

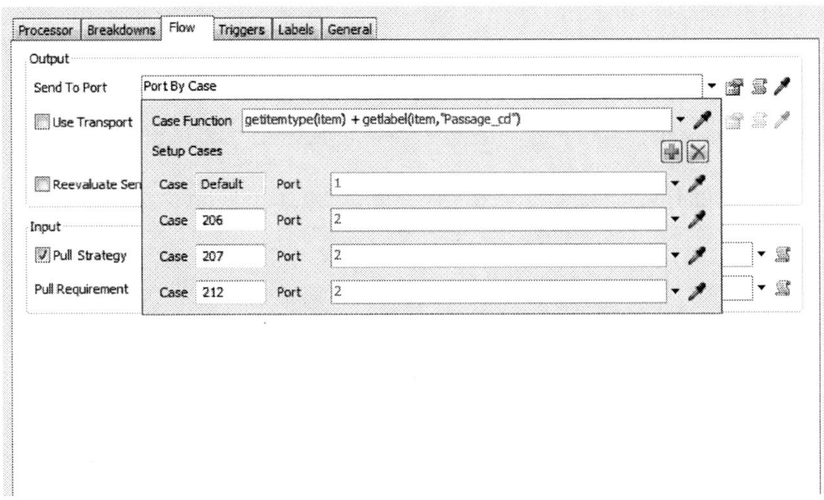

Figure 2: The part of flow of the Output of the machine

3.1.3 Queues:

We use a set of queues to either group the batches together to wait for the order to pass to the machine or to direct the batch to its next step. Here is the model in 3D view:

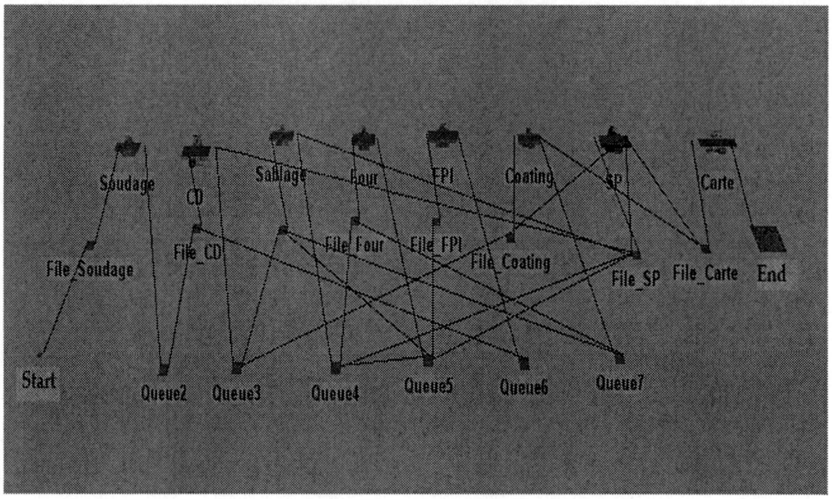

Figure 3: 3D view of the repair shop model.

4 Experimentation results

In the following, we present the experiments that have been established on our resolution approach. We performed several experiments on real instances, and we performed tests by simulating the application of a single rule in the entire studied part of the workshop, to then analyze and compare them with the results obtained by the proposed approach. Then, we compared between these and the real results obtained in the workshop, to be able to evaluate the effectiveness of the proposed approach.

The aim is to follow the evolution of the optimization through the different iterations as well as the comparison of the results obtained by our resolution approach with the real results of the workshop. For this we carried out experiments on an instance composed of 20 *jobs* that were launched for repair in 2015 to 2016 whose repair was completed in 2016.

For each job we have the following data that are entered into the simulator:
- The date of entry into the system.
- The operating range that represents the path of a job in the workshop.
- The processing time on each machine.
- Due date.

Job number	Job description	Repair starting date	Due date	Repair end date	Real time in the system
SB01135	Bucket HP MS5002	3/24/2015	6/21/2015	6/22/2016	456
SB01393	Bucket LP MS5002	3/24/2015	6/22/2015	2/23/2016	336
SB00910	Bucket LP MS5002	3/24/2015	6/23/2015	2/21/2016	334
SB01117	Bucket LP MS5002	8/18/2015	11/18/2015	12/1/2016	471
SB01411	Bucket LP MS5002	9/2/2015	12/5/2015	12/1/2016	456
SB01196	Bucket S2 MS6001	9/20/2015	2/17/2016	9/26/2016	372
SB01484	Bucket S2 MS6001	9/23/2015	2/21/2016	9/25/2016	368
SB01481	Bucket S2 MS6001	9/23/2015	2/22/2016	9/5/2016	348
SB01571	Bucket LP MS5002	10/6/2015	1/7/2016	4/28/2016	205
SB00862	Bucket HP MS5002	10/18/2015	1/21/2016	3/24/2016	158
SB00884	Bucket HP MS3002	10/21/2015	2/18/2016	7/31/2016	284
SB01357	Bucket HP MS5002	10/22/2015	3/23/2016	4/7/2016	168
SB01568	Bucket HP MS5002	11/8/2015	2/12/2016	9/24/2016	321
SB01301	Bucket HP MS5002	11/8/2015	2/6/2016	3/24/2016	137
SB01626	Bucket LP MS5002	11/16/2015	2/21/2016	10/6/2016	325
SB00669	Bucket HP MS5002	11/22/2015	2/28/2016	10/25/2016	338
SB01215	Bucket HP MS5002	11/22/2015	2/29/2016	8/18/2016	270
SB01621	Bucket HP MS5002	11/22/2015	2/18/2016	6/26/2016	217
SB01686	Bucket LP MS5002	3/2/2016	6/10/2016	9/26/2016	208
SB01696	Bucket HP MS5002	3/8/2016	6/17/2016	5/25/2016	78

Figure 4: Instance tested by the simulator

Two similar simulation models were programmed, with a different objective function for each.

The tests were run on an Intel(R) Core(TM) i5 CPU 2.50 Ghz and 4.00 Gb of RAM. After several preliminary tests, the following values were empirically chosen as parameters of our genetic algorithm: the population size *populationsize* is equal to 100 chromosomes. The crossover probability is equal to 0.90 and the mutation probability is equal to 0.1. The number of generations *Maxgeneration* (i.e., the stopping test is given by Maxgeneration is equal to 50).

We give an example of a test on an instance with simulation model 1. The optimality criterion that was programmed on this model is the minimization of the completion time of all jobs (the makespan). This instance is composed of 20 jobs of different ranges. The last column in Figure 4 represents the real time in the system calculated from the repair start date of the first job and the repair end date of the last job. The total time of the repair that was necessary in the workshop is: **618** days.

After launching the GA and the simulator, we obtain the solution of makespan is equal to 499. The simulator provides the following Gantt chart with the solution found to the scheduling problem posed.

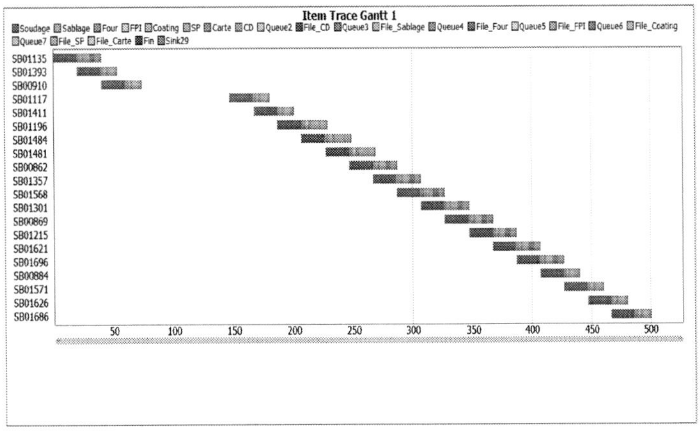

Figure 5: Gantt chart of the best solution Mod1.

The makespan obtained during this experiment is equal to **499** days. The number of days may seem large because this is due to the arrival dates of the last two jobs which are 345 and 350 days respectively after the arrival of the first job, see figure 5. But by comparing it with that achieved in the workshop which is **618** days, the number of working days optimized with our resolution approach on this instance of jobs is **119** days.

Our method has shown the performance of genetic algorithms in solving our job shop problem in the workshop which is a very complex problem. As well as the simulation of several management strategies by combining several priority rules. Note also that this method gives a solution in a very reasonable time (a few minutes), especially since the number of scenarios applied for each instance is enormous.

5 Conclusion

The main contribution of this study lies in the diverse solutions provided to the company's planners. In fact, this model makes it possible to act at any moment in case of change or unavailability of resources, urgency on a job or modification its due date. In addition, the simulator will be a powerful decision-support tool since it provides a Gantt chart, which is a way of modeling a solution to a scheduling problem. and visualize the entire system by giving an idea of the job order, and the dates of start of each job.

There are several possible extensions to this research work. Analyze different models related to the characteristics of the workshop for example: the dynamic arrival of jobs, unavailability of the spare part for machine maintenance as well as management of the human factor. It would also be interesting to develop other methods and compare them with the genetic algorithm. Also another direction of research is to take into account the stochastic aspect of our problem.

REFERENCES

Goldberg, D. E., and V. Corruble. 1994. *Algorithmes génétiques: exploration, optimisation et apprentissage automatique*. Ed. Addison-Wesley France.

Holland, J. 1975. "Adaptation in artificial and natural systems". *Ann Arbor: The University of Michigan Press*.

Lopez, P., and F. Roubellat. 2001. *Ordonnancement de la production*. Hermès science publications.

Luo, J., and D. El Baz. 2018. "A survey on parallel genetic algorithms for shop scheduling problems". In *2018 IEEE International Parallel and Distributed Processing Symposium Workshops (IPDPSW)*, 629–636. IEEE.

Phanden, R. K., A. Jain, and R. Verma. 2012. "A Genetic Algorithm-based Approach for Job Shop Scheduling". *International Journal of Production Research* 50 (24): 7318–7331.

Vaghefinezhad, S., and K. Y. Wong. 2012. "A genetic algorithm approach for solving a flexible job shop scheduling problem". *arXiv preprint arXiv:1207.2253*.

Wang, Y., B. van Stein, M. Emmerich, and T. Bäck. 2020. "A tailored NSGA-III instantiation for flexible job shop scheduling". *arXiv preprint arXiv:2004.06564*.

AUTHOR BIOGRAPHIES

Chakib Medjkane is an Algerian professional currently serving as the Inventory Control and Quality Audit Manager at Amazon. He obtained a Master's degree in Operational Research from the University of Sciences and Technology Houari Boumedienne (USTHB) in Algeria. He worked on a topic related to scheduling in a production environment and investigated optimization techniques to enhance operational efficiency.

Yasmine Rihane has obtained her Master's degree in Operational Research from the University of Science and Technology Houari Boumediene (USTHB) in Algeria. She worked on a topic related to scheduling in production environnement, where she explores optimization techniques to improve operational efficiency.

Nacira Chikhi is an Associate Professor in the Department of Operational Research at the University of Science and Technology Houari Boumediene (USTHB) in Algeria. She received her Habilitation in Operational Research from USTHB. Her research focuses on various aspects of Operational Research, particularly scheduling problems, mathematical modeling, and optimization techniques. She has published numerous research papers in leading international journals and conference proceedings, addressing topics in Operational Research, transportation, manufacturing, and healthcare.

Proceedings of the Operational Research Society Simulation Workshop 2025 (SW25)
M. Luis, A. Harper, T. Monks and N. Mustafee, eds.
https://doi.org/10.36819/SW25.008

SIMULATION MODELING FOR SURGERY ROOM SCHEDULING PROBLEM

Mr. Ibrahim Kridi

Khemis Miliana University
i.kridi@univ-dbkm.dz

Mr. Tawfiq Tabouche

Khemis Miliana University
t.tabouche7@gmail.com

Dr. Imène Ait Abderrahim

Khemis Miliana University
LIM laboratory, University of Tiaret
i.aitabderrahim@univ-dbkm.dz

ABSTRACT

The Operating Room Scheduling Problem (ORSP) is a complex NP-hard optimization challenge that significantly impacts the efficiency and effectiveness of healthcare systems. This problem involves allocating surgical cases to available operating rooms while adhering to multiple constraints, such as the availability of surgeons, nurses, and facilities, as well as meeting diverse operational objectives. In this study, we simulate the feasibility of surgical schedules under varying resource availability and management scenarios. Using real-world data from a hospital in Algeria, we evaluate the performance of the schedule through a series of scenario-based experiments. The findings provide valuable insights into managing limited resources and mitigating the challenges posed by resource unavailability, offering practical implications for improving operating room scheduling and overall healthcare delivery.

1 INTRODUCTION

The Operating Room Scheduling Problem (ORSP) poses a significant challenge in combinatorial optimization, revolving around the allocation of surgical procedures to available operating rooms within a specified timeframe (Cardoen, Demeulemeester, and Beliën 2010). The primary objective of ORSP is to maximize resource utilization while minimizing patient waiting times, thereby enhancing overall healthcare efficiency. Effective scheduling strategies play a pivotal role in hospital management, offering potential cost reductions and improvements in care quality (Xiang, Yin, and Lim 2015).

ORSP entails consideration of various constraints, including the availability of operating rooms, surgical staff, and equipment, as well as factors like surgery priorities, duration, and postoperative recovery needs. Particularly in scenarios involving numerous surgical cases, the complexity of the scheduling problem escalates, necessitating the incorporation of case interdependencies (Gu, Liu, and Xiang 2015) (Toub, Souissi, and Achchab 2022).

This problem is proven to be NP-hard in the strong sense which means that, in most cases (excluding instances of small size), it is not possible to find the optimal solution (i.e. the optimal project schedule) within an acceptable processing time. Additionally, in practice, hospitals or healthcare centers need to manage not only a single schedule but several schedules for the different days of the week (Rahimi and Gandomi 2021). To address these challenges, researchers have turned to algorithmic solutions for surgery schedules by framing them as a combinatorial optimization problem. However, the feasibility of the obtained schedule by this algorithm is not reliable if some resources become unavailable at some point in the schedule (Ait Abderrahim, Kridi, and Tabouche 2024).

In this paper, we present a simulation study for scheduling surgeries based on resource availability and its impact on the initial schedule, which is basically based computation of some numerical parameters related to resources availability and surgery durations.

2 DATASET DESCRIPTION

Due to the ORSP's diverse constraints and goals, researchers have created various instance sets tailored to their models. The current data were collected manually from "Boukhroufa Abdelkader" hospital in Ben Aknoun, Algiers, Algeria. The dataset includes the following information:

- **Index**: A unique identifier for each surgery.
- **Name**: Name or description of the surgery.
- **Duration**: Duration of the surgery(per min).
- **Professeur**: Number of professors required per surgery.
- **Surgeon doctor**: Number of Surgeon doctors required per surgery.
- **Resident doctor**: Number of resident doctors required/surgery.
- **Surgery room**: The block or the room where the surgery is scheduled to take place.
- **Anesthetist**: Number of anesthesiologists required.
- **Nurse** : Number of Nurse staff required.

3 EXPERIMENTAL RESULTS: EXAMPLE OF AN APPLICATION

In these experiments, we study the impact of different resource availability on the efficiency of a schedule of one day for a real work application. The base schedule is a schedule from the Hospital of Algiers mentioned previously. In the simulations, we consider the absence or unavailability of certain resources and evaluate their impact on the schedule. This study considers 12 scenarios.

Note that, in the current study, we consider that the total available working time per day is 8 hours (From 8 am to 4 pm), with no scheduled break time for planned surgeries. Additionally, the hospital considered in the case study does not operate 24-hour surgeries, meaning that all procedures must be completed within the available working hours mentioned previously.

Moreover, this study does not take into account dynamic emergency surgeries; we perform only the scheduled surgeries planned in advance by the hospital staff. The average duration time per surgery is about 193 minutes .

The number of resources used in these experiments is described in Table 1 as follows:

Table 1: Dataset details

Resources	Total number
Professor	3
Surgeon doctor	4
Reseident doctor	8
Surgery room	3
anesthetist	6
Nurse	9

For this study, we consider twelve (12) scenarios. These scenarios were chosen based on the provided information by the hospital managers where they explain that sometimes the hospital go through difficult situations when a few resources are not available without prior notice. Therefore, to generate new schedules they do it manually, which is time consuming and exhausting task and from the other hand influences on the scheduled surgeries time. With this study, our aim is to provide a simpler and better way to simulate these situations in a quicker way for better decision making. The considered scenarios for these experiments are described as follows:

- S1: Reduce one *Professor* resource.
- S2: One *Professor* resource is unavailable from 08h00 to 12h00.
- S3: One *Professor* resource is unavailable from 14h00 to 17h00.
- S4: Reduce one (1) *Room* resource.
- S5: Reduce two (2) *Room* resource
- S6: One *Room* resource is unavailable from 08h00 to 12h00
- S7: One *Room* resource is unavailable from 14h00 to 17h00
- S8: Reduce one (1) *Nurse* resource.
- S9: Reduce two (2) *Nurse* resource

- S10: Reduce one (1) *Surgeon* resource and one (1) *Nurse* resource.
- S11: A surgery x has 30 min delay.
- S12: A surgery x has 60 min delay.

For the experimental part, to evaluate the scenarios, we use the simulator "SimPy", a process-based discrete-event simulation framework based on standard Python [1]. The obtained results (schedules) for all the tested scenarios are illustrated in Figure 2. Additionally, for comparison study, we illustrate the original schedule for 1 day in Figure 1.

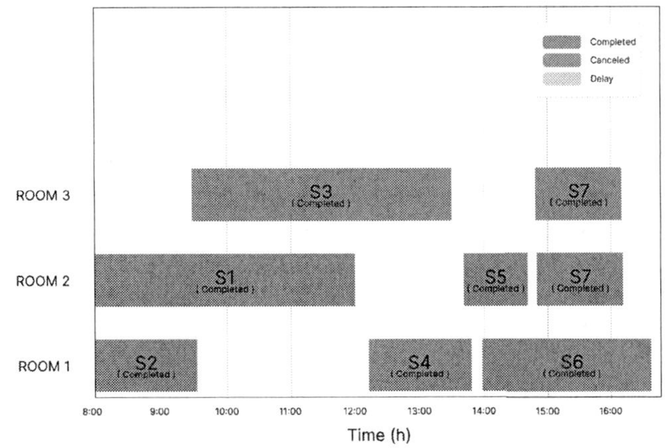

Figure 1: Original Schedule for 1 day

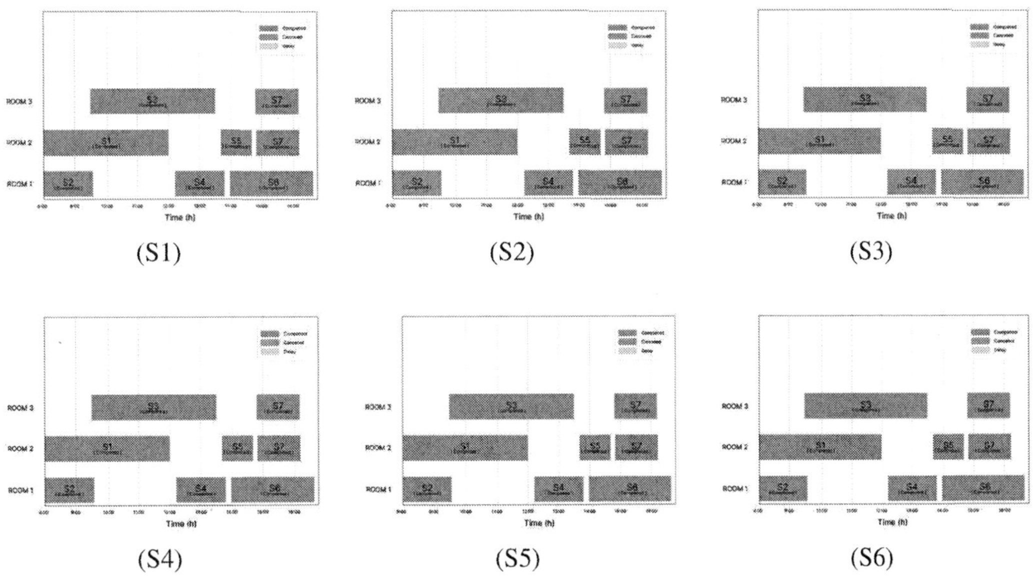

(S1) (S2) (S3)

(S4) (S5) (S6)

Figure 2: Professors, Nurses and Surgeon Scenarios

The results presented in Figure 2 illustrate the impact of different scenarios involving the removal or unavailability of professors, nurses, and surgeons (S1-S6) on the scheduling of surgeries across multiple operating rooms. Despite these disruptions, the overall schedule appears to maintain feasibility, showing that the system has some resilience to moderate resource unavailability.

[1] https://simpy.readthedocs.io/en/latest/index.html

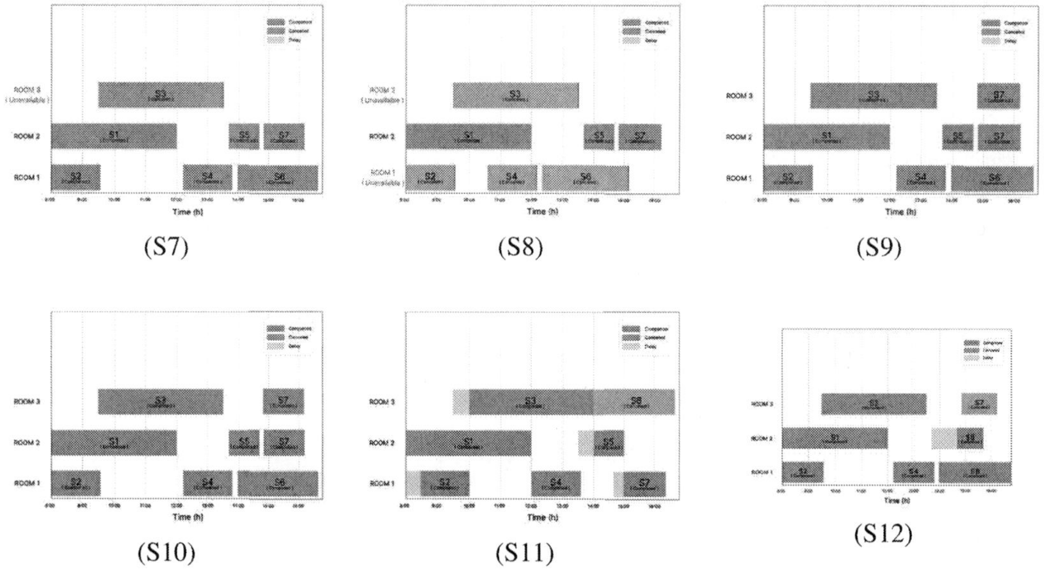

(S7) (S8) (S9)

(S10) (S11) (S12)

Figure 3: Rooms and delays Scenarios

The results in Figure 3 illustrate the effects of different resource constraints on operating room scheduling. S7 to S10 depict the impact of unavailable surgery rooms, for the whole day or for a period of time during the day. Notably, in scenarios S7 and S8, where one or more surgery rooms are removed, a clear reduction in available scheduling slots is observed, leading to increased cancellations of surgeries. Scenarios S11 and S12 focus on surgery delays, where delayed surgeries (highlighted in grey and orange) indicate bottlenecks in resource allocation. S11, in particular, shows a more significant delay impact compared to S12, which maintains schedule stability despite minor delays. Overall, the results emphasize that while the scheduling system is resilient to moderate constraints, severe disruptions, such as multiple staff unavailabilities or extended delays, pose significant operational challenges.

Table 2: Simulation Results for Scheduling Scenarios

Scenario	Affected Resources	Makespan (Overtime/min)	Completed	Canceled	Delayed
Professor Scenarios					
S1	1 professor removed	8h (0)	7	0	0
S2	1 professor (4-hour unavailability)	8h (0)	7	0	0
S3	1 professor (3-hour unavailability)	8h (0)	7	0	0
Nurse and Surgeon Scenarios					
S4	1 nurse removed	8h (0)	7	0	0
S5	2 nurses removed	8h (0)	7	0	0
S6	1 surgeon, 1 nurse removed	8h (0)	7	0	0
Surgery Room Scenarios					
S7	1 surgery room removed	8h (0)	6	1	0
S8	2 surgery rooms removed	8h (0)	3	4	0
S9	1 surgery room (4-hour unavailability)	8h (0)	7	0	0
S10	1 surgery room (3-hour unavailability)	8h (0)	7	0	0
Surgery Delay Scenarios					
S11	1 surgery delayed	8.5h (30)	6	1	4
S12	1 surgery delayed	8h (0)	6	1	1

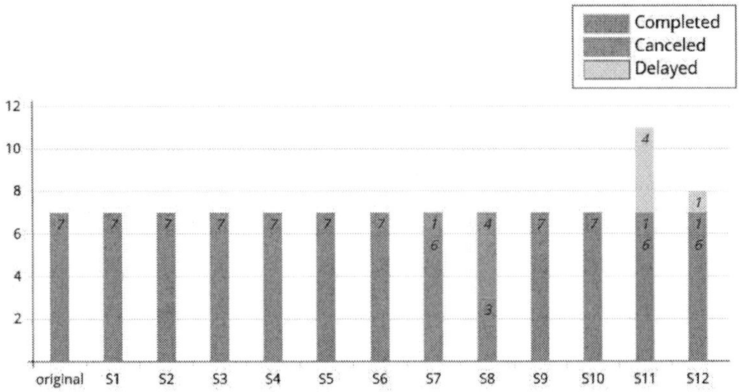

Figure 4: Surgery outcomes accross scienarios

The results in Table 2 and Figure 4 summarize the full experiments and demonstrate that the proposed scheduling is robust to certain resource constraints, such as temporary unavailability of professors, nurses, and surgeons, as no surgeries were canceled or delayed in these scenarios. However, surgery room availability emerged as a critical bottleneck, with the removal of one or more rooms significantly reducing the number of completed surgeries such as in scenarios S7 and S8. This highlights the need for contingency planning, such as allocating backup rooms or implementing flexible scheduling strategies.

Additionally, scenarios involving surgery delays such as S11 and S12 revealed the schedule's sensitivity to disruptions, leading to overtime, cancellations, and delays. These findings emphasize the importance of minimizing delays through improved preparation processes or incorporating buffer times into the schedule. Overall, the study underscores the need to prioritize critical resources, such as operating rooms, while maintaining sufficient redundancy in staffing.

4 CONCLUSION

This study proposed an effective approach for managing resources in operating room scheduling while adhering to critical availability constraints. We considered twelve scenarios showcasing the delay or unavailability of a few resources such as professor, surgery room, nurses. The results from the application example demonstrate the robustness and efficiency of the proposed schedule, with the primary schedule remaining largely stable across various scenarios. However, minor adjustments were observed in a few scenario cases where critical constraints, such as operating room availability, or delays in surgeries were more restrictive. Although this work is ongoing, the initial findings underline the potential of the approach in addressing resource management challenges in healthcare settings. Future work should focus on testing the approach with larger-scale scenarios and exploring adaptive rescheduling algorithms to enhance flexibility and resilience.

5 DISCLAIMER (ARTIFICIAL INTELLIGENCE)

Author(s) hereby declare that generative AI technology like ChatGPT has been used during writing or editing part of this manuscript. The ChatGPT, version GPT-3.5 was used, model developed by OpenAI. The source of this technology is OpenAI, a research organization focused on artificial intelligence. This generative AI technology was utilized to assist in drafting and refining the text. The use of this AI tool included providing language suggestions and ensuring coherence and clarity throughout the manuscript.

Prompts used included the following

- Reformulate the following paragraph
- Improve the quality of the the text
- summarize the text into shorter paragraphs

REFERENCES

Ait Abderrahim, I., I. Kridi, and T. Tabouche. 2024. "Ant Colony Optimization for Operating Room Scheduling: Improved Efficiency and Resource Management". In *2024 International Conference of the African Federation of Operational Research Societies (AFROS)*, 1–5.

Cardoen, B., E. Demeulemeester, and J. Beliën. 2010. "Operating room planning and scheduling: A literature review". *European journal of operational research* 201 (3): 921–932.

Gu, C., Q. Liu, and W. Xiang. 2015. "A Modified Ant Colony Optimization for the Multi-Objective Operating Room Scheduling". In *Advances in Swarm and Computational Intelligence: 6th International Conference, ICSI 2015, held in conjunction with the Second BRICS Congress, CCI 2015, Beijing, China, June 25-28, 2015, Proceedings, Part I 6*, 197–204. Springer.

Rahimi, I., and A. H. Gandomi. 2021. "A comprehensive review and analysis of operating room and surgery scheduling". *Archives of Computational Methods in Engineering* 28 (3): 1667–1688.

Toub, M., O. Souissi, and S. Achchab. 2022. "Operating room scheduling 2019 survey". *International Journal of Medical Engineering and Informatics* 14 (1): 1–30.

Xiang, W., J. Yin, and G. Lim. 2015. "An ant colony optimization approach for solving an operating room surgery scheduling problem". *Computers & Industrial Engineering* 85:335–345.

IMENE AIT ABDERRAHIM holds a PhD in Computer Science (2020) from the University of Oran1, Oran, Algeria. She works as an Associate Professor at Khemis Miliana University, Ain Defla, Algeria. Her research area is about Operations Research, Combinatorial Optimization, Swarm Intelligence, Automatic Algorithm Configuration and Machine Learning. She is especially interested in investigating the automatic algorithm configuration for different problems especially the real world cases. She is also interested in combining metaheuristics with artificial intelligence and machine learning methods to solve problems in operations research and optimization.

IBRAHIM KRIDI is a Computer Science engineer and holds a Master's degree in Computer Science (2023) from Khemis Miliana University, Ain Defla, Algeria. He works as an assistant teacher at Khemis Miliana University. His research focuses on Operations Research, Combinatorial Optimization, Swarm Intelligence, and Simulation Modeling. He is also skilled in programming for mobiles, web, and desktop applications.

TAWFIQ TABOUCHE is a PhD student at Tambov State Technical University,Tambov, Russia. He earned his Master's degree in Computer Science from Khemis Miliana University, Ain Defla, Algeria, in 2023. His research specializes in Operations Research, Swarm Intelligence, and problem-solving, with a particular focus on integrating metaheuristics with artificial intelligence techniques to tackle complex optimization challenges.

Proceedings of the Operational Research Society Simulation Workshop 2025 (SW25)
M. Luis, A. Harper, T. Monks and N. Mustafee, eds.
https://doi.org/10.36819/SW25.009

OPTIMIZING WASTE TREATMENT CENTER LOCATIONS: A MATHEMATICAL MODELING AND SIMULATION APPROACH

Younes Abderrahim

LAP Laboratory
University of Batna 2
Batna, Algeria
younes.abderrahim@univ-batna2.dz

Salah Eddine Bellal

LAP Laboratory
University of Batna 2
Batna, Algeria
s.bellal@univ-batna2.dz

M'hammed Sahnoun

CESI LINEACT
Rouen, France
msahnoun@cesi.fr

ABSTRACT

Waste management is becoming increasingly important for developing countries due to its impact on the environment, health, and economy. Challenges in waste management are often attributed to inefficient collection systems and poorly planned installations. This underscores the need for strategic decisions, beginning with the optimal location of waste treatment centers, particularly in the context of rapidly expanding urban areas. This paper examines the placement of waste treatment centers in the city of Tlemcen, Algeria. It includes various types of centers and considers strategic and operational constraints. A mathematical model was developed to determine the optimal locations, and its feasibility was verified through simulations that introduced more realistic constraints. Key aspects include minimizing transportation costs, complying with regulations, and gaining social acceptance. The study highlights the importance of simulation in strategic planning and provides valuable insights for policymakers to improve waste management practices in developing countries.

1 INTRODUCTION

Waste management has become an increasingly urgent global challenge due to the continual rise in waste generation and its consequential impacts on the environment and public health. The world generates billions of tons of municipal solid waste annually, yet only a fraction is managed sustainably. Poorly handled waste contaminates water bodies, undermines ecosystems, spreads diseases, and contributes to climate change through greenhouse gas emissions (Nichols and Smith 2019, Wong, Surampalli, Zhang, Tyagi, and Selvam 2016).

In many developing countries, including Algeria, these challenges are particularly acute. Rapid urbanization—characterized by the emergence of new cities and expansions of existing urban areas—strains existing waste treatment infrastructures. In Tlemcen, for instance, the exponential growth of new housing projects and the limited capacity of its traditional treatment centers have led to a pressing need for strategic studies focusing on where to locate new treatment facilities. Complying with national environmental regulations and gaining community acceptance further complicates these location decisions (Abderrahim, eddine Bellal, and Sahnoun 2023, Cheniti, Kerboua, Sekiou, Aouissi, Benselhoub, Mansouri, Zeriri, Barbari, Gilev, and Bouslama 2024).

Simulation methods have long been used to evaluate the performance of waste management systems under various scenarios. Among these, discrete-event simulation (DES) has been the dominant technique, largely because it excels at modeling logistical processes such as truck routing, scheduling, and processing times at facilities (de Oliveira, Fagundes, da Silva Lima, and Montaño 2020, Knapčíková, Behúnová, and

Behún 2020). DES models, however, often fall short when the problem involves complex interactions between human behavior, environmental factors, and spatial dynamics. For example, DES typically treats waste flows and generation rates as pre-defined and static, making it less suited to scenarios where waste production patterns evolve over time or where community behavior (e.g., recycling participation rates, illegal dumping) significantly influences system performance.

In contrast, agent-based modeling (ABM) provides a more flexible framework for representing these dynamic and heterogeneous behaviors. ABMs simulate the actions and interactions of individual agents—such as households, collection vehicles, and facility operators—allowing the model to capture the emergent effects of local decisions on system-wide outcomes. For instance, ABM can represent how a new facility's proximity to a neighborhood might influence local recycling rates or how changes in waste disposal fees alter household behavior(Tian, Peng, Wei, Xiao, Ma, Hu, and Liu 2025, Ribeiro-Rodrigues and Bortoleto 2024, Ceschi, Sartori, Dickert, Scalco, Tur, Tommasi, and Delfini 2021).

While DES offers a well-established foundation for logistics-focused analyses, ABM opens new possibilities for integrating human and environmental dimensions into waste management models. By incorporating both behavioral variability and spatial heterogeneity, ABMs can complement optimization approaches by providing a richer understanding of how strategic decisions perform under real-world conditions(Ding, Gong, Li, and Wu 2018).

Despite the demonstrated strengths of ABM in modeling dynamic human-environment interactions, its use in waste management remains relatively limited. Most waste facility location studies still rely on optimization methods and, to a lesser extent, DES for performance evaluation. There is a lack of research that systematically combines ABM's ability to capture evolving waste behaviors with optimization models' capacity to identify cost-effective facility locations(Anvari and Turkay 2017)

Moreover, existing hybrid approaches have primarily focused on integrating DES with optimization, leaving a gap in the literature for ABM-based methods. This gap is particularly notable in the context of developing countries, where the need to account for community behaviors and rapidly changing urban conditions is critical.

1.1 Contributions

To address these gaps, this paper introduces a hybrid framework that combines an integer linear programming (ILP) model for optimizing waste treatment center locations with an agent-based model for dynamic system evaluation. This framework provides the following contributions:

1. **Novel integration of ABM and optimization:** By leveraging ABM's capacity to simulate human behavior, we extend the capabilities of optimization models to capture dynamic and spatially variable conditions.
2. **Application in a developing country context:** We demonstrate the framework's relevance by applying it to the Tlemcen region in Algeria, offering insights into how strategic decisions interact with local social and environmental factors.
3. **Comparison of simulation approaches:** We highlight the advantages of ABM over DES for certain aspects of waste management, providing guidance for future researchers and practitioners on when to use one method versus the other.

The remainder of this paper is structured as follows: Section 2 presents the mathematical optimization model, detailing the objective function, decision variables, and constraints. Section 3 introduces the ABM framework, explaining the agent interactions, parameterization, and validation methods. Section 4 discusses the experimental setup and the results of the hybrid approach, comparing it to traditional simulation methods. Finally, Section 5 concludes the paper and outlines future directions for research on hybrid simulation-optimization models in waste management.

2 MATHEMATICAL MODEL

The objective of the optimisation model is to minimize the total cost associated with waste management, which includes variable costs such as collection costs, CO2 pollution costs, and truck usage costs, as well as fixed costs defined by treatment center implementation costs, while also considering the distances between treatment centers, cities and sensitive zone.

Sets and Indices

- I: Set of cities, indexed by i.
- K: Set of potential treatment center sites, indexed by k.
- SZ: Set of sensitive zones, indexed by z.

Parameters

- T_i: Daily waste quantity generated by city i.
- DT_{ik}: Cost of collecting and transporting one unit of waste from city i to a treatment center at location k.
- CAP_k: Capacity of the treatment center located at the location k (in units of waste per day).
- COC_k: Fixed (setup) cost of opening or implementing a treatment center at location k.
- CTT_k: Cost of treating one unit of waste (tonne) at center k.
- u: Pollution cost coefficient (CO_2 cost per distance/waste unit).
- D_{ik}: Distance between city i and treatment center k.
- Dk: Minimum acceptable distance between centers and any city (e.g., regulatory or social constraint).
- DP_{kz}: Distance between potential center site k and sensitive zone z.
- Dz: Minimum required distance from sensitive zones.
- CP: Capacity of one truck (in units of waste per trip). We assume that all the trucks have the same capacity.
- QT: Cost of operating a single truck (daily or monthly basis, depending on time horizon).
- $\mathscr{Y}$: Total number of available trucks in the system.
- DT: Daily time window for collecting waste (hours per day).

Decision Variables

- $X_{ik} \in \{0,1\}$: Binary variable, equals 1 if city i is served by a treatment center at location k, and 0 otherwise.
- $Y_k \in \mathbb{N}$: Integer variable representing the number of trucks assigned to center k.
- $Z_k \in \{0,1\}$: Binary variable, equals 1 if a treatment center at location k is opened, and 0 otherwise.

Objective Function

$$\min \underbrace{\sum_{k\in K} COC_k \cdot Z_k}_{\text{(Fixed center setup costs)}} + \underbrace{\sum_{i\in I}\sum_{k\in K} (DT_{ik} + u\cdot D_{ik})\, T_i X_{ik}}_{\text{(Transport and pollution costs)}} + \underbrace{\sum_{i\in I}\sum_{k\in K} CTT_k T_i X_{ik}}_{\text{(Treatment costs)}} + \underbrace{\sum_{k\in K} Y_k \cdot QT}_{\text{(Truck usage costs)}} \quad (1)$$

Where :

- Fixed center setup costs: $\sum_{k\in K} COC_k Z_k$ captures the cost of opening a treatment center at site k.
- Transport and pollution costs: $\sum_{i\in I}\sum_{k\in K}(DT_{ik} + u\cdot D_{ik}) T_i X_{ik}$ combines both distance-based transport cost and CO_2 pollution cost, scaled by the waste quantity T_i sent from city i to site k.
- Treatment costs: $\sum_{i\in I}\sum_{k\in K} CTT_k T_i X_{ik}$ covers the cost of processing/disposing of waste at the treatment center.
- Truck usage costs: $\sum_{k\in K} Y_k \cdot QT$ reflects the total cost for the number of trucks assigned to each center.

Constraints
Facility Activation and Serving Constraint

$$X_{ik} \leq Z_k, \quad \forall i \in I, \forall k \in K \quad (2)$$

If the center k is not opened ($Z_k = 0$), no city can be served by that center.

Capacity Constraints

$$\sum_{i \in I} T_i\, X_{ik} \;\leq\; CAP_k \cdot Z_k, \quad \forall k \in K \tag{3}$$

The total waste going to center k cannot exceed its capacity. If $Z_k = 0$, no waste can be sent there.

Minimum Distance to Sensitive Zones

$$DP_{kz} \geq D \cdot Z_k, \quad \forall k \in K, \forall z \in Z \tag{4}$$

If $Z_k = 1$, site k must respect the regulatory distance D from each sensitive zone z.

Minimum Distance from Cities

$$D_{ik} X_{ik} \;\geq\; D_{\min} \cdot X_{ik}, \quad \forall i \in I, \forall k \in K \tag{5}$$

Truck Allocation Constraints

$$\sum_{k \in K} Y_k \leq \mathscr{Y} \tag{6}$$

The total number of trucks used across all centers cannot exceed the total available $\mathscr{Y}$.

Truck Capacity and Time Window Constraints

To ensure the assigned trucks at center k can collect T_i from each city i.

$$Y_k \geq \sum_{i \in I} \left(\frac{T_i X_{ik}}{CP} \right) \cdot \left(\frac{\text{Travel Time}(\text{dist}_{ik})}{DT} \right), \quad \forall k \in K \tag{7}$$

where Travel Time(dist_{ik}) is some function of D_{ik}, possibly $\frac{D_{ik}}{\text{average speed}}$.

Each city i must be assigned to one or more treatment centers.

To ensure that the assigned city at center k can collect T_i, we have:

$$\sum_{k \in K} T_i \cdot X_{ik} \geq 1, \quad \forall i \in I \tag{8}$$

With:

$$X_{ik} \in \{0,1\}, \quad Z_k \in \{0,1\}, \quad Y_k \in \mathbb{N} \tag{9}$$

2.1 Discussion

Z_k governs whether a treatment center is opened at location k, while X_{ik} specifies if city i is assigned to center k. Including both variables enables a clear separation between center-opening decisions (fixed costs, capacity) and city assignments. This approach is a common standard in facility location problems *[add relevant references here]*.

The objective function in (1) balances "fixed setup costs", "transportation/pollution costs", "waste treatment costs", and "truck operations costs", facilitating an integrated view of the strategic decision. Constraints (2) and (3) ensure logical consistency of the assignment, while constraints (4) and (5) handle environmental and social acceptance criteria.

3 SIMULATION

Our objective of the simulation is to develop an approach that minimizes costs associated with waste collection, treatment, and transportation, while also reducing CO_2 emissions in realistic situation and see the long term effect of the proposed solution. This will be achieved by optimizing the spatial arrangement of waste treatment centers, using the mathematical modelling and and simulate this solutions using the multi-agent simulator. This section presents details of the development of this simulator.

The simulation model can evaluate the solution with the consideration of a stochastic value of the generated stage and a dynamic model of population growth and urban extension. In this case, the problem of the quantity of generated waste will grow with the number of population and the distance between the treatment center and the cities (collection points) will variate because of the urban extension. We used a multi-agent modelling of the process where each important element in the considered system is considered as an agent that have his own behaviour and it interacts with the rest of the elements of the system. The Figure 1 is our process model for the problem of locating waste treatment centers. In the rest of this section, we explain the role of each agent and its interactions.

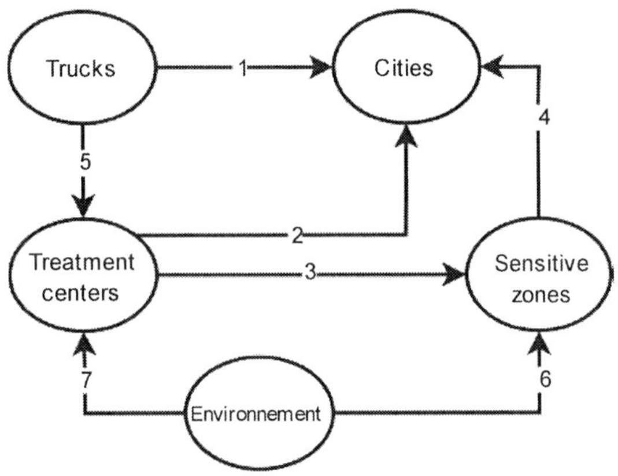

Figure 1: multi-agent conceptual model

- Cities: Urban areas where waste is generated and collected. Each city has specific waste management needs and capacities that must be considered in the optimization model.
- Trucks: Vehicles used for the collection and transportation of waste from cities to treatment centers. The number of trucks and their capacity are critical factors in the efficiency of the waste management system.
- Treatment Centers: Facilities where waste is processed, treated, or disposed of. These centers have specific capacities and associated costs that impact the overall waste management strategy.
- Sensitive Zones: Areas that require special consideration due to environmental, health, or regulatory concerns. Waste management operations near these zones must adhere to stricter guidelines to minimize negative impacts.
- Environment: The natural surroundings affected by waste management activities, including air, water, and land. Environmental considerations are essential for ensuring sustainable practices and minimizing pollution and ecological damage.

The different interactions are as follows:

- **Interaction (1):** *Trucks collect waste from cities:* Trucks collect waste from cities, with their efficiency depending on factors like capacity, fuel consumption, and routing strategies. As cities generate waste stochastically, the system must adapt to varying waste quantities and urban growth. Poor routing or insufficient truck capacity can lead to delays, increased costs, and overflow in cities, while optimized strategies reduce emissions and improve service levels.
- **Interaction (2):** *Treatment centers affect cities (through emissions and disease transmission):* Treatment centers impact nearby cities through emissions (e.g., CO, methane) and potential disease transmission. Proximity to urban areas exacerbates these effects, degrading air quality and increasing health risks. Over time, urban expansion may bring cities closer to treatment centers, intensifying these negative impacts unless mitigated by emission control technologies or strategic location planning.
- **Interaction (3):** *Treatment centers affect sensitive zones (via visual pollution, odor, and disease):* Treatment centers negatively affect sensitive zones, such as natural reserves or water bodies, through visual pollution, odors, and disease vectors. Environmental factors like wind direction and water flow determine the spread of pollutants, potentially harming ecosystems and biodiversity. Buffer zones and pollution dispersion models can help minimize these impacts.
- **Interaction (4):** *Direct and indirect effects on cities and populations, regardless of distance:* Waste management practices have far-reaching effects, impacting cities and populations even at considerable distances. For example, contaminated water sources or air pollution from treatment centers can affect regions far beyond their immediate vicinity. These indirect effects highlight

the need for comprehensive waste management strategies that consider regional and long-term environmental consequences.

- **Interaction (5):** *Trucks transport waste from cities to treatment centers:* Waste collection trucks transport waste from cities to treatment centers, with their efficiency depending on factors such as road infrastructure, traffic conditions, and transportation distances. Urban sprawl increases these distances, leading to higher fuel consumption, costs, and emissions. Increasing the number of collection routes while optimizing them can minimize the number of trucks needed, reducing environmental and operational impacts. Additionally, using eco-friendly vehicles can further enhance efficiency and sustainability.
- **Interaction (6):** *Rate of effect of sensitive zones and the environment:* The impact of treatment centers on sensitive zones and the environment depends on factors like wind patterns, water flow, and topography. Pollutants can travel long distances, affecting ecosystems and increasing transportation costs due to poor road conditions. Modeling pollutant dispersion and improving infrastructure can mitigate these effects
- **Interaction (7):** *Environmental influence on treatment centers and cities:* The environment plays a crucial role in determining the impacts of treatment centers on cities, particularly concerning health and ecological effects. Factors such as climate, geography, and local biodiversity can modulate how waste management practices affect urban areas and surrounding ecosystems.

4 EXPERIMENTATION AND RESULTS

In this section, we evaluate the performance of our hybrid approach under three distinct scenarios. First, we present the experimental setup, including data sources and model parameters. We then summarize the results in a single compact table, followed by a concise discussion comparing key performance indicators across scenarios.

4.1 Experimental Setup

We consider three scenarios reflecting different waste management strategies in the Tlemcen region:

- **Scenario 1:** Single existing waste treatment center using traditional methods.
- **Scenario 2:** Addition of a second, partially modernized center to supplement the existing one.
- **Scenario 3:** Replacement of the original center with an advanced facility featuring technologies such as pyrolysis, gasification, or incineration with energy recovery.

Each scenario is simulated over a predefined planning horizon (e.g., one year). Key parameters include city populations, daily waste generation rates, truck capacities, treatment center capacities, and distances between cities and centers. *[Add references or details on any additional assumptions or data sources here.]*

4.2 Consolidated Results

Table 1 provides a succinct overview of the primary outcomes across all three scenarios. We measure:

- *Coverage Rate:* Percentage of total waste collected and routed to an official treatment center.
- *Treatment Efficiency:* Proportion of collected waste successfully processed, disposed of, or recovered.
- *Energy Recovery (where applicable):* Approximate electricity generated (kWh per ton of treated waste), relevant only for technologies in Scenarios 2 and 3.
- *Estimated Cost:* Includes capital, operational, and transportation costs.

4.3 Discussion of Findings

Scenario 1 achieves a moderate treatment efficiency but exhibits the lowest coverage rate, indicating that a significant portion of waste remains uncollected or unmanaged. This gap can lead to environmental degradation, public health issues, and illegal dumping.

Table 1: Comparison of Scenarios: Key Indicators

Scenario	Coverage Rate (%)	Treatment Efficiency (%)	Energy Recovery (kWh/ton)
1. Traditional Center	55.6	99.99	–
2. Improved Center	74.5	99.99	50
3. Advanced Center	92.6	99.99	70

Scenario 2 improves coverage by adding a second center with partial technological enhancements. Although this scenario still leaves areas underserved, it significantly reduces the uncollected waste volume compared to Scenario 1.

Scenario 3 presents the best coverage rate and incorporates advanced treatment technologies, including energy recovery. Despite a higher initial investment and operational complexity, the system mitigates environmental impacts and enhances sustainability by generating electricity from waste. However, the overall energy balance may remain negative when factoring in the cost of technology, logistics, and maintenance, underscoring that the main benefit is improved waste management rather than profitable energy production.

By evaluating each scenario's coverage, treatment efficiency, and cost implications, decision-makers can balance economic, environmental, and social criteria. Adopting advanced technologies, as seen in Scenario 3, appears to offer the most effective long-term solution—particularly in rapidly urbanizing regions—although higher short-term costs and infrastructural requirements must be accounted for.

Key Takeaways:

- Adding even a partially modernized facility significantly improves coverage, reducing negative externalities.
- Advanced technologies in Scenario 3 yield superior performance in terms of coverage and potential energy recovery.
- Policymakers must consider upfront costs, funding mechanisms, and community acceptance, especially in developing regions.

4.4 General discussion

The results of the three scenarios can be analyzed along three axes, as shown in the Figure 2 :

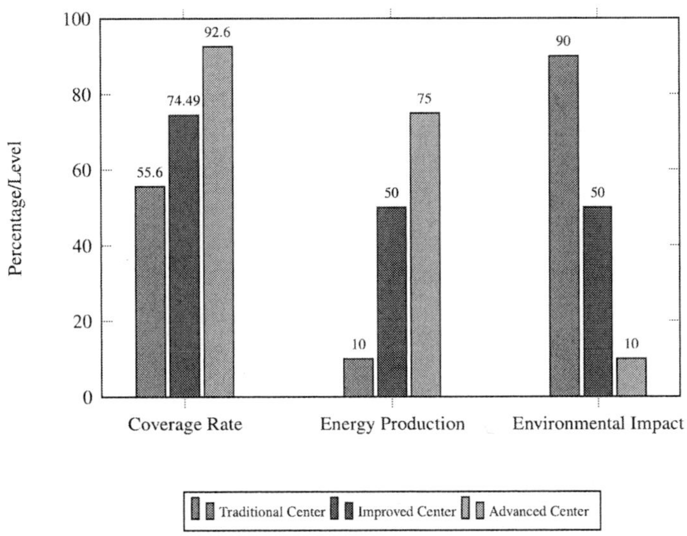

Figure 2: Comparison of scenario results

From the figure 2, it is clear that the coverage rate is closely linked to the technologies used in the treatment centers. A more advanced technology makes it possible to achieve a significantly higher treatment rate than that obtained with traditional methods such as landfill or open-air incineration. In addition, advanced technologies offer major benefits in terms of social and environmental impact, considerably reducing the nuisances for local populations and ecosystems.

In terms of energy, although energy production is still moderate with these technologies, their adoption in Algeria has significant advantages. Indeed, in a country where the cost of energy production is relatively low, the interest does not lie solely in energy recovery but more in reducing environmental impacts and improving the quality of life of residents. These modern technologies thus contribute to more sustainable waste management while aligning national practices with international environmental protection standards.

4.5 Perspectives

The three studied scenarios highlight the limitations of waste management systems in Tlemcen, particularly regarding geographical coverage and environmental impact. The originality of this research lies in the introduction of new performance indicators that provide a more detailed assessment of the social and environmental impacts of waste treatment centers. The following index can be included in the evaluation of the solution:

- Risk level of each sensitive zone
- Rate of the protected zone affected by the policy of waste management
- Coverage rate of each treatment center
- Quality of life index that can be a rated sum of the previous indicators.

Also, we aim to develop other behaviours related to the population behaviour in terms of selective sorting and consumption behaviour.

5 CONCLUSION

This paper highlights the critical importance of strategically locating waste treatment centers in the Tlemcen region of Algeria. In the face of rapid population growth and urban expansion, waste management has become a major concern for both the environment and public health. The results from the simulations demonstrate that, despite existing efforts, the current infrastructure is insufficient to handle the total waste generated.

The three scenarios analyzed underscore the need to optimize waste collection and treatment systems by integrating advanced technologies and considering environmental and social constraints. Improving the coverage rates of treatment centers, along with adopting sustainable management practices, is essential to minimize negative impacts on residents' quality of life.

Ultimately, this work provides valuable insights for policymakers, equipping them with analytical tools for informed decision-making. A strategic and integrated approach is vital for transforming waste management in Algeria, ensuring a more sustainable and resilient future for local communities.

REFERENCES

Abderrahim, Y., S. eddine Bellal, and M. Sahnoun. 2023. "Comparative Study of Waste Management Systems in Algeria and Other Countries: a literature review". In *2023 International Conference on Decision Aid Sciences and Applications (DASA)*, 164–169. IEEE.

Anvari, S., and M. Turkay. 2017, 06. "The facility location problem from the perspective of triple bottom line accounting of sustainability". *International Journal of Production Research* 55:1–22.

Ceschi, A., R. Sartori, S. Dickert, A. Scalco, E. M. Tur, F. Tommasi, and K. Delfini. 2021. "Testing a norm-based policy for waste management: An agent-based modeling simulation on nudging recycling behavior". *Journal of Environmental Management* 294:112938.

Cheniti, H., K. Kerboua, O. Sekiou, H. A. Aouissi, A. Benselhoub, R. Mansouri, I. Zeriri, K. Barbari, J. B. Gilev, and Z. Bouslama. 2024. "Life Cycle Assessment of Municipal Solid Waste Management within Open Dumping and Landfilling Contexts: A Strategic Analysis and Planning Responses Applicable to Algeria". *Sustainability* 16 (16): 6930.

de Oliveira, R. L., L. D. Fagundes, R. da Silva Lima, and M. Montaño. 2020. "Discrete event simulation to aid decision-making and mitigation in solid waste management". *Mitigation and Adaptation Strategies for Global Change* 25:67–85.

Ding, Z., W. Gong, S. Li, and Z. Wu. 2018, 07. "System Dynamics versus Agent-Based Modeling: A Review of Complexity Simulation in Construction Waste Management". *Sustainability* 10:2484.

Knapčíková, L., A. Behúnová, and M. Behún. 2020. "Using a discrete event simulation as an effective method applied in the production of recycled material". *Advances in Production Engineering & Management* 15 (4): 431–440.

Nichols, W., and N. Smith. 2019. "Waste generation and recycling indices 2019: Overview and findings". *Verisk Maplecroft: London, UK*:3–18.

Ribeiro-Rodrigues, E., and A. P. Bortoleto. 2024. "A systematic review of agent-based modeling and simulation applications for analyzing pro-environmental behaviors". *Sustainable Production and Consumption* 47:343–362.

Tian, X., F. Peng, G. Wei, C. Xiao, Q. Ma, Z. Hu, and Y. Liu. 2025. "Agent-based modeling in solid waste management: Advantages, progress, challenges and prospects". *Environmental Impact Assessment Review* 110:107723.

Wong, J. W., R. Y. Surampalli, T. C. Zhang, R. D. Tyagi, and A. Selvam. 2016. "Sustainable solid waste management". American Society of Civil Engineers Reston, VA.

AUTHOR BIOGRAPHIES

Younes ABDERRAHIM Currently a PhD candidate at Mostefa Ben Boulaïd University Batna 2, his research focuses on the localization of waste treatment centers around Algerian cities. He holds a Master's degree in Organization and Management of Logistics Systems from Paris-Saclay University and an engineering degree in Industrial Engineering, specializing in Industrial Management and Logistics, from the Higher School of Applied Sciences in Tlemcen. His expertise encompasses operational research, supply chain management, and information systems.

Dr. Salah Eddine BELLAL is an Associate Professor at the University of Batna 2 in Algeria. He earned his Ph.D. in Industrial Engineering in 2022, focusing on the development of wheelchairs for disabled persons in Algeria. Holding an engineering diploma in Information Technology from the same university, he teaches Information Systems and Enterprise Resource Planning (ERP). Dr. Bellal supervises Ph.D. candidates and has guided several master's students in their research.

Dr. M'hammed SAHNOUN is a Research Director at CESI LINEACT. His research primarily focuses on the modeling, simulation, and optimization of complex systems, particularly in the areas of manufacturing systems and renewable energy. He holds his Habilitation to Supervise Research (HDR) in Industrial Engineering from Normandy university, a PhD in Automation, and a Master's degree in Organization from the University of Metz, as well as a Master's degree in Robotics and Intelligent Systems from the University of Paris 6. He also earned an Engineering degree in Automation from the National Polytechnic School of Algiers. Dr. Sahnoun previously worked as a Research Engineer at the Grenoble Institute of Technology and served as a Lecturer at the University of Lorraine. He has supervised several PhD students, with research topics covering industrial data exploitation, complex systems management, and dynamic scheduling of flexible manufacturing systems. Additionally, he manages and coordinates various European and national research projects, including Optiman, CoRoT, AntiHpert, and UV-Robot.

Proceedings of the Operational Research Society Simulation Workshop 2025 (SW25)
M. Luis, A. Harper, T. Monks, N. Mustafee, eds.

https://doi.org/10.36819/SW25.012

IMPROVING DIABETES TREATMENT OUTCOMES: AN AGENT-BASED MODEL OF PATIENTS' SELF-MANAGEMENT BEHAVIOURS AND TREATMENT OUTCOMES IN GHANA

Eunice Twumwaa Tagoe
University of Strathclyde
199 Cathedral Street
Glasgow, G4 0QU
eunice.adwubi@strath.ac.uk

Dr Itamar Megiddo
University of Strathclyde
199 Cathedral Street
Glasgow, G4 0QU
itamar.megiddo@strath.ac.uk

Prof. Robert Van Deer Meer
University of Strathclyde
199 Cathedral Street
Glasgow, G4 0QU
robert.van-der-meer@strath.ac.uk

ABSTRACT

Despite Ghana's national health insurance coverage for diabetes (DM) care, many patients struggle to achieve adequate blood glucose control due to challenges with medication access, affordability, and adherence. This study explores type 2 diabetes patients' self-management behaviour and how it influences blood glucose control, medicine adherence and admissions within Ghana's public health system. The study uses health behaviour theories, clinicians' expertise, and evidence from published literature to build an agent-based model for improving understanding and examining the benefits of selected public health interventions: a 20% sugar-sweetened beverage (SSB) tax, increasing medicine availability and insurance coverage. Experiment results indicate that a 10% increase in insurance coverage for five consecutive years is more effective at improving blood glucose, reducing admissions and increasing medicine adherence than implementing a 20% SSB tax or a 10% increase in medicine availability. The results have implication for national insurance operation and diabetes service planning and delivery.

Keywords: Diabetes, Agent-based Modelling, Self-Management Behaviour

1 INTRODUCTION

Diabetes mellitus (DM), particularly type 2, accounts for a significant proportion of morbidity, mortality, health resource consumption, lost productivity due to illness, and financial hardship to individuals and households (American Diabetes Association, 2024). DM burden in Africa is significant, with 24 million cases in 2023 and an additional 9 million expected by 2030 if current trends continue (Magliano and Boyko, 2021). Ghana is the first African country to institute national health insurance (NHIS) for achieving universal health coverage and improving health (Government of Ghana, 2012). Although DM services are covered under the NHIS, the disease burden keeps increasing with roughly 0.9% – 8.3% of adults aged 20 – 79 years living with DM, and 77,400 – 286,800 undiagnosed (Magliano and Boyko, 2021). DM is associated with reduced productivity, increased demand for health services, and catastrophic health expenditures, leading many households into poverty (American Diabetes Association, 2024).

The World Health Organisation recommends public health (PH) interventions, within the Best-buy policies, for their far-reaching positive impact on modifiable risk factors (World Health Organisation, 2022, 2017). PH interventions include fiscal policies and legislative changes in, but not limited to, trade, agriculture and urban planning that can influence health behaviours. The NHIS and the 20% SSB tax (World Health Organisation, 2023) are examples of PH interventions in Ghana.

However, inadequate funding for health, few trained health providers, and inadequate health technology are among the many mutually influencing factors inhibiting NHIS operation and DM control in the country.

Even the most well-designed interventions can fail if patients do not adhere to treatment regimens or adopt recommended lifestyle changes. Therefore, understanding patient self-management behaviour provides valuable insights for modelling and is crucial for developing and implementing successful DM control interventions. Agent-based modelling (ABM) is a viable methodology for improving understanding of complex individual and system behaviours. It can represent heterogeneous patients' characteristics and complex behaviour in a dynamic environment, using decision rules from logic, theories, and empirical data (Macal, 2016). A developed ABM offers an opportunity to perform "what-if" analysis for predicting and examining the impact of interventions on DM control (Pollard et al., 2025).

The study uses ABM to describe DM patients' SMB and test the effectiveness of selected PH interventions–increasing public insurance coverage, a 20% SSB tax and increasing medicine availability–for improving blood glucose control, admissions, and medicine adherence among T2DM patients within Ghana's public health service. The research generates evidence to support policy decision-making on DM control in Ghana. The methodology used in developing and validating the model, interventions, experiments, and outcomes assessed are in Section 2. Section 3 presents results from uncertainty and sensitivity analysis and experiments. Discussions are presented in Section 4, and conclusion and limitations in Section 5.

2 METHODS

2.1 ABM Model Description

The ABM model represents T2DM patients receiving treatment within Ghana's public health system. Detailed model descriptions, including parameterisation and calibration, are openly available from the University of Strathclyde KnowledgeBase at https://doi.org/10.15129/e0d78b33-152f-44dc-9d8e-07886db72288. Using data from empirical studies conducted in Ghana, the model initialised patients with sociodemographic variables (age, insurance and wealth) and DM-related variables (blood glucose, comorbidity, clinical state, and lifestyle). Patients use these variables in decisions making on medicine adherence and health. Lifestyle is proxied from obesity and overweight prevalence, and comorbidity prevalence proxied from hypertension prevalence. Health Belief Model (HBM) (Strecher and Rosenstock, 1997) and Theory of Planned Behaviour (TPB) (Ajzen, 1991) are used to conceptualise and design patients' behaviour rules. Health facilities are in patients' environments. Clinical service delivery rules are designed based on clinicians' opinions and Ghana's DM treatment guidelines. For example, patients with poorly controlled blood glucose who seek care are admitted. Figure 1 shows the relationship between model variables and blood glucose control. Medicine adherence, lifestyle and health services directly influence blood glucose control in our model. Figure 2A shows patients' transition states in the model.

The scheduling of model procedures is in Figure 2B. Timesteps are counted in weeks, and each simulation lasts for ten years. In a timestep, outpatients decide on lifestyle (i.e., eating a healthy diet and engaging in recommended physical activity), taking medicines as prescribed, and attending review appointments if due, in the order presented in Figure 2B. Based on HBM and TPB, inpatients are assumed to adhere to medications and live a healthy lifestyle during admission. After discharge, patients may revert to prior lifestyle upon recovery from the complication that led to admission. Figure 2B shows patients' transition between blood glucose states and what tiggers transition. DM-specific deaths are included in crude mortalities because blood glucose alone rarely causes deaths in DM. The modelled cohort is a close; there were no births, but patients died from the model.

Blood glucose control is estimated from medicine adherence and lifestyle, using simple heuristic (Figure 2A): medicine adherence and healthy lifestyle result in good control, either one results in moderate control, and neither of them results in poor control. Based on the HBM and TPB, insured patients or those within middle to high-wealth quintile are assumed to afford medicines. Poor uninsured patients may be insured in subsequent years and then afford medicines. If medicines are available, patients who can afford them are assumed to take medicines. Otherwise, patients do not take medicines regardless of their ability to buy them. Aside from comorbid patients who are admitted to health facilities if presenting with poorly controlled blood glucose, all patients receive prescriptions and new appointments when they attend review appointments. Poor blood glucose without comorbidity receives the next appointment scheduled after glucose is brought under control. Patients stay a maximum of two weeks in admission.

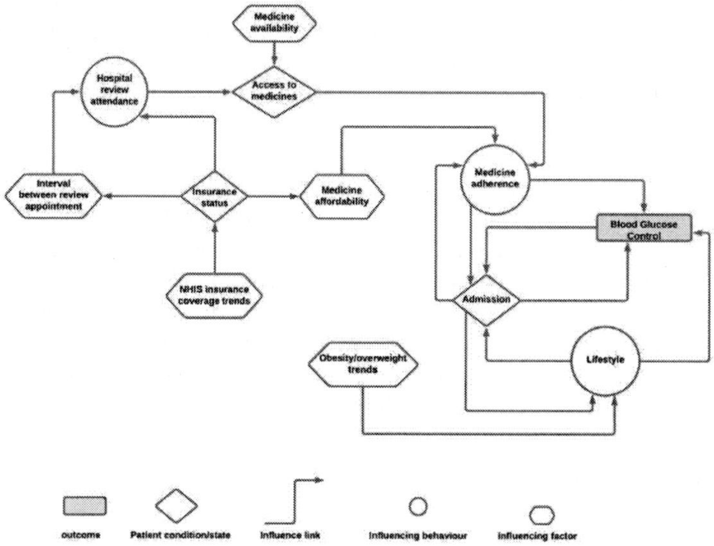

Figure 1 *Relationships between model variables and blood glucose outcome*

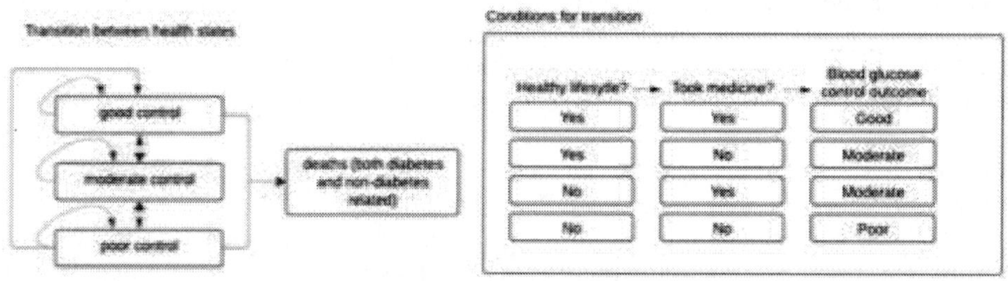

A: Transition between blood glucose states and conditions for transition

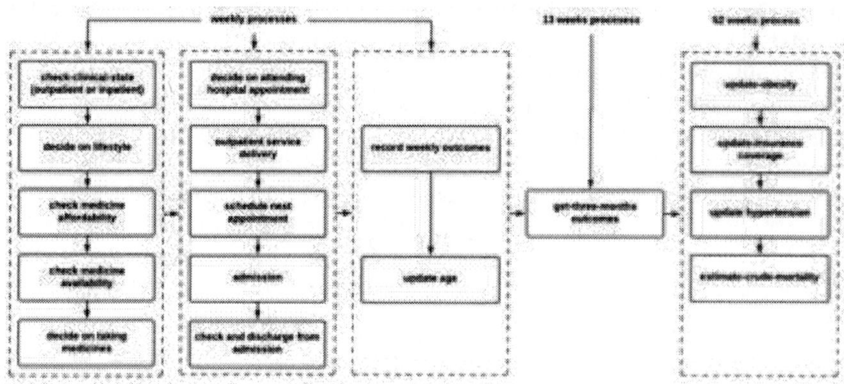

B: Overview and scheduling of model procedures

Figure 2 *Transition between diabetes states and scheduling of model procedures*

2.2 Data Collection and Parameterisation

The model uses data from literature, expert opinions and calibration techniques to define and quantify the model parameters. The researcher (ETT) had periodic discussions with physicians and nurses to scope the problem, build and validate the model structure and assumptions. Using a semi-structured interview approach and informal discussions, clinicians were asked about the model assumptions relating to lifestyle and medicine adherence, when and what clinical services are provided, and the relationship between medicine adherence, lifestyle and blood glucose control. The researcher ran model iterations and asked clinicians to comment on model outcomes. Section 7.6 summarises findings from our engagement with clinicians.

2.3 Model Confidence Building

The model components were tested incrementally: 1) individual patient behaviours, first validating medicine adherence decisions based on insurance status and medicine availability; appointment attendance based on blood glucose control state and appointment 2) health care delivery, testing appointment scheduling, and admissions. The health service delivery processes were validated based on service providers' opinions of how services are ordered (e.g., during an appointment, poor glycemic control is improved, and a new appointment is rescheduled if a patient is not comorbid. Otherwise, the patient is admitted). The Sigmoid function was used to calibrate insurance coverage, lifestyle, and the prevalence of comorbidity in the model, ensuring that they matched observed real-world patterns in the data sources. The predicted values were compared to observed prevalence to ensure a close match with observed data before incorporating the parameters of the predictive models into the ABM model to predict prospective years. Also, a probabilistic sensitivity analysis around model parameters was conducted using Latin Hypercube Sampling and partial ranked correlation (McKay, 1992). Aside from medicine adherence and lifestyle used in the base case to estimate blood glucose control, an uncertainty analysis was conducted around the model for estimating blood glucose control. Specifically, the study examined the effect if we reported weekly blood glucose outcomes (Model 1) or if comorbidity (Model 2) and DM duration (Model3) were included in the model for estimating blood glucose outcome. The model was built in NetLogo 6.3, and experiments and analysis in R version 4.2.2.

2.4 Interventions Examined

The study examined three main PH interventions: a 10% increase in the proportion of times patients found medicines available in their communities (Inter1), a 10% increase in active NHIS coverage for five consecutive years (Inter2) and a 20% SSB tax (Inter3). The researcher also examined a combined Inter2 and Inter3 (Inter4), based on the motivation that tax-generated revenue could be invested in expanding insurance coverage. Interventions were compared to baseline/current practice (Inter0). The interventions are based on the WHO Global Diabetes Targets 2022 and World Obesity Target, Ghana's recent 20% SSB tax policy. They are refined based on discussions with government officials in NHIS about the feasibility in term of implementation.

2.5 Experiments, Number of Simulations and Outcomes Reported

Due to stochasticity in ABMs, several simulations are required to understand the system's behaviour. the researchers defined the outcomes converged for our purpose when the 95% confidence intervals of the mean annual outcomes were within ± 5 incidence of good blood glucose control. The outcomes converged after 465 simulations but to be conservative 500 simulation was used in all experiments and 1000 runs in the sensitivity analysis. The model starts from 2024, using the year's prevalence in obesity and overweight, hypertension and insurance coverage. Thus, there is no warm-up period. The study reported the mean and 95% confidence interval of the difference in the mean incidence of blood glucose control and medicine adherence, admissions, and outpatient attendance across interventions over ten years. Based on clinicians' opinions, the study reported the 13-week frequent blood glucose control outcome in patients, representing the concept of glycated haemoglobin instead of the weekly outcomes. Medicine adherence is also assessed over 13 weeks and categorised as good–80% of medicines taken as prescribed, moderate–50% but less than 80%, poor–less than 50%. Admissions are counted weekly and accumulated over time.

3 RESULTS

3.1 Results of Confidence Building

3.1.1 Clinicians' opinion and NHS operations

Clinicians provided feedback on our model assumptions, procedure scheduling and interventions. According to clinicians, outpatient appointments are scheduled considering availability and the mode of payment. Even when available, appointments in insured patients are capped at six times in 12 months, per the NHIS operational manual (National Health Insurance Authority, 2022). Patients who miss outpatient appointments are not rescheduled. They set their next appointment to any random week between when they missed an appointment and 13 weeks (i.e., the interval between outpatients' review appointments). Insured patients are set to have a maximum of six appointments in 12 months.

Clinicians explained that lifestyle effectively controls blood glucose in the early stages of T2DM. Medicine stockout influences medicine adherence but not as much as the ability to afford medicines. They explained that patients could find medicine in private pharmacies, but high prices prevent access. Clinicians expected that in the short term (i.e., 5years) expanding insurance coverage would improve medicine adherence more than increasing medicine availability. They expected that an intervention that improves affordability or a healthy lifestyle would improve cohort-level blood glucose control more than an intervention that increased medicine availability.

After incorporating clinicians' opinions, the model is run under three different scenarios and asked clinicians to validate the model mechanism that led to medicine adherence, outpatient attendance and blood glucose control outcomes. The parameters representing prevalence of unhealthy lifestyles in rural and urban areas, insurance coverage, and medicine availability are varied (Figure 3). The model is then ran 5 times, each five years long, and patterns reported. There were, on average, 5 outpatient service attendance per patient; the minimum number of visits was one, occurring in 0.04% of the patient cohort (Figure 3A). The results confirmed the pattern clinicians described, and clinicians confirmed the model mechanism and outcomes.

3.1.2 Uncertainty

Models 1 – 3 led to a significant increase in the incidence of poor blood glucose outcomes, admissions and outpatient attendance and a decrease in the incidence of poor medicine adherence compared to the base case model. There was no significant difference in the outcomes in Models 1 – 3.

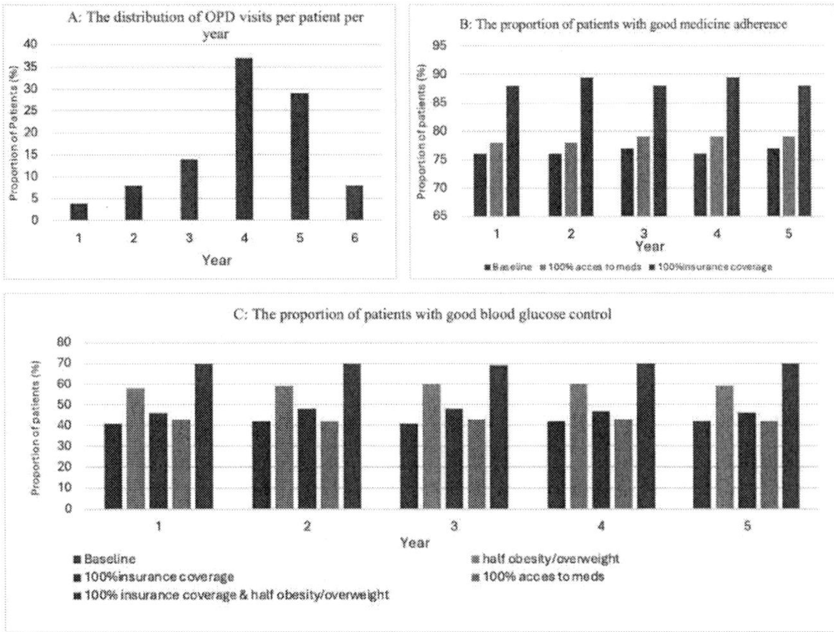

Figure 3 *Model Outcomes after Face Validation. OPD = outpatient department attendance. In the baseline, the percentage of times patients found medicines in urban and rural communities was 80% and 70%, respectively. In Figure 3C, the proportion of insured patients in the baseline ranged from 50% to 65%; obesity/overweight is a proxy for unhealthy lifestyle behaviours.*

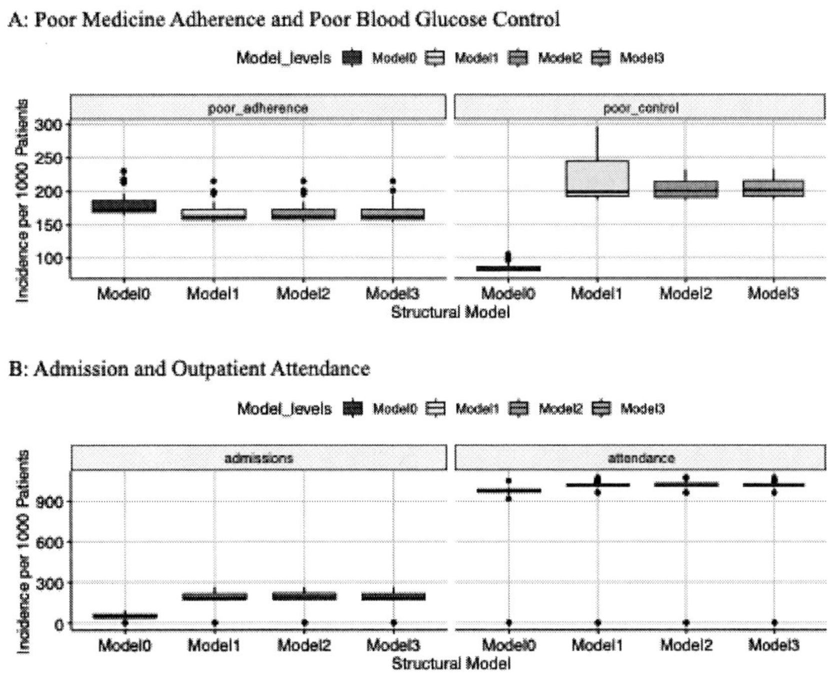

Figure 4 *Outcomes of Structural Sensitivity Analysis on Models for Estimating Blood Glucose Control. Model0 represented the base case model, which estimated blood glucose control from medicine adherence and lifestyle. Model1 uses the weekly blood glucose control measure instead of a 3-month average to estimate control. Model2 estimates blood glucose control from medicine adherence, lifestyle and comorbidity. In Model3, the duration of diabetes is added to medicine adherence and lifestyle to estimate blood glucose control.*

3.1.3 Sensitivity Analysis Results

Table 1 highlights the partial ranked correlation coefficient of the parameters that were sensitive to the model outcomes in probabilistic sensitivity analysis. If we increase the proportion of outpatient attendance, there will be a corresponding substantial decrease in incidences of poor control, admissions, and poor medicine adherence. Increasing the interval between review appointments beyond 13 weeks moderately increases the incidence of poor blood glucose, poor medicine adherence and admissions. Increasing the prevalence of unhealthy lifestyles in rural and urban areas led to a moderate increase in the incidence of poor blood glucose control. The incidence of poor medicine adherence marginally reduces if unhealthy lifestyles in rural areas increase.

Table 1 *Key outcomes of probabilistic sensitivity analysis*
PRCC = Partial ranked correlation coefficient. 95% confidence intervals of the PRCC are presented.

Parameters	PRCC	P.value	95%CI lower	95%CI upper
Poor blood glucose control				
Unhealthy lifestyle - Urban	0.2586	0.0118	0.0595	0.5011
Unhealthy lifestyle - Rural	0.4274	0	0.2448	0.6119
Outpatients Attendance Proportion	-0.7841	0	-0.8894	-0.7097
Interval between review appointment	0.3256	0.001	0.1323	0.5448
Poor medicine adherence				
Poor lifestyle - Rural	-0.1945	0.0539	-0.4549	-0.011
Outpatients Attendance Proportion	-0.8078	0	-0.8866	-0.7416
Interval between review appointment	0.3237	0.0038	0.1096	0.5141
Incidence of admissions				
Interval between review appointment	-0.8078	0	-0.8866	-0.7416
Interval between review appointment	0.3237	0.0038	0.1096	0.5141

3.2 Results of Experiments

3.2.1 Blood Glucose Control

In the baseline (Inter0), the incidence of good and poor control declined steadily and marginally, while moderate control increased as the patient cohort advanced in age. Inter2 and Inter4 more effectively improved blood glucose control than Inter1 and inter3 when compared to Inter0 (Figure 4A). The effectiveness of Inter4 was largely due to Inter2. Inter2 led to a substantial decrease in the incidence of poor control and an increase in good control compared to Inter0 over ten years (mean of difference in poor control = 24; 95%CI of the difference 22 – 26; mean of difference in good control = 22; 95%CI of the difference 21 – 24). Inter1 and Inter3 were no more effective than Inter0.

3.2.2 Medicine Adherence Behaviour

The incidence of good medicine adherence increased steadily, while moderate and poor adherence decreased over time in Inter0. Inter2 and Inter4 were more effective at improving medicine adherence behaviours than Inter0 (Figure 4B). Again, the effectiveness of Inter4 was due to Inter2. Inter2 led to a substantial increase in the incidence of good adherence (mean of difference in incidence = 94, 95% CI of the difference: 86 - 101) and a decrease in the incidence of poor adherence (mean of difference in incidence = 52, 95% CI of the difference: 48 - 57) compared to Inter0 after ten years. Inter1 and Inter3 did not reduce the incidence of poor medicine adherence outcomes in Inter0.

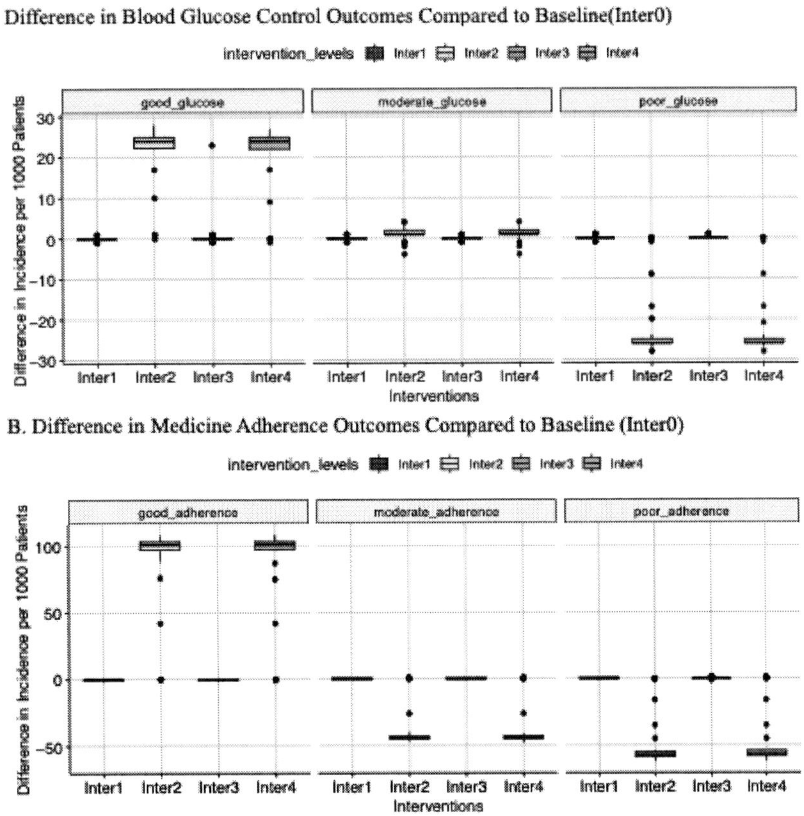

Figure 5 *Blood Glucose and Medicine Adherence Outcomes by Interventions. Box plot of the outcomes after ten years under intervention scenarios. Inter0 = baseline, Inter1 = 10% increase in the percentage of times patients found medicines in rural and urban areas; Inter2 = 10% annual increase in the proportion of patients actively insured under the National Health Insurance Scheme for five consecutive years; Inter3 = 20% tax on sugar-sweetened beverages; Inter4 = combined Inter2 and Inter3. Good = incidence of good blood glucose control/ medicine adherence; moderate = incidence of moderately controlled blood glucose/ medicine adherence; poor = incidence of poorly controlled blood glucose/ medicine adherence. Lower hinge: 25% quantile; lower whisker: smallest observation greater than or equal to lower hinge − 1.5×IQR; middle: median; upper hinge: 75% quantile; upper whisker: largest observation less than or equal to upper hinge + 1.5×IQR; black dot: outlier.*

3.2.3 Admissions and Outpatient Attendance

Inter 2 and Inter4 more effectively reduced the incidence of admissions but increased outpatient attendance in Inter0 (Figure 5). Again, Inter2 drove the effectiveness observed in Inter4. After ten years, Inter2 had an average of 14 fewer admissions (95% CI of the difference: 11 – 16) and 23 more outpatient attendance (95% CI of the difference: 20 – 27) compared to Inter0. Inter3 and Inter1 were no more effective at reducing admissions than Inter0.

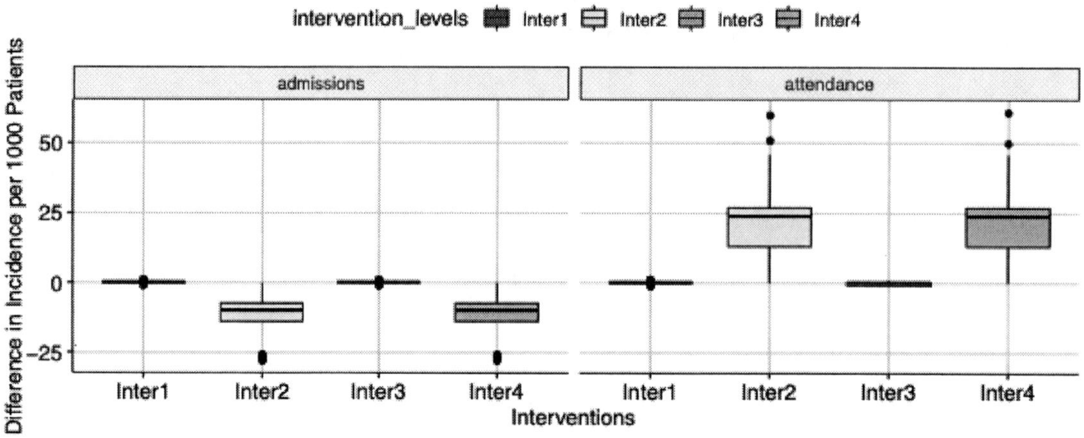

Figure 6 *Admissions Avoided and Additional Outpatient Attendance Relative to Baseline. Box plot of the outcomes ten years under intervention scenarios. Inter0 = baseline, Inter1 = 10% increase in the percentage of times patients found medicines in rural and urban areas; Inter2 = 10% annual increase in the proportion of patients actively insured under the National Health Insurance Scheme for five consecutive years; Inter3 = 20% tax on sugar-sweetened beverages; Inter4 = combined Inter2 and Inter3. Lower hinge: 25% quantile; lower whisker: smallest observation greater than or equal to lower hinge − 1.5×IQR; middle: median; upper hinge: 75% quantile; upper whisker: largest observation less than or equal to upper hinge + 1.5×IQR; black dot: outlier.*

4 DISCUSSIONS

This study sought to improve understanding of T2DM patients' SMB and blood glucose control outcomes and to investigate the health effect of PH interventions for blood glucose control in a cohort of T2DM patients receiving treatment within the Ghana public health system. Our analysis indicates that increasing the proportion of actively insured patients was the most effective at improving medicine adherence and blood glucose control. Expanding insurance coverage reduces admissions as more patients at least adhere to medications due to increase affordability. The finding is consistent with studies in Ghana (Aryeetey et al., 2016) and Nigeria (Oseni et al., 2023), where the odds of medication adherence in insured patients were 4.5 times the odds in uninsured hypertension patients. Similar findings are reported in other countries (Guindon et al., 2022). Nevertheless, the feasibility of this intervention is worth considering, given that the NHIS encounters operational and financial challenges.

Implementing a 20% SSB tax and increasing medicine availability did not improve the blood glucose outcomes any further in the baseline scenario. The study is the first to examine the impact of a 20% SSB tax on blood glucose outcomes in T2DM in Ghana. Although the model does represent the details of the tax design and implementation, the results can be important for health outcomes and SMB of T2DM. The study applied the effect of a 20% SSB tax on obesity and overweight from modelling studies in India and South Africa (Basu et al., 2014; Manyema et al., 2014). As the policy was recently implemented in Ghana, data on its effect is sparse. Data collection and further studies on the policy's effect could improve understanding of the policy's impact on food choices, consumption behaviours and obesity, which can improve our model outcomes.

A 10% increase in the proportion of times medicines were available to patients does not improve blood glucose control in T2DM any further than the current practice. This is because scaling medicine availability alone addresses the availability problem, leaving concerns about medicine costs to patients. The analysis shows that affordability, through NHIS coverage, influences good medicine adherence behaviours more than availability. Medicine stockout in Ghana has been associated with transportation from central and regional medical stores, poor inventory management and poor management of the revolving drug fund (Sarley et al., 2003). The Ghana Medicines Policy is an example of a local intervention for addressing the challenge (Ministry of Health, 2017). Strengthening the medicine supply chain and transportation systems in the country could improve access to medicines in the country (Sarley et al., 2003).

Changes in these model parameters: the prevalence of obesity and overweight in rural and urban resident patients, the interval between outpatient appointments, and the proportion of patients who attended scheduled outpatient appointments led to significant changes in cohort-level blood glucose control, medicine adherence, admissions, and outpatient attendance. This implies that accurate and representative data on these factors and their relationship with SMB is important for improving our understanding of PH intervention's effect on T2DM control and supporting intervention design.

5 CONCLUSION AND LIMITATION

In conclusion, the ABM study improves the understanding of the interaction of SMB and clinical services and PH interventions in controlling blood glucose among T2DM patients A 10% annual increase in the proportion of patients with active NHIS insurance for five consecutive years is the most effective at improving blood glucose control and medication adherence. Increasing medicine availability and a 20% SSB tax policy did not significantly change the health outcomes observed in the baseline. Our model results indicate the expanding insurance coverage increases outpatient services utilisation but reduces admissions. This insight can inform discussions about DM service planning and NHIS operations for DM control. Key study findings are being drafted into a policy brief for dissemination to policymakers in Ghana.

The model's accuracy and level of detail are restricted by the quality of the input parameters. It does not capture all potentially relevant covariates. Improving the model parameters would improve the model's estimates. Despite uncertainty analysis of the model's structure for blood glucose estimation, the complexity surrounding blood glucose regulations in the individual body would limit the generalisation of our findings. The model assumed that intentions led to behaviour when applying HBM and TPB, which is not always the case and thus affects the ability to general our model outcomes. The researchers aim extend the model to include service provider behaviours and health facility resources constraints. The extension will capture knowledge, expertise and performance, availability of appointments and beds, which influence DM service delivery, patients SMB and blood glucose control.

REFERENCES

Ajzen, I., 1991. The theory of planned behavior. Organizational Behavior and Human Decision Processes, Theories of Cognitive Self-Regulation 50, 179–211. https://doi.org/10.1016/0749-5978(91)90020-T

American Diabetes Association, 2024. Standard of Care in Diabetes-2024. Diabetes care 47, S1–S322. https://doi.org/doi:10.2337/dc24-Sint.

Aryeetey, G.C., Nonvignon, J., Amissah, C., Buckle, G., Aikins, M., 2016. The effect of the National Health Insurance Scheme (NHIS) on health service delivery in mission facilities in Ghana: a retrospective study. Global Health 12, 32. https://doi.org/10.1186/s12992-016-0171-y

Basu, S., Vellakkal, S., Agrawal, S., Stuckler, D., Popkin, B., Ebrahim, S., 2014. Averting Obesity and Type 2 Diabetes in India through Sugar-Sweetened Beverage Taxation: An Economic-Epidemiologic Modeling Study. PLoS Med 11, e1001582. https://doi.org/10.1371/journal.pmed1001582

Government of Ghana, 2012. National insurance act, 2012 (ACT 852).

Guindon, G.E., Fatima, T., Garasia, S., Khoee, K., 2022. A systematic umbrella review of the association of prescription drug insurance and cost-sharing with drug use, health services use, and health. BMC Health Serv Res 22, 297. https://doi.org/10.1186/s12913-022-07554-w

Macal, C.M., 2016. Everything you need to know about agent-based modelling and simulation. J Simulation 10, 144–156. https://doi.org/10.1057/jos.2016.7

Magliano, D.J., Boyko, E.J., 2021. IDF Diabetes Atlas, 10th edition. ed, IDF Diabetes Atlas. International Diabetes Federation, Brussels.

Manyema, M., Veerman, L.J., Chola, L., Tugendhaft, A., Sartorius, B., Labadarios, D., Hofman, K.J., 2014. The Potential Impact of a 20% Tax on Sugar-Sweetened Beverages on Obesity in South

African Adults: A Mathematical Model. PloS one 9, e105287. https://doi.org/10.1371/journal.pone.0105287
McKay, M.D., 1992. Latin hypercube sampling as a tool in uncertainty analysis of computer models, in: Proceedings of the 24th Conference on Winter Simulation - WSC '92. Presented at the the 24th conference, ACM Press, Arlington, Virginia, United States, pp. 557–564. https://doi.org/10.1145/167293.167637
Ministry of Health, 2017. Ghana National Medicines Policy 3rd Edition 2017-2021.
National Health Insurance Authority, 2022. National health insurance scheme tariffs operational manual. National Health Insurance Authority, Accra, Ghana.
Oseni, T.I.A., Blankson, P.-K., Dele-Ojo, B.F., Duodu, F., Echieh, C.P., Alabi, S.B., Tayo, B.O., Sarpong, D.F., Amoakoh-Coleman, M., Boima, V., Ogedegbe, G., 2023. Medication adherence and blood pressure control: A preliminary assessment of the role of health insurance in Nigeria and Ghana. SAGE Open Med 11, 20503121231152324. https://doi.org/10.1177/20503121231152324
Pollard, D., Pidd, K., Breeze, P., Brennan, A., Thomas, C., 2025. Sheffield Type 2 Diabetes Treatment Model version 3: with the Embedding RCT health economic analyses implemented. https://doi.org/10.15131/SHEF.DATA.23545995.V2
Sarley, D., Abdallah, H., Rao, R., Gyimah, P., Azeez, J., Garshong, B., 2003. Pharmaceutical Pricing Study. Arlington, Va.: John Snow, Inc./DELIVER.
Strecher, V.J., Rosenstock, I.M., 1997. The health belief model. Cambridge handbook of psychology, health and medicine 113, 117.
World Health Organisation, 2023. Global report on the use of sugar-sweetended beverage taxes 2023. World Health Organisation, Geneva.
World Health Organisation, 2022. Fiscal policies to promote healthy diets: policy brief. WHO.
World Health Organisation, 2017. Tackling NCDs: best buys and other recommended interventions for the prevention and control of noncommunicable diseases. World Health Organization, Geneva.

AUTHOR BIOGRAPHIES

EUNICE TWUMWAA TAGOE holds a Master of Public Health from the University of Ghana and is completing a PhD in Management Science with Strathclyde University. She is currently a research assistant at the NHIR Policy Research Unit Behavioural and Social Sciences based at Newcastle University.

DR ITAMAR MEGIDDO is a Senior Lecturer at Strathclyde Business School where he teaches a range of modules, including agent-based modelling. He holds a PhD in Management Science, specialising in modelling for healthcare policy.

PROF. ROBERT VAN-DEER-MEER is Professor of Management Science at Strathclyde Business School. He has a PhD in Operational Research and teaches many courses including Healthcare Operations Management.

Proceedings of the Operational Research Society Simulation Workshop 2025 (SW25)
M. Luis, A. Harper, T. Monks, N. Mustafee, eds.
https://doi.org/10.36819/SW25.013

EVALUATING POOLED PROCUREMENT AND INVENTORY MANAGEMENT FOR ESSENTIAL MEDICINES IN NIGERIA

Mr. Viraj Joshi

Arizona State University,
Ira A. Fulton School of Engineering,
Industrial Engineering Department,
699 S Mill Ave #119, Tempe, AZ 85281
vvjoshi3@asu.edu

Dr. Mikaella Polyviou

Arizona State University,
W. P. Carey School of Business,
Department of Supply Chain Management,
300 E Lemon St, Tempe, AZ 85281
Mikaella.Polyviou@asu.edu

Dr. John Fowler

Arizona State University,
W. P. Carey School of Business,
Department of Supply Chain Management,
300 E Lemon St, Tempe, AZ 85281
John.fowler@asu.edu

Dr. Gene Schneller

Arizona State University,
W. P. Carey School of Business,
Department of Supply Chain Management,
300 E Lemon St, Tempe, AZ 85281
Gene.Schneller@asu.edu

Dr. Adegoke Oke

Arizona State University
Department of Supply Chain Management,
W. P. Carey School of Business,
300 E Lemon St, Tempe, AZ 85281
Adegoke.oke@asu.edu

ABSTRACT

This study examines how pooled procurement and a shared stock system across four states in Nigeria can lower costs and improve access to essential medicines. Our study first reviews existing sourcing and inventory practices in these states. Then, it introduces a pooled procurement approach integrated with a Continuous Review Policy (CRP). By comparing the current state with our suggested approach, we identify potential benefits, including cost reduction and improved stock management. We then design two simulation scenarios: the four states adopting the CRP model but operating independently and the four states following CRP with access to shared stock. Both scenarios were tested under normal demand and a 100% surge in demand in one state. The results demonstrate the significant advantages of pooled procurement and shared stock systems, particularly in mitigating the impact of demand spikes and improving inventory availability.

Keywords: Pooled procurement, Shared stock system, Continuous Review Policy (CRP), Essential medicines

1 INTRODUCTION

In this study, we collaborated with four states in Nigeria, State A, State B, State C, and State D, to evaluate their current procurement and inventory management practices for a critical list of essential medicines for child and maternal health. Each state currently manages these activities independently without any coordination or collaboration with other states. Our objective was to evaluate the potential benefits of shifting to a pooled procurement and inventory management model. By collaborating with the four states and a third-party supply chain association in Nigeria, we collected data on 14 essential medicines that include a combination of antibiotics, antimalaria drugs, hydration solutions, and others: Artemether-Lumefantrine (ACT) 20/120; Artemether-Lumefantrine (ACT) 80/480; Amoxicillin suspension; Artesunate; Gentamycin sulfate; Magnesium sulfate; Malaria rapid diagnostic test (RDT); Misoprostol; Normal saline; Oral rehydration solution (ORS); Oxytocin; Paracetamol syrup; Ringer's lactate solution; and Sulphadoxine pyrimethamine. Our analyses revealed the following: Each state currently manages its procurement independently and its inventory using a different inventory policy. At the same time, each state seems to adopt the same inventory policy for all 14 medicines. The four states can achieve significant savings if they (a) pool procurement, (b) adopt a Continuous Review Policy (CRP) with a 90% or 99% service level, and (c) pool their inventory management.

Finally, a simulation of different scenarios was carried out to demonstrate further the benefits of collaboration across states under "normal" and "disrupted" conditions. The analyses focused on one form of collaboration: the states maintain an amount of stock that can be shared among them. For example, when a state has understocked, it can receive inventory from the shared stock instead of placing an order with the supplier. The simulation results show that the states benefit from fewer stockouts when there is a shared stock not only under normal demand conditions but also under demand surges (e.g., a disease outbreak in one state that requires a much higher volume than normal). Hence, cross-state collaboration via inventory sharing can help mitigate severe stockouts due to demand disruptions.

1.1 Background and Initial Analysis – Current Inventory vs. Continuous Review Policy

The Federal Republic of Nigeria comprises 36 states and a Federal Capital Territory in Abuja. Nigeria's national health guidelines encourage states to establish Drug Management Agencies (DMAs). A DMA is a legal entity responsible for sourcing, warehousing, selling, and distributing drugs and medical consumables for all public health commodities in a specific state (Chemonics, 2023). Currently, 20 states have a DMA. Each DMA handles supply chain activities independently, which means it also independently negotiates and enters into contractual agreements with local manufacturers and distributors of these commodities. This procurement model results in independent purchasing agreements between DMAs and manufacturers/ distributors with differences in pricing and other terms (e.g., product brand, quality, delivery) for each state. Furthermore, each state independently manages its inventory of these commodities. As a result, the states lack scale and bargaining power when negotiating with suppliers, do not communicate or collaborate, for example, by sharing inventories when one state overstocks and another one understocks, and forgo important opportunities for sharing information about products and suppliers with each other and achieving better contractual terms. Therefore, our study examined the potential for pooling procurement and inventory management across the states.

Pooled procurement is a "formal arrangement where financial and non-financial resources are combined across various purchasing authorities to create a single entity for purchasing health products (e.g., medicines) on behalf of individual purchasing authorities" (WHO, 2020). This central entity distributes health products to next-level buyers (Institute of Medicine, 2002). In other words, and our project's context, pooled procurement means that the DMAs would join their resources and create a single entity for purchasing drugs and other medical disposables on behalf of the individual states. This central entity would then distribute the products to each DMA, responsible for serving its state.

Pooling procurement and inventory management should bring about several benefits for the states (i.e., the buyers) and their suppliers. For the states, pooled structures that consolidate purchasing and inventory management help reduce unit purchase prices, improve product quality, improve procurement efficiency and reduce administrative costs, increase equity among the participating members, and improve access to essential medicines (Huff-Rousselle, 2012; Parmaksiz et al., 2022). For suppliers, pooled procurement and inventory management structures enable them to access more buyers and higher volumes and improve the stability of their supply chain by smoothing out individual demand fluctuations (Balakrishnan et al., 2004).

In this section, we estimate each state's annual inventory costs using its reported inventory policy and evaluate whether each state would achieve savings by following a different inventory policy, such as a CRP. A CRP is a dynamic method of inventory control where inventory levels are constantly monitored (Chopra and Meindl, 2019). We will consider (a) the cycle stock, which is used during the regular production or purchasing cycle and must be replaced as the organization sells its products (Silver et al., 2016) and (b) the safety stock, which is the additional quantity of inventory that an organization holds to buffer against any uncertainties in demand (e.g., demand surges) or supply (e.g., supply delays) (Silver et al., 2016). Finally, we consider the savings when the four states pool their inventory management instead of managing inventories independently.

In inventory management, two key decisions need to be made by organizations: (a) How much to order? and (b) When to place an order? Answers to these questions determine the costs highlighted in the equations given below. We consider the (a) order placement cost, which is the fixed cost of placing an order; (b) inventory holding cost, which is the cost of physically storing the inventory; and (c) the procurement spend, which is the actual cost paid to suppliers to purchase the product. The following equations are considered for calculating the inventory costs.

$$\textit{Annual order placement cost} = \textit{No. of orders} \times \textit{Order cost per order} \quad (1)$$

$$\textit{Annual inventory holding cost} = \textit{Unit rate} \times \textit{Inventory holding cost percentage} \times (\textit{Safety stock} + \textit{Average inventory level}) \quad (2)$$

$$\textit{Annual procurement spend} = \textit{Unit rate} \times \textit{Annual spend} \quad (3)$$

1.1.1. Annual Costs Under Current Inventory Policy

In this section, we estimate the costs (order placement, inventory holding, and procurement spend) associated with the states' current inventory policy. Table 1 shows each state's current inventory policy. State A holds one month's worth of inventory (min. stock) and re-orders two months' worth of inventory (i.e., max. stock minus the re-order level). We interpreted the inventory policies of State C and State D similarly. State B reported following a CRP but provided no other information; hence, we assumed that State B had calculated the optimal order quantity (Economic Order Quantity - EOQ) and managed its inventory in that manner. These policies are based on ad-hoc practices rather than formal inventory control methods and resemble an (s, S) policy. Since the review intervals were not specified, we assumed that the states follow the typical restocking timelines used by each state. Finally, we applied this current inventory policy to all 14 medicines considered in the project, as the states have not specified different inventory policies for the various medicines.

Table 1: Current Inventory Policy Across States

	Current Inventory Policy		
States	**Min. Stock**	**Re-order Level (Order Quantity)**	**Max. Stock**
State A	1 month	2 months	4 months
State B	Continuous Review Policy		
State C	2 months	4 months	8 months
State D	1 month	2 months	4 months

Table 2: Average Unit Rate by Healthcare Product and State

	Average unit rate for each state			
Healthcare Product	**State A**	**State B**	**State C**	**State D**
ACT 20/120	₦498.82	₦275.28	₦250.00	₦431.22
ACT 80/480	₦601.88	₦497.65	₦345.90	₦435.58
Amoxicillin	₦447.35	₦382.24	₦433.33	₦376.68
Artesunate	₦1,566.12	₦720.00	₦1,050.00	₦848.43
Gentamycin sulphate	₦473.33	₦344.12	-	₦335.00
Magnesium sulphate	₦403.33	₦480.00	₦1,127.12	₦350.00
Malaria RDT	₦5,117.65	₦4,072.94	₦2,771.38	₦2,528.50
Misoprostol	₦324.47	₦448.52	₦274.00	₦386.00
Normal saline	₦379.41	₦525.88	₦437.22	₦409.17
ORS	₦226.67	₦277.50	₦198.90	₦226.67
Oxytocin	₦204.76	₦142.06	₦117.00	₦130.00
Paracetamol syrup	₦219.39	₦205.50	₦155.00	₦219.39
Ringer's lactate solution	₦519.29	₦525.88	₦454.00	₦425.00
Sulphadoxine pyrimethamine	₦303.76	₦217.80	₦150.00	₦200.95

To estimate the three cost components outlined above, we made the below assumptions. We based these assumptions on discussions with representatives from the DMAs and other key stakeholders involved in the project:

- Unit rate = Average unit rate for each drug for each state (data provided by the states), as presented in Table 2.
- Fixed order cost per order = $100 (₦162,500) [currency exchange: $1 = ₦1,625].
- Inventory holding cost percentage = 25% of the unit rate.

Using equations (1), (2), (3), and average unit rates by healthcare product shown in Table 2, we estimated each state's current annual costs, as shown in Table 3.

Table 3: Annual Costs Based on Current Inventory Policy

State	Annual Inventory Holding Cost	Annual Order Placement Cost	Annual Procurement Spend	Annual Total Cost
State A	₦10,943,261	₦13,643,212	₦175,074,454	₦199,660,927
State B	₦27,896,763	₦11,469,141	₦1,017,556,729	₦1,056,922,633
State C	₦6,987,504	₦6,355,631	₦55,904,611	₦69,247,746
State D	₦10,860,147	₦13,656,178	₦173,766,665	₦198,282,990
Total	**₦56,687,675**	**₦45,124,162**	**₦1,422,302,459**	**₦1,524,114,296**

1.1.2. Annual Costs Under Continuous Review Policy (Independent States Without Pooling and States with Pooling)

Based on the given consumption data for the products, we evaluated the total cost under a CRP with a 99% service level, as shown in Table 4. Our analyses are based on the below assumptions:

- Unit rate = Average unit rate for each medicine for each state.
- Fixed order cost per order = $100 per order (₦162,500) [currency exchange: $1 = ₦1,625].
- Inventory holding cost % = 25% of the unit rate.
- Lead time (average) = 15 days (i.e., on average, it takes about 15 days from placing an order with the supplier until the time the items are ready to be sold to customers).
- Lead time (standard deviation) = 5 days (i.e., variations due to production delays, shipping delays, or other transportation problems).
- Service level = 90% or 99% (i.e., the probability that a stockout will not occur is either 90% or 99%).
- Note that the procurement spend remains the same across the three policies as we assumed the same average unit rate for all policies.

Due to limited space, we only show the table of costs for the 99% service level. Figure 1 compares the annual inventory holding costs and order placement costs under the states' current inventory policy with those under a CRP a 99% service level. We conclude that the states can save millions by adopting a CRP policy: the annual inventory holding cost decreases by more than ₦5 million under a CRP of 99% and more than ₦16 million under a CRP with a 90% service level. Similarly, the states can save more than ₦18 million in order placement costs by switching from their current inventory policy to a CRP.

Table 4: Annual Costs Across All States Under a Continuous Review Policy (99% Service Level)

Healthcare Product	Annual Inventory Holding Cost	Annual Order Placement Cost	Annual Procurement Spend	Annual Total Cost
ACT 20/120	₦2,697,258	₦1,696,609	₦67,995,163	₦72,389,030
ACT 80/480	₦2,745,648	₦1,759,556	₦46,853,896	₦51,359,100
Amoxicillin	₦3,365,597	₦2,342,617	₦69,160,555	₦74,868,769
Artesunate	₦1,491,756	₦1,119,629	₦20,639,774	₦23,251,159
Gentamycin sulphate	₦4,561,102	₦2,325,335	₦126,062,170	₦132,948,607
Magnesium sulphate	₦1,986,442	₦1,116,068	₦30,783,288	₦33,885,798
Malaria RDT	₦847,875	₦615,129	₦6,098,102	₦7,561,106
Misoprostol	₦1,544,203	₦1,068,454	₦20,098,844	₦22,711,501
Normal saline	₦5,208,267	₦2,830,086	₦111,861,443	₦119,899,796
ORS	₦5,177,985	₦2,440,755	₦151,686,602	₦159,305,342
Oxytocin	₦1,959,896	₦1,276,861	₦21,087,992	₦24,324,749
Paracetamol syrup	₦15,464,850	₦5,303,164	₦695,631,095	₦716,399,109
Ringer's lactate solution	₦2,287,605	₦1,481,937	₦34,629,648	₦38,399,190
Sulphadoxine pyrimethamine	₦1,434,838	₦1,037,333	₦19,713,887	₦22,186,058
Total	**₦50,773,322**	**₦26,413,533**	**₦1,422,302,459**	**₦1,499,489,314**

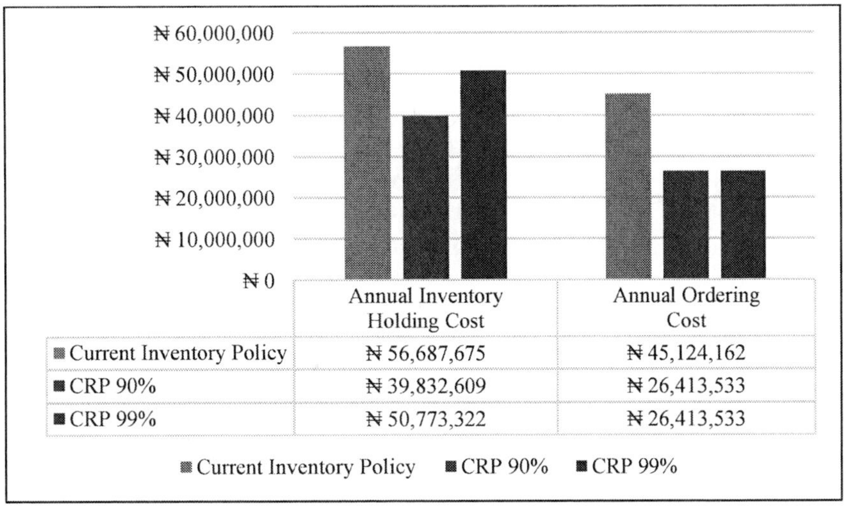

Figure 1: Cost Comparison: Current Inventory Policy vs. Continuous Review Policy (CRP) Across All States

Table 5 summarizes the different cost components and annual costs under the various policies. The last two rows of Table 5 show the results of pooling procurement and inventory management across the four states. In addition to savings in procurement spend, states can save in their annual order placement and inventory holding costs when pooling. As shown in Table 5, pooling inventory across states saves them ₦42,870,499 (₦1,524,114,296 - ₦1,481,243,797) or ₦256,646,429 ((₦1,524,114,296 - ₦1,267,467,867) when using a CRP with a 99% service level and the weighted average unit rate or the minimum unit rate, respectively.

Table 5: Cost Comparison: Current Inventory Policy of Individual States vs. Continuous Review Policy Without and With Pooling

Inventory Policy	Unit Rate	Annual Inventory Holding Cost	Annual Order Placement Cost	Annual Procurement Spend	Annual Total Cost
Current Inventory Policy	Average unit rate for each state	₦56,687,675	₦45,124,162	₦1,422,302,459	₦1,524,114,296
Individual States – CRP (90% Service Level)	Average unit rate for each state	₦39,832,609	₦26,413,533	₦1,422,302,459	₦1,488,548,601
Individual States – CRP (99% Service Level)	Average unit rate for each state	₦50,773,322	₦26,413,533	₦1,422,302,459	₦1,499,489,314
Pooled CRP (99% Service Level)	Minimum unit rate across 4 states	₦35,013,483	₦16,036,305	₦1,216,418,079	₦1,267,467,867
Pooled CRP (99% Service Level)	Weighted average unit rate across 4 states	₦40,597,137	₦18,344,681	₦1,422,301,979	₦1,481,243,797

2 METHODOLOGY – SIMULATING INDEPENDENT STATE PROCUREMENT VS. POOLED PROCUREMENT SCENARIOS

We developed a simulation model using the Arena simulation software to evaluate the dynamic behavior of the current state of independent procurement and inventory management versus a collaborative procurement and inventory management model. The simulation was run to compare the CRP under two cases: (a) each state operating independently under a CRP with a 95% service level[1] and (b) the four states each operating under a CRP with 90% service level and collaborating by keeping an amount of stock that can be shared among them (i.e., shared stock). The shared stock was calculated considering the difference of the sum of re-order points (ROPs) of the states considering 95% service level and 90% service level. This shared stock can be tapped by each state when it runs out of its own inventory. The scenarios were evaluated based on stockout days and stockout quantities under normal and surge demand conditions.

$$\textit{Shared Stock Inventory} = 2 \times (\textit{Sum of State ROPs under a 95\% service level} - \textit{Sum of State ROPs under a 90\% service level}) \tag{4}$$

We considered the following data for the analysis. The simulation focused on four states: State A, State B, State C, and State D. The drug Oxytocin was considered for illustration purposes. All the states consume Oxytocin, and specific characteristics, such as consumption patterns and inventory parameters, were used to model real-time inventory flows in each state. The following simulation parameters were considered for each state: Economic Order Quantity (EOQ), Re-order Point (ROP), State Warehouse Inventory, Ordering Frequency, Stockout Frequency, and Stockout Quantity. Note that EOQ, ROP, state warehouse inventories, and ordering frequencies were calculated based on the assumptions discussed in Section 1.1.1 and Section 1.1.2. We collected monthly demand data for a year from each state and forecasted demand for the next 9 years using a 2% annual growth rate (compounded yearly). We assumed that the monthly demand was normally distributed with a ±10% variability factor from the average monthly value for that year. The daily demand was then generated from a normal distribution with the mean equal to the monthly demand divided by 30 and the standard deviation equal to 25% of the mean. The simulation runs for 3,653 days (i.e., 10 years) and 10 replications.

The flowchart in Figure 2 represents the CRP inventory management system for an individual state

[1] This service level inventory level was instead of the 99% service level from the previous section to create a more realistic scenario, as a 99% service level would account for higher inventory levels

warehouse that operates independently from the other states. The simulation logic works as follows. Medicine consumption is created daily as a "demand entity" for each state to simulate the arrival of demand at a state warehouse. The demand pattern for each state is based on the historical consumption data the states provided to the research team. The simulation begins by assigning the daily demand in a state; this demand is subtracted from the state warehouse's current inventory. If the inventory level drops below or reaches the ROP, and there are no orders for the supplier currently outstanding, a new order is placed to the supplier. This new order also factors in the supplier's stochastic lead time, namely the time between when the order is sent out and when the state warehouse receives the order. Once the stochastic lead time passes, the inventory is replenished, increasing the warehouse stock. The stochastic lead time is modeled using a delay block with a triangular distribution of (10,15,20) days. If an order is already in progress and the inventory level is zero, the simulation tracks a stockout and resets the inventory level for further operations. Hence, the process ends with one of the two outcomes of demand fulfillment or stockout based on the inventory levels and order status.

The flowchart in Figure 3 represents the CRP inventory management system for an individual state warehouse under a shared stock policy. . In this scenario, the state can request inventory from a shared stock that is kept in collaboration with the other states. The simulation begins with a state fulfilling its demand from its warehouse. If the state's warehouse inventory is insufficient, the system checks if shared stock is available. If available, the state's demand is fulfilled from the shared stock. If the shared stock is also low (below its ROP), the system places an order with the supplier to replenish the shared stock inventory, given that there is no outstanding order already. A stochastic lead time is factored in for the delivery of this shared stock, after which the shared stock is replenished. The stochastic lead time is modeled using a delay block with a triangular distribution of (6, 7, 8) days, which is shorter than the state warehouse replenishment lead time.

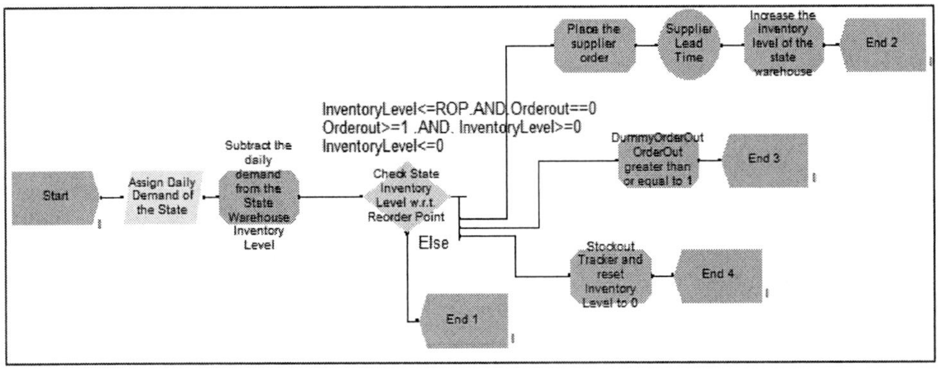

Figure 2: Simulation Logic Diagram for Inventory Management for Individual States

This reduction in lead time is assumed to result from the shared stock being managed at a central location, enabling faster restocking due to simplified logistics. We also assumed that suppliers can expedite the orders for the shared stock, ensuring quicker delivery to the warehouse. A stockout is recorded if neither the state's warehouse nor the shared stock can fulfill the state's demand. As before, the simulation runs for 3,653 days and tracks the number of days and number of units in stockouts for each state.

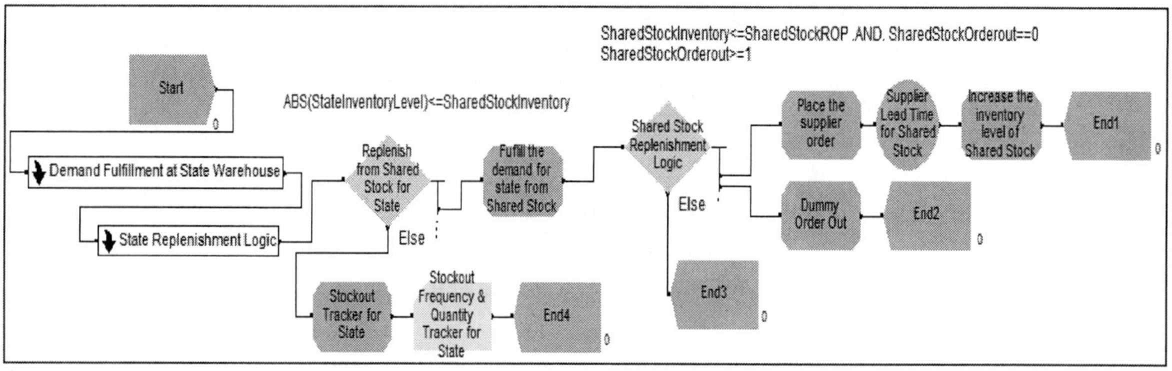

Figure 3: Simulation Logic Diagram for Inventory Management with Collaboration Across States via Shared Stock

3 RESULTS & DISCUSSION

3.1 Simulation Results I: The Benefits of Shared Stock Under Normal Conditions

Table 6 shows the results under the scenario where each state operates independently and where the states collaborate via maintaining a shared stock. The table represents the average replication values with the half-width of a 95% confidence inverval shown in parentheses. As we can observe, State D had the highest number of stockouts and, on average, stocked out for 33.9 (±5.09) days and 19,177 (±3,064) units when operating independently. In contrast, when there is a shared stock, State D tapped into the shared stock and reduced its stockout days to an average of 25.2 (±3.30) days and an average stockout quantity of 15,265 (±2,061) units. Similarly, States A, B, and C also incurred stockouts when operating independently but reduced or eliminated stockouts when using the shared stock. Paired t-test results support these findings. For State A, the p-value (0.176) was greater than 0.05, meaning the reduction in stockouts was not statistically significant. In contrast, State B ($p = 0.0057$), State C ($p < 0.0001$), and State D ($p = 0.0388$) all showed statistically significant reductions in stockout quantity, suggesting that shared stock had a noticeable impact in these cases. Evidently, even under normal operating conditions (i.e., normal demand), the states can mitigate stockouts by collaborating and having some common inventory they can tap when they stock out at their warehouses.

Table 6: Comparison of Stockouts without and with Collaboration Across States Via Shared Stock (Regular Demand Conditions)

Each state operates independently					
	State A	**State B**	**State C**	**State D**	**Shared Stock**
No. of orders to the supplier	17 (0)	19.9 (0.23)	19 (0)	28.2 (0.30)	0 (0)
Stockout days	1 (1.12)	2.6 (1.85)	4.1 (1.41)	33.9 (5.09)	NA
Stockout quantity	55.32 (89.06)	245.9238 (105.50)	275.57 (78.12)	19177.24 (3064.12)	NA
The states collaborate by maintaining a shared stock					
No. of orders to the supplier	17 (0)	19.3 (0.34)	19 (0)	27.5 (0.37)	3.42 (0.79)
Stockout days	0.1 (0.23)	0 (0)	0 (0)	25.2 (3.30)	NA
Stockout quantity	14 (Insufficient**)	0 (0)	0 (0)	15264.96 (2060.90)	NA

** not enough observations to create a confidence interval

3.2 Simulation Results II: The Benefits of Shared Stock Under a Demand Surge

Perhaps the real value in shared stock is when there is a surge in demand in one or more states. In this section, we tested the model under demand surge conditions in one state. We conducted the same analysis as in Section 3.1 but doubled the demand in State C. Note that if two or more states need shared stock, the shared stock is allocated on a first-in-first-out basis. Demand surges can occur if there is a disease outbreak in a state, a natural or other disaster, an accident, or a mass casualty event, such that a state needs to access a higher stockpile of specific medications or medical devices. Table 7 demonstrates the results under the scenario where each state operates independently and where the states collaborate via maintaining shared stock. When each state operates independently, State C faced the most severe impact(as expected), experiencing an average of 166 (±4.91) stockout days and average stocking out by 16,575 (±433) units per year. State D also suffered high shortages with an average of 38.2 (±3.47) stockout days and an average stockout quantity of 21,036 (±780) units per year. While this is larger than that of State C, this is because this is the state with the largest population.

State A and State B had minimal stockouts compared to State C and State D. With collaboration via shared stock, the situation improved. State C reduced its stockout days from an average of 166 (±4.91) to just an average of 1.4 (±1.52), and stockout quantity decreased from an average of 16,575 (±433) units to an average of 364 (±212). State D reduced its stockout days from an average of 38.2 (±3.47) to an average of 26.5 (±3.79) and its stockout quantity from an average of 21,036 (±780) units to an average of 15,441 (±2,369). State B eliminated stockouts. State A's stockout days decreased from an average of 0.7 (±0.9) to an average of 0.1 (±0.23), while stockout quantity slightly increased to 80 units, indicating minor shortages. The paired t-test results generally confirm these trends. State A ($p = 0.416$) did not see a statistically significant reduction in stockouts. However, for State B ($p = 0.0068$), State C ($p < 0.0001$), and State D ($p = 0.0003$), the reductions in stockout quantity were significant, showing that shared stock helped meet demand more effectively. Collaboration among states via a shared stock allows the states that experience demand disruptions through demand surges to reduce stockouts. As in the no-surge scenario, it also allows the other states that do not experience any demand surges to tap the shared stock and mitigate or even eliminate stockouts.

Table 7: Comparison of Stockouts Without and With Collaboration Across States via Shared Stock (Demand Surge in State C)

Each state operates independently					
	State A	**State B**	**State C**	**State D**	**Shared Stock**
No. of orders to the supplier	17 (0)	19.5 (0.38)	36.9 (0.23)	28 (0)	0 (0)
Stockout days	0.7 (0.90)	4.7 (2.86)	166 (4.91)	38.2 (3.47)	NA
Stockout quantity	73 (170.68)	373.28 (228.91)	16,574.89 (433.13)	21,036.23 (780.36)	NA
The states collaborate by maintaining a shared stock					
No. of orders to the supplier	17 (0)	19.3 (0.35)	36.5 (0.38)	27.4 (0.37)	7.10 (1.14)
Stockout days	0.1 (0.23)	0 (0)	1.4 (1.52)	26.5 (3.79)	NA
Stockout quantity	80 (Insufficient)	0 (0)	363.7083 (212.20)	15,441.11 (2368.76)	NA

4 CONCLUSIONS AND FUTURE RESEARCH

Our analyses lead to the following conclusions. The four states in Nigeria currently manage their procurement and inventory management of essential medicines for child and maternal health independently. Furthermore, they follow a different inventory policy from other states but seem to have adopted the same policy for all medicines included in our analyses. The four states can achieve significant savings if they adopt a CRP with a 90% or 99% service level and even higher savings if they pool their procurement and inventory management.

A simulation of different scenarios was carried out to demonstrate the benefits of collaboration across states. The analyses focused on one form of collaboration: the states maintain an amount of stock that can be shared among them, for example, when a state does not enough stock to satisfy demand. The simulation results show that the states benefit from fewer stockouts when there is shared stock not only under normal demand conditions but also under demand surges (e.g., a disease outbreak in one state that requires a much higher volume than normal). Hence, cross-state collaboration can help mitigate severe stockouts due to demand disruptions.

Going forward, we plan to expand our analysis to include multiple medicines and more states. When multiple medicines are considered it is possible to also reduce transportation costs by consolidating shipments of the medicines. This will allow us to also compare the costs of the policies, in addition to considering service performance.

ACKNOWLEDGMENTS

We sincerely thank Ms. Azuka Okeke, the CEO of the Africa Resource Center for Excellence in Supply Chain Management (ARC-ESM), for facilitating the communication with the four states and the states for participating in the data collection.

REFERENCES

Balakrishnan, A., Geunes, J., & Pangburn, M. S. (2004). Coordinating supply chains by controlling upstream variability propagation. Manufacturing & Service Operations Management, 6(2), 163-183.

Chemonics (2023). *Nigeria's Drug Revolving Fund: A Conversation with Tukur Ibrahim*. URL: https://chemonics.com/blog/nigerias-drug-revolving-fund-a-conversation-with-tukur-ibrahim/.

Chopra S. and Meindl P. (2019). *Supply Chain Management: Strategy, Planning, and Operation*. 7th Ed. Pearson, 325-370.

Huff-Rousselle, M. (2012). The logical underpinnings and benefits of pooled pharmaceutical procurement: a pragmatic role for our public institutions? *Social Science & Medicine*, *75*(9), 1572-1580.

Institute of Medicine (US) Committee on the Economics of Antimalarial Drugs (2002). *Saving Lives, Buying Time: Economics of Malaria Drugs in an Age of Resistance*. Arrow, K. J., Panosian, C., & Gelband, H. (Eds.). National Academies Press (US). URL: https://www.ncbi.nlm.nih.gov/books/NBK215633/.

Parmaksiz, K., Pisani, E., Bal, R., & Kok, M. O. (2022). A systematic review of pooled procurement of medicines and vaccines: identifying elements of success. *Globalization and Health*, 18(1), 59.

Silver, E. A., Pyke, D. F., & Thomas, D. J. (2016). *Inventory and Production Management in Supply Chains*. 4th Ed. CRC Press, pp. 26-28.

World Health Organization (WHO) (2020). *WHO Guideline on Country Pharmaceutical Pricing Policies*. URL: https://www.who.int/publications/i/item/9789240011878.

AUTHOR BIOGRAPHIES

VIRAJ JOSHI is currently pursuing a Master's in Industrial Engineering at Arizona State University, having previously completed his undergraduate degree in Industrial Engineering from Savitribai Phule Pune University.

MIKAELLA POLYVIOU is an Associate Professor in the Department of Supply Chain Management at the W. P. Carey School of Business, Arizona State University.

JOHN FOWLER is the Motorola Professor of Supply Chain Management in the Department of Supply Chain Management at the W. P. Carey School of Business, Arizona State University.

EUGENE SCHNELLER is a Professor and Dean's Council of 100 Distinguished Scholars in the Department of Supply Chain Management at the W. P. Carey School of Business, Arizona State University.

ADEGOKE OKE is Department Chair and Professor in the Department of Supply Chain Management at the W. P. Carey School of Business, Arizona State University, and a Hal Fearon Distinguished Fellow.

Proceedings of the Operational Research Society Simulation Workshop 2025 (SW25)
M. Luis, A. Harper, T. Monks, N. Mustafee, eds.

https://doi.org/10.36819/SW25.014

CHIP AWAY EVERYTHING THAT DOESN'T LOOK LIKE AN ELEPHANT

Dr John D Salt

Cranfield Defence and Security
Cranfield University
Defence Academy of the United Kingdom
Shrivenham, SN6 8LA
United Kingdom
j.salt@cranfield.ac.uk

ABSTRACT

This paper addresses the question of how conceptual models are created in a simulation modelling activity. Assuming an entity-based approach to simulation, some techniques for discovering good entity classes are considered, including personation. Also considered are the notations by which a conceptual model can be represented, and the modes of thought required for good conceptual modelling. Specifically excluded from consideration is the idea of applying a cut-and-dried method. The shortcomings of computers for conceptual modelling are remarked upon.

Keywords: Conceptual modelling, Stochastic discrete-event simulation, best practice

1 INTRODUCTION

Making a conceptual model remains one of the most mysterious parts of the art of simulation modelling.

An old joke of indeterminate origin (https://quoteinvestigator.com/2014/06/22/chip-away accessed 20 Oct 2024) has someone asking a sculptor how he produces a lifelike sculpture of an elephant from a block of marble. The answer is to take a hammer and chisel, and chip away everything that doesn't look like an elephant. Such advice may be true, but it is hardly helpful.

The intention of this paper is to offer a few ideas on the means of representation and modes of thought that the author has found to be helpful in developing a conceptual model. It is hoped that these might prove slightly more useful than "chip away everything that doesn't look like an elephant".

2 PREVIOUS RESEARCH

Since being introduced to stochastic discrete-event simulation modelling in 1987, the author has seen little written about the way simulation modellers make conceptual models. This is disappointing; the initial stage of deciding what simulation to write is surely one of the most important parts of any simulation modelling project. The first book on the topic was published by Robinson et al (2010), and Robinson has clearly maintained an interest in the question (Robinson 2011, Robinson 2013, Robinson 2020) and has done a fine job of identifying the existing literature and persuading simulation academics to get together to discuss the matter.

Despite being an academic, the author's interest is more from the perspective of the practitioner than the academic. This paper will therefore offer a few observations on how conceptual models are constructed, based on his own experience over several decades writing simulation models for the defence, oil, transport, and aerospace industries.

3 DISCOVERING THINGS

Practically all the simulation modelling the author has ever done is entity-based. Indeed, the idea of entity-based simulation is so widespread that it might not occur to people that there is any other way of doing it.

3.1 The Idea of Thingness

Philosophers – specifically, ontologists – have agreed for over two thousand years that the physical universe is made up of things. Typically these things have properties, and may be divided into classes or categories. The idea of thingness extends beyond the physical universe. Abstract objects can exist without physical reality; the idea of a triangle, a Thursday, or a kingdom.

Despite the popularity of this view, it is not the only one possible. In the novel "The Third Policeman", Flann O'Brien (O'Brien 1967) refers to the imaginary substance raw omnium. This is the stuff everything in the universe is made from, but before it is made into things. It seems to me that the task of the conceptual modeller is not unlike sculpting omnium.

Entities have been part of the software representation of simulation models at least since the 1960s. The idea of object-oriented programming using classes (Dahl and Nygaard 1968) was devised specifically for the purpose of creating discrete-event simulation models, a point often forgotten now that it is the dominant approach to software development everywhere. Even earlier, Tocher's idea of activity-cycle diagrams (ACDs) (Tocher, 1963) implicitly assumed the existence of entity classes whose entity life-histories were depicted in the diagrams.

A large part of conceptual modelling, therefore, lies in deciding what classes of things should be present in the model.

3.2 Beings and Doings

One of the pioneers of object-oriented techniques in mainstream software development, Peter Coad (Coad and Yourdon 1990) observed a tendency in the analysis phase of projects he had been involved with for the development team to split into two parties, one pursuing initially a functional decomposition, and the other a data-based decomposition. In his experience, the latter was generally a sounder basis for development, but took longer to put together. Usually, therefore, the functional decomposition was pursued, often leading to problems later on.

Not everyone would agree with Coad's observation. There exists a considerable family of purely functional programming languages, such as ML, its offspring, OCaml and Standard ML, and Haskell, Curry, and Clojure. These represent a minority sport in practical computer programming, and as far as I have been able to tell have made little impression on practice in simulation modelling.

Still, simulation modellers, unlike database designers or enterprise architects, cannot get away with just defining what things there are and how they are related. The relations in a simulation model are necessarily dynamic. The data must be made to dance. In the classic object-oriented view, the distinction between "beings" and "doings" is traditionally between instances of classes (objects) and their methods (including multi-methods).

A popular method for discovering candidate classes is known as "grammatical dissection". This is done by taking a short textual description of the system under study, and underlining the nouns. These then become the initial set of candidate classes. Underlining the verbs might be done to give an idea of some potential methods. It seems highly optimistic to rely on a language with such informal grammar as English to make such a distinction. On the one hand, any verb phrase can be replaced by one using a noun ("John gave Mary a kiss" rather than "John kissed Mary"), and, on the other, "there's no noun in the language that can't be verbed". Bertrand Meyer (Meyer, 1997) rightly mocks the naïveté of this approach, and offers more useful advice based on the idea that classes are implementations of abstract data types. What is more, it can be argued that the distinction between an object and a process (which one might think of as representing a noun and a verb respectively) is a false dichotomy. Any entity in your simulation can be thought of as a permanent thing, or as a transient process, depending solely on the timescale under consideration. For example, while it may be unusual to consider a building as a process, rather than an entity, it seems more process-like when one considers that there was a time when it did not exist, and there will be a time when it does not exist again.

3.3 Discovering Classes

Having decided on a set of candidate classes from which one might start to construct a working model, the conceptual modeller(s) will need to decide which to keep, which to discard, and how they interact. A popular way of doing this is by using CRC (Class-Responsibility-Collaborator) cards. CRC cards were originated by Kent Beck and Ward Cunningham (Beck and Cunningham 1989) as a way of helping students to experience an object perspective. They have since proven themselves useful for responsibility-driven design (Wirfs-Brock et al, 1990) and enjoyed a certain amount of popularity with the agile programming movement.

Some of the strengths of the CRC card technique are that it requires minimal equipment (a few file cards and some writing tools) and is intrinsically participative. Since it is an avowedly informal approach, it can be understood by subject-matter experts (SMEs) and operators of the real system who may have no great simulation modelling expertise. This is reminiscent of the HOCUS (Hand or Computer Universal Simulator) approach devised by Hills (Hills 1968) where ACDs would be developed by hand before being translated into computerized form. The advantage of ACDs is that the execution syntax is more formal than with CRC cards. What matters, it seems to me, is to develop a "cardboard model" in collaboration with SMEs before attempting to implement the thing on a computer.

3.4 The Naming of Parts

During the process of class discovery, whether using the CRC card technique or not, naming is important. Scott Ambler has described the art of object-oriented programming as extending the programming language into the problem domain. If the people who use the real system do not have a name for something, that thing seems unlikely to be important to the functioning of the system. On the other hand, if they have fine distinctions in naming between things that seem similar, further investigation is merited.

3.5 Personation: The Big Secret

The idea behind CRC cards, and behind Peter Coad's "Object Game", was to get people to experience an object perspective. This is more like a "first-person shooter" view, from the perspective of a single object, than a "God's-eye view" taking in the whole of the system at once.

I often think that the big secret about simulation modelling is that there is no big secret, but, if there is one, it is this. When acting out the interactions between objects during a CRC card or similar "cardboard modelling" session, the participants pretend to be the objects. This approach was taught to me by Peter Coad in a short course on Object-Oriented Analysis, but I have found no mention of it in the associated book. I believe he called it "personation", and he gave the impression that other analysts used a very similar technique. Whether because it has no agreed name, or because it involves imaginative play that risks appearing childish, I have not seen it referred to in either the simulation modelling or more general software development literature. It would be very interesting to know if other simulation modellers employ such an approach.

4 NOTATIONS

There are a number of diagrammatic notations associated with simulation modelling. ACDs have long been established in the UK and go back at least to Keith Tocher's foundational work (Tocher 1963). whereas Event graphs (Buss 1996) seem to have been first put forward by Evans, Wallace and Sutherland in 1967 (Evans et al 1967), are now associated mostly with the name of Schruben (Schruben 1983) and have more recently been referred to as Simulation Graphs (Schruben & Yücesan 1993). The author has experimented with Role Activity Diagrams (Holt et al 1983) and Petri nets (Petri 1963) but found neither of them satisfactory.

4.1 OMG Standards

The Object Management Group (OMG) has published a standard for the Business Process Model and Notation (BPMN) (https://www.omg.org/spec/BPMN accessed 21 Oct 2024), but I have yet to see it used for simulation modelling.

Better known, for mainstream software development, is OMG's standard for the UML (Unified Modeling Language) (https://www.omg.org/spec/UML/ accessed 21 Oct 2024). This includes a large number of diagram types. Probably the most useful for the simulation modeller are the Statechart, which resembles the traditional State Transition Diagram, and the Activity Diagram, which has execution semantics resembling those of a Petri net, and, given its use of swimlanes rather than overlapping activities, appears to be a rather clumsier version of the Tocher-style ACD. Class diagrams, an extension of the classic Entity Relationship Diagram, are useful for showing the static structure and relationships between classes, but do not help to capture dynamic behaviour.

Before the arrival of the UML, numerous authors had their own diagramming methods for object-oriented software development. Some of these could become quite complex. Grady Booch (Booch 1991) proposed a notation with more than 50 symbol types. There were also various extensions of existing diagramming methods proposed in PhD theses (including the author's). None of these seems to have endured.

4.2 Visual Interactive Modelling: "Visual GPSS"

Probably the most frequently-encountered diagram style in discrete-event simulation is the network consisting of service points, queues, entry and exit points, and resources. Notations of this kind are found in the various VIM (Visual Interactive Modelling) tools such as Simul8 or ExtendSim that offer the user the ability to construct and run simulation models "with no programming" (although I would argue that what is happening is visual programming).

These notations strongly resemble the block diagrams (originally sequence charts) associated with GPSS (Gordon 1969). While this "visual GPSS" approach lends itself admirably to job-shop queueing systems that are suitable for modelling lots of problems in transport, manufacturing, and telecommunications, the forced distinction between temporary entities (transactions) and permanent entities (service points and resources) makes it hard to model multi-party collaborations, something at which ACDs excel. It is a mystery to me why, with so many VIS tools on the market, none seems to implement the ACD approach.

4.3 Others

Still other notations have been suggested for conceptual modelling. Influence diagrams, ideally suited to systems dynamics modelling, seem to me to be ill-adapted to entity-based modelling. Rich Pictures, from the Soft Systems Methodology (SSM), may prove useful because they do not limit what the modeller includes in them, but, lacking any specified execution semantics, they may end up producing undesirably static models.

Some software development notations seem to me to be quite unsuitable. The Input-Processing-Output (IPO) approach embodied in Data Flow Diagrams (DFDs) has never struck me as a natural way of conceptualizing systems. The fact that Ed Yourdon, the person most associated with popularizing DFDs, abandoned them for an object-oriented approach suggests that better things are available. Control flow charts have scarcely been used in software development for many decades now, but remain unaccountably popular with some managers. Teaching on the Discrete and Continuous Simulation course at Shrivenham, I have noticed that a fairly common mistake among students is to try to specify the behaviour of a simulation using a traditional flowchart. This usually works very badly. The emphasis on branching decisions is less likely to be of interest in a simulation than questions of timing and randomness, neither of which a control flowchart can show. Flowcharting does not address the question of what entities exist, cannot deal with several things going on at once, and implies the God's-eye view that is seldom helpful to the modeller.

5 MODES OF THOUGHT

The trick a simulation modeller is trying to pull off is to find and express a useful correspondence (or metaphoresis) between the problem-owner's system of abstractions and some set of precise and executable mathematical constructs. This is not a trivial task of transposition, but, in the same way as translating from one human language to another, it is often perceived as such and seen as trivial by those with no skill or experience in it. This failure to regard simulation modelling as a distinct skill is a failing I have seen have dire effects on a simulation project. Ed Russell listed the skills necessary to a successful simulation project as being software development, project management, subject matter expertise, and modelling skill (Russell 1983). Of course, I am not a disinterested party in the matter, but it seems to me that modelling skill should command greater regard, and of course more lavish emoluments. Certainly nobody would be silly enough to attempt a simulation project with no attempt to provide for any of Russell's other categories of needful skill.

In order to do an adequate job of conceptual modelling, it seems to me that the simulationist should cultivate certain habits of mind.

5.1 Simplifying

The essence of simulation modelling is simplification. The modeller therefore needs to be able to distinguish those parts of the system under study that can be idealized, or left out entirely. The more experienced the modeller, the greater is likely to be the confidence with which they will make sometimes quite brutal simplifications. It is always easier to add complication to a model than to take it out. I have seen simulation models fail because they were too complicated; I cannot recall having seen one do so because it was too simple.

It is a commonplace that simulation modelling is used to address "what if?" questions. I suggest that the conceptual modeller should often ask themself "what if not?" – what would happen if we left something out? This is in accordance with the principle enunciated by Saint-Exupéry (Saint-Exupéry 1939): *"Il semble que la perfection soit atteinte non quand il n'y a plus rien à ajouter, mais quand il n'y a plus rien à retrancher"* (It seems that perfection is attained, not when there is nothing left to add, but when there is nothing left to take away). Economy of expression is much to be desired. Simulationists should be software poets, rather than software novelists.

One great aid to simplifying is a clear idea of the ultimate purpose of the simulation study. Here the old cyberneticist's question, "it is a machine to do what?", can be very helpful. If the modeller is unclear as to what the simulation is supposed to achieve, it becomes impossible to tell whether any particular element is or is not important, so it is included just in case, and the model grows like Topsy. As John Sterman puts it (Sterman 1991), "The art of model building is knowing what to cut out, and the purpose of the model acts as the logical knife".

5.2 Clarity and Concretion

It seems to me that simulation modellers, at least for entity-based simulation, must of necessity be fairly concrete thinkers. Not for them the numinous and grandiloquent utterances of managers seeking to impress. For a conceptual model to be useful, it is necessary that all parties understand its elements in the same way. While it might be tempting to let people understand things each in their own different way for the sake of a quiet life, things will go badly when the disagreement is detected.

I try to impress upon my students that there are often times when it is more important to be clear than to be correct. If you are clearly in error, the error can then be corrected; if it is not clear what you mean, such correction might be deferred indefinitely.

5.3 Tolerance of Uncertainty

It is a natural human tendency to desire psychological closure. Once things are done and dusted, one can stop worrying about them. This is the sort of thinking the conceptual modeller should avoid.

Here I am not thinking of the aleatory uncertainty of randomness, although of course simulationists should be comfortable with that. Rather, it is the suspension of final judgement on what is the right way to proceed. Even at the conceptual modelling stage, simulation modellers should expect to use an iterative approach that requires re-visiting elements of the model at frequent intervals. Conceptual modellers should have the flexibility of mind to consider several different representations of the system under study, to think in different categories.

Note that this point is not in conflict with the previous one. It is possible to be clear, concrete, and provisional, just as it is possible to be vague, abstract, and final.

5.4 Dealing with Ignorance

Simulation modellers often need to become instant experts in areas that are new and strange to them. Obviously, this needs them to be quick learners, and it has already been mentioned that it is a good idea to try to learn and speak the language of the problem domain. It also means that they need to become accustomed to being ignorant.

One aspect of wrestling with one's ignorance is a willingness to ask questions which may, in retrospect, sound stupid. Better to expose your ignorance with the stupid question than to preserve it, and attempt to preserve your dignity, by not asking.

Another natural human tendency is to stick to what one knows, and it can be tempting to concentrate on those parts of the system under study that are well understood, and for which the best data is available. This is likely to prove a mistake: the greatest benefit from a simulation study will come from improving our understanding of poorly-understood areas. Too often have I seen students scope a simulation model so as to exclude matters they were not comfortable with.

5.5 Spirit of Play

The technique of personation requires playing games of make-believe in a manner easily seen as childish. Collaborative sessions creating cardboard models, using CRC cards or otherwise, therefore run best if animated by the spirit of play. If everybody is at play, then they will feel comfortable exposing outlandish creative ideas, and have an environment in which it is safe to explore, and safe to fail.

Although it probably does not count as a business benefit, this will also make conceptual modelling a lot more enjoyable.

6 METHODS AND MACHINES

It will not have gone unnoticed that I have not recommended either a method for the construction of conceptual models, nor any computer software to assist with it.

6.1 Methods

I do not believe that it is possible to devise a fixed method to carry out creative, artistic work such as conceptual modelling. The idea that methods can be prescribed for activities of all kinds smacks of a Fordian attempt to de-skill creative workers. This is defined as "creationism" in the Jargon File (http://www.catb.org/jargon/html/C/creationism.html accessed 21 Oct 2024) in the following terms:

> *The (false) belief that large, innovative software designs can be completely specified in advance and then painlessly magicked out of the void by the normal efforts of a team of normally talented programmers. In fact, experience has shown repeatedly that good designs arise only from evolutionary, exploratory interaction between one (or at most a small handful of) exceptionally able designer(s) and an active user population — and that the first try at a big new idea is always wrong. Unfortunately, because these truths don't fit the planning models beloved of management, they are generally ignored.*

As Albert Camus (Camus, 1956) had it, *"Quand on n'a pas de caractère, il faut bien se donner une méthode"* (when one has no character, one is obliged to resort to a method). Conceptual modellers should have sufficient character not to need a method. A more recent aphorism expressing the same thought comes from Nassim Nicholas Taleb (Taleb 2016), who says "Your brain is most intelligent when you don't instruct it on what to do."

6.2 Machines

Given these beliefs, it will come as no surprise that I do not think a computer will help much in the conceptual modelling phase. While Hill's HOCUS was born at a time when extensive paper-based preparation was done for all programming activities before consuming any expensive computing resources, the idea of restricting conceptual modelling to paper or cardboard media remains a good one. For one thing, paper or card models are much easier to throw away and re-do. Also, despite the advances in other aspects of performance, computers remain miserable at allowing more than a couple of people to work on the same task simultaneously. Where a group of people might be able to conduct a conceptual modelling session with rich multi-party interactions between all members of the group, introducing a computer screen into the proceedings will transmute the richness of many-to-many human interactions to a limited number of human-to-computer interactions. This is not what we want.

It must be admitted that simulation modelling has pioneered the application of visual programming in VIM. However, the universality of the "visual GPSS" paradigm means that the conceptual modelling has largely been done beforehand. This is bad luck if the model you need does not fit neatly into the limited "job shop" view.

7 CONCLUSION

Conceptual modelling does not appear to be very well understood, even by acknowledged experts in simulation. It does not seem to be accorded the same respect by management as other skills. As successful conceptual modelling seems to depend on freely admitting to ignorance, and on a child-like spirit of play, this is perhaps unsurprising. Popularity with management is not helped by the fact that conceptual modelling is not amenable to automation or codification. I would, however, contend that it is the most critical skill needed to conduct a useful simulation project. Without a good conceptual model, the rest of the project will be built on a base of sand.

ACKNOWLEDGMENTS

The author would like to acknowledge a vast debt to the profound thinkers who have influenced his thinking about simulation modelling over the last 37 years, including notably Prof Isi Mitrani, Colin Grey, the late Jim Barr, Chris Carrigan, Ron Belanger, Peter Coad, Prof Mike Pidd, Dr Paul Syms, Phil Barker, and most of all my good friend the late Prof Ray Paul.

REFERENCES

Beck, K and Cunningham, W (1989). A Laboratory For Teaching Object-Oriented Thinking. In: Meyrowitz, N K (ed), *OOPSLA'89 Conference Proceedings,* New Orleans, LA, pp. 1-6.

Booch G (1991). Object Oriented Design with Applications, Benjamin Cummings.

Budd, T (1994). Multi-paradigm programming in Leda, Addison-Wesley.

Buss, A H (1996). Modeling with Event Graphs. In: Charnes, J M, Morrice, D J, Brunner, D T, and Swain J J, *Proceedings of the 1996 Winter Simulation Conference*, San Diego, CA, pp. 153-160.

Camus, A (1956). La Chute, Gallimard.

Coad, P, and Yourdon, E (1990). Object-Oriented Analysis (2nd ed), Yourdon Press.

Dahl, O-J, and Nygaard, K (1968). Class and subclass declarations. In: Buxton, J N (ed), IFIP Working Conference on Simulation Programming Languages, North Holland.

Evans, G; Wallace, G; Sutherland, G (1967). Simulation Using Digital Computers", Prentice-Hall.

Gordon, G (1969). System Simulation, Prentice-Hall.

Hills, P R (1968). HOCUS: A Simple Approach to Simulation. In: *Data Processing*, May 1968.

Holt A W, Ramsey H R, and Grimes J D (1983). Coordination System Technology as the Basis for a Programming Environment. Electrical Communication 57-4, pp. 308-314.

Meyer, B (1997). Object-Oriented Software Construction (2nd ed), Prentice Hall.

O'Brien, F (1967). The Third Policeman, MacGibbon and Kee.

Petri, C A (1963). Fundamentals of a Theory of Asynchronous Information Flow, 1st IFIP World Computer Congress, Munich 1962, North Holland, pp. 386-390.

Saint-Exupéry, A (1939). Terre des Hommes, Gallimard.

Robinson S, Brooks R, Kotiadis K, and van der Zee D-J (eds) (2010). Conceptual Modelling for Discrete-Event Simulation, CRC Press.

Robinson S (2011). Choosing the right model: Conceptual modeling for simulation. In: Jain S, Creasey R R, Himmelspach J, White K P, and Fu M (eds). *Proceedings of the 2011 Winter Simulation Conference.* Piscataway, NJ, pp. 1428–1440.

Robinson S (2013). Conceptual modeling for simulation. In: Pasupathy R, Kim S-H, Tolk A, Hill R, and Kuhl M E (eds). *Proceedings of the 2013 Winter Simulation Conference.* Washington DC, pp. 377-388.

Robinson S (2020). Conceptual modelling for simulation: Progress and grand challenges. Journal of Simulation 14(1): 1-20.

Russell, E C (1983). Building simulation models with SIMSCRIPT II.5. CACI, La Jolla, CA.

Schruben, L (1983). Simulation Modeling with Event Graphs, Communications of the ACM, 26(11), pp. 957–963.

Schruben L, and Yücesan, E (1993) Complexity of simulation models: a graph theoretic approach, In: Evans, G W, Mollaghasemi, M, Russell, E C, and Biles, W E (eds), *Proceedings of the 1993 Winter Simulation Conference.* Los Angeles, pp. 641–649.

Sterman, J D (1991). A Skeptic's Guide to Computer Models. In: Barmey, G O, et al (eds.), Managing a Nation: The Microcomputer Software Catalog, Westview Press, pp. 209-229.

Taleb, N N (2016). The Bed of Procrustes: Philosophical and Practical Aphorisms, Penguin.

Tocher, K (1963). The Art of Simulation, English Universities Press.

Wirfs-Brock, R, Wilkerson, B, and Wiener, L (1990). Designing Object-Oriented Software, Pearson.

AUTHOR BIOGRAPHY

JOHN D SALT received a BA (Comb Hons) in French and Russian from the University of Exeter in 1982, a MSc in Computing Science from the University of Newcastle-upon-Tyne in 1988, and a PhD in Computer Science from Brunel University in 1999. With over 35 years of experience as a simulation practitioner, he has created and maintained simulation models on a great variety of topics for organisations such as Hunting Engineering Limited, Eurotunnel, the European Space Agency, Shell International, Saudi Aramco, The Norwegian Defence Research Establishment, General Dynamics UK, DERA and DSTL. He is a member of the SSAISB, ACM, MCA, UKSS and RUSI, and is a Fellow of the Operational Research Society. He expects to retire next year from his post as a lecturer in simulation, OR and analytics with Cranfield Defence and Security at the Defence Academy of the UK, Shrivenham. https://www.cranfield.ac.uk/people/dr-john-salt-493715

Proceedings of the Operational Research Society Simulation Workshop 2025 (SW25)
M. Luis, A. Harper, T. Monks, N. Mustafee, eds.
https://doi.org/10.36819/SW25.015

DEVELOPING A CONCEPTUAL MODEL TO EVALUATE SHELF-LIFE EXTENSION AS A RESILLIENT STRATEGY IN HUMAN MILK BANKS

Mrs. Marta Staff
Prof. Navonil Mustafee

Centre for Simulation, Analytics & Modelling
The Business School
University of Exeter
Exeter, EX4 4PU, UK
Ms670@exeter.ac.uk
N.Mustafee@exeter.ac.uk

Dr. Natalie Shenker

Department of Surgery and Cancer
Faculty of Medicine
Imperial College London
London, W12 0HN, UK
Natalie.Shenker@imperial.ac.uk

ABSTRACT

The COVID-19 pandemic and higher levels of uncertainty due to climate change have emphasised the need for resilient and secure supply chains. This is also true for Human Milk Banks (HMBs), which are responsible for providing screened and safe Donor Human Milk (DHM) to neonatal hospital infants. Given the perishable nature of human milk, current UK operations are constrained by practices yielding a maximum shelf-life of six months. For improved resiliency and improved adverse event preparedness we present a conceptual model of HMB operations, which is an augmented version of one previously communicated, incorporating an additional process pathway yielding DHM with an extended shelf-life of 18 months. To address the associated operational constraints, our new conceptual model provides a framework for exploring the potential benefits of extended shelf-life on supply chain performance, especially related to inventory management and an enhanced ability for human milk banks to face future disruptions.

Keywords: Conceptual Model, Perishable Inventory, Shelf-life Extension

1 INTRODUCTION

In the context of medical and food products, ensuring safety and effectiveness at the point of consumption is an essential consideration. For perishable products, factors such as the perishability itself, and the associated inventory management, logistics, and transportation are central considerations for resilient and efficient supply chains. The need to maintain product quality during transit (where controlled conditions could be required), and to manage shelf-life, and respond to unpredictable disruptions in supply and/or demand, creates a complex decision-making environment. Agricultural produce is often regarded as higher quality the fresher it is at the point of use. This is also true for some medical products of human origin. For instance, even though red blood cells are typically considered to be viable for up to 42 days, some studies suggest that the transfusion of fresh blood may lead to improved health outcomes (Grasas et al, 2015). On the other hand, effective management of perishable inventory, especially when subject to stochastic demand, favours products with longer shelf-lives, as these can ease inventory management and lead to a reduction in waste.

Broadly speaking, advancements in technologies to extend the shelf-life of various perishable products are ongoing. Beyond "simply" controlling product temperature or high-heat treatments, alternative methods are being developed and deployed such as chemical treatment to control microbiological growth. Given these novel technologies, the extension of shelf-life for products like platelets has become a key area of study. A recent review by Rebulla and Prati (2022) highlights technologies such as pathogen reduction and bacterial detection as effective methods to extend platelet shelf-life. The review emphasizes the importance of a careful cost-benefit analysis at both the inventory management and clinical levels to ensure these technologies are implemented effectively and sustainably.

The particular perishable inventory field considered in this contribution is that of donor human milk (DHM) within the human milk banking supply chain. DHM offers important health benefits as an alternative in the event of the absence of mother's own milk. Depending on the jurisdiction, DHM is known to be classified differently as either a medical or a food product (Klotz et al, 2021). Human milk banks (HMBs) aim to provide a safe supply of DHM primarily to hospital neonatal settings. For detailed information on UK HMB operations see Staff et al (2024). Currently, all the demand that gets satisfied in the UK is in the form of frozen DHM. However, subjecting human milk to the freeze-drying process, dehydrates it, meaning that it no longer needs storing under frozen conditions, but instead can be stored at room temperature. Additionally, the freeze-drying process extends shelf-life characteristics over the frozen form of DHM, albeit with additional production costs. These characteristics make the freeze-dried form of particular interest when it comes to disaster preparedness.

In the recent workshop proceedings "Improving resilience in human milk banking" (Shenker et al, 2024, in press) several steps were suggested for how to ensure service provision during adverse events. Notably, it was highlighted that NHS milk banks, despite their critical role, remain outside of the NHS Emergency Preparedness, Resilience and Response (EPRR) Framework (https://www.england.nhs.uk/ourwork/eprr/ accessed 20 October 2023). This underscores an important gap in structured disaster preparedness and risk management specific to the unique requirements of HMBs. These operations include donor recruitment, milk screening, pooling, pasteurisation and more (for more details please refer to Sun et al 2022 and Staff et al 2024). Given the essential need for supply continuity of DHM, by focussing on the trade-offs between production costs and wastage when incorporating a freeze-dried component to varying degrees, our current study constitutes an initial phase of a larger programme of work on disaster preparedness.

Clearly the inventory management of perishable products is far from simple, however it is worth noting that associated studies presented previously have focused on those problems inherently constrained by a small number of time periods (namely, shelf-life measured in a small number of days). This constraint makes mathematical modelling a feasible option for capturing the core dynamics. In order to generate more robust results, through rich "*what-if*" scenario testing, simulation models that can track the age of individual items over an extended time horizon (such as discrete-event simulation (DES)), are likely to offer additional benefits.

Our work aims to make contributions by: (i) developing a conceptual model as a foundation for discussion with wider stakeholders including HMBs, medical professionals and disaster preparedness scholars, followed by iterative development of an associated computer-based DES model; (ii) modelling the flow of milk units through two processing and preservation paths- one yielding frozen products, and the other freeze-dried products with extended shelf-life- to assess their impact on overall inventory performance and to provide actionable insights into inventory management.

In Section 2 we discuss previous studies that aimed to assess shelf-life extensions in adjacent fields of perishable products. This is followed by a presentation of the problem description in Section 3 and the conceptual model in Section 4. Finally, discussion and conclusions are presented in Section 5.

2 LITERATURE REVIEW

A significant body of research has previously focused on blood products, as they are of a life-saving nature and exhibit high perishability. Blood products hold a resemblance to human milk as both products are of human origin and collected based on voluntarily donations, which translates into stochastic supply. As they are challenging to manage due to their short shelf-life, blood platelets have received considerable attention. Examples of recent studies examining the operational impacts of extending platelet shelf-life include works by Prioli et al (2018), Earnshaw at al. (2021), and Dillon et al (2023). Briefly, the study by Earnshaw at al. (2021) compares two platelets processing technologies that extend platelets shelf-life (5 days to 7 days). Beyond assessing clinical function, including adverse events and platelets efficacy, the aspects relating to extended availability, reduced waste and overall economic impact are also considered. By using the decision tree approach the study simulated platelet shelf-lives within a decision-analytic framework differentiated by processing method. By comparing the shelf-life performance across simulations, the model generates data on wastage rates (due to expiry), unit availability and transfusion cost. Linking the shelf-life extension to transfusion capacity reveals substantial benefits. Fewer units are required when the extended shelf-life is simulated in the scenario of high-demand, and this was identified as a cost-effective strategy. Similar conclusions when assessing the technology for shelf-life extensions of platelets were reached in the studies by Prioli et al (2018) and Dillon et al (2023). Prioli et al (2018) developed a budget impact model and reported that while pathogen-reduced platelets incur slightly higher costs, they offer benefits such as reduced wastage due to earlier availability and elimination of additional bacterial testing. Dillon et al (2023), by using a case study from Finland, developed a stochastic programming model that facilitated incorporation of demand uncertainty and included an optimisation element for defining optimal policy for the management of platelets. While the overall notion that these technologies enable better inventory management remains unchanged, it is evident that the latest study by Dillon et al (2023) makes greater efforts to incorporate uncertainty compared to the earlier studies.

While mathematical models, including analytical models, can offer valuable insights into the system being investigated, their ability to capture the complexity of real-world systems can be challenging for certain types of investigations. In particular, the analytical models, in order to ensure tractability, must incorporate simplified assumptions from the onset. While it is also true that simulation models require assumptions to facilitate meaningful decision-aiding, they are far more flexible and adaptive in nature.

In the field of perishable inventory management, Discrete Event Simulation represents a useful and relatively low-cost way to model complex systems to aid decision-making processes. Beyond being able to capture the stochastic nature of supply and demand, and hence incorporate a more realistic representation of system uncertainty, DES allows entities to represent individual units along with their so called attributes (i.e. individual characteristics), in this case including those related to age and perishable constraints. This allows a convenient and meaningful tracking of individual inventory units over time, which in turn allows a deeper, more granular understanding of how expiration impacts product availability and wastage. Importantly, DES facilities scenario testing, including inventory policies, without the need to disturb real-life operations, which not only is likely to be lees financially intensive, but also, in some cases, a safer option- for instance, when dealing with life-saving products such as blood. Since the publication of our review on the use of DES for perishable inventory management in the Simulation Workshop Proceedings (Staff and Mustafee, 2023), we have extended our search to include a wider range of literature in preparation for a full journal paper. This extended search, conduced in September 2023, did not identify any existing publications specifically addressing the extension of shelf-life for perishable products using DES. However, a more recent exploration of related fields led to the identification of a single study conducted by Moussavi, Sahin and Riane (2024), which relates to the agri-food supply chain. The study reports a DES model which simulates the inventory of strawberries at the retail level that aims to assess the effectiveness of the introduction of new packaging designed to extend the product's shelf-life. The study considers different shelf-life scenarios and reports that the longer shelf-life (2 days to 3 days) translates into a reduction of waste as well as providing a better buffer against stock-outs. However, it is worth noting that while the demand is modelled as stochastic, the replenishment policy follows the *"periodic review, order-up-to-level policy"* – also referred to as (T,S) policy. Such a replenishment policy would not be a realistic assumption for the donated product of human milk, for which supply is stochastic in nature. Additionally, the fact that the shelf-life of DHM is measured in months rather than days also differentiates our problem from those involving rapidly perishing products. This distinction is likely to alter the dynamics of inventory management, potentially easing certain time-sensitive pressures, while introducing challenges such as long-term storage and the requirement for more robust tracking mechanisms to monitor inventory age and ensure efficient stock rotation.

3 EXTENDING THE SHELF-LIFE OF HUMAN MILK

Human milk, upon expression, is highly perishable, and needs to be consumed almost immediately, otherwise it gets spoiled through natural biological processes (e.g. product degradation, microbiological contamination). However, as per UK NHS recommendations (https://www.nhs.uk/conditions/baby/breastfeeding-and-bottle-feeding/breastfeeding/expressing-breast-milk/ accessed 1 November 2023), lowering its temperature to fridge temperature (approx. 4°C) or freezer temperature (approx. -20°C) extends its shelf-life to eight days and six months, respectively. However, when milk gets donated to HMBs rather than being used to feed a mother's own child, handling practices become more strictly controlled to ensure safety. Rigorous protocols are followed to minimise the risk of contamination and degradation, thereby maintaining the milk quality for the recipient infant (often premature and/or otherwise vulnerable).

Globally, there is no consensus of what constitutes a safe storage duration and temperature for DHM, with some protocols recommending storing milk at -80°C for up to 12 months prior to pasteurisation (anecdotal accounts), and another study by de Waard et al (2018) showing that storing at -20°C for a duration of 8 months post-pasteurisation is a safe approach. In the UK it is required that "*donor milk awaiting pasteurisation in the freezer at the milk bank (at −20°C)* [is stored] *for no longer than 3 months from the date of expression*" and to be stored re-frozen post-pasteurisation "*for no longer than 6 months after the date of expression*" (https://www.nice.org.uk/guidance/cg93 accessed 10 September 2024).

Given these varied protocols and storage limitations, innovations in preservation methods are being explored to achieve an extended shelf-life in order to enhance supply chain resilience. For emergency preparedness, as well as for improving efficiency (such as waste reduction, better allocation etc.) of perishable inventory management, the technology of freeze-drying DHM has been utilised in some countries (e.g. Australia, Israel), however this has not so far been utilised in the UK.

As well as the additional post-pasteurisation step of the freeze-drying itself, careful tracking of the weights pre- and post- freeze-drying is also required in order that the freeze-dried product can be reconstituted by mixing with the correct volume of water (this is more important for DHM due to the biochemical heterogeneity of the human based product, than for to standardised infant formula). The water for rehydration is measured and bottled and stored along with the freeze-dried DHM. The additional steps of freeze-drying, weighing and measuring/bottling of water for re-hydration represent additional costs in the production process relative to frozen DHM. However, the freeze-dried product is reported to have a considerably longer shelf-life than the frozen DHM, and as such could lead to lower waste due to shelf-life timeouts. Additionally, with the freeze-dried product the costs associated with storage freezers are avoided, and beyond the cost savings, the ability to store in an unfrozen state represents an environmentally more sustainable, and resilient option. Clearly, these considerations remain valid for the transportation and subsequent supply chain echelons. Moreover, these characteristics are likely to enhance agility in disaster preparedness, as they allow for easier stockpiling and dispatch under ambient conditions.

Another aspect of relevance is that the demand for DHM is stochastic in nature, and as highlighted in the literature review section, it has been shown that extending the shelf-life allows for improved fulfilment rates as well as reduction in waste. Note finally that from a biological point of view, the two forms (frozen and freeze-dried) are considered equivalent in terms of nutritional function.

4 CONCEPTUAL MODEL

As discussed in the Introduction section, simulation-based studies of perishable inventory problems are likely to offer advantages over approaches based on mathematical modelling, and therefore, referring to Figure 1, we present a conceptual model, in the IDEF SIM (Integrated Definition Methods-Simulation) syntax, for simulation modelling of HMB operations in the case that DHM is produced in both frozen and freeze-dried forms. The IDEF-SIM technique was developed to facilitate the seamless translation of conceptual models into computer models, ensuring consistency and clarity in communication in the modelling process (Montevechi et al 2014). This is an extension of the conceptual model for milk bank operations as previously presented by the authors (Staff et al, 2023). Briefly, the paper presented at the Winter Simulation Conference 2023 developed a conceptual model for human milk banking, focusing on structural representation of donor milk processing and flow, related inventory management, and hospital demand fulfilment. Using a UK based case study, it identified key challenges within the human milk supply chain, including supply variability, perishability constraints, and demand uncertainty, emphasising the need for tailored inventory control strategies. The conceptual model provided a structured foundation for future simulation- based analysis, and in the case of this paper, it has been extended to incorporate the process for freeze-dried DHM. In Figure 1, the elements shown in black represent the elements as previously presented solely for frozen DHM, while those in blue represent the extensions for the freeze-dried DHM. Both forms share common batch handling processes (prior to pasteurization), pasteurization and testing steps (as shown in the upper section of Figure 1).

The different processing steps of frozen and freeze-dried DHM results in the two parallel processing paths, as shown in the lower section of Figure 1. The splitting of batches between the two paths is determined by a parameter *R* which is defined as the ratio of the volumes of DHM sent to the frozen and freeze-dried paths. By keeping the demand and supply parameters the same between experiments, experimenting with *R*, we aim to gain an understanding of system behaviour related to the trade-offs between production costs and wastage when introducing the freeze-dried component in varying degrees. Returning to Figure 1, both processing paths share some common features, including the discard of batches upon failed test results. For this it is noteworthy that the freeze-drying processing must immediately follow pasteurization for all batches, without waiting to receive test results back from the testing laboratory (typically a small number of days). This means that freeze-drying costs are incurred even for batches which are eventually discarded due to failed test results. Referring to Figure 1 and Table 1, in our Conceptual Model, the relevant costs to be modelled are shown as C1 through C6, with C1 and C2 being common to both processing paths, and the remaining ones being specific to a particular path. For the initial explorations those will remain fixed. Together with the different maximum shelf-life of the products on each path (L1 for frozen DHM, L2 for freeze-dried DHM as shown in the figure), and the aforementioned *R*, those constitute the parameters of the model.

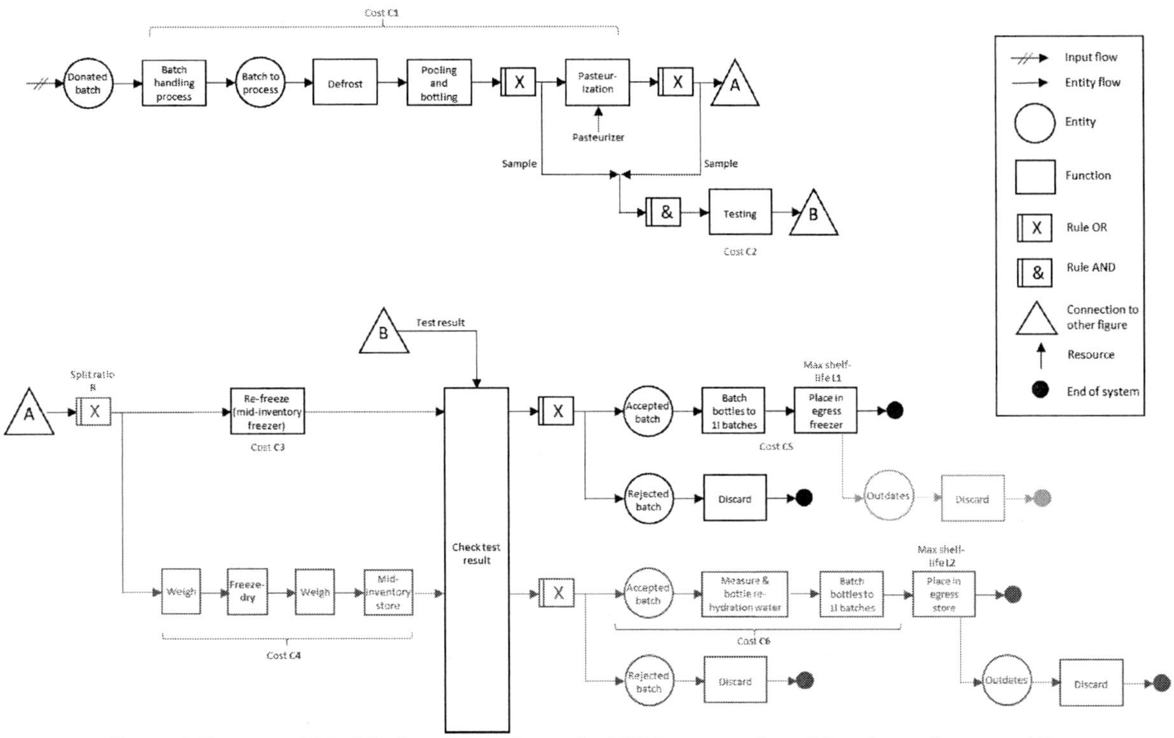

Figure 1 Conceptual Model of current pathway for DHM preservation of freezing and proposed freeze-drying pathway within HMB, using the IDEF-SIM notation. Elements in **black** represent those previously described in (Staff et al, 2023) for frozen product alone. Elements in grey correspond to elements added to the frozen DHM arm relative to previously presented Conceptual Model. Elements in **blue** represent additional processing required for the freeze-dried processing path.

Table 1 *Cost and Latency Parameters*

Parameter	Description
C1	Cost for batch processing from reception through to Pasteurisation
C2	Microbiological testing
C3	Frozen DHM – mid inventory freezer storage
C4	Freeze-dried DHM – freeze drying and associated weighing procedures

C5	Frozen DHM – assembly to 1*l* product batches and egress freezer storage
C6	Freeze-dried DHM – measure and bottle water for re-hydration, and assembly to 1*l* product batches
L1	Frozen form shelf-life
L2	Freeze-dried form shelf-life

The conceptual modelling stage is an intermediate process for developing the abstraction of a real-life problem in hand, prior to computer model development. To effectively communicate the project's current direction, we go beyond presenting a conceptual model artifact in the form of the IDEF SIM syntax represented graph (Figure 1). Building on Robinson's framework- which encompasses "understanding the problem situation, determining the modelling and general project objectives, identifying the model outputs, identify the model inputs, and determining the model content" (2008)- we also provide tables describing elements of the system. These elements are defined, as far as possible, according to the current state of the *"modeller's mind*", a concept emphasised by Robinson (2023) as good practice in capturing and documenting understanding during early stages of conceptualisation and implementation. Table 2 summarises the *inputs and outputs* of the simulation model, which is an augmented (changes/additions in bold font) version of the conceptual model previously developed by the authors (Staff et al, 2023). Stochastic supply and demand will be modelled. The demand assumption is that the decision to satisfy demand is general/common across processing paths, in other words, that there is no distinction/preference between frozen and freeze-dried forms of DHM at the point of dispatch or at the point of use in the hospital setting. The outputs are designed in order to be able to assess the aforementioned trade-offs to be investigated, and as such comprise statistics on fulfilment rates, wastage rates, stockout rates and costs, within both processing paths.

Turning to the aspects of *Components*, Table 3 shows that while all *Activities* and *Queues* will be modelled, only those *Entities* important for the study in hand (namely milk units and bottles) will be included. In terms of *Resources*, while we include all relevant equipment, these will only be modelled in terms of processing times and capacity. Also, as the processes involved in the two processing paths, as well as in the stages prior to processing path split, are likely to be labour-intensive, human resources will be modelled, but only to the extent that they contribute to the costs directly associated with the process.

Table 2 Inputs and Outputs. Aspects beyond Staff et al (2023) shown in bold

Model Input-
- Donor milk supply and demand-related parameters (statistical model parameters)

Model Output-
- Order fulfilment rate
- Shelf-life characteristics of dispatched batches **separately for frozen and freeze-dried DHM**
- **Wastage separately for frozen and freeze-dried DHM**
- **Stockout characteristics**
- **Cost metrics**

Model Output to support the establishment of a possible scenario when aims were not met-
- Shelf-life distribution profile within egress inventory **separately for frozen and freeze-dried DHM**

Table 3 Component Inclusion. Components beyond Staff et al (2023) shown in bold

Component	Milk Bank Component	Inclusion
Entities Physical or information components with defined characteristics that pass through the system (e.g., patients, phone calls, food units etc.). They undergo *Activities*, compete for potentially limited *Resources*, and can form the *Queues* when needed.	Milk Units Bags Jugs **Pasteurization bottles** **Rehydration bottles**	Included Excluded Excluded **Included** **Included**
Activities Actions to the *Entities* that refers to the state transition.	Batch Handling Process Defrosting, Pooling and Bottling Testing Pasteurization Refreezing and Batching Moving to egress freezer for frozen arm	Included Included Included Included Included Included

	Weighing for freeze-dried arm **Freeze-drying** **Bottling of water for rehydration**	**Included** **Included** **Included**
Queues Aggregation of *Entities* which await *Activities*.	Ingress Freezer Mid-inventory Freezer (frozen arm) **Mid-inventory Store (freeze-dried arm)** Egress Freezer (frozen arm) **Egress Store (freeze-dried arm)**	Included Included **Included** Included **Included**
Resources Human or equipment that is required for *Activities* to get completed and allow *Entities* to progress through the system.	External Microbiology testing facilities On-site equipment (e.g., pasteurizers, freeze-drier, freezers) **Human resources**	Excluded Included **Included***

Note*: Human resources included in terms of costs **C1** through **C6**.

5 DISCUSSION AND CONCLUSION

This paper presents a conceptual model of operation processes within a human milk bank, with a specific focus on exploring the potential introduction of a freeze-drying pathway to produce a product with extended shelf-life. The conceptual model extends the previously communicated conceptual base model (Staff et al, 2023) and forms the basis for a discrete-event simulation model currently in development, which will be used as a tool for experimentation. The simulation approach is designed to compare the process flow of the current (base) system with that of the proposed future system under identical conditions. By utilising the consistent random number streams, the same demand, supply and other parameters will be applied to both systems, to ensure a reliable comparison. Developing such a model aligns well with a broader aim of exploring and establishing resilient inventory management for HMBs. Resilience in this context refers to the ability of milk banks to maintain consistent supply and service delivery despite disruptions, such as increased demand, donor supply fluctuations, or external crisis. By enabling the production of freeze-dried milk with an extended shelf-life, milk banks could reduce wastage, improve storage flexibility, and enhance their capacity to respond to emergencies. Given the fact that the freeze-drying pathway is currently non-operational in any of the UK milk banks, and is only under consideration, developing a computer model to facilitate experimentation of "*what-if*" scenarios offers the potential for valuable insights before committing fully to real-world implementation. While our collaboration allows access to data associated with the current system including cost data, the lack of an operational freeze-drying process means we will need to rely on synthetic data, with characteristics assumed to be plausible by the stakeholders.

At this early stage, our focus remains on refining and validating the conceptual model through collaboration with Hearts Milk Bank, a medium-sized milk bank within the UK. Hearts Milk Bank shares both expertise on the operational system and data on supply and demand, ensuring that the model is grounded in practical realities. The computer model development stage currently involves iterative refinement based on discussions with stakeholders, that is to ensure the key operational processes and decision points are accurately represented. The validation by stakeholders will continue to play a crucial role in aligning the model with real-world practices.

For the simulation experiments, the model will be run over the timeframe including a warm-up period followed by a timeframe intended to capture a realistic cycle of supply, demand and expiry. While the exact timeframe is yet to be determined, we envisage that approx. three years of simulated operations should capture the system behaviour efficiently, given the longer time to expiry of the freeze-dried product and the seasonal differences observed within the system. Multiple scenarios, still to be agreed upon, will be tested. The simulation experiments will address two key questions (i) whether the introduction of a longer shelf-life freeze-dried product is likely to facilitate waste reduction of human milk and, if so, (ii) what proportion or combination of frozen and freeze-dried products would yield a financially sustainable mix.

Overall, this conceptual model, which represents an initial step in a larger resilience and disaster preparedness project, provides a framework for experimentation to understand how the introduction of a product variant with different shelf-life characteristics is likely to affect operations of HMBs. It will enable us to assess potential benefits in terms of perishable inventory management related to fulfilment, stockout and outdates. Additionally, assessment of financial implications of any transition to include freeze-dried DHM in the supply chain will provide valuable insights, ensuring informed decisions before committing to implementation.

ACKNOWLEDGMENTS

The authors would like to thank Dr. Simon Cameron and Simran Cheema, both of Queen's University Belfast, for helpful and informative discussions on the technical aspects of freeze-drying of human milk.

REFERENCES

Dillon M, Vauhkonen I, Arvas M, Ihalainen J, Vilkkumaa E and Oliveira F (2023). Supporting platelet inventory management decisions: What is the effect of extending platelets' shelf life?. *European Journal of Operational Research*, **310(2)**: 640-654.

Earnshaw S, Beyhaghi H, McDade C, Purser M, Marriott R, Daane L, Le Coent V, Yang J and Toback S (2021). Clinical and economic impacts of large volume delayed sampling and pathogen reduction technology platelet processing strategies in the United States. *Transfusion*, **61(10)**: 2885-2897.

Grasas A, Pereira A, Bosch M A, Ortiz P and Puig L (2015). Feasibility of reducing the maximum shelf life of red blood cells stored in additive solution: a dynamic simulation study involving a large regional blood system. *Vox sanguinis*, **108(3)**: 233–242.

Klotz D, Wesołowska A, Bertino E, Moro G E, Picaud J C, Gayà A and Weaver G (2022). The legislative framework of donor human milk and human milk banking in Europe. *Maternal & child nutrition,* **18(2)**: e13310.

Montevechi J A B, de Oliveira M L M, Leal F and de Pinho A F (2014). Analysis of the applicability of the IDEF-SIM modeling technique to the stages of a discrete event simulation project. In: Tolk A, Diallo S D, Ryzhov I O, Yilmaz L, Buckley S and Miller J A (eds). *Proceedings of the 2014 Winter Simulation Conference (WSC)*. Piscataway, NJ: IEEE, pp. 950–961.

Moussavi S E, Sahin E and Riane F (2024). A discrete event simulation model assessing the impact of using new packaging in an agri-food supply chain. *International Journal of Systems Science: Operations & Logistics*, **11(1)**: 2305816.

Prioli K M, Karp J.K, Lyons N.M. Chrebtow V, Herman J H and Pizzi L T (2018). Economic Implications of Pathogen Reduced and Bacterially Tested Platelet Components: A US Hospital Budget Impact Model. *Appl Health Econ Health Policy* **16**: 889–899.

Rebulla P and Prati D (2022). Pathogen Reduction for Platelets-A Review of Recent Implementation Strategies. *Pathogens*, **11(2)**: 142.

Robinson S (2008). Conceptual Modelling for Simulation Part II : A Framework for Conceptual Modelling. *Journal of the Operational Research Society* **59**:12–21.

Robinson S (2023). A Tutorial on Conceptual Modellingg For Disctere-Event Simulation In: Currie C and Rhodes-Leader L (eds). *Proceedings of the Operational Research Society Simulation Workshop 2023 (SW23)*, Southampton, UK, pp. 12-21.

Shenker N, et al (in press). Improving resilience in human milk banking: Workshop Proceedings, 11th November, London UK. *BMC Proceedings*

Staff M and Mustafee N (2023) Discrete-Event Simulation to support the management of perishable inventory-a review. In: Currie C and Rhodes-Leader L (eds). *Proceedings of the Operational Research Society Simulation Workshop 2023 (SW23)*, Southampton, UK, pp. 206–217.

Staff M, Mustafee N and Shenker N (2023). Conceptual Modeling for Perishable Inventory: A Case Study in Human Milk Banking. In: Corlu C G, Hunter S R, Lam H, Onggo B S, Shortle J and Biller B, (eds). *Proceedings of the 2023 Winter Simulation Conference (WSC)*. San Antonio, TX: IEEE IEEE, pp. 1208-1219.

Staff M, Mustafee N, Shenker N and Weaver G (2024). Ensuring neonatal human milk provision: A framework for estimating potential demand for donor human milk. *European Journal of Operational Research*. **318(2)**: 642-655.

Sun R, Maillart LM, Valeva S, Schaefer A J, Starks S and Milk, H (2022). Optimal pooling, batching, and pasteurizing of donor human milk optimal pooling, batching, and pasteurizing of donor. *Service Science,* **4(1)**: 13-34.

de Waard M, Mank E, van Dijk K, Schoonderwoerd A and van Goudoever J B (2018). Holder-pasteurized human donor milk: How long can it be preserved?. *Journal of pediatric gastroenterology and nutrition* **66(3)**: 479-483.

AUTHOR BIOGRAPHIES

MARTA STAFF received a BSc (Hons) in Biology from the University of London, and an MBA from the University of Exeter. She is studying for an ESRC-funded PhD at the University of Exeter Business School, UK. The focus of her research is operations management and simulation in healthcare. Her email address is ms670@exeter.ac.uk.

NAVONIL MUSTAFEE is a Professor of Analytics and Operations Management at the University of Exeter Business School, UK. His research focuses on M&S methodologies and Hybrid Modeling and their application in healthcare, supply chain management, circular economy and resilience and adaptation due to climate change. He is a Joint Editor-in-Chief of the Journal of Simulation. His email address is n.mustafee@exeter.ac.uk.

NATALIE SHENKER BM BCh, MSc, PhD, MRCS (Eng) is currently a UKRI Future Leaders Fellow and co-founder of the Human Milk Foundation, which supports families to feed their babies with human milk. The charity is enhancing access to screened donor milk when breastfeeding is impossible or delayed and is working towards creating equitable milk banking services. Her email is natalie.shenker09@imperial.ac.uk.

Proceedings of the Operational Research Society Simulation Workshop 2025 (SW25)
M. Luis, A. Harper, T. Monks, N. Mustafee, eds.
https://doi.org/10.36819/SW25.016

DEVELOPING HYBRID KIDNEY CARE MODELS WITH FACILITATED MODELLING

Stacey Croft

CORDA, BAE Systems

Preston, UK
stacey.croft@baesystems.com

Sally Thompson, Dr Lucy Morgan

The Strategy Unit,
NHS Midlands and Lancashire CSU
Birmingham, UK
sally.thompson37@nhs.net, lucy.morgan48@nhs.net

Prof. Antuela Tako, Dr Yun He

Nottingham Business School, Nottingham
Trent University
Nottingham, UK
Antouela.takou@ntu.ac.uk, yun.he@ntu.ac.uk

Prof. Mark Lambie

School of Medicine,
Keele University
Keele, UK
lambiem@doctors.org.uk

ABSTRACT

This paper presents a simulation modelling study aimed at supporting capacity planning of kidney replacement therapy services offered to patients at different stages of kidney failure. The model consists of a combined discrete-event simulation (DES) and system dynamics (SD) model, representing two different aspects of kidney care. The SD model represents the demand for kidney care by modelling disease progression in patients over time, whereas the DES models the provision of care including kidney transplantation and different types of dialysis offered either in hospital or at home. A facilitated modelling approach is adopted to engage with a range of stakeholders representing kidney care services to ensure the development of a relevant and representative model. To the best of our knowledge, this is the first facilitated modelling study of a combined (hybrid) simulation presented in the literature. We present the approach, followed by reflections and future work.

Keywords: Facilitated simulation, kidney care, health services, system dynamics, discrete-event simulation, hybrid simulation.

1 INTRODUCTION

Chronic kidney disease (CKD) is a long-term condition, where patients' kidneys become increasingly less able to filter waste from the blood. This progressively worsening kidney function is classified from stage 1 to stage 5. Kidney replacement therapies (KRT) are treatments given to people with CKD which has progressed to kidney failure, replacing their normal kidney functions. The main types of KRT are dialysis (at home or in-centre) and kidney transplantation (from a living or deceased donor). Nearly 71,000 adult patients were receiving KRT for end stage kidney disease at the end of 2022, among which 56.2% were transplant recipients (UK Renal Registry 2024). Patients can also receive conservative care to manage symptoms while maintaining the quality of life, especially those whose frailty suggests that KRT may be counterproductive.

Dialysis is expensive, with costs estimated at around £36,000 per patient per year for in-centre treatment, although mortality remains high, and quality of life remains significantly impaired. Dialysis at home is cheaper (between £17,000 and £24,000 per patient per year), and it can be associated with better quality of life, but the uptake of this option is variable. Kidney transplantation provides better quality and length of life at reduced cost but is not possible when the peri-operative mortality risk is too high, and the availability of donor organs remains a rate-limiting step. The number of patients on in-centre dialysis has been inexorably rising in the UK for several decades now (UK Renal Registry 2024). The growth curbed during COVID-19, although this is likely due to high mortality rates from COVID-19, so estimates foresee the growth in demand for dialysis to continue (UK Renal Registry 2024).

These issues make the management of KRT services challenging, with an urgent need to minimise future demand for in-centre dialysis, along with the associated ill-health, environmental cost and healthcare expenditure. This highlights the need for the optimisation of transplantation and dialysis-at-home services, as well as reducing the progression of CKD to kidney failure. In addition, predicting the increased capacity needed for unavoidable in-centre dialysis can support decisions for new dialysis units to be built and staffed. Achieving this will require realistic and evidenced estimates of the impact of investments in different possible strategies, taking population changes in size, ethnicity and age into account. This also calls for an approach that integrates primary, secondary and tertiary care of patients with kidney disease within the UK National Health Service (NHS), ensuring appropriate co-ordination across the different NHS organisations and structures.

The aim of this paper is to present the simulation modelling study undertaken to support capacity planning decisions for KRT services. This study is undertaken as a collaboration between The Strategy Unit (SU), Nottingham Trent University and Midlands Kidney Network (MKN). The model is intended to be used by the Midlands Kidney Network to support capacity planning decisions at a centre- and unit- level, as well as by other NHS kidney networks and KRT providers in England. The model combines two modelling approaches, discrete-event simulation (DES) and system dynamics (SD), to ensure that the kidney care system is represented effectively. The SD model represents the demand for kidney care by modelling disease progression in patients over time, and the DES model represents the provision of care services including kidney transplantation and different types of dialysis, to cater for future patient demand. We adopt a facilitated modelling approach to engage with a diverse group of stakeholders involved in kidney care services to ensure that a relevant and representative model is developed that can support decisions and future capacity planning for the NHS.

The contribution of this paper is twofold. First, the model developed extends existing kidney care simulation models as it provides a comprehensive and more accurate representation of the kidney care provision systems and current care pathways in the DES model, including diversion to conservative care, pre-emptive transplant and home haemodialysis (HHD). Furthermore, demand for kidney care is more accurately represented as it is generated by a separate model component (the SD model) that tracks disease progression in the population over long time. Such a model that operates at both service provision and demand levels for kidney care is not available in the existing literature. Secondly, it contributes towards the facilitated modelling methodology by presenting a novel study that adopts a facilitated approach for developing a combined (hybrid) simulation study. To the best of our knowledge, this is the first facilitated modelling study of hybrid simulation presented in the literature.

The outline of the paper is as follows. Section 2 briefly reviews existing models on kidney care and the state of art in facilitated hybrid simulation modelling. Section 3 explains the methods and the novel facilitated modelling process adopted. Section 4 presents the preliminary SD and DES models developed, while section 5 concludes the paper.

2 BACKGROUND ON KIDNEY CARE MODELLING

2.1 Kidney Care Modelling

A range of approaches have been used to model both the disease progression of CKD and the demand for KRT in the current literature.

An early DES was previously developed to model future demand for KRT in England (Roderick et al. 2004). The model utilised prevalence data, acceptance rates, survival rates, and transitions between haemodialysis (HD) and peritoneal dialysis (PD) treatment modalities. It used national population and mortality statistics, literature, and data from the UK Renal Registry and UK Transplant to assess unmet needs, demographic changes, and the impact of Type 2 diabetes on patient survival and transplant availability. An adapted version of the model was used in 2007 to inform plans for future kidney care services in the West Midlands (Warwick Business School 2007). These models and patient pathways are now outdated and were created in a software which is no longer available. The "Inside CKD" programme (Chertow et al. 2024) used a microsimulation model to project the CKD prevalence and costs over time, with country-specific analyses based on diagnosis rates, disease progression, comorbidities, treatment and mortality. A UK-based case study predicted 9.2 million CKD cases over 6 years to 2027, with a 5% rise in costs for diagnosed CKD and KRT (Tangri et al., 2023). Allen et al. (2020) developed a DES to support the organisation of dialysis services during the COVID-19 pandemic in the South of England.

SD models are useful in shaping health policy and representing population dynamics. Ansah et al. (2021) used an SD model to investigate the impact of interventions on the prevalence of CKD, end stage kidney disease patients needing dialysis, and the cost of dialysis in Singapore up to 2040. With projected increases in CKD and dialysis, the cost of dialysis care was projected to more than double in the base case. The interventions investigated showed that significant savings could be made. Another SD model, constructed by the Department of Health in 2009 and later updated in 2011, supported policymaking and commissioning for KRT services for adults in England (Wild & Etim 2011). It projected the number of patients by dialysis modality and transplant over a ten-year period for use by Specialist Commissioning Groups at high level residence-based areas.

The age of the software these models were built in, password protected files, lack of licenses for commercial software within the NHS and lack of open access to adapting externally commissioned models, meant that Kidney Networks around the UK were mostly using excel-based forecasting models to plan future demands for services. HHD, pre-emptive transplant and conservative care needed to be added, as well as addressing other factors that may influence CKD's progression to a stage requiring KRT, such as increased use of medications to slow the progression of CKD. A model was needed that would reflect the current patient pathways and give insight to relevant scenarios of future demand. The model needs to be scalable, with adaptable parameters, and available for use across the NHS.

2.2 Facilitated Hybrid Simulation

Hybrid simulation combines various methods, techniques, and/or paradigms for a more comprehensive understanding of complex socio-technical systems in real-world settings (Tolk et al. 2024; Brailsford et al. 2019). The development of hybrid simulation models requires the involvement of expertise from various stakeholders who are part of these complex systems. This means that modellers in the team must engage effectively with heterogeneous groups of external stakeholders while working with a collection of simulation methods and techniques efficiently. Like facilitated modelling, facilitated hybrid simulation includes the design of workshop sessions with interactive activities to engage stakeholder groups into the modelling process (Tako and Kotiadis 2015). It aims to achieve common modelling objectives between the modelling team and the stakeholders responsible for the systems under study via mutual understanding, group discussions, and consensus reaching activities (Eldabi et al. 2019). The PartiSim framework (Tako and Kotiadis 2015 and 2018) offers a structured approach for stakeholder engagement while also being flexible to involve other simulation techniques and paradigms.

Recent hybrid modelling and simulation studies applied to healthcare has mainly focused on emergency departments and acute care, long-term condition services and elderly care units, integrating simulation and modelling with policy development (Cassidy et al. 2019). The combination of simulation approaches (DES and SD) for healthcare has emerged since the 2010s (Kar et al. 2024). Existing literature guiding hybrid model development consists primarily of a toolkit for the design of the combination (Morgan et al 2017) and a framework for conceptual modelling development (Ngyuen et al 2024). There is however, little guidance on how to effectively engage stakeholders in the modelling process in hybrid modelling, apart from a study by Jones et al (2022) applied to the transport sector.

2.3 METHODS

We develop a hybrid model that combines SD and DES that leverages the strengths of both approaches to offer the a holistic view of kidney care services . SD lends itself well to population-level disease modelling. It provides a high-level, aggregated view of the system, capturing feedback loops and long-term trends, such as the impact of interventions and health policy changes on patient populations. People in various stages of CKD are modelled as stocks, and their progression through these stages are represented by flows. DES is chosen due to its ability to model future prevalence of KRT based on patient demographics, clinical outcomes, and resource availability. It allows for detailed simulation of patient entities through healthcare processes over time. It can account for the duration between events of change in treatments and mortality. It can also represent resource-constrained processes and the prioritisation in queues such as transplant waiting lists. Additionally, DES can incorporate uncertainties in patient outcomes and treatment practices, providing scenario analysis and supporting decision-making in kidney care with a measure of variability in the results rather than a single output. A sequential design (Morgan et al. 2017) describes how the SD and DES models link conceptually (Figure 1). The SD model that tracks the progression of disease at population level, feeds the number of patients with CKD into the DES model, which in turn tracks the service capacity levels for KRT .

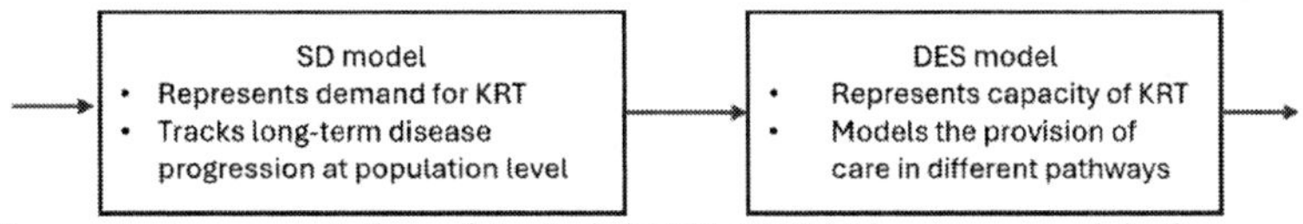

Figure 1: Conceptual representation of the hybrid SD-DES kidney care model of a sequential design

This hybrid SD-DES model can simulate both individual patient pathways and system-wide dynamics, enabling a comprehensive understanding of the future demands for KRT services, while considering the impacts of both upstream and downstream interventions. By assessing the long-term impacts, policymakers and healthcare providers can determine resource allocation and plan for changes in demand across treatment modalities. One challenge of developing such a hybrid model lies in how to facilitate a diverse stakeholder group to participate in defining and developing a model that operates across differing time scales and levels of granularity.

To tackle this challenge, this study combines three key elements to support the model development: participative modelling workshops, evidence mapping and patient experience pathways.

The evidence mapping provided an overview of the evidence base to inform the modelling team of the kidney care, covering aetiology, diagnosis, treatment, prognosis, prevention, as well as past modelling approaches. The patient experience pathway explores the way that patients understand and experience their pathway, which is broader than their traditional engagement with individual services, extending further the work of Tako et al (2019). The patient experience pathway will be used to validate the modelling work, improve our understanding of early intervention, accessibility and inequity issues, and identify changes to models of care that might be the most suitable.

We develop a customised participative modelling approach that combine elements from Partisim (Tako and Kotiadis 2015), Simtegr8 (Tako et al 2019) and Scriptapaedia (https://en.wikibooks.org/wiki/Scriptapedia, accessed 17th Nov 2024) to inform the approach and activities included in the facilitated workshops with a diverse group of stakeholders.. Based upon existing models in the literature and pre-understanding of the problem from the initial evidence mapping, the team developed preliminary models prior to the facilitated workshops. These models served as prompts to facilitate the discussion and analytical thinking at the workshops, where the modelling team gathered feedback from the stakeholders to further develop these models. Refined models were then presented back to the stakeholders and validated with the stakeholder group. The following section presents an overview of the facilitation process.

2.4 The Facilitation process

Five workshops are planned in total, of which three have already taken place. A summary of the three workshops held so far is provided in Table 1.

Table 1: Summary of workshops 1-3, detailing the participants, workshop format and outcomes

Items	Workshop 1	Workshop 2	Workshop 3
Number of participant	10	11	11

Duration	3 hours	6 hours	3 hours
Location	In person	In person	Online
Structure	1. Introduction and setting the scene (30') 2.Objective elicitation (30') 3. Developing problem definition (40') 4. Demand and capacity problems in current kidney services (60') 5. Summary and close (5')	1. Introduction and recap (25') 2. Causal loop diagram explanation and exercise (15') 3. SD modelling exercise (95') 4. DES modelling exercise (70') 5. Model objectives 'How to measure success' (60') 6. Summary and close (5')	1. Introduction and recap (20') 2. SD model part walkthrough (70') 3. DES model walkthrough (50') 4. Group reflections and discussion (30')
Workshop Aims	-Identify and formulate the problem; - Develop a common understanding of the problem situation with the model build group; - Agree on overall study objectives.	- Further developed two detailed diagrams of: a) KRT services and b) kidney disease progression in the population; - Define the model objectives.	- Validate/Review/Adjust the assumptions adopted by the conceptual models with stakeholders; - Refine data requirements and identify data sources.
Preliminary model	A simple DES model based on previous studies	Two high level models DES and SD models were presented to help conceptualisation.	Two more detailed DES and SD models developed by the team were presented to gather feedback and for verification.
Workshop Outcomes	A problem statement under the CATWOE framework is formulated and important factors to consider for demand and capacity are discussed.	Revised causal loop diagrams and simulation models are created, pathways of care for different categories of kidney patients discussed.	Revision/Confirmation of DES model assumptions; References of data sources; Testing scenarios to experiment identified; Stakeholders gain a clear understanding of model outcomes.

3.2.1 Preliminary problem formulation workshop

The Strategy Unit and the Midlands Kidney Network met virtually for a preliminary problem formulation workshop in May 2023. The aims of this workshop were to: 1) Consider the purpose of the modelling work and to create engagement amongst the stakeholder group for the next steps.

The discussions during this workshop helped inform the modelling team to gain insight into differing perspectives on how kidney care services may change. Participants were guided through facilitated discussion in 3 steps using questions to guide their thinking through the past, current and future of kidney care services. Notes and comments were added virtually to an online note board. There was a brief discussion of potential methods and questions that the model could potentially explore. There was a significant pause whilst waiting for the funding for the project to be secured.

3.2.2 Workshop 1: Defining the problem

Workshop 1 focused on problem definition, which consisted of a 3-hour in-person facilitated session. Various activities were designed to help the participants identify current problems faced by kidney care services and consider changes needed. In the end, a problem statement using the CATWOE framework was formulated and important factors to consider for demand and capacity were discussed. The participants identified issues such as demand/capacity mismatch, inequality in outcomes compared to ethnicity, as well as additional bottlenecks in the KRT pathway. Prevention and slowing disease progression were identified amongst the main interventions to improve future kidney care service provision. Members of the evidence team were included in both in-person workshops (Workshops 1 & 2) to understand the context of the evidence required so they could support the parameterisation and assumptions made in the modelling.

3.2.3 Workshop 2: Defining the model

Workshop 2 took place two weeks after Workshop 1 as a whole-day in-person event that focused on scoping the conceptual model of the CKD progression and kidney care services using causal loop diagrams (CLDs) for the SD model and process flow diagrams (PFD) for the DES model. The modelling team prepared one preliminary CLD depicting the different stages of kidney disease progression in the patient population and one preliminary PFD depicting the whole kidney care system for kidney replacement therapy services and asked participants for comments and additions.

3.2.4 Workshop 3 Model Refinement

Workshop 3 took place online, 2.5 months after Workshop 2. It focused on model validation, testing and scenario identification, lasting approximately 3 hours. Between Workshop 2 and 3, the modelling team worked on refining the SD and DES models based on the comments received in Workshop 2. In this workshop, the participants and the modelling team discussed the model assumptions, data requirements, data sources, model outcomes and 'what-if' scenarios. The modelling team and stakeholders also agreed on the next action plans. Two additional SD and DES model validation workshops were planned, followed by a final model implementation workshop.

3 THE KIDNEY CARE SD AND DES MODELS

The two preliminary DES and SD models developed iteratively with the input of the stakeholder group in the first three workshops are next described.

3.1 System dynamics model of kidney disease progression

Due to difficulties in recognising and diagnosing early-stage CKD (stages 1 and 2), the disease progression SD model focused on the more advanced stages of CKD, from stage 3 through to stage 5 and then to those needing KRT. Figure 2 shows a simplified structure of the SD model, built using Stella Architect (isee systems, https://www.iseesystems.com/, accessed 28 January 2025). The four stocks on the left-hand side represent people with CKD at stages 3-5 and are split between diagnosed and undiagnosed. The flows indicate progression through the various stages and diagnosis states. The 'KRT' stock represents people who are either on dialysis or who have received a kidney transplant. Auxiliary variables affect the flow rates in and out of the model, and between the stocks. Interventions can also be incorporated into the model. For instance, a 'primary prevention' intervention would influence the 'CKD incidence', whereas a disease management intervention would slow progression between CKD stages and decrease the mortality at each stage.

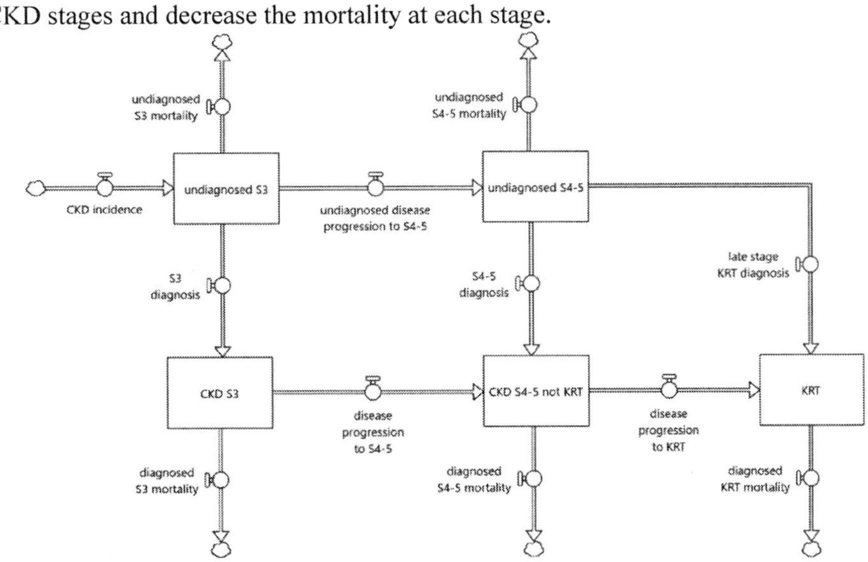

Figure 2: Overall structure of the SD model: key stocks and flows representing the various stages of chronic kidney disease

The model is parameterised using data from many sources, identified together with stakeholders in the participative workshops. Data sources include CVD Prevent (https://www.cvdprevent.nhs.uk/), the UK Renal Registry (2024), and findings from the Inside CKD microsimulation (Chertow et al. 2024). The flow rates were approximated by calibrating the model to fit the historical reported prevalence, using a Powell Optimization algorithm. The simulation runs for a time span of 20 years, from 2016 to 2035. The baseline model assumes the status quo that is no intervention is implemented.

3.2 Discrete-event simulation model of kidney replacement therapies services

The DES models the incidence of kidney transplant and the prevalence of different modes of dialysis and functioning kidney grafts to allow for service planning over a 20-year period. A high-level representation of the DES model is illustrated in Figure 3. The model integrates the prevalence of patients by dialysis modality, the number of live and deceased donor transplants and the prevalence of functioning grafts for each simulated year. The model extends the prevalence of dialysis and kidney transplant model developed by (Roderick et al. 2004) to allow the investigation of additional interventions such as increasing home therapies through a combination of HHD and PD, diverting additional patients to conservative kidney care management, increasing live kidney donations, improvements to the speed of transplant work up, decreasing late presentation and increasing pre-emptive transplants (before dialysis is required).

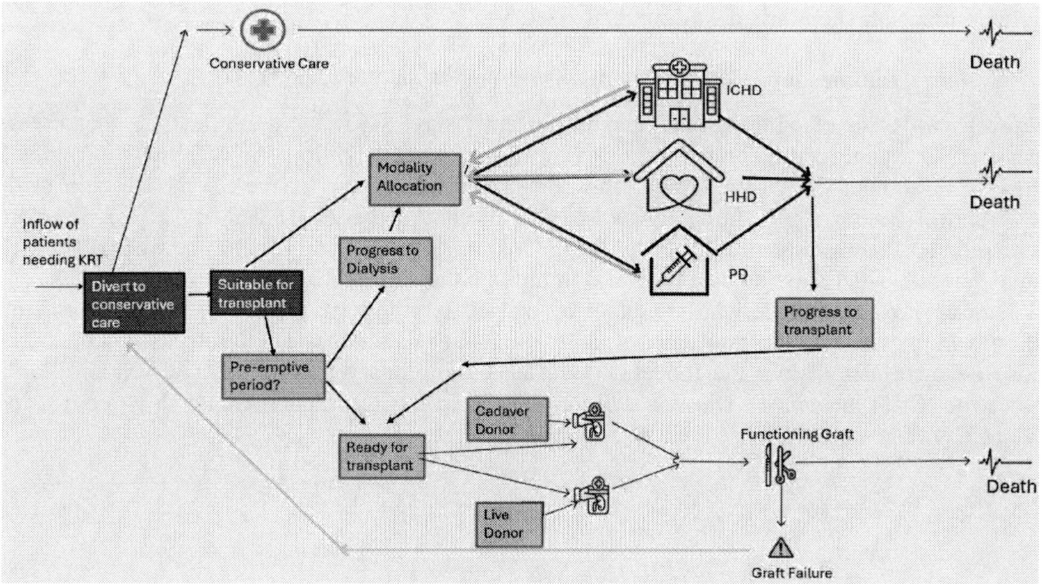

Figure 3: A high-level representation of the DES model

The DES model commences at the point when a patient requires KRT. It allows a proportion of patients to be diverted to conservative kidney management. Those who are not diverted to conservative care and unsuitable for transplant go on to receive dialysis. Those suitable for transplant can either a) receive dialysis whilst awaiting transplant, b) wait for transplant without needing dialysis initially and then require dialysis before being transplanted or c) pre-emptively receive kidney transplant without requiring dialysis. When functioning grafts fail, the patients may either die or re-enter the KRT pathway in the model. During the receipt of dialysis or a functioning graft and in conservative kidney management, it is possible for patients to leave the model through mortality. The DES model was constructed in Simul8 Professional (build no. 31.0.4730).

The model is parameterised using an example kidney care centre and drawing on data from published reports from UK Renal Registry (2024) and NHS Blood and Transplant (2024), historic parameters from the West Midlands version of the previous model, unpublished analysis of UK Renal registry data, and estimates from discussions with subject matter experts following the facilitated workshops.

4 CONCLUSIONS AND FUTURE WORK

This paper presents a simulation modelling study carried out to support capacity planning of care services for Chronic Kidney disease (CKD) in the UK. The aim of the study was to develop a generic model that can be customised with data to be used by local kidney care services across the UK. The study adopts a hybrid modelling approach combining SD and DES models. It offers an effective and detailed representation of the whole kidney care system including both kidney disease progression that triggers demand for kidney care (SD part of the model) and capacity requirements for KRT from a service level perspective (DES part of the model).

The study is the first to offer a hybrid simulation model that leverages the strengths of both approaches to analyse the future demand for KRT. The SD-DES model has potential to simulate both individual patient pathways and system-wide dynamics. It can offer a comprehensive representation of the future demands for KRT services, while considering the impacts of both upstream and downstream interventions at patient population level and at care service delivery level. Developing such a model that operates across different time units and levels of granularity poses challenges in facilitating and engaging a diverse stakeholder group.

The study combined a wide range of stakeholders including clinicians, commissioners, service managers, nurses and patients to draw diverse perspectives into the models and the scenarios tested. Four workshops have so far taken place, with three more planned. A preliminary workshop established appetite for the project. Workshop 1 considered the wider kidney care system and issues affecting efficient provision of services. Workshop 2 scoped out the conceptual model. It is noted that the simulation models were developed iteratively by the modelling team from pre-workshop 1, while more details were added as information was elicited at the two workshops. The format of workshops varied, with Workshop 1 and 2 in person while Workshop 3 online to fit into stakeholders' time and availability. The workshop activities were varied to ensure effective involvement of the stakeholder group using individual and group activities, including objective cards, whiteboard, post-it, flipchart, pre-printed conceptual models. These interactive activities guided the communication during the workshops and enhanced stakeholder engagement. Questionnaires distributed after workshops 1 and 2 measured the participants' perception about the communication, commitment, consensus and usefulness of the model and the workshops. Participants gave very positive feedback across all categories of questions. This paper illustrates a novel example of adopting a facilitated approach for co-creating hybrid simulation models with a group of stakeholders. To our knowledge so far this is the only hybrid SD-DES model developed adopting a fully facilitated mode. The facilitation process adopted differs to that of existing facilitated studies in the literature to suit the data and conceptual model elicitation requirements of the two modelling approaches we use.

It is acknowledged that the study faced several limitations, including issues with data availability. The model currently does not include capacity data for both staff and dialysis slots. The UK Kidney Network is currently undertaking a capacity audit which we hope will inform conversion of demand to capacity requirements. The models presented are still at a preliminary stage and will need to be linked to feed data into each other. Whilst commercial software has been used to aid stakeholder interaction with the development of the models and their validation, the intent is for these preliminary models to be developed into a free and open-source tool for wider use within the NHS. Plans to redevelop and combine the models in open-source python modelling tool (Palmer and Tian 2021) are in place to enable further validation, deployment and embedding into service planning. The NHS aim to develop a web interface using Shiny (https://shiny.posit.co/, accessed 23rd Jan 2025) to enable wider sharing of the model by other Kidney Networks across the UK.

ACKNOWLEDGMENTS

The authors would like to thank the workshop participants for offering their valuable insights and time to shape the model development. Special thanks go to Marie Atkins, from the Midlands Kidney Network who supported the study and the smooth running of the workshops. We acknowledge the support provided by members of the Strategy Unit, Jennifer Wood, Alison Turner, Richard Ward, Freddie Finlay, Jane Greenstock, Mahmoda Begum for contributing to the study, and Stewart Loughlin, Maciej Waszak-Hayes, Deborah Mabbley, for their assistance with organising the workshops and contracting. The project has also benefitted from the advice provided by Prof. Sally Brailsford and Dr Steffen Bayer from the University of Southampton.

REFERENCES

Allen M, Bhanji A, Willemsen J, Dudfield S, Logan S, Monks T. A simulation modelling toolkit for organising outpatient dialysis services during the COVID-19 pandemic. *PLoS One*. 2020 Aug 13;15(8):e0237628. doi: 10.1371/journal.pone.0237628. PMID: 32790773; PMCID: PMC7425906.

Ansah J P, Hng K L S, Ahmad S, Goh C. Evaluating the impact of upstream and downstream interventions on chronic kidney disease and dialysis care: a simulation analysis. First published: 19 April 2021. *System Dynamics Review* 37(1). https://doi.org/10.1002/sdr.1676

Brailsford, S.C., Eldabi, T., Kunc, M., Mustafee, N., Osorio, A.F. (2019). Hybrid simulation modelling in operational research: A state-of-the-art review, *European Journal of Operational Research*, Volume 278, Issue 3, Pages 721-737, ISSN 0377-2217, https://doi.org/10.1016/j.ejor.2018.10.025.

Cassidy, R., Singh, N.S., Schiratti, PR. *et al.* Mathematical modelling for health systems research: a systematic review of system dynamics and agent-based models. *BMC Health Serv Res* **19**, 845 (2019). https://doi.org/10.1186/s12913-019-4627-7.

Chertow, G. M., Correa-Rotter, R., Eckardt, K.-U., Kanda, E., Karasik, A., Li, G., Christiansen, C.F., Stafylas, P., Holt, S.G., Hagen, E.C., Garcia Sanchez, J.J., Barone, S., Cabrera, C., Nolan, S., Coker, T., Webber, L., Retat, L. (2024) eClinicalMedicine, Volume 72, 102614, https://doi.org/10.1016/j.eclinm.2024.102614

Eldabi, T., Tako, A. A., Bell, D., Tolk, A. (2019). Tutorial on Means of Hybrid Simulation," 2019 *Winter Simulation Conference (WSC)*, National Harbor, MD, USA, pp. 33-44, doi: 10.1109/WSC40007.2019.9004712.

Jones, W., Kotiadis, K., & O'Hanley, J. R. (2022). Maximising stakeholder learning by looping again through the simulation life-cycle: a case study in public transport. *Journal of the Operational Research Society*, *73*(12), 2640-2659.

Kar, E., Fakhimi, M., Turner, C., Eldabi, T. (2024) Hybrid simulation in healthcare: a systematic exploration of models, applications, and emerging trends, *Journal of Simulation*, DOI: 10.1080/17477778.2024.2354250

Morgan, J.F., Howick, S., Belton, V. (2017) A toolkit of designs for mixing Discrete Event Simulation and System Dynamics, European Journal of Operational Research, Volume 257, Issue 3, Pages 907-918, ISSN 0377-2217, https://doi.org/10.1016/j.ejor.2016.08.016.

Nguyen, L.K.N., Howick, S., Megiddo, I. A framework for conceptualising hybrid system dynamics and agent-based simulation models, *European Journal of Operational Research,* Volume 315, Issue 3, 2024, Pages 1153-1166, ISSN 0377-2217, https://doi.org/10.1016/j.ejor.2024.01.027.

NHS Blood and Transplant (2024) Annual Report on Kidney Transplantation Report for 2023/2024, Available from: https://nhsbtdbe.blob.core.windows.net/umbraco-assets-corp/34295/nhsbt-kidney-transplantation-report-2324.pdf

Kidney Research UK. (June 2023) Kidney disease: A UK public health emergency https://www.kidneyresearchuk.org/wp-content/uploads/2023/06/Economics-of-Kidney-Disease-full-report_accessible.pdf

Palmer, G. I., Tian, Y. (2021). Implementing hybrid simulations that integrate DES+SD in Python. *Journal of Simulation*, *17*(3), 240–256. https://doi.org/10.1080/17477778.2021.1992312

Roderick, P, Davies, R, Jones, C, Feest, T, Smith, S & Farrington, K 2004, 'Simulation model of renal replacement therapy: predicting future demand in England', *Nephrology Dialysis Transplantation*, vol. 19, no. 3, pp. 692-701.

Tangri N, Chadban S, Cabrera C, Retat L, Sánchez JJG. Projecting the Epidemiological and Economic Impact of Chronic Kidney Disease Using Patient-Level Microsimulation Modelling: Rationale and Methods of Inside CKD. *Adv Ther*. 2023 Jan;40(1):265-281. doi: 10.1007/s12325-022-02353-5. Epub 2022 Oct 28. PMID: 36307575; PMCID: PMC9616410.

Tako, A.A., Kotiadis, K. (2015). PartiSim: A multi-methodology framework to support facilitated simulation modelling in healthcare, *European Journal of Operational Research*, Volume 244, Issue 2, Pages 555-564, ISSN 0377-2217, https://doi.org/10.1016/j.ejor.2015.01.046.

Tako, A.A. Kotiadis, K. (2018). Participative simulation (PARTISIM): a facilitated simulation approach for stakeholder engagement, 2018 *Winter Simulation Conference* (WSC), Gothenburg, Sweden, 2018, pp. 192-206, doi: 10.1109/WSC.2018.8632434.

Tolk, A., Richkus, J.A., Shaikh, Y. (2024). Towards Hybrid Modelling and Simulation Concepts for Complex Socio-technical Systems. In: Fakhimi, M., Mustafee, N. (eds) *Hybrid Modeling and Simulation. Simulation Foundations, Methods and Applications*. Springer, Cham. https://doi-org.ntu.idm.oclc.org/10.1007/978-3-031-59999-6_4.

Tako, A.A, Robinson, S., A. Gogi, Z. Radnor and Ch. Davenport (2019) "Evaluating Community-based Integrated Health and Social Care Services: The SIMTEGR8 Approach". In *Proceedings of the 2019 Winter Simulation Conference*, N. Mustafee, K.-H.G. Bae, S. Lazarova-Molnar, M. Rabe, C. Szabo, P. Haas, and Y-J. Son (eds), IEEE, pp 1220- 1231, Maryland, USA.

UK Renal Registry (2024) UK Renal Registry 26th Annual Report – data to 31/12/2022, Bristol, UK. Available from https://ukkidney.org/audit-research/annual-report

Warwick Business School. (2007). *Adult renal replacement therapy in the West Midlands: Current and projected need 2007–2017.* Prepared on behalf of the West Midlands Renal Network and the West Midlands Strategic Commissioning Group.

Wild, D., & Etim, A. (2011). *MORRIS v2 user guide: Model for optimising renal replacement investment and services.* Clinical Quality & Efficiency Analytical Team, Department of Health.

AUTHOR BIOGRAPHIES

STACEY CROFT is a Principal Consultant at the Centre for Operational Research and Defence Analysis (CORDA) at BAE Systems. This work was conducted in her prior role in the NHS, as Analytics Manager (Simulation) at the Strategy Unit where she provided analytical support to major health and care change programmes. She worked for the NHS for over 20 years and has a master's degree in public health from the University of Birmingham. She is a member of the Operational Research Society and the UK Chapter of the System Dynamics Society. Her interests include the use of participative methods in Discrete Event Simulation and System Dynamics simulation models to aid understanding of the impact of proposed changes to services.

ANTUELA TAKO is a Professor of Operations Research at Nottingham Business School, Nottingham Trent University. She holds a PhD in Simulation and an MSc in Management Science and Operational Research from the University of Warwick. Her research interests include alternative simulation approaches (discrete-event simulation, system dynamics, agent-based simulation and hybrid simulation), facilitated and participative simulation, conceptual modeling, behavioural simulation, applied primarily in healthcare, supply chains, emergency services, sustainability and circular economy. She is an Associate Editor of the Journal of the Operational Research Society and Journal of Simulation and Area Editor of Health Systems.

YUN HE is a Senior Research Fellow in Nottingham Business School, Nottingham Trent University. Her research interests lie in modelling, optimisation and management of sustainable operations in complex systems, such as transport and logistics, supply chain and healthcare.

SALLY THOMPSON completed her MSc in Operational Research at the University of Strathclyde. She now works as a Senior Healthcare Analyst at the Strategy Unit, where she focuses on simulation modelling.

LUCY MORGAN is an Analytics Manager (Simulation) for the Strategy Unit and a Visiting Researcher at Lancaster University. Her research interests are simulation modelling in healthcare and advancing simulation methodology in the areas of uncertainty quantification and simulation analytics.

MARK LAMBIE is a Professor of Nephrology at Keele University, and a Consultant Nephrologist at University Hospitals of North Midlands NHS Trust. His research interests cover clinical trials and observational research incorporating epidemiological and translational approaches related to dialysis. As co-chair of the Midlands Kidney Network he is engaged with optimising the outcomes for patients with kidney disease, including sustainability and service planning, and delivery of value-based healthcare.

Proceedings of the Operational Research Society Simulation Workshop 2025 (SW25)
M. Luis, A. Harper, T. Monks and N. Mustafee, eds.
https://doi.org/10.36819/SW25.017

CONCEPTUALISING A DISCRETE-EVENT SIMULATION MODEL OF TURNAROUND OPERATIONS TO EVALUATE AIRLINE SCHEDULE ROBUSTNESS

Elisa Guardo-Martinez

University of Southampton
Southampton, SO16 7QF, UK
e.guardo-martinez@southampton.ac.uk

Stephan Onggo

University of Southampton
Southampton, SO16 7QF, UK
b.s.s.onggo@southampton.ac.uk

Martin Kunc

University of Southampton
Southampton, SO16 7QF, UK
martin.kunc@southampton.ac.uk

Maurizio Tomasella

University of Edinburgh
Edinburgh, EH8 9JS, UK
maurizio.tomasella@ed.ac.uk

Silvia Padron

TBS Business School
Toulouse, 31068, France
s.padron@tbs-education.fr

ABSTRACT

Turnaround operations at an airport are important factors affecting airline schedule reliability. This paper introduces a discrete-event simulation (DES) conceptual model that simulates daily turnaround operations at an airport terminal to evaluate the reliability of the schedules of a dominant airline i.e. the owner of the majority of turnarounds in the terminal. The simulation model is designed to provide a high-fidelity representation of the turnaround operations that captures the interactions between the schedule (including aircraft and crew assignments) and turnaround resources and activities. The model is designed to be used to more accurately estimate the schedule punctuality performance in the airport terminal and identify resource assignments prone to delays, which may be used to guide retiming. Additionally, search experiments may produce insight to support collaboration and negotiation between the airline and ground handling service providers (GHSP).

Keywords:

DES, airline scheduling, turnaround operations, operational resilience.

1 INTRODUCTION

Airline scheduling determines future operations specifying date, time and resources (aircraft and crew) assigned to each flight (De Neufville et al. 2013, Belobaba et al. 2009). The optimisation problem associated with airline scheduling seeks to maximise profitability and is typically decomposed into four optimisation stages, namely flight scheduling, fleet assignment, aircraft routing, and crew pairing (Barnhart and Talluri 1997, Barnhart et al. 2003). Flight scheduling decides the markets to be served, the frequency of flights per route, and the planned departure and arrival time for each flight leg, i.e. the timetables. Fleet assignment allocates an aircraft type to each flight in the schedule aiming to satisfy market demand at minimum cost. The aircraft routing assigns a specific aircraft to each flight in the timetable given the fleet types determined in the fleet allocation. Crew pairing creates work schedules to cover the flights for multiple days while minimising cost. Traditionally, airline planners have used deterministic models, assuming favorable conditions for operations. However, modern approaches increasingly incorporate robust scheduling, which accounts for unexpected operational disruptions.

Airlines aim to plan robust schedules that will most likely operate despite potential disruptions, minimising the need for costly recovery actions (Ball et al. 2007, Wu 2010). The objective of robust scheduling is to determine the departure time and flight resources, accounting for the uncertainties of the operation (Barnhart and Smith 2012). Since even minor schedule deviations (i.e. delays) may propagate, leading to infeasible aircraft or crew assignments, most robustness approaches focus on absorbing delays to foster punctuality and make the schedule more *reliable* (Burke et al. 2010). This type of approach, named *absorption robustness* (Clausen et al. 2010), inserts buffer times in aircraft routes (Marla et al. 2018, Cui et al. 2019) and crew itineraries (Wen et al. 2020). The buffers may be inserted either during the assignment of resources, when planners decide the aircraft routes and the crew pairings, or after the schedule is complete. The latest applies a *retiming* strategy (Lan et al. 2006, Ahmadbeygi et al. 2010, Sanjeevi and Venkatachalam 2021, Rhodes-Leader et al. 2022), which adjusts the departure time of selected flights to increase the time between consecutive assignments where the probability of delay is high. Appropriate slacks effectively enhance schedule robustness; however, they reduce resource productivity and increase *planned costs*. Therefore, decisions regarding buffers, i.e. duration and location, need accurate estimates of uncertainties. Although uncertainty affects resources during airborne and ground time, airline operations at airports, including aircraft turnaround (i.e. preparation of an aircraft for the next flight), contribute significantly to punctuality variability (De Neufville et al. 2013).

As an integral part of operations, the turnaround process (Schmidt 2017, Wu and Caves 2004) is essential to airlines because it affects the costs and quality of the services offered to passengers (Graham 2018). The turnaround encompasses services required between two consecutive flights including passengers disembarking and boarding, aircraft fuelling, cabin cleaning, baggage unloading and loading, catering, toilet servicing and potable water servicing. The airline schedule sets the starting and finishing time of the turnaround, that is, the scheduled in-block time (SIBT) and the scheduled off-block time (SOBT), respectively. Because the turnaround is performed while the aircraft is on the ground standing in the apron i.e. the area in the terminal airside between the gates and the taxiway (Ashford et al. 2012), it is also named aircraft ground handling or apron operations. Since airline deregulation and liberalisation made the industry operate mostly under commercial competition, the turnaround services are typically outsourced to third-party organisations, the ground handling service providers (GHSP) (Graham 2018). This means that the turnaround human resources and the ground service equipment (GSE) they use, such as catering trucks and baggage carts, are shared among multiple airlines. As a consequence, one airline's delayed flights can impact not only its subsequent flights — sharing aircraft or crew— but also the turnaround operations of other airlines relying on the same GHSP resources. The contribution of this paper is to design a simulation model that can be used to evaluate the reliability of airline schedules at a hub airport. The model measures the propagation of flight arrival delays through the turnaround operations considering the interaction between crew assignments and the boarding activity as well as the availability of GHSP resources for the turnarounds of the airline under study.

In Section 2, we introduce the conceptual model for the simulation study. Implementing the DES paradigm (Robinson 2014), the model represents the resources and queues of the system to capture the mechanism of delay propagation. The simulation model outputs correspond to the key performance indicators (KPI) that this research aims to study and improve, such as maximum and total delay across turnarounds. Section 3 summarises the main characteristic of the model and its potential academic and practical use.

2 SIMULATION CONCEPTUAL MODEL

Our model aims to support airline scheduling decisions by studying the aircraft turnaround performed at hub airports, where a significant part of their operations is concentrated. By operating a hub-and-spoke network, some airlines increase the number of passengers and cities they serve harnessing economies of scale and traffic density (IATA 2023). This type of airline can significantly improve overall performance by reducing delays in hubs. The model considers that the turnaround operational system involves multiple stakeholders, including airlines that own and operate the aircraft, the GHSP in charge of servicing the aircraft, and the airport manager of the physical space. The decision-maker that this model will inform is the airline demanding the majority of all turnarounds performed in the apron, that is, the dominant airline (Calzada and Fageda 2023). Our study simulates all turnarounds handled by the GHSP that serves the dominant airline including those operated by other airlines. The decision maker is a full-service carrier that operates a hub-and-spoke network but the other airlines may be full-service or low-cost carriers (LCC) operating hub-and-spoke or point-to-point networks.

Because GHSPs have limited resources and rely on plans that maximise resource use, their operation is prone to delay propagation (Gök et al. 2023), affecting the performance of their client airlines. Dominant airlines may have resources at their hubs to recover from schedule disruptions, such as back up aircraft or crew, but recovery may not be practical in some cases. For example, a delayed inbound aircraft may affect multiple outbound aircraft due to passenger itineraries. In addition, reliability has proven more effective in improving schedule performance compared to flexibility to recover (Burke et al. 2010).

The model introduced in this section is a simplified representation of the operational system in which aircraft turnaround is performed. Airport turnaround operations take place *airside*, while aircraft are parking at a gate or a remote stand position. Typically, multiple aircraft are serviced simultaneously. When the turnaround finishes, the aircraft is normally pushed back into the taxiway (especially if parked at a terminal gate) to start its transit towards the runway for take-off. Figure 1 illustrates the elements of an airport terminal. Most airports have only one or two runways and manage access to this resource using time slots, therefore, delayed aircraft may need to wait for a new time slot. The simulation model is intended to be used in a terminating simulation study to analyse a day of operations in the apron of a specific terminal in a medium or large-sized airport.

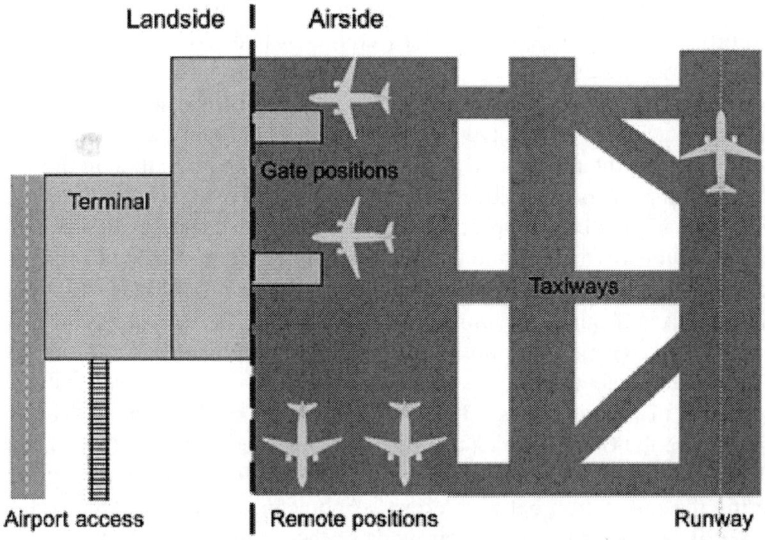

Figure 1: Terminal airside elements, source: Schmidt (2017)

The turnaround encompasses ground handling services required to prepare an aircraft for its next flight. Figure 2 illustrates the turnaround business process, including only the activities on the critical path (Wu and Caves 2004, Evler et al. 2022). We provide more details on this simplification in section 2.8. The figure shows the activities, the precedence relationships between them, and the type of resource in charge of every activity (lanes in the diagram). Multiple GHSP may handle an aircraft as they typically specialise in one or two types of service. Each GHSP develops their own plan assigning resources (i.e. GSE and the staff who operate it), to every turnaround activity in their schedule.

2.1 Objectives

The following objectives drive the conceptualisation of the simulation model:

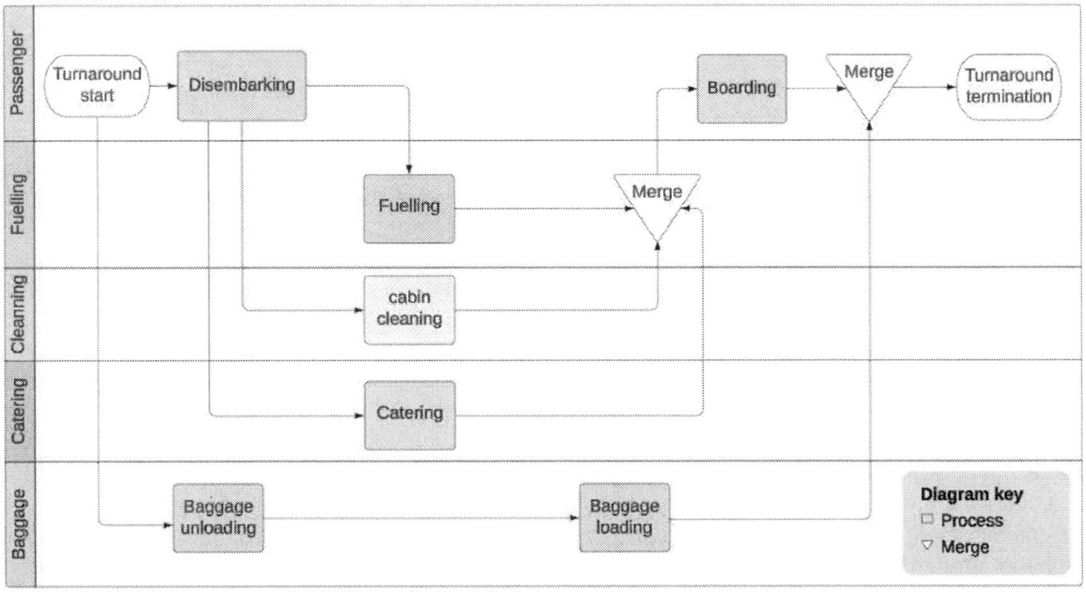

Figure 2: Turnaround Process Diagram

- Study the propagation of flight arrival delays through the shared resources and connected activities of turnaround process.
- Evaluate the robustness of airline schedules considering the uncertainties that affect aircraft turnaround.

2.2 Boundaries

This simulation model replicates the most relevant characteristics of the apron operational system to attain the previous objectives. The scope includes the activities in the critical path of the turnaround process (see Figure 2), and the resources needed to perform those activities (staff, GSE and stands). In this model, the waiting time in queues will account for the delays associated with a lack of staff. Therefore, the model captures the impact of other airlines' turnarounds on the availability of GHSP staff to perform the dominant airline's turnaround activities. Additionally, we model the dependencies between activities of different turnarounds specified in the airline schedule. That is, we model crews and passengers who disembark from an aircraft and need to board another. By modelling these dependencies and shared resources we can study the mechanisms of delay propagation, including airline schedule tightness and turnaround inefficiencies.

This approach aims to provide a more realistic representation of the turnaround operational system compared to models that rely on delay codes (Wu and Caves 2004, Wu 2006, Wu and Wu 2018). Delay codes are the standardisation of delay causes produced by the International Air Transport Association (IATA), used by airlines to report their delays (Eurocontrol 2023). Examples of delay causes are late crew boarding, for which the airline is accountable; and lack of staff or GSE, for which the GHSP is accountable. Not surprisingly, the delay code reports are a source of controversy between the two organisations and are, therefore, unreliable to accurately describe the system characteristics. Our model considers most of the delay causes in the two groups directly associated to the turnaround: passenger and baggage, and aircraft and ramp handling.

The processes performed on the landside of the airport terminal, e.g. passenger and baggage security screening, are not in the scope of this model. Similarly, all airside activities not included in the turnaround are excluded from our model, particularly those related to taxiway and runway management. The push-back, which moves the aircraft onto the taxiway after all turnaround services are complete, is not modelled because it depends on the congestion on taxiways. Therefore, in future research our model will be used to estimate the propagation and possible amplification of delays up to the push-back. It can be assumed that the propagated delay at departure is higher than that at push-back because delayed aircraft may miss their assigned slot for departure and need to wait for a new slot. This analysis is out of the scope of our model.

2.3 Entities and Attributes

The entities that flow through the system are the aircraft that arrive at and depart from the airport terminal. Their attributes are:

Airline: Specifies the airline that owns the aircraft being handled, whether it is the dominant airline or other airlines.

Arrival time: Corresponds to the SIBT of every incoming flight. It is represented as the number of minutes from the start of the operations to the scheduled arrival time of the aircraft to the apron. For example, if the terminal opens at 5:00 am and an aircraft arrives at 5:05 am, the arrival time is 5.

Turnaround duration: The scheduled turnaround duration in minutes, equals the SOBT minus the SIBT, which are both deterministic values specified by the airline schedule.

Dependencies: Delay propagates across the airline schedule through the resources shared between consecutive flights, including aircraft, crew and passengers (Ahmadbeygi et al. 2010). When an outbound flight needs to board passengers or crew who deboard from an inbound flight, there is a dependency between the two turnarounds. This attribute allows the model to capture the propagation of delays through these dependencies. For the aircraft carrying a crew or passengers that need to board another aircraft, this attribute equals the identifier of the destination aircraft and vice versa.

2.4 Resources

The system is operated by five types of teams, each responsible for a specific activity: disembarking and boarding (passenger handling), fueling, cabin cleaning, catering, and baggage processing (loading and unloading). In our model, a team includes all staff and GSE required to complete the designed activity e.g. cleaning, in the standard time. In addition to teams, we model the stand or gate where aircraft are handled because, expectedly, delay propagates through this airport resource.

2.5 Queues

The model includes eight queues, one queue per turnaround activity and one for stands as listed below:

1. Passenger and crew disembarking
2. Passenger and crew boarding
3. Fuelling
4. Cabin cleaning
5. Catering
6. Baggage loading
7. Baggage unloading
8. Stand

All queues in the model are assumed to work under the First-in First-out discipline (Law 2015).

2.6 Events

The events to be monitored during the simulation are:

1. Arrival of aircraft at the stand and each of the queues
2. Start of each service or activity
3. Termination of each service or activity
4. Termination of turnaround
5. Termination of disembarking of a crew or passenger that must board another aircraft

2.7 Variables

An input to the model is the schedule of all turnarounds serviced during the simulation horizon i.e. a day of operations at the airport. The schedule has three components: the scheduled time of arrival (STA); SOBT, which helps calculate the scheduled turnaround duration; and the assignments of crews and passengers to aircraft (for the dominant airline). The STA corresponds to the SIBT when the model is used to study delay propagation. In future research, the schedule can be used as a decision variable in a simulation optimisation approach to retime the schedule and improve reliability. Other inputs to the model are the number of resources per type of service, the number of available gates and the processing time for each turnaround activity.

Some inputs are stochastic values realised from probability distributions. For instance, we estimate the processing time of activities using a triangular distribution where the scheduled processing time (SPT) is the most likely value (see Table 1). The (SPT) of each turnaround service is a deterministic value defined by the aircraft manufacturer. This reflects the effect of aircraft size on turnaround duration. All variables, including the probability distributions, are parameters that can be changed to calibrate the model or conduct experiments. For example, weather conditions and seasonality affecting processing times can be investigated changing the variability of the respective probability distributions (Gök et al. 2023). Table 1 shows the distributions associated with every stochastic input.

Table 1: Input variables and probability distributions

Variable	Probability distribution and parameters	Source
Arrival time	Triangular The lower limit is STA – 5 min The upper limit is STA + 5 min The most likely value is STA	(Gök et al. 2023)
Processing times	Triangular The lower limit is 20% below SPT The upper limit is 30% above SPT The most likely value is the SPT	(Gök et al. 2023) SPT is determined by the aircraft's technical manual

Our model outputs aim to support the research objectives. To measure the robustness of the schedule and understand the propagation of flight arrival delays through the turnaround, the following KPIs are calculated:

- $totalD^A$ and $totalD^{SP}$: are the total overall delay with respect to the SOBT.
- $maxD^A$ and $maxD^{SP}$: are the 90th percentile of the maximum operational delay with respect to the SOBT.

The superscript denotes the analysis that the KPI is intended for. For example, $totalD^A$ measures the robustness of the dominant airline schedule and is calculated over its turnarounds. In contrast, $totalD^{SP}$ calculates the delay over the turnarounds of other airlines i.e. other GHSP clients. Analysing $totalD^{SP}$ may produce insights to foster cooperation from external actors i.e. GHSP and airport.

2.8 Assumptions and Simplifications

The basic configuration of the system includes the number of teams available per service, as well as the number of stands. We assume this information is shared by the GHSP and the airport through a collaborative framework which will be introduced in a future study. We also assume that there are no personnel absences or prolonged GSE malfunctions, therefore, the uncertainties of processing times are accounted for as explained in Table 1.

Typically, airports operate using their gate positions (i.e. stands in the apron next to a gate), however, sometimes they need to allocate remote stands, for example at peak times. We simplify the model assuming all stands are gate positions and we model travel times as a median value. We further simplify the model by excluding turnaround activities that are not in the critical path, such as toilet and potable water servicing. This may reduce the computation time of our model without significantly impacting the accuracy of delay estimation (Wu and Caves 2004, Evler et al. 2022). We support these assumptions with insights from industry experts.

Assumptions need to be made regarding the number of flights the dominant airline operates across the terminal, as well as the proportion of GHSP turnarounds that correspond to the dominant airline.

3 CONCLUDING REMARKS

The DES model introduced in this paper is designed to simulate daily turnaround operations at an airport terminal to estimate the propagation of flight arrival delays through shared ground resources (GSE, personnel and stands). It aims to evaluate the robustness of the schedules operated by the dominant airline i.e. owner of the majority of turnarounds in the terminal. The main hub airport of an airline operating a hub-and-spoke network manages a significant part of the airline flights, therefore, improving the punctuality performance of those flights, can make a difference on the schedule overall punctuality.

The simulation model is designed to be a realistic simplification of apron operations, which combines network level and ground level inputs. The former includes the scheduled arrival and departure times of every aircraft i.e. multiple airlines, and optionally, the crew assignments of the dominant airline. The latter encompasses the number of resources allocated by the GHSP, the number of stands (gates) available, as well as the standard processing time per service per aircraft type. Overall, the model captures the availability of resources for the dominant airline turnaround activities and conversely, the delays due to resource limitations can be captured without relying on delay codes.

By combining network and ground level inputs, the model enables airline planners to produce insight for various decisions. First, it may offer a high fidelity estimation of the schedule performance in the hub. Second, considering the interactions between crew assignments and the turnaround boarding activity is useful to more accurately identify aircraft routes and crew pairings prone to delay. Third, search experiments can inform the negotiations with GHSPs regarding the requisite staffing that ensures the target schedule performance.

In a future research, we will implement the simulation model using Python and use it in our simulation optimisation algorithm that improves a schedule robustness applying retiming of vulnerable aircraft routes and crew connections. The simulation optimisation model will iteratively evaluate the robustness of candidate solutions and to reduce the computation time we will consider approaches such as multifidelity modelling (Rhodes-Leader et al. 2022)) and simheuristics (Gök et al. 2023). Since the modelled system involves the operative configuration of GHSP, which is unknown by the airline, a practical implementation assumes GHSP cooperation to share operational data (number of resources and turnarounds of other airlines in their plan). Because such information is sensitive, potential cooperation is unlikely unless the retiming generates value for GHSP. For that reason, the study will analyse the value of retiming for other GHSP clients.

REFERENCES

Ahmadbeygi, S., A. Cohn, and M. Lapp. 2010. "Decreasing airline delay propagation by re-allocating scheduled slack". *IIE Transactions* 42 (7): 478–489.

Ashford, N., P. Coutu, and J. Beasley. 2012. *Airport Operations - Third Edition*. McGraw-Hill Publishing.

Ball, M., C. Barnhart, G. Nemhauser, and A. Odoni. 2007. "Air transportation: Irregular operations and control". *Handbooks in operations research and management science* 14:1–67.

Barnhart, C., P. Belobaba, and A. R. Odoni. 2003. "Applications of operations research in the air transport industry". *Transportation Science* 37 (4): 368–391. Cited By :222.

Barnhart, C., and B. Smith. 2012. *Quantitative problem solving methods in the airline industry : a modeling methodology handbook*. New York: Springer (International series in operations research and management science, v. 169).

Barnhart, C., and K. Talluri. 1997. "Airline operations research". In *Design and operation of civil and environmental engineering systems*, edited by C. ReVelle and A. E. McGarity, 453–469. New York, USA: Wiley.

Belobaba, P., A. Odoni, and C. Barnhart. 2009. *The airline global industry*. John Wiley and Sons, Ltd.

Burke, E. K., P. De Causmaecker, G. De Maere, J. Mulder, M. Paelinck, and G. Vanden Berghe. 2010. "A multi-objective approach for robust airline scheduling". *Computers and Operations Research* 37 (5): 822–832.

Calzada, J., and X. Fageda. 2023, FEB. "Airport dominance, route network design and flight delays". *Transportation Research Part E - Logistics And Transportation Review* 170.

Clausen, J., A. Larsen, J. Larsen, and N. J. Rezanova. 2010. "Disruption management in the airline industry-Concepts, models and methods". *Computers and Operations Research* 37 (5): 809–821.

Cui, R., X. Dong, and Y. Lin. 2019, NOV. "Models for aircraft maintenance routing problem with consideration of remaining time and robustness". *Computers & Industrial engineering* 137.

De Neufville, R., A. Odoni, P. Belobaba, and T. G. Reynolds. 2013. *Airport Systems Planning, Design, and Management - Second edition*. McGraw-Hill Education.

Eurocontrol 2023. "All-causes delays to air transport in Europe". Accessed: 27.07.2024.

Evler, J., M. Lindner, H. Fricke, and M. Schultz. 2022. "Integration of turnaround and aircraft recovery to mitigate delay propagation in airline networks". *Computers and Operations Research* 138.

Graham, A. 2018. *Managing Airports: An International Perspective*. Routledge.

Gök, Y. S., S. Padron, M. Tomasella, D. Guimarans, and C. Ozturk. 2023. "Constraint-based robust planning and scheduling of airport apron operations through simheuristics". *Annals of Operations Research* 320 (2): 795–830.

IATA 2023. "Chart of the week: airlines-operate-key-hubs-for-growth-and-connectivity". Accessed: 3.02.2025.

Lan, S., J. . Clarke, and C. Barnhart. 2006. "Planning for robust airline operations: Optimizing aircraft routings and flight departure times to minimize passenger disruptions". *Transportation Science* 40 (1): 15–28.

Law, A. M. 2015. *Simulation modeling and analysis*. McGraw-Hill.

Marla, L., V. Vaze, and C. Barnhart. 2018. "Robust optimization: Lessons learned from aircraft routing". *Computers and Operations Research* 98:165–184.

Rhodes-Leader, L., B. L. Nelson, B. S. Onggo, and D. J. Worthington. 2022. "A multi-fidelity modelling approach for airline disruption management using simulation". *Journal of the Operational Research Society* 73 (10): 2228–2241.

Robinson, S. 2014. *Simulation: The Practice of Model Development and Use*. Bloomsbury Publishing Plc.

Sanjeevi, S., and S. Venkatachalam. 2021. "Robust flight schedules with stochastic programming". *Annals of Operations Research* 305 (1-2): 403–421.

Schmidt, M. 2017, JUL. "A review of aircraft turnaround operations and simulations". *Progress in Aerospace Sciences* 92:25–38.

Wen, X., H. . Ma, S. . Chung, and W. A. Khan. 2020. "Robust airline crew scheduling with flight flying time variability". *Transportation Research Part E: Logistics and Transportation Review* 144.

Wu, C. L. 2006. "Improving airline network robustness and operational reliability by sequential optimisation algorithms". *Networks and Spatial Economics* 6 (3-4): 235–251.

Wu, C.-L. 2010. *Airline Operations and Delay Management*. Ashgate Publishing, Ltd.

Wu, C. L., and R. E. Caves. 2004, FEB. "Modelling and optimization of aircraft turnaround time at an airport". *Transportation Planning and Technology* 27 (1): 47–66.

Wu, W., and C. L. Wu. 2018. "Enhanced delay propagation tree model with Bayesian Network for modelling flight delay propagation". *Transportation Planning and Technology* 41 (3): 319–335.

AUTHOR BIOGRAPHIES

ELISA GUARDO-MARTINEZ is a doctoral candidate at the University of Southampton within the Decision Analytics and Risk department of Southampton Business School. Previously, she was a consultant and project manager for various sectors including government, health and transport. She is interested in researching methodologies to streamline operations and transform businesses, such as simulation-optimisation, data analytics, machine learning and artificial intelligence. Her email address is e.guardo-martinez@soton.ac.uk.

STEPHAN ONGGO is a Professor of Business Analytics at Southampton Business School, the University of Southampton. He is a member of the Centre for Operational Research, Management Sciences and Information Systems (CORMSIS). His research interests lie in the areas of simulation modelling methodology (symbiotic simulation/digital twin, hybrid modelling, agent-based simulation, discrete-event simulation) with applications in supply chain, health care and disaster management. He is the area editor for the Flexible Services and Manufacturing Journal and Associate EDitor for the Journal of Simulation. His website is https://bsonggo.wordpress.com. His email address is b.s.s.onggo@soton.ac.uk.

MARTIN KUNC is a Professor of Business Analytics/Management Science at Southampton Business School, the University of Southampton. previously to becoming an academic, he was a consultant at Arthur Andersen. He has also had independent consulting projects in the media, pharmaceutical, financial services, consumer goods, cement and wine industries. He is a member of the Centre for Operational Research, Management Sciences and Information Systems (CORMSIS). He is interested in the intersection of management science, behavioural science and strategic management. He is interim Director of the Centre for Healthcare Analytics and is Editor-in-Chief of the Journal of the Operational Research Society. His email address is M.H.Kunc@soton.ac.uk.

MAURIZIO TOMASELLA is a Reader (Associate Professor) in Management Science at the University of Edinburgh Business School. Previously at the University of Cambridge Engineering Department and Politecnico di Milano, Maurizio's work employs Simulation-Optimization and Multi-Criteria Decision Analysis techniques to address applications in airport operations management. His e-mail address is maurizio.tomasella@ed.ac.uk.

SILVIA PADRON is an Associate Professor at TBS Business School (Toulouse, France). Her research is focused on metaheuristics and the hybridisation of optimisation methods with simulation techniques to solve stochastic and complex combinatorial problems in application areas such as transportation, aviation, and supply chain management. Her e-mail address is s.padron@tbs-education.fr.

Proceedings of the Operational Research Society Simulation Workshop 2025 (SW25)
M. Luis, A. Harper, T. Monks and N. Mustafee, eds.
https://doi.org/10.36819/SW25.018

Isochrone Maps for Military Ground Movement: Information Inference by Intersection

Alexander Roman

University of the Bundeswehr
Munich, GERMANY
alexander.roman@unibw.de

Prof. Dr. Oliver Rose

University of the Bundeswehr
Munich, GERMANY
oliver.rose@unibw.de

Abstract

A primary objective in contemporary military operations is to streamline planning processes, enabling faster and more informed decision making while easing the burdens on military and civilian personnel. Our work aims to facilitate this planning, particularly for resupply operations, asset coordination, and predicting enemy troop movements. We use isochrones on a geospatial road network to represent ground unit movement and visualize possible interactions between assets in a given timeframe. How isochrones are shaped and whether they overlap is information the planner can use for his decision-making. We improve existing approaches by implementing a way to represent off-road travel possibilities of ground assets. The resulting software can be used in military training simulations. Furthermore, we plan to utilize isochrones as action-space representations for battlefield simulations.

1 Related Work

Isochrone maps are widely acknowledged as essential tools for planning urban infrastructure and civilian transportation systems. Consequently, the body of literature addressing civilian applications is extensive, and a thorough review of this area extends beyond the aims of the present paper. Instead, this study concentrates on the military applications of isochrone maps and the specific adaptations required within this research domain.

Building upon the focus on military applications, an illustrative example is provided by Galar and Sadowski (2023). They employ isochrone maps to assess the vulnerability of Polish cities to hypothetical surprise attacks. Their study concentrates on the feasibility of reaching a city center from the border within a designated time frame, such as one hour from border crossing to establishing a defendable position with political significance. The underlying premise is that if a force can secure even a medium-sized city center, it could occupy and maintain control over such a position for weeks, thereby compelling political negotiations.

Marciuska and Gamper (2010) presents methods for determining objects within isochrones in spatial network databases. It introduces two algorithms to transform an isochrone network into an isochrone area. The first constructs a spatial buffer around each edge, the link-based approach (LB). The second creates a polygon from the outermost edges, using the surface-based approach (SB). These methods are compared with a precise baseline algorithm using real-world data, demonstrating high efficiency and precision. LB is more accurate, but has a longer runtime, and SB is faster, but does not evaluate off-road areas within a closed network loop.

Several existing software solutions offer implementations of those two approaches. GeoApiy https://www.geoapify.com/ accessed 30.07.2024, implements an adaptation LB. However, given the sensitive nature of military applications, relying on commercially hosted software is not preferable. OpenRouteService, for example, https://github.com/GIScience/openrouteservice?tab=readme-ov-file accessed 30.07.2024, implements an adaptation of SB, but lacks the functionality to compute the desirable LB variant.

Our solution incorporates both approaches, can run completely offline, and improves upon the LB approach by implementing a decreasing buffer area around reachable roads, representing diminishing off-road-travel possibilities.

2 Method

Our approach does not simulate road traffic, nor does the algorithm prescribe specific actions; instead, it identifies potential locations for troop assembly by calculating the area reachable within a predetermined time frame for a given asset navigating road networks. Consequently, if a decision-maker opts to reposition troops based on our model's outputs, it remains their responsibility to manage any resulting congestion from troop movements. Potential overcrowding resulting from excessive overlapping of isochrones in specific areas is considered negligible within the framework of our assumptions.

We utilize Python alongside a suite of packages to calculate isochrones. Initially, OSMnx facilitates access and downloading Open Street Map data as needed. GeoPandas is employed for geospatial data operations, ensuring precise plotting of isochrones. For visualization, TkinterMapView integrates map functionality within Python applications. The resulting GUI allowed us to validate or approach with military subject matter experts (SMEs). Our enhanced LB approach computes the reachable sub-graph of a given road network, splits edges as necessary to achieve higher resolution, and applies buffering to these edges. The buffer thickens edge lines by orthogonally adding the remaining travel budget at each edge, scaled down by a predetermined factor to represent slower offroad travel speeds. Additionally, forests, wetlands, water bodies, and other inaccessible areas can be excluded if the respective ground asset cannot traverse them.

3 Results

Overlapping isochrones of different groups, whether friendly or hostile, provide valuable tactical insights. For instance, overlapping friendly isochrones can indicate optimal locations for establishing supply posts, while intersections between friendly and enemy isochrones may identify potential engagement zones within a specified timeframe. Isochrone-based analysis offers a more realistic solution compared to simple straight-line assessments and is particularly applicable to ground troop movements. Figure 1 illustrates an output of our method and its analysis using SB, whereas Figure 2 showcases our enhanced LB approach, depicting a vehicle traveling at 60 km/h for six minutes.

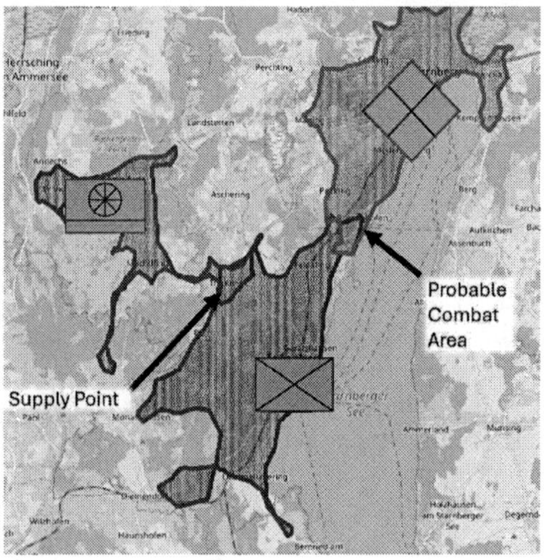

Figure 1: An example of three SB isochrones, two friendly blue units, and an enemy red unit. The blue supply unit on the top left is trying to find a supply point for the infantry unit on the bottom right, which is planning an engagement with the enemy infantry unit on the top right. The isochrones clearly show where it can lead to planned contacts.

Figure 2: As a ground asset travels, the remaining travel distance gets shorter. If an asset decides to go offroad this results in a reduced travel speed. This logic forms wedges of offroad reachable areas along the edges of the road network. Inaccessible areas are cut out of the reachable area.

4 Runtime Performance

As previously discussed, this study concentrates on the military applications of isochrone mapping and the specific modifications required within this research area. These modifications inherently result in a higher computational burden compared to civilian applications. For instance, military applications necessitate the precise calculation of off-road reachability and the exclusion of terrains inaccessible to armored vehicles, such as swamps. Consequently, a quantitative comparison between civilian and military algorithms is not meaningful, as the algorithms under evaluation do not process the same types of surfaces. To assess our approach, we analyze the runtime performance. The objective is to ensure a computation that is sufficiently rapid while maintaining the high quality required for military use.

When data caching is not utilized and the radius is small (e.g., 6km), data fetching operations consume a significant portion of the total processing time, particularly fetching land use data. As the radius increases or when caching is implemented, the time spent on data retrieval decreases substantially. Consequently, the computational focus shifts toward polygon creation and geometric processing tasks, such as creating wedge-shaped buffered polygons and adjusting land use geometries. Figure 3 shows the relative computational burden for different isochrone sizes. Table 6 in the appendix shows the absolute runtime for chosen example sizes (6, 12, and 60 km).

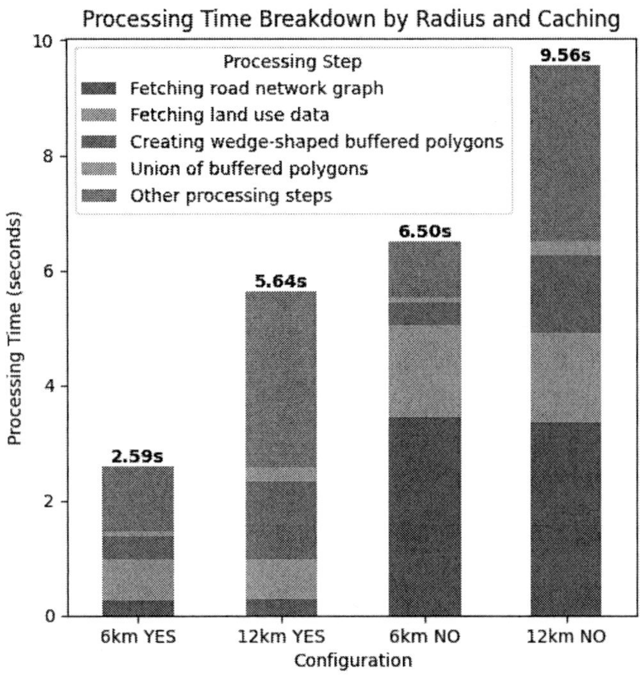

Figure 3: The biggest difference with a higher travling budget is the computation of the Wedge Shapes as this is a computationally expensive task.

5 Conclusion and Future Work

Our isochrone-based approach qualitatively enhances military planning by visualizing potential troop movements and interactions. Subject Matter Experts (SMEs) found our concept appealing, suggesting potential benefits, although further studies are needed to confirm its effectiveness. Our improved Link-Based (LB) method offers a more realistic approach compared to established link-based approaches but demands higher runtimes.

Looking ahead, several extensions and refinements are already under active investigation:

1. **Probabilistic Enemy Positioning:** Formulating a probabilistic state of enemy positions based on sparse observation data.

2. **Detailed Terrain Classification:** Integrating higher-resolution land-cover datasets and refining off-road speed profiles, including field trials to better match actual vehicle speeds in varied terrains.
3. **Elevation-Aware Modeling:** Incorporating Digital Elevation Models (e.g., SRTM or Copernicus DEM) to account for slope-based speed adjustments.
4. **Scalability and Parallelization:** Developing tile-based and parallelized approaches for larger operational radii or simultaneous computations to reduce runtime.
5. **Multi-Agent and Congestion Effects:** Simulating multiple units concurrently to factor in congestion on narrow roads or choke points.
6. **Firing Zones and Threat Overlays:** Experimenting with overlay methods to subtract or highlight high-threat regions, facilitating safer route planning.
7. **Empirical Validation and Calibration:** Conducting structured real-world trials in collaboration with military training centers to gather GPS data for iterative refinements of off-road speed assumptions and overall model accuracy.

Our ongoing optimization efforts also focus on automating the analysis of intersecting isochrones and enhancing geometric computations to reduce overall processing time for larger areas or cached scenarios.

6 Appendix

Table 1: Processing times [s] for each step with 6km, 12km, and 60km Travel Budget

Travel Distance/Budget	**6km**	**12km**	**60m**	**6km**	**12km**	**60km**
Cached Data	NO	NO	NO	YES	YES	YES
Number of land use geometries	1466	1466	10130	1466	1466	10130
Number of possible land use matches	235	1114	10130	235	1114	10130
Fetching road network graph	**3.44**	**3.35**	**44.20**	**0.27**	**0.28**	**3.19**
Finding start node	0.01	0.01	0.06	0.05	0.07	0.05
Generating ego graph	0.01	0.03	0.70	0.01	0.03	0.86
Converting graph to GeoDataFrames	0.02	0.05	1.08	0.02	0.05	1.19
Calculating shortest path lengths	0.00	0.01	0.12	0.00	0.00	0.10
Mapping shortest paths to edges	0.00	0.00	0.03	0.00	0.00	0.02
Calculating travel budget and filtering edges	0.00	0.00	0.02	0.00	0.00	0.02
Transforming geometries to UTM	0.02	0.04	0.93	0.02	0.04	0.89
Creating wedge-shaped buffered polygons	0.39	1.34	**29.48**	0.39	1.34	**29.09**
Union of buffered polygons	0.09	0.26	5.20	0.09	0.26	5.30
Fetching land use data	**1.60**	**1.56**	**29.13**	**0.71**	**0.70**	**3.13**
Converting land use geometries to UTM	0.22	0.23	1.08	0.23	0.23	1.09
Spatial indexing and union of land use geometries	0.10	0.50	7.95	0.10	0.48	7.92
Eroding land use areas	0.10	0.37	11.20	0.10	0.36	11.32
Adjusting land use geometries	0.40	1.29	**37.82**	0.40	1.27	**37.86**
Subtracting land use areas	0.08	0.35	7.33	0.09	0.35	7.21
Setting up Mapview	0.10	0.17	3.60	0.10	0.16	3.51
Total processing time before GUI	**6.52**	**9.56**	**179.91**	**2.59**	**5.64**	**112.73**

REFERENCES

Galar, Z., and A. Sadowski. 2023. "Threat/risk assessment tool to assess vulnerability of Polish cities to Russian attacks". *Defense amp; Security Analysis*.

Marciuska, S., and J. Gamper. 2010. "Determining Objects within Isochrones in Spatial Network Databases". In *Advances in Databases and Information Systems*, edited by B. Catania, M. Ivanović, and B. Thalheim, 392–405. Berlin, Heidelberg: Springer.

Proceedings of the Operational Research Society Simulation Workshop 2025 (SW25)
M. Luis, A. Harper, T. Monks and N. Mustafee, eds.
https://doi.org/10.36819/SW25.019

NETLOGOPY: UNLOCKING ADVANCED SIMULATION AND INTEGRATION FOR NETLOGO USING PYTHON

Nourddine Bouaziz

CESI LINEACT
Saint-tienne-du-Rouvray, France
nbouaziz@cesi.fr

Belgacem Bettayeb

CESI LINEACT
Lille, France
bbettayeb@cesi.fr

M'hammed Sahnoun

CESI LINEACT
Saint-tienne-du-Rouvray, France
msahnoun@cesi.fr

Adnan Yassine

LAMH, University of Le Havre Normandie
Le Havre, France
adnan.yassine@univ-lehavre.fr

ABSTRACT

NetLogo is widely recognized as one of the most popular software tools for agent-based simulation. However, it has notable limitations, particularly the lack of advanced libraries in specialized areas such as optimization, artificial intelligence (AI), and mechanical or electrical modeling. On the other hand, Python is a feature-rich programming language that is increasingly used in various research domains. This study explores the integration of NetLogo and Python to leverage the strengths of both tools. The result of this integration is the Netlogopy library, which allows direct control of NetLogo agents from Python, providing greater flexibility through Pythons ecosystem. Netlogopy is a freely available library that adds an additional layer to existing NetLogo models, enhancing simulation capabilities and making them more accessible to researchers.

Keywords:

Agent-based simulation, NetLogo, Python, Netlogopy, Integration

1 INTRODUCTION

Agent-based simulation (ABS) is a powerful technique for modeling complex systems across various fields, such as biology, economics, and operations management (Wilensky 2015). NetLogo, an agent-based simulation environment, is a popular choice due to its free availability and its ability to model systems with numerous agents (Wilensky 2015). However, while NetLogo excels in handling agents and interactions within complex simulations, it has limitations when it comes to performing more advanced computations, such as optimization, artificial intelligence (AI), or physical process modeling. Python, on the other hand, has emerged as a versatile programming language with a vast range of libraries and capabilities in various scientific fields (Oliphant et al. 2006, McKinney et al. 2010, Pedregosa, Varoquaux, Gramfort, Michel, Thirion, Grisel, Blondel, Prettenhofer, Weiss, Dubourg, Vanderplas, Passos, Cournapeau, Brucher, Perrot, and Duchesnay 2011). This observation has led many researchers to explore ways of combining the user-friendly simulation features of NetLogo with Python's computational power in other domains.

Several attempts to integrate Python and NetLogo have been explored mainly over the last decade. The most common method relies on client-server architectures, where Python controls certain predefined functions in NetLogo by sending commands and retrieving results via scripts (Thiele 2014, Jaxa-Rozen and Kwakkel 2018). While useful, this approach has a significant limitation: it does not allow direct control of agents or manipulation of their behavior from Python. This forces users to switch between the two programming environments, making the integration complex and less flexible.

Previous research to link NetLogo with other programming environments have focused on extending NetLogo's capabilities through external interfaces. For instance, Thiele et al. (Thiele 2014) developed RNetLogo, an interface between NetLogo and R, allowing for advanced statistical analysis of NetLogo models. Similarly, Jaxa-Rozen and Kwakkel (Jaxa-Rozen and Kwakkel 2018) introduced pyNetLogo, a connector that allows NetLogo to be controlled from Python, enabling users to perform simulations and retrieve results within a Python environment.

Py4J provides a bridge between Python and Java, enabling Python programs to dynamically access Java objects. This capability allows developers to directly control NetLogoa Java-based simulation environmentfrom Python. By using Py4J, users can seamlessly interact with NetLogo simulations at the agent level, efficiently managing models without requiring deep expertise in Java. However, despite its efficiency, Py4J may present challenges in more complex interactions and require an in-depth understanding of the underlying Java-Python bridge.

While these integration efforts have expanded the capabilities of NetLogo, significant gaps remain, particularly regarding the direct control of NetLogo agents from Python. Existing interfaces generally allow for running simulations and collecting results but lack the ability to manipulate individual agents or modify their behaviors during runtime directly from Python. This limitation hampers the ability to leverage Python's extensive libraries for machine learning, optimization, and data analysis, which could enhance agent behaviors and decision-making processes within simulations.

In this paper, we introduce **Netlogopy**, an innovative Python library that bridges the gap between NetLogo and Python, allowing for enhanced agent-based simulations by leveraging the strengths of both tools.

The remainder of this paper is structured as follows: The next section introduces the Netlogopy library, detailing its functionality and providing illustrative examples of its application. Section 3 evaluates the performance and feasibility of the library through a comparative analysis. Finally, Section 4 concludes the paper by summarizing the findings and discussing potential future directions for this work.

2 THE NETLOGOPY LIBRARY

In this section, we provide a detailed explanation of the Netlogopy library, including installation instructions and usage examples. The *Netlogopy* library is released as open-source software under the MIT License.[1] This license grants users the freedom to use, modify, and distribute the code under permissive terms. The source code is publicly available on PyPI[2] and GitHub[3]. We encourage the community to contribute to the development of `Netlogopy` by opening issues, submitting pull requests, and sharing feedback. For more information on best practices for open-source simulation code, please see the guidance provided in (Monks, Harper, and Mustafee 2024).

2.1 Installation

To use Netlogopy, it is recommended to create a dedicated Conda virtual environment to avoid conflicts with existing packages and ensure reproducibility. Netlogopy supports Python versions **3.6 and above**, ensuring compatibility with a wide range of Python environments. Follow the steps below:

1. **Install Conda**: If you do not already have Conda installed, download and install Anaconda or Miniconda.
2. **Clone the Repository**: Clone the Netlogopy repository from GitHub to access the `environment.yml` file and other resources.
   ```
   git clone https://github.com/yourusername/netlogopy.git
   cd netlogopy
   ```
3. **Create the Conda Environment**: Use the provided `environment.yml` file to create a new Conda environment:
   ```
   conda env create -f environment.yml
   ```
4. **Activate the Environment**:
   ```
   conda activate netlogopy-env
   ```

[1] `https://opensource.org/licenses/MIT`
[2] `https://pypi.org/project/netlogopy`
[3] `https://github.com/Bouaziz19/netlogopy`

5. **Install Netlogopy**:
   `pip install netlogopy`
6. **Install NetLogo**: Download and install NetLogo from the official site.
7. **Configure Your IDE**: If using Visual Studio Code or another IDE, set the default terminal to the Command Line Interface (CLI) for compatibility.

Note: An example `environment.yml` file is shown below:

```
name: netlogopy-env
channels:
  - defaults
  - conda-forge
dependencies:
  - python=3.9
  - openjdk=11
  - pip
  - pip:
    - netlogopy
```

2.2 Features

Netlogopy provides several key features:

- **Direct Agent Manipulation**: Create and control NetLogo agents (turtles) directly from Python.
- **World Configuration**: Resize the NetLogo world, set backgrounds, and customize patches.
- **Integration with Python Libraries**: Use Python's scientific libraries for computation and analysis within the simulation.
- **Simplified Syntax**: Abstracts the complexity of NetLogos language, allowing users to focus on simulation logic.

2.3 Main Functionalities

Below are examples demonstrating how to use Netlogopy for agent-based simulations through its main functionalities.

2.3.1 Creating and Controlling Agents

```python
import time
from netlogopy.netlogopy import *

if __name__ == "__main__":
    # Specify the NetLogo installation path
    netlogo_home = "path/to/netlogo_home/NetLogo 6.2.2"
    n = run_netlogo(netlogo_home)

    # Resize the NetLogo world
    resize_world(n, 0, 60, 0, 60)

    # Create a turtle agent
    car01 = pyturtle(n, x=20, y=20, shape="car",
            size_shape=4, color=15,
            name="car01", labelcolor=15)

    # Simulation loop
    for i in range(10):
        time.sleep(1)
        print(f"Step {i}")
```

```
  n.close_model()
```

2.3.2 Moving Agents

```
# Move the agent forward by 1 unit each step
for i in range(10):
  time.sleep(1)
  car01.fd(1)
  print(f"Agent moved to position {getxyturtle(n, car01)}")
n.close_model()
```

2.3.3 Interacting Between Agents

```
# Create a second turtle agent
car02 = pyturtle(n, x=5, y=5, shape="car",
         size_shape=4, color=55,
         name="car02", labelcolor=55)

# Create a link (street) between agents
street(n, fromm=car01, too=car02, label="street",
    labelcolor=35, color=35, thickness=0.5)

# Move agent car01 towards car02
for i in range(10):
  time.sleep(1)
  car01.face_to(car02)
  car01.fd(1)
  distance = car01.distanceto(car02)
  print(f"Distance to car02: {distance}")

n.close_model()
```

2.3.4 Setting Background and Customization

```
# Set a background image
background_image = "path/to/image/nelogopy.png"
set_background(n, background_image)
```

2.3.5 Accessing Agent Properties

```
# Get the agent's position
position = getxyturtle(n, car01)
print(f"Agent position: {position}")

# Set the agent's position
car01.setxy(10, 10)
```

2.3.6 Additional Examples

Moving to Another Agent

```
# Move car01 to the position of car02
car01.move_to(car02)
```

Hiding and Showing Agents

```
# Hide the agent car01
car01.hideturtle()
```

Changing Agent Shape

```
# Change the shape of car01 to 'default'
car01.set_shape('default')
```

Calculating Distance Between Agents

```
# Calculate the distance between car01 and car02
distance = distancebetween(n, car01, car02)
print(f"Distance: {distance}")
```

2.3.7 Integrating an Existing NetLogo Model

Netlogopy allows you to layer Python-controlled agents on top of older NetLogo models:

```
import time, os, sys
from netlogopy.netlogopy import *

if __name__ == "__main__":
  netlogo_home = "C:/Program Files/NetLogo 6.2.2"
  path_model = os.path.join(os.path.dirname(__file__),
                 "Wolf Sheep Predation.nlogo")
  n = run_netlogo(netlogo_home, path_model)

  # Resize world
  resize_world(n, 0, 70, 0, 55)

  # Initialize the original NetLogo model
  run_command(n, "setup")

  # Add Python-controlled agents
  car01 = pyturtle(n, x=20, y=20, shape="car",
           size_shape=4, color=15,
           name="car01", labelcolor=15)
  car02 = pyturtle(n, x=5, y=5, shape="car",
           size_shape=4, color=55,
           name="car02", labelcolor=55)
  street(n, fromm=car01, too=car02,
      label="street", labelcolor=35,
      color=35, shape="default", thickness=0.5)

  for i in range(100):
    run_command(n, "go") # Run the NetLogo model step
    time.sleep(0.1)
    print(f"*********** {i} ********")
    car01.fd(1)
    if i % 20 == 0:
      car01.setxy(10, 10)
```

2.4 Application Examples

Below are illustrative scenarios demonstrating how Netlogopys integration can enhance simulation capabilities:

Ecological Simulation In ecological modeling, agent-based simulations are used to study interactions between predator-prey species (Wilensky 2015). By integrating Pythons reinforcement learning libraries, predator agents can adapt hunting strategies in real-time (Gunaratne and Garibay 2020).

Industrial Production Systems Agent-based models in operations research help simulate manufacturing processes and supply chains (Bouaziz, Bettayeb, Sahnoun, and Yassine 2024, Siebers, Macal, Garnett, Buxton, and Pidd 2010, Sahnoun, Xu, Belgacem, Imen, David, and Louis 2019). Python-based optimization (e.g., genetic algorithms) can be combined with NetLogos agent structures (Fortin, De Rainville, Gardner, Parizeau, and Gagné 2012).

Robotics Simulation Combining NetLogos agent approach with Pythons ML libraries (e.g., *scikit-learn* (Pedregosa, Varoquaux, Gramfort, Michel, Thirion, Grisel, Blondel, Prettenhofer, Weiss, Dubourg, Vanderplas, Passos, Cournapeau, Brucher, Perrot, and Duchesnay 2011)) allows advanced behaviors for virtual robots (Sahnoun, Xu, Abdelaziz, and Baudry 2019).

3 EVALUATION AND COMPARISON WITH EXISTING LIBRARIES

Our work was inspired by existing libraries such as NL4Py, which parallelizes NetLogo simulations. Netlogopy builds on these concepts by adding richer agent-level commands and a more Python-focused workflow.

To evaluate the feasibility, we implemented a production-line simulation with six machines and six operators in both **Netlogopy** and **pure NetLogo** (same underlying logic). Development in Netlogopy took around 16 hours while building the same logic purely in NetLogo required around 25 hours. Further scenario additions also proved faster in Netlogopy (about one hour) versus NetLogo (around six hours). The more complex the model or the greater the number of inputs, the larger the speed and flexibility gap in favor of Netlogopy.

Table 1: List of Libraries Linking Python and NetLogo

Library	**URL**
pyNetLogo	`https://pynetlogo.readthedocs.io`
Py4J	`https://www.py4j.org`
NL4Py	`https://github.com/chathika/NL4Py`
Netlogopy	`https://pypi.org/project/netlogopy/`

3.1 Comparison of Features

- **pyNetLogo** (Jaxa-Rozen and Kwakkel 2018): Focuses on running NetLogo simulations from Python and retrieving results but lacks direct agent-level manipulation.
- **Py4J**: General-purpose Java-Python bridge; powerful but requires deeper knowledge of NetLogo internals.
- **NL4Py** (Gunaratne 2019): Allows parallelized NetLogo simulations but does not provide fine-grained agent control.
- **Netlogopy**: Direct agent creation/manipulation in Python, plus integrated simulation management.

	Netlogopy	pyNetLogo	Py4J	NL4Py
Language required	Python only	Python, NetLogo code	Python & Java	Python, NetLogo code
Integration w/ Python libs	✓	Limited	Limited	✓
Python-based sim management	✓	-	-	-
Direct agent manipulation	✓	-	-	-

Table 2: Feature Comparison of PythonNetLogo Libraries

4 CONCLUSION

Netlogopy represents a significant advancement in integrating Python and NetLogo for agent-based simulations. By allowing direct manipulation of NetLogo agents and leveraging Pythons extensive libraries, Netlogopy greatly enhances modeling flexibility, reduces development time, and enables more rapid iteration of sophisticated simulators. This seamless interaction between Python and NetLogo opens the door to more powerful and adaptable simulations across various fieldssuch as ecology, social sciences, industrial optimization, and complex systems analysis.

Furthermore, the accessibility of a Python-driven interface broadens the user base by lowering technical barriers. Researchers, educators, and students who may not have deep expertise in Java or NetLogo can now easily engage with advanced agent-based modeling, fostering interdisciplinary collaboration and the adoption of cutting-edge simulation methods.

Ensuring the long-term sustainability and maintainability of Netlogopy is a key priority. We have implemented strategies such as modular code design, comprehensive documentation, open-source collaboration, and continuous integration practices to maintain code quality and reliability. Looking ahead, future developments of Netlogopy could include support for more advanced modeling scenarios (3D simulations, parallel processing, GPU acceleration) and deeper integration with Python-based data analysis and machine learning tools. We also plan to cultivate a vibrant user community to exchange best practices, promote collaboration, and further expand Netlogopy's capabilities.

ACKNOWLEDGEMENT

Acknowledgment is made to the Normandy region and the European Union for supporting this research through the RIN regional research program by funding the AntiHpert project.

REFERENCES

Bouaziz, N., B. Bettayeb, M. Sahnoun, and A. Yassine. 2024. "Incorporating uncertain human behavior in production scheduling for enhanced productivity in Industry 5.0 context". *International Journal of Production Economics*:109311.

Fortin, F.-A., F.-M. De Rainville, M.-A. G. Gardner, M. Parizeau, and C. Gagné. 2012. "DEAP: Evolutionary algorithms made easy". *The Journal of Machine Learning Research* 13 (1): 2171–2175.

Gunaratne, C. 2019. "Evolutionary model discovery: Automating causal inference for generative models of human social behavior".

Gunaratne, C., and I. Garibay. 2020. "Evolutionary model discovery of causal factors behind the socio-agricultural behavior of the ancestral Pueblo". *Plos one* 15 (12): e0239922.

Jaxa-Rozen, M., and J. H. Kwakkel. 2018. "Pynetlogo: Linking netlogo with python". *Journal of Artificial Societies and Social Simulation* 21 (2): 28–31.

McKinney, W. et al. 2010. "Data structures for statistical computing in Python.". In *SciPy*, Volume 445, 51–56.

Monks, T., A. Harper, and N. Mustafee. 2024. "Towards sharing tools and artefacts for reusable simulations in healthcare". *Journal of Simulation*:1–20.

Oliphant, T. E. et al. 2006. *Guide to numpy*, Volume 1. Trelgol Publishing USA.

Pedregosa, F., G. Varoquaux, A. Gramfort, V. Michel, B. Thirion, O. Grisel, M. Blondel, P. Prettenhofer, R. Weiss, V. Dubourg, J. Vanderplas, A. Passos, D. Cournapeau, M. Brucher, M. Perrot, and E. Duchesnay. 2011. "Scikit-learn: Machine learning in Python". *the Journal of machine Learning research* 12:2825–2830.

Sahnoun, M., Y. Xu, F. B. Abdelaziz, and D. Baudry. 2019. "Optimization of transportation collaborative robots fleet size in flexible manufacturing systems". In *2019 8th International Conference on Modeling Simulation and Applied Optimization (ICMSAO)*, 1–5. IEEE.

Sahnoun, M., Y. Xu, B. Belgacem, B. Imen, B. David, and A. Louis. 2019. "Fractal modeling of cyber physical production system using multi-agent systems". In *2019 International Conference on Applied Automation and Industrial Diagnostics (ICAAID)*, Volume 1, 1–6. IEEE.

Siebers, P.-O., C. M. Macal, J. Garnett, D. Buxton, and M. Pidd. 2010. "Discrete-event simulation is dead, long live agent-based simulation!". *Journal of Simulation* 4 (3): 204–210.

Thiele, J. C. 2014. "R marries NetLogo: introduction to the RNetLogo package". *Journal of Statistical Software* 58:1–41.

Wilensky, U. 2015. *An Introduction to Agent-Based Modeling: Modeling Natural, Social, and Engineered Complex Systems with Netlogo*. The MIT Press.

AUTHOR BIOGRAPHIES

NOURDDINE BOUAZIZ is a PhD student at CESI LINEACT in Rouen, France. His research interests include human behavior, production scheduling, optimization, and simulation. He can be reached at nbouaziz@cesi.fr

BELGACEM BETTAYEB, Ph.D., MSc-MEng, is an Associate Professor of Industrial Engineering at CESI LINEACT in Lille, France. He obtained his M.Eng. in Industrial Systems Engineering and M.Sc. in Optimization and Systems Safety from the University of Technology of Troyes, France. He later earned his Ph.D. in Industrial Engineering from the University of Grenoble Alps, France. His research interests include Industry 4.0/5.0, Production Planning & Control, Quality Control, and Maintenance Planning. He can be reached at bbettayeb@cesi.fr

M'HAMMED SAHNOUN is a Research Director at CESI LINEACT, specializing in modeling, simulation, and optimization for manufacturing and renewable energy systems. He holds an HDR in Industrial Engineering (Normandy University), a Ph.D. in Automation, and master's degrees in Organization (University of Metz) and Robotics/Intelligent Systems (University of Paris 6), plus an Engineering degree in Automation (National Polytechnic School of Algiers). Formerly a Research Engineer at Grenoble Institute of Technology and Lecturer at the University of Lorraine, he has supervised several PhD theses on industrial data exploitation, complex system management, and dynamic scheduling. He also leads European and national R&D projects applying simulation and optimization across diverse domains. Email: msahnoun@cesi.fr

ADNAN YASSINE is a Full Professor at the Le Havre Normandy University in France and a member of the Laboratory of Applied Mathematics of Le Havre (LMAH). He teaches optimization, Operational Research, and logistics at the Superior Institute of Logistic Studies (ISEL). He is the author and co-author of numerous international publications in numerical and combinatorial optimization, among which some concerning scheduling and logistics problems. He obtained a Ph.D. in Applied Mathematics at the University of Grenoble (France) in 1989 and a Habilitation to Supervise Research (HDR) at the University of Nancy (France) in 1998. Email: adnan.yassine@univ-lehavre.fr

Proceedings of the Operational Research Society Simulation Workshop 2025 (SW25)
M. Luis, A. Harper, T. Monks and N. Mustafee, eds.
https://doi.org/10.36819/SW25.020

SIMULATION METAMODELLING VIA LOCAL LINEAR INTERPOLATION

Varun Ramamohan
Deep Bansal
Harsh Vardhan Singh
Yash Sarju Shah
Department of Mechanical Engineering, Indian Institute of Technology Delhi
Indian Institute of Technology, Hauz Khas, New Delhi 110016, INDIA
varunr@mech.iitd.ac.in; {deep.2016.bansal, harshv27, shahyash0531}@gmail.com

ABSTRACT

Simulation metamodels are constructed by fitting a model to a dataset wherein each dataset sample typically consists of a set of inputs (metamodel 'design points'), and estimates of one or more simulation outputs that forms the dependent variable for the metamodel. In this paper, we present a novel approach for constructing simulation metamodels that involves working directly with the simulation replications generated for each metamodel design point. Simulation outcome estimates corresponding to a test point - a set of simulation inputs not part of the design space - are generated by computing a convex combination of replicate outcome estimates from a set of nearest 'neighbours' of the test point in the design space. This approach eliminates the curve-fitting step in the metamodel construction process, and because multiple realisations of outcomes for a single test point are generated, possesses the potential of preserving the stochasticity associated with simulation outcomes.

1 INTRODUCTION

Discrete-event simulations (DESs) are widely used to model the (stochastic) operations of a vast variety of manufacturing and service systems. DESs help capture the variability in outcomes of interest associated with the typically complex systems being simulated (Law and Kelton 2007). When the complexity and computational expense of the simulation increases, models that more succinctly capture the simulated input-output relationship may be useful for fast and computationally inexpensive generation of the outcomes of interest. Such models are built using a dataset generated from the simulation in question, and hence are called 'metamodels' given that they are models of a simulation model (Barton 2023). Therefore, any model $y = f(x|\beta)$, where $x \in \mathbb{R}^n$ represents the set of simulation inputs of interest and $y \in \mathbb{R}^m$ represents the set of simulation outputs to be estimated as a function of x, is a metamodel of the simulation in question. In the above expression, $f : \mathbb{R}^n \rightarrow \mathbb{R}^m$ is the metamodel function with parameter set $\beta \in \mathbb{R}^d$. Metamodel outputs y are typically estimates of central moments associated with simulation outcomes, such as expectations or variances. Often, $y \in \mathbb{R}$, implying that a different metamodel $f(.)$ would need to be fit for each simulation output (Barton 2023).

Metamodels vary widely in form; however, most metamodels are deterministic in that they yield point estimates of the simulation output of interest as a function of a set of simulation inputs. For example, commonly used metamodels may be linear regression models, higher-order polynomials (Barton 2023), or even methods that originated in machine learning such as artificial neural networks (Dunke and Nickel 2020) or support vector regressors. A landmark method in simulation metamodelling is the stochastic kriging method (Ankenman et al. 2010). This method also yields point estimates of the simulation output by assuming that the simulation output random variable is a summation of a realisation of a Gaussian process response surface relating the simulation input and output and a realisation of a mean-zero random field. The use of Gaussian process regression lends the method its versatility in capturing general nonlinear simulation input-output behaviour. However, this method, like most regression methods, also involves matrix inversion, which may be computationally expensive and be prone to issues with singularities when design points are highly correlated due to, for example, their spatial closeness. More recent work around stochastic kriging has focused on generating quantile-based output estimates such as value-at-risk (Chen and Kim 2016), and integrating this method with neural networks to generate prediction intervals for the output associated with each design point (Lam and Zhang 2021). This latter kriging and neural network based method captures to some extent the uncertainty associated with the prediction by utilising the notion of the expected coverage rate associated with neural network predictions (Khosravi et al. 2010).

Another relatively recently developed method involves dynamic Bayesian networks (DBN) that also attempts to answer probabilistic questions around the simulation outcomes of interest (Poropudas and Virtanen 2007, Kelleher et al. 2018). DBN based metamodels attempt to predict the distribution of the system state via a network of conditional distributions of the system state at different time instants. Prediction of simulation output is achieved by loading the observed simulation state at a particular instant of time and updating the conditional distributions of the simulation state at network nodes (Poropudas and Virtanen 2011). These methods also involve curve-fitting of a sort given that the conditional distributions of the system state at network nodes must be estimated using simulation data. More recent work around DBNs for metamodels involves their enhancements with the integration of causal graphical models (Amaranath et al. 2023).

All of the metamodels discussed above, in our understanding, involve a curve-fitting procedure at some stage. In this study, we propose a new approach towards simulation metamodelling that eliminates the need for curve-fitting and can potentially, at minimum, accurately estimate the variance or standard deviation of the simulation outcome of interest (in addition to its expectation).

Our proposed metamodelling method involves performing, for a given set of simulation inputs for which a simulation output estimate is desired (i.e., a 'test point'), local linear interpolations of simulation replication data associated with the 'neighbours' of the test point. A metamodel is developed using a set of 'design points', each of which is a set of simulation inputs, and for which simulation outputs are generated for constructing the metamodel. That is, once the analyst developing the metamodel has decided upon the choice of $f(.)$, then its parameter set β is estimated using simulation data (i.e., estimates of simulation outputs y) generated for the design space. Most metamodels are developed using point estimates of the outputs y calculated from replicate values (e.g., averaged where y is an expectation) of the simulation outcome random variable of which y is a function. In contrast, our method works directly with the replicate values of the outcome generated by the simulation. For estimating the simulation output associated with a test point, a set of 'neighbours' of the test point in the design space is first constructed. Then convex combinations of the replicate values of the outcomes corresponding to these neighbours is computed to in turn generate 'replicate' values of the outcome for the test point. The output y for the test point (i.e., y) is then estimated as a function of these replicates.

Therefore, our proposed method estimates outputs of interest via linear interpolation between outcome replicate values of its neighbours, and hence we refer to it as the local linear interpolation (LLI) metamodel. It is also evident that other statistics, such as the variance, can be estimated from the replicate values of the simulation outcome generated by our proposed metamodelling approach.

We now provide a detailed description of our proposed LLI metamodelling approach.

2 LOCAL LINEAR INTERPRETATION METALMODELLING

We begin by introducing the terminology associated with our proposed LLI metamodelling approach.

– Simulation outcome. A random variable capturing some aspect of the performance of the system being simulated. Each replication of the simulation generates a realisation of the outcome. For example: utilisation of a machine in a DES of a production line. Denoted by Y.

– Simulation output. A parameter of the distribution of a simulation outcome of interest estimated via a simulation experiment. For example, the expectation or variance of a simulation outcome. Denoted by y, where y is a statistic associated with Y.

– Design point. A set of simulation inputs for which simulation outcomes are generated and the associated simulation output is estimated, done for constructing the metamodel. Denoted by x_d.

– Design space. The set of all design points used in constructing the metamodel. Denoted by $\mathbb{D}$, where $L = |\mathbb{D}|$ is the cardinality of the design space.

– Test point. A set of simulation inputs not in $\mathbb{D}$ for which an estimate of the simulation output in question is desired. Denoted by x_t, with its ith element $x_{t,i}$ representing a single simulation parameter.

– Response matrix A. An $R \times L$ matrix wherein the dth ($d \in \{1,\ldots,L\}$) column of A stores the R replicate realisations of the outcome Y_d corresponding to design point x_d. Thus the element A_{rd} of A represents the rth realisation of the outcome Y_d for the dth design point.

The LLI metamodelling process can be split into two phases: (a) construction and (b) test point evaluation. The construction phase involves generation of the design matrix A, and the evaluation of a test point x_t using the design space $\mathbb{D}$ and the design matrix A is the LLI phase.

LLI metamodel construction phase.

1. The first step in this phase involves identifying the design points x_d that populate the design space $\mathbb{D}$. This may be done following standard design point selection practice for metamodel construction, such as the use of factorial or fractional factorial designs (Barton 2023, Sanchez et al. 2020). However, our proposed approach is applicable for an arbitrarily constructed design space.

2. The second step involves generating, for each $x_d \in \mathbb{D}$, the R replicate values of Y_d to populate the dth column of the response matrix A. Note that a response matrix A needs to be generated for each simulation outcome Y.

Test point evaluation phase.

The key novelty in our proposed LLI metamodelling approach is associated with the test point evaluation phase. The procedure to be followed to estimate the output y_t associated with a test point x_t is depicted in Algorithm 1 below.

Algorithm 1 Test point evaluation under the local linear interpolation metamodelling method with the distance based neighbourhood construction approach.

```
Initialize with the response matrix A, size of neighbourhood m, design space 𝔻
L ← cardinality of design space 𝔻
Initialize empty list 𝒱
/*Construct neighbourhood of x_t: distance based approach*/
for d = 1 to L do
    Compute distance v_d of design point x_d from x_t    ▷ Example: Euclidean distance can be used
    Store v_d in 𝒱
end for
Initialize empty list N_t
Sort 𝒱 in ascending order
Store the first m elements of 𝒱 in N_t    ▷ Find the m closest elements to x_t
/*Output estimation for x_t*/
for x_d ∈ N_t do    ▷ Compute weights
    Compute weight W_d as Euclidean distance between neighbour x_d and test point x_t
end for
for r = 1 to R do    ▷ Estimate replicate value of simulation outcome Y_t corresponding to x_t
    Y_{t,r} = (Σ_{d=1}^{m} W_d A_{rd}) / (Σ_{i=1}^{m} W_d)    ▷ Use replicate values of simulation outcomes stored in response matrix A
end for
Compute output estimate as ŷ_t = (Σ_{r=1}^{R} Y_{t,r}) / R    ▷ Assumption: output y_t is an expectation
```

As depicted in Algorithm 1, the first step in the test point evaluation phase involves construction of the neighbourhood N_t of x_t. We propose two possible approaches for construction of the neighbourhood of x_t. The first approach (outlined in Algorithm 1), which we refer to as the *distance based* neighbourhood construction approach, in that it can be used for any design space - e.g., even for spaces that are not factorial or fractional factorial designs. This approach simply involves computing the m closest design points to the test point using some measure of distance (e.g., Euclidean distance). As will be demonstrated in the subsequent section, the choice of the neighbourhood size m is important.

The second approach for constructing N_t, which we term the *component Cartesian product* approach, is outlined in Algorithm 2. This approach, while technically applicable for arbitary design spaces, is primarily suitable for factorial or fractional factorial designs. It involves taking the Cartesian product N_t^C of two sets: first, the n-tuple of nearest neighbours of individual components of x_t that are smaller (x_t^l); and second, the ordered n-tuple of nearest neighbours of individual components of x_t that are larger. All the elements in this Cartesian product N_t^C may not belong also to the design space $\mathbb{D}$, and hence the neighbourhood N_t is set to be the intersection of N_t^C and $\mathbb{D}$. Note that for design spaces that are not constructed using factorial approaches, the intersection of N_t^C and $\mathbb{D}$ - that is, N_t - is not guaranteed to be non-empty.

Algorithm 2 Test point component Cartesian product approach for neighbourhood construction.

$n \leftarrow$ length of test point vector x_t
Initialize empty lists x_t^l and x_t^u
for i = 1 to n **do**
    $x_{t,i}^l \leftarrow \sup\{x_{d,i} \in \mathbb{D} : x_{d,i} < x_{t,i}\}$ ▷ Find nearest simulation input parameter in design space smaller than i^{th} component of x_t
    Store $x_{t,i}^l$ in x_t^l
    $x_{t,i}^u \leftarrow \inf\{x_{d,i} \in \mathbb{D} : x_{d,i} > x_{t,i}\}$ ▷ Find nearest simulation input parameter in design space larger than i^{th} component of x_t
    Store $x_{t,i}^u$ in x_t^u
end for
$N_t^C \leftarrow x_t^l \otimes x_t^u$ ▷ Construct Cartesian product of x_t^l and x_t^u
$N_t \leftarrow N_t^C \cap \mathbb{D}$ ▷ Obtain neighbourhood of x_t as intersection of N_t^C and design space $\mathbb{D}$

Once N_t is constructed, then linear interpolation of replicate values A_{rd} associated with each design point $x_d \in N_t$ is performed using weights calculated for each x_d. The most general approach for calculating these weights involves using a measure of distance between each neighbourhood design point (i.e., each $x_d \in N_t$) and the test point x_t. For instance, the distances (e.g., Euclidean distance) computed for the x_d during the construction of N_t may be used as weights for those $x_d \in N_t$.

In addition, we propose an alternate approach for calculating neighbourhood design point weights that is applicable when the metamodel input variables of interest (i.e., the variables that change between design and test points) are restricted to distributional parameters. In our knowledge, existing metamodels do not allow for the distribution itself (as opposed to its parameters) to change between test points and the design points used to construct the metamodel. For instance, consider a case where interarrival times of jobs to a production line are uniformly distributed - i.e., $X \sim U(a,b)$ - and an experimenter wishes to estimate the simulation output when X becomes normally distributed (e.g., $X \sim N(\mu, \sigma^2)$). Here some comparability between the uniform and normal distributions may be assumed (e.g., the limits a and b of the uniform distribution may be comparable to the extreme quantiles of the normal distribution). Alternatively, consider a case where the distribution changes from $U(a,b)$ to $U(c,d)$. In this case, under existing metamodel construction approaches, unless both the lower and upper limits of the distribution are included separately as independent variables in the metamodel, the impact of a change such as this on the simulation output cannot be estimated.

We propose a method for computing weights associated with the neighbours of the test point and the test point itself that allows for the distribution of the test point component to change. We suggest using as weights two statistical quantities designed to quantify how 'different' one distribution is from another: (a) the Kullback-Leibler (KL) divergence, and (b) the Kolmogorov-Smirnov (KS) statistic.

The KL divergence measures the 'difference' between the distributions of two continuous random variables A and B (with density functions $a(x)$ and $b(x)$) defined on the same sample space (the real line in this case) via the calculation below (Kullback and Leibler 1951).

$$KL_{AB} = \int_{-\infty}^{\infty} a(x) \log\left(\frac{a(x)}{b(x)}\right)\, dx$$

The above expression represents the expectation of the logarithmic difference between the probabilities associated with A and B across the sample space. The expectation is computed using the density function $a(.)$ of A, and hence A is the (often empirical) distribution being evaluated against the hypothesized distribution B. Thus $KL_{AB} \neq Kl_{BA}$, and if the weight $w_{i,d}$ for the ith component (e.g., the random variable $A \sim U(a,b)$) of the design point x_d with respect to the ith component of the test point x_t (e.g., the random variable $B \sim U(c,d)$) is calculated using this approach, then $w_{i,d}$ is calculated as $0.5 \times (KL_{AB} + KL_{BA})$.

The KS statistic is used as part of the KS test for determining whether two random samples are identically distributed (Berger and Zhou 2014). In case random samples are not provided, as in this case, they can be generated from the distributions to be compared. The KS statistic measures the 'distance' between the cumulative distribution functions $F_A(x)$ and $F_B(x)$ of random variables A and B defined on the same sample space χ_x, and is calculated as follows:

$$KS_{AB} = \sup_{x \in \chi_x} |F_A(x) - F_B(x)|$$

When using the KL divergence or KS statistic to compute the weights $w_{i,d}$, we note that the 'component' $x_{i,t}$ of x_t or $x_{i,d}$ of x_d may not be a single parameter (e.g., the parameter of an exponential distribution), but may be a tuple (e.g. (a,b) for the uniform distribution or (μ, σ) for the normal distribution). Once the weight $w_{i,d}$ for each component of the design point x_d is computed against the corresponding i^{th} component of the test point, the weight W_d for the design point x_d can be computed as the l_2-norm of the vector of component-wise weights $w_{i,d}$.

We now discuss the computational experiments conducted to illustrate the implementation of the LLI metamodelling approach.

3 LLI METAMODELLING APPROACH: COMPUTATIONAL ILLUSTRATION

In order to demonstrate the implementation of the LLI metamodelling approach, we first conduct a relatively more comprehensive set of experiments associated with a simple $M/G/$ system with one or two servers. We then present a limited set of experiments for a DES of a queueing system with three workstations in series, each with a single server. We use the first set to illustrate the more general distance measure based neighbourhood construction approach and the second set for the component Cartesian product based neighbourhood construction approach for factorial designs.

For the first set of experiments, we consider a single workstation with an average interarrival time of 10 minutes. We consider two design variables: the number of servers, and the average service time of the workstation servers, wherein service time is modelled as a uniform random variable given by $U(\mu - 1, \mu + 1)$ and μ is the average service time. A full factorial design was constructed wherein the average service time was varied between 2 minutes and 9.5 minutes in increments of 0.5 minutes, yielding 16 levels, and the number of servers had two levels: 1 and 2. This yielded a design space with cardinality 32, wherein each design point was two-dimensional. Three simulation outcomes - average wait time, the average length of stay (LOS) and the utilisation (occupancy) of the workstation - and six simulation outputs (the mean and standard deviation of each simulation outcome) were considered.

Given that the LLI method involves constructing linear combinations of replicate output values associated with design points, it was important to examine the method's performance in regions of the output - input relationship with significant nonlinearity. In order to do this, with the parent DES of the worsktation, we examine the relationship between average wait time and average LOS and workstation utilisation. These relationships are depicted in Figure 1 below.

(a) Average wait time (in minutes) versus utilisation. (b) Average length of stay (in minutes) versus utilisation.

Figure 1: The relationship between wait time and length of stay and utilisation.

From Figure 1, it can be seen that nonlinearity in the relationship appears to become significant starting with utilisation levels larger than approximately 0.55. Thus we need to evaluate LLI performance for test points yielding utilisation significantly larger than 0.5: for example, with a test point (7.5, 1).

We performed this evaluation for a set of test points yielding expected utilisation values between 0.0625 and 0.925. These included test points with component values falling outside the range of values considered for the corresponding design point component (e.g., where extrapolation was performed). The response matrices for the three simulation outcomes of interest were generated by executing the parent simulation for 15,000 minutes of simulation time, and recording outcomes after a warm-up period of 3,000 minutes. 60 replications were performed, yielding three 60×32 response matrices. A neighbourhood size (m from Algorithm 1) of four with the Euclidean distance measure was used for test point evaluation, and all of the 60 replications were used to construct output replications for test points. The LLI estimates of the outputs for each test point were compared to the corresponding outputs from the parent simulation. Estimates of the outputs from the parent simulation were generated for the test points in the same manner as done for the design points. The performance of the LLI method was quantified via the absolute percentage error, denoted by PE_{abs} where $PE_{abs} = \frac{|Simulation\ estimate - LLI\ estimate| \times 100}{Simulation\ estimate}$.

The results of the validation exercise for the LLI method for this queueing system DES are provided in Table 1. Table 1 provides, for 18 test points, the LLI estimates of both the mean and standard deviation of the simulation outcomes of interest. Simulation estimates of the outputs on a Intel *i7* workstation with 16 gigabytes of memory and 1.90 gigaHertz base clock speed required on average 9.14 seconds (standard deviation 1.89 seconds) whereas LLI estimates required an average runtime of 0.0075 seconds (standard deviation 0.0039 seconds).

Table 1: Local linear interpolation metamodel performance for an $M/G/$ queueing system simulation.

Test point	Wait time: Mean (SD)		LOS: Mean (SD)		Average Utilisation	
	Simulation	LLI	Simulation	LLI	Simulation	LLI
(1.25, 1)	0.11 (0.012)	0.21 (0.021)	1.36 (0.021)	2.41 (0.029)	0.13 (0.004)	0.18 (0.005)
(1.25, 2)	0.00 (0.002)	0.15 (0.015)	1.26 (0.014)	2.35 (0.024)	0.06 (0.002)	0.16 (0.005)
(2.25, 1)	0.34 (0.031)	0.36 (0.035)	2.59 (0.034)	2.68 (0.042)	0.23 (0.006)	0.22 (0.007)
(2.25, 2)	0.02 (0.005)	0.04 (0.006)	2.27 (0.015)	2.37 (0.018)	0.11 (0.003)	0.13 (0.004)
(3.25, 1)	0.80 (0.064)	0.84 (0.070)	4.05 (0.067)	4.09 (0.072)	0.33 (0.008)	0.33 (0.009)
(3.25, 2)	0.05 (0.010)	0.05 (0.011)	3.31 (0.018)	3.31 (0.019)	0.16 (0.004)	0.16 (0.005)
(4.25, 1)	1.58 (0.130)	1.66 (0.145)	5.83 (0.134)	5.91 (0.144)	0.43 (0.011)	0.43 (0.011)
(4.25, 2)	0.12 (0.018)	0.12 (0.020)	4.37 (0.024)	4.37 (0.026)	0.21 (0.005)	0.21 (0.006)
(5.25, 1)	2.86 (0.282)	3.06 (0.299)	8.12 (0.285)	8.31 (0.297)	0.52 (0.014)	0.53 (0.014)
(5.25, 2)	0.22 (0.033)	0.22 (0.033)	5.47 (0.037)	5.47 (0.038)	0.26 (0.007)	0.26 (0.008)
(6.25, 1)	5.17 (0.661)	5.45 (0.628)	11.4 (0.664)	11.7 (0.627)	0.62 (0.015)	0.63 (0.017)
(6.25, 2)	0.38 (0.051)	0.38 (0.056)	6.63 (0.054)	6.63 (0.058)	0.31 (0.008)	0.31 (0.009)
(7.25, 1)	9.33 (1.300)	9.92 (1.242)	16.6 (1.299)	17.2 (1.241)	0.72 (0.017)	0.72 (0.018)
(7.25, 2)	0.60 (0.075)	0.61 (0.078)	7.85 (0.080)	7.86 (0.079)	0.36 (0.008)	0.36 (0.010)
(8.25, 1)	18.9 (3.451)	20.4 (4.20)	27.1 (3.449)	28.7 (4.193)	0.83 (0.019)	0.82 (0.021)
(8.25, 2)	0.92 (0.115)	0.92 (0.104)	9.17 (0.118)	9.16 (0.104)	0.41 (0.010)	0.41 (0.011)
(9.25, 1)	50.5 (18.59)	49.6 (23.76)	59.7 (18.59)	58.7 (23.76)	0.92 (0.020)	0.87 (0.019)
(9.25, 2)	1.33 (0.173)	4.71 (1.12)	10.6 (0.174)	13.8 (1.115)	0.46 (0.012)	0.50 (0.012)

From Table 1, aside from 4 out of 18 test points, we see that the LLI method provides reasonably accurate estimates of both outputs associated with each simulation outcome. The average PE_{abs} values for each output associated with these 14 test points is provided in Table 2 below.

The LLI method performance is reasonable even in regions with significant nonlinearity - for example, for almost all test points with utilisation exceeding 0.6. The test points $(1.25, 1), (1.25, 2)$ and $(2.25, 2)$ all involve extrapolation in terms of the range of utilisation levels considered in the design space, hence the high PE_{abs} values are unsurprising. However, even though the PE_{abs} is high for these test points, the practical impact of the differences between the predicted and actual values (e.g., very low wait

Table 2: PE_{abs} values for LLI output estimates for 14 test points of the $M/G/$ system simulation.

Average wait time		Average length of stay		Utilization	
Mean	SD	Mean	SD	Mean	SD
3.974	11.191	1.629	9.62	1.61	12.042

times) is likely to be negligible, implying that the LLI estimates also contain information similar to that of the simulation estimates.

The performance of the LLI method at test point $(9.25,2)$ requires more investigation. Given that the performance of the method at test point $(9.25,1)$ and other test points with 2 servers appears acceptable, the poor performance at this test point is unexpected. Upon investigation, we noted that the four neighbours identified for $(9.25,2)$ were, in decreasing order of distance: $(9.0,2),(9.5,2),(8.5,2)$ and $(9.0,1)$. While the first three neighbours yield utilisation values (and therefore, wait times and LOSs) that are comparable to that of the test point, the design point $(9.0,1)$ yields a utilisation value that is nearly twice that of the test point. The wait times and LOSs associated with this design point are nearly 20 to 30 times those of the other neighbours; however, the weight associated with this neighbour is only 4 to 1.5 times lesser than that of the other neighbours. Thus, the distance-based weights in such cases require adjustment to reflect the sensitivity of outputs to each independent variable.

A potential method of adjustment could involve computation of a square symmetric matrix with each off-diagonal element representing the reciprocal of the average of the absolute value of the differences between replicate values of the output in question for each pair of design points. This matrix could then be multiplied with the distance-based weights vector. For example, in this case, a 4×4 matrix for the average wait time output may be computed wherein each off-diagonal element a_{ij} $(i \neq j)$ represents the reciprocal of the average of the absolute differences (e.g., the l_1-norm) between the replicate average wait time values associated with the ith and j^{th} neighbouring design points (e.g., between the wait time replicates of $(9.0,2)$ and $(9.5,1)$). Implementing this weight adjustment for the test point $(9.25,2)$ dramatically improved the performance of the LLI method for this test point: the PE_{abs} values for the average wait time, LOS and utilisation reduced to 0.91%, 3.00% and 3.20%. Applying the adjustment to the three other test points also yielded similar substantial improvements. For the test point $(1.25,1)$, the maximum PE_{abs} value reduced from approximately 91% to 41%, and for the test point $(1.25,2)$, the maximum PE_{abs} value (computed across outputs) reduced from approximately 144% to 80%. However, this method has potential pitfalls: in regions with significant nonlinearity, outputs can change substantially with small increments in variable values (e.g., when service time increases from 9.4 to 9.5). In such regions, applying this weight adjustment method yields greater weight on neighbouring design points at a larger distance from the test point in question, but have smaller pairwise distances between outputs associated with other neighbours close to them. Thus a more comprehensive investigation of when this adjustment method may be adopted is required, which we leave for future work.

An alternative approach for the test point $(9.25,2)$ could simply involve reducing the number of neighbours to three for this test point and recalculated the LLI estimates. This reduced the PE_{abs} values for the mean outputs to less than 4%, and to less than 20% for the standard deviations of the simulation outcomes. It is thus evident that the size of the neighbourhood becomes an important parameter for the LLI method. If the above weight adjustment method described above is not used, some approach for automatically selecting the size of the neighbourhood such that prediction accuracy is maximized must be developed.

We conclude the description of the experiments with the $M/G/$ system simulation by depicting the distributions of the average wait time and LOS outputs generated by the LLI approach in comparison with those from the parent simulation. These are provided for the test point $(8.25,1)$ in Figure 2. From the figure, the LLI method appears to provide reasonable approximations of the outcome distributions, even if there is potential for improvement.

We now describe a brief set of experiments with the 3-workstation queueing system and the component Cartesian product based neighbourhood construction approach. The queueing system is depicted in Figure 3 below.

The arrival of 'jobs' to this queueing system is Poisson, with the mean interarrival time being an independent variable for the metamodel. The service time in Workstation 1 (henceforth W/S1) is exponentially distributed. For Workstation 2 (W/S2), the service time follows the triangular distribution,

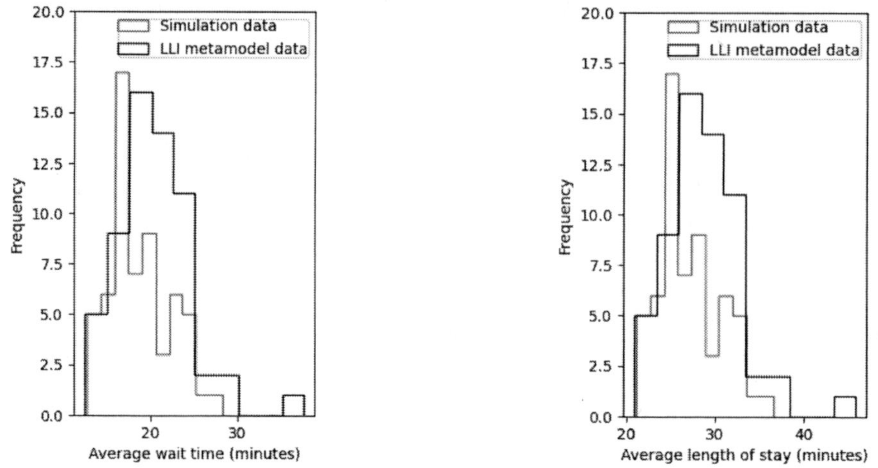

(a) Average wait time: $(8.25,1)$. (b) Average length of stay: $(8.25,1)$.

Figure 2: Distributions of outcomes for the test point $(8.25,1)$.

Figure 3: Three workstation queueing system simulated for LLI demonstration.

and for Workstation 3 (W/S3), it is the uniform distribution. Thus a single set of inputs for any metamodel of this system can be represented as $x = (\lambda_1, \lambda_2, (a,b,c), (u,l))$. Here the first two components are the parameters of W/S1 (an $M/M/1$ queueing system), the tuple (a,b,c) with $a < c < b$ represents the parameters of the triangular distribution of the service time of W/S2, and the tuple (u,l) similarly parameterizes the service time distribution of W/S3. We consider the following six simulation outputs for metamodel construction: the expected wait times at each workstation and the expected utilisation of each workstation.

The DES and its LLI metamodel were implemented on a workstation with an Intel *i*7 processor with 3.4 GHz clock speed and 128 gigabytes of memory. In order to construct the LLI metamodel for the DES of this queueing system, we first constructed the design space $\mathbb{D}$ with cardinality 24. A factorial design approach was used in the construction of $\mathbb{D}$, with the constraint that the expected utilisation of each workstation must be less than 1 to ensure stability of the system. At each design point, 500 replications of the DES were run and output estimates - average wait times at each workstation and the utilisation recorded at each workstation - were recorded for each replication. For each simulation output, a response matrix of dimensions 500×24 was created. The mean and variance of the relevant outcomes from the DES were also estimated from the data generated as part of the metamodel construction, and were used for benchmarking the performance of the LLI metamodel constructed.

Five test points were used to evaluate the performance of the LLI metamodelling approach, wherein only the parameters of the triangular distribution describing the service time of W/S2 change in each test point with respect to each other. However, all three of the parameters of the triangular distribution change. This scenario was constructed in order to illustrate the use of the KL divergence and the KS statistic approaches towards neighbourhood design point weights calculation, which we recall can be used when the only parameters that change between a test point and a design point are distributional parameters. Note that the neighbourhood for each of these test points was constructed via with the component Cartesian product neighbourhood construction approach.

The PE_{abs} values for each output and for the Euclidean distance and KL-divergence based weight calculation approaches, averaged across all 5 test points, is provided in Table 3.

We see from Table 3 that average PE_{abs} values for all outputs except the average wait time at W/S3 appear to be acceptable, especially when the Euclidean distance weights calculation approach

Table 3: Local linear interpolation metamodel performance for mean values of key outcomes from the 3-workstation queueing system DES.

Outcome	Average PE_{abs}		
	Euclidean distance	KL divergence	KS statistic
Wait time W/S 1	0.230	0.250	0.250
Wait time W/S 2	7.730	11.430	11.430
Wait time W/S 3	52.340	71.280	71.280
ρ W/S 1	0.120	0.080	0.080
ρ W/S 2	1.160	1.660	1.660
ρ W/S 3	0.080	0.070	0.070

Notes. All average wait times are in minutes. ρ = utilisation, W/S = workstation, PE_{abs} = absolute value of percentage error, KL = Kullback-Leibler, KS = Kolmogorov Smirnov.

is used. The simulation estimate of the average wait time for W/S3 is very low (< 0.1 minutes) across all 5 test points, and the LLI estimates are also correspondingly very low, conveying the same information, but yielding larger PE_{abs} values due to the low denominator. The PE_{abs} values for outcome variances are approximately around 80%, once again due to very low baseline values of variance given the large number of replications used. With regard to the weight calculation approach used for test point evaluation, we see that the Euclidean distance based approach appears to outperform the other measures; however, this requires more comprehensive investigation.

Overall, it appears that the LLI metamodelling approach demonstrates reasonable performance at least in the case of the simple queueing system simulations considered in this section. However, several open questions remain regarding the method that require further investigation, as will be discussed in the following section.

4 DISCUSSION

In this study, we present a novel methodology, which we refer to as the local linear interpolation (LLI) approach, for the development of metamodels of discrete-event simulations. For a given set of input parameters (a test point) for which simulation outputs are desired, the LLI approach involves computing a convex combination of the replicate values of the outputs associated with the design points (used to construct the metamodel) within a neighbourhood of the test point. The metamodel construction itself does not involve any curve-fitting procedure or model parameter estimation; it instead only involves generation (and storage) of replicate outcome values for each design point, which will likely also be done as part of other metamodelling approaches.

The LLI approach, in addition to eliminating the curve-fitting step, also is nonparametric in nature in that no assumptions around the distribution of the simulation outcomes are made. Further, given that the evaluation of a test point involves working directly with replicate outcome values of its neighbourhood, the LLI approach can potentially also estimate higher moments of the simulation outcome in question. Our approach using the KL divergence and the KS statistic towards calculation of the weights associated with each design point as part of the test point evaluation process also is novel for scenarios wherein the distribution associated with a simulation input (e.g., the service time of a workstation server) to change in its entirety. For example, the service time distribution can change from uniform random variable to a beta random variable.

Several questions remain to be answered with respect to this model. For instance, the LLI approach appears to work well even in regions of the simulation input-output relationship that exhibit significant nonlinearity for the simple queueing system DES considered in this simulation. However, for more complex types of nonlinearity (e.g., periodic behaviour as observed for trigonometric functions) the density of the design space in such regions may need to be substantial. A key question thus arises - how does the additional number of design points in such regions scale with increasing nonlinearity (e.g., as the degree of the Taylor series polynomial approximation increases)? Further, the efficacy of the LLI approach has been demonstrated for DESs of simple queueing systems. The efficacy of the LLI approach for more complex DESs or for DESs of complex real-world systems may be explored.

REFERENCES

Amaranath, P., P. J. Haas, D. Jensen, and S. Witty. 2023. "Causal Dynamic Bayesian Networks for Simulation Metamodeling". In *Proceedings of the 2023 Winter Simulation Conference*, 746–757. IEEE.

Ankenman, B., B. L. Nelson, and J. Staum. 2010. "Stochastic kriging for simulation metamodeling". *Operations Research* 58 (2): 371–382.

Barton, R. R. 2023. "Tutorial: Basics of Metamodeling". In *2023 Winter Simulation Conference (WSC)*, 1516–1530. IEEE.

Berger, V. W., and Y. Zhou. 2014. "Kolmogorov–Smirnov test: overview". *Wiley Statsref: Statistics Reference Online*.

Chen, X., and K.-K. Kim. 2016. "Efficient VaR and CVaR measurement via stochastic kriging". *INFORMS Journal on Computing* 28 (4): 629–644.

Dunke, F., and S. Nickel. 2020. "Neural networks for the metamodeling of simulation models with online decision making". *Simulation Modelling Practice and Theory* 99:102016.

Kelleher, C. T., R. R. Hill, K. W. Bauer, and J. O. Miller. 2018. "Using dynamic Bayesian networks as simulation metamodels based on bootstrapping". *Computers & Industrial Engineering* 115:595–602.

Khosravi, A., S. Nahavandi, D. Creighton, and A. F. Atiya. 2010. "Lower upper bound estimation method for construction of neural network-based prediction intervals". *IEEE Transactions on Neural Networks* 22 (3): 337–346.

Kullback, S., and R. A. Leibler. 1951. "On information and sufficiency". *The Annals of Mathematical Statistics* 22 (1): 79–86.

Lam, H., and H. Zhang. 2021. "Neural predictive intervals for simulation metamodeling". In *Proceedings of the 2021 Winter Simulation Conference*, 1–12. IEEE.

Law, A. M., and W. D. Kelton. 2007. *Simulation Modeling and Analysis*, Volume 3. Mcgraw-hill New York.

Poropudas, J., and K. Virtanen. 2007. "Analyzing air combat simulation results with dynamic Bayesian networks". In *Proceedings of the 2007 Winter Simulation Conference*, 1370–1377. IEEE.

Poropudas, J., and K. Virtanen. 2011. "Simulation metamodeling with dynamic Bayesian networks". *European Journal of Operational Research* 214 (3): 644–655.

Sanchez, S. M., P. J. Sanchez, and H. Wan. 2020. "Work smarter, not harder: A tutorial on designing and conducting simulation experiments". In *Proceedings of the 2020 Winter Simulation Conference*, 1128–1142. IEEE.

AUTHOR BIOGRAPHIES

VARUN RAMAMOHAN is an Associate Professor in the Department of Mechanical Engineering at the Indian Institute of Technology Delhi. He holds a PhD in Industrial Engineering from Purdue University (USA) and a B.Tech. from the National Institute of Technology Tiruchirappalli. More information regarding his research and teaching activities can be found on his webpage: web.iitd.ac.in/ varunr.

Deep Bansal is an undergraduate student in the Department of Mechanical Engineering at the Indian Institute of Technology Delhi. He can be reached at deep.2016.bansal@gmail.com.

Harsh Vardhan Singh is an undergraduate student in the Department of Mechanical Engineering at the Indian Institute of Technology Delhi. He can be reached at harsh27v5@gmail.com.

Yash Sarju Shah is an undergraduate student in the Department of Mechanical Engineering at the Indian Institute of Technology Delhi. He can be reached at shahyash0531@gmail.com.

Proceedings of the Operational Research Society Simulation Workshop 2025 (SW25)
M. Luis, A. Harper, T. Monks, N. Mustafee, eds.

https://doi.org/10.36819/SW25.021

ONTOLOGICAL GRAPH BASED MODELLING AND SIMULATION

Steven Jones
Leading Professional Simulation, RHDHV
Cornerblock, Birmingham
Steve.Jones@rhdhv.com

César A. Mardomingo Alonso
Digital Twin Solutions Consultant, RHDHV
Contactweg 47, Amsterdam
Cesar.Mardomingo@rhdhv.com

Ben Lomax Thorpe
Leading Professional Digital Twin, RHDHV
Cornerblock, Birmingham
Ben.Lomax.Thorpe@rhdhv.com

Nicola J Farrer
Simulation Project Manager & Consultant RHDHV
Cornerblock, Birmingham
Nicola.Farrer@rhdhv.com

ABSTRACT

We examine the benefits of using an ontology and knowledge graph (KG) approach in developing and maintaining discrete-event simulation (DES) models. Ontologies provide a standardised language, enabling a structured representation of domain knowledge and enhancing model accuracy, reliability, and knowledge transfer. Ontologies applied in Knowledge Graphs represent physical assets and processes, enabling the integration of diverse data sources, maintaining the model's relevance. Together, they enable the creation of digital twins to support advanced analytics and informed decision-making. In conjunction the Digital Twin Ontology (DTO) and Digital Twin Graph (DTG) form the foundation of a data model, providing a formalized language and digital representation of entities. Using Microsoft Azure Digital Twins (ADT), we enable automation of the development of a brewery process simulation, highlighting the benefits of ontologies and knowledge graphs for building and maintaining simulation models, ensuring accurate representations of physical assets and processes, and enabling use cases.

Keywords: ontology, knowledge graph, discrete event simulation, witness, digital twin

1 INTRODUCTION

We look to show that discrete event simulation (DES) model development can benefit from an ontology and KG approach to structurally define knowledge relevant to the process being modelled. We discuss the reasons why this approach has benefits and demonstrate a worked example.

Using an ontology and KG approach to develop and maintain a DES model offers several significant advantages. Firstly, ontologies provide a structured and formal representation of the domain knowledge, which ensures consistency and clarity in the model (Sapel et al, 2024). The first steps in any sound simulation study are to define the problem and define a conceptual model (Law,2014).

This structured representation helps in defining the entities, relationships, and rules within the simulation environment, making it easier to understand and communicate the model's components and their interactions (Ezzell et al, 2011). By leveraging ontologies, researchers can ensure that the DES model is built on a solid foundation of well-defined concepts and relationships, reducing ambiguities, and enhancing the model's accuracy and reliability. Secondly, the use of ontologies facilitates better documentation and knowledge transfer of the conceptual model (Robinson, 2008; Onggo 2009), making it easier for new team members to understand and contribute to the model. Beyond DES, the employment of reusable models and domain specific modelling languages also has demonstrable value for agent-based simulation approaches (Zschaler et al, 2023; Godfrey et al 2022; Godfrey et al, 2023; Parunak et al, 2022).

Third, knowledge graphs (KG) complement ontologies by enabling the integration and linking of diverse data sources (Jurasky et al, 2021; Listl et al, 2023). In a DES model, various data inputs are often required to simulate real-world scenarios accurately. Knowledge graphs facilitate the seamless integration of these heterogeneous data sources, allowing for a more comprehensive and interconnected representation of the simulation environment. This interconnectedness not only enhances the richness of the simulation but also enables dynamic updates and data integration, which are crucial for maintaining the model's relevance and accuracy over time. As new data becomes available, the knowledge graph can be updated, ensuring that the DES model remains current and reflective of the latest information.

This capability is particularly valuable for organizations that rely on diverse data inputs to simulate complex processes. By integrating these data sources, organizations can achieve a more holistic view of their operations, leading to better-informed decision-making and more effective problem-solving.

Lastly, the use of ontologies and knowledge graphs in DES models supports advanced analytics and reasoning capabilities. Ontologies enable the application of logical reasoning and inference, allowing researchers to derive new insights and identify hidden patterns within the simulation data. Knowledge graphs, with their rich semantic relationships, further enhance these capabilities by providing a framework for complex queries and analyses. This combination of ontologies and knowledge graphs empowers researchers to perform sophisticated analyses, optimize simulation parameters, and make informed decisions based on the insights gained from the model.

Overall, the integration of ontologies and knowledge graphs in DES model development leads to more robust, flexible, and insightful simulations, ultimately advancing the field of discrete event simulation. By leveraging the power of ontologies and knowledge graphs, organizations can transform their simulation models into powerful tools for strategic planning and operational excellence.

2 CHALLENGE

Discrete Event Simulation (DES) is generally agreed to provide a better understanding of:

1. **Process performance behavior** and its causes.
2. **Complex interactions**, **decision points** and **trigger levels**
3. **The effect of variability** and testing for **robustness**
4. **Prediction of performance** under given constraints and resourcing
5. **Risk-free environment** to test ideas without disrupting real systems.

Some of the challenges of using Discrete Event Simulation are:

1. **Reaching a common understanding** of how a process works or will work
2. **Speed to answer** business questions in time using DES approach
3. **Maintaining and documenting** complex DES models, especially when knowledge leaves with people and is not retained in systems
4. Going from **Strategic to Operational questions** about the same process
5. **Alignment and interoperability** with other models, planning tools and data systems
6. **Self-serve modular decision support** – reliance of skilled DES modellers to also be business analysts using these tools

2.1 Common Understanding

Many of the issues and challenges of using DES in practice come back to the understanding of stakeholders of the simulation results and the modelling approach when compared to reality. Many approaches in the field address this with methodologies to align stakeholders' views of the modelling approach and assumptions, for example, using conceptual models (Robinson, 2024).

One challenge with these conceptual models or simpler descriptions of assumptions is that they rely on natural language which has the inherent potential for ambiguity, inconsistency, and variability of meaning to different people. This can include different understanding of the same words or phrases or different understanding of the strength of importance.

One of the major benefits of going through the process of development a DES model is the discovery of shared understanding of the process and data, some of which is lost if this information is not captured and shared clearly to all currently involved, but also those that may pick up the work in future. Typically, data involved in documenting the process is structured as it relates to simulation elements, or in the format in which the business already stores process data but in many different tables which are unstructured in their relation to one another. Ontologies provide one way to structure the relationships between this process data.

2.2 Speed to Answer

If a DES is not built and utilized in time to influence decision-making, then static analysis and gut feel will be used for decision-making. DES as an approach may take time to develop and the re-use of concepts from one model to another can accelerate the deployment of simulation within business decision windows.

2.3 Maintenance and Documentation

Maintaining and documenting DES models is an often neglected or avoided step in the project process. It takes time and effort to succinctly describe the process, modelling assumptions and simplifications and interpret the results, for future users of the project assets. That knowledge is generally current and available at the point the project moves from model development phase to validation and experimentation phases, but if the model is not in constant use by the same people then the knowledge can be lost.

Re-developing model understanding by new modelers or analysis teams can be onerous. While software can often be used to trace connections and assumptions back to their root, and to auto-document models, some of the reasoning and semantic meaning behind modelling decisions cannot necessarily be retrieved.

2.4 Strategic to Operational

Often DES models start their life in the design and strategic phases of projects, where risk and CAPEX budgets are high, and decision support can have a big impact. These then often mature into assets which are used in setup, transition and on into operational phases of project lifecycles. In doing so they typically need to be adapted, refactored or the scope breadth or depth changed in reaction to changing requirements. Additionally, the DES model may need connections to new data, or more frequently updated data, to enable certain operational use cases.

This requires the conceptual model to be understood by new stakeholders and potentially modellers. Transferring this knowledge base and adapting the models requires clarity in the foundation of the model. Often the frequency and fidelity of data requirements will change but many of the concepts and assumptions remain.

2.5 Alignment and Interoperability

DES models are frequently used alongside other modelling disciplines through data exchange or through software APIs. Along with other modelling disciplines, DES needs to be able to integrate with Digital Twins (Karabulut et al, 2024), planning or optimization approaches and data systems such as Enterprise Resource Planning (ERP, Chiroma et al, 2016). Commonly this is done through custom interfaces taking time and effort to create and leaving legacy code that is difficult to maintain.

2.6 Self-serve Decision Support

A common criticism of DES as a decision support approach is the requirement for a skilled user of the software, and of the model in question to be available to perform experimentation and develop analysis based on simulation results. This is often because the assumptions of the data and model are required to be understood to interpret the results.

3 HYPOTHESIS

3.1 Hypothesis

Our hypothesis is that an ontological approach to DES conceptual modelling can go some way to addressing the above challenges. We demonstrate this with a worked example. We believe the approach could have the following benefits to DES stakeholders:

- **Cost savings** - speed of search, identify inconsistencies, less use of analyst time
- **Control** - compliance, governance, reporting
- **Capability enhancement** - data quality leading to better or different data science outcomes
  - Digital Twin ready simulation
  - Modeling approach interoperability
  - Strategic to operational capability – freq. and fidelity + availability of structured data
- **Improved customer service** - innovation, ability to map customer journey or touch points

3.2 Addressing the challenges

3.2.1 Shared Understanding

Ontologies and knowledge graphs give us a better way to reach a point of "shared understanding," based on formal language with clear entity identification, and the ability to rank on connectivity, quantifiable similarity metrics and a visual representation of concepts that is readily understood.

Some of this can be done with hierarchy and taxonomy/classification but not all relationships are hierarchical, and semantic meaning is important to the interpretation of real world to simulation model in development, as of simulation results back to the real world based on this foundation.

3.2.2 Speed to Answer

While developing an ontology and knowledge graph may feel like an extra set of workflow steps, we believe the clarity and effectiveness of the approach for all but the smallest models can benefit the speed and validity of the project, increasing trust in results. Time is often spent in DES projects explaining relationships, assumptions, and the source of data.

Using the KG approach improves DES model build automation possibilities, since the representation of the physical assets and relationships sits in this KG and is using a standard format.

3.2.3 Maintenance and Documentation

The approach makes for maintenance of those models to be faster as documentation of the process is clearer to new team members, and refreshing memory of concepts and assumptions after a gap in model development can be achieved through visual representation of the ontology/knowledge graph and through querying for relationships that meet certain criteria. Positioning the model of the assets and relationships outside of the DES tool enables more collaborative and concurrent model development.

3.2.4 Alignment and Interoperability

The ontological approach leads to a formalized language which can be interpreted by other systems. We see this as a crucial link between Digital Twins and simulation. The Digital Twin environment provides further links to other analysis tools (statistics, dashboards, machine learning, etc.), visualizations, documentation in document form or in data form (such as Building Information Models

(BIM)) and process control systems. This is particularly aided by the accelerated movement for BIM standards such as Industry Foundation Classes (IFC). We suggest the development of the ontology and knowledge graph of a system should be developed with the real world and other systems in mind, but with clear simulation-focused components.

3.2.5 Strategic to Operational

Transferring the knowledge basis of one simulation project with a simulation asset designed to answer strategic questions to the next phase of a project lifecycle requires clarity of design and assumptions. The ontology and knowledge graph encode these in machine and human readable form.

Using this simulation asset to answer a further set of questions normally requires adaptation in the scope breadth or depth, particularly as the simulation becomes focused on shorter planning windows. That adaptation will often be done by different people to the original creator and requires a thorough understanding of the rules and logic implied. For simulation models to continue to have impact long past the initial strategic value phase, to be re-used regularly in operational planning, it is vital for the knowledge not to be lost in documents or in the minds of modelers who may move on. Additionally, knowledge graphs, for example hosted in Azure Digital Twins, can enable event-based data interfaces to achieve a higher fidelity or frequency for model input data used.

3.2.6 Self-serve Decision Support

The users of simulation models, experimenting to answer business questions, must understand the basis of those models, and often that knowledge only resides with the modeler. In taking the knowledge and relating it to real world and the Digital Twin of the system, we enable more analysts access to the benefit of using the simulation model. The increased interoperability also means that others can develop decision support systems without being an expert in the DES software itself.

3.3 Use Cases

Addressing these challenges also allows us to access more use cases for simulation and Digital Twins, with a move towards more operational use cases such as:

- Daily/weekly production scheduling
- Best course of action when equipment fails
- Re-planning supply chains due to weather disruptions
- Allocating resources to minimize bottlenecks.

These use cases can be challenging to address without the speed-to-answer and alignment with other software and data that this approach can deliver.

4 WORKED EXAMPLE

Royal HaskoningDHV (RHDHV) is developing new ways to manage changes to simulation models, as processes and systems change over time and enable better co-development opportunities.

Building on our experience with standard languages for process modelling and simulation (e.g. BPMN BP-Sim and the Witness DES software package) we are investigating the rise of Digital Twin technology, as it presents an opportunity for new simulation model architectures, automation, and valuable use cases.

Two key concepts lay the foundation for this:

- **Digital Twin Ontology (DTO)**: a standard, *formalised language* to define the entities that can exist in the Digital Twin, including their properties, their mutual relationships, and their behaviour, and how we represent all those in data.
- **Digital Twin Graph (DTG)**: *the digital representation of entities from a physical system*. The Graph is created using the standard defined in the ontology, and data and information is attributed to the assets, processes, and systems in the Digital Twin Graph.

A DTG, based on a relevant DTO, becomes the digital twin of the physical asset, process, or system.

A best practice architecture for simulation models uses this digital twin to automatically build (and in later stages maintain), the simulation model, populating:

- the assets in the model & relevant meta data for those assets
- relevant properties and attribute data associated with these assets.

In order to test our hypothesis we needed to choose software tooling and a domain process topic for the example, but we expect that many of the fundamentals of this approach would be true if using other software or domain processes as a subject.

4.1 Process topic

To demonstrate the approach, we built a brewery process simulation (Figure 1). This concept had previously formed the basis of our web app model (https://breweryapp.azurewebsites.net/, accessed 12th January 2025). It was suitable due to its simplicity, scale, and modular structure.

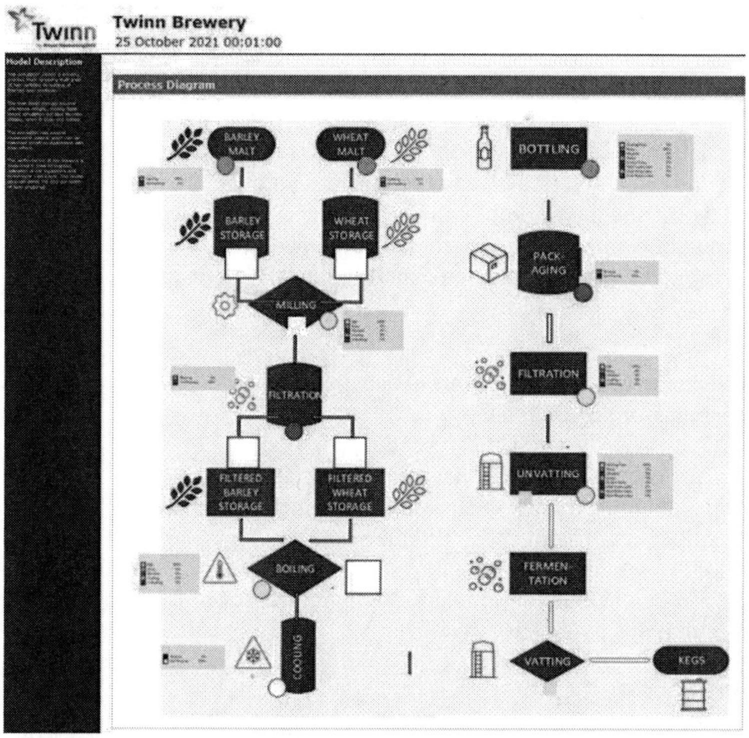

Figure 1 *Fictional Brewery Process Simulation in Witness*

4.2 Ontology and Knowledge Graph Software

We used Microsoft Azure Digital Twins (ADT) to create and host the DTO and DTG. We already use ADT as part of Digital Twin projects and understood its capabilities for presenting the Ontology in a visual way, storing relationship and property data and ability to upload and download relationships as data or via an API. The software has both a browser-based and a desktop interface that use common cloud sources (based on wider Azure services), allowing team members to collaborate on live data. It also allows for graphs to be queried using a proprietary but SQL-like query language.

There are many other graph and Digital Twin software packages that could perform this role in our approach. We also investigated the neo4j graph database (Neo4j Cypher Query Language. https://neo4j.com/product/cypher-graph-query-language./, accessed: 15 January 15, 2025) which demonstrates good data input/output and querying capabilities and a powerful querying language in Cypher. Neo4j is also used in the AI and machine learning world, leading to increased interoperability with those tools, whereas ADT is more focused on Digital Twins. We also considered the widely cited and open-source ontology editor Protégé (A free, open-source ontology editor and framework for Building Intelligent Systems, Protégé. https://protege.stanford.edu/, accessed: 15 January 2025). Given our desire to connect the simulation to other systems and data streams in future work, the cloud-based ADT service was found to be more applicable than the exclusively desktop-based Protégé.

4.3 Simulation Software

For the example we used the Witness DES software, as it provided excellent functionality in modularity, data-driven simulation and options around creating models from data. The options available to us to create model elements included:

- **At run time:** using the Witness function CreateFromDesigner and custom Designer Element templates
- Through the **Witness API**
- In an **XML text-based** representation

We used the XML text-based representation as this aligns very well with the form of data produced from the knowledge graph. A reference model enabled us to create reusable components much like the Designer Elements in the Witness software, copying the text-based representation from the reference model to the new model version. The API option had the benefit of verifying model changes before implementation, but lacked the ability to change visuals, as it was developed to create visual-less DES models as part of simulation-based applications. The run time option had many of the same benefits as the XML version but required a further data-to-sim-interface, such as a separate Excel or CSV file, in addition to the DES software which we wished to abstract to Python for non-Witness users to be able to work with.

4.4 Data Exchange and Client Application

For the exchange of data between ADT and Witness we chose Python for its ease of use, flexibility and interoperability with both ADT and Witness.

4.5 Ontology Standards

Developing an ontology from scratch may have benefits but one of the prime reasons for our adoption of this approach is interoperability and this is best served by re-using and adapting existing ontologies from industry standards. We researched potential options for our foundation ontology and found no de-facto standard for industry or simulation concepts.

Different industries and different approaches used different ontologies – for example in the brewing industry there may be a standard for process description, but this may be different to the standard for building or asset description.

Our use of Microsoft ADT led us to use RealEstateCore (RealEstateCore. https://www.realestatecore.io/, accessed: 15 January 15, 2025). (See Figure 2) as a basis ontology, as it included many of the aspects of the concepts we wished to represent. Almost any starting point would have required further development for simulation-based concepts.

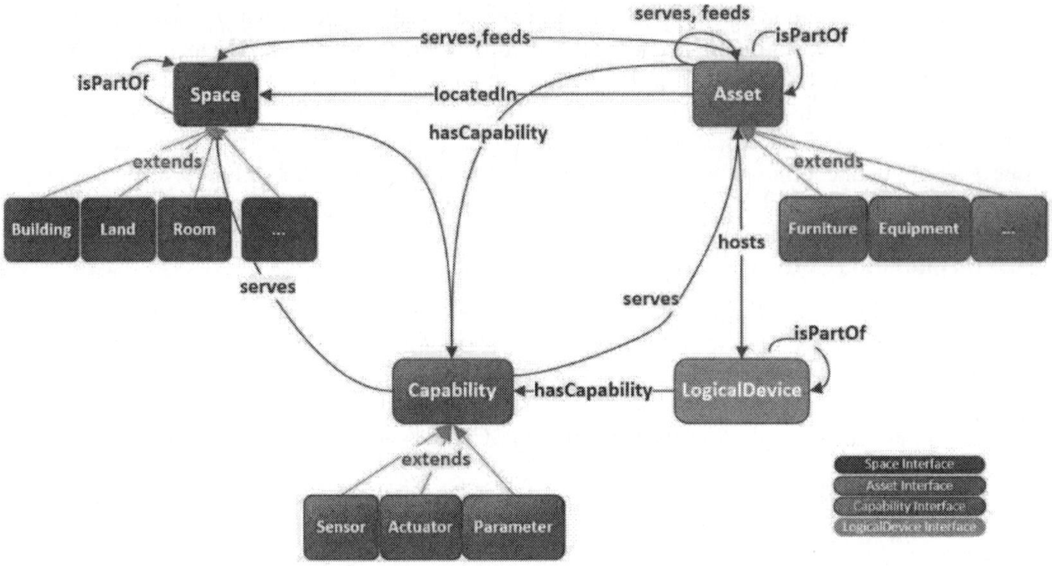

Figure 2 *RealEstateCore Ontology*

Alternative ontologies that were considered included:

- Discrete-event Modeling Ontology (DeMO, Silver et al, 2011) covers the simulation conceptual model well, with concepts of state, events, activity and process, but relies on domain specific ontologies.
- Brick has many similarities to RealEstateCore and work has been ongoing to align them. (Brick: A Uniform Metadata Schema for Buildings. https://brickschema.org, accessed: 15 January 2025).
- The Industrial Ontologies Foundry Core ontology has a focus on manufacturing and so will have applicable concepts to many DES models (IOF ontology. https://spec.industrialontologies.org/iof/, Accessed: 15 January 2025).

Other ontologies which can be used in conjunction with ADT can be found in the Microsoft Learn documentation for ADT (Microsoft Learn, learn.microsoft.com). (Adopting a DTDL industry ontology.https://learn.microsoft.com/en-us/azure/digital-twins/concepts-ontologies-adopt, accessed: 15 January 2025).

More broadly, ontologies used in conjunction with simulation include DESO (Guizzardi, 2011) based on Universal Formal Ontology (UFO), and Rube for 3D XML based modelling (Fishwick, 2002; Fishwick et al, 2004). Object Management Group's Systems Modeling Language (OMG SysML™,) has been used to combine a simulation ontology with domain knowledge (McGinnis et al, 2011).

4.6 Ontology Approach

The ontology and KG development was proven on previous IoT and Digital Twin projects. In those projects, the base ontology was extended to represent the real-world system, and in the twin domain. In Digital Twin projects we extended the real world domain with sensors and sensor data and in the simulation domain with the concepts of events, states, and the concept of an industrial asset having a matching sim model which would be composed with other sim models.

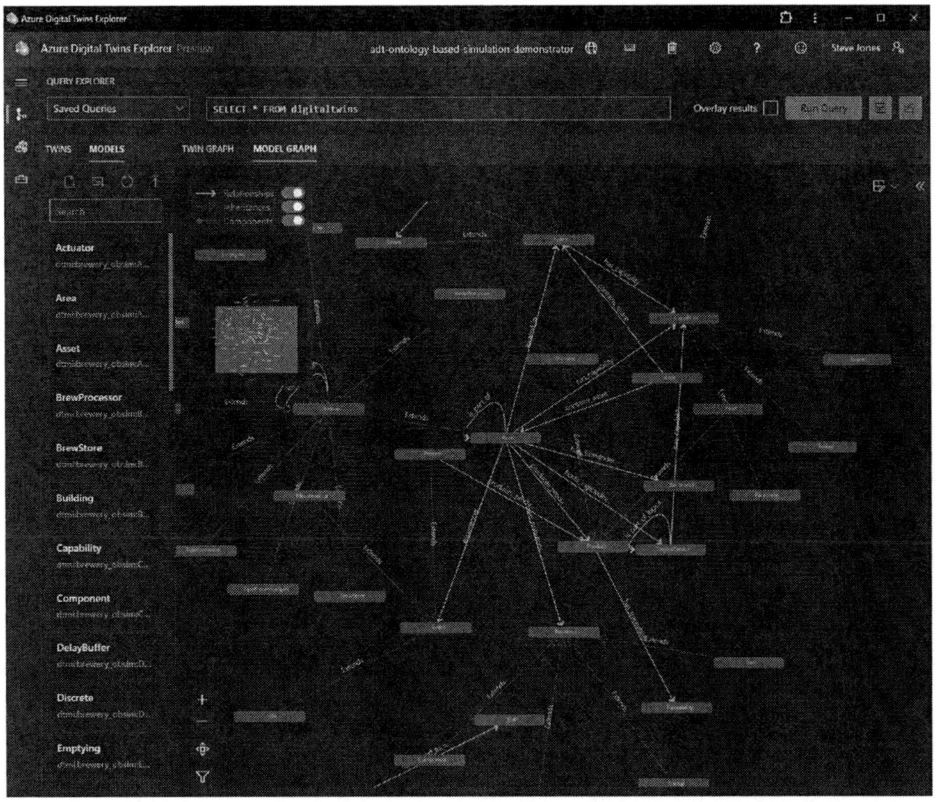

Figure 3 *Azure Digital Twin Explorer software with customised RealEstateCore ontology.*

Our customised ontology based on RealEstateCore shown in Figure 3 was extended to include concepts from simulation including Model, Product, Resource, Shifts, Events, and event states such as Idle and Busy. Figure 4 shows the colour-coded similarity between modules of the simulation model which can be represented using a Ontology concept, and a module from the reference model.

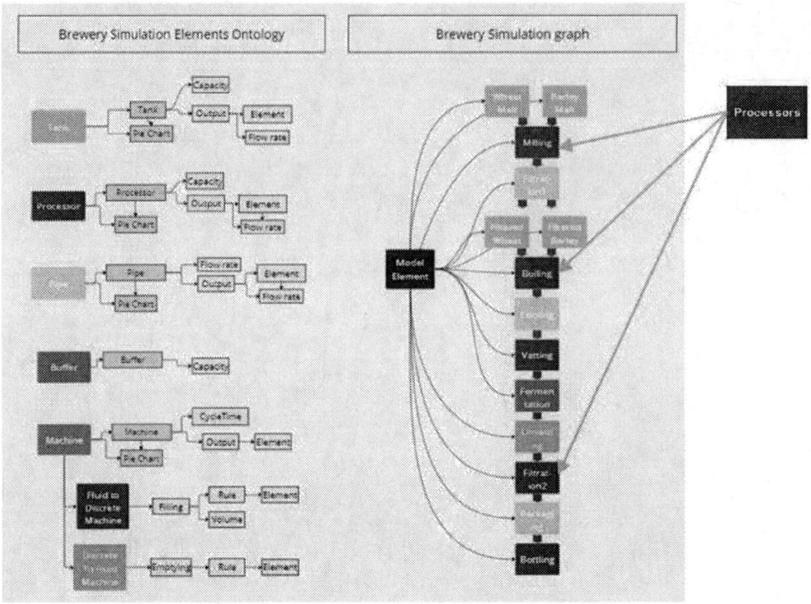

Figure 4 *Brewery Ontology and Knowledge Graph simulation components.*

4.7 General Description of Approach

The approach was developed with two workflows in mind:

- Developing the initial simulation model from the KG
- Maintaining the simulation model after a change to the KG

We query the graph to build datasets in XML to automate the development of the simulation model by composing elements of sim model XML to match the KG. For maintaining the model, which may have been altered by a simulation modeler, we query the KG to first identify the updates from the previous version. The new information is then incorporated in the latest user version of sim XML, updating only the target fields while keeping the rest of the model unchanged. The information of the new version of the model is then pushed to the KG for version tracking.

If the sim model differs from the KG after manual changes, then it is possible to alert the user to avoid KG changes overwriting manual changes, or to allow them. This is more flexible than other methods that would rely on automatic model build every time the model is used.

There are currently no flows in our workflow from the sim model back into the KG. The KG is considered to be a representation of the real world, so should only be updated (via ADT) if the changes should be considered from the real world, not based on "what-if" changes in simulations.

4.8 Approach specifics

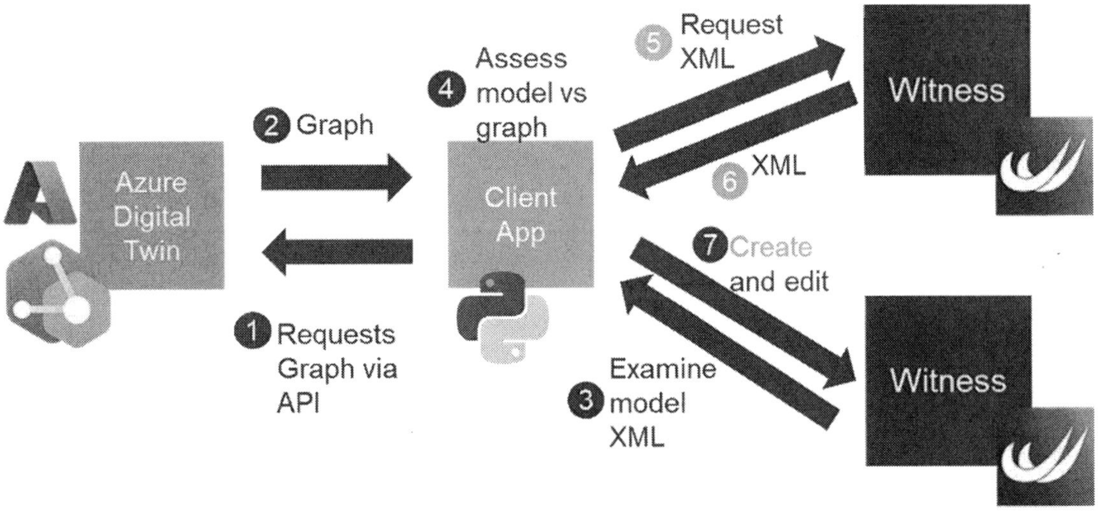

Figure 5 *Workflow steps.*

In general, the workflow to create or update the simulation from the KG follows the same workflow steps (Figure 5):

1. Query Graph: Client app (Python) requests Graph information via the ADT API
2. Return Graph: Graph is returned according to structured query in request in JSON form (**Figure 6**).
3. Query Sim XML: Retrieves Sim XML.
4. Assess changes: Client app assesses simulation model against the data returned from KG.
5. Request Sim Reference: If changes are required, then the reference model XML is queried from the client app.
6. Return Reference XML: reference model XML is required (Figure 7).
7. Create or edit sim: Any new elements or changes to properties are either created in a new version of the sim or edited in an existing version and saved with new version number, based on a property flag of the Model node in the KG.

```
{"@id":"dtmi:brewery_obsim:PipeProcessor;1",
"@type":"Interface",
"@context":"dtmi:dtdl:context;2",
"displayName":"PipeProcessor",
"extends":"dtmi:brewery_obsim:Station;1",
"contents":[{"@type":["Property","Volume"],
"name":"pipe_process_capacity",
"displayName":"Pipe process capacity",
"schema":"double",
"unit":"litre"},
{"@type":["Property","Volume"],
"name":"pipe_capacity",
"displayName":"Pipe capacity",
"schema":"double","unit":"litre"},
{"@type":["Property","VolumeFlowRate"],
"name":"flow_rate",
"displayName":"Flow rate",
"schema":"double",
"unit":"litrePerSecond"}]}
```


Figure 6 *Example of JSON returned from ADT.*

```xml
<userElement type="module">
        <module name="PipeProcessor" isOptimisable="true" title="" walkToModule="0" linkToFile="0" linkFileName="" inputElement="NONE
                <userElements>
                        <userElement type="pipe">
                                <pipe name="P_PipeOut" isOptimisable="true" quantity="1" priority="Undefined" capacity="250" initialF
                                        <flow rate="fr_FlowOutRate ()" withNoInput="1"> </flow>
                                        <displayItems>
                                                <displayItem type="displayPipe" drawAs="individual" displayOrder="21">
                                                        <displayPipe surface="0" label="Pipe">
                                                                <members>
                                                                        <member index="1">
                                                                                <position x="56" y="625"/>
                                                                                        <points>
                                                                                                <point x="352" y="625" index="1"/>
                                                                                                <point x="352" y="624" index="2"/>
                                                                                        </points>
                                                                                </position
                                                                        </member>
                                                                </members>
                                                                <outline color="21885" status="0"/>
                                                        </displayPipe>
                                                </displayItem>
                                        </displayItems>
                                </pipe>
                        </userElement>
```


Figure 7 *Example of Witness XML from reference module.*

5 RESULTS

By applying this method, the Python script can create or update a brewery sim model from an ADT KG in approximately 4 seconds. Since the DTO relationships are included in the workflow, the result of the workflows is a functional model (e.g. flow of parts and fluids to the target stations). More complex logic is also preserved when updating the model, only changing the target values of the target elements.

This result shall provide confidence in the feasibility and low risks involved when applying this approach compared to traditional modelling.

The speed to develop the Ontology and Knowledge graph clearly depends on the size and complexity of the process but the process steps and relationships captured within the graphs also need to be understood using a traditional model development approach and here are captured in a clear, logical, structured way for future users to pick up.

Automation of simulation model builds from data has long been an approach for systems with many components, especially where those can be codified into building blocks or re-usable models. The advantages of our approach in this example include alignment, interoperability, and self-service by non-DES aware users.

6 DISCUSSION

6.1 Benefits

Alignment and Interoperability: This approach has benefits to simulation alignment and interoperability, with an increasing need to align simulation with digitalisation in industry and other techniques and toolsets. This can only be achieved through speaking the same language and clarity of concepts.

Reconfigurability: The approach we have used above allows us to create simulation models of the whole process to chain or to select sub-sets of the process to be simulated, given assumption about upstream and downstream availability. This flexibility could allow more targeted answering of business questions.

Scalability: The example we give has relatively few processes, or building blocks in the reference model, but for larger scale processes with large volumes of inter-connected systems, this approach could be scaled.

6.2 Drawbacks to approach

- Ontology change requires sim modelers to build new reference models: KG changes can be automatically incorporated into an updated sim model but new ontology elements or new relationship types would require experienced simulation modellers to be involved.
- XML verification: The XML version of the model is unverified until run, and for this we see a role for use of the Witness API with verification steps built in, once the API is developed to allow better customisation of model visuals. This work is already underway.
- Client App User Interface: A generic user interface to take any ontology/KG to simulation model without Python knowledge is required for non-Python users to take advantage of the approach.

6.3 What next

Firstly, we believe there is a requirement for more co-operation and alignment on standards in the Digital Twin and DES space. Customisation of Ontologies may always be a feature of this approach, but as much standardisation between projects in similar industries would be beneficial to understanding across the spectrum of stakeholders.

Secondly, we believe there is a requirement for more guidance to be developed on how to implement this approach on DES projects. Despite ontology frameworks being available for many years, this is often not the starting point even for complex processes.

Thirdly, developing ontologies and knowledge graphs can be time-consuming but we believe this process could be automated. AI, such as Large Language Models (LLMs) approaches, also use KG representations to structure the relationships they find in their training data, and this close alignment should mean that LLMs could be used to automatically extract Ontologies and Knowledge Graphs from data such as sensors, process documentation (such as P&ID diagrams), maintenance and training manuals and corporate information such as sales brochures for equipment.

The Brewery simulation model and associated code is available on request from the authors.

ACKNOWLEDGMENTS

We would like to thank and acknowledge the contributions of the following people: Kent Bader and team for constant inspiration, John Beadsmoore for guidance, Martijn Stroeven for Ontology and Architecture support, Andy Chandler for Witness support and Jeremy Horgan for Witness and Python support.

REFERENCES

Chiroma E, Ladbrook J and Abdalla H (2016) Investigation into ERP-based symbiotic simulation project implementation on Ford engine production line: challenges, opportunities, and prospects. In: Bruzzone, De Felice, Frydman, Massei, Merkuryev and Solis (Eds), *Proceedings of the 15th International Conference on Modelling and Applied Simulation, Cyprus.*

Ezzell Z, Fishwick P, Lok, B, Pitkin A and Lampotang S (2011). An ontology-enabled user interface for simulation model construction and visualization, *Journal of Simulation*, **5(3)**, 147-156.

Fishwick, P. (2002). Using XML for Simulation Modeling. In: Snowdon J L, Charnes J M (eds). *Proceedings of the 2002 Winter Simulation Conference:Exploring New Frontiers*, San Diego, California, USA; pp. 616-622.

Fishwick P A and Miller J A (2004). Ontologies for modeling and simulation: issues and approaches. In: Ingalls R G, Rossetti M. D., Smith J. S. and Peters B. A. (eds) *Proceedings of the 2004 Winter Simulation Conference.*, vol. 1. IEEE, 2004, pp. 259–264.

Godfrey T, Zschaler S, Batra R., Douthwaite S T, Edgeworth J, Edwards M, and Miles S. (2023) Supporting Emergency Department Risk Mitigation with a Modular and Reusable Agent-Based

Simulation Infrastructure. In: Corlu C G, Hunter S R, Lam H, Onggo, B S, Shortle J and. Biller B (eds), *2023 Winter Simulation Conference (WSC), San Antonio, TX, USA, 2023, pp. 162-173.*

Godfrey T, Batra R, Douthwaite S, Edgeworth J, Miles S and Zschaler S (2022). A Methodology for DSML-assisted Participatory Agent-Based Enterprise Modelling. In: Barn B S, Sandkuhl K. (eds) *The Practice of Enterprise Modeling.* PoEM 2022. *Lecture Notes in Business Information Processing*, Springer, Cham, **456**, pp 201-215.

Guizzardi, G and Wagner G (2011). Towards an ontological foundation of discrete event simulation. In Johansson B, Jain S, Montoya-Torres J, Hugan J and Yücesan E.(eds*) Proceedings of the 2010 Winter Simulation Conference*, Baltimore, MD, USA; pp. 652–664.

Jurasky W, Moder P, Milde M, Ehm H, Reinhart G (2021)."Transformation of semantic knowledge into simulation-based decision support" *Robotics and Computer-Integrated Manufacturing*, **71**,102174.

Karabulut E, Pileggi S F, Groth P and Degeler V (2024). Ontologies in digital twins: A systematic literature review. *Future Generation Computer Systems,* **153**, 442 – 456.

Law, A M (2014). Simulation modeling and analysis. McGraw-Hill, Boston.

Listl F. G., Fischer J. and Weyrich M. (2023). "An Architecture for Knowledge Graph based Simulation Support," *2023 IEEE 28th International Conference on Emerging Technologies and Factory Automation (ETFA)*, Sinaia, Romania, 2023, pp. 1-8.

McGinnis L, Huang E, Kwon K S and Ustun V (2011). Ontologies and simulation: a practical approach. *Journal of Simulation,* **5(3),** 190-201.

Onggo, B S (2009). Towards a unified conceptual model representation: A case study in healthcare. *Journal of Simulation*, **3(1)**, pp. 40–49.

Parunak H V D (2022). Social simulation for non-hackers *Multi-Agent-Based Simulation XXII* 2022, Cham Springer, 1-14.

Robinson, S (2024). Conceptual modelling for simulation: Definition and requirements. In: Robinson S, Brooks R J, Kotiadis K and van der Zee, D.-J. (eds.), *Conceptual modeling for discrete-event simulation*, Boca Raton, FL: CRC Press, pp 3-30.

Robinson S (2008). Conceptual Modelling for Simulation Part II: A Framework for Conceptual Modelling. *Journal of the Operational Research Society,* **59(3)**, 291-304.

Sapel, P, Molinas Comet, L, Dimitriadis, I. *et al.* (2024) A review and classification of manufacturing ontologies. *J Intell Manuf.* https://doi.org/10.1007/s10845-024-02425-z

Silver, G A, Miller J A, Hybinette, M, Baramidze G, and York W S (2011). An ontology for discrete-event modeling and simulation." *Simulation,* **87(9)**, 747-773.

Zschaler S and Polack F A C (2023). Trustworthy agent-based simulation: the case for domain-specific modelling languages. *Software and Systems Modelling*, **22(2)**, 455-470.

AUTHOR BIOGRAPHIES

STEVEN JONES is Leading Professional Simulation with Royal Haskoning DHV, Birmingham, UK. Steven received a BSc (Hons) Mathematics from the University of Surrey in 2006. In 2005 he became an Operational Research Analyst working in System Dynamics at HM Revenue and Customs, as part of the Government Operational Research (GORS) group, modelling the housing market and self-assessment tax filing. This was followed by period at CORDA, BAE Systems working in fleet management of fast jets, and discrete-event simulation. Since 2011 Steven has been working across a range of industries with Lanner/Royal Haskoning DHV including in manufacturing, logistics, food and drink, and energy.

CÉSAR A. MARDOMINGO ALONSO is a Digital Twin Solutions Consultant at Royal HaskoningDHV in Amsterdam, Netherlands. He pursued his studies in Industrial Engineering with a Bachelor's degree in Industrial Technologies Engineering from Universidad Carlos III de Madrid. Concurrently, he worked for Quilosa - Selena Iberia, S.L.U., where he developed an innovative thermodynamic simulator, which earned him the highest score for his thesis. César then pursued a Master's degree in Industrial Engineering, also at Universidad Carlos III de Madrid, completing it in 2020. During this period, he worked for Mapal, leading a R&D project team focused on applying industrial process simulation to the hospitality sector. His master's thesis, which showcased an innovative approach and yielded tangible results, received the highest recognition from the thesis board. Since then, César has been involved in the digitalization and simulation of various sectors, including hospitality, industry, water, and aviation. In 2023, he furthered his expertise by completing a Master's degree in Digital Product Management.

BEN LOMAX THORPE is Leading Professional and Director Advisory Group Digital Twin, and as such leads the Royal HaskoningDHV Digital Twin agenda and business. Ben studied Mechanical and Automotive Engineering, receiving a First Class BEng (Hons) from the University of Bradford before joining Cummins, where he focused on Global Operations Excellence. Ben then moved to Lanner (now RHDHV) in 2016 as a simulation consultant, working on projects across a range of industries and additionally was awarded an MSc (with Distinction) in Engineering Business Management at the University of Warwick. In more recent years, Ben has focussed on Digital Twins across sectors such as Water, Maritime, Industry, Energy, Aviation and Rail.

NICOLA J. FARRER is a Simulation Project Manager and Consultant with Royal Haskoning DHV, Birmingham, UK. She was awarded a first-class degree in Natural Sciences from the University of Cambridge in 2003, followed by a PhD in Chemistry in 2007, before undertaking postdoctoral work at the University of Warwick. She led an academic research group for 8 years in the Department of Chemistry at the University of Oxford. She has 38 peer-reviewed research papers and book chapters across a range of scientific, medical, and technological disciplines, with an h index of 22. She is a Chartered Chemist and since joining RHDHV in 2024 she has worked with multiple sectors including manufacturing, food and drink, and energy.

Proceedings of the Operational Research Society Simulation Workshop 2025 (SW25)
M. Luis, A. Harper, T. Monks and N. Mustafee, eds.
https://doi.org/10.36819/SW25.022

TOWARDS CONTAINER-BASED SIMULATION: A CONCEPT FOR A DISTRIBUTED AND SCALABLE SIMULATION FRAMEWORK

Daniel Seufferth
Falk Stefan Pappert
Oliver Rose

University of the Bundeswehr Munich
Werner-Heisenberg-Weg 39, 85579 Neubiberg, Germany
daniel.seufferth@unibw.de
falk.pappert@unibw.de
oliver.rose@unibw.de

ABSTRACT

Popular methodologies such as machine learning, simulation-based optimization, and data farming depend on simulation environments capable of handling scalable workloads and enabling access to distributed computational resources. Containerization and container orchestration offer promising approaches to establishing a generalized way for distributing simulation workload across various computing nodes. To this end, we propose a concept for a distributed, scalable, container-based simulation environment designed to meet the evolving requirements of diverse simulation and optimization techniques. We describe the core components of our concept with focus on the *Scenario Manager*, how it works and interacts with the remaining components.

1 INTRODUCTION

Several fields of study in and adjacent to the broader simulation domain, e.g. Simulation-based Optimization (SBO), Machine Learning (ML), or data farming, experience a significant rise in demand for computational power to evaluate large numbers of simulation runs.

Combining simulation and optimization algorithms, SBO aims to find optimal or near-optimal solutions for problems (Fowler et al. 2023). A wide range of approaches utilize SBO to especially assist in decision-making processes and optimise real-world systems based on the insights gathered from experiments (Lidberg et al. 2020, Nikolopoulou and Ierapetritou 2012, Nguyen et al. 2014). Since many optimization algorithms require multiple iterations of simulation computation to find solution candidates, increasing the number of concurrently running model instances can significantly accelerate the optimization process.

A recent study by Van Noorden and Perkel (2023) asked 1600 researchers how they think ML and Artificial Intelligence (AI) in general will affect their future research. Among the main benefits stated are improvements in data processing and increased productivity, showing the importance of ML as a research field. To create comprehensive ML-tools, a prolific amount of training and test data is needed. As shown in examples for different ML approaches by Can et al. (2014), Pappert and Rose (2021) and Zhang et al. (2018), simulation is a well-working approach to generate synthetic data to be used as training data. For large training sets, scalable simulation has the potential to provide this system-specific data in a timely manner, by distributing multiple simulation runs across different computing nodes.

Simultaneously, the increasing complexity of simulation models and the number of simulation experiments place significant demands on the simulation environment. As computational resources remain limited, the workload required for large-scale, complex simulations can restrict the feasibility of conducting these experiments efficiently. These constraints challenge the ability to scale simulation-based studies and, therefore, to provide timely decision support to users. Distributing simulation workload across multiple computation nodes enables a large number of simultaneously running simulation models, which helps to finish simulation tasks faster and thereby accelerates timely decision-making.

Speeding up simulation experiments has been an active field of research since the 1970s (Taylor 2019). As Lechler et al. (2021) stated, distributing simulation workload onto multiple compute nodes efficiently addresses the increased need for resources. The ongoing trend of cloud computing, virtualization, and containerization offers an exciting opportunity to efficiently provide computing resources and create a scalable simulation framework. The research in this field is diverse and growing. Król et al. (2013) developed their own framework, Scalarm, to bring simulation workloads into a distributed and heterogeneous environment. In more recent work, Anagnostou et al. (2019) evaluated a microservice- and deadline-based simulation approach utilizing the MiCADO framework. MiCADO focuses on efficiently utilizing cloud resources. It extends Kubernetes' Application Programming Interface (API) objects with its own Application Description Templates (https://micado-scale.github.io/adt/ accessed 28 October 2024), making it less universal. Großmann et al. (2024) show how they distribute simulation workload on a Raspberry Pi cluster using KNIME and Kubernetes.

Although the research shows the benefits of scalable and distributed simulation environments, no significant uptick in adopting these methods is visible in the broader simulation community, neither from the practitioner nor the software developer side. We attribute this to the perceived steep learning curve of using containers and container management. Although some simulators support the distribution of simulation workloads across cloud or on-premise infrastructures, their applicability is significantly limited. This can have various reasons, e.g., restrictive licensing models or enforcing the usage of special cloud infrastructures. This restricts integrating massiv amounts of simulation into a larger decision-support system. To approach this, we discussed the characteristics required of simulation software to be easy to scale in (Seufferth et al. 2023) and discussed the use of container orchestration as a means to easily distribute simulation workloads on different infrastructures from grid computing to purpose build simulation clusters in Seufferth et al. (2024).

Building on our previous work (see (Seufferth et al. 2023), (Pappert et al. 2024), and (Seufferth et al. 2024)), this paper focuses more on how scenarios get processed in the *Scenario Manager* (*SM*) and, thus, how the *SM* itself works and interacts with the remaining components of our concept. The concept presented here aims at distributing multiple simulation runs over hardware resources and does not focus on the challenges of distributed models. These difficulties should be addressed by the simulation software, which in turn can be deployed as containers within the discussed infrastructure. For this, we structure the paper as follows: First, we give an introduction to the core technology utilized by our concept: containerization and container orchestration. Next, we provide an overview of our concept for a container-based simulation environment. Following this, we explain the terms project, scenario, and replication in the context of our projects and the different states a scenario can be in. We close the paper with a brief summary and an outlook of our future research.

2 INTRODUCTION TO CONTAINERIZATION AND CONTAINER ORCHESTRATION

Container technology is a type of operating system virtualization that isolates a part from the underlying host Operating System (OS) for the process of the software packaged in the container. In contrast to a Virtual Machine (VM), containers utilize this isolated part of the OS and directly access the host computer's hardware.

Containers are commonly created using a container image using a specific software called a container engine. There are several different container engines that all follow a similar approach during image creation, utilizing a descriptive file that defines all steps necessary to containerize a software package. As a generalization, we call this file the containerization file. It typically defines the base image and the more specific parts of the container built atop.

As highly portable software packages, containers are can run on various hardware configurations, from edge devices to office PCs and full-scale server computers with high Central Processing Unit (CPU) count. Container orchestrators are used to manage large amounts of containers. They are, therefore, a vital component for highly scalable simulation environments, where they handle large numbers of simultaneously running simulator instances.

There are several different container orchestrators; one of the most prominent ones is Kubernetes, with which Google launches about 4 billion containers per week (https://cloud.google.com/blog/products/containers-kubernetes/why-choose-gke-as-your-kubernetes-service accessed 6 April 2024). More information on containers and Kubernetes can be found in Hitchcock (2022), Huawei Technologies Co. Ltd. (2023), and Poulton and Joglekar (2022).

Utilizing containers for Discret Event Simulation (DES) has two effects: first, providing a Simulation-as-a-Service platform for distributing large numbers of simulation runs across a bigger calculation infrastructure, as we discuss in this paper. A second effect is also the possibility to provide auxiliary capabilities to the simulation model with the help of microservices, which eases modeling and may be an essential approach for larger distributed simulation models. As an example, in a combat simulation, information regarding weapon effect, the terrain of the operation or possible weather conditions could be provided as independent services, with which the simulator communicates. This approach allows for modular simulation models and takes complexity away from the basic model and distributes it to external services. In the context of battle simulation, this is an important requirement for connecting multiple simulation models into a larger shared simulation as these shared services allow for defining a shared global ground truth across all model parts an therefore provides fair simulation conditions.

3 CONTAINER-BASED SIMULATION ENVIRONMENT

Figure 1 visualizes our architecture, which consists of five major components, all designed as service-based applications. The *Design of Experiment Service* (*DoES*) is the main entry point to the simulation environment. It combines multiple important tasks in one comprehensive software: in the *DoES* the complete configuration of the simulation experiment is situated. For methodologies utilizing dynamically generating new scenarios as solution candidates like SBO, the *DoES* provides the optimization algorithms, which create new solution candidates and add them to the *Scenario Detail Database*. The *SM* is the management component of the concept and is responsible for the four auxilliary databases and the creation of other components. With the experiment definition configured by the *DoES*, the *SM* deploys and initializes the *Scenario Detail Database* and *Result Database* based on the provided database schemes, creates entries for the *Scenario Status Database* and adds the project to the *Project Database*. In addition, the *SM* starts the *Translators* and *Simulation Runners* (*Runners*). The *Translator* is responsible for providing executable simulation models for each scenario in the form of container images stored in a *Container Image Repository*. Depending on the complexity of the simulation project and model, the *Translator* may create full container images for each individual scenario or create a base image to be parameterized with scenario specific parameters later on when initializing the *Runners*. This streamlines the creation process of the *Runners*, which are solely managed by the *SMs*. The *Runners* execute the containerized simulation model with the settings required for each scenario of the project. After execution, they report their results to the *Result Database*. Finally, the *PostProcessingService* (*PPS*) is responsible for aggregating and assessing the results of the finished *Runners*.

DoES, *Translator*, *PPS*, *Runner*, *Scenario Detail Database*, and *Result Database* are project-specific components which have to be individually built and tailored to the requirements of the simulation project. This separation is also indicated in the colour scheme of Figure 1, with the project-specific components coloured blue and the project-agnostic components coloured yellow.

3.1 Design of Experiment Service

As mentioned above, the *DoES* represents the scenario-creating element of our simulation-environment. Depending on the project needs, it only provides a prepared set of scenario data or acts as a fully-fledged experimental design tool, allowing various popular experimentation methods, e.g., parameter variation, factorial design, etc. In addition, the *DoES* also sets necessary meta-data for the *SM*, e.g., providing database schemes, information regarding hardware resources, the *Translator* to be used for the project, or the initial number of replications for each scenario. Moreover, the *DoES* implements optimization algorithms and automatically creates new solution candidates during simulation execution. It is, therefore, the interface to the remaining part of the environment and necessary to configure and start simulation workloads.

3.2 Scenario Manager

The *SM* is the central management component of our system. It keeps track of the status of all scenarios on the platform, which we describe in detail in Section 4. After configuring a simulation project via

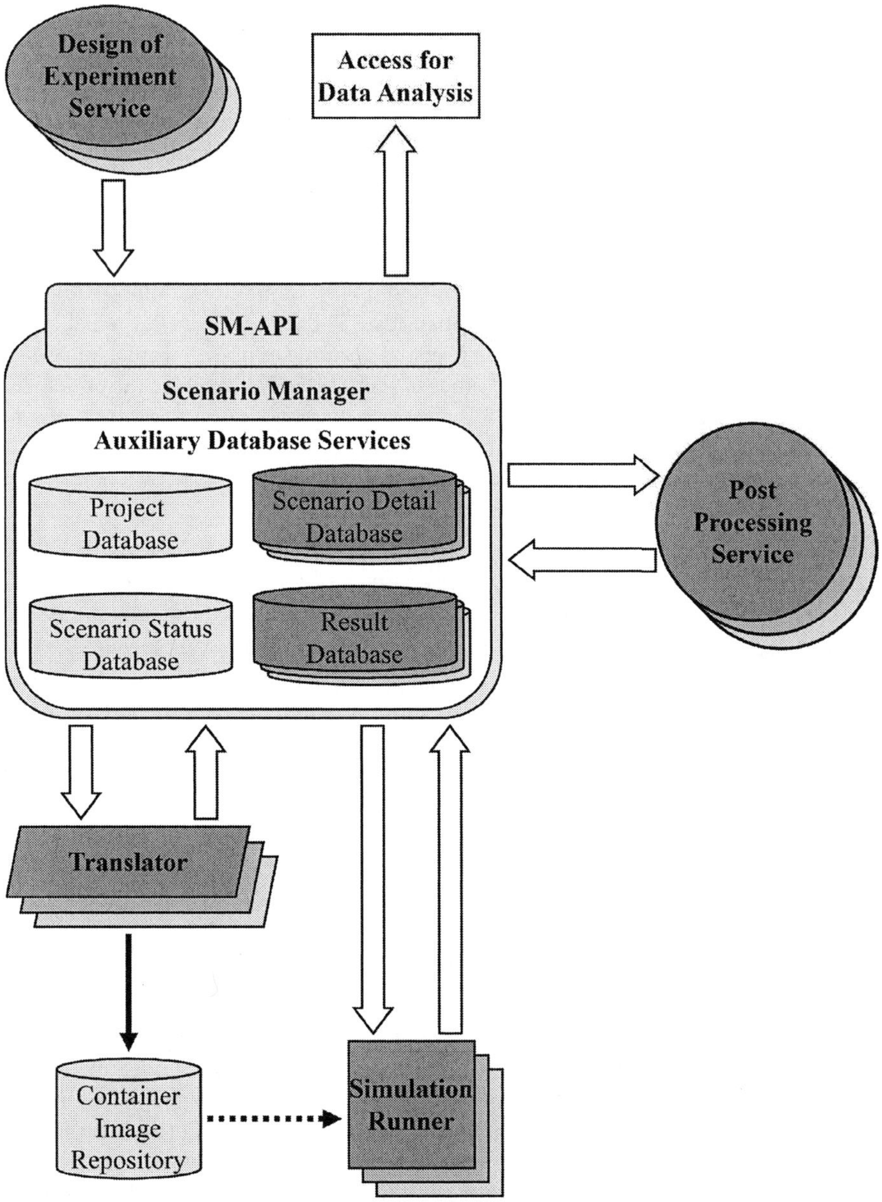

Figure 1: Concept of a container-based simulation environment, consisting of five main components: *Design of Experiment Service* (*DoES*), *Scenario Manager* (*SM*), *Translator*, *Simulation Runner* (*SR*), and *PostProcessingService* (*PPS*).

DoES, the *SM* is responsible for creating a project entry in the *Project Database*, adding the new scenarios to the *Scenario Status Database*, and starting the remaining two auxiliary databases for this project and filling them with data provided by *DoES*. When the *SM* schedules a scenario, a chain of processes is started, leading to the starting of *Translators*, *Runner*s and *PPS*s. Therefore, the *SM* not only manages the execution of scenarios and its data but also the starting of the remaining three components. The *SM* allows for easy access to simulation result data for external data analysis via an API.

3.3 Translator

The *Translators* are started by the *SM* when scheduling a scenario. Depending on the complexity of the simulation project, the scenario data stored in the *scenario detail database* can consist of simple parameters or very complex descriptions with which the *Translators* have to generate executable simulation models. Depending on the complexity of the model, the *Translator* either creates a base image that can be parameterized and used for several scenarios or creates a scenario-specific simulation model. In both cases, the resulting model is containerized and provided as a container image to be later used to create the *Runners* executing the simulation model. These container images are stored in a *Container Image Repository*.

3.4 Simulation Runner

The *Runners* are the executing component and are based on the simulation container images created by the *Translator* wrapped inside a Kubernetes Pod manifest. The *Runners* are responsible for executing the simulation model and writing the result data in the *Result Database*. Finished *Runners* will be deleted. A significant concern with *Runners* is process stability and, therefore, the ephemeral nature of Pods. This is addressed in Seufferth et al. (2023), where we discussed simulation software requirements to enable a beneficial use in such environments.

3.5 PostProcessingService

The *PPS* is utilized after all currently planned replications of a scenario have been completed and their results have been written by the *Runners* to the *Result Database*. The component fulfils two main purposes. First, it allows us to calculate aggregated Key Performance Indicators (KPIs) based on performed simulation runs, thereby providing the overall results for a given scenario.

Another important aspect of post processing is result quality assurance. As we typically run stochastic simulation runs, predetermining the number of replications required to reach a desired confidence before starting simulations is difficult. To this end, Law and Kelton (2004) proposed an iterative approach to solve this issue. Instead of predetermining the number of replications before starting, a small number of replications is used as a starting point. After these few replications have concluded, the result quality is calculated, and if not within the desired range, another set of replications is triggered. This is repeated until a sufficient result quality is achieved. We, therefore, allow the *PPS* to adapt the required number of simulation runs for a scenario, leading to the start of additional *Runners* and thereby increasing the sample size.

4 SCENARIO STATES

In our concept, we use the terms project, scenario, and replication. All three have a specific meaning in the context of our container-based simulation architecture, which we will describe in the following. A project is a collection of scenarios and additional information for one specific research or business purpose. Each project is independent, meaning there is no communication between projects. A scenario is one distinct configuration of the simulated system. Figure 2 shows two scenarios of a simplified model of a manufacturing system discussed by Law and McComas (2002) with one workstation and one buffer. The first scenario is operating the workstations with three machines and has two buffer

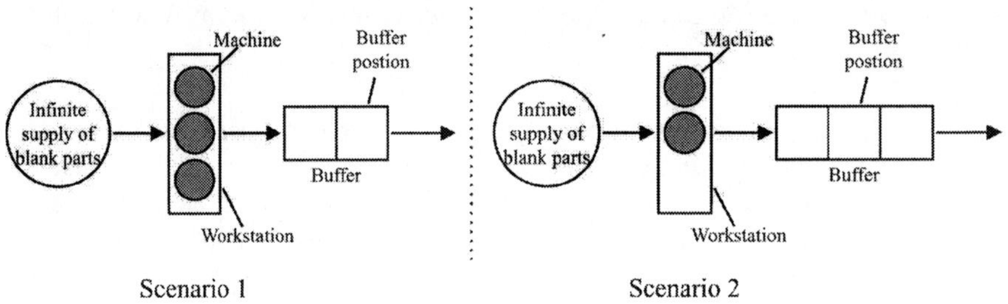

Figure 2: A scenario is a distinct configuration of the modeled system (example inspired by Law and McComas (2002)).

positions, while the second scenario operates the same workstation with only two machines and has three positions in its buffer. Additional scenarios might add more workstations and buffers or completely new objects. Scenarios can be generated at the project start or during project execution, as is common in SBO when generating new solution candidates. The last term we have to define is replication. A common practice is to simulate the specific scenario multiple times to determine the behaviour of a scenario with confidence, depending on the targeted confidence intervals. Therefore, each distinct simulation run of one scenario is called a replication of this scenario.

To simplify the management of scenarios, we define six possible states they can be in:

- CREATED: This is the initial state of every scenario. At the beginning of an experiment, every scenario of the project is in this state.
- SCHEDULED: The scenario is selected for execution, and all prerequisite tasks are initiated.
- STARTING RUNNERS: The execution of the scenario started, yet the number of started *Runners* is not equal to the required amount of scenario replications.
- IN PROCESSING: The number of started *Runners* is equal to the demanded number of replications for this scenario. The count of running *Runners* is either equal or smaller than the number of replications.
- POSTPROCESSING: The results of the *Runners* are undergoing aggregation and evaluation by the *PPS*. In this state, no *Runners* are active.
- FINISHED: The scenario is completed, and its results are available with sufficient stochastic confidence.

Figure 3 visualizes the life cycle of a scenario in the context of our concept. A scenario is typically created by the *DoES* and starts in the CREATED state. This state is mainly for initialization and setup. During this state, the required entries in the databases are created, and the scenarios defining parameters are set. Once the scenario setup is finished, it transitions to the SCHEDULED state and awaits the computing resources being assigned to it. Depending on the system load and its priority, the scenario may idle in this state for some time. As soon as computing resources are available, a container image for the execution of the scenarios replications is generated with the *Translator's* help and stored within the *Container Image Repository*. With the container image created, the scenario transitions to the STARTING RUNNERS state. In this state, the *Runners* are instantiated and started, performing one replication of the scenario each. Once all demanded replications are started, the scenario transitions to the IN PROCESSING state. While in this state, no further action is required from the *SM*, as IN PROCESSING is primarily a state in which the completion of the *Runner* is awaited. As soon as all currently demanded replications have been completed, the scenario transitions to the POSTPROCESSING state. During this state, simulation results are aggregated to KPIs, providing the information desired from the scenario's execution. A second but not less important aspect of POSTPROCESSING is the evaluation of the results with regard to their significance. Suppose the number of replications performed does not provide sufficient sample data to achieve the intended confidence. In that case, additional replications may be requested, transitioning the scenario back to the STARTING RUNNERS state. If the result quality is acceptable, the scenario transitions to the FINISHED state, indicating the completion of this scenario's calculation.

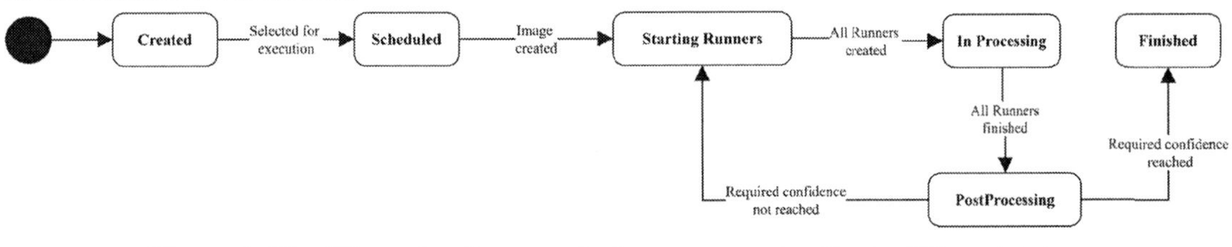

Figure 3: The life cycle of a scenario in our concept with six different states.

5 SUMMARY AND OUTLOOK

This paper described the components of a distributed and scalable simulation environment designed to support large-scale, resource-intensive workloads. We briefly introduced the core concept of containerization and container orchestration. Then, we described the terms project, scenario and replication in the context of our project and the different states a scenario can be in. Lastly, we gave a concise outline of our project as a whole and presented the five main components of it in detail. This concept is the foundation for a portable, distributed and scalable simulation platform. In future research, we will fine-tune our concept and naturally implement our thoughts in a usable simulation framework that utilizes Kubernetes. Moreover, we want to focus more on essential components in future work, e.g., the *DoES*.

REFERENCES

Anagnostou, A., S. J. E. Taylor, N. T. Abubakar, T. Kiss, J. DesLauriers, G. Gesmier, G. Terstyanszky, P. Kacsuk, and J. Kovacs. 2019, January. "Towards a Deadline-Based Simulation Experimentation Framework Using Micro-Services Auto-Scaling Approach". In *2019 Winter Simulation Conference (WSC)*, edited by Navonil Mustafee, Ki-Hwan G. Bae, Sanja Lazarova-Molnar, Markus Rabe, C. Szabo, Peter Haas, and Young-Jun Son, 2749–2758. Piscataway, New Jersey: Institute of Electrical and Electronics Engineers, Inc.

Can, B., C. Heavey, and K. E. Kabak. 2014, December. "Generating Operating Curves in Complex Systems Using Machine Learning". In *Proceedings of the Winter Simulation Conference 2014*, 2404–2413.

Fowler, J., S. E. Sawah, and H. H. Turan. 2023, January. "Recent Advances in Simulation-Based Optimization for Operations Research Problems". *Annals of Operations Research* 320 (2): 545–546.

Großmann, M., M. Leißau, and C. Laroque. 2024. "Entwicklung Einer Verteilten Simulationinfrastruktur Auf Einem Raspberry Pi-Cluster Mit Kubernetes Und KNIME". In *ASIM SST 2024 Tagungsband Kurzbeiträge*, 13–16. Wien: ARGESIM Verlag.

Hitchcock, K. 2022, January. "Containers". In *Linux System Administration for the 2020s*, 155–200. Berkeley, CA: Apress.

Huawei Technologies Co. Ltd., n. 2023, January. "Container Technology". In *Cloud Computing Technology*, 295–342. Springer, Singapore.

Król, D., M. Wrzeszcz, B. Kryza, Ł. Dutka, and J. Kitowski. 2013, January. "Massively Scalable Platform for Data Farming Supporting Heterogeneous Infrastructure". In *The 4th International Conference on Cloud Computing, Grids, and Virtualization: (Cloud Computing 2013) ; Valencia, Spain, 27 May - 1 June 2013 ; Held at ComputationWorld 2013*, edited by W. Zimmermann, 144–149. Wilmington: IARIA.

Law, A., and M. McComas. 2002, December. "Simulation-Based Optimization". In *Proceedings of the 2002 Winter Simulation Conference*, Volume 1, 41–44 vol.1. Piscataway, New Jersey: Institute of Electrical and Electronics Engineers, Inc.

Law, A. M., and W. D. Kelton. 2004. *Simulation Modeling and Analysis*. 3. ed., internat. ed. ed. McGraw-Hill Series in Industrial Engineering Und Management Science. Boston: McGraw-Hill.

Lechler, T., M. Sjarov, and J. Franke. 2021, January. "Data Farming in Production Systems - A Review on Potentials, Challenges and Exemplary Applications". *Procedia CIRP* 96:230–235.

Lidberg, S., T. Aslam, L. Pehrsson, and A. H. C. Ng. 2020, December. "Optimizing Real-World Factory Flows Using Aggregated Discrete Event Simulation Modelling". *Flexible Services and Manufacturing Journal* 32 (4): 888–912.

Nguyen, A.-T., S. Reiter, and P. Rigo. 2014, January. "A Review on Simulation-Based Optimization Methods Applied to Building Performance Analysis". *Applied Energy* 113:1043–1058.

Nikolopoulou, A., and M. G. Ierapetritou. 2012, December. "Hybrid Simulation Based Optimization Approach for Supply Chain Management". *Computers & Chemical Engineering* 47:183–193.

Pappert, F. S., and O. Rose. 2021, January. "Reducing Response Time with Data Farming and Machine Learning". *SNE Simulation Notes Europe* 31 (2): 87–94.

Pappert, F. S., D. Seufferth, H. Stein, and O. Rose. 2024, February. "Using Kubernetes to Improve Data Farming Capabilities". In *Proceedings of the 2023 Winter Simulation Conference*, WSC '23, 2052–2063. Piscataway, New Jersey: Institute of Electrical and Electronics Engineers, Inc.

Poulton, N., and P. Joglekar. 2022, January. *The Kubernetes Book*. January 2022 ed. [United Kingdom]: Nigel Poulton.

Seufferth, D., F. S. Pappert, H. Stein, and O. Rose. 2024. "Container-Based Simulation: A Concept For Large-Scale Simulation Environments". In *ASIM SST 2024 Tagungsband Langbeiträge*, 151–158. Wien: ARGESIM Verlag.

Seufferth, D., H. Stein, F. Pappert, and O. Rose. 2023, September. "On the Usage of Container and Container Orchestrators as a Computational Infrastructure for Simulation Experiments". *20. ASIM Fachtagung Simulation in Produktion und Logistik 2023*:393–401.

Taylor, S. J. 2019, January. "Distributed Simulation: State-of-the-Art and Potential for Operational Research". *European Journal of Operational Research* 273 (1): 1–19.

Van Noorden, R., and J. M. Perkel. 2023, September. "AI and Science: What 1,600 Researchers Think". *Nature* 621 (7980): 672–675.
Bandiera_abtest: a Cg_type: News Feature Subject_term: Machine learning, Mathematics and computing, Technology, Computer science

Zhang, T., S. Xie, and O. Rose. 2018, December. "REAL-TIME BATCHING IN JOB SHOPS BASED ON SIMULATION AND REINFORCEMENT LEARNING". In *2018 Winter Simulation Conference (WSC)*, 3331–3339.

AUTHOR BIOGRAPHIES

DANIEL SEUFFERTH is research assistant and PhD student at University of the Bundeswehr Munich as a member of the scientific staff of Prof. Dr. Oliver Rose at the Chair of Modeling and Simulation. His focus is on the usage of virtualization and containerization for distributing simulation execution. He has received his M.Eng. degree in Mechanical Engineering from Coburg University of Applied Sciences and is a member of VDI. His email address is daniel.seufferth@unibw.de. ORCID: 0009-0000-2831-7761.

FALK STEFAN PAPPERT is a research assistant and PhD student at the Chair of Modeling and Simulation of the University of the Bundeswehr Munich. His focus is on using data farming to support the development of proxy models for production systems to be used in planning, and short term decision making. He is a member of GI. He has received his M.S. degree in Computer Science from Dresden University of Technology. His email address is falk.pappert@unibw.de. ORCID: 0009-0006-6541-3924.

OLIVER ROSE holds the Chair for Modeling and Simulation at the Department of Computer Science of the University of the Bundeswehr Munich, Germany. He received a M.S. degree in applied mathematics and a Ph.D. degree in computer science from Würzburg University, Germany. His research focuses on the operational modeling, analysis and material flow control of complex manufacturing facilities and supply chains. He is an experienced teacher of modeling and simulation, as well as the mathematical and practical background, and shares his experiences for example as a member of INFORMS Simulation Society, ASIM, and GI. His email address is oliver.rose@unibw.de. ORCID: 0000-0003-3365-1611.

Proceedings of the Operational Research Society Simulation Workshop 2025 (SW25)
M. Luis, A. Harper, T. Monks, N. Mustafee, eds.
https://doi.org/10.36819/SW25.023

THE SIMPLEST, BUT NO SIMPLER, AGENT-BASED MODEL

Charles M. Macal

Argonne National Laboratory
9700 South Cass Avenue, Lemont, IL 60439
USA
macal@anl.gov

ABSTRACT

In this paper, we describe what we believe to be the simplest agent-based model. More specifically we define the class of the simplest agent-based simulation model formulations, referred to as SABM. We describe the nine essential elements of agent-based simulation models in the class SABM and give an example of such a model. We find that the simplest ABM formulation provides a basis for a transparent, compact and elegant description of agent-based modeling. The design illustrates the essential characteristics of agent-based modelling as a field of research and application and facilitates the explanation of agent-based modeling. We hope that the simplest formulation demystifies agent-based modeling for those within the simulation community, as well as those new to the field such as researchers from other disciplines and application communities.

Keywords: agent-based model, simulation, model design, design patterns, conceptual modelling, model complexity, model simplicity

1 INTRODUCTION

Agent-based modeling has taken its place as an accepted simulation technique alongside discrete event simulation (DES), System Dynamics (SD), and Monte Carlo (MC) simulation. Many people have an intuitive understanding of what is meant by an agent-based model, and many continue to be drawn to do agent-based modeling, recognizing the well-known benefits that ABM can provide. Many come to ABM from non-traditional modeling disciplines, such as social sciences, ecology, economics, transportation and supply chains, to name a few, and are often not formally trained in traditional modeling and simulation techniques. ABM has the potential to truly be an accepted scientific method of creating new knowledge, supporting real-time business decision-making for a wide range of business functions, and supporting policy makers in ways that other simulation techniques have not been able to realize.

Nonetheless many barriers stand in the way of adopting ABM and limit ABM from realizing its full promise. The perceptions that ABM is too complex, takes too long to implement, is too data intensive, takes too long to learn, is too difficult to model behavior, is too opaque of an approach to be useful, does not add value over existing modeling techniques, or is not a rigorous enough approach are just a few objections that are routinely voiced. Work on ABM has begun to address some of these issues, but there is much work to do until the field can advance to reach its full potential. There is a need for a rigorous and constructive description of ABM's essential features, in the simplest possible form, so that ABM can be understood by the widest possible audience.

This paper attempts to simplify and demystify agent-based modeling. The paper explains and describes the essential elements of ABM, focusing on ABM design and eschewing the additional complications associated with ABM implementation. Nonetheless, the results presented here also have direct implications for providing a simple path for implementing ABMs and is a foundation for how the simplest ABM form may systematically be made more complex, and possibly more realistic, by adding key elements of simulation modeling.

Many agent-based modelers are self-taught by attending on-line courses, reading key publications (Wilensky and Rand, 2015; Railsback and Grimm, 2013; Epstein and Axtell, 1996, Borshchev, 2013), and adopting an agent-based modeling toolkit of choice (e.g., NetLogo, Repast, AnyLogic, MASON, Mesa, etc.). ABM toolkits provide structure and capabilities common to all agent-based models, such as agent representation, agent-interaction scheduling, data input and output formatting, etc. (Macal and North, 2010). Often, the purpose of a toolkit is for the user to avoid programming in a particular computer language that they may not know. Yet, each toolkit requires learning its own language based on the programming paradigm on which it is based. For example, NetLogo is based on the Logo turtle-patch paradigm, and has a set of language constructs (essentially functions) to apply in building an ABM. Many other ABM toolkits are based on the class-method paradigm of object-oriented programming and provide agent-specific class extensions as a foundation to implement specific models. Thousands of people have successfully learned to do ABM by following the instructions and examples that come with an established ABM toolkit.

However, learning ABM through the examples provided by an ABM toolkit may obscure the essential features of what an agent-based model actual is as well as the purpose of agent-based modeling. This creates a gap for many in terms of a deep understanding of ABM in the broader context of the simulation and modelling knowledge corpus, as well as a gap in understanding of simulation and modeling good practice (Oren et al, 2023).

In this paper, we focus on the design part of the agent-based modeling process to express a general and simple representation that applies to all agent-based models. Separation of design from implementation is one of the foundational principles of modern software engineering and this principle is directly applicable to modelling. The goal is to make the modeling process simpler by reducing the complexity of interactions across the modeling process. Model designs can be expressed separately and in advance of model implementation (coding). A documented model design can be handed over to a coder who proceeds to implement the model with minimal interaction with the model designer . We propose here the simplest design representation for an agent-based model that captures the essential and defining features of any agent-based model.

This paper is organized as follows. We discuss design principles of simplicity and minimalism in Section 2. We describe the simplest agent-based model design or form that applies to the entire class of agent-based models, referred to as the simplest agent-based model, SABM. We state the essential characteristics of SABM in Section 3. We give a concrete example of a model in the class SABM in Section 4.

2 SIMPLICITY IN MODELING

2.1 Simplicity in Design

What do we know about simplicity in modeling? And how do we measure model simplicity? Modeling is the process of translating what we see in the world around us into a systematic and widely understandable representation or form that can be communicated effectively and unambiguously to model stakeholders. There is a natural distinction between model design and model implementation, just as in software engineering. Design is the creative modeling process (often referred to as the "art of modeling") and the implementation (coding) is the engineering, (building) part of the modeling process. A good model design is a standalone entity that can be easily documented, communicated and understood. Ideally, a good model design can be implemented in computer code with minimal interaction between coders and model designers. This is akin to an architect creating the design for a house with a blueprint that is turned over to a builder for construction.

A natural part of design is simplicity or minimalism in which only the necessary and essential features are included in the model design. According to the Oxford English Dictionary simplification is "the action, process, or result of making something less complex or elaborate, or of becoming less complex," and minimalism is "the practice of using the minimum means necessary to achieve a desired result, especially in literature, design, etc. (OED, 2024). Anecdotal notions of simplicity and minimalism abound and are widespread in contemporary society, in architecture, in art, in psychology, in Zen, as well as in simulation modeling. Effectively, the goal of good modeling is to create models that are as "simple as possible, but no simpler" (Einstein, 2010) than is necessary to serve their intended purpose and credibly answer the questions for which they were designed.

2.2 Simplicity in Simulation

Robinson and Brooks (2024) survey the definitions and aspects of simplification for discrete-event simulation models. Many definitions, as well as metrics, related to model simplification have been proposed (Birta and Arbez, 2013; Innis and Rexstad, 1983; Maile et al., 2010; Robinson, 2008; van der Zee et al., 2018; Ward, 1989). Paraphrasing the benefits of model simplification in this literature: "simpler is shorter, simpler is more efficient, simpler improves transparency, simpler is easier to understand, simpler enables more rapid model development, simpler enables easier and more rapid use, simpler can reduce the cost of a simulation study, etc.," while recognizing there can sometimes be tradeoffs among these factors.

In agent-based modeling, simplicity and minimalism are also regarded as desirable features. Sun et al (2016) address simplicity, complexity, and complicatedness for all aspects of agent-based modeling. Grimm et al (2020) present the ODD protocol, a standard for describing ABMs and their implementation. For the most part, these are the same treatments as one would have for any modeled system.

Simplicity and smallness are not the same but are related concepts. A small model often connotes a model of limited extent that can be explained easily. For example, Brailsford's notion of a small model is "a model is small if you can describe it within 15 minutes." (Brailsford, 2024). A simple model may be small or large. For example, an ABM that is simple in form and structure, with few operations but that has millions of simply structured agents could be regarded as a simple ABM. This is illustrated by the example in Section 4.

Overall, the literature does not suggest a ready-made metric for model simplicity. In this paper we take an informal simplicity metric as being the number of defining concepts for an ABM. The simplest ABM is then an ABM that is defined by the fewest essential concepts, which are stated in the next section.

3 THE SIMPLEST AGENT-BASED MODEL FORM

In this section, we discuss the basic constructs, concepts, essential elements, and paradigms common to any agent-based model and formally define these notions in mathematical notation. In practice, there is not a standard, agreed-upon formal definition of an agent-based model. Individual-based model (IBM) and multi-agent systems (MAS) are terms that are also used in various modeling communities, but for all practical purposes, these are the same as ABM (Railsback and Grimm 2013). Next, we precisely define an agent-based model.

3.1 Agent-Based Model

There is widespread agreement on at least four key elements of an agent-based model (Macal, 2016), with the caveat noted below:

1. A set of *agents,* their attributes and behaviours. Agents have individual states and behaviours update agent states. Behaviors extend to individual agents as well as to groups of interacting agents. Agents are defined in an ABM depending on the model purpose and the questions the model is designed to answer as an *in silico* experimental platform. An agent may be any natural or designed entity having autonomous or semi-autonomous behaviors.
2. *Agent interactions* and a set of relationships and methods for agents to interact. A defining characteristic of agent-based modeling is that agents interact with each other. At least one agent interacts with at least one other agent at some step in the simulation. An underlying topology of connectedness defines who the agents interact with. Agent interactions can be described by simple sets or by networks.
3. The agents' *environment*: The environment consists of everything in the modeled system besides the agents. Agents interact with their environment in addition to interacting with other agents.

4. A simulation mechanism for stepping the model forward by animating the agent interactions and managing updates to the agent states and the environment.

Everything in an agent-based model (variables, parameters, data) is associated with one of these items above (Macal and North, 2005). An exception to these defining elements of an agent-based model worth noting concerns the second element—agent interactions. Many useful agent-based models have been published that do not have agent interaction. In these models, the emphasis is on modeling agent behaviors and the heterogeneity of the agent attributes and behaviors across the entire population. The lack of agent interaction makes these models much easier to solve, especially through distributed computation. ABMs without agent interaction can be considered a special, even simpler, case of the ABM form presented here.

Effectively, an agent-based model works by simulating the dynamic state of each agent as it changes over time due to its own behaviors and interactions with other agents and the environment.

In the most general case of an agent-based model, the following conditions are present:

1. *Limited Interactions:* An agent may interact at a particular time or within a time period with any other agents in its common social interaction group, often referred to as the agent's neighbors. An agent's *neighborhood* and is often represented as a *social network*. Groups are limited in scope-- any agent only interacts with a limited number of other agents at any time.
2. *Exogenous and Endogenous Group Formation:* The size, composition, and number of interaction groups may change over time. Agent social interaction groups may be constant over the simulation—i.e., be exogenously specified--or may change during the simulation based on conditions in the simulation -- i.e., endogenously emerge.
3. *Agent Population*: The agent population may change over the simulation as agents are created (born) and destroyed (die).

3.2 ABM Formalism

In this section, we formalize the essential elements of an ABM as described above. We take an object-oriented approach with references to class, attributes for members of a class, methods that operate on classes, and instances of specific members of a class. The nine key elements of any ABM consist of 6 entities, items 1-6 below, and 3 methods, items 7-9 below, that operate on the entities (Figure 1 shows an entity-relationship diagram relating these concepts):

1. environment
2. agents
3. agent
4. groups
5. group
6. model
7. create
8. update
9. simulate

The *environment* is a list of one or more environmental attributes and a set of methods that operates on the environment. The agent population, *agents*, is built upon the environment. Without loss of generality, we assume there is a single environment. For an ABM in which there are multiple environments, such as land, atmosphere, hydrological layer, etc., *environment* would represent a composite or a superclass of these many environments (note, # denotes "number of"):

$$\text{environment} = [\text{attE}_{[i]}, \text{metE}_{[j]}] \text{ for } i = 1, \ldots, \#\text{ attributes}, j = 1, \ldots, \#\text{ methods}. \quad (1)$$

agents is a list of one or more agents:

$$\text{agents} = [\text{agent}_{i}\,..] \text{ for } i = 1, \ldots, \#\text{ agents}. \quad (2)$$

An *agent* is a list of one or more attributes associated with the agents and a set of methods (agent behaviors):

agent$_i$ = [attA$_{\{i\}}$, behA$_{\{j\}}$] for i =1,…, # agent attributes, j =1,…, # agent behaviors. (3)

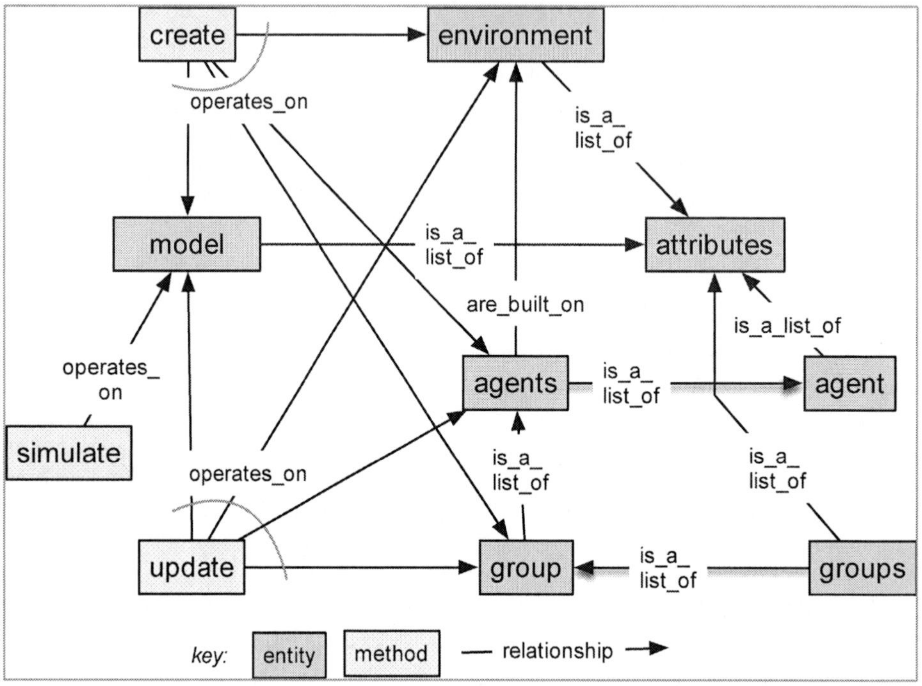

Figure 1 Entity Relationship Diagram for the Simplest Agent-Based Model

The *groups* are a list of one or more groups.

groups = [group$_i$,..] for i =1,…, # groups. (4)

A *group* is a list of one or more agents:

group$_i$ = [agent$_j$,..]   for j =1,…, # agents in group i. (5)

A *model* is a list of attributes which are model parameters that control the simulation.

model = [attM$_{\{i\}}$, metM$_{\{j\}}$] for i =1,…, # attributes, j =1,…, # methods. (6)

For example, key attributes of *model* are *step* and *log*. A *step* is an index for labeling and tracking agent interactions. For example, in a discrete time model, *step* may represent a discrete time point, t. At step t, we record essential information of the ABM at time t in a log.

step = t (7)

A *log* is a list of information extracted from the simulation at step t:

log = [attL$_j$,..] for j =1,…, # steps in the simulation. (8)

There are 3 key methods applied to the entities (1)-(6): *create*, *update*, and *simulate*. *create* creates the entities environment, agents, groups and model to initialize the simulation. *update* updates the entities environment, agents, groups and model at each step of the simulation. *simulate* updates the state of the simulation at each step by updating the agents, groups, and the environment, as well as the model itself.

The nine concepts above (1)-(9) comprise the simplest representation for a general ABM that captures its essential elements. We term (1)-(9) as the *simplest ABM form* or design, and the class of such models as denoted *SABM*. Figure 2 shows how these concepts are related to operationalize the most general form for an agent-based model. In Section 4 we give an example of a useful but minimal model in the class SABM.

4 A SIMPLEST ABM EXAMPLE

4.1 SIR ABM Model Description

In this section we present an example of one of the simplest, but useful, models in the minimalist ABM form described above. The SIR compartmental model, a differential equation model often set up as a system dynamics simulation, is widely used in the field of epidemiology for modeling the dynamics of infectious diseases and predicting possible disease spread through a population (Dhar 2020). The SIR model and its more complex variants was the basis for epidemiological models forecasting the spread of the CoV-2 virus in the recent COVID-19 Pandemic.

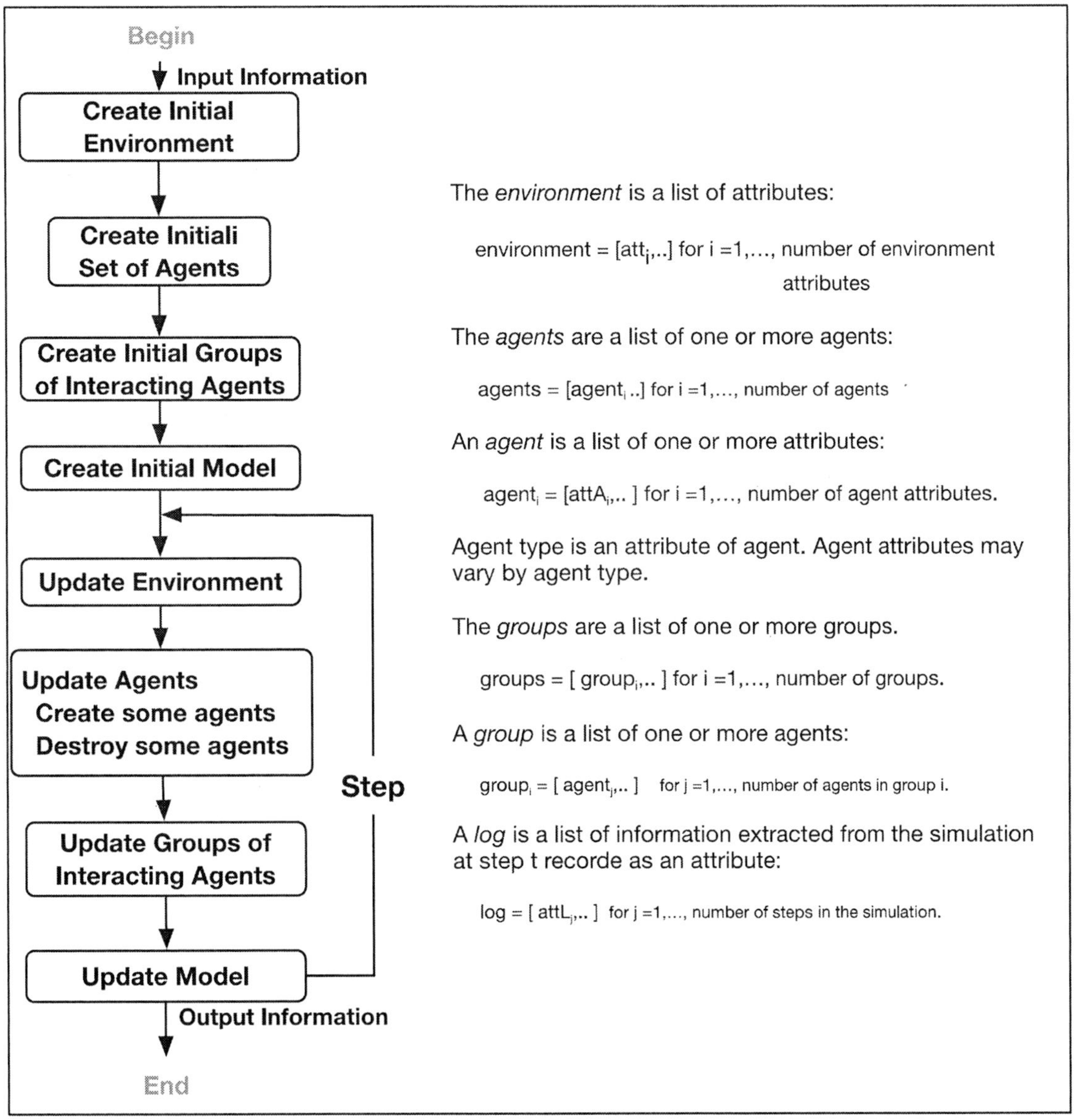

Figure 2 The Simplest Agent-Based Model Form, SABM

The SIR model considers three population segments: susceptible (S), infected/infectious (I), and recovered (R). Any individual is in one of these three states at any time. As the disease spreads the numbers of individuals in each disease state varies as individuals move through the disease states in the order S, I, and R . Transitions between states are effectively modeled as: S => I (a portion of the susceptible population transitions to the infected state after contact with infected individual(s) in the population), and I => R (a portion of the infected population transitions to the recovered state after the disease runs its course in the individual. The duration for an individual in the I state is a model parameter implicitly assumed to be exponentially distributed. Typical use of the model is to initially set a single the population with one infected individual and the rest of the population as susceptible.

Here we formulate we formulate the simplest SIR ABM model by the 9 design concepts. The pseudocode for initializing and running the SIR ABM simulation is shown in Figure 3.

Pseudocode for SIR ABM:

```
environment = createEnvironment[probInfect, meanDurI]
agents = createAgents[nAgents, nIAgents]
model = {nSteps}
groupParameters = {groupType, beta}
simulate[groups,agents,environment]:
   simulationLog = Do[
     (
     groups = createGroupsOfAgents[groupParameters, step]
     agents = updateAgentsInGroups[environment, groups, step];
     environment = updateEnvironment[environment, agents, step];
     ),
     {step, nSteps}
  ]
```

Model Input (Model Parameters):

```
probInfect = 0.2
meanDurI = 3
nAgents = 2790344 (*$chicagoPopulation*)
nIAgents = 50000
nSteps = 21
groupParameters={"ConstantSize", contacts=10}
```

Model Output:

`simulationLog`: log of number of agents in each disease states for all steps of the simulation.

Methods (Functions):

`createEnvironment`: creates an environment that is simply a list of environmental parameters, `probInfect`, and `meanDurI`.

`createAgents`: creates a list of agents where an agent is reoresented by its disease state, e.g., "S","I", or "R".

`createGroupsOfAgents`: creates groups of interacting agents, e.g., groups = {{ "I", "S","S"}, { "S","S","S","S"}}.

`simulate`: runs the simulation for `nStep` steps, creating groups, updating agents, and updating the environment at each step (see above).

`updateAgentsInGroups`: updates the disease states of the agents in a group at step.

`updateEnvironment`: updates the environment, as necesary, at step.

Figure 3 Pseudocode for Simplest SIR ABM

We note a subtlety here, which leads to a further simplification. Since there is only one agent type, *agent*, an agent's state does not need to include the attribute agent type. The agent state simplifies to only its disease state. Further, no other agent attributes, such as a tag or identifier, is needed, because it is not necessary to access a specific agent to update the agent states *en masse*.

The pseudocode can be implemented directly in the computer language of choice. To complete the implementation, one would write the programs `createEnvironment`, `createAgents`, `createGroupsOfAgents`, `updateAgentsInGroups`, and `updateEnvironment`. Or, the model could be implemented based on the 9 basic ABM design concepts in an agent-based modeling toolkit.

4.1.1 SIR ABM Model Simulation Results

The results from a run of the simulation are shown in Figure 4. The SIR ABM simulation results are directly comparable to the form of the results from the basic SIR model (not shown here).

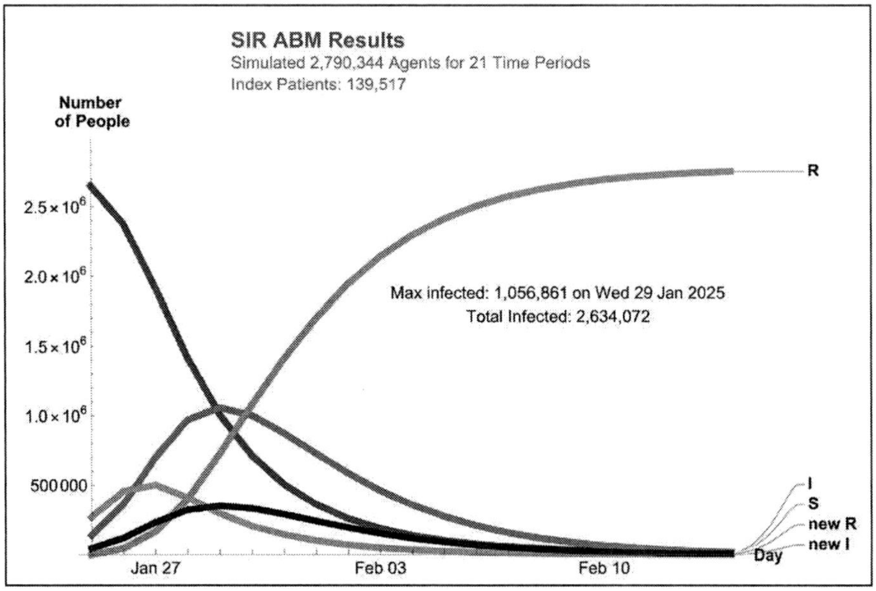

Figure 4 Results Simplest SIR ABM Simulation

5 SUMMARY AND CONCLUSIONS

We have shown how to formulate and design an agent-based model using the fewest number of constructs and termed the class of simplest agent-based models as SABM. We have provided an example of a System Dynamics model implemented in the SABM framework and argued that the framework applies to any agent-based model. Future work will show how the SABM framework can be used to model the broadest class of simulation and other kinds of models. Future work will provide a development pathway for increasing model complexity through incorporation of additional simulation modelling features such as stochasticity, events, and dynamic scheduling.

ACKNOWLEDGMENTS

This material is based upon work supported by the U.S. Department of Energy, Office of Science, under contract DE-AC02-06CH11357.

REFERENCES

Birta L G and Arbez G (2013). *Modelling and simulation: Exploring dynamic system behaviour* (2nd ed.). Springer-Verlag.

Borshchev A (2013). *The Big Book of Simulation Modeling: Multimethod Modeling with AnyLogic 6*. Oakbrook Terrace, IL USA, AnyLogic North America.

Brailsford S (2024). Titan Talk at the Winter Simulation Conference, December 16, 2024, Orlando, FL USA.

Dhar A (2020). *What one can learn from the SIR model*, Indian Academy of Sciences Conference Series (2020) 3:1, DOI: 10.29195/iascs.03.01.0016.

Einstein, A (2011). *The Ultimate Quotable Einstein*, Alice Calaprice, ed., Princeton, NJ:Princeton University Press.

Epstein J M and Axtell R (1996). *Growing artificial societies: Social science from the bottom up.* Washington D.C., Brookings Institution Press.

Grimm V, Railsback S F, Vincenot C E, Berger U, Gallagher C, Deangelis D L, Edmonds B, Ge J, Giske J, Groeneveld J, Johnston A S A, Milles A, Nabe-Nielsen J, Polhill J G, Radchuk V, Rohwäder M-S, Stillman R A, Thiele J C and Ayllón D (2020). The ODD Protocol for Describing Agent-Based and Other Simulation Models: A Second Update to Improve Clarity, Replication, and Structural Realism. *Journal Of Artificial Societies and Social Simulation* 23(2).

Innis G and Rexstad E (1983). Simulation model simplification techniques. *Simulation*, 41(1), 7–15. https://doi. org/10.1177/003754978304100101

Macal, C M (2016). Everything You Need to Know About Agent-based Modeling and Simulation, *Journal of Simulation*. 10: 144. doi:10.1057/jos.2016.7.

Macal, C M and North, M J (2010). Tutorial on Agent-Based Modelling and Simulation, *Journal of Simulation, Special Issue: Agent-Based Modelling* 4(3): 151–162 (Sept.).

Maile T, Fischer M, Haymaker J and Bazjanac V (2010). *Formalising approximations, assumptions, and simplifications to document limitations in building energy perfor- mance simulation.* Center for integrated facility engineering (CIFE). Working paper #WP126. Stanford University.

Oren T, Zeigler B P and Tolk A, (Eds.) (2023). *Body of Knowledge for Modeling and Simulation: A Handbook by the Society for Modeling and Simulation International.*

OED (Oxford English Dictionary Online) (2024). oed.com, Accessed 5 December 24.

Railsback, S F and Grimm V (2013). *Agent-based and Individual-based Modeling: A Practical Introduction.* Princeton NJ:Princeton University Press. http://www.railsback-grimm-abm-book.com/.

Robinson S and Brooks R (2024). Assumptions and simplifications in discrete-event simulation modelling, *Journal of Simulation*: 1-18.

Sun Z, Lorscheid I, Millington J D, Lauf S, Magliocca N R, Groeneveld J, Balbi S, Nolzen H, Müller B, Schulze J and Buchmann C M (2016). Simple or Complicated Agent-Based Models? A Complicated Issue. *Environmental Modelling Software* 86: 56-67.

van der Zee D-J, Tako A, Robinson S, Fishwick P and Rose O (2018). Panel: Education on simulation model simplification – beyond rules of thumb. In Rabe M, Juan A A, Mustafee N, Skoogh A, Jain S and Johansson B (Eds.), *Proc. 2018 Winter Simulation Conference* (pp. 3987–4001). IEEE, Piscataway, NJ.

Ward S C (1989). Arguments for constructively simple models. *The Journal of the Operational Research Society*, 40(2), 141–153. https://doi.org/10.1057/jors.1989.19

Wilensky U and Rand W (2015). *An Introduction to Agent-Based Modeling: Modeling Natural, Social, And Engineered Complex Systems With NETLOGO.* Cambridge, Massachusetts MIT Press.

AUTHOR BIOGRAPHY

CHARLES MACAL, Ph.D., is a senior systems engineer and distinguished fellow at Argonne National Laboratory, where he is group leader for Social and Behavioral Systems. He has authored and co-authored articles on agent-based model development methods and novel large-scale applications ranging from energy, environment, infrastructure, socio-technic systems and healthcare. He is a Fellow of the Society for Computer Simulation International (SCS). He holds a Ph.D. from Northwestern University, and Master's degree from Purdue, both in Industrial Engineering.

Proceedings of the Operational Research Society Simulation Workshop 2025 (SW25)
M. Luis, A. Harper, T. Monks and N. Mustafee, eds.
https://doi.org/10.36819/SW25.024

HIERARCHICAL HYBRID SIMULATION MODELING OF BACTERIAL DISEASE INFECTION

Mr. Avi Roy Chowdhury

Department of IEOR, IIT Bombay
Mumbai, India 400076
aviroychowdhury@iitb.ac.in

Dr. Jayendran Venkateswaran

Department of IEOR, IIT Bombay
Mumbai, India 400076
jayendran@iitb.ac.in

Dr. Om P Damani

Department of CSE, IIT Bombay
Mumbai, India 400076
damani@cse.iitb.ac.in

ABSTRACT

Modeling complex global health systems, such as infectious disease dynamics, requires balancing details with abstraction. A hybrid simulation approach combining System Dynamics (SD) and Agent-Based Modeling (ABM) to study bacterial infection spread at both individual(person) and community levels respectively is presented. SD model captures within-host(individual) dynamics, focusing on bacterial growth, immune responses, and antibiotic treatment. ABM introduces individual variability and interactions, enabling the simulation of infection spread among a population of agents(Community). This integrated framework connects within-host and population-level dynamics, providing a foundation for adding layers of complexity. By simulating different scenarios, the model offers insights into infection dynamics and strategies for managing bacterial infections and antibiotic resistance at the community level.

1. INTRODUCTION

Balancing abstraction and complexity in global health systems modeling is necessary to capture key dynamics without overwhelming the model. Too much complexity can make the model difficult to understand and computationally expensive, while too much abstraction risks losing important details. A balanced approach ensures the model remains both accurate and usable for decision-making. Hence modeling such complex health systems needs to combine several methods to get a useful result.

Several bacterial infections models in the literature describe the complex interaction between immunity and pathogens (Quintela et al. 2014), (Mayer et al. 1995), (Cantone et al. 2017), (Talaei et al. 2021). While many studies focus on the role of various immune cells in providing immunity, few address the issue of how a person becomes infected. Quintela et al. (2014) proposed a mixed PDE-ODE model to capture immunity dynamics. Their model illustrated how the innate immune response reacts to bacterial load and highlighted the role of macrophages. They also showed how immunity cells from neighboring tissues migrate to the infection site to fight off infection. Building on this work, Talaei et al. (2021) expanded the model by incorporating additional assumptions to capture the complexity of the immune response. Their model included sensitivity analysis and parameter estimation using clinical data, combining cellular and cytokine responses for a more comprehensive understanding of immune behavior. Shi et al. (2015) explored both innate and adaptive immunity in their modeling and identified conditions leading to either recovery or organ dysfunction.

Cantone et al. (2017) reviewed different modeling approaches, such as compartmental, individual-based, and stochastic models, providing examples and discussing their limitations. They stressed the importance of hybrid models for accurately representing immune responses. In Mayer et al. (1995), a basic mathematical model was introduced to capture the interactions between the bacterial population and the immune response. Ibargüen-Mondragón et al. (2014) expanded on this by presenting the dynamics of the bacterial population in the presence of antibiotics. They divided the bacterial population into sensitive and resistant groups, demonstrating that the current antibiotic dosages recommended by the WHO can lead to resistance in the case of tuberculosis. Building on this, Daşbaşı and Öztürk (2016) incorporated the immune response into the model and obtained similar results. Despite the extensive literature exploring immune responses, there remains a lack of comprehensive system modeling approaches in the current body of research.

Hybrid simulation has recently been used for healthcare-related problems and gives insightful results. In hybrid simulation, different types of simulation techniques such as System dynamics (SD), Agent-based Modeling (ABM), and Discrete Event Simulation (DES), are combined. Each of these simulation techniques has its own strengths and limitations. Several hybrid simulation models capture different aspects of the healthcare sector, planning of resource allocation, pandemic response, etc. (Caudill and Lawson 2013) investigated patient-healthcare worker interactions in hospitals using a hybrid simulation model that combines intra-host and inter-host dynamics. Bacterial population dynamics within hosts were modeled using differential equations, while hosts were represented as heterogeneous agents. A Bacterial Population Vector (BPV) was introduced to track multiple bacterial populations with varying resistance profiles, updated via differential equations for computational efficiency, and agent-based modeling captured inter-agent interactions. Infection transmission was categorized into six types, influencing spread. Later, (Caudill and Lawson 2017) integrated immune response dynamics and included antibiotic treatment history to model the evolution of antibiotic resistance. In Bobashev et al. (2007), the authors combined two simulation techniques: Agent-Based Simulation and Equation-Based Modeling. This hybrid model was used to study the spread of disease on a global scale. By implementing a switching threshold policy, the model alternated between the simulation methods to gain computational efficiency without losing important micro-level details. Similarly, Zulkepli et al. (2012) developed a hybrid simulation framework that combined DES and SD to simulate an integrated care setup. In their model, DES was used to capture individual-level variables, while SD provided a more holistic view. The models were integrated sequentially: the output of the DES model fed into the SD model to continue the simulation. It captures the overall dynamics of an integrated care setup which is not possible for the single simulation approach. Elliott et al. (2020) created a hybrid simulation model combining agent-based and discrete-event approaches to study hospital ward dynamics, pathogen transmission, and outbreak management. Their model evaluated seven scenarios, including various timings of genome sequencing, and was calibrated to reflect real-world outcomes. The results indicated that early sequencing helped control outbreaks and reduce hospital costs.

Banerjee (2017) emphasized that pathogen spatial distribution and stochasticity significantly affect infection outcomes, especially during the early stages when rare immune cells must encounter specific antigens. They developed a stage-structured hybrid model, using ABMs in the early stages and transitioning to ODEs later. This method balances computational efficiency with complexity, offering insights into pathogen behavior and strategies for distributed systems inspired by immune responses. Djanatliev et al. (2012) combining System Dynamics (SD) and Agent-Based Modeling (ABM), are increasingly used in healthcare technology assessments. These models merge the benefits of SD for system-level behaviors and ABM for individual variability, enabling detailed simulations of complex healthcare innovations. The loosely coupled model structure allows for the integration of diverse healthcare scenarios, providing insights into the economic, demographic, and health outcomes before full-scale technology deployment. Finally, Kang et al. (2021) proposed a hybrid simulation model and simulation-based optimization to study the effects of social distancing policies on the COVID-19 epidemic.

In this paper, we propose a hybrid simulation approach to model within-host bacterial infection dynamics and investigate the emergence of infection in the community. We use SD-ABM together to investigate bacterial infection dynamics at both individual and population levels. An individual's bacterial dynamics are governed by an SD model (aggregate level). Each agent having its own SD model reflecting its bacterial dynamics. Agents possess unique physical and behavioral traits that influence their SD model, and their interactions drive population-level infection dynamics. ABM is used to address heterogeneity among individuals and to study the effects of their interactions. SD captures aggregate dynamics but struggles with heterogeneity, while ABM handles variability but is computationally expensive (Hunter and Kelleher 2022). By combining both, we overcome their limitations for a more realistic framework. We first explore individual infection dynamics under different scenarios, then extend the model to multi-agent infection spread.

2. PROBLEM STATEMENT

We investigate the role of the environment and individual interactions in the spread of antibiotic resistance. While viral and bacterial infections share similarities, their modeling differs. Viral models focus on intracellular replication, immune evasion, and burst-like growth, often requiring delay or discrete-time dynamics. Bacterial models emphasize population growth, immune responses, and antibiotic effects, typically using continuous-time models. Unlike viruses, which rely on host cells, bacteria reproduce independently, influencing transmission and treatment modeling.

For bacterial infection, it is important to consider the individual bacterial dynamics and then build the community-level model. A susceptible agent becomes infected if its bacterial population exceeds a threshold, driven by external factors like environmental contamination. Once infected, the immune response activates to fight the bacteria. If immunity can control the bacteria within a given time, the agent returns to a susceptible state. If not, the agent seeks treatment, where antibiotics reduce the bacterial load. If treatment is successful, the agent becomes susceptible again; otherwise, the agent may die if treatment fails or is delayed too long. Each individual has this dynamics and infected individuals come in contact with susceptible individuals and infect them with some probability. We also consider the environmental contamination.

In this paper, we present a robust framework designed to model bacterial infections. With appropriate parameter configurations, it can be adapted to represent specific diseases caused by particular pathogens (e.g., E. coli). This model effectively captures infection spread within a community, serving as a foundation for further exploration. In the future, we aim to refine it for specific pathogens by selecting suitable parameters. We can add the individual's behavior and the surrounding environment into the model to capture the real aspects of the spreading of infection. Also, we can add the healthcare setting into the model to observe the importance of quality treatment to treat the infected people efficiently. Food intake is a source of the pathway of the pathogens to enter the individual's body. Food preparation practices and hygiene level contribute to the infection. Many more components can be added to the model to capture the real infection dynamics at the community level.

3. SINGLE AGENT FRAMEWORK

In this paper, we use the SD-ABM framework for infection dynamics. For within-host bacterial infection dynamics, we consider the bacterial population, immunity cells, and antibiotics. If the bacterial population is greater than some threshold then we consider the administration of antibiotics. To capture the individual's behavior we use the Agent-based modeling (ABM) simulation to incorporate the micro-level details of the individual. The hybrid SD-ABM model is given in Figure 1.

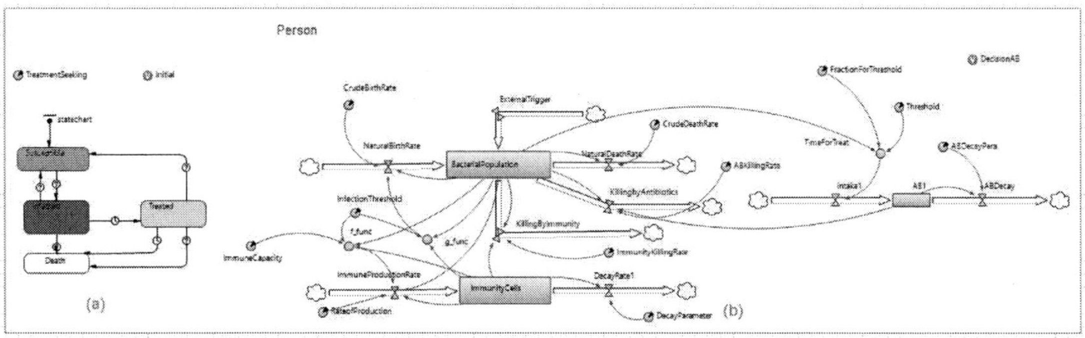

Figure 1: Single Agent Framework. Implemented in AnyLogic (a) State chart of individual agent (b) System Dynamics model of bacterial population

3.1. STATECHART REPRESENTATION OF BACTERIAL INFECTION

The agent-based model captures the individual aspects of the host. The model is based on the statechart model of Susceptible, Infected, Treated, Susceptible, and Death (SITSD), which can be seen in Figure 1(a). Every human's gut contains some amount of bacteria but the person becomes infected when due to some external triggers the bacterial load increases suddenly. Initially, the agent is in the susceptible state. A susceptible agent becomes infected in our model if its bacterial population exceeds the threshold (depending on *FractionForThreshold* and BacterialPopulation) assigned. Here, the bacterial population dynamics are governed by the SD model. The bacterial population in susceptible agent increases due to external influences like contaminated environment, contact with infected individuals, etc. We didn't mention the source of external triggers for single-agent setup.

Once the agent gets infected then the agent's immunity is also activated according to the bacterial load. Infected agent wait for some time before treatment. Meanwhile, two possible scenarios can occur. If immunity can suppress the increased bacterial population in the given time then the agent be cured and moved to susceptible state. Another case is when the immunity can't cure the infection within the tolerance time and the agent opts for the treatment. In this case, the agent moves to the treatment state. When the agent is in the treatment state then antibiotics are administered to decrease the bacterial load. If the treatment is effective then bacterial load decreases and the agent becomes susceptible again. it is possible that in some cases the treatment is not effective so the bacterial population growth can't be controlled in that scenario the agent dies (for single agent cases it is not considered), also for the case of prolonged treatment we consider the agent dies. Here, the *FractionForThreshold*, *TreatmentSeeking* and *ToleranceLevel* are the parameters. *FractionForThreshold* defines the threshold fraction for the infection, *TreatmentSeeking* is the waiting time before going to treatment and *ToleranceLevel* for the transition time from infection to death constrained to the excessive bacterial load.

3.2. SYSTEM DYNAMICS SUB-MODEL FOR BACTERIAL INFECTION

Each agent is associated with an SD model and it captures the infection dynamics. The model can be seen in Figure 1(b). The bacterial population stock captures the total bacteria within the host (e.g. E.Coli in the gut). The stock has two inflows and three outflows. The inflow (NaturalBirthRate) of the birth of the bacteria is assumed to be proportional to the bacterial population. The other inflow (ExternalTrigger) represents the bacterial intake from external sources and captures the scenario of getting another infection from the environment or an infected individual. There is a natural death rate (NaturalDeathRate) associated with the bacterial population. The other outflows of the bacteria population include the killing by immunity cells (killingbyImmunity) and the killing by antibiotics (killingbyAntibiotics).

In this model, the immune response is triggered by the presence of the bacterial population. The immune response is activated in the presence of the bacteria. The killing rate by immunity is a function of the immune cell count, bacterial population, and immunity killing rate. A carrying capacity of the immune cells is considered which limits the effectiveness of the immunity cells against a large population of bacteria. The decay of immunity is assumed to be proportional to the immune cell count. For simplicity, we assume the aggregated immune response for the proposed model.

The model also includes one stock of antibiotics, to capture the scenario when antibiotics may be administrated when an infection occurs.

Here x, y, a, and t represent the bacterial population, the immunity, the antibiotics stock, and the simulation time. The model parameters are given in Table 1. The governing equations are as follows:

$$\frac{dx}{dt} = rxg(x, K, y) - \frac{\alpha xy}{p+x} - \mu x + \sum_{j=1}^{N} M_j \delta(t) - k_a xa \tag{1}$$

$$\frac{dy}{dt} = -\lambda y + \frac{\beta xy}{p+x}\left(1 - \frac{y}{f(x, K, I_{\max})}\right) \tag{2}$$

$$\frac{da}{dt} = \Delta - d_e a \tag{3}$$

where the auxiliary functions are:

$$f(x,K,I_{\max}) = \begin{cases} x+1 & \text{if } x<K \text{ and } x<I_{\max} \\ I_{\max} & \text{otherwise} \end{cases}$$

$$g(x,K,y) = \begin{cases} 1-\frac{x}{K} & \text{if } \frac{x}{K} \leq 1 \text{ and } y>0 \\ 1-\frac{x}{10K} & \text{otherwise} \end{cases}$$

Table 1: SD parameter table

Parameter	Model Variable	Parameter Range	Units
r	CrudeBirthRate	[0.7, 1]	Cells/day
μ	CrudeDeathRate	0.02	Cellss/day
K	InfectionThreshold	[1000,2000]	Cells
α	ImmunityKillingRate	0.6	Cells/day
M_j	External bacterial Intake	[50,1000]	Cells
β	RateofProduction	[0.3,0.75]	Cells/day
λ	DecayParameter	0.01	Cells/day
I_{max}	ImmuneCapacity	[750,1200]	Cells
p	Shape Parameter	50	Cells
Δ	Intake1	20	ml/day
d_e	ABDecayPara	0.09	ml/day
k_a	ABKillingRate	0.009	Cells/day/ml

In Eq(1), the first term denotes the natural birth depending on bacterial birth rate, bacterial population, and infection threshold. The second term denotes the killing by immunity depends on bacterial population and immunity cells. The third term is related to the natural death rate. The fourth term for quantifying the external triggers. The fifth term is related to the antibiotics killing rate, depending on the bacterial population and antibiotics.

In Eq(2), the first term is related to the natural decay rate of immunity. The second term denotes the immunity production rate that depends on bacterial population and variable immunity-carrying capacity.

In Eq(3) denotes the intake and decay of antibiotics.

In this study, single-agent dynamics are not isolated but serve as essential building blocks for understanding and predicting population-level phenomena. The single-agent model provides details about infection mechanics. Understanding single-host bacterial dynamics better, can help design find appropriate interventions to manage community-level disease dynamics. Adding several agents with different parameter configurations exhibits different individual dynamics and their interactions.

4. MULTI AGENT FRAMEWORK

The multi-agent framework consists of a population of agents. The statechart is similar to the single-agent framework but some more components are added, which can be seen in Figure 2. For infection spreading mechanism, we consider contact with infected individuals along with the environmental components which can be further classified into water sanitation and food practices. Every individual interacts with the environment each day, if the environment is contaminated then the infection can spread through it.

In this section, we consider a population of individuals. Each agent has its within-host dynamics and interacts with each other with some contact rate. If infected persons contact with susceptible people then there is a probability that the susceptible person becomes infected. In this work, we consider that the infected person will pass some bacterial load on to the susceptible person. Depending on the susceptible person's immunity and external bacterial load the person may become infected or may not change its state. This way modeling helps us to connect the within-host infection dynamics to the population-level model. It can help us to examine the effects of individual infection dynamics on spreading the infection in the community. In this model, an infected person can contact any random individual from the population. We incorporated a seasonal pattern in bacterial growth within the environment. Additionally, we tested intervention strategies, such as environmental clearing and preventing infected individuals from contaminating the environment, to analyze their impact on disease spread within the

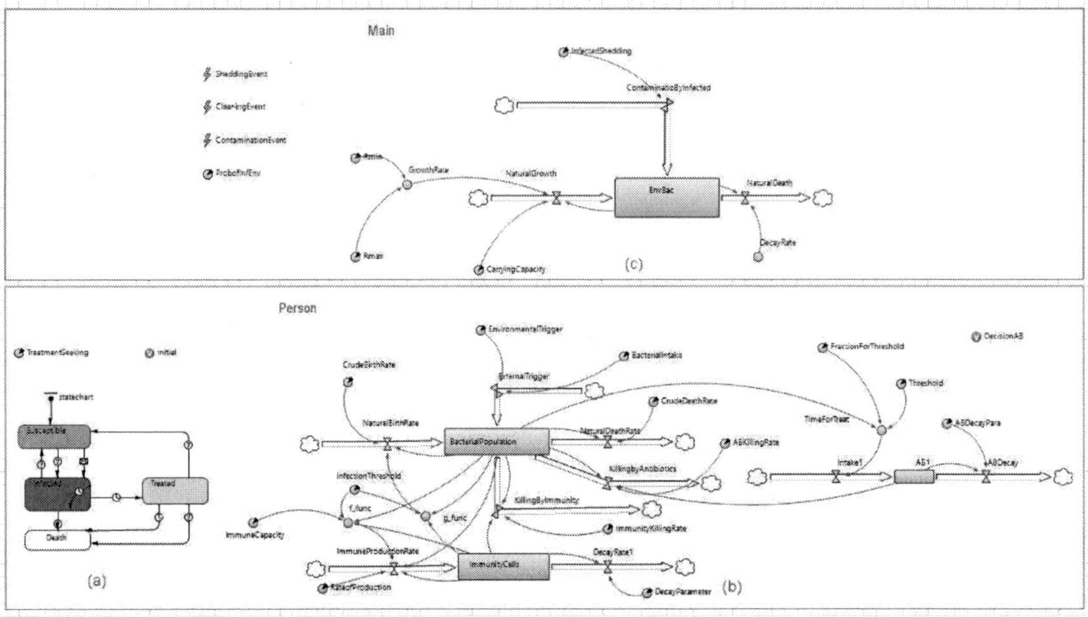

Figure 2: Multi Agent Framework. Implemented in AnyLogic (a) State chart of individual agent (b) System Dynamics model of bacterial population (c) Environmental Model for bacterial growth in community.

population. We didn't include the healthcare sub-model to reduce complexities and better analyze the model's structure. In ongoing work, we include the sub-model to capture more realistic scenarios. We consider a population of 200 agents with a fixed contact rate and infectivity. Each agent has its SD model within it and the parameters are taken from the uniform distribution from a specified range. We consider the scenario with treatment (antibiotics are used). Only one antibiotic is considered for treatment. In the healthcare sub-model, multiple antibiotics can be used but we didn't include it here. We also include the environmental contamination here. Here are the parameters of the multi-agent model Table 2. For the multi-agent model, the parameters are initialized based on the parameter values given by Table 1.

Table 2: Parameters for Multi-Agent Model

Model Variable	Parameter Range	Units
Initial number of agents	2-10^8	Person
ProbofInfEnv	0.6	unit less
EnvironmentalTrigger	0-10^7	Cells
BacterialIntake	0-15000	Cells
GrowthRate (v)	0.2-1	Cells/day
InfectedShedding (B_i)	0-10^7	Cells
CarryingCapacity (K_E)	10^7	Cells
DecayRate (d_E)	0.5-0.75	Cells/day
ToleranceLevel	2-10	days
TreatmentSeeking	2-5	days

The "Event Based" parameters change values from the events associated with them and "Variable" depends on other parameter values.

4.1. ENVIRONMENTAL SUB-MODEL

In this sub-model, we examine how a contaminated environment influences infection spread. It can be seen in the Figure 2(c). The model includes a bacterial stock representing the total bacteria present in the environment, with two inflows and one outflow. The bacterial growth rate in the environment

is influenced by climate, so a seasonal pattern is applied to model this growth. Additionally, infected individuals are assumed to contribute bacteria to the environment. The outflow is governed by an environmental decay parameter, and each person who interacts with the contaminated environment receives a certain bacterial load. This framework includes two scenarios for analysis.
The governing equation is as follows:

$$\frac{dE}{dt} = \nu E(1 - \frac{E}{K_E}) + \sum_{i=1}^{Infected} B_i \delta(t) - d_E E \quad (4)$$

where E represents the Environmental bacterial Stock, K_E is the carrying capacity of the environment. The natural growth of bacteria in the environment, ν is given by

$$\nu_{min} + ((\nu_{max} - \nu_{min})/2)(1 + \sin(2\pi t/360))$$

, ν_{min} and ν_{max} are the minimum and maximum growth rates in environment respectively. The second term denotes the bacterial load (B_i) received from the infected persons. The third term represents the natural death rate in the environment, d_E is the natural death rate of bacteria in the environment.

5. SIMULATION RESULTS

All simulations were conducted using AnyLogic 8.9.2 Personal Learning Edition (Borshchev 2013). In the case of the single-agent model, we consider three scenarios depending on the parameter values of β, *TreatmentSeeking* and *ToleranceLevel*. Two external bacterial loads in time stamps are 50 and 80. The first bacterial load is smaller in quantity and the second one is sufficiently large. When treatment starts 5 days of antibiotics are given and assume that the individual completes the dose. For visualization purposes, we scale up antibiotics by 20 times. In the multiagent setting, we consider the disease transmission by contacts and environmental contamination. Here, we consider three scenarios with environmental clearing, preventing infected individuals from contaminating the environment and allowing infected people to contaminate the environment with regular interval cleaning of the environment. A single run of the model is performed as there are no stochastic parameter.

5.1. SCENARIOS - SINGLE AGENT DYNAMICS

Parameter Values		Observations
Scenario 1	β = 0.6 ToleranceLevel = 10 TreatmentSeeking = 5	Higher tolerance level with stronger immunity production rate leads to more severe infection (Figure 3).
Scenario 2	β = 0.3 ToleranceLevel = 10 TreatmentSeeking = 5	Re-infection observed due to low immunity production rate (Figure 3).
Scenario 3	β = 0.6 ToleranceLevel = 2 TreatmentSeeking = 5	Low ToleranceLevel causes immunity to fail in suppressing bacterial load. (Figure 4). Sudden increase in bacterial load leads to death.

The interplay between β, ToleranceLevel, and TreatmentSeeking behavior significantly affects infection dynamics. A very low tolerance level triggers early treatment-seeking behavior, but it may also indicate a fragile immune response incapable of managing bacterial proliferation. This suggests that both tolerance and immunity need to be balanced to prevent fatal outcomes. The results match our intuition and validate the model.

5.2. SCENARIOS FROM THE MULTI-AGENT DYNAMICS

Here, we discuss three multi-agent dynamics scenarios.

- **No Spillover:** In this scenario, we consider that the infected person would not contaminate the environment (Figure 5(a)). It implies that $B_i = 0$. Here, we can observe the seasonal pattern of

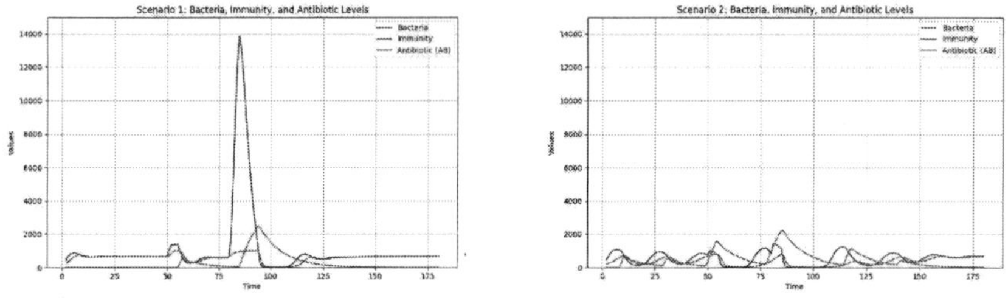

(a) Infection dynamics of individual when β:0.6, *ToleranceLevel*:10 (b) Infection dynamics of individual when β:0.3, *ToleranceLevel*:10

Figure 3: Some Scenarios from the Single-Agent Model

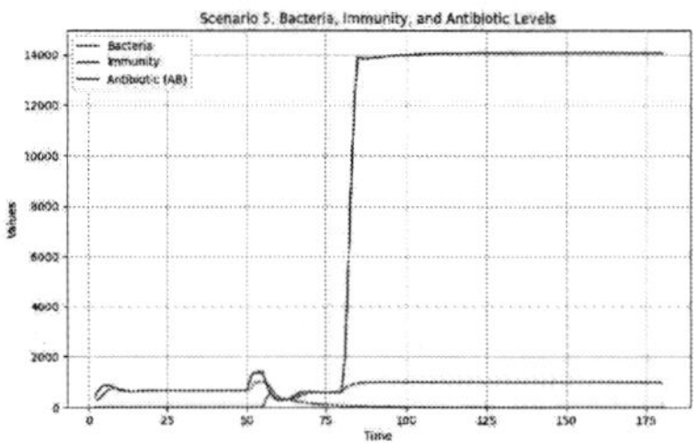

Figure 4: Infection dynamics of individual when β:0.6,*TreatmentSeeking*:5, *ToleranceLevel*:2.

the infection spreading through environmental contamination. It highlights the role of climate conditions in the spread of the infection.

- **Clearing Contaminated environment:** In this scenario, we consider some cleaning of the contaminated environment. After 120 days we clean the contaminated environment (Figure 5(b)). So, the expression be $E = 0$ and $B_i = 0$ when $\mod(t, 120)$ is 0. We observe the effect of clearance on environmental contamination from the reduced number of infected individuals.
- **Spillover with no cleaning:** In this case, we don't clear the environment but allow the infected people to contaminate the environment (Figure 6). It shows that the number of infected people is high and so are the people with treatment. Here, due to the contaminated environment, the disease spreads faster and becomes more severe.

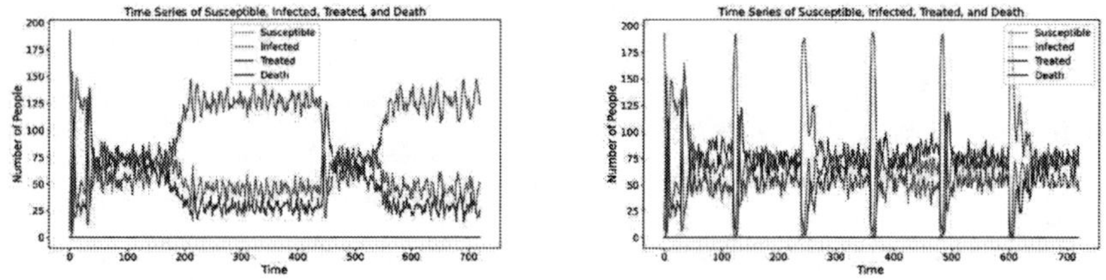

(a) No spillover from Infected people (b) Clearing of Contaminated environment

Figure 5: Some Scenarios from the Multi-Agent Model

In the multi-agent model, environmental contamination significantly impacted the spread and severity of infections. When infected individuals contaminate the environment without regular cleaning, the infection spreads more rapidly and affects a larger population. However, implementing periodic environmental cleaning effectively reduced the number of infections, highlighting the importance of environmental management in controlling disease spread. Scenarios without environmental spillover demonstrated a seasonal infection pattern, indicating that environmental contamination is a crucial

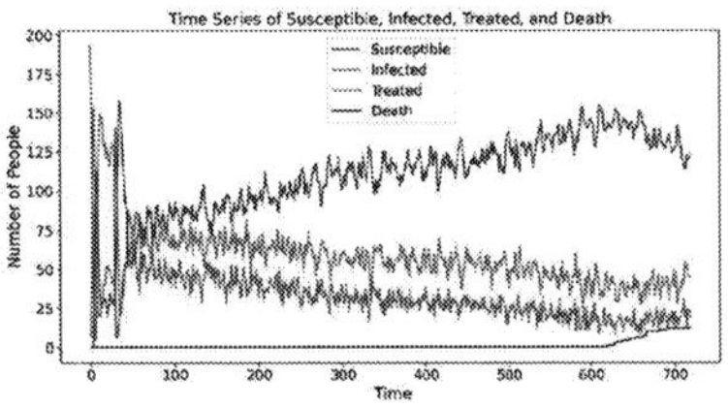

Figure 6: Multi-Agent Model States with Spillover and No Cleaning

factor in sustaining infection dynamics.

6. CONCLUSIONS AND FUTURE WORK

We explore the within-host infection dynamics of individuals and the spread of infection in the community. We explored infection dynamics in both single-agent and multi-agent models to assess the effects of treatment-seeking behavior, immunity production, and environmental contamination on infection spread and severity. In the single-agent model, results validate our intuition and the multi-agent model shows environmental contamination significantly amplifies infection spread and severity, but periodic cleaning effectively reduces infections, emphasizing the importance of environmental management. Without spillover, infections follow a seasonal pattern, underscoring contamination's role in sustaining infection dynamics.

We have not yet differentiated between sensitive and resistant bacteria. Given the significance of antibiotic resistance, this differentiation would enable the model to better address the emergence and spread of antibiotic resistance at the population level.

The current model presented is logically consistent and aligned with existing literature. In the system dynamics modeling step, we logically capture infection scenarios and explore various possibilities for a single agent, ensuring a detailed representation of individual-level processes. The model intuitively reflects infection dynamics and produces results consistent with known facts and established patterns, reinforcing its validity. Further empirical validation of the data for a specific case is left as future work.

Additionally, more healthcare factors should be included, such as healthcare infrastructure, accessibility of doctors, number of untrained doctors, awareness level regarding antibiotics, sanitation levels etc. Incorporating the movement of individuals within and between communities can provide insights into how mobility affects infection spread. We could also model different antibiotic usage scenarios, such as overuse or misuse. Including factors like income level or access to healthcare may shed light on disparities in infection outcomes across different population groups. We aim to integrate individual behaviors into the model, such as hygiene practices, attitudes toward antibiotic use, and knowledge about antibiotics and treatment procedures. This integration will allow the model to more accurately reflect real-world behaviors.

REFERENCES

Banerjee, S. 2017. "A stage structured hybrid model for within-host emerging infectious disease modelling". *Network Biology* 7 (4).

Bobashev, G. V., D. M. Goedecke, F. Yu, and J. M. Epstein. 2007. "A hybrid epidemic model: combining the advantages of agent-based and equation-based approaches". In *2007 winter simulation conference*, 1532–1537. IEEE.

Borshchev, A. 2013. *The Big Book of Simulation Modeling: Multimethod Modeling with AnyLogic 6*. Chicago, IL: AnyLogic North America.

Cantone, M., G. Santos, P. Wentker, X. Lai, and J. Vera. 2017. "Multiplicity of Mathematical Modeling Strategies to Search for Molecular and Cellular Insights into Bacterial Lung Infection". *Frontiers in Physiology* 8:264848.

Caudill, L., and B. Lawson. 2013. "A hybrid agent-based and differential equations model for simulating antibiotic resistance in a hospital ward". In *2013 Winter Simulations Conference (WSC)*, 1419–1430. IEEE.

Caudill, L., and B. Lawson. 2017. "A unified inter-host and in-host model of antibiotic resistance and infection spread in a hospital ward". *Journal of theoretical biology* 421:112–126.

Daşbaşı, B., and İ. Öztürk. 2016. "Mathematical Modelling of Bacterial Resistance to Multiple Antibiotics and Immune System Response". *SpringerPlus* 5:1–17.

Djanatliev, A., R. German, P. Kolominsky-Rabas, and B. M. Hofmann. 2012. "Hybrid simulation with loosely coupled system dynamics and agent-based models for prospective health technology assessments". In *Proceedings of the 2012 winter simulation conference (WSC)*, 1–12. IEEE.

Elliott, T. M., X. J. Lee, A. Foeglein, P. N. Harris, and L. G. Gordon. 2020. "A hybrid simulation model approach to examine bacterial genome sequencing during a hospital outbreak". *BMC Infectious Diseases* 20:1–12.

Hunter, E., and J. D. Kelleher. 2022. "Understanding the assumptions of an SEIR compartmental model using agentization and a complexity hierarchy". *Journal of Computational Mathematics and Data Science* 4:100056.

Ibargüen-Mondragón, E., S. Mosquera, M. Cerón, E. M. Burbano-Rosero, S. P. Hidalgo-Bonilla, L. Esteva, and J. P. Romero-Leitón. 2014. "Mathematical Modeling on Bacterial Resistance to Multiple Antibiotics Caused by Spontaneous Mutations". *Biosystems* 117:60–67.

Kang, B. G., H.-M. Park, M. Jang, and K.-M. Seo. 2021. "Hybrid model-based simulation analysis on the effects of social distancing policy of the COVID-19 epidemic". *International Journal of Environmental Research and Public Health* 18 (21): 11264.

Mayer, H., K. Zaenker, and U. An Der Heiden. 1995. "A Basic Mathematical Model of the Immune Response". *Chaos: An Interdisciplinary Journal of Nonlinear Science* 5 (1): 155–161.

Quintela, B. d. M., R. W. dos Santos, and M. Lobosco. 2014. "On the Coupling of Two Models of the Human Immune Response to an Antigen". *BioMed Research International* 2014 (1): 410457.

Shi, Z., C.-H. J. Wu, D. Ben-Arieh, and S. Q. Simpson. 2015. "Mathematical Model of Innate and Adaptive Immunity of Sepsis: A Modeling and Simulation Study of Infectious Disease". *BioMed Research International* 2015 (1): 504259.

Talaei, K., S. A. Garan, B. d. M. Quintela, M. S. Olufsen, J. Cho, J. R. Jahansooz et al. 2021. "A Mathematical Model of the Dynamics of Cytokine Expression and Human Immune Cell Activation in Response to the Pathogen Staphylococcus Aureus". *Frontiers in Cellular and Infection Microbiology* 11:711153.

Zulkepli, J., T. Eldabi, and N. Mustafee. 2012. "Hybrid simulation for modelling large systems: An example of integrated care model". In *Proceedings of the 2012 winter simulation conference (WSC)*, 1–12. IEEE.

ACKNOWLEDGEMENTS

The author would like to thank KCDH,IIT Bomabay for their support.

AUTHOR BIOGRAPHIES

AVI ROY CHOWDHURY is a PhD scholar in the IEOR Dept., IIT Bombay. His research interest consists of System dynamics, Agent-based Simulation, Data Science, and Epidemiology.

JAYENDRAN VENKATESWARAN is an Institute Chair Professor in the IEOR Dept., IIT Bombay. His current research and teaching interests are in systems thinking, system dynamics, agent-based modeling & simulation, discrete-event simulation, supply chain & sustainability and OR for development.

OM P DAMANI is a professor in the CSE Dept. at IIT Bombay with research interests in System Dynamics and Data Science. His work focuses on solutions for water and agriculture issues.

Proceedings of the Operational Research Society Simulation Workshop 2025 (SW25)
M. Luis, A. Harper, T. Monks, N. Mustafee, eds.
https://doi.org/10.36819/SW25.025

APPLICATION OF HYBRID AGENT-BASED MODELING AND SYSTEM DYNAMICS SIMULATION: COLLABORATION TO IMPROVE SUPPLY CHAIN RESILIENCE

Davoud Hosseinnezhad

University of Limerick
Limerick, Ireland
Davoud.Hosseinnezhad@ul.ie

Cathal Heavey

University of Limerick
Limerick, Ireland
Cathal.Heavey@ul.ie

Mrs. Fooroogh Goodarzi

Czstochowa University of Technology
Czstochowa, Poland
Forooogh.Goodarzi@yahoo.com

ABSTRACT

This paper explores the application of a hybrid Agent-Based Modeling (ABM) and System Dynamics (SD) simulation to address collaboration within supply chains, focusing on evolving interactions between individual entities. By integrating ABM and SD, the model captures both the dynamic decisions of the collaborating entities as well as the decision-making processes of each individual. Using AnyLogic, the hybrid approach is applied to analyze supply chain collaboration in the manufacturing and semiconductor industries and examine the consequences of disruptions in primary suppliers. The findings indicate that the proposed model effectively captures supply chain entities' complex interactions and individual preferences. The results also show that the stability of collaboration between companies is impacted by disruption and the duration of disruption. The proposed model can be expanded to examine intertwined supply chains and assess the resilience of multi-player supply chains.
Keywords: Hybrid Simulation, System-Dynamics, Agent-based Modeling, Collaboration, Disruption

1 INTRODUCTION

Simulation modeling methods such as System Dynamics (SD), Discrete Event Simulation (DES), and Agent-Based Modeling (ABM) are widely used in the literature to support decision-making in complex systems. Each simulation method offers distinct advantages (Howick and Megiddo, 2020). However, using any single approach can pose significant limitations in representing the multi-dimensional nature of complex systems. As a result, there is an increasing shift towards hybrid simulations that integrate multiple simulation methods (Brailsford et al 2019; Swinerd, 2014). Of particular interest is the combination of the SD approach with ABM, which can be used for representing complex adaptive systems. While SD allows for a macro-level view of systemic interactions through feedback loops, ABM enables a detailed examination of individual agents' decisions and actions within the system.

Supply chain resilience involves the identification of strategies that enable a supply chain to react and recover from disruptions (Nikookar and Yanadori, 2022). It focuses on the ability to withstand and recover from disruptions, especially when a disturbance at one point in the chain cascades downstream, impacting overall performance. By using simulation to model complex interactions and test resilience strategies, one can provide insights into designing supply chains that can better absorb shocks and maintain stability in the face of disruptions (Ivanov, 2018).

In response to the dynamic market environment and the need for swift recovery from disruptions, companies are boosting the importance of collaboration to enhance resilience (Duong and Chong,

2020). The main motivation for this study is to examine how the hybrid simulation approaches could be used to examine the impact of collaboration to boost supply chain resilience under disruption. Accordingly, this paper aims to answer the following research question. *Does collaboration (specifically horizontal collaboration) between companies (competing manufacturers in this paper) improve supply resilience?* The novelty of this paper lies in developing an integrated SD and ABM approach to examine the impact and stability of collaboration between companies in response to changes in external parameters and potential disruptions. This work further contributes to the literature by analyzing the behavior of cooperating companies as they negotiate with each other for additional access to the shared capacities. The remainder of this paper is organized as follows: Section (2) reviews the literature on the application of simulation and collaboration for enhancing supply chain resilience. Section (3) introduces a hybrid ABM and SD simulation approach designed to capture the dynamics of collaboration from a strategic perspective. Section (4) proposes how to build the proposed hybrid simulation mode using AnyLogic simulation software. Section (5) analyzes the performance of the proposed model under disruption scenarios, with conclusions presented in Section (6).

2 LITERATURE REVIEW

The literature review in this section is organized into two main streams. The first stream examines the application of ABM and SD simulation in supply chains, focusing on their roles in enhancing supply chain resilience and collaboration. The second stream focuses on collaboration for resilience.

2.1 ABM simulation

It is commonly useful for analyzing supply chain risk management and inter-organizational integration. It enables a representation of supply chain participants' behaviors, cooperation processes, coordination, and adaptable network structures within supply chains. Recent literature reviews also highlight the integration of digital twins with ABM to enhance supply chain management (Orozco-Romero et al 2019). ABM is also a powerful tool for modeling collaborative supply chain processes. It supports decentralized negotiation and information sharing, enhancing decision-making and planning (Dorigatti et al 2016). Additionally, ABM has been applied to evaluate cooperation in non-profit networks, using cooperative game theory to optimize logistics and assess the benefits of collaboration (Hosseinnezhad et al 2023). ABM has been used to simulate disruption management in supply chains to develop strategies to minimize disruption impacts (Rahman et al 2022). ABM can highlight high-risk areas and support the development of mitigation strategies, improving supply chain resilience (Blos et al 2015)

2.2 SD simulation

It is applied to simulate supply chain behaviors on a more strategic level, focusing on feedback loops and time delays (Rebs et al 2019). SD is also used to improve sustainability in supply chains by optimizing resources and reducing waste (Kaur and Kander, 2023). There is also an increasing focus on implementing SD simulation for collaboration in supply chains. Xu et al (2021) used SD to model an information-collaborative supply chain, analyzing market demand and inventory levels before and after implementing information sharing. Recent reviews also emphasize the growing use of SD focusing on sustainability and disruptions (Eudave-Mercado et al 2024). Zhu et al (2021) explore various collaborative strategies to improve supply chain resilience against disruptions. They examined how different collaboration approaches can mitigate specific types of disruptions. Despite SD simulation's benefits, there is a need for hybrid simulation models including SD-ABM modeling to examine complex interactions (Hosseinnezhad et al 2022; Azizsafaei et al 2022).

2.3 Collaboration for supply chains resilience

Supply chain collaboration involves partners working together, planning to generating mutual values beyond what each firm could achieve independently (Scholten and Schilder, 2015). Collaboration within supply chains fosters synergies among partners, facilitates joint planning, and actions to effectively respond to, and recover from disruptions. Current literature underscores the role of collaboration in building a resilient supply chain (Azadegan and Dooley, 2021; Zhou et al 2024). Collaboration in supply chains includes but is not limited to joint planning, resource pooling, and information sharing, where the extraction and integration of information from multiple sources can enhance supply chain resilience in response to disruptions (Hosseinnezhad and Saidi-Mehrabad, 2018).

Figure 1 illustrates the scope of collaboration within supply chains. Internal collaboration encompasses collaboration across different departments within a company. External collaboration could be in vertical and/or horizontal types. Vertical collaboration involves partnerships with companies at different echelons in the supply chain. Horizontal collaboration involves cooperation among companies operating at the same echelon in the supply chain (Kessa et al 2021). For example, in the semiconductor or automotive industry, two manufacturers at the same echelon of the supply chain may collaborate to share a reliable source of production capacity, ensuring continuity during demand surges or supply constraints[1]. In contrast, vertical collaboration occurs between firms at different echelons, such as when a manufacturer partners with a supplier to secure critical components. Notably, internal collaboration falls outside the scope of the hybrid simulation modeling proposed in this paper.

Regarding capacity sharing as a horizontal collaboration, Xie and Han (2020) introduced game models to assess the efficiency of capacity sharing between competing firms with limited capacity. Cockx et al (2019) developed an Osotua-based resource-sharing approach to aid financially distressed companies facing shortages. Ouhader and Kyal (2017) examined suppliers who jointly delivered products through shared depots and vehicles. Ma et al (2017) developed a resource-sharing model to enhance sustainability in the garment industry. For a comprehensive review of the current studies on horizontal collaboraitn, see Mrabti et al (2022). Also, see Lotfi and Larmour (2022) to examine how vertical and horizontal collaboration could boost supply chain resilience in the presence of uncertainty.

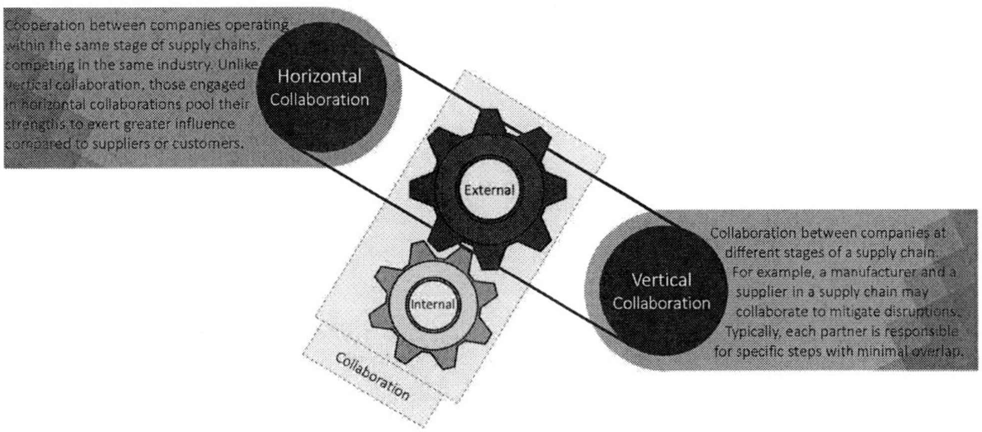

Figure 1 The scope of collaboration in the supply chain

Despite the consensus on collaboration for supply chain resilience, understanding the precise mechanisms through which collaboration influences resilience remains an interesting research topic. The literature suggests varying perspectives on the relationship between collaboration and reducing vulnerability to disruptions (Kessler and Arlinghaus, 2022). While some argue that single-sourcing increases vulnerability, others posit that increased collaboration and information-sharing, serve as mitigators by expediting risk response processes (Holgado and Niess, 2023). Thus, understanding how to collaborate and identifying crucial collaborative activities are imperative for bolstering supply chain resilience under uncertainties and disruptions. Collaboration in the supply chain provides multiple advantages. However, it may not always be feasible, desirable, or stable to establish collaboration. The literature on collaboration for supply chain resilience lacks insights into new approaches. This paper

[1] https://www.cisco.com/c/dam/en_us/about/annual-report/cisco-annual-report-2022.pdf

focuses on applying hybrid simulation modeling to address the importance of collaboration in supply chain resilience. It also explores how collaboration helps supply chains bounce back from disruptions.

3 PROPOSED HYBRID SIMULATION MODEL OF COLLABORATION

This section develops a hybrid SD-ABM simulation model to capture the dynamics of collaboration between two companies in response to disruption. Disruptions affecting one company can impact other connected companies, potentially destabilizing the entire supply chain network; a phenomenon referred to as risk transmission or ripple effects in the literature (Ivanov et al 2019). For instance, if suppliers fail to deliver materials, manufacturers may face raw material shortages, thereby disrupting regular production. In practice, a company that loses a supplier can mitigate the impact by finding a replacement or by strengthening collaboration with other companies to reduce the risk of shortages (Shi et al 2022). Accordingly, this paper assumes a supply chain that initiates collaboration to enhance resilience. The collaborating partners may represent companies at different stages of the supply chain. The proposed model is adaptable to both horizontal and vertical collaboration types. However, this paper focuses on modeling collaboration between two competing manufacturers.

The model includes two manufacturers with their initial suppliers prone to disruption. Hence, they agree to invest mutually and share a secure supplier to enhance their resilience during disruptions. This collaborative approach reduces individual investment costs, addressing the reluctance often observed among companies when it comes to expanding their capacity independently (Hu et al 2017). Figure 2 illustrates a schematic view of the supply chain and collaboration between the manufacturers and the application of the proposed hybrid simulation approach. The proposed hybrid simulation model of collaboration between the manufacturers consists of two sections: ABM and SD simulation.

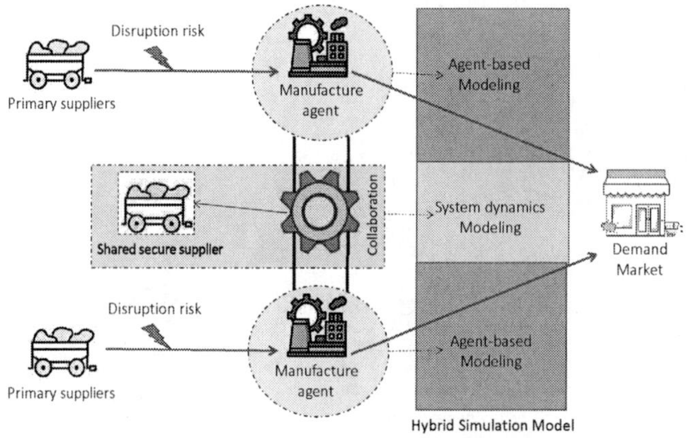

Figure 2 Application of hybrid simulation approach for collaboration in the proposed supply chain problem

3.1 Agent-Based Modeling

ABM enables capturing the individual decision-making processes of collaborating entities within the proposed model; i.e. manufacturers. The processes can vary based on the characteristics of collaborators in the supply chain. This study examines a simplified scenario with two similar agents, both manufacturers, which share an identical decision-making framework for fulfilling demand in their respective markets. It is important to note that if agents possess distinct decision-making processes, these differences would yield different decision-making processes for each agent. Figure 3 illustrates the decisions of each manufacturer as the agents of the model, detailing the sequence of steps through which they assess and respond to demand. ABM is applied to address the individual decision-making of each manufacturer as follows. When a new demand is received, each manufacturer first assesses their normal capacity to determine if they can fulfill the order. If their initial capacity from primary suppliers is inadequate, they then attempt to fulfill the order using the shared secure capacity. If they have already exhausted their access to the shared capacity but still struggling to meet the total demand, they start negotiating with the other manufacturer for additional access to the shared capacity. If these negotiations fail, the unfulfilled demand will be added to the backorders and returned to the incoming demand queue.

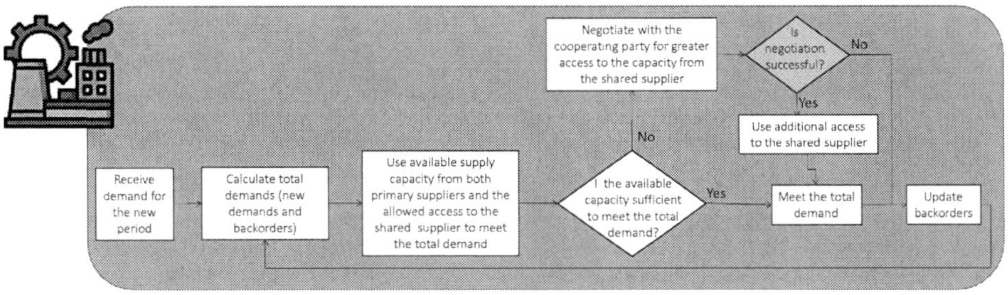

Figure 3 Decision-making process of the agents (manufacturers)

3.2 Systems-Dynamics Modeling

This simulation section examines the dynamics of collaboration between the agents (manufacturers). The decision variable of this SD simulation section is the probability of adopting a cooperative strategy by the agents in the negotiation stage in Figure 3. This decision impacts the likelihood of negotiation success as a part of the decision-making process of each agent, as shown in Figure 4. Accordingly, two possible stocks have been considered for each agent in the SD section; i.e. cooperative versus non-cooperative strategy. The model utilizes a flow between stocks to determine the rate of change from a non-cooperative strategy to a cooperative strategy. This rate of change is determined based on cost-related parameters, disruption in the primary suppliers, the behavior of the other agent, incentives versus penalties, and the price offered for additional access to the shared supply capacity.

To determine the rate of change from a non-cooperative to a cooperative approach, it is required to calculate the profit function for each agent under both cooperative and non-cooperative strategies. The rate of change from a non-cooperative to a cooperative strategy will be positive only if the expected profit from a cooperative approach exceeds that of a non-cooperative approach. Various methods, such as the Replicator Dynamics Equation, can be applied to analyze how the agents' strategies evolve during the negotiation stage (Hofbauer and Sigmund, 2003).

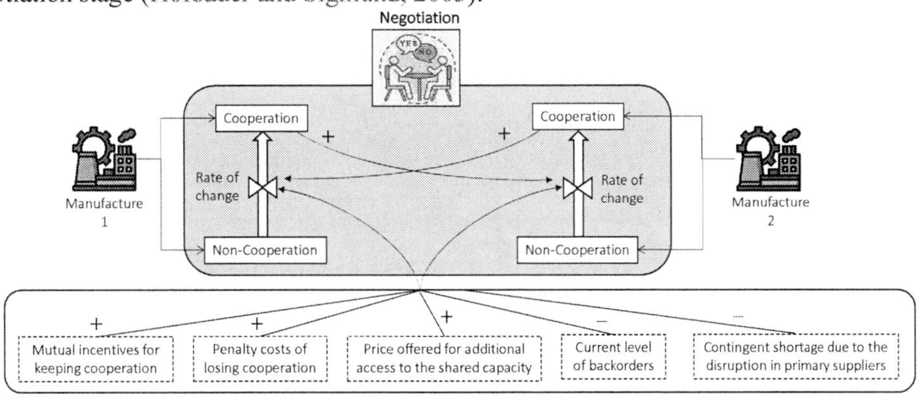

Figure 4 SD simulation of the dynamics of agents' (manufacturers) behavior in the negotiation stage

3.3 Hybrid ABM and SD model interactions

Figure 5 illustrates how the decisions of each agent in the ABM in Figure 3 are linked to the dynamics of interactions during the negotiation stage in the SD model in Figure 4. This linkage could be explained for Manufacturer 1 and similarly applies to Manufacturer 2. When Manufacturer 1 seeks additional access to the shared capacity in the ABM section, the success of this access depends on Manufacturer

2's strategy, and whether Manufacturer 2 adopts a cooperation approach. Note that the probability of a cooperative approach by the manufacturer in the negotiation stage is a dynamic value that updates based on the parameters and mutual interactions shown in Figure 4. It determines if the negotiation is successful and whether Manufacturer 1 could get additional access to the shared capacity.

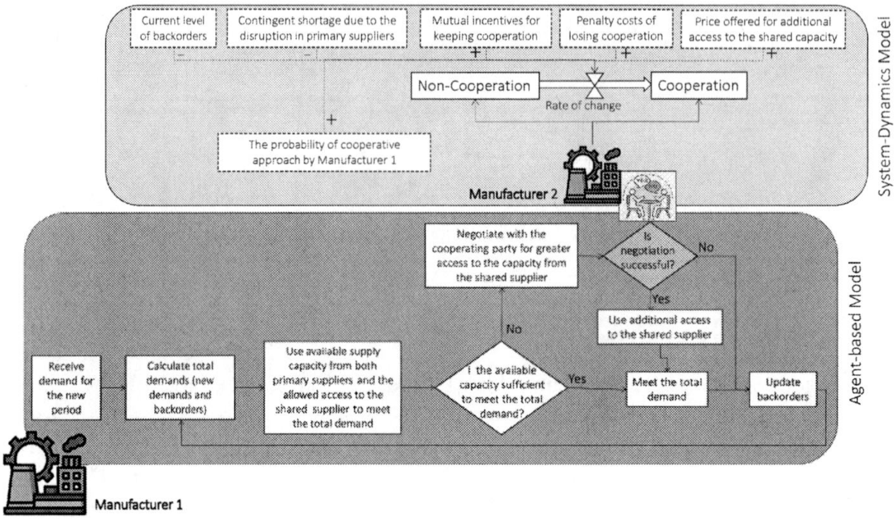

Figure 5 Hybrid simulation connecting decisions in the ABM to the SD model

4 PROPOSED HYBRID SIMULATION MODE IN ANYLOGIC

We constructed a simulation model using AnyLogic software to assess the model and the stability of collaboration. AnyLogic is a widely employed tool in the literature for simulating supply chains (Ren et al 2019). In this study's simulation approach, we connect the ABM decision-making process of manufacturers with an SD model, which evaluates the likelihood of negotiation success. Consequently, the likelihood of manufacturers adopting a cooperative strategy will be utilized in the negotiation stage within the proposed ABM of manufacturers' decisions.

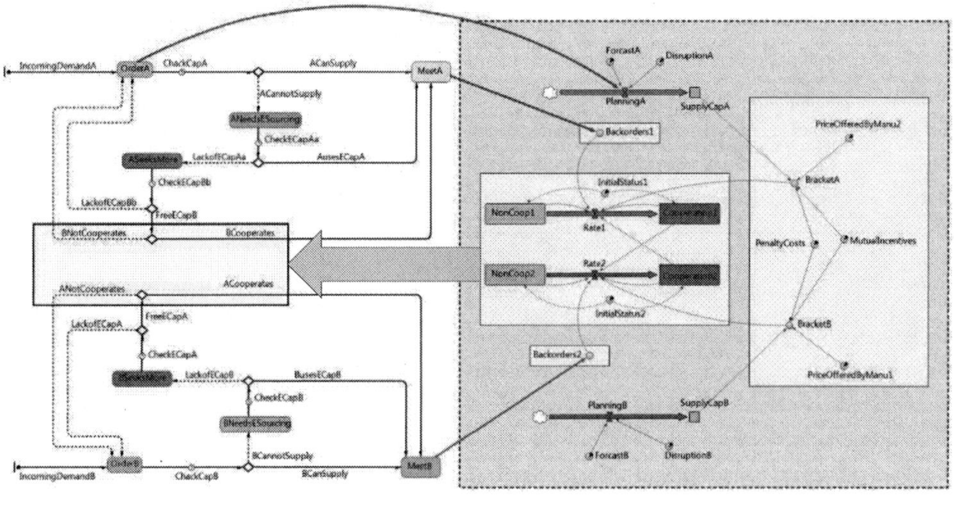

Figure 6 AnyLogic model of the proposed hybrid simulation

The integration of these two modeling approaches is crucial for accurately capturing the individual decision-making processes of manufacturers as well as the SD analysis of collaborative interactions between competing manufacturers. The hybrid model integrates these two approaches by linking the decisions in the ABM to the dynamic probabilities calculated in the SD model. As shown in Figure 6, the decision-making process for each manufacturer is directly influenced by the outcomes of the SD model. The dynamic probability of cooperation is calculated within the SD model and fed back into the ABM to determine the success of negotiation efforts. On the other hand, the stability of the collaborative approach during the negotiation stage modeled as an SD simulation depends on the current level of backorders (see Figure 4). The level of the backorders is decided in the ABM section and therefore the stability of collaboration in the SD section is also linked to the level of backorder in the ABM section.

5 DISRUPTION ANALYSIS USING THE PROPOSED HYBRID SIMULATION MODEL

The proposed hybrid simulation model incorporates disruption scenarios by creating events within the SD components of the model. As depicted in Figure 7, which is built on the model framework in Figure 6, disruptions are introduced using the *Event* element in AnyLogic. This software enables the exploration of both recurring and one-time disruption events. This paper assumes a one-time disruption as shown in Figure 7. Additionally, the severity of each disruption and the associated recovery plan can be modeled using Java code within the *Action* section of each event's properties.

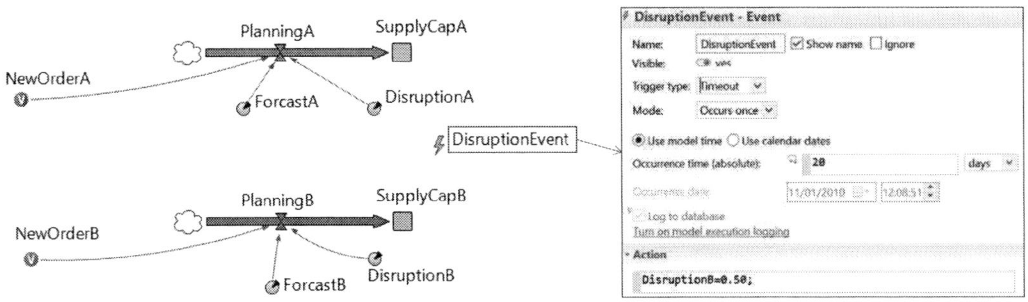

Figure 7 Disruption modeling using an event element in the proposed hybrid simulation model

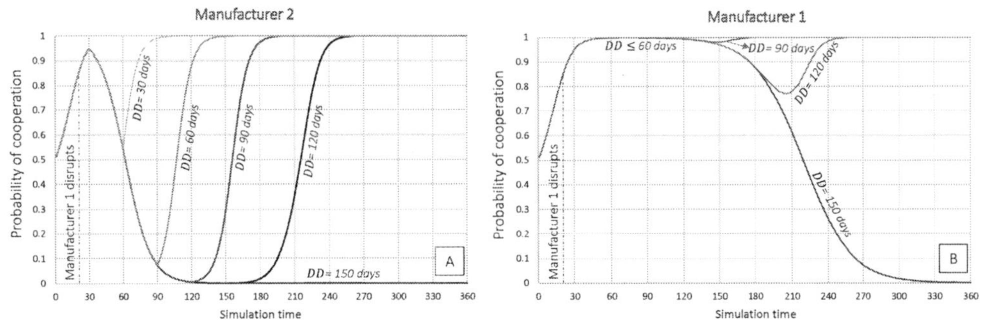

Figure 8 Stability analysis of collaboration under different disruption durations (*DD*)

The disruption scenario in this section assumes a 50% reduction in the supply capacity for manufacturer 2 from its primary suppliers starting at time 20, but this disruption has the potential to persist for a longer duration. Consequently, we aim to investigate the impact of this disruption's duration (*DD*) on the stability of the cooperative relationship between the manufacturers. Figure 8 illustrates how the behavior of the manufacturers evolves in response to varying disruption durations (*DD* = 30, 60, 90, 120, 150 days) for manufacturer 2. As depicted in Figure 8-A over a simulation period of one year, shortly after the disruption occurs, manufacturer 2 opts for a non-cooperative strategy, seeking increased access to the shared capacity to mitigate shortages. This graph showcases the alterations in manufacturer 2's behavior under different *DD* values. In this scenario, if the disruption persists for 150 days or longer, manufacturer 2 continues with the non-cooperative approach, subsequently pushing manufacturer 1 towards adopting a non-cooperative strategy as well. However, for shorter *DD* periods, manufacturer 2 eventually reverts to a cooperative approach after some time.

6 CONCLUSIONS AND MANAGERIAL INSIGHTS

The issue of promoting stable collaboration as a collaborative recovery strategy for disruption management has attracted the attention of both scholars and practitioners. Nonetheless, concerns remain regarding the challenges associated with collaboration especially horizontal collaboration with competitors, as this can potentially allow competitors to gain a larger market share. There is a gap in the existing literature when it comes to the dynamic analysis of the stability of collaboration within supply chains considering the individual profit-seeking decisions of collaborating parties. Simulation approaches are applied in the literature for modeling complex supply chain problems under uncertainty. However, there is a need for studies on the application of simulation models for collaborative networks.

This study proposes a novel simulation approach to examining collaboration between two competing manufacturers by focusing on mutual investment in a secure supplier, both hesitant to invest individually. A hybrid simulation model, integrating SD simulation and ABM simulation, was developed to capture the complex dynamics inherent in such collaborative interactions. The model was executed in the AnyLogic software, leveraging ABM to simulate the decision-making processes of individual manufacturers as autonomous agents. Each agent's decisions are influenced by the likelihood of successful negotiation for additional access to shared capacity when required. Simultaneously, the SD component of the model captures the evolution of agents' strategies in the negotiation stage. Additionally, the proposed model considers the risk of disruption in primary suppliers, which examines the uncertainty that firms may face in collaborative networks under disruptions.

Collaboration through capacity sharing allows competing companies to pool their resources, reduce individual investment costs, and provide mutual support during disruptions. This approach not only improves supply resilience but also creates economic opportunities for collaborating companies to capitalize on their excess capacity. If one manufacturer faces a disruption, they can negotiate with the other party for additional access to the shared capacity at an agreed price. This collaborative approach fosters a win-win scenario where manufacturers support each other during disruptions. This study offers insights for future research aimed at developing cooperative relationships among competitors for disruption recovery. It underscores the importance of the application of hybrid simulation models to analyze technical parameters and formulate well-crafted agreements to ensure the stability of collaborative recovery strategies. However, it is worth noting that this study has certain limitations that warrant further consideration in future research endeavors. This study has not addressed cooperative relationships between manufacturers considering the decisions of a buyer. Future research could develop multi-agent hybrid SD-ABM simulation models to create a comprehensive model encompassing both horizontal and vertical collaboration relationships.

REFERENCES

Azadegan, A., & Dooley, K. (2021). A typology of supply network resilience strategies: complex collaborations in a complex world. *Journal of Supply Chain Management*, 57(1), 17-26.

Azizsafaei, M., Hosseinian-Far, A., Khandan, R., Sarwar, D., & Daneshkhah, A. (2022). Assessing risks in dairy supply chain systems: a system dynamics approach. *Systems*, 10(4), 114.

Blos, M. F., Da Silva, R. M., & Miyagi, P. E. (2015). Application of an agent-based supply chain to mitigate supply chain disruptions. *IFAC-PapersOnLine*, 48(3), 640-645.

Brailsford, S. C., Eldabi, T., Kunc, M., Mustafee, N., & Osorio, A. F. (2019). Hybrid simulation modelling in operational research: A state-of-the-art review. *European Journal of Operational Research*, 278(3), 721-737.

Cockx, R., Armbruster, D., & Bendul, J. C. (2019). Resource sharing as supply chain disruption risk management measure. *IFAC-PapersOnLine*, 52(13), 802-807.

Dorigatti, M., Guarnaschelli, A., Chiotti, O., & Salomone, H. E. (2016). A service-oriented framework for agent-based simulations of collaborative supply chains. *Computers in Industry*, 83, 92-107.

Duong, L. N. K., & Chong, J. (2020). Supply chain collaboration in the presence of disruptions: a literature review. *International Journal of Production Research*, 58(11), 3488-3507.

Eudave-Mercado, S. E., Román-del-Valle, M. A., & Hernández-González, J. C. (2024). System Dynamics for Local Supply Chain Management: A Literature Review. *Saudi J Eng Technol*, 9(7), 280-289.

Hofbauer, J., & Sigmund, K. (2003). Evolutionary game dynamics. *Bulletin of the American mathematical society*, 40(4), 479-519.

Holgado, M., & Niess, A. (2023). Resilience in global supply chains: Analysis of responses, recovery actions and strategic changes triggered by major disruptions. *Supply Chain Management: An International Journal*, 28(6), 1040-1059.

Hosseinnezhad, D., & Saidi-mehrabad, M. (2018). Data fusion and information transparency in disaster chain. *International Journal of Innovation, Management and Technology*, 9(4), 152-159.

Hosseinnezhad, D., Heavey, C., & Nugroho, Y. K. (2022). Resource sharing between suppliers for a flexible recovery during disruption. *IFAC-PapersOnLine*, 55(10), 655-660.

Hosseinnezhad, D., Nugroho, Y. K., & Heavey, C. (2023). Horizontal collaboration between suppliers to mitigate supply chain disruption: A secure resource sharing strategy. *Computers & Industrial Engineering*, 177, 109088.

Howick, S., & Megiddo, I. (2020, March). A hybrid simulation modelling framework for combining system dynamics and agent-based models. *Operational Research Society Simulation Workshop 2020.*

Hu, S., Wan, Z., Ye, Q., & Chi, W. (2017). Supplier behavior in capacity investment competition: An experimental study. *Production and Operations Management*, 26(2), 273-291.

Ivanov, D. (2018). Revealing interfaces of supply chain resilience and sustainability: a simulation study. *International Journal of Production Research*, 56(10), 3507-3523.

Ivanov, D., Dolgui, A., & Sokolov, B. (2019). The impact of digital technology and Industry 4.0 on the ripple effect and supply chain risk analytics. *International journal of production research*, 57(3), 829-846.

Kaur, G., & Kander, R. (2023). Supply Chain Simulation of Manufacturing Shirts Using System Dynamics for Sustainability. *Sustainability*, 15(21), 15353.

Kessa, R., Sadiq, A. A., & Yeo, J. (2021). The importance of vertical and horizontal collaboration: United States' response to COVID-19 pandemic. *Chinese Public Administration Review*, 12(1), 61-71.

Kessler, M., & Arlinghaus, J. C. (2022). Managing Supply Chain Disruption by Collaborative Resource Sharing. In Supply Network Dynamics and Control (pp. 79-93). *Cham: Springer International Publishing.*

Lotfi, M., & Larmour, A. (2022). Supply chain resilience in the face of uncertainty: how horizontal and vertical collaboration can help?. *Continuity & Resilience Review*, 4(1), 37-53.

Ma, K., Wang, L., & Chen, Y. (2017). A resource sharing mechanism for sustainable production in the garment industry. *Sustainability*, 10(1), 52.

Mrabti, N., Hamani, N., & Delahoche, L. (2022). A comprehensive literature review on sustainable horizontal collaboration. *Sustainability*, 14(18), 11644.

Nikookar, E., & Yanadori, Y. (2022). Preparing supply chain for the next disruption beyond COVID-19: managerial antecedents of supply chain resilience. *International Journal of Operations & Production Management*, 42(1), 59-90.

Orozco-Romero, A., Arias-Portela, C. Y., & Saucedo, J. A. M. (2020). The use of agent-based models boosted by digital twins in the supply chain: a literature review. *Proceedings of the 2nd International Conference on Intelligent Computing and Optimization 2019* (ICO 2019), 642-652.

Ouhader, H., & El Kyal, M. (2017). Combining facility location and routing decisions in sustainable urban freight distribution under horizontal collaboration: how can shippers be benefited?. *Mathematical Problems in Engineering*, 2017(1), 8687515.

Rahman, M. M., Nguyen, R., & Lu, L. (2022). Multi-level impacts of climate change and supply disruption events on a potato supply chain: An agent-based modeling approach. *Agricultural Systems*, 201, 103469.

Rebs, T., Brandenburg, M., & Seuring, S. (2019). System dynamics modeling for sustainable supply chain management: A literature review and systems thinking approach. *Journal of cleaner production*, 208, 1265-1280.

Ren, J., Zhao, Q., Liu, B., & Chen, C. (2019). Selection of pallet management strategies from the perspective of supply chain cost with Anylogic software. *PloS one*, 14(6), e0217995.

Scholten, K., & Schilder, S. (2015). The role of collaboration in supply chain resilience. *Supply Chain Management: An International Journal*, 20(4), 471-484.

Shi, X., Yuan, X., & Deng, D. (2022). Research on supply network resilience considering the ripple effect with collaboration. *International Journal of Production Research*, 60(18), 5553–5570

Swinerd, C. (2014). On the design of hybrid simulation models, focussing on the agent-based system dynamics combination.

Xie, L., & Han, H. (2020). Capacity sharing and capacity investment of environment-friendly manufacturing: Strategy selection and performance analysis. *International Journal of Environmental Research and Public Health*, *17*(16), 5790.

Xu, W., Bo, H., & Chen, Y. (2021). System dynamics-based model for supply chain organizational collaboration. *Journal of Intelligent & Fuzzy Systems*, 40(2), 3085-3095.

Zhou, J., Hu, L., Yu, Y., Zhang, J. Z., & Zheng, L. J. (2024). Impacts of IT capability and supply chain collaboration on supply chain resilience: empirical evidence from China in COVID-19 pandemic. *Journal of Enterprise Information Management*, 37(2), 777-803.

Zhu, N. J., Ahmad, R., Holmes, A., Robotham, J. V., Lebcir, R., & Atun, R. (2021). System dynamics modelling to formulate policy interventions to optimise antibiotic prescribing in hospitals. *Journal of the Operational Research Society*, 72(11), 2490-2502.

AUTHOR BIOGRAPHIES

DAVOUD HOSSEINNEZHAD received an MSc in Industrial Engineering from the University of Tehran. He completed his PhD at the University of Limerick in 2024. His research interests include simulation, operations research, and game models. His Email address is Davoud.Hosseinnezhad@ul.ie.

CATHAL HEAVEY is a Professor in the School of Engineering at the University of Limerick. His research interests include simulation modeling of discrete-event systems; modeling and analysis of supply chains and manufacturing systems; process modeling; and decision support systems. His email address is Cathal.Heavey@ul.ie.

FOOROOGH GOODARZI received an MSc in Logistics from the Czestochowa University of Technology in Poland. Her main research interests are Simulation, Bioenergy supply chains, and Multi-criteria Decision-Making systems. Her Email address is Foroogh.Goodarzi@yahoo.com.

Proceedings of the Operational Research Society Simulation Workshop 2025 (SW25)
M. Luis, A. Harper, T. Monks, N. Mustafee, eds.
https://doi.org/10.36819/SW25.026

MULTI-OBJECTIVE AIRPORT SIMULATION-BASED OPTIMISATION USING DES AND RESPONSE SURFACE METAMODELS

Ahmad Attar

Exeter Digital Enterprise Systems Laboratory
Department of Engineering
University of Exeter
Streatham Campus, Exeter EX4 4QF, UK
a.attar@exeter.ac.uk

Mahdi Babaee

Department of Industrial Engineering
Islamic Azad University, South Tehran Branch
N. Iranshahr St., Tehran, Iran 11518-63411
babaei@behpardakht.com
mahdibabaee21@gmail.com

Sadigh Raissi

Department of Industrial Engineering
Islamic Azad University, South Tehran Branch
N. Iranshahr St., Tehran, Iran 11518-63411
raissi@azad.ac.ir

Majid Nojavan

Department of Industrial Engineering
Islamic Azad University, South Tehran Branch
N. Iranshahr St., Tehran, Iran 11518-63411
m_nojavan@azad.ac.ir

ABSTRACT

The aviation industry has always faced uncertainties and vulnerabilities from all aspects, making planning and optimising its components quite challenging. This paper addresses some of these complexities by investigating civil airports that act as the main components of this industry. We develop a discrete event simulation (DES) model to estimate key performance indicators (KPIs) of such systems while considering both takeoff and landing operations. This model is then used to propose a set of metamodels that link the KPIs of the system to the input parameters through some mathematical equations. Using these metamodels, a multi-objective mathematical optimisation model is developed and solved by the well-known LP-metrics method to assist airport managers in identifying the best improvement direction for the system. The proposed approach is implemented on a real airport case study, demonstrating promising avenues by discovering improvements that could outperform existing methods by 70%.

Keywords: Metamodel, Aviation Simulation, Design of Experiments, Performance Predictions

1 INTRODUCTION

Airport optimisation has long been a fundamental challenge in the aviation industry. Expansion and marketing strategies are among other decisions that require a thorough understanding of the airport subsystems' behaviour. The dominant theoretical approaches for estimating these behaviours are the analytical methods available in civil engineering references for airport design (Ashford et al., 2011; Horonjeff et al., 2010). However, airports are complex systems, encompassing multiple interactive components, and these analytical methods severely suffer from estimation errors, lacking support for realistic uncertainties in the input demand for the airport services or any fluctuations in the time consumed by any of the airport operations (Attar et al., 2024). This has led to the establishment of a series of alternative methods based on computer simulation (Attar et al., 2024; Dönmez et al., 2023; Feng and Johnson, 2021; Lau et al., 2021; Manataki and Zografos, 2010; Hunter et al., 2019).

On the other hand, envisioning the airport as a service provider positions the airlines as consumers of the service, and what the airport offers would be some available capacity for accommodating the takeoff and landing operations of its customers' planes. By viewing the airport from this angle, customer satisfaction would be associated with lower airport-imposed delays, and productivity would be defined as the number of possible operations (i.e., takeoffs and landings) with the available facilities. This is the segment of the airport that is commonly known as airside, consisting of the key assets and infrastructure of the airport such as the runway, the taxiway system, the apron, and the control tower. In such a system, the tower acts as the brain, controlling and monitoring the airspace of the airport with all the incoming and outgoing flow. Similar to any other service providers with random incoming flows and stochastic process times, some queues are defined in this system that can be aerial (e.g., flying a hold) or on the ground (e.g., departure queue).

The amount of time spent in these queues is the major portion of the airport-related delays that would reflect managerial decisions and should be minimised to attain higher levels of customer (i.e., airline) satisfaction. Meanwhile, maximising the overall productivity of the airport is one of the vital goals that the management team is expected to seek when making decisions for this business. However, the time complexity reported by other studies that used simulation modelling (e.g., Attar et al., 2024; Sadono et al., 2021) renders such a multi-objective optimisation task even more challenging. For complex systems whose simulation process suffers from high execution costs, a class of mathematical methodologies, known as metamodels, can be employed to approximate the simulation model (Barton et al., 2006; Gonzalez et al., 2020; Li et al., 2010). This class seeks to predict the simulation outcomes by identifying a mathematical relationship between the system's performance indicators and the values of the input factors (Amaral et al., 2022; Attar et al., 2016; Dellino et al., 2015; Kleijnen, 2014).

In general, various techniques can be applied for metamodeling, including Kriging, polynomial and quadratic regression, artificial neural networks (ANN), and ensemble methods (e.g., random forest and gradient-boosted trees) (Amaral et al., 2022; Dellino et al., 2015). The thorough reviews performed by Amaral et al. (2022) and Barton et al. (2006) revealed the popularity of regression-based metamodels, especially those involving the response surface methodology (RSM) for designing the required experiments. Therefore, in this paper, we offer RSM metamodels for predicting the outcome of managerial decisions on the main performance indicators of civil airports. These metamodels form the set of objective functions of a mathematical optimisation problem, using which we suggest the optimal decisions for this system. For the multi-objective optimisation side of this study, several exact, heuristic, and metaheuristic methods are available in the literature (Attar et al., 2015, 2017; Osorio, 2019; Li et al., 2024; Sousa-Junior, 2019). In this study, we deploy the well-known LP-metrics method that was successfully applied in various contexts and problems including simulation-based optimisations (Kabiri et al., 2022; Pasandideh et al., 2015).

The rest of the paper is organised as follows: The system description and the definition of the proposed models are provided in Section 2. The multi-objective mathematical model is presented in Section 3. This section also includes the proposed solution approach, the optimal solution, and the related discussions on the archived results. Eventually, some concluding remarks and future research directions are presented in Section 4.

2 MODELING METHODOLOGY

The proposed modelling approach for this system is divided into two phases: (i) simulation modelling, and (ii) the development of metamodels. Each of these phases is described in detail in this section.

2.1 Simulation Model

The system under study comprises multiple components including the control tower, holding stack, common glide path, runway, taxiway, apron, and the departure queue. Figure 1 graphically illustrates these key elements in the airport area. The airside of the airport is under direct control of the control tower and when an aircraft enters the airport's airspace, the pilot is expected to follow all the commands of the control tower until the plane exits the airfield upon its succeeding departure. When an airplane enters the airfield, it informs the tower and joins an aerial queue (i.e., holding stack), waiting for the tower's permission to approach the runway. This stage is symbolised by *Queue 1* in the process flowchart of Figure 2. The duration each plane spends flying a hold depends on many factors, including the number of flights already waiting in the airfield for takeoff or landing operations, airport conditions,

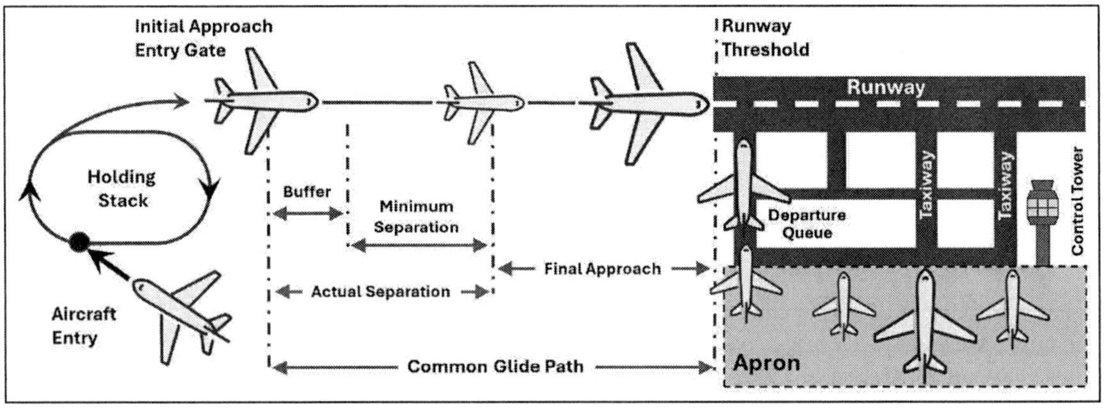

Figure 1 Components of the airside in a civil airport (aspect ratios are for demonstration purposes).

etc. Once the approach clearance is given to a plane, it can enter the common glide path and eventually reach the runway for landing.

One of the main decisions a control tower should make for the landing operations is to determine the right moment for granting approach permissions to each plane; for which the tower takes a set of factors into account. The main factors for this permission are the existing planes in the common glide path and the ones waiting in the takeoff queue. For each type of plane, a minimum separation distance should be maintained with its succeeding and proceeding planes to avoid any hazards on the flight. These separation standards are defined by global aviation administration organisations, such as the Federal Aviation Administration (FAA) in which three groups of aircraft are usually considered: small and medium (A&B), large (C), and heavy (D). Table 1 summarises this mandatory minimum separation for landing and takeoff operations (Ashford et al., 2011; Attar et al., 2024; Dixit and Jakhar, 2021; Horonjeff et al., 2010).

Table 1 Minimum separation for different types of aircraft during takeoff and landing operations.

Aircraft	**Type**	**Arrival – Arrival (nautical miles)**						**Departure – Departure (seconds)**					
	Trailing	D		C		A&B		D		C		A&B	
Leading	*Rules*	*IF*	*VF*	*IF*	*VF*	*IF*	*VF*	*IF*	*VF*	*IF*	*VF*	*IF*	*VF*
D		4	2.7	5	3.6	6	4.5	120	90	120	120	120	120
C		3	1.9	3	1.9	4	2.7	60	60	60	60	60	50
A&B		3	1.9	3	1.9	3	1.9	60	50	60	45	60	35

As seen in Table 1, the separation varies based on the vision conditions of the airport. That is, the aircraft are expected to maintain a farther distance from each other if they need to apply instrumental flight rules (IFR) rather than the normal visual flight rules (VFR) (Lau et al., 2021). In addition to the minimum policies stated in this table, the tower controller may impose a buffer time for takeoff and landing operations. This buffer is normally set based on the airport conditions and the controller's experience. In order to convert the distance separation presented in Table 1 for the landing operations into a time distance (i.e., a delay time) the following equations are usually utilised (Horonjeff et al., 2010):

$$MTS_{ij} = \text{Max}\left(ROT_i,\ \Delta_{ij}\right) + \text{Buffer Time} \tag{1}$$

$$\Delta_{ij} = \frac{\delta_{ij}}{V_i} + \text{Max}\left(\frac{1}{V_i} - \frac{1}{V_j}, 0\right) \times (\varphi - \delta_{ij}) \tag{2}$$

where, for a leading aircraft i and a trailing aircraft j, V is the approach speed, δ_{ij} is the distance separation from Table 1, φ is the common glide path length, ROT_i is the runway occupancy time of the leading aircraft, and eventually, MTS_{ij} represents the arrival-arrival minimum time separation.

After receiving the permission to enter the glide path, it takes the plane φ/V seconds to travel the distance to the runway and arrive at the runway for landing. Here, the operation time on the runway (i.e., ROT) is a function of the takeoff weight of the plane, its type, and the airport conditions. As shown in the flowchart of Figure 2, the runway is one of the components of the airside that are used both in the landing operations and in the takeoff. Landing planes are expected to vacate the runway after the successful landing by taking the available sideroads, i.e., taxiways. These taxiways lead the aircraft to the apron area where the planes are parked. For a return flight, with a departure already scheduled, the plane should unload its passengers and shipments and load/board new shipments/passengers during the apron operation. Refuelling, cleaning, safety inspection, and maintenance are also covered in this portion of the process. After completing the apron operations, the pilot has another permission required from the tower to initiate the pre-departure procedures, start the plane's engines, and (if necessary) request a pushback.

For the departure operations, the tower controller should take the minimum separation time (stated in Table 1) and the aircraft type into account when granting departure permissions, and just as we had for the landing, it may also apply the time buffer. Once the taxiway operation time (TOT) elapsed, the aircraft enters the runway, performs the takeoff operation, and eventually leaves the airport's airspace. As demonstrated in Figure 2, the taxiway is capable of handling the flow in both directions (from/to the apron), and the status of the flight determines the next step in the simulation process. However, to avoid conflicts and congestion, it is common to assume that each taxiway only has one function in each decision period, i.e., either used for landing or departure flights. Thus, without losing generality, we implement this assumption in the simulation model and consider two separate taxiways for departure and landing flights.

The process is modelled using the discrete event simulation (DES) technique in INCONTROL's Enterprise Dynamics (ED) simulation software which benefits from a wide range of features including a realistic 3D visualisation. This software was successfully utilised by several studies for developing simulation models in various industries (e.g., Ghasemi et al., 2023; Attar et al., 2015, 2016, 2017, 2024). Figure 3 shows a snapshot of the developed simulation model in this software. To build this simulation model, we collected the process time data from a civil airport in the northwestern part of Iran and

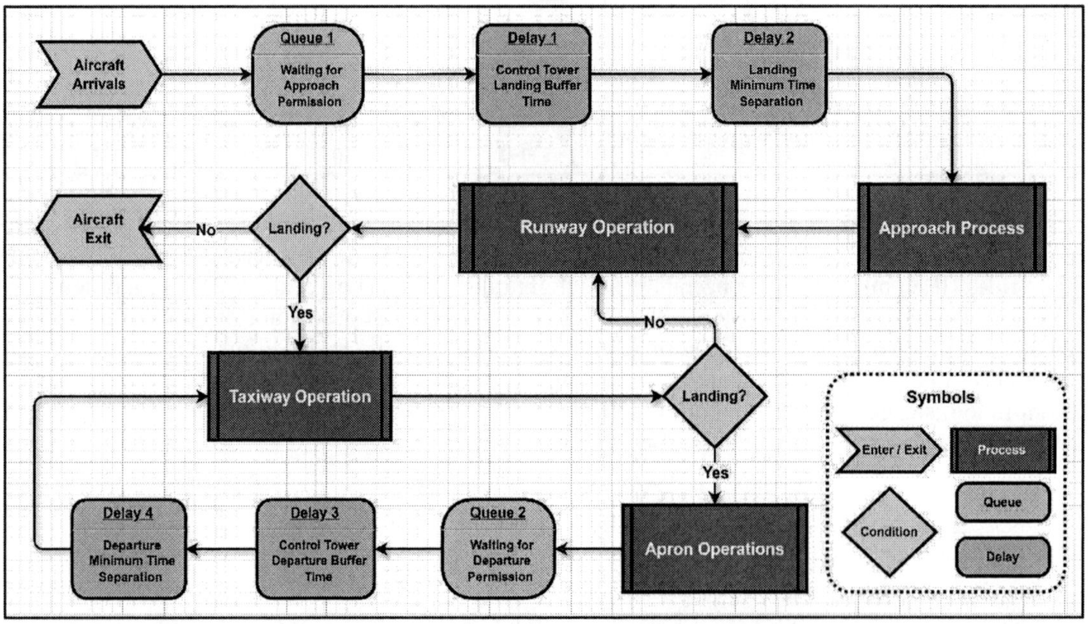

Figure 2 Process chart of the simulation model for mixed takeoff and landing operations in a civil airport.

estimated the distribution functions for the approach speed (V), landing ROT (LROT), departure ROT (DROT), TOT, the time between aircraft arrivals to the holding stack (TBHS), and the apron operation time (AOT). This data is presented in Table 2 for each type of aircraft, together with the corresponding p-value of the goodness-of-fit tests for each of the parameter distributions reported for this case study. In this table, $N(\mu,\sigma)$, $W(\alpha,\beta,\theta)$, $LN(\gamma,\beta,\theta)$ and $G(\alpha,\beta,\theta)$ represent normal, Weibull, lognormal, and gamma distributions, respectively; in which θ is used as the threshold parameter.

Figure 3 A snapshot of the simulation model developed in Enterprise Dynamics simulation software.

Table 2 Time distribution of the components of the airside in the case study.

Aircraft Type	**A / B**		**C**		**D**	
Parameter	*Distribution*	p-value	*Distribution*	p-value	*Distribution*	p-value
V (m/s)	$N(52, 3)$	0.175	$N(68, 5)$	>0.25	$N(75, 7)$	>0.25
LROT (s)	$N(54, 10)$	>0.25	$N(60, 8)$	>0.25	$N(65, 5)$	0.130
DROT (s)	$N(55, 3)$	>0.25	$N(49, 5)$	0.130	$N(43, 7)$	0.240
TOT (s)	$N(200, 12)$	0.133	$N(180, 13)$	>0.25	$N(173, 10)$	>0.25
TBHS (h)	$W(24.1, 0.7, 0)$	0.207	$LN(3.9, 413, 0)$	>0.25	$G(11.4, 1.2, 0)$	>0.25
AOT (s)	$N(2700, 80)$	>0.25	$N(3300, 95)$	>0.25	$N(4000, 122)$	0.118

For this model, we assume that all flights are normally leaving the system with no fatal failure and major maintenance expected in the planning horizon. The records of this airport show significant use of the IFR rules. Thus, in our analysis, we assume that all flights are using instruments for both landing and takeoff operations. The length of the common glide path of this airport is 15 kilometres, the apron can currently accommodate up to 5 planes, simultaneously, and the gates accept all types of aircraft with no preemptions applied. In the existing state of the airport, the buffer time applied by the control tower is approximately 20 seconds. As an extra safety rule for the departure, the control tower does not allow any departure flights to use the runway if there exists a landing flight in the approach area in less than two nautical miles distance of the runway.

2.2 The Proposed Metamodels

In this section, we propose a mathematical metamodel for the system under study. By consulting the management team and staff of this airport, we have identified a set of KPIs, symbolized by $Y_1 - Y_4$, that are defined respectively as follows: (i) average waiting time in the holding stack, (ii) utilisation rate, (iii) maximum hourly capacity, and (iv) average waiting time for departure. Here, the last KPI is the total time between completion of the apron operation and when the plane starts the final taxi for departure. Furthermore, the airport consultants believe that four factors, namely, approach speed, runway occupancy time, buffer time, and apron occupancy time, are of high importance and impact for these KPIs. Hereinafter, we refer to these selected factors as $x_1 - x_4$, respectively.

In order to form the mathematical equations for these KPIs, we deploy the DOE-based approach applied by Attar et al. (2016). In this approach, a full two-level factorial, face-centred central composite design method is used to generate the specifications of the required experiments. Unlike Box-Behnken designs, this method also includes designs that involve the extreme points for all factors. This design method is a sub-group of the response surface methods that generates 62 experiments (i.e., $2^6 - 2$) for the four factors of the defined problem (i.e., $x_1 - x_4$). The upper and lower bounds of the decision factors for these experiments are provided in Table 3, and Table 4 shows the first 10 experiments designed by this method using Minitab statistical software together with the corresponding simulated values of the defined KPIs. These bounds are chosen based on our preliminary experiments as well as the opinions received from the airport experts. For each of these experiments, the results represent one simulation run, for which (on average) a CPU time of 20 seconds was spent.

Table 3 The range of values for the selected factors.

Decision Factor	Lower Bound	Midpoint	Upper Bound
x_1	41.5	64.0	86.5
x_2	30	60	90
x_3	0	20	40
x_4	600	1800	3000

Table 4 A sample of the experiments derived using the DOE method.

Experiment No.	Factor Value				KPI			
	x_1	x_2	x_3	x_4	Y_1	Y_2	Y_3	Y_4
1	75.0	75	10	2400	5344	23.0	19	8.2233
2	52.0	75	30	1200	3126	39.4	26	16.850
3	52.0	75	10	2400	5493	22.4	18	0.0006
4	52.0	45	30	2400	5390	17.4	17	2.5840
5	86.5	60	20	1800	4341	24.6	20	1.9772
6	75.0	75	30	1200	2965	40.5	26	6.2246
7	75.0	75	10	1200	2945	40.8	27	6.2242
8	63.5	30	20	1800	4217	19.1	20	0.0002
9	86.5	60	20	1800	4341	24.6	20	1.9772
10	75.0	75	30	2400	5364	22.4	18	6.2235

In the next step for establishing the desired cause-and-effect relationship between the response values and the factors, we use the regression method to derive the mathematical functions for each of the KPIs. In this study, we examined the third-order polynomial regression functions using Minitab software, allowing both positive and negative exponents. The final response functions are given in Eqs. (3)-(6) for $Y_1 - Y_4$, respectively. These functions featured very high R-square values, ranging from 0.82 to 0.99, indicating the adequate fit of these equations to the data collected in the DOE stage.

$$Y_1 = 920.76 - 2.7025\, x_1 + 1.9297\, x_4 \quad (3)$$

$$Y_2 = 34.9640 + 0.2208\, x_2 - 0.0124\, x_4 - 3.1800 \times 10^{-13}\, x_3^{-1} \quad (4)$$

$$Y_3 = 13.261 - 137.83\, x_1^{-1} + 16697\, x_4^{-1} \quad (5)$$

$$Y_4 = 701.72 - 1.1134\, x_4 + 5.6149 \times 10^{-4}\, x_4^2 - 9.03 \times 10^{-8}\, x_4^3 \quad (6)$$

As an extra statistical step in checking the validity of the derived functions, we test the normality of the residuals for each function. As shown in Figure 4, the residuals of all functions are properly normal with their p-values noticeably above the typical 0.05 value for α. This further indicates that the

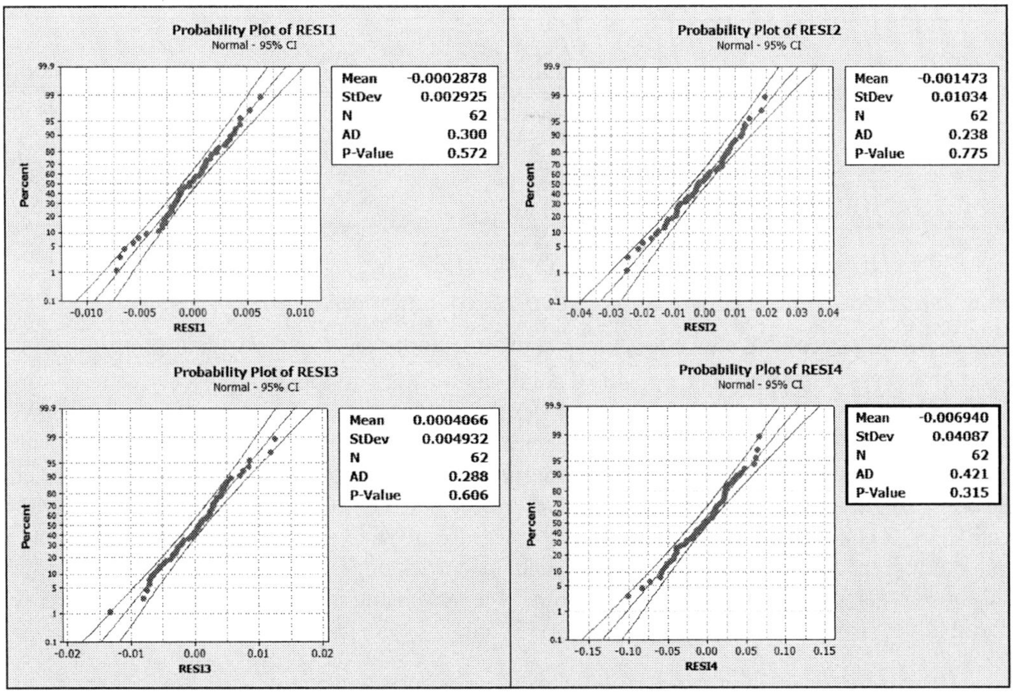

Figure 4 Normal probability plots for the residuals of Y_1-Y_4 represented as RES 1-4, respectively.

metamodels derived in this section are statistically suitable for predicting the outcome of the simulation model in the defined ranges and can be used reliably for optimisation purposes.

3 MULTI-OBJECTIVE OPTIMISATION

In this section, we utilise the metamodels from the last section to develop a comprehensive multi-objective mathematical optimisation model. We also explain our proposed method for solving the system to optimality together with some discussion on the archived numerical results.

3.1 Mathematical Model

Among the considered KPIs, only the hourly capacity (i.e., Y_3) is expected to be maximised and for the other indices lower values are more desirable. Thus, we can declare the objectives of the mathematical model as stated in (7)-(8). Constraints (9)-(12) are exactly the limits we defined for the DOE in Table 3. It is notable that, as stated earlier by Attar et al. (2016), the derived KPI equations are accurate even slightly outside these limits. However, since these limits were set after consulting the aviation staff and experts, we use the main conservative and practical limits for optimisation purposes as well.

$$\text{Minimize} \left\{ Y_1, \quad Y_2, \quad Y_4 \right\} \tag{7}$$

$$\text{Maximize} \left\{ Y_3 \right\} \tag{8}$$

Subject to:

$$41.5 \leq x_1 \leq 86.5 \tag{9}$$

$$30 \leq x_2 \leq 90 \tag{10}$$

$$0 \leq x_3 \leq 40 \tag{11}$$

$$600 \leq x_4 \leq 3000 \tag{12}$$

$$x_i \in Z^+, \forall\, i \in \{1,2,3,4\} \tag{13}$$

3.2 Solution and Discussion

The LP-metrics method is widely adopted to address multi-objective models which seeks to identify the optimal solution that minimises the distance from the ideal solution of each objective (Pasandideh et al., 2015; Kabiri et al., 2022). This metric can be calculated using the following function:

$$Lp = \left\{ \sum_{j=1}^{k} w_j \times \left[\frac{f_j(x^{*j}) - f_j(x)}{f_j(x^{*j}) - f_j(\bar{x}^j)} \right]^p \right\}^{1/p} \tag{14}$$

where $f_j(\cdot)$ is the jth objective function, w_j is its relative importance degree in the optimisation process, x^{*j} and $\bar{x}^j$ represent the ideal and anti-ideal solutions for the jth objective, respectively, and p is the degree of emphasis on the available deviations (Kabiri et al., 2022). For this study, we assume equal importance levels for all objectives and consider a degree of emphasis of 3 for this model. The ideal and anti-ideal values of each objective were derived by solving the proposed nonlinear model eight times as a single-objective model using exact solvers in GAMS software (i.e., twice with each objective). Subsequently, the LP-metrics function was formed and solved to optimality, resulting in the overall optimal scenario. The optimal solution and the corresponding KPI values are presented in Table 5. This table reports the KPI values for the optimal scenario using the metamodel as well as the average values obtained using the simulation model for 25 runs.

Table 5 The optimal solution and the KPI values obtained using the proposed models.

Optimal Solution		Response (KPI)	Value		Relative Deviation (%)
Factor	Value		Metamodels	Simulation Model	
x_1	86.0	Y_1	1846.17	1977.64	6.65
x_2	30.0	Y_2	34.15	36.70	6.95
x_3	21.23	Y_3	39.49	38.82	1.73
x_4	600	Y_4	216.31	226.81	4.63

Similar to Attar et al. (2016), in Table 5, we also report the relative deviation of the metamodel from the simulation model. These results reveal that the proposed metamodels have effectively predicted the simulation model performance with less than 7% deviation for this new scenario. The minimum deviation belongs to the average hourly capacity (Y_3) which was less than 2%. Moreover, a comparison of the optimal scenario outcomes from this study with the current system conditions reported by Attar et al. (2024) indicates that, theoretically, by altering the identified factors, this airport's hourly capacity can be augmented from approximately 18 to as high as 39. Given that the expected capacity reported for the best scenario by Attar et al. (2024) does not surpass 23, our approach demonstrates a 70.26% relative improvement compared to the best available solution in the literature.

4 CONCLUSION

Airport optimisation and management is one of the substantial challenges in the aviation industry, which is approached in this study from the airside perspective. This paper features a discrete event simulation model that covers all components of the airside with realistic assumptions. Since comprehensive models for the airport are known to be relatively complex, we integrated this simulation model with a metamodeling technique to facilitate the analysis, optimisation, and decision-making. The metamodels are derived by designing a set of experiments using the well-known response surface methodology and collecting the related response values from the simulation model. Moreover, we adopted a real case study of a civil airport in Iran to demonstrate the performance of the proposed approach.

By consulting the airport managers and experts, a set of four factors was identified as important input parameters, together with four main response KPIs. The derived metamodel functions are employed to build a multi-objective mathematical model and subsequently solved using the LP-metrics method. The achieved results for the hourly airport capacity of the optimal scenario revealed the superiority of the proposed optimisation approach by over 70% compared to the best-found solution in the literature. Given the significant improvements achieved in this study, a possible extension can involve deploying this approach for the landside of the airport. Analysing disruptions in airport operations and considering sudden or long-lasting failures and the related maintenance operations is another possible direction for future research, for both landside and airside. This paper presented a single-solution method for the proposed multi-objective model. Exploring the Pareto optimal solutions and their possible advantages is another interesting extension for this work. The variation of aircraft mix is one of the main factors that may affect the estimated KPI equations. Therefore, another extension avenue for this research may involve analysing the robustness of the coefficient estimations for changes in the incoming mix of aircraft.

REFERENCES

Ashford N J, Mumayiz S, and sWright P H (2011). Airport Engineering: Planning, Design, and Development of 21st Century Airports; *John Wiley & Sons: Hoboken*, NJ, USA.

Amaral J V S and Montevechi J A B, de Carvalho Miranda R. and de Sousa Junior W T (2022). Metamodel-based simulation optimization: A systematic literature review. *Simulation Modelling Practice and Theory*, *114*, 102403.

Attar A, Babaee M, Raissi S, and Nojavan M (2024). Airside Optimization Framework Covering Multiple Operations in Civil Airport Systems with a Variety of Aircraft: A Simulation-Based Digital Twin. *Systems 12*(10): 394.

Attar A, Jin Y, Luis M, Zhong S, and Sucala V I (2023). Simulation-Based Analyses and Improvements of the Smart Line Management System in Canned Beverage Industry: A Case Study in Europe. In *2023 Winter Simulation Conference (WSC)*: 2124-2135.

Attar A, Raissi S, and Khalili-Damghani K (2015). Multi-Objective Reliability-Redundancy Allocation for Non-Exponential Multi-State Repairable Components. In *11th International Conference of Industrial Engineering - IIEC2015*, Jan 7-8, Tehran, Iran: 1–8.

Attar A, Raissi S, and Khalili-Damghani K (2016). Simulation–optimization approach for a continuous-review, base-stock inventory model with general compound demands, random lead times, and lost sales. *Simulation*, *92*(6): 547-564.

Attar A, Raissi S, and Khalili-Damghani K (2017). A simulation-based optimization approach for free distributed repairable multi-state availability-redundancy allocation problems. *Reliability Engineering & System Safety*, *157*: 177-191.

Barton R R and Meckesheimer M (2006). Metamodel-based simulation optimization. *Handbooks in Operations Research and Management Science* 13: 535-574.

Dellino G, Kleijnen J P, and Meloni C (2015). Metamodel-based robust simulation-optimization: An overview. *Uncertainty Management in Simulation-Optimization of Complex Systems: Algorithms and Applications*, 27-54.

Dixit A, and Jakhar S K (2021). Airport capacity management: A review and bibliometric analysis. *J. Air Transp. Manag.* 91:102010.

Dönmez K, Aydoğan E, Çetek C, and Maraş E E (2022). The Impact of Taxiway System Development Stages on Runway Capacity and Delay under Demand Volatility. *Aerospace 10*(1): 6.

Feng Y and Johnson M E (2021). Simulation Analyses of End-Around Taxiway Operations under Four Different Runway and Taxiway Choices. *Transportation Research Record*: 1-10.

Ghasemi P, Goodarzian F, Simic V, and Tirkolaee E B (2023). A DEA-based simulation-optimisation approach to design a resilience plasma supply chain network: A case study of the COVID-19 outbreak. *Int. J. Syst. Sci. Oper. Logist* (10): 2224105.

Gonzalez S R, Jalali H, and Van Nieuwenhuyse I (2020). A multiobjective stochastic simulation optimization algorithm. *European Journal of Operational Research 284* (1): 212-226.

Horonjeff R, McKelvey F X, Sproule W J, and Young S B (2010). Planning and Design of Airports, 5th ed.; *McGraw-Hill*: New York, NY, USA, Volume 4.

Hunter S R, Applegate E A, Arora V, Chong B, Cooper K, Rincón-Guevara O, and Vivas-Valencia C (2019). An introduction to multiobjective simulation optimization. *TOMACS*, 29(1):1-36.

Kleijnen J P (2014). Simulation-optimization via Kriging and bootstrapping: a survey. *Journal of Simulation, 8* (4), 241-250.

Lau M E C, Lam A J G, and Alam S (2021). Predicting runway configuration transition timings using machine learning methods. In *2021 Winter Simulation Conference (WSC)*, 1-12.

Li Q, Huang S, Zhang X, Li W, Wang R, and Zhang T (2024). Topology Design and Operation of Distribution Network Based on Multi-Objective Framework and Heuristic Strategies. *Mathematics 12*(13): 1998.

Li Y F, Ng S H, Xie M, and Goh T N (2010). A systematic comparison of metamodeling techniques for simulation optimization in decision support systems. *Applied Soft Computing 10* (4): 1257-1273.

Manataki I E and Zografos K G (2010). Assessing airport terminal performance using a system dynamics model. *Journal of Air Transport Management 16*(2): 86-93.

Osorio C (2019). High-dimensional offline origin-destination (OD) demand calibration for stochastic traffic simulators of large-scale road networks. *Transportation Research Part B,* 124: 18-43.

Pasandideh S H R, Niaki S T A, and Asadi K (2015). Optimizing a bi-objective multi-product multi-period three echelon supply chain network with warehouse reliability. *Expert Systems with Applications 42* (5): 2615–2623.

Sadono M, Putra D Y and Harahap S A (2021). Development of Aircraft Movement Simulation in Airport Airside Area. *AVIA 2*(1): 9-19.

Sousa-Junior W D, Montevechi J A B, Miranda R D C, Rocha F, and Vilela F F (2019). Economic lot-size using machine learning, parallelism, metaheuristic and simulation. *International Journal of Simulation Modelling 18*(2): 205-216.

AUTHOR BIOGRAPHIES

AHMAD ATTAR is a postgraduate teaching associate with the Dep. of Eng., University of Exeter, UK, mainly delivering System Modelling, Simulation, and Mathematical Programming. He received his M.Sc. and B.Sc. degrees as the top student in Industrial Engineering from IAU-STB and joined Exeter in 2022 as a Ph.D. student in Engineering, focusing on the simulation of resilient, sustainable, and cost-efficient supply chains. He has about a decade of experience in the industry, and his main areas of research interest include simulation modelling, digital twinning, supply chain, reliability, airport management, inventory, healthcare systems, and offshore wind energy.

MAHDI BABAEE received his M.Sc. degree from IAU-STB in 2014 and holds a B.Sc. in Industrial Engineering from Amirkabir University of Technology (2010) and a Data Science certificate from Tose'e Higher Education Institute, Tehran, Iran. He has over 20 years of experience in process management and planning in top companies in the country and various industries including civil infrastructures and fintech. Mahdi is currently the Vice-President of Planning at BehPardakht Mellat, the nation's largest Payment Service Provider (PSP). His main research interests are simulation modelling, meta-models, digital twins, transportation optimisation, and airport systems management.

SADIGH RAISSI is a Professor at the Department of Industrial Engineering, IAU-STB. He received a Ph.D. in industrial engineering from IAU-SRB in 2002. Since 1988, he has been engaged in many industrial engineering consultancy projects and held different management positions including the Vice Chancellor for Education and Graduate Studies, IAU-STB. He has published over 200 articles, and more than ten scientific journals were initiated through his efforts. His main research interests include quality & reliability engineering, system simulation, and statistical methods in engineering. He also acts as the Editor-in-Chief of Journal of Industrial Engineering International (JIEI).

MAJID NOJAVAN is an Associate Professor in the Department of Industrial Engineering, IAU-STB. He received a BSc from Isfahan University of Technology, Iran (1989), MSc from Iran University of Science and Technology, Tehran, Iran (1994) and PhD from Islamic Azad University, Science & Research Branch, Tehran, Iran (2004) all in the field of Industrial Engineering. His research interests are quality engineering, expert systems, fuzzy theory and multiple criteria decision-making.

Proceedings of the Operational Research Society Simulation Workshop 2025 (SW25)
M. Luis, A. Harper, T. Monks and N. Mustafee, eds.
https://doi.org/10.36819/SW25.027

GENERATORS FOR LARGE-SCALE STOCHASTIC SIMULATION-OPTIMIZATION EXPERIMENTS

Renee Oswalt

Mays Business School
Texas A&M University
4113 TAMU
College Station, TX 77843, USA
reneeoswalt@tamu.edu

Dr. David J. Eckman

Department of Industrial and Systems Engineering
Texas A&M University
3131 TAMU
College Station, TX 77843, USA
eckman@tamu.edu

ABSTRACT

Running stochastic simulation-optimization solvers on a testbed of diverse problem instances allows users to evaluate their empirical performance, but obtaining meaningful results requires executing many replications. When problem instances feature realistic simulators, the associated computational costs are often prohibitively expensive. Cheaper, synthetic problem instances generally fail to preserve essential aspects of simulators, and a solver's performance on them may not be representative of its performance in practice. We propose a novel class of problem instance designed to imitate important features of simulation test problems and generate representative solver performance data at relatively low computational cost. We augment existing models predominantly used for emulation, namely, Gaussian processes, generalized lambda models, and kernel regression models, with an approximation of a Gaussian copula process. This adaptation facilitates efficient coordinated sampling across solutions (via common random numbers) and across solvers (via the sharing of sample-path functions) while keeping the number of user-specified parameters manageable.

Keywords:

simulation-optimization experiments, Gaussian processes, generalized lambda models, kernel regression, common random numbers

1 INTRODUCTION

Simulation optimization (SO) is the practice of finding optimal configurations, or designs, of a complex real-world system by systematically manipulating the inputs of a computer simulation model of the system and observing its performance estimates. In a supply chain setting, SO can be used to identify inventory control policies that minimize expected costs—e.g., a combination of order, holding, and re-order costs—while keeping customer order fill rates above some target threshold. This paper concerns *stochastic* simulation models, which internally generate random quantities, e.g., production yields and customer demands, in the execution of a replication. Given fixed inputs, e.g., an inventory control policy, the outputs of such models are stochastic, varying from replication to replication. Consequently, multiple replications must be performed when evaluating the performance of the model under a given set of inputs, henceforth referred to as a *solution*. SO solvers are algorithms designed to search a space of possible inputs to find solutions having better and better performance. One way to evaluate an SO solver's performance on a given problem is to fix a computation budget, measured in terms of CPU or wall-clock time or the number of replications, and track the improvement in the performance (objective function value) of the solutions it recommends over time (Eckman et al. 2023a). To assess a solver's overall performance, one needs to apply it on many problems, with many runs (macroreplications) performed on each problem.

SimOpt is an open-source library of SO solvers and test problems equipped with experiment design and analysis tools for studying the empirical performance of SO solvers (Eckman et al. 2024, Eckman et al. 2023b). SimOpt's library of SO problems is primarily populated with Monte Carlo or discrete-event simulation (DES) models, the latter of which can be especially computationally intensive for realistic or even semi-realistic models. Even though SimOpt's current design enables solver macroreplications to be run in parallel, large-scale experiments in SimOpt remain computationally demanding. Some empirical studies of SO solvers on DES models have been conducted (Dong et al. 2017, Boonsiriphatthanajaroen et al. 2024), but the high computation costs have, by and large, hindered more comprehensive experiments.

Problem testbeds have been an important resource for benchmarking and standardizing comparisons of solvers in deterministic optimization communities (Gould 2024, GAMS Software. 2024). Some testbeds of stochastic optimization problems have been built from deterministic optimization problems by adding mean-zero noise to objective functions that are typically polynomials or other algebraic functions (Ali et al. 2005, Surjanovic and Bingham 2024). These *synthetic* stochastic optimization problems offer certain advantages over more *realistic* SO problems built around DES models: namely, objective function evaluations are extremely cheap to evaluate, structural properties of the objective function are known, and the optimal solution may be known.

Synthetic problems also have serious downsides. First, unlike in simulations of real systems, the added noise is often homoskedastic, meaning the variance is common across solutions. When attempting to evaluate solvers that employ common random numbers (CRN) across different solutions, this property has the unintended effect of making all sample-path functions vertically shifted versions of the objective function. (As used in this paper, the term *sample-path function* refers to how the output of a single simulation replication varies as a function of the solution when the same realizations of the random primitives are used to drive the simulation for all solutions.) Any solver that leverages sample-average approximation will therefore reduce what was ostensibly a stochastic problem to a deterministic one *with the true optimizer and true gradients*. The performance of some SO solvers on such problems may therefore not be truly representative of their performance in practice. Second, certain intrinsic properties of stochastic simulation models are distorted or altogether absent in synthetic problems. In particular, gradient estimates and any effects of CRN—namely, the notion of a sample-path function—are artificial, divorced from the underlying dynamics of the simulator.

Motivated by the relative strengths and weaknesses of realistic and synthetic problems, this paper proposes an intermediate class of SO test problems that attempts to achieve the benefits of both. Specifically, problem instances should be extremely computationally efficient so as to enable large-scale experiments with SO solvers, while also capturing the stochastic sample-path behavior exhibited by SO problems involving complex simulators, e.g., DES models. This is accomplished by replacing the prototypical simulation model around which SO problems are framed with another, more primitive, stochastic model that mimics the input-output relationship of a simulation model, yet is significantly cheaper to evaluate. We refer to this simpler model as an *approximator* to indicate that its purpose is to approximate the behavior of a more complex stochastic simulation model.

Approximators have predominantly been used as *emulators* of a particular system under study (Gramacy 2020). Consequently, much of the related literature concerns the statistical problem of how to *fit* these models to data generated from simulation experiments, i.e., how to specify parameters of the approximator. In the emulation context, the focus is typically on accurately capturing the *marginal* output distributions at different solutions, with any correlation across systems usually arising incidentally from an extrinsic spatial covariance function. In this paper, we investigate three classes of models that have been used as emulators in the operations research, statistics, and applied mathematics communities: Gaussian processes (GPs) (Ankenman et al. 2010), generalized lambda models (GLaMs) (Zhu and Sudret 2021), and kernel regression models (KRMs) (Moutoussamy et al. 2015). The marginal distributions associated with these classes are normal distributions, generalized lambda distributions, and convex combinations of fixed probability distributions, respectively. More recently, machine learning techniques have also been leveraged for emulation tasks, e.g., generative neural networks (Cen et al. 2020), but we do not pursue this line of investigation here.

This paper is fundamentally concerned with the use of approximators for *generating* stochastic simulation outputs rather than emulating a particular simulator. We seek a generic class of models that are described by a modest number of user-specifiable parameters or parameters functions and are flexible enough to reflect the diversity of real-world SO problems. We use the term *generator* when referring to the targeted use of approximators for generating outputs, similar to how one interacts with stochastic simulators, that is, the ability to generate independent and identically distributed outputs at a given solution and correlated outputs across solutions via CRN. As far as we are aware, the problem of modifying approximators to serve as generators has received scant attention, yet is critically important if they are to catalyze experiments comparing SO solvers. Our efforts in this direction are similar in spirit to those of McDaniel and Ankenman (2000), who developed a testbed for randomly generating simulation response surfaces taking the form of polynomials.

We encounter two technical challenges when re-purposing existing approximators for generation rather than emulation: generating sample-path functions by implementing some functional equivalent of CRN across solutions, and synchronizing randomness across solvers so that they can work with a common set of sample-path functions. Gaussian processes offer a partial solution to the former through the specification of a covariance function, but more effort is required to achieve the desired sample-path sampling and cross-solver synchronization. On the other hand, GLaMs and KRMs were originally defined without regard for correlating outputs from different solutions. To fill this gap, we propose embedding an underlying *Gaussian copula process*, specified by the user, that yields correlated outputs across solutions. For cross-solver synchronization, we outline a bookkeeping scheme that enables sampling conditional on the outputs observed by previous solvers at previously queried solutions. This approach introduces its own computational challenges that we overcome by turning to approximate kernel methods, specifically *random Fourier features*, to approximate the Gaussian copula process.

The remainder of the paper is organized as follows: Section 2 articulates the problem statement, detailing the properties desired in generators and the challenges that accompany these demands. Section 3 examines the potential for GPs, GLaMs, and KR models to serve as generators and lays out existing knowledge gaps. In Section 4, we present our approach to address these gaps through the embedding of a Gaussian copula process, coordinated conditional sampling, and approximate kernel methods. We conclude with future research directions in Section 5.

2 DESIDERATA OF GENERATORS

Let $Y(x,\xi)$ denote the (random) output associated with a generic replication of a stochastic simulation model at a given solution x, where ξ represents the random primitives, e.g., the underlying pseudo-random numbers, required to execute a replication. Analyzing how the distribution of $Y(x,\xi)$ differs across solutions is fundamental to decision making under uncertainty, as this distribution often reflects certain risks associated with the simulated system described by x. For ease of exposition, we restrict our attention to the case where $Y(x,\xi)$ is a scalar; the setting in which replication outputs are vector valued introduces additional interesting challenges, which we leave for future research. We do not distinguish between cases where $Y(x,\xi)$ is real valued or integer valued, but note that GPs and GLaMs can handle only real-valued outputs whereas KR models can accommodate both real- and integer-valued outputs. For convenience, we assume that $x \in \mathscr{X} \subseteq \mathbb{R}^d$ for some finite $d > 0$ so that standard definitions of spatial covariance and gradients apply, but the framework presented here can apply much more generally to settings where x is integer valued or even categorical, as arises in ranking-and-selection problems.

To faithfully mimic the essential aspects of stochastic simulation models, an approximator should possess the following properties and capabilities:

Solution-dependent output distributions. Outputs from different solutions x and x', denoted by $Y(x,\xi)$ and $Y(x',\xi)$, should be able to have different *marginal* distributions, including different variances, a.k.a. heteroskedasticity.

Common random numbers across solutions. An approximator should be able to mimic the effects of implementing CRN within a simulator. CRN is a computational technique in which the same sequences of pseudo-random numbers are used to drive a simulation model under two or more different settings, i.e., at different solutions. More precisely, outputs from the jth replications at solutions x and x' are denoted by $Y(x,\xi_j)$ and $Y(x',\xi_j)$ for $j = 1,2,\ldots$, where a common realization of the random primitives, represented here by ξ_j, appears in both terms. In the supply chain setting, CRN could entail using the same realizations of the random production yields and customer demands for the jth replication of any inventory control policy. When successful, CRN induces a positive correlation between $Y(x,\xi)$ and $Y(x',\xi)$ and thereby reduces the variance associated with their difference, making it easier to correctly determine which solution has a better expected performance, e.g., a lower expected cost. Broadly speaking, an SO solver stands to benefit from the use of CRN across solutions it visits, hence this will be a valuable capability when performing SO experiments. More generally, a *sample-path* *function* of the form $Y(\cdot,\xi_j)$ characterizes how the simulation model's output on a given replication j varies across solutions as a result of using CRN. When working with an approximator, we would ideally like to be able to evaluate the same sample-path function at different values of x, but at a minimum we need to be able to sample the outputs at different solutions from the correct joint distribution.

Direct gradient estimation. Some stochastic simulators admit so-called *direct* gradient estimators, which refers to any estimator $G(x,\xi) \in \mathbb{R}^d$ of the gradient of some functional of the distribution of $Y(x,\xi)$, such as $\nabla_x \mathbb{E}[Y(x,\xi)]$, that can be obtained from a single replication. An example is the infinitesimal perturbation analysis (IPA) estimator (Glasserman 1991), which involves differentiating the realized sample-path function $Y(\cdot,\xi_j)$ with respect to x. When executing the jth replication of an approximator at a solution x, we would like to be able to simultaneously obtain a performance estimate $Y(x,\xi_j)$ and gradient estimate $G(x,\xi_j)$. Moreover, any effects of CRN in terms of influencing the geometry of the sample-path functions should extend to gradient estimates $G(x,\xi_j)$ and $G(x',\xi_j)$ as well. Both objectives will be achieved when using approximate kernel methods, as discussed further in Section 4.2.

The three classes of approximators we study all natively support solution-dependent output distributions through user-specified inputs. In this paper, we mainly focus on facilitating correlated sampling across solutions and obtaining direct gradient estimates. For GPs, all three properties listed above have been extensively studied, often from the perspective of fitting GPs to simulation experiment data.

We investigate what is additionally required of approximators for them to be used as generators within large-scale SO experiments. A standard SO problem formulation is

$$\min_{x\in\mathscr{X}} \{\mu(x) := \mathbb{E}[Y(x,\xi)]\}, \tag{1}$$

where $\mathscr{X}$ is some feasible region described by one or more deterministic constraints. The objective function, $\mu(\cdot)$, is defined as the expected performance of the system associated with the output, $Y(\cdot,\xi)$, e.g., the expected costs of different inventory control policies in the supply chain setting. We concern ourselves with SO problems of the form (1) for the sake of grounding our discussion, but our main results pertain to generating outputs, not strictly objective function estimates, and thus should extend to SO problems in which other functionals, e.g., quantiles, appear in the objective. Many SO solvers approach Problem (1) by visiting a sequence of solutions that hopefully possess better and better objective function values. Hence, a run of a solver, also called a *macroreplication*, entails executing many replications of the simulation model in the course of the search over the solution space. Moreover, because a solver's trajectory of visited solutions depends on the random objective function estimates it observes, one must perform multiple macroreplications.

For approximators to effectively replace realistic stochastic simulators in experiments comparing SO solvers, they should possess several properties and capabilities other than those previously discussed. In what follows, it will be useful to re-express a simulator's output at a given solution x as the unknown objective function value plus some mean-zero noise (henceforth referred to as error):

$$Y(x,\xi) = \mu(x) + \varepsilon(x,\xi). \tag{2}$$

At a high-level, throughout the remainder of the paper we will exploit Equation (2) by treating the objective function $\mu(\cdot)$ as user specified and focusing on approximators of the error stochastic process, $\{\varepsilon(x,\xi) : x \in \mathscr{X}\}$, rather than the output stochastic process, $\{Y(x,\xi) : x \in \mathscr{X}\}$.

Few user-specified parameters. The user should be able to directly or indirectly control important characteristics of a problem instance through a manageable number of parameters or parameter functions. This property enables large sets of *random* problem instances to be created by randomly generating values of these parameters. Important characteristics include the objective function $\mu(\cdot)$; the number of local or global optima; structural properties of the objective function and sample-path functions such as convexity, Lipschitz continuity, and smoothness; the marginal distributions of $\varepsilon(x,\xi)$ at any solution x; and the strength of any correlation between outputs at different solutions on a given replication, i.e., between $\varepsilon(x,\xi_j)$ and $\varepsilon(x',\xi_j)$ for $x \neq x'$.

Common random numbers across solvers. To achieve more standardized comparisons between solvers, it can be beneficial to control the underlying randomness so that on any given macroreplication, if two solvers ever simulate the same solution, they see the same sequence of outputs from replication to replication. In other words, different solvers should be able to work from the same universe of indexed sample-path functions when run on a common problem instance. This synchronization helps ensure that comparisons of solvers' performances are based more on the differences in how the solvers operate and less on the intrinsic randomness of the simulator or generator.

Computationally inexpensive. Large-scale experiments with SO solvers require many replications, hence obtaining observations of $Y(x,\xi)$ and $G(x,\xi)$ for any given solution x should be cheap. Moreover, any methods employed to imitate common random numbers and synchronize sample-path functions across solvers should be relatively inexpensive and scale well with the number of solutions visited by the solvers.

In Section 3, we present three existing classes of approximators and evaluate how they can be adapted for use as generators in SO experiments. All three classes require the user to specify a few parameters, but each requires some additional effort to permit solvers to work from the same sample-path functions. In Section 4, we comment on how the computational costs associated with our initial approach for coordinated sampling scale with the number of solutions visited by the solvers and explore an approximation scheme that offers considerable improvements in efficiency. The generator class we ultimately propose, which combines a Gaussian copula process and random Fourier features, satisfies all of the desired properties outlined above.

3 THREE CLASSES OF APPROXIMATORS

We give an overview of three classes of approximators and discuss the ways in which they do or do not inherently possess the desired properties described above.

3.1 Gaussian Processes

Gaussian processes are extensions of multivariate normal distributions to functions defined over real-valued domains. GPs are widely used to build metamodels of the expected outputs of stochastic simulation models for both optimization and inference (Ankenman et al. 2010). An example of the former is the use of GPs within SO solvers as surrogates of the objective function, e.g., within the context of Bayesian optimization (Frazier 2018). For the latter purpose, many important extensions and enhancements have been investigated, including gradient information (Chen et al. 2013), the effects of CRN (Chen et al. 2012), and diagnostics (Bastos and O'Hagan 2009).

Prior work involving GPs for SO commonly models the unknown objective function $\mu(\cdot)$ as being drawn from a GP and seeks to quantify uncertainty about the value of this function at any solution of interest. In contrast, we treat the stochastic process for the simulation error that yields a sample-path function as being drawn from a GP with mean zero and covariance function $K\colon \mathscr{X} \times \mathscr{X} \mapsto \mathbb{R}$, i.e.,

$$Y(\cdot,\xi) \sim \mu(\cdot) + \mathrm{GP}(0, K(\cdot,\cdot)), \tag{3}$$

from which it follows that $\mu(x) = \mathbb{E}[Y(x,\xi)]$ and $K(x,x') = \mathrm{Cov}(\varepsilon(x,\xi), \varepsilon(x',\xi))$ for all $x,x' \in \mathscr{X}$. We can also see from Equation (3) that the GP governing the error process specifies both the marginal distribution for the output, namely, $Y(x,\xi) \sim N(\mu(x), K(x,x))$, and the joint distribution for the outputs across solutions, namely, a multivariate normal distribution. When using a GP to generate simulation output data in this manner, the covariance function is to be specified by the user. The covariance function describes the covariance between outputs at different solutions and can take various well-known forms, e.g., variants of the radial basis function kernel and the Matèrn kernel, many of which impose some form of spatial correlation, dictating that the correlation between solutions that are closer to one another in the input space is stronger (more positive) than that between solutions that are far apart. Heteroskedasticity is incorporated into the model through the specification of the covariance function.

Among the classes of approximators we consider, GPs most readily satisfy the properties put forward in Section 2. A relative advantage of GPs is that they naturally impose a joint distribution on outputs from different solutions via the covariance function. Even so, it can be unwieldy to work directly with sample-path functions from GPs, as is desired for experiments with SO solvers. When working with simulators, a sample-path function follows from fixing the sequence of pseudo-random numbers fed into the simulator. As far as we are aware, however, GPs do not permit the fixing of a sample-path *upfront, across all solutions*. Instead, when wanting to generate $Y(x,\xi)$ at a new solution x, one samples from its *conditional* distribution given the outputs previously observed at other solutions on that same replication. This process is repeated, at growing computational expense, as a solver queries more solutions, and the sample-path function is incrementally revealed though never completely realized. As we will see in Section 4.1, this creates certain difficulties with coordinating sampling in SO experiments while keeping computation costs in check.

3.2 Generalized Lambda Models

Generalized lambda models (GLaMs) are a class of approximator used by the statistics and applied mathematics communities (Karian and Dudewicz 2000, Zhu and Sudret 2021). For GLaMs, the marginal distribution of $\varepsilon(x,\xi)$ at a given x follows a generalized lambda distribution (GLD) that is most cleanly described through its quantile function

$$F^{-1}_{\varepsilon(x)}(u) = \lambda_1(x) + \frac{1}{\lambda_2(x)}\left(\frac{u^{\lambda_3(x)}-1}{\lambda_3(x)} - \frac{(1-u)^{\lambda_4(x)}-1}{\lambda_4(x)}\right) \text{ for } u \in [0,1], \tag{4}$$

where $\lambda_1(\cdot), \lambda_2(\cdot), \lambda_3(\cdot)$, and $\lambda_4(\cdot)$ are commonly modeled as polynomials. As seen in Equation (4), the parameter $\lambda_1(x)$ controls the location, the parameter $\lambda_2(x) > 0$ controls the spread, and the parameters $\lambda_3(x)$ and $\lambda_4(x)$ together control the symmetry of the distribution. Generalized lambda distributions are a flexible family of continuous distributions that can well approximate many standard distributions including uniform, normal, and Weibull. However, the GLD family only accommodates unimodal distributions, which in some contexts may be an unworkable limitation.

When GLDs are used for emulation, the fitting of their parameter functions $\lambda_1(\cdot)$, $\lambda_2(\cdot)$, $\lambda_3(\cdot)$, and $\lambda_4(\cdot)$, typically involves the use of truncation sets and polynomial chaos expansions (Zhu and Sudret 2021). In our intended use of GLaMs as generators, the parameter functions would be specified by the user in a way that ensures $\varepsilon(x,\xi)$ is mean zero for all $x \in \mathscr{X}$. From Karvanen and Nuutinen (2008), this can be accomplished by having the user specify $\lambda_2(x)$, $\lambda_3(x)$, and $\lambda_4(x)$ and setting

$$\lambda_1(x) = \frac{1}{\lambda_2(x)}\left(\frac{1}{1+\lambda_4(x)} - \frac{1}{1+\lambda_3(x)}\right) \text{ for all } x \in \mathscr{X}.$$

For the purposes of generating simulation outputs, the fact that GLDs are most cleanly described through their quantile function as opposed to their probability density function (pdf) or cumulative distribution function (cdf), is a strength rather than a weakness, because it implies GLD random variates can be efficiently generated via inversion. To the best of our knowledge, GLaMs have not been equipped with a joint distribution across solutions. In Section 4, we induce correlation across solutions by embedding a Gaussian copula process within the generation of the simulation error.

3.3 Kernel Regression Models

The third class of approximators we consider is kernel regression models (KRMs) (Moutoussamy et al. 2015). As we apply them here, KRMs model the distribution of the simulation error at a given solution x as a convex combination (mixture) of mean-zero distributions $F_1, F_2, \ldots, F_n$ associated with a fixed set of solutions $x_1, x_2, \ldots, x_n$. For a given solution x, the mixture weights are related to the distance between x and each x_i as described by some kernel function, $K_R(\cdot,\cdot)$. More precisely, the cdf of the error term $\varepsilon(x,\xi)$, denoted by $F_{\varepsilon(x)}\colon \mathbb{R} \to [0,1]$, can be expressed as

$$F_{\varepsilon(x)}(\cdot) = \sum_{i=1}^{n} \frac{K_R(x_i,x)}{\sum_{j=1}^{n} K_R(x_j,x)} F_i(\cdot). \tag{5}$$

KRMs offer more flexibility than GPs and GLaMs in terms of the distribution of the simulation error. Users can specify a KRM generator by picking $\mu(\cdot)$, the pairings $\{(x_i,F_i)\colon i = 1,2,\ldots,n\}$, and the kernel function. One can engineer problem instances possessing almost any problem characteristic using KRM. For example, problems with highly unstable optima could be produced by associating a mean-zero error distribution having a large variance near the known optimizer of $\mu(\cdot)$. A realization of the simulation error at a given solution x can be generated from the mixture distribution given in Equation (5) by first randomly choosing a distribution from among $F_1, F_2, \ldots, F_n$ according to their associated weights and then evaluating the corresponding inverse cdf at a random value $U \sim \text{Uniform}(0,1)$. As was the case with GLaMs, KRMs do not prescribe a joint distribution on the simulation errors from different solutions; we address this shortcoming in the next section.

4 ENABLING COMPUTATIONALLY EFFICIENT CORRELATED SAMPLING

Motivated by the need to remedy the aforementioned limitations of GLaMs and KRMs, we propose two generalizable approaches that together enable efficient correlated sampling across solutions in a broad class of generators. The first approach, Gaussian copula processes, constructs a joint distribution on the simulation error associated with different solutions, but also creates certain computational issues that the second approach, approximate kernel methods, seeks to resolve.

4.1 Gaussian Copula Processes

Our first approach entails embedding a *Gaussian copula process* (Wilson and Ghahramani 2010) within the generator to induce correlation in the error terms from different solutions on a given replication. The main idea is that by allowing the user to specify the covariance function of an underlying GP, they can produce a similar, though not identical, correlation structure on the simulation errors and, by extension, the simulation outputs.

Like a GP, a Gaussian copula process describes the covariance between two normally distributed random variables associated with any pair of solutions x and x'. However, the normal random variables in question all have mean 0 and variance 1, hence the covariance is equal to the correlation. More concretely, we consider a collection of standard normal random variables $\{Z(x) : x \in \mathscr{X}\}$, where $\text{Cov}(Z(x), Z(x'))$ is described by a covariance function $K_Z(\cdot,\cdot)$. The user specifies the covariance function $K_Z(\cdot,\cdot)$, typically via a few parameters, and in doing so indirectly influences the resulting covariance function for the simulation errors.

We proceed to elaborate on how Gaussian copula processes fit within our framework in the context of a single macroreplication of a single solver and a single replication index j. To generate the output $Y(x,\xi_j)$ at a newly visited solution x, we will generate the associated error term $\varepsilon(x,\xi_j)$ *conditional* on the errors that have been generated at solutions for which we have previously evaluated their jth replication. For a Gaussian copula process, this conditional sampling is done on the underlying normal random variables as follows: Let $\mathbb{X}$ denote the set of solutions for which we have previously obtained the jth replication, and let $Z_j(\mathbb{X})$ be the vector of associated standard normal random variables from these solutions. According to the Gaussian copula process, the conditional distribution of $Z_j(x)$ conditional on $Z_j(\mathbb{X})$ being a particular realization $z_j(\mathbb{X})$ is given by

$$(Z_j(x) \mid Z_j(\mathbb{X}) = z_j(\mathbb{X})) \sim N(K_Z(x,\mathbb{X})K_Z(\mathbb{X},\mathbb{X})^{-1}z_j(\mathbb{X}), 1 - K_Z(x,\mathbb{X})K_Z(\mathbb{X},\mathbb{X})^{-1}K_Z(\mathbb{X},x)), \quad (6)$$

where $K_Z(x,\mathbb{X}) = K_Z(\mathbb{X},x)^T$ is a row vector containing the covariances between x and each $x' \in \mathbb{X}$, and $K_Z(\mathbb{X},\mathbb{X})$ is the covariance matrix associated with solutions in $\mathbb{X}$ (Glasserman 2004). If x were the first solution for which we needed to generate the jth replication, i.e., if $\mathbb{X} = \emptyset$, then one simply generates $Z_j(x) \sim N(0,1)$.

The error term $\varepsilon(x,\xi_j)$ is generated by first generating $Z_j(x)$ according to Equation (6), applying the cdf for a standard normal, $\Phi(\cdot)$, to produce a Uniform(0, 1) random variable, and then transforming that variable into one having the desired marginal distribution of $\varepsilon(x,\xi_j)$ by applying inversion, i.e., hitting the uniform random variable with the inverse marginal cdf of $\varepsilon(x,\xi_j)$. The transformations described above imply that the jth simulation output at x can be expressed as

$$Y(x,\xi_j) = \mu(x) + F^{-1}_{\varepsilon(x)}(\Phi(Z_j(x))), \quad (7)$$

where $F^{-1}_{\varepsilon(x)}(\cdot)$ is the inverse marginal cdf, or quantile function, of $\varepsilon(x,\xi)$.

The ease of evaluating $F^{-1}_{\varepsilon(x)}(\cdot)$ in a way that preserves the correlation structure given by the Gaussian copula process varies by approximator class. For Gaussian processes, the embedded copula process described above is unnecessary, and one can directly obtain $\varepsilon(x,\xi_j)$ conditional on the simulation errors at other previously evaluated solutions using an expression similar to (6) where $K_Z(\cdot,\cdot)$ is replaced with the GP's covariance function $K(\cdot,\cdot)$. For GLaMs, the quantile function $F^{-1}_{\varepsilon(x)}(u)$ is defined in closed form in Equation (4), allowing the correlation structure to be preserved through the inversion. For KRMs, the quasi-inversion method described in Section 3.3 will not preserve the correlation structure. An alternative approach is to numerically invert $F_{\varepsilon(x)}(\cdot)$ by reformulating it as an optimization problem $\min_{y \in \mathbb{R}}(F_{\varepsilon(x)}(y) - u)^2$ and solving using available derivative information from differentiating Equation

(5). This method incurs a small computational cost, one which is to be paid for each objective function evaluation, but is crucial to achieving correlated sampling.

From Equation (7), it can be seen that the smoothness of the sample-path functions produced by using a Gaussian copula process will depend on the smoothness of the objective function, the covariance function, the marginal distributions of the errors, and how $F^{-1}_{\varepsilon(x)}(\cdot)$ is evaluated. For the inversion approaches described above, smooth objective functions, and continuous marginal distributions that change continuously across the solution space, the resulting sample-path functions will generally be smooth. Due to the discrete nature of DES models, it is perhaps reasonable to expect that for many SO problems formulated around DES models, their sample-path functions will be discontinuous, and therefore not well-modeled by some of the models we propose that are built upon Gaussian copula processes. Further study on how to incorporate discontinuities into our proposed generators is left for future research, but Mohammadi et al. (2019) offers some promising approaches in this direction.

The conditional sampling routine described above can be extended to achieve correlated sampling across solvers, as part of a larger SO experiment. This is accomplished by retaining a complete history of the outputs, or more specifically, the $Z(x,\xi_j)$s, that have been observed thus far by any solver on a given macroreplication. In terms of Equation (6), this entails redefining $\mathbb{X}$ as the set of all solutions previously visited *by any solver* and for which the jth replication has been obtained. A consequence of this scheme is that in any experiment, solvers must be run serially, i.e., one after the other, on a given problem. Nevertheless, it is still possible to take advantage of parallel computing resources to accelerate the experiments by distributing the set of macroreplications of all solvers to different processors.

4.2 Approximate Kernel Methods

The conditional sampling scheme introduced in Section 4.1 enables correlated sampling across solutions and across solvers but entails computing the inverse of a covariance matrix whose size grows with the number of simulated solutions. The Schur complement can be used to accelerate block updates of matrix inverses, but the resulting cost still grows with the number of simulated solutions. An alternative approach is to sample from an approximate conditional distribution by conditioning on only a subset of the previously simulated outputs. This approach has several shortcomings relative to what we will propose, namely, solvers cannot be run in parallel, matrix inverses must still be repeatedly computed, and the approximation error may not be easily controlled.

Adopting a popular idea from the machine learning community, we propose using *random Fourier features* (RFF) (Rahimi and Recht 2007) to approximate the covariance function of the Gaussian copula process and ultimately generate approximate sample-path functions. As we will see, relative to the conditional sampling approach, RFF offers several significant benefits: faster, albeit inexact, sampling from the Gaussian copula process; the ability to fix full sample-path functions and share them across solvers; and effortless direct gradient estimates. In related work, RFF has also been leveraged to generate approximations of the flow map of a deterministic dynamic simulator (Mohammadi et al. 2024).

In the following analysis, we assume that the covariance function governing the Gaussian copula process is stationary, i.e., $K_Z(x,x') = K_Z(x-x')$, and positive definite. Random Fourier features approximates such a covariance (kernel) function by the inner product of a randomized map that maps solutions to a finite-dimensional space of randomized features. Applying RFF to the task of inexactly sampling from the Gaussian copula process at a given solution x on a given replication j, we can obtain the following approximation using a Bayesian linear model with Gaussian random weights:

$$\widetilde{Z}_j(x) := \sum_{i=1}^{m} w_{ij}\sqrt{\frac{2}{m}}\cos(\omega_{ij}^{\top}x + \tau_{ij}), \tag{8}$$

where $w_{ij} \sim N(0,1)$, $\tau_{ij} \sim \text{Uniform}(0,2\pi)$, and $\omega_{ij} \sim p(\omega)$ for $i = 1,2,\ldots,m$, all mutually independent, and $p(\omega)$ is the normalized Fourier transform of $K_Z(\cdot)$ (Wilson et al. 2021). A proxy simulation output $\widetilde{Y}(x,\xi_j)$ can then be obtained by substituting $\widetilde{Z}_j(x)$ for $Z_j(x)$ in Equation (7). We do not view the inexactness of the resulting proxy sample-path functions as a serious concern within our context, as we would like the generator to approximate the behavior of SO models *collectively*, rather than emulate a particular system. In light of the many benefits offered by RFF, we consider this to be an acceptable trade-off, noting that the accuracy of the approximation can be controlled through the choice of m. We intend to further study this approximation error and how it propagates through the copula.

A consequence of Equation (8) is that upon sampling $\{(w_{ij}, \tau_{ij}, \omega_{ij}) \colon i = 1, 2, \ldots m\}$, the proxy sample-path function associated with replication j is fully determined and can be evaluated at any solution x, in any order. The proxy sample-path functions can also be shared across solvers, allowing solvers to be run in parallel. Furthermore, direct gradient estimates can be obtained by differentiating the proxy version of Equation (7) with respect to x. Assuming the user-specified objective function $\mu(\cdot)$ is differentiable, the remaining task is to differentiate $F^{-1}_{\varepsilon(x)}(\Phi(\widetilde{Z}_j(x)))$. For GPs, this calculation simplifies on account of the Gaussian copula process being superfluous, whereas for GLaMs and KRMs, it is necessary to apply the chain rule twice. In the case of GLaMs, $F^{-1}_{\varepsilon(x)}(\cdot)$ is easily differentiated with respect to x as seen in Equation (4). As for KRMs, the desired gradient can be obtained via standard rules for differentiating inverse functions and applying the aforementioned numerical inversion routine.

5 CONCLUSION

This paper explored several classes of models that approximate stochastic simulators and proposed ways to adapt them to effectuate the kind of controlled, correlated sampling needed to carry out well-designed large-scale SO experiments. Of the proposed generators, each has distinct competencies and shortcomings. GPs readily achieve most desiderata with the exception of computational scalability, whereas GLaMs and KRMs require augmentation with copulae and random Fourier feature approximations, but support broader classes of simulation error distributions. We view this study as a preliminary attempt to frame the most crucial requirements of these models when used for data generation within SO experiments and address some of the technical challenges presented in the case of scalar-valued outputs. We intend to extend the framework to vector-valued simulation outputs and thereby broaden its scope to encompass other classes of SO problems, such as those with multiple objectives or stochastic constraints. Furthermore, we will study settings in which the objective or constraints feature functionals other than expected values. An anticipated concern with extending in these directions is a proliferation in the number of parameters that the user must specify to describe a problem instance, though at present we see this being unavoidable. We also plan to more thoroughly investigate the use of approximate kernel methods and the benefits they offer, as sketched out in Section 4.

On the coding front, we plan to implement the three classes of approximators in SimOpt for dual use as emulators paired with existing problems in the library or as generators for users to specify through the choice of their parameters. We will also build out capabilities for coordinating sample-path functions across solvers, as described in this paper, and for randomly generating problem instances.

ACKNOWLEDGMENTS

This work was partially supported by National Science Foundation Grant OAC-2410948. We also thank Shane Henderson, Barry Nelson, Rui Tuo, and William Taylor for helpful conversations.

REFERENCES

Ali, M. M., C. Khompatraporn, and Z. B. Zabinsky. 2005. "A numerical evaluation of several stochastic algorithms on selected continuous global optimization test problems". *Journal of Global Optimization* 31:635–672.

Ankenman, B., B. L. Nelson, and J. Staum. 2010. "Stochastic kriging for simulation metamodeling". *Operations Research* 58 (2): 371–382.

Bastos, L. S., and A. O'Hagan. 2009. "Diagnostics for Gaussian process emulators". *Technometrics* 51 (4): 425–438.

Boonsiriphatthanajaroen, N., R. He, L. Liu, T. Ye, and S. G. Henderson. 2024. "Evaluating solvers for linearly constrained simulation optimization". In *Proceedings of the 2024 Winter Simulation Conference*, 3482–3493. IEEE.

Cen, W., E. A. Herbert, and P. J. Haas. 2020. "NIM: modeling and generation of simulation inputs via generative neural networks". In *Proceedings of the 2020 Winter Simulation Conference*, 584–595. IEEE.

Chen, X., B. E. Ankenman, and B. L. Nelson. 2012. "The effects of common random numbers on stochastic kriging metamodels". *ACM Transactions on Modeling and Computer Simulation (TOMACS)* 22 (2): 1–20.

Chen, X., B. E. Ankenman, and B. L. Nelson. 2013. "Enhancing stochastic kriging metamodels with gradient estimators". *Operations Research* 61 (2): 512–528.

Dong, N. A., D. J. Eckman, X. Zhao, S. G. Henderson, and M. Poloczek. 2017. "Empirically comparing the finite-time performance of simulation-optimization algorithms". In *Proceedings of the 2017 Winter Simulation Conference*, 2206–2217. IEEE.

Eckman, D. J., S. G. Henderson, and S. Shashaani. 2023a. "Diagnostic tools for evaluating and comparing simulation-optimization algorithms". *INFORMS Journal on Computing* 35 (2): 350–367.

Eckman, D. J., S. G. Henderson, and S. Shashaani. 2023b. "SimOpt: A testbed for simulation-optimization experiments". *INFORMS Journal on Computing* 35 (2): 495–508.

Eckman, D. J., S. G. Henderson, S. Shashaani, and R. Pasupathy. 2024. "SimOpt". https://github.com/simopt-admin/simopt.

Frazier, P. I. 2018. "A tutorial on Bayesian optimization". *arXiv preprint arXiv:1807.02811*.

GAMS Software. 2024. "GAMS World model library". https://github.com/GAMS-dev/gamsworld.

Glasserman, P. 1991. *Gradient Estimation Via Perturbation Analysis*. The Netherlands: Kluwer.

Glasserman, P. 2004. *Monte Carlo Methods in Financial Engineering*, Volume 53. Springer.

Gould, N. 2024. "CUTEst". https://github.com/ralna/CUTEst. Version 2.3.

Gramacy, R. B. 2020. *Surrogates: Gaussian Process Modeling, Design, and Optimization for the Applied Sciences*. Boca Raton, FL: Chapman and Hall/CRC.

Karian, Z. A., and E. J. Dudewicz. 2000. *Fitting Statistical Distributions: The Generalized Lambda Distribution and Generalized Bootstrap Methods*. Boca Raton, FL: Chapman and Hall/CRC.

Karvanen, J., and A. Nuutinen. 2008. "Characterizing the generalized lambda distribution by *L*-moments". *Computational Statistics & Data Analysis* 52 (4): 1971–1983.

McDaniel, W. R., and B. E. Ankenman. 2000. "A response surface test bed". *Quality and Reliability Engineering International* 16 (5): 363–372.

Mohammadi, H., P. Challenor, and M. Goodfellow. 2024. "Emulating complex dynamical simulators with random Fourier features". *SIAM/ASA Journal on Uncertainty Quantification* 12 (3): 788–811.

Mohammadi, H., P. Challenor, M. Goodfellow, and D. Williamson. 2019. "Emulating computer models with step-discontinuous outputs using Gaussian processes". *arXiv preprint arXiv:1903.02071*.

Moutoussamy, V., S. Nanty, and B. Pauwels. 2015. "Emulators for stochastic simulation codes". *ESAIM: Proceedings and Surveys* 48:116–155.

Rahimi, A., and B. Recht. 2007. "Random features for large-scale kernel machines". *Advances in Neural Information Processing Systems* 20.

Surjanovic, S., and D. Bingham. 2024. "Virtual library of simulation experiments: Test functions and datasets". https://www.sfu.ca/~ssurjano/index.html.

Wilson, A. G., and Z. Ghahramani. 2010. "Copula processes". *Advances in Neural Information Processing Systems* 23.

Wilson, J. T., V. Borovitskiy, A. Terenin, P. Mostowsky, and M. P. Deisenroth. 2021. "Pathwise conditioning of Gaussian processes". *Journal of Machine Learning Research* 22 (105): 1–47.

Zhu, X., and B. Sudret. 2021. "Emulation of stochastic simulators using generalized lambda models". *SIAM/ASA Journal on Uncertainty Quantification* 9 (4): 1345–1380.

AUTHOR BIOGRAPHIES

RENEE OSWALT is pursuing degrees in Applied Mathematics, Business, and Industrial Engineering at Texas A&M University. She will work at Texas Instruments as a pricing specialist upon graduation.

DAVID J. ECKMAN is an Assistant Professor in the Wm Michael Barnes '64 Department of Industrial and Systems Engineering at Texas A&M University. His research interests deal with optimization and output analysis for stochastic simulation models. He is a co-creator of SimOpt, a testbed of simulation optimization problems and solvers.

Proceedings of the Operational Research Society Simulation Workshop 2025 (SW25)
M. Luis, A. Harper, T. Monks and N. Mustafee, eds.
https://doi.org/10.36819/SW25.028

DO WE NEED SIMULATION OPTIMISATION FOR QUEUEING ALLOCATION PROBLEMS?

Dr. Luke A. Rhodes-Leader

Department of Management Science
Lancaster University
Lancaster, UK
l.rhodes-leader@lancaster.ac.uk

Ms. Yu-Ting Lin

Department of Management Science
Lancaster University
Lancaster, UK
y.lin52@lancaster.ac.uk

ABSTRACT

As computational resources get cheaper and more convenient, largely through cloud technologies, the general trend is to solve larger simulation optimisation problems with more complex/realistic simulation models, sometimes in an exhaustive manner. This is despite the need for the computing sector and thus the simulation sector to reduce its carbon emissions. This paper advocates for using simpler models to aid the optimisation, particularly in queueing network problems, where many analytical models have been developed and system behaviours can make simulation optimisation more difficult. We focus on Jackson Networks for multi-fidelity optimisation of a server allocation problem, and set up a series of experiments to examine how well these models can aid simulation optimisation.

1 INTRODUCTION

The purpose of this paper is two-fold. The first is to contribute to the discussion around the impact of Operational Research techniques on the environment through its intensive use of computing resources, and our responsibility to tackle this. The second is to show the scope for significant computational savings when facing queueing network design problems.

Simulation is an inherently computational discipline. It relies on computing hardware and resources, the use of which has an environmental impact, particularly through data centres and cloud computing that are an increasingly prominent resource for simulation analysis. High power computing resources are becoming more widely available, as well as more efficient in their individual energy consumption.

Greater availability is leading to more usage, overwhelming the efficiency savings. As Knowles et al. (2022, p. 39) put it: "Greater efficiency leads, almost always, to growth in overall carbon emissions, as efficiency gains are quickly swamped by the desire to do more; hence we see global emissions increasing decade after decade despite continual efficiency gains in every sector." This can be observed within the Operational Research/Management Science (ORMS) field and how simulation is used. For example, simulation optimisation (SO) that utilises a large number of parallel processors (often accessed through a cloud server) has meant that Ranking & Selection algorithms (SO algorithms that exhaustively evaluate the solution space) are now being designed for problems with millions of solutions, such as PASS (Pei, Nelson, and Hunter 2024), rather than applying a searching procedure that is more selective but with more chance of missing the global optimum.

The result of this growth in ICT usage is a sector that accounts for a reasonable proportion of global CO_2 emissions. Exact percentages range considerably, depending on the assumptions made, but Freitag et al. (2022) place the figure between 1.8% and 2.8% for 2020. The acceleration towards "big data" in many sectors, including simulation, is likely to lead to a growth in these CO_2 emissions, especially as large amounts of data need to be processed in energy intensive data centres (Freitag et al. 2022). Whilst computing as a field is beginning to recognise that it needs to work on reducing its impact (Knowles et al. 2022), perhaps the ORMS community should also be considering how our use of simulation contributes to this. Obviously, simulation is a small part of this big picture, but is likely to be a large part of the ORMS carbon footprint.

Fujimoto (2020) studied this issue in detail, discussing the various aspects of power consumption when developing, running and analysing a discrete-event simulation model. Contributing factors include the model complexity, the way in which the event calendar is handled (though this is likely outside a user's control) and the number of replications required on a particular model, whether this is for experimenting with different system configurations, sensitivity analysis for estimated or unknown parameters, or just using multiple sets of random numbers to estimate the variability in the system.

This paper considers the final of these points, in the context of SO. Often, the main consideration in reducing the time to solve an optimisation problem is linked to the fact that some decisions need to be made quickly. Implicitly, this suggests that computation time is not that important when a decision is not required in real-time. Adding the energy usage dimension highlights the importance of computational efficiency even for strategic decision making optimisation problems. We aim to promote the use of simpler and much less computationally expensive queueing models to significantly reduce the number of replications in a queueing optimisation problem. We do not claim this is a new idea, the use of multiple models of differing fidelity has been proposed in multiple places (Xu et al. 2016, Cao et al. 2021). Rather, we aim to demonstrate that this is particularly appropriate for queueing systems. We do this through a set of experiments in which we start with the simplest queueing network, a Jackson Network, and move the service times further away from Exponential, to examine the alignment between the Jackson Network and the simulation model.

There are other benefits to multi-fidelity modelling, beyond the computational aspects. Henderson (2021) advocates for it as a method of learning more about the system and what makes a good solution, as lower fidelity models can highlight general system behaviours (particularly if the model is analytically tractable). The author actually goes further, suggesting that each model should be optimised on its own, to help gain this insight.

The remainder of this paper is structured as follows. Section 2 briefly describes some existing multi-fidelity optimisation approaches, both in general and those using queueing models. Section 3 defines the queueing optimisation problem of interest and its particular challenge for SO. Jackson Networks are discussed in Section 4. The experiments and results are detailed and analysed in Sections 5 and 6, respectively, before Section 7 concludes and mentions further considerations.

2 RELATED LITERATURE

Multi-fidelity simulation optimisation has been advocated in multiple papers. There are general algorithms and those targeted at particular problems. Xu et al. (2016) made the important point that utilising the high-fidelity model as part of the optimisation, so as to avoid bias. Jian and Henderson (2015) and Rhodes-Leader et al. (2022) tackle specific problems, bike sharing and airline disruption problems, and in both cases optimise the low-fidelity model(s) and use those optimal solutions as a starting point for SO.

Xu et al. (2016) propose a general method, MO^2TOS, that first orders all solutions by the low-fidelity model and groups them. High-fidelity simulation effort is allocated to the groups using OCBA (Chen et al. 1997). The choice of these groups has been developed to include clustering approaches. Cao et al. (2021) perform a clustering algorithm, and then group clusters in such a way that the best groups have a small number of solutions that are likely to be good, whilst the worst groups have a large number of solutions that are likely to be poor. Cao et al. (2023) also propose a clustering approach, but do not then group these clusters, and alter the high-fidelity simulation effort allocation.

Each of these algorithms are based around Ranking & Selection, in which all solutions can be simulated. When this is not possible, a search is required. Many of the algorithms in this realm draw upon Bayesian Optimisation, such as the MFGMIA algorithm proposed by Li et al. (2022) for discrete SO problems, generalising the GMIA algorithm (Salemi et al. 2019) to handle multiple fidelities.

The experimental results in both Xu et al. (2016) and Li et al. (2022) involve a manufacturing line, where the low-fidelity model is chosen to be a Jackson Network. However, they do not experiment directly with the system, as the purpose of those experiments is to test their optimisation methods.

There are several examples in the literature where ideas from queueing theory are utilised to aid the SO of the configuration of a queueing network. In an Emergency Department setting, Izady and Worthington (2012) use a network of $M(t)/G/\infty$ queues as a low-fidelity model (which is analytically tractable despite time-dependent arrivals and general service times) to indicate the number of servers needed at each node to achieve a target quality of service. This suggestion is then simulated using a discrete event simulation model, and if the service level is too low (or high) the target quality of service is adjusted in the low-fidelity model to suggest an alternative solution.

Osorio and Bierlaire (2013) investigate the problem of setting traffic-light signal timings to minimise congestion in a city using a microscopic traffic simulator. These simulation models can be extremely expensive. The authors note that the city is effectively a large queueing network, and so utilise a network of $M/M/1/c$ queues. This model requires solving a large number of non-linear simultaneous equations, but is still considerably faster than the simulation model. The output from the simulation model is then assumed to be related to the low-fidelity model with a multiplicative and quadratic additive error. This enabled the SO procedure to be very selective as to which solutions are simulated. Osorio and Chong (2015) continued this work by making some approximations in the queueing network, enabling the model evaluation to be sped up considerably.

Dieker, Ghosh, and Squillante (2017) also note that SO can be very expensive, and argue that knowledge from queueing theory should be used as part of the optimisation. They propose an approximation to the system that assumes its steady-state distribution will have a product form, and using the general queueing behaviour at each node - typically performance behaves approximately as $1/(1-\rho)$ (where ρ is the traffic intensity). This generates an initial solution for a Stochastic Approximation (SA) algorithm to improve upon without the product form assumption. This beats straightforward SA when changing rates in a single-server queueing network, and can be adapted to server allocation.

3 SIMULATION OPTIMISATION OF QUEUEING NETWORKS

Consider the problem of trying to optimise a queueing network by changing the server allocation. In particular, let the network consist of K service nodes. "Customers" (or jobs, patients, clients etc.) arrive to service node k at a rate λ_k. If all of the s_k servers at service node k are busy, the customer has to wait until a server becomes available. The time it takes to serve a customer at node k is random, with a mean of $\tau_k = 1/\mu_k$ (where μ_k is the service rate) and a variance σ_k^2. Following the completion of service at node k, a customer could go to another node, l, with probability q_{kl} or leave the network, with probability r_k. Such a network is known as a Generalised Jackson Network. The optimisation problem is to allocate servers across the service nodes so as to minimise some performance metric of the system, $f(\mathbf{s}) = f(s_1, s_2, ..., s_K)$, whilst sticking to a particular budget, B.

For simplicity, this paper will make some assumptions about the queueing network. Firstly, the arrivals from outside the system are from a stationary Poisson arrival process (so that inter-arrival times are exponentially distributed with constant rate λ_k). We also assume that the desired performance measures are steady-state and can be written as the expectation of a random variable, such as expected number in the system. For the servers, we assume that the number of servers at each node will not change over time, that all servers have cost 1, and that they cannot be shared between service nodes once allocated.

We can write our optimisation problem as:

$$\min_{\mathbf{s}\in\mathbb{N}^K} f(\mathbf{s}) = f(s_1, s_2, ..., s_K) \tag{1}$$

$$\text{subject to} \quad \sum_{k=1}^{K} s_k \leq B \tag{2}$$

Despite a wide array of analytical queueing models based on stochastic processes, in all but a few cases, $f(\mathbf{s})$ cannot be directly calculated, and so must be estimated using a simulation model. Therefore, this is a discrete SO problem, in a relatively simple form. However, it has a particular structure that can prove a challenge for quickly finding an optimal solution.

By means of demonstration, consider a popular, and very effective, Ranking & Selection algorithm, KN (Kim and Nelson 2001). This algorithm aims to filter out bad solutions quickly by doing a series of pairwise comparisons to see if there is sufficient statistical evidence to remove a solution. Whether solution i eliminates solution j after r iterations of the algorithm is based on the following comparison:

$$\bar{Y}_j \geq \bar{Y}_i + V_{ij} = \bar{Y}_i + \max\left(0, \frac{\delta}{2r}\left(\frac{t^2 S_{ij}^2}{\delta^2} - r\right)\right). \tag{3}$$

Here, t is a constant dependent on the number of solutions, the required probability of correct selection (PCS) and the number of initial replications, whilst δ is the indifference zone parameter, which specifies how much better the best must be to achieve the PCS (often selected to be the smallest practically significant difference). The threshold term, V_{ij}, is linked to the variance of the difference between the outputs, $S^2_{ij} = \mathrm{Var}(Y_i - Y_j)$. In turn, this is linked to the variance of the two solutions.

This is where the nature of a queueing system can harm the SO process. A better performing solution, i.e., one that controls the queue lengths more effectively, results in a less variable system. If there is low variability, as there would be in good performing solutions, we can potentially remove these quite quickly. However, badly performing systems are highly variable, making them harder to eliminate, as the V_{ij} value is larger. Thus, additional effort can be wasted on simulating poor solutions. This can be aided by using common random numbers, but the effect is still there.

A similar argument would be made for algorithms based on OCBA (Chen et al. 1997), where the budget allocation is in part linked to the observed variance of the solution output (a more variable solution will warrant more budget allocated to it). Indeed, the variability makes all SO problems harder. In Section 6, we will show the extent of these issues, demonstrating how much the variance can increase for some queueing networks, and how this impacts the allocation of budget using the KN algorithm.

However, the area of queueing theory could be utilised to force structure onto the optimisation problem that is lacking from a generic SO algorithm. One way of doing that is using one of the simplest analytical queueing network models available: a Jackson Network.

4 JACKSON NETWORKS

A Jackson Network (Jackson 1957) is a network of queues in which all arrival processes are stationary Poisson, all service times are exponentially distributed, the queueing discipline is first-in-first-out and there is no limit on the number of customers who can be waiting at any queue. That is, each of the service nodes are $M/M/s$ queues. This is a Markov process, with the state being the vector saying how many customers are waiting or being served at each service node. The important result from Jackson (1957) is that, at steady state, each of the queues act independently, meaning that they can be analysed separately and then combined to give the full network performance. The analysis therefore reduces to simply using the well known steady-state formulas for an $M/M/s$ queue (Hillier and Lieberman 1986, pp. 554–557) and e.g. combining these together across the nodes.

The first step is to calculate the effective arrival rate at each queue (as arrivals will come from both an external source, with rate λ_k, and from other queues). Let Γ_k be the effective arrival rate at node k, which satisfies the following set of simultaneous equations:

$$\Gamma_k = \lambda_k + \sum_{l=1}^{K} \Gamma_k q_{lk} \qquad \forall k = 1, ..., K. \tag{4}$$

Note that steady-state requires that $\Gamma_k < s_k \mu_k$, giving a lower bound for the number of servers required. If this is not achieved by a solution, the variance of the simulation estimate will be extremely large, making optimisation even more difficult. In some networks, an analyst may naturally analyse the situation and come up with this result - arguably using insight from a low-fidelity model to help the optimisation. In other cases, such as when there are feedback loops, getting to Γ_k is not so straightforward, and a more explicit use of these equations to create the constraints is helpful.

Suppose the performance metric of interest is the sum of the steady-state average waiting times at each of the nodes. Then, in a Jackson Network, this can be calculated using:

$$W = \sum_{k=1}^{K} W_k \tag{5}$$

where W_k can be calculated using the steady-state formulae for the $M/M/s_k$ waiting time:

$$W_k = \frac{1}{\Gamma_k} \frac{\rho_k (s_k \rho_k)^{s_k}}{s_k!(1-\rho_k)^2} \left[\sum_{n=0}^{s_k - 1} \frac{(s_k \rho_k)^n}{n!} + \frac{(s_k \rho_k)^{s_k}}{s_k!(1-\rho_k)} \right]^{-1}$$

where $\rho_k = \Gamma_k / s_k \mu_k$ is the effective traffic intensity for service node k.

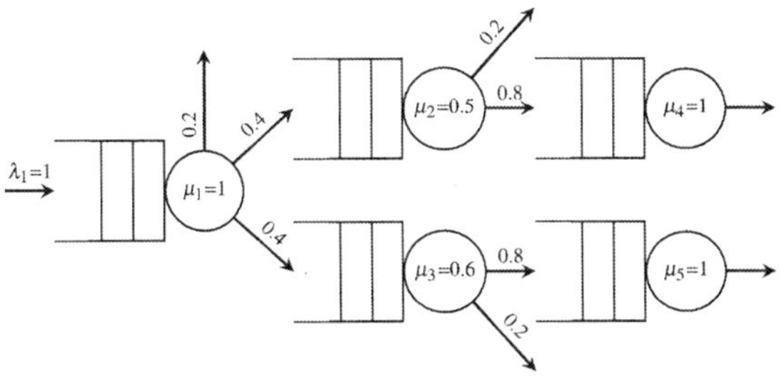

(a) System 1 - Tree network

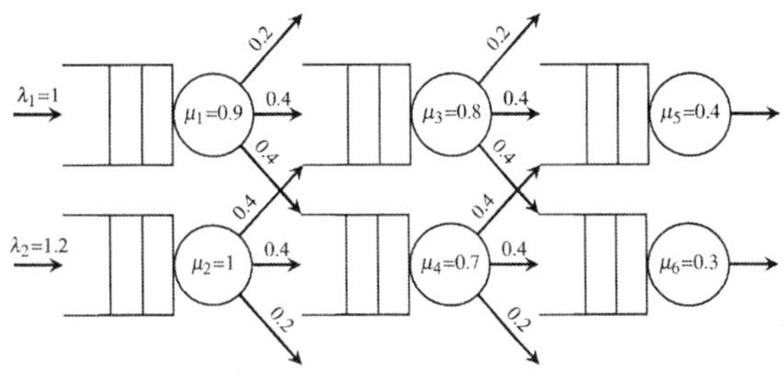

(b) System 2 - non-tree feed-forward network

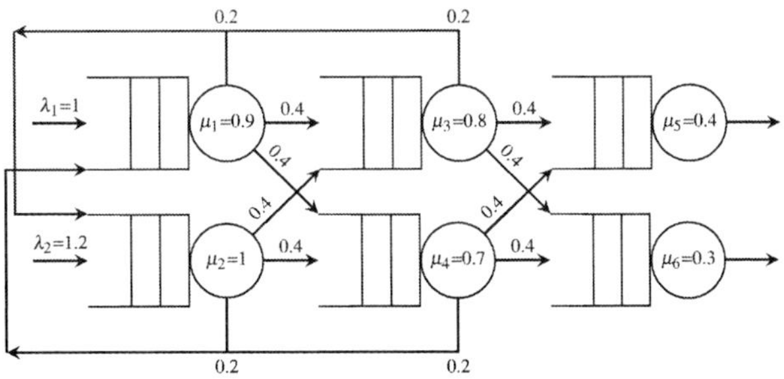

(c) System 3 - non-tree non-feed-forward network

Figure 1: Queueing networks used for the experimentation.

Due to its assumptions, using a Jackson Network to approximate the function $f(\mathbf{s})$ may not give accurate results for systems without Exponentially distributed service times (or inter-arrival times). The simulation is still needed to provide a prediction of performance. But, the results might be good enough to capture the relative performance of solutions, and thus the shape of the objective function.

5 EXAMPLE QUEUEING NETWORK ALLOCATION PROBLEMS

The specific queueing systems considered in this paper are displayed in Figure 1. System 1 and 2 are used in the experiments of Dieker, Ghosh, and Squillante (2017) (though the service rates have been altered). System 3 is an extension of System 2 in which customers can re-enter the system. All service times follow a Weibull distribution, with a mean $\tau_k = 1/\mu_k$. This allows us to control the mean and variance of the service times, which are typically the dominant features on queueing performance, in line with the Pollaczek-Khintchine formula for an M/G/1 queue (Hillier and Lieberman 1986, p. 563).

The aim is to minimise the sum of the expected waiting time at each node, as in equation (5). For System 1, at least 6 servers are required in the network (allocated as $\mathbf{s} = (2,1,1,1,1)$) to keep each node stable ($\Gamma_k < s_k\mu_k$). The budget is set to 10, and we assume all 10 servers will be used (as this will minimise the objective). This results in 70 feasible solutions. For Systems 2 and 3, a minimum of 13 and 15 servers are required to achieve stability at each node, and the budgets are 18 and 20, respectively. There are an additional 5 servers available, meaning that there are 252 feasible solutions.

To experiment with non-exponential service times, the shape parameter, α_k, of the Weibull distribution was altered, with values $0.3, 0.5, 0.8, 1, 2, 5, 10$ (note that $\alpha_k = 1$ is equivalent to the Exponential distribution). Due to computation time restrictions, the $\alpha_k = 0.3$ cases were omitted for Systems 2 and 3. Shape parameters less than one increase the variability of the service time, whilst values greater than one lead to distributions with a non-zero mode and lower variance. Increasing variance will increase the congestion at a service node, and vice versa. These settings were applied to (a) all nodes simultaneously; (b) just at the bottleneck node (node 2 in System 1, node 5 in System 2 and node 4 in System 3, identified as the node with the highest effective traffic intensity under the minimum staffing case); and (c) at a non-bottleneck node (nodes 1, 6 and 3 for Systems 1, 2 and 3).

The simulation model was implemented in Python using the SimPy 3.0 package (SimPy 2020, Monks and Harper 2023), making use of the sim-tools package (Monks 2021), which was also used

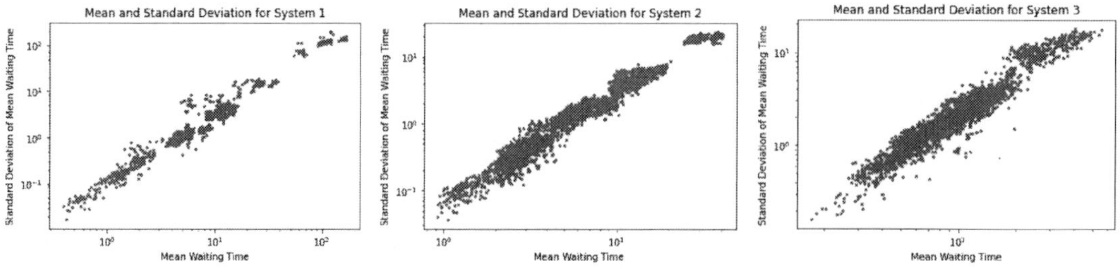

Figure 2: Plots of the relationship between mean waiting times and standard deviation of the simulation output. All solutions across all settings of α_k are included. For clarity, both axes are on the log scale.

for the implementation of the KN algorithm. Warm-up periods were selected using the Fixed Precision method described in Nelson and Pei (2021), evaluated with a staffing level just sufficient for steady-state to exist (i.e. $\Gamma_k/s_k\mu_k < 1$ for all nodes), meaning this was a conservative measure. The results collection period was set at 2000 time units.

Two sets of experiments were performed. The first was an evaluative experiment in which every solution for each problem was simulated so that a direct comparison between the Jackson Network results and the simulation results could be considered. Each solution was simulated until the confidence interval width was within 5% of the estimated mean.

The second experiment was running the KN algorithm on a selection of problems for each system, firstly on the whole solution space, and secondly on a solution space only containing the best 50% of solutions. (Some settings with very high variance, e.g. $\alpha_k = 0.3$, were excluded due to computational time constraints.) This experiment was intended to compare the computational effort between the two methods, and explore the extent to which poorly performing solutions are simulated. The algorithm was repeated 10 times for each problem to give an indication of the variability of performance.

6 EXPERIMENTAL RESULTS

6.1 Comparison Between Jackson Network and Simulation

First, we examine how the performance predictions of the Jackson Network and the simulation model compare over the range of service time distributions. Figure 2 demonstrates the relationship between the mean waiting time and the standard deviation of the simulation output. This grows approximately linearly in all three systems. This demonstrates the extent of the issue that could be caused to a Ranking & Selection procedure like KN. The full impact on the algorithm will be explored in the next section.

To see whether the Jackson Network is a useful low-fidelity model, we plot the Jackson Network performance from Equation (5) against the simulated performance for some example problems. These can be seen in Figure 3. The rows refer to different systems, and the columns are where non-exponential service times are applied to all service nodes, the bottleneck or a non-bottleneck service node.

For System 1 (S1), Figures 3a-3c, each of these settings lead to a different optimal solution, either through moving resources from node 5 to node 2 or from node 4 to node 1. The difference is small in 3a, but when the service times become considerably more variable than Exponential, more resource is moved to that node. These are amongst the most extreme settings tested, and yet the Jackson network still provides useful (but not perfect) information. In only five of the nineteen settings did the optimal solution differ (in a statistically significant way).

Example results for System 2 (S2) are shown in Figures 3d-3f. In the sixteen cases, there were only four examples when the optimal solutions differed by a statistically significant amount. However, there were many cases where another solution was indistinguishable from the Jackson Network optimal. The cases where the optimal solution changed were either when $\alpha_5 > 1$, i.e. the bottleneck service node had lower variance, or when a non-bottleneck node (6) became considerably more variable.

For System 3 (S3), only 3 settings led to a differing optimal solution. All of these occurred when non-bottleneck node 3 had a lower variance, as in 3i. In these cases, a server is moved from here to node 2. For cases where all α_k change, the deviation from a straight line is minimal, as in 3g. When the bottleneck is altered, there are clear bands, as in 3h, but this does not change the optimal solution.

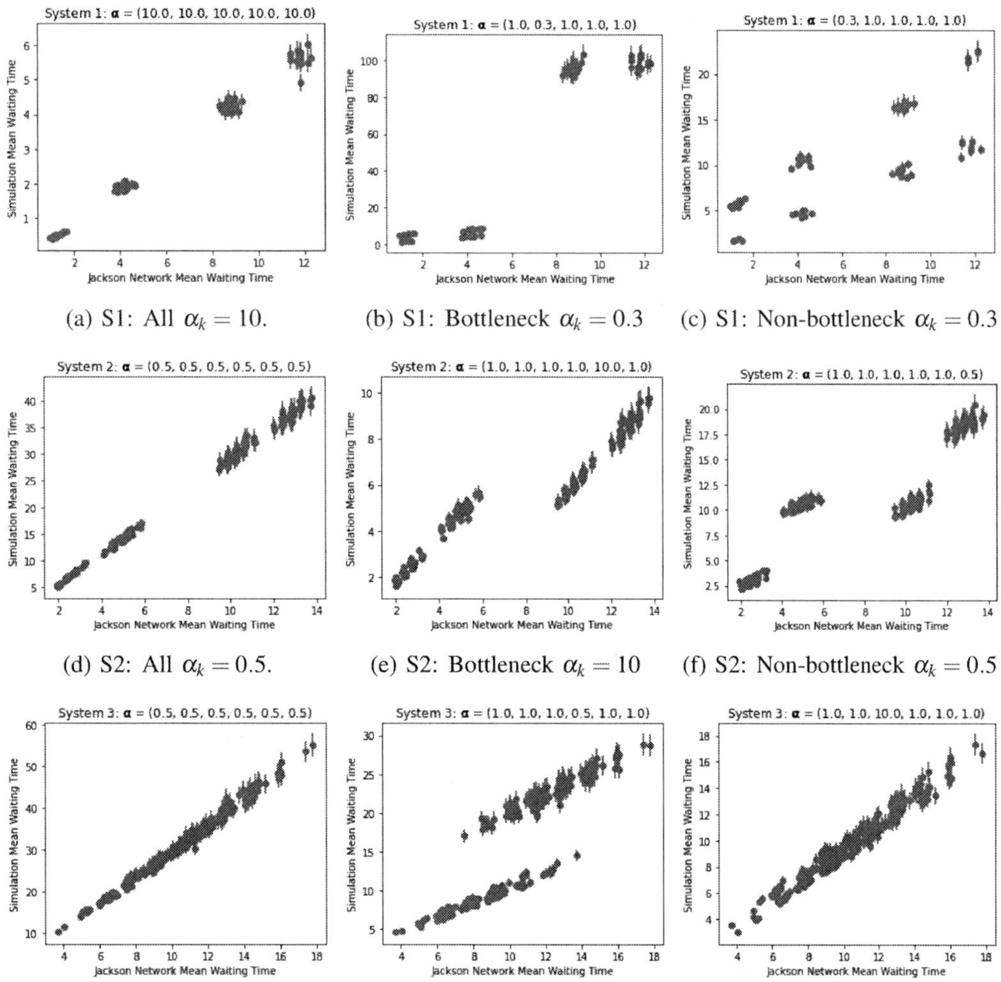

(a) S1: All $\alpha_k = 10$. (b) S1: Bottleneck $\alpha_k = 0.3$ (c) S1: Non-bottleneck $\alpha_k = 0.3$

(d) S2: All $\alpha_k = 0.5$. (e) S2: Bottleneck $\alpha_k = 10$ (f) S2: Non-bottleneck $\alpha_k = 0.5$

(g) S3: All $\alpha_k = 0.5$. (h) S3: Bottleneck $\alpha_k = 0.5$ (i) S3: Non-bottleneck $\alpha_k = 10$

Figure 3: Scatter plots of Jackson Network performance against simulated performance for each feasible solution in a problem. Error bars show a 95% confidence interval.

It is interesting to note that a clustering structure is evident in many of the scatter plots for Systems 1 and 2. This would indicate that the clustering approaches to ordinal optimisation proposed by Cao et al. (2021) and Cao et al. (2023) would perform particularly well. This structure, however, is less obvious for System 3.

Table 1 summarises a few key measures, averaged over all α_k settings. Because exact performance metrics differ between the models, we measure the similarity in objective function by correlation. Whilst this is not a perfect measure, as it does not consider the nature of the deviation, such as the two bands shown in Figure 3h, it does give some indication of whether optimising one system is equivalent to optimising the other. Most of the correlations were close to 1, indicating a reasonable agreement between the objective functions, and thus suggesting the Jackson Networks are a useful low-fidelity model. We report the optimality gap as a multiple of the indifference zone used in the KN algorithm, δ, as this is linked to the objective function range over the solution space (2.5% for Systems 1 and 3, 5% for System 2). In all cases, the mean optimality gap is less than δ, and the median is very close to 0. This indicates that in many of the test cases, difference between the solution provided by a Jackson Network and SO is not practically significant. However, there are cases where the gap is more significant, as demonstrated by the maximum column.

To conclude this section, it is clear that a Jackson Network does not necessarily provide a good prediction of performance. In some cases, it also does not provide the optimal solution, in which case

Table 1: Summary of comparison between Jackson Network and simulated performance.

	Correlation			Optimality Gap (multiple of δ)		
Problem	Mean	Median	Minimum	Mean	Median	Maximum
System 1	0.972	0.996	0.769	0.60	0	7.33
System 2	0.979	0.992	0.864	0.19	0.07	0.79
System 3	0.955	0.986	0.807	0.23	0	1.42

SO is required. However, in all cases tested it was able to identify good and bad solutions, with the correlation often being close to 1 demonstrating this.

6.2 Performance of Ranking and Selection Algorithm

This section looks at the results from the SO. Figure 4 shows the average proportion of the replications used by KN on the full solution set within a macro-replication for each solution, by rank. For the first two systems, it is clear that a substantial proportion of the simulation effort is focussed on the poor solutions, meaning that these solutions are harder to eliminate, in part due to their increased variance. The same is not true for System 3, where the budget is more equally spread across the solutions. This still indicates that poor solutions are being simulated as much as good solutions, on average. Thus, if these were removed before we got to the SO, considerable savings could be made.

We now turn to a comparison of the number of simulation replications needed by KN on the full problem and limited to the best 50% of solutions according to the Jackson Network model. Figure 5 shows all settings of α_k for each system. In all cases, the total budget required decreases when you reduce the solution space by half, as expected. In many of the cases, the reduction is by over half and the consistency increases. The largest gains are in cases with increased service time variability (i.e. α_k is small for at least one service node). The smallest gains are in System 3, which tallies with the message from Figure 4. This result demonstrates the value of the Jackson Network as an aid to the optimisation in these settings.

7 CONCLUSIONS

This paper has explored the effectiveness of a Jackson Network as a low-fidelity model for queueing allocation problems. This is motivated by the need for the ORMS community to reduce its energy consumption to a more sustainable level. The results suggest that these very simple queueing models can lead to good, though perhaps not optimal, solutions even when the system deviates significantly from a Jackson Network (in service time distribution). A simple heuristic of taking the top 50% also indicates that significant savings can be made in SO.

The experiments here are limited, and would benefit from a theoretical analysis to support the argument, as well as more extensive experimentation with different network structures. Examples based on real-world systems would help to improve the generalisability of these results.

There are many ways that a queue can deviate from a steady-state Jackson Network, beyond service time distribution. These include service nodes having a capacity on the number waiting, or time dependent behaviour. Servers may be able to serve multiple service nodes. Each of these

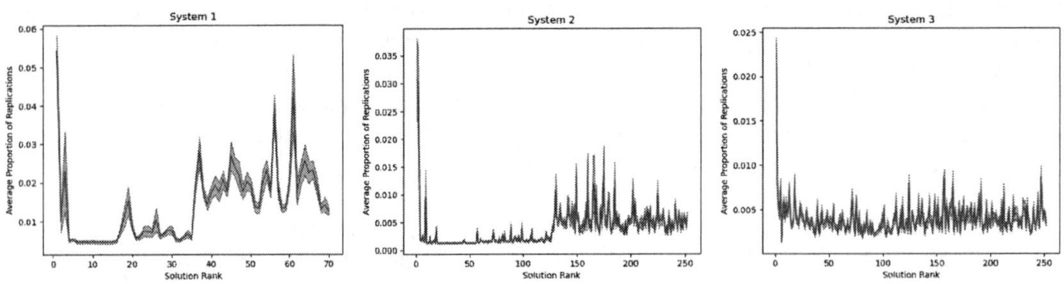

Figure 4: The average proportion of the budget spent on each solution, by rank, with a 95% confidence interval. Averaged over all macro-replications and settings of α_k.

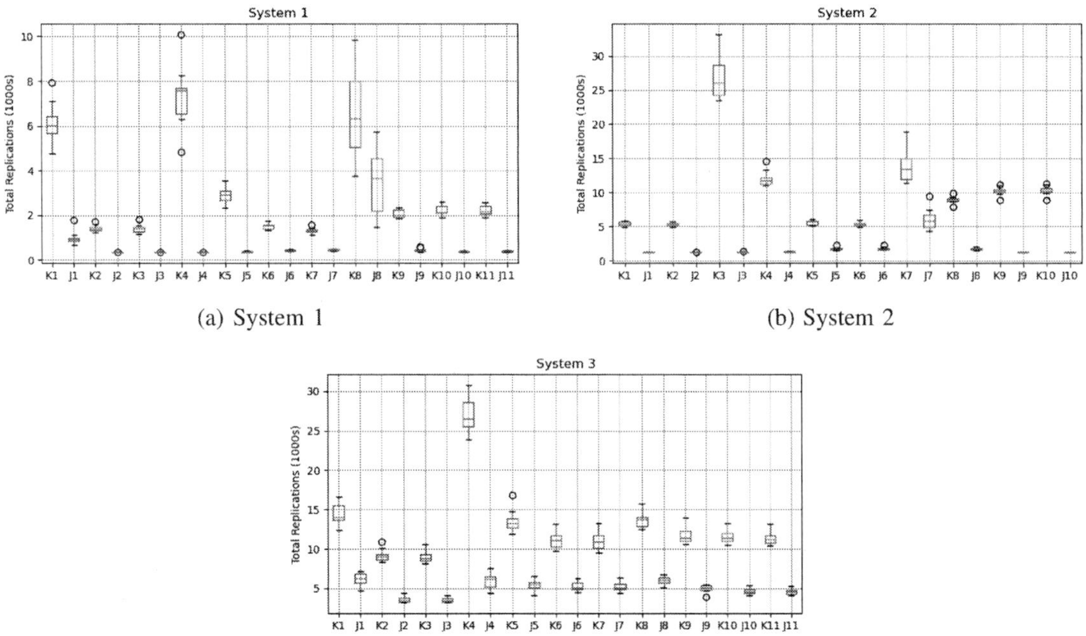

(a) System 1

(b) System 2

(c) System 3

Figure 5: Box plots of the total number of replications needed by KN. K1 and J1 refers to using KN on the full solution space or the reduced solution space for the first setting of α_k, respectively.

would further break the assumptions of the Jackson Network model. Further work should investigate whether a Jackson Network remains effective, or whether more complex queueing network models (that remain computationally tractable) could be developed/applied instead. On possible method would be to generalise Discrete-Time Modelling (Wall and Worthington 2007) approaches to a network.

REFERENCES

Cao, Y., C. Currie, B. S. Onggo, and M. Higgins. 2021. "Simulation optimization for a digital twin using a multi-fidelity framework". In *Proceedings of the 2021 Conference on Winter Simulation*, edited by S. Kim, B. Feng, K. Smith, S. Masoud, Z. Zheng, C. Szabo, and M. Loper, 1–12. Piscataway, NJ, USA: IEEE.

Cao, Z., H. Li, E. P. Chew, H. Wang, and K. C. Tan. 2023. "Cluster-Based Sampling Allocation for Multi-Fidelity Simulation Optimization". In *Proceedings of the 2023 Conference on Winter Simulation*, edited by C. G. Corlu, S. R. Hunter, H. Lam, B. S. Onggo, J. Shortle, and B. Biller, 3448–3459. Piscataway, NJ, USA: IEEE.

Chen, H.-C., L. Dai, C.-H. Chen, and E. Yücesan. 1997. "New development of optimal computing budget allocation for discrete event simulation". In *Proceedings of the 1997 Conference on Winter Simulation*, edited by S. Andradóttir, K. J. Healy, D. H. Withers, and B. L. Nelson, 334–341. Piscataway, NJ, USA: IEEE.

Dieker, A. B., S. Ghosh, and M. S. Squillante. 2017. "Optimal Resource Capacity Management for Stochastic Networks". *Operations Research* 65 (1): 221–241.

Freitag, C., M. Berners-Lee, K. Widdicks, B. Knowles, G. S. Blair, and A. Friday. 2022. "The real climate and transformative impact of ICT: A critique of estimates, trends, and regulations". *Patterns* 3 (8): 100576.

Fujimoto, R. M. 2020. "Power consumption in modelling and simulation". *Journal of Simulation* 14 (3): 157–168.

Henderson, S. G. 2021. "Reflections On Simulation Optimization". In *Proceedings of the 2023 Conference on Winter Simulation*, edited by S. Kim, B. Feng, K. Smith, S. Masoud, Z. Zheng, C. Szabo, and M. Loper, 1–15. Piscataway, NJ, USA: IEEE.

Hillier, F. S., and G. J. Lieberman. 1986. *Introduction to Operations Research*. 4th ed. London: McGraw-Hill, Inc.

Izady, N., and D. Worthington. 2012. "Setting Staffing Requirements for Time Dependent Queueing Networks: The Case of Accident and Emergency Departments". *European Journal of Operational Research* 219 (3): 531–540.

Jackson, J. R. 1957. "Networks of Waiting Lines". *Operations Research* 5 (4): 518–521.

Jian, N., and S. G. Henderson. 2015. "An Introduction to Simulation Optimization". In *Proceedings of the 2015 Winter Simulation Conference*, edited by L. Yilmaz, W. K. V. Chan, I. Moon, T. M. K. Roeder, C. Macal, and M. D. Rossetti, 1780–1794. Piscataway, NJ, USA: IEEE.

Kim, S.-H., and B. L. Nelson. 2001. "A Fully Sequential Procedure for Indifference-Zone Selection in Simulation". *ACM Transactions on Modeling and Computer Simulation* 11 (3): 251–273.

Knowles, B., K. Widdicks, G. Blair, M. Berners-Lee, and A. Friday. 2022, May. "Our house is on fire: The climate emergency and computing's responsibility.". *Commun. ACM* 65 (6): 38–40.

Li, D., H. Liu, X. Jin, H. Li, E. P. Chew, K. C. Tan, and Y. H. Lin. 2022. "Multi-Fidelity Discrete Optimization via Simulation". In *Proceedings of the 2022 Conference on Winter Simulation*, edited by B. Feng, G. Pedrielli, Y. Peng, S. Shashaani, E. Song, C. Corlu, L. Lee, E. Chew, T. Roeder, and P. Lendermann, 3170–3181. Piscataway, NJ, USA: IEEE.

Monks, T. 2021. "sim-tools: fundamental tools to support the simulation process in python".

Monks, T. and A. Harper 2023, July. "SimPy and StreamLit Tutorial Materials for Healthcare Discrete-Event Simulation".

Nelson, B. L., and L. Pei. 2021. *Foundations and Methods of Stochastic Simulation: A First Course*. Second Edition ed, Volume 187 of *International Series in Operations Research & Management Science*. Cham, Switzerland: Springer Cham.

Osorio, C., and M. Bierlaire. 2013. "A Simulation-Based Optimization Framework for Urban Transportation Problems". *Operations Research* 61 (6): 1333–1345.

Osorio, C., and L. Chong. 2015. "A Computationally Efficient Simulation-Based Optimization Algorithm for Large-Scale Urban Transportation Problems". *Transportation Science* 49 (3): 623–636.

Pei, L., B. L. Nelson, and S. R. Hunter. 2024. "Parallel Adaptive Survivor Selection". *Operations Research* 72 (1): 336–354.

Rhodes-Leader, L. A., B. L. Nelson, B. S. Onggo, and D. J. Worthington. 2022. "A Multi-fidelity Modelling Approach for Airline Disruption Management using Simulation". *Journal of the Operational Research Society* 73 (10): 2228–2241.

Salemi, P., E. Song, B. L. Nelson, and J. Staum. 2019. "Gaussian Markov Random Fields for Discrete Optimization via Simulation: Framework and Algorithms". *Operations Research* 67 (1): 250–266.

Team SimPy 2020. "SimPy 3.0".

Wall, A., and D. Worthington. 2007. "Time-dependent analysis of virtual waiting time behaviour in discrete time queues". *European Journal of Operational Research* 178 (2): 482–499.

Xu, J., S. Zhang, E. Huang, C.-h. Chen, L. H. Lee, and N. Celik. 2016. "MO^2TOS: Multi-Fidelity Optimization with Ordinal Transformation and Optimal Sampling". *Asia-Pacific Journal of Operational Research* 33 (3): 1650017:1–26.

AUTHOR BIOGRAPHIES

LUKE A. RHODES-LEADER is a Lecturer in Management Science at Lancaster University, UK. His research interests include applications of simulation optimisation and methodological aspects of digital twins. His email address is l.rhodesleader@lancaster.ac.uk, and his website is https://www.lancaster.ac.uk/lums/people/luke-rhodes-leader.

YU-TING LIN is s a graduate of Lancaster University, UK, where she earned an MSc degree in Business Analytics in 2024. Her research interests include simulation optimisation and queueing theory, with a particular focus on the application of Markovian queues. Her Master's dissertation is titled 'Use of Markovian Queues to Improve Simulation Optimisation of Queueing Networks.' She is committed to advancing analytical techniques for complex network systems. Her email address is y.lin52@lancaster.ac.uk

Proceedings of the Operational Research Society Simulation Workshop 2025 (SW25)
M. Luis, A. Harper, T. Monks and N. Mustafee, eds.
https://doi.org/10.36819/SW25.029

A DES-BASED ONLINE DIGITAL TWIN FRAMEWORK FOR FESTO'S CYBER-PHYSICAL SYSTEM: INDUSTRY 4.0

Muhammad Alfas

Department of Mechanical Engineering
Indian Institute of Technology Delhi
New Delhi, India 110016
mez208100@iitd.ac.in

Yanyan Tian

Exeter Digital Enterprise Systems Laboratory
Department of Engineering
University of Exeter
Streatham Campus, Exeter EX4 4QF, UK
yt401@exeter.ac.uk

Ahmad Attar

Exeter Digital Enterprise Systems Laboratory
Department of Engineering
University of Exeter
Streatham Campus, Exeter EX4 4QF, UK
a.attar@exeter.ac.uk

Martino Luis

Exeter Digital Enterprise Systems Laboratory
Department of Engineering
University of Exeter
Streatham Campus, Exeter EX4 4QF, UK
m.luis@exeter.ac.uk

Voicu Ion Sucala

Exeter Digital Enterprise Systems Laboratory
Department of Engineering
University of Exeter
Streatham Campus, Exeter EX4 4QF, UK
i.sucala@exeter.ac.uk

ABSTRACT

This paper proposes a digital twin framework for the Festo Cyber-Physical Factory through the discrete event simulation (DES) method. As a virtual representation of a physical system, such a twin facilitates seamless bidirectional communication between the physical and virtual components. This integration enables real-time monitoring, predictive maintenance, and process optimization, particularly in production lines. The proposed framework deploys Open Platform Communications Unified Architecture (OPC UA) to establish a reliable connection between the physical factory and its digital counterpart, ensuring effective data exchange. This paper explores the technical facets of developing this digital twin, examining its functionalities, prospective applications, and its practical contribution to improving operational efficiency and decision-making.

Keywords: Online Digital Twin, Cyber-Physical Systems, Industry 4.0, Discrete Event Simulation

1 INTRODUCTION

Industry 4.0, also known as the Fourth Industrial Revolution, aims to utilize advancements in digitalization to increase productivity, flexibility, and efficiency in the manufacturing sector. The key components of Industry 4.0 include the Internet of Things (IoT), cyber-physical systems (CPS), smart factories, and the latest advancements in technology, such as cloud computing, big data, and machine learning (Lasi et al. 2014). Smart factories are a kind of implementation of Industry 4.0 for manufacturing, which uses tools and techniques like sensors, actuators, embedded programmable logic controllers (PLCs), automated guided vehicles (AGVs), and other network-connected objects to track, monitor, and analyze the data collected from the production lines to develop more efficient and productive systems (Chen et al. 2018).

The CPS refers to a system that combines the digital and physical worlds by combining computational capabilities with real-world physical systems. Such an integrated structure enables the CPS to continuously monitor, control, and improve physical operations in real time. This fusion of computation, communication, and control provides opportunities in diverse areas like transportation, healthcare, and aerospace (Baheti and Gill 2011). In fact, CPS is the layer in smart factories that facilitates the integration of digital technologies into manufacturing through interconnectivity, data utilization, and autonomous operations; yielding better flexibility, customization, enhanced efficiency, and broader socio-economic implications (Sinha and Roy 2020). The availability of real-time data and feedback mechanisms in such CPS structures paves the way for a digital twin that is a virtual replica of physical systems that differs from the traditional simulation models by providing real-time interaction with the physical system and the potential for continuous improvements (Attar et al. 2023, 2024). The development and implementation of digital twins in a CPS lead to a more efficient system with minimal additional infrastructure requirements (Tao et al. 2019).

The major components of a digital twin include a set of physical elements (e.g., machines and related parts), a set of virtual models that mimic the physical elements, and a communication and integration layer (Grieves and Vickers 2016). Digital twins provide every advantage a typical simulation model offers, i.e., it can be used to forecast and predict possible downtime and maintenance, perform experiments and what-if scenarios, and optimize operations. Additionally, digital twins provide bidirectional communication, thus enabling continuous improvement of the physical system using feedback loops. These twins generate valuable data that may be used to enhance the performance and productivity of the real system in multiple ways. The data can be used for optimization, data analytics, simulation analysis, forecasting models, machine learning, and predictive maintenance (PdM) (Liu et al. 2023). Some PdM-related applications that would benefit from having such a digital twin are health indicators, reinforcement learning for improving maintenance schedules and predicting remaining useful life (Chen et al. 2023).

In this study, we develop a digital twin framework for a cyber-physical system by utilizing the discrete event simulation (DES) method with a special focus on Festo's cyber-physical factory (FesCPF). FesCPF is an Industry 4.0 integrated, modular, and flexible manufacturing production system with a research platform designed for academic institutes. This paper also lays out major components, development details, applications, and future extension plans of the proposed framework. The rest of the paper is organized as follows: The next section explores the major, recent, and most related studies in the domain of digital twins. Section 3 details the methodology and developmental framework of the online twin, followed by some discussion on the developed twin in Section 4. Finally, the conclusion and future research directions are provided in Section 5.

2 RELATED LITERATURE

Although the concept of creating a digital model that integrates real-time data from physical devices has existed for a long time, the term "Digital Twin" was first introduced during a Product Life-cycle Management course at the University of Michigan in early 2002 (Grieves 2014). Following that, NASA presented one of the earliest definitions of the digital twin, with their initial models found to be in the domain of aerospace engineering (Negri et al. 2017, Attar et al. 2024). Based on the idea of real-time feedback and control, digital twins have found applications in healthcare, urban planning, energy, airspace, agriculture, climate, and transportation (Rasheed et al. 2020). For instance, digital twins in the energy industry have numerous successful implementations in all stages, i.e., generation, storage, transmission, distribution, and management (do Amaral et al. 2023). In industrial settings, where real-time data can be gathered from stations and equipment, digital twins depend on these data collection and feedback systems. Nevertheless, real-time data collection is not directly implemented in many of the aforementioned fields, necessitating frequent data update mechanisms (Fuller et al. 2020).

In the mid-2010s, as a part of Industry 4.0 adoption, the manufacturing industry also started proceeding in the direction of digital twins and real-time feedback systems. Schroeder et al. (2016) are considered the pioneers of digital twin implementation in the field of CPS that integrates both virtual and physical systems through communication, computing, and control. As CPS provides a better infrastructure for real-time feedback and data collection, digital twins became the tool to leverage the data generated and acted as a decision support system (Esterle et al. 2021). Josifovska et al. (2019) presents a five-level reference framework for digital twin implementation in CPS, which starts with connecting sensors to the digital model and evolves into a plug-and-play mode in level five. This implementation also calls to look into big data handling, lifecycle perspective, and semantic modeling (Negri et al. 2017). Recently, Michael et al. (2024) discussed how digital twins can be implemented to interpret the behavior of CPS akin to how explainable artificial intelligence (AI) models work.

Among these studies, there have been a few attempts to develop a digital twin for the Festo cyber-physical factory (FesCPF) from an academic perspective. Mihai et al. (2021) developed a digital twin for the Festo CP factory using the Unity game engine. This work focuses on the two production cells in the factory and discusses the applications and challenges. Onaji et al. (2022) provides a comprehensive literature review and a framework for digital twins as well as three case studies. The case studies investigated by Onaji et al. (2022) included a FesCPF, a pharmaceutical continuous crystallization system, and a virtual x-ray of electric motors. Furthermore, a recent study by Teimoori et al. (2023) used Siemens Tecnomatix Plant Simulation (TPS) software and developed a monitoring system for a small FesCPF with only two production cells. Our study extends the existing models and digital twins for the FesCPFs to cover a more complex structure that involves three production cells, robotic assembly, and multiple products.

3 METHODOLOGY

As stated by Grieves and Vickers (2016), a digital twin comprises three core components: (i) physical objects that constitute a physical system we want to model, (ii) digital objects that constitute a virtual replica of the physical system, and (iii) connections between physical and digital objects. Besides these core components, digital twins may also have an intelligence layer, which includes databases, algorithms, and control programs to provide insights into the performance of the physical system. Figure 1 demonstrates a schematic overview of these components and their interaction. In the figure, the physical objects are connected to their digital counterparts using a layer based on a communication protocol like OPC-UA (Open Platform Communications Unified Architecture). On top of the digital objects, we can employ an intelligence layer that constitutes databases, control programs to manage manufacturing, and algorithms to predict and forecast maintenance and other activities. The proposed framework has five major stages that are summarized in Figure 2. As seen in this figure, these stages are:

1. **Conceptual design:** This step mainly focuses on planning the work, defining modeling objectives, and deciding which processes and data need to be collected.

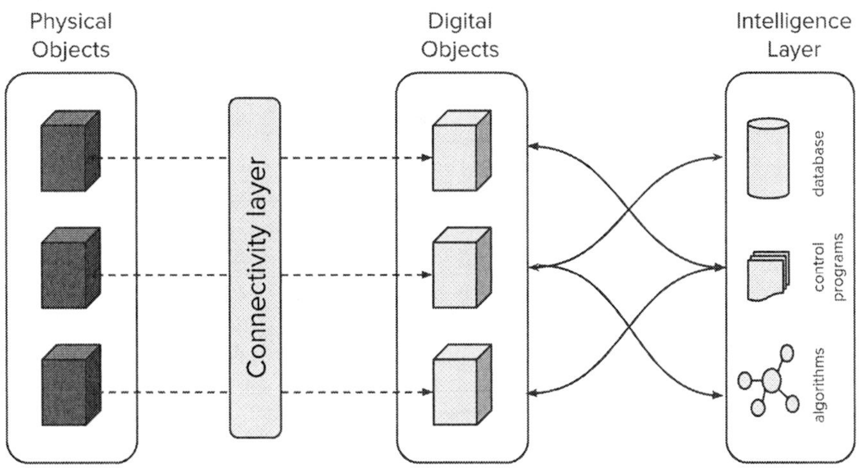

Figure 1: Overview of the digital twin components.

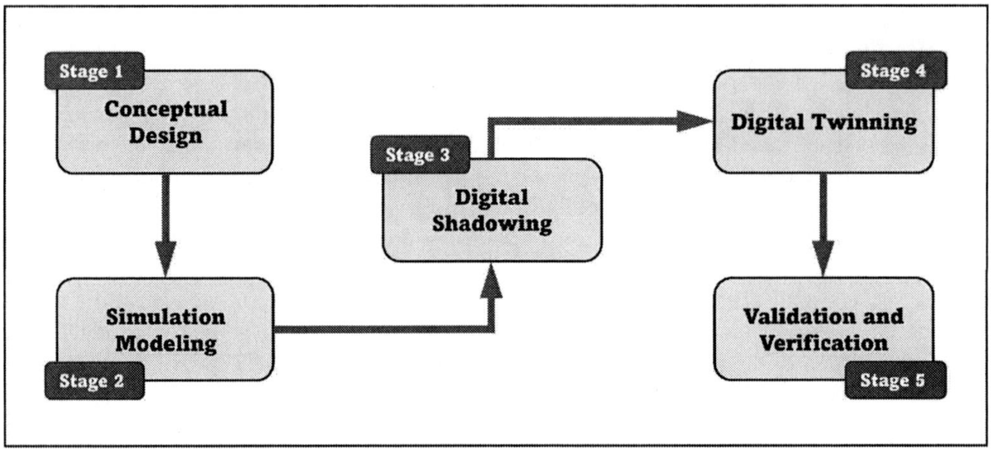

Figure 2: Summary of all stages of the applied framework.

2. **Simulation modeling:** The simulation model is the digital copy of the physical system. The simulation model is developed based on the discrete event simulation method using a simulation software. Service times of the stations, as well as the travel times of the conveyors, are collected from the Manufacturing Execution System (MES) software and provided in the model.
3. **Digital shadowing:** In this phase, the workstations and components in the simulation model are connected to the physical objects using the available communication protocols. Then, the data is collected and sent to the simulation model in real-time.
4. **Digital twinning:** In this stage, the data transfer is enabled in both directions, enabling data transfer from the simulation model to the actuators of the physical objects to control the production flow.
5. **Validation and verification:** This step ensures that the digital twin mimics the actual behaviors of the objects in the FesCPF production line.

In the following subsections, we detail the components and process sequence of the FesCPS located in the Exeter Digital Enterprise Systems (ExDES) Laboratory, Department of Engineering, University of Exeter, UK, and describe our proposed digital twin.

3.1 FesCPF System Description

The studied FesCPF system contains 13 main modules: Top Magazine Station (TM), Measuring Station (MS), Drilling Station (DS), Pressing Station (PS), Bottom Magazine Station (BS), Output Station (OS), Automatic Storage and Retrieval System (ASRS), Robot Assembly Station (RASS), Pick by Light (iP), Branches to transfer from and to the islands (B1, B2, and B3), and an automated guided vehicle (AGV) called Robotino. Please note that Branch 3 (B3) is on Island 1, and Branch 1 (B1) is on Island 3. The layout of the studied FesCPF system is schematically visualized in Figure 3, in which all transportation within the islands is carried out via conveyor belts, and the inter-island transportation is performed by the AGV. The proposed digital twin aims to monitor and control the two products of the CP factory, namely, Products A and B. In this system, production orders are sent and managed by a Manufacturing Execution System (MES) software, coupled with an AGV fleet manager software for the required communication with Robotino.

Product A production starts at Island 1 when the top magazine station (TS) loads the top cover of the product to the workpiece carrier/pallet. Then, the carrier is moved to MS to check whether the top cover is in the proper orientation. Subsequent to passing this test, the workpiece is carried to the DS via a conveyor belt to drill four holes precisely in the top cover. Then, the pallet is moved to B3, waiting for the AGV to transfer it to Island 2. The AGV, Robotino, delivers the carrier to B2 on Island 2, where the first process is the pre-assembly of the back cover of the product, carried out in BS. The final assembly of the bottom cover is performed in the PS station, where a pneumatic press assures proper attachment of all components. In all production cells of this system, the carrier's movement is possible only in one direction. That is, based on the current layout of the system in Figure 3, the pallet has to complete one loop to reach PS from the BS station. Successful pressing in the PS station concludes the production of Product A, following which it leaves the system via the output station (i.e., OS).

For Product B, however, the process starts at Island 3, where the top cover is loaded to the pallet by the ASRS from its existing stock. Then, it is transferred to Island 1 (by Robotino) for the measuring and drilling operations. Upon completion of the required operations on Island 1, the AGV carries the workpiece back to Island 3 for circuit board assembly in the RASS station. This station uses an advanced robotic arm to assemble the printed circuit board (PCB) and the required fuse units on the workpiece. The only operation remaining on this island is to fit the bottom cover of the product, which is done manually in the iP station. The product is then carried by the AGV to Island 2 for final pressing and output, and this completes one production cycle for Product B.

3.2 Proposed Digital Twin

The simulation model in this study follows a DES paradigm that involves modeling events at discrete time points. The entities in this model are machines, stations, robots, conveyors, and storage units. Events and processes in this model are the processing and transfer of the product at different stations. Occasional breakdowns and maintenance are also counted towards events and need to be considered. Throughput rate, processing times, resource utilization, bottleneck statistics, and process cost are among the performance metrics collected using these models to analyze the state of the system, providing insights for decision-makers.

The simulation model is developed using the Siemens Tecnomatix Plant Simulation (TPS) software that has been successfully used in various industries and applications (Attar et al. 2023, Cortés et al. 2021, Pekarcikova et al. 2021, Teimoori et al. 2023). This object-oriented modeling platform enables detailed representation of different segments of the production system, such as workstations, material flows, and logistical processes. In this model, the default object classes available in the software are used for modeling stations, conveyors, assembly processes, and robotic assembly. Furthermore, we use the class worker for a better representation of the autonomous behavior of Robotino in the system. While an order is running, MES tracks how much time each machine spends on processing activities and provides a preliminary comparison with the expected time. Thus, the simulation parameters (e.g., the transit times along the conveyors and the service times at each station) are collected directly from

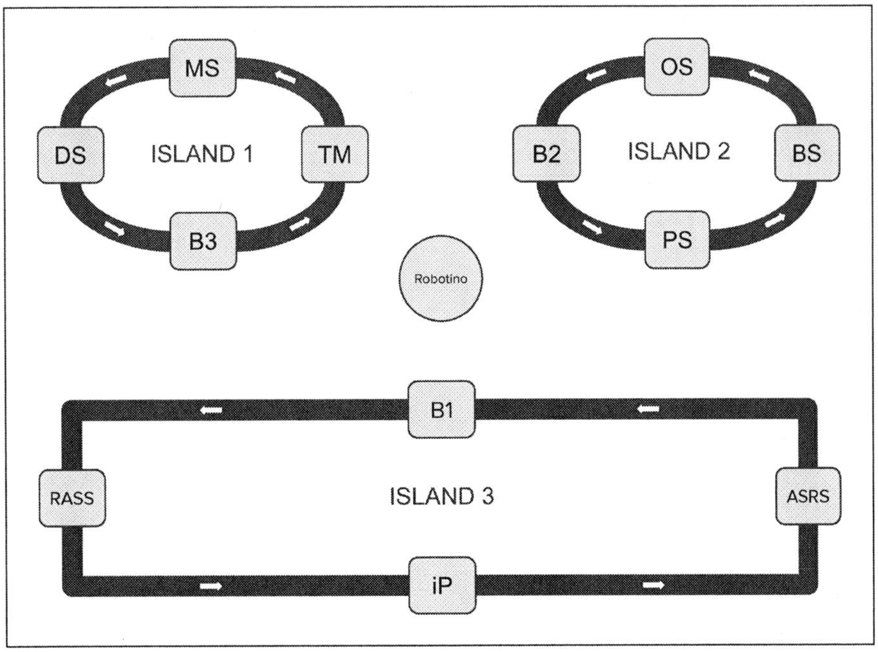

Figure 3: Layout of the studied FesCPF system.

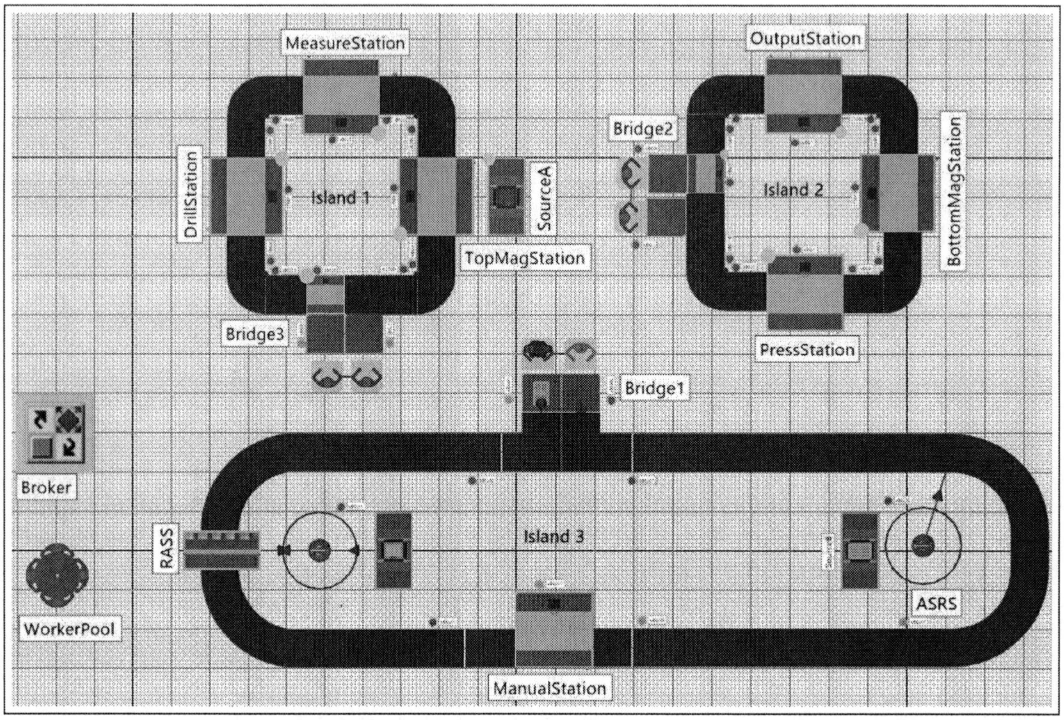

Figure 4: The 2D representation of the proposed model for the FesCPF in the TPS software.

the MES software. A snapshot of the proposed model is presented in Figure 4. Please note that the Pick by the Light station is the same as the Manual Station.

In order to transform this model into a digital shadow of the FesCPF, it should be linked to the activities of the physical system. This task is accomplished by deploying the OPC-UA available in the TPS software which creates a communication link between the simulation model and the real system. It is notable that the used OPC-UA is a widely adopted industrial communication standard known for its robust security features and ability to handle real-time data exchange between disparate systems. This fact generalizes the application of the proposed framework to a broader application area in the industry, beyond laboratory equipment. Each station and conveyor has a set of sensors and instruments that gather operational data, including machine performance, production counts, and system statuses, continuously fed into the simulation model through the OPC-UA protocol. Therefore, this digital shadow replicates the behavior of the FesCPF system realistically and can be used effectively as a monitoring and analysis tool.

The proposed shadow evolves into a proper digital twin when data transfer occurs in both directions between the simulation model and the physical system, for which we still utilize the same OPC-UA protocol. However, unlike the digital shadow, the twin uses the protocol to send control signals and commands back to the physical system. This bidirectional communication enables adjustment of production speeds, rerouting of material flows, or activation of specific workstations based on real-time data and analyses. That leads to one of the primary benefits of these digital twins, which is to facilitate ongoing enhancements to the physical system by utilizing the data generated through the application of certain decision algorithms.

4 DISCUSSION

The present model offers a wealth of opportunities for creating PdM models and identifying possible solutions for optimizing performance, thanks to the current twin's ability to simulate and capture all relevant sensor data, as well as the existing control systems. Strengthening this aspect of the proposed twin can result in a more realistic digital twin experience. As seen in Figure 4, the visual objects used in the proposed digital twin to represent the stations and equipment are not the exact representation of the real systems. With reference to the benefits highlighted by Attar et al. (2024) for 2D and 3D representation of digital twins on the management audience, this can be a potential weakness for our digital twin. This underscores a practical extension avenue for the current study that would involve importing the realistic 3D models of the machines as well as their realistic animations to the digital twin.

The major advantage of such digital twins is adding the possibility of continuous improvements to the physical system based on the generated data using some decision algorithms. However, observations during the development of this digital twin reveal that the digital model may occasionally encounter latency relative to the physical system due to the extensive data collection and computational demands. Thus, another technical aspect that might need addressing based on this finding is employing such twins on high-performance multi-core servers. This would guarantee a smooth running of the program. Such a smooth real-time connection will facilitate the above-mentioned continuous improvement process and enhance the user experience of this digital twin.

On the other hand, digital twins themselves also necessitate ongoing enhancements to keep up with system evolution, especially when dealing with a modular system like FesCPF. The modular nature of the hardware and software is one of the greatest advantages of the FesCPF, as it facilitates the installation of new machines and reconfiguration of the line. Such situations, however, call for reconfiguration and recalibration of the proposed digital twin and may necessitate further testing of the data collected from the previous version or some reevaluations before proceeding to develop the decision algorithms. With operational systems, sensors, and devices producing massive amounts of data in real-time, another aspect to address in this digital twin is the deployment of advanced data storage solutions, e.g., databases, cloud storage, or distributed storage systems, that could help speed the storage and retrieval of data from and to the physical system, the digital model, and decision algorithms.

5 CONCLUSION

The development of digital twins for modular smart production lines of well-known equipment manufacturers has long been important for both academics and industrial practitioners. This paper addresses this need by proposing a digital twin framework for a smart line from Festo's cyber-physical factory (FesCPF) class installed in the ExDES laboratory at the University of Exeter, United Kingdom. Our study outlines the methodology and components that are required in the development of such a digital twin using the Siemens Tecnomatix Plant Simulation software. The proposed procedure begins by defining the modeling objectives and developing an offline model based on the existing production data. The next stage in this framework is digital shadowing, where a real-time data collection mechanism is deployed using the OPC-UA protocol. Eventually, enabling bidirectional data transfer turns the digital shadow into a digital twin. Validation and verification experiments were also carried out to ensure the reliability of the developed model. The current twin, which simulates and captures all requisite sensor data alongside actual management systems, offers substantial possibilities for system optimization purposes.

The implementation of digital twins in a smart factory extends beyond the creation of the digital twin. An intelligence layer is also essential, which incorporates advanced data storage solutions, algorithms, and programs on top of the developed twin. However, this layer was out of the scope of this study, as we were laying the foundations for the proposed digital twin framework and its technicalities in such systems. An interesting future research avenue may involve leveraging the complete capabilities of this intelligence layer that contains data analytics, machine learning, and other algorithms and techniques to act as a decision support system. Working on this can lead to comprehensive predictive maintenance (PdM) models and performance optimization. Deploying efficient algorithms for anomaly detection, fault diagnosis, and remaining useful life prediction, as well as data analytics solutions like pattern recognition models and trend analyzers, are all among the possible future applications of the proposed framework that can be applied to similar Festo factories or other smart production lines.

ACKNOWLEDGMENTS

The authors would like to thank Dr. Igiri Uko Onaji, AMRC Wales, UK, whose initial model, insights, and contributions significantly guided the early stages of this research. The first author also extends his sincere gratitude to the Department of Engineering, University of Exeter, UK, for providing technical and financial support and to Dr. Shaurya Shriyam, Department of Mechanical Engineering, Indian Institute of Technology Delhi, India, for facilitating his visit to ExDES to accomplish this project.

REFERENCES

Attar, A., M. Babaee, S. Raissi, and M. Nojavan. 2024. "Airside Optimization Framework Covering Multiple Operations in Civil Airport Systems with a Variety of Aircraft: A Simulation-Based Digital Twin". *Systems* 12 (10): 394.

Attar, A., Y. Jin, M. Luis, S. Zhong, and V. I. Sucala. 2023. "Simulation-Based Analyses and Improvements of the Smart Line Management System in Canned Beverage Industry: A Case Study in Europe". In *2023 Winter Simulation Conference (WSC)*, 2124–2135. IEEE.

Baheti, R., and H. Gill. 2011. "Cyber-physical systems". *The impact of control technology* 12 (1): 161–166.

Chen, B., J. Wan, L. Shu, P. Li, M. Mukherjee, and B. Yin. 2018. "Smart Factory of Industry 4.0: Key Technologies, Application Case, and Challenges". *IEEE Access* 6:6505–6519.

Chen, C., H. Fu, Y. Zheng, F. Tao, and Y. Liu. 2023, December. "The advance of digital twin for predictive maintenance: The role and function of machine learning". *Journal of Manufacturing Systems* 71:581–594.

Cortés, D., J. Ramírez, L. E. Villagomez, R. Batres, A. Velilla, E. Gonzalez, J. Puente, G. Esparza, N. Cruz, and A. Molina. 2021. "Semi-automatic simulation modelling. Results with Tecnomatix Portfolio in the automotive sector". *IFAC-PapersOnLine* 54 (1): 576–581.

do Amaral, J., C. dos Santos, J. Montevechi, and A. de Queiroz. 2023, December. "Energy Digital Twin applications: A review". *Renewable and Sustainable Energy Reviews* 188:113891.

Esterle, L., C. Gomes, M. Frasheri, H. Ejersbo, S. Tomforde, and P. G. Larsen. 2021, September. "Digital twins for collaboration and self-integration". In *2021 IEEE International Conference on Autonomic Computing and Self-Organizing Systems Companion (ACSOS-C)*, 172–177. IEEE.

Fuller, A., Z. Fan, C. Day, and C. Barlow. 2020. "Digital Twin: Enabling Technologies, Challenges and Open Research". *IEEE Access* 8:108952–108971.

Grieves, M. 2014. "Digital twin: manufacturing excellence through virtual factory replication". *White paper* 1 (2014): 1–7.

Grieves, M., and J. Vickers. 2016, August. *Digital Twin: Mitigating Unpredictable, Undesirable Emergent Behavior in Complex Systems*, 85–113. Springer International Publishing.

Josifovska, K., E. Yigitbas, and G. Engels. 2019, May. "Reference Framework for Digital Twins within Cyber-Physical Systems". In *2019 IEEE/ACM 5th International Workshop on Software Engineering for Smart Cyber-Physical Systems (SEsCPS)*, 25–31. IEEE.

Lasi, H., P. Fettke, H.-G. Kemper, T. Feld, and M. Hoffmann. 2014, June. "Industry 4.0". *Business & Information Systems Engineering* 6 (4): 239–242.

Liu, Z., E. Blasch, M. Liao, C. Yang, K. Tsukada, and N. Meyendorf. 2023, April. "Digital twin for predictive maintenance". In *NDE 4.0, Predictive Maintenance, Communication, and Energy Systems: The Digital Transformation of NDE,* 6. SPIE.

Michael, J., M. Schwammberger, and A. Wortmann. 2024, January. "Explaining Cyberphysical System Behavior With Digital Twins". *IEEE Software* 41 (1): 55–63.

Mihai, S., W. Davis, D. Hung, R. Trestian, M. Karamanoglu, B. Barn, R. Prasad, H. Venkataraman, and H. Nguyen. 2021. "A digital twin framework for predictive maintenance in industry 4.0". In *HPCS 2020: 18th Annual Meeting*. IEEE.

Negri, E., L. Fumagalli, and M. Macchi. 2017. "A Review of the Roles of Digital Twin in CPS-based Production Systems". *Procedia Manufacturing* 11:939–948.

Onaji, I., D. Tiwari, P. Soulatiantork, B. Song, and A. Tiwari. 2022, January. "Digital twin in manufacturing: conceptual framework and case studies". *International Journal of Computer Integrated Manufacturing* 35 (8): 831–858.

Pekarcikova, M., P. Trebuna, M. Kliment, and M. Dic. 2021. "Solution of bottlenecks in the logistics flow by applying the kanban module in the tecnomatix plant simulation software". *Sustainability* 13 (14): 7989.

Rasheed, A., O. San, and T. Kvamsdal. 2020. "Digital twin: Values, challenges and enablers from a modeling perspective". *IEEE access* 8:21980–22012.

Schroeder, G. N., C. Steinmetz, C. E. Pereira, and D. B. Espindola. 2016. "Digital Twin Data Modeling with AutomationML and a Communication Methodology for Data Exchange". *IFAC-PapersOnLine* 49 (30): 12–17.

Sinha, D., and R. Roy. 2020, June. "Reviewing Cyber-Physical System as a Part of Smart Factory in Industry 4.0". *IEEE Engineering Management Review* 48 (2): 103–117.

Tao, F., Q. Qi, L. Wang, and A. Nee. 2019, August. "Digital Twins and Cyber–Physical Systems toward Smart Manufacturing and Industry 4.0: Correlation and Comparison". *Engineering* 5 (4): 653–661.

Teimoori, O., M. Ateeq, and A. Alexoulis-Chrysovergis. 2023, December. "Implementing and Enhancing Monitoring System on the Edge of a Smart Factory: A Case Study with FESTO's Cyber-physical System". In *2023 16th International Conference on Developments in eSystems Engineering (DeSE)*, 177–182. IEEE.

AUTHOR BIOGRAPHIES

MUHAMMAD ALFAS is a Ph.D student at the Department of Mechanical Engineering, Indian Institute of Technology Delhi, India. His research work focuses on modeling complex systems, resource allocation, and optimization using heuristics, as well as reinforcement learning.

YANYAN TIAN is a Ph.D. student at the Department of Engineering at the University of Exeter, UK. Her research focuses on predictive maintenance in the field of smart manufacturing.

AHMAD ATTAR is a postgraduate teaching associate with the Dep. of Eng., University of Exeter, UK, mainly delivering System Modeling, Simulation, and Mathematical Programming. He received his M.Sc. and B.Sc. degrees as the top student in Industrial Engineering from IAU-STB and joined Exeter in 2022 as a Ph.D. student in Engineering, focusing on the simulation of resilient, sustainable, and cost-efficient supply chains. He has about a decade of experience in the industry, and his main areas of research interest include simulation modeling, digital twinning, supply chain, reliability, airport management, inventory modeling, healthcare systems, and offshore wind energy.

MARTINO LUIS is a Senior Lecturer at the Department of Engineering, University of Exeter, UK. He holds a Ph.D. in Operations Research from Kent Business School, University of Kent. His research interests are the applications of Exact Methods, (Meta)-Heuristics optimization and a combination of both, as well as simulation modeling in manufacturing systems, facility location problems, sustainable supply chain design networks, and inventory routing problems that focus on environment and sustainable operations.

VOICU ION SUCALA is a Professor in Engineering Management and the Head of Engineering at the University of Exeter. He holds a Ph.D. in Industrial Engineering (TU Cluj-Napoca) and a Ph.D. in Social Sciences (University of Glasgow), serves as vice-chair of the Research, Innovation and Knowledge Transfer committee at Engineering Professors' Council, and leads Exeter Digital Enterprise Systems (ExDES) laboratory. His research focuses on modeling, simulation, digital twinning and optimization of manufacturing processes, technology innovation and entrepreneurship, industrial organization management, and engineering education.

Proceedings of the Operational Research Society Simulation Workshop 2025 (SW25)
M. Luis, A. Harper, T. Monks, N. Mustafee, eds.
https://doi.org/10.36819/SW25.030

FROM BLUE-SKY CONCEPT TO INDUSTRIAL DEPLOYMENT: HOW OCADO TECHNOLOGY USED SIMULATION TO GUIDE THE DEVELOPMENT OF THE WORLD'S MOST ADVANCED GROCERY PICKING ROBOT

Robert Backhouse

Ocado Technology
Hatfield, United Kingdom
r.backhouse@ocado.com

Sean Schrauben

Ocado Technology
Hatfield, United Kingdom
sean.schrauben@ocado.com

Gareth Siret

Ocado Technology
Hatfield, United Kingdom
gareth.siret@ocado.com

ABSTRACT

Ocado Technology recently released On-Grid Robotic Pick (OGRP) - the world's most advanced grocery picking robot. Simulation played a significant role in guiding several years of research and development for this product.

In this paper, we discuss how the simulation of OGRP was built in parallel with the development of the product itself, and how having an integrated model enabled us to better search the large and complex design space of possible implementations. We describe the benefits of this approach around business alignment and product development speed, which could be applicable to other large industrial simulation projects.

Keywords: Simulation Development Practice, Design Optimisation, Hardware Development

1 INTRODUCTION

Simulations have become an integral part of decision-making processes across many different industries. From manufacturing and healthcare to finance and logistics, simulation models of complex systems allow businesses to compare scenarios and predict outcomes without costly real-world experiments.

At Ocado Technology, the innovation factory behind the technology used by 13 online grocery operations around the world, we have a long history of using simulation. Starting with the first simulation of our conveyor-based Customer Fulfilment Centre (CFC) in 2006, we now have long-established simulations that cover a range of business areas - from warehouse automation and in-store picking, to supply chain and last-mile delivery. Simulation is embedded across the business, integrated into everything from strategic decision making down to low-level product development.

Grocery fulfilment is a challenging market, with thin margins, large orders and tens of thousands of different products. In order to pick customer orders as efficiently as possible, our CFCs are built around the Hive, a proprietary warehouse automation technology with a fleet of robots (or "bots") that moves stock and customer orders around a storage grid to pick 50-item orders in just a few minutes. Coordinating hundreds of bots to pick thousands of orders means that simulation is essential to understand the complex emergent behaviours of the system, and to predict how these behaviours lead to system performance across business KPIs. For this reason, the AI orchestration software that coordinates the Hive has always been developed alongside its sister simulation, so we have a well-established model of our warehouse automation. This simulation is developed in-house using our own Java simulation libraries, in order to fully embed the production control code alongside models of the hardware, software and human processes that interact with the Hive[1]. It is used extensively to support strategic and tactical decision making for concept development, CFC design and operational deployment.

Figure 1 The Hive, with bots driving on the grid and stacks of storage bins underneath

While the Hive automation already offered market-leading productivity for fulfilling grocery orders, as a Goods-to-Person system the manual step of packing customer shopping bags still accounted for a significant proportion of the total CFC labour costs. Automating the final picking process itself promised another step-change in the efficiency of our CFCs. However, the rigidly programmed robotic systems that are widely used in other industries are unsuitable for grocery, for several reasons. We have 13 global partners each with a unique and ever-changing range of tens of thousands of products, so we need to be able to pick products that we have never seen before. Grocery products are highly heterogeneous, often need careful handling, and they need to be densely packed for efficient delivery. This is why the physical picking and packing of stock has only recently been automated, with the development of Ocado Technology's On-Grid Robotic Pick (OGRP) solution, the world's most advanced picking robot designed specifically for the grocery use case.

Robotic arms are used for automation in many industries, frequently for manufacturing and processing but also for picking. There has been a range of research into the hardware, software and deployment of robotic pick in academia and business, including at Ocado Technology. Due to the particular challenges of grocery, we have been at the forefront of how to deploy many new innovations at scale, with over 1200 technology patents granted. Developing the OGRP arm included research in areas such as in computer vision, soft manipulation and imitation learning, with many different approaches being developed in parallel as the technology matured towards a practical and cost-effective solution.

A significant part of the development of OGRP was integrating this technology into the overall Hive solution. Instead of bots taking bins to people at pick stations, they deposit stock next to a robotic arm to be packed into bags on the grid. So the robotic arms need to coordinate seamlessly with our fleet

[1] We have separate simulations at different levels of detail, from low-level simulation to test the bot hardware controllers through to high-level models of the end-to-end flow of work through CFCs. The simulation discussed lies between these, where we build up from hardware specifications and control logic to understand the emergent behaviour of the Hive system itself.

of bots, while operating in the same physical space. Designing a great OGRP product required informed end-to-end decisions taking the whole system into account. Simulation enabled us to reason about the system far in advance of having a physical prototype, significantly reducing the amount of costly real-world experimentation.

Figure 2 An Ocado Technology OGRP arm in the Hive

In this paper, we present a case study outlining how simulation[2] was integral to the development and delivery of Ocado Technology's On-Grid Robotic Pick solution, and how simulation supported the journey from blue-sky research to a productionised industrial technology.

2 THE PROBLEM: EXPLORING A COMPLEX DESIGN SPACE

The OGRP product combines many different individual components, each of which had to be developed and adapted as part of the overall solution. For the robotic arms themselves, there was completely new research in areas such as computer vision, soft manipulation and imitation learning. Some of these areas featured the parallel development of alternative implementations, such as different ways to build an AI that can safely and efficiently pick products it has never seen before. As well as the arm itself, the product needed to be developed in areas such as installation process, design of the Hive layout, and software integration with the bot orchestration system, which are all coupled.

For example, consider the question of where best to place OGRPs in the Hive, which depends heavily on how well bots can supply bins to different locations in alternative layouts. Assessing the congestion and constraints that drive this performance requires a detailed view of the arm behaviour and its interaction with the bot movements. A difference in how the bots coordinate with the robotic arms could affect congestion under one layout but not in another, so decisions on arm placement need to be made with a complete view of the system. Similarly, we want to design the bot orchestration algorithms around the overall system constraints, which depend on where OGRPs will be in the Hive.

The development of the OGRP solution is therefore analogous to exploring a large design space, where the space is uncertain, complex and tightly coupled. We needed to search this space for an overall design that could reliably pick many different products, interact effectively with our bot orchestration

[2] Similarly to our bot hardware simulation, we also have an independent physics-based simulation of our robotic arms, "RoboSim", which we use for developing and testing the arm itself, machine learning, and training remote operators who help our OGRPs recover from exceptional cases in production. Here, we refer to only our mid-level systems simulation of OGRP and its interaction with our bot orchestration AI.

AI, and remain cheap and easy to install and maintain. Efficient searching required rapid iteration, evaluating local decisions in the context of all of the other development streams, and we needed this evaluation from the start of the project, long before having an integrated prototype to experiment with. Our simulation model provided this evaluation function. By providing fast, consistent feedback on how local decisions would affect the overall performance, our simulation allowed us to optimise the development of OGRP by focusing our resources on the most promising directions, avoiding dead ends, and collectively moving towards a better end product.

3 DEVELOPING A SIMULATION MODEL ALONGSIDE THE PRODUCT

The first OGRP simulation was a quick prototype added to our existing bot orchestration simulation, built to test whether on-grid picking was a sensible concept to pursue. We had already experimented with robotic arms in pick stations, where conveyors line up the stock bins and customer orders that bots have dropped off. The idea behind OGRP was for bots to deposit stock next to arms on the grid, and retrieve it after picking along with the completed orders. OGRP promised not only to save picker labour, but also station hardware and space requirements. However, there were significant risks if the interaction between bots and robotic arms led to congestion or poor pick performance.

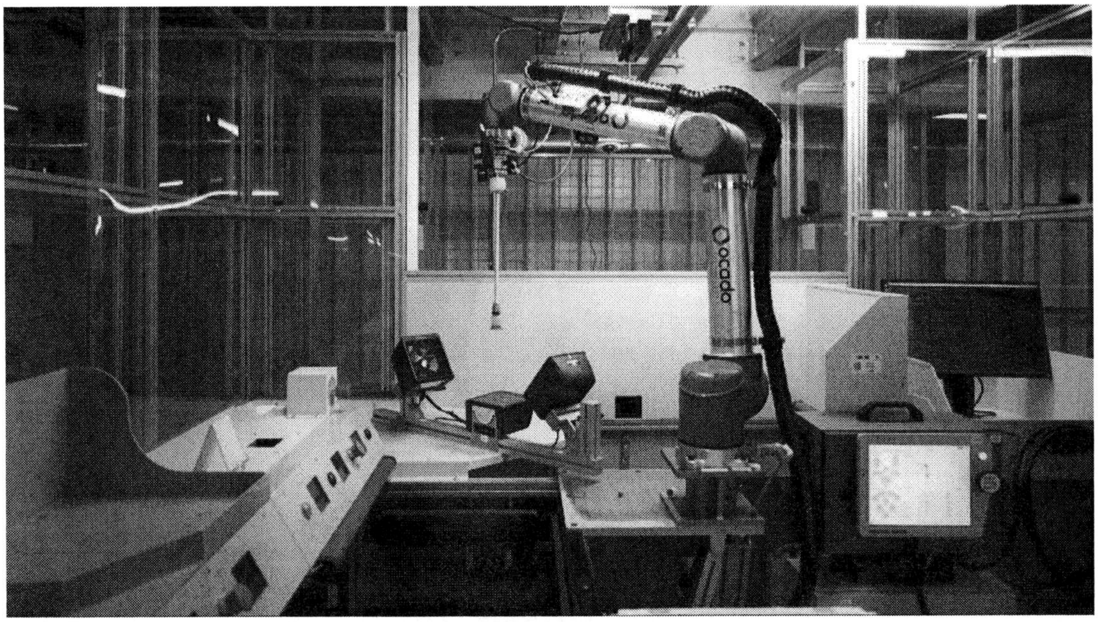

Figure 3 A prototype robotic arm deployed in a pick station

To build a useful simulation at this early stage, we needed to put together a consistent conceptual model for how the final solution might look, aligned with all the different product teams and their planned direction. Some teams had a clear implementation vision or target metric that was straightforward to include in the model. In other cases, we needed to negotiate a suitable assumption with the relevant product team, which could be a placeholder rather than a realistic end behaviour.

An example of such a placeholder was the robotic arm performance. We could model the existing behaviour, but wanted to simulate a future state where we had developed new features and algorithms, with a specific target throughput. Setting a physical timing to zero is a physically impossible model of end-game behaviour, but one that can give an upper bound for an algorithm improvement that improves that process or reduces the need for it. In some cases we used unrealistic timings in our model of end-game behaviour, when everyone agreed that this was equivalent to a planned improvement, and when we could reason that it was appropriate to design other parts of the system against it.

Despite the high level of uncertainty, the early simulation demonstrated that with our placeholder model of arm behaviour and a basic algorithm for bot interaction we could achieve a reasonable throughput. This high-level view was enough to confirm that the fundamental OGRP concept was sound, and to give the business confidence to invest in the product's development. The simulation model was also good enough for the bot orchestration team to start developing against it, providing rapid feedback as they started developing more sophisticated algorithms.

From this point, we always had a provisional model for how an OGRP end-game could look, which evolved alongside the product itself. The assumptions were continually changing, as each strand of research progressed and the overall product evolved, but they were always agreed with stakeholders and we could always model the interaction of the different systems. At first, the low fidelity of the simulation meant that we could only give approximate answers to large questions. As development progressed and we included more refined models and confident assumptions, we could give increasingly precise answers to subtler questions, which naturally became important in the later stages of development. But at any point in time, the assumptions could be confirmed and the simulation used to provide a timely, data-driven answer for questions on the overall system behaviour.

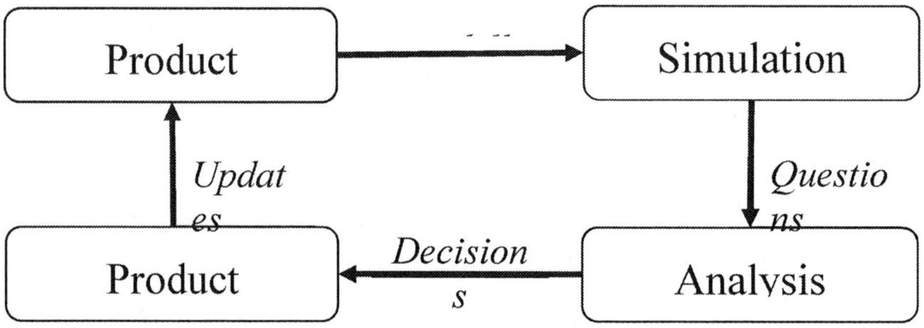

Figure 4 The iterative cycle of simulation development

4 BENEFITS OF THIS APPROACH

4.1 Simulation Credibility

Having product teams responsible for providing modelling assumptions and updating them throughout the project meant that it was relatively easy to build trust in our simulation model. We started the project with a well-established simulation of our warehouse orchestration system, which was already integrated into business decision making. Having explicit product owners for each OGRP assumption on top of this meant that decision makers could easily confirm that assumptions were up-to-date, and discuss these with the relevant teams if they had any concerns, giving the simulation credibility despite the uncertainty and complexity of the system.

The first time our CFC design team used the simulation was to understand how many OGRP arms we would need in different scenarios. This number was largely driven by assumptions for how much of the product range we would be able to pick, but it needed a buffer to cope with natural fluctuations, and there were complex tradeoffs between adding arms or bots to get higher throughput. Since the CFC design team already knew the bot orchestration part of the simulation, and we could break down assumptions into different product areas, we could focus the modelling discussions on the big picture and the key assumptions for this specific question. This meant that we could more easily assess the appropriateness of the model for the new use case and quickly start generating answers.

4.2 Business Alignment

The conceptual modelling phase of a simulation can help to surface inconsistencies even before any simulations are run. In our case, having an early simulation evolving in parallel with the OGRP product meant that valuable modelling conversations took place throughout the project lifecycle, revealing many potential problems much earlier than they would otherwise have been discovered.

This continual alignment of assumptions was particularly valuable for the interface between the arms and bots. The bots are deterministic and predictable, passing within 5mm of each other at speeds of 4m/s with precision measured in milliseconds. OGRP arms need to cope with however the stock is presented, adjusting their movements based on real-world feedback, all while fitting in with the precise movement of the bots. Today, the bots and arms collaborate seamlessly, but reaching this point required detailed planning and negotiation between the two domains. Since the simulation used sufficiently detailed models of both arms and bots (including the production orchestration code), we could use it to facilitate discussions on the best way for the systems to interact, even while the rest of the system was regularly changing.

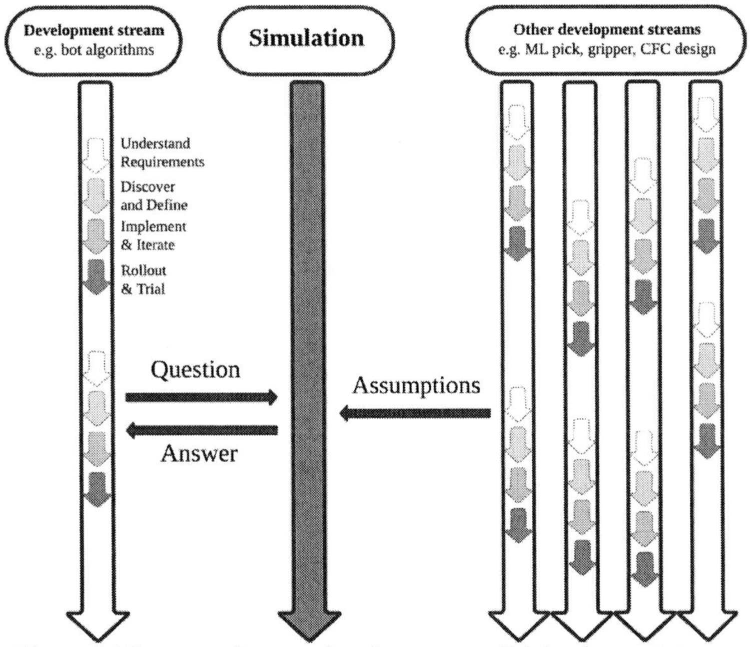

Figure 5 Alignment of assumptions between parallel development streams

Updating the simulation model also served as a clear point of commitment that could align multiple development streams. At one stage, the plan was to mount a camera on a gantry at the edge of the picking footprint. The downside of this was losing space for bot routing and storage. By comparing simulations with and without the lost space, we could estimate the value of recovering it if we could remove the need for the gantry. This value turned out to justify the engineering effort in a wrist-mounted camera on the arm itself, which required development across areas such as the computer vision system, hardware design and installation process. Explicitly agreeing to update the end-game simulation model was a clear commitment to deliver the feature, which helped to rapidly align all of the development streams behind the new direction.

4.3 Early Decision Making

We discussed earlier that our simulation model gave straightforward, consistent feedback on how local decisions would affect the overall system performance. Analysing a range of scenarios gave us insight into how sensitive the overall performance was to different metrics or assumptions, which allowed teams to shift their focus to the most important drivers. Simulations quickly highlighted when a target was incompatible with other areas or when it wouldn't achieve the necessary performance, avoiding development dead ends. Building the simulation early and developing it in parallel meant that we could provide valuable feedback from the start of the project and give more precise answers in the later stages of development.

On top of faster iteration and more effective searching, we could also deliver the overall product earlier by starting development against the simulation. By testing against the model before we had built a full prototype, we could bring forward decisions, development and feedback, allowing us to deliver the end result sooner[3].

The tightest feedback loops were with the bot orchestration system, which needed to be adapted in order to work effectively with OGRP. This was a significant piece of work, which needed a detailed

[3] Another example of using simulation in this way is Nvidia's graphics card development, as described in Rumelt R (2012) *Good Strategy/Bad Strategy: The Difference and Why It Matters*, Profile Books Ltd.

view of the arm behaviour for designing control strategies. The orchestration developers have always built algorithms against the simulation, and were able to start as soon as we had the first OGRP model. The simulation allowed them to test each iteration of control code against the best available view of end-game behaviour, and get feedback on both the headline performance and the detailed drivers behind it. By starting early and developing alongside the rest of the product, we had a proven control system before fitting OGRPs in production, saving time that would otherwise have been needed to test and fix the system after the arm was ready.

Having an early simulation model also gave us a chance to identify new challenges and opportunities earlier in the project. Examining the model outputs could reveal constraints or potential improvements as soon as the end behaviour was sufficiently clear, and the simulation was complete and accessible enough that new teams could apply the resulting insight in their areas.

One improvement that was identified and developed earlier as a result of simulation was a change to how we pack products together. In our CFCs, smart "cubing" algorithms determine how products should be packed into totes for delivery. Reducing the number of bags needed is crucial for saving space in vans and efficient delivery, but it is a hard problem when considering real-world grocery constraints (such as not packing bleach and apples together). As soon as our simulation had a detailed enough view of the system constraints, we could see the potential value of consolidating robotically pickable products in the same tote. Despite the cubing team not being involved in OGRP development until that point, they could understand the wider impact of potential optimisations in this area and start assessing how to adapt the overall cubing algorithm.

5 OUTCOMES

OGRPs are now in active use, and being installed in CFCs around the world. The arms can already pick a large proportion of our UK products, and at full capacity we expect this to exceed 70% of an extensive grocery range. The orchestration system coordinating the arms and bots was developed against many different versions of the simulation before its successful deployment in production. Our Luton CFC was designed using one of the early versions of the OGRP simulation, and the design is successfully handling the picking of over a million items per week by robotic arms. The OGRP technology and its deployment are still being improved, and the simulation model is still being updated as the product itself changes.

Figure 6 OGRP arms deployed in Luton CFC

Stakeholders continue to explore OGRP behaviour to help guide new features, optimisations and deployments. The use cases are expanding to cover an even wider range of scenarios, including generalising to a wide range of industry contexts as a new business unit, Ocado Intelligent Automation, starts to apply our automation technology in many different non-grocery domains. Our simulation model of our Hive warehouse automation is still crucial to our understanding of OGRP performance.

6 CONCLUSION

OGRP was a challenging project for decision making, due to the uncertain implementation, multiple streams of development, and the complexity of their interaction. Ocado Technology's simulation approach was to build a provisional model of the end-to-end system, and to continually refine this in parallel with the product development itself.

This allowed local decisions to be taken with visibility of how these would affect the combined product, and allowed such decisions to be taken throughout the development process. Having a unified model with clear ownership of individual modelling decisions made it easier for the business to align on direction, and gave decision makers confidence in the analysis that was coming from the simulation. This approach drove a faster delivery of OGRP by saving wasted effort and bringing forward development, and ultimately led to a better end product.

AUTHOR BIOGRAPHIES

ROBERT BACKHOUSE is the technical lead for Simulation Research at Ocado Technology, focused on the techniques and practice of using simulation for business insight. He has ten years at the company working across the development, tooling and analysis of many different simulations. He previously worked in a variety of roles at the intersection of algorithms, analysis and software development. He holds an MA in Mathematics from Cambridge University.

SEAN SCHRAUBEN is Principal Product Manager for Simulation at Ocado Technology, where he focuses on building simulation products and tooling used by teams across the business. His previous experience spans various software products at the intersection of analytics, data, and platforms. He holds a MSci in Chemical Engineering from Université Catholique de Louvain and an MSci in Management from University College London.

GARETH SIRET is Head of Data for Simulation at Ocado Technology. His background is in software engineering, algorithmic research, simulation practice and data science. He has led collections of teams developing simulations and related software across domains including warehouse automation, in-store picking, supply chain and last-mile logistics. He holds a MSci in Physics from Imperial College London.

Proceedings of the Operational Research Society Simulation Workshop 2025 (SW25)
M. Luis, A. Harper, T. Monks, N. Mustafee, eds.

https://doi.org/10.36819/SW25.031

DISCRETE EVENT SIMULATION WITH REINFORCEMENT LEARNING FOR ADVANCED MANUFACTURING DECISION-MAKING

Dr. Cansu Kandemir

Advanced Manufacturing Research Centre,
University of Sheffield
Western Bank, Sheffield S10 2TN
c.kandemir@amrc.co.uk

Mr. Scott Herod

Advanced Manufacturing Research Centre,
University of Sheffield
Western Bank, Sheffield S10 2TN
s.herod@amrc.co.uk

Mr. Matin Ghojogh

School of Electrical and Electronic Engineering,
University of Sheffield
Western Bank, Sheffield S10 2TN
mghojogh1@sheffield.ac.uk

Mr. Ali Naraghipour

School of Electrical and Electronic Engineering,
University of Sheffield
Western Bank, Sheffield S10 2TN
anaraghipour1@sheffield.ac.uk

Mr. Marco Franchino

Advanced Manufacturing Research Centre,
University of Sheffield
Western Bank, Sheffield S10 2TN
m.franchino@amrc.co.uk

Dr. Payam Soulatiantork

School of Electrical and Electronic Engineering,
University of Sheffield
Western Bank, Sheffield S10 2TN
p.soulatiantork@sheffield.ac.uk

ABSTRACT

The manufacturing sector increasingly relies on Artificial Intelligence (AI) to improve decision-making and streamline processes. Discrete Event Simulation (DES) is a valuable tool for simulating manufacturing operations, providing a safe environment to train and test AI for rapid decision-making. This paper explores how DES integrates with Reinforcement Learning (RL), an AI technique that learns through trial and error, to address challenges such as job scheduling in complex production systems. This study reviews RL models applied in DES-based manufacturing and presents a practical implementation. A proof-of-concept is demonstrated through an Automated Guided Vehicle (AGV) job scheduling case, where a communication framework integrates AI with the simulation model. The MQTT messaging protocol ensures seamless interaction between the AI agent and DES for state-based decision-making. Initial experiments with Deep Q-Network (DQN) and Proximal Policy Optimisation (PPO) show promising results, improving scheduling efficiency through optimal routing and task allocation. These findings highlight RL-DES integration's potential to enhance manufacturing adaptability and productivity.

Keywords: Artificial Intelligence, Reinforcement Learning, Discrete Event Simulation

1 INTRODUCTION

With increasing product complexity and fluctuating market demands, optimising manufacturing processes has become more critical than ever. Consequently, organisations are turning to innovative methods and tools, such as machine learning, data mining, data farming, process mining, and big data analytics to address contemporary challenges, enhance efficiency, and improve adaptability within their operations. Among these, Artificial Intelligence (AI) has emerged as a key technology for predictions, production planning, and production flow optimisation, enabling manufacturers to make more informed decisions and boost operational performance (Del Gallo et al., 2023).

However, despite AI's growing integration in manufacturing decision-making, significant challenges remain in acquiring and preparing the necessary data for training and testing AI models. Data availability is often limited, and existing datasets may be incomplete, noisy, or contain errors that hinder model accuracy (Fiona Zhao et al., 2024). Privacy regulations further complicate access to sensitive information, while biases and imbalances in datasets can result in AI models that perform poorly on underrepresented cases. Additionally, the costs associated with data acquisition, ethical concerns, and the need to keep datasets updated pose further obstacles (European Commission, 2019). Literature and industry reports consistently emphasise data preparation and management as crucial steps in successfully deploying AI (Christiaens, 2023; Roh et al., 2021).

In contrast, Discrete Event Simulation (DES) presents a promising solution for generating clean and synthetic data to train and test AI agents (Chan et al., 2022). DES provides a controlled, flexible, and scalable environment where AI agents can interact with simulated real-world processes, allowing them to learn from complex systems and make decisions without the risks and costs of real-world experimentation. It facilitates the modelling of dynamic behaviours, system constraints, and stochastic events, helping AI agents adapt to various scenarios and uncertainties. By generating large amounts of synthetic data, DES addresses data scarcity issues, enabling agents to train across diverse situations and policies. These capabilities make DES a powerful tool for developing robust AI solutions, particularly in sectors such as manufacturing, logistics, and healthcare.

There are several approaches to combining AI with DES, including using DES for AI-driven predictions and employing reinforcement learning (RL) to train AI agents. In the first approach, DES can generate synthetic data or simulate various scenarios, which is then used to train AI algorithms for predictive tasks, such as forecasting production outcomes or identifying optimal process configurations. This allows AI models to learn from a wide range of simulated conditions and make accurate predictions without relying solely on real-world data. On the other hand, RL involves training AI agents to make sequential decisions by interacting with the DES environment, where they receive feedback in the form of rewards or penalties. This approach enables agents to adapt and improve policies over time, optimising decision-making for tasks such as dynamic scheduling or resource allocation.

RL's ability to adapt to changing conditions is particularly advantageous for manufacturing, where fluctuations in demand, machine performance, and other factors are common. By continuously learning from new data and adjusting its policies, RL can help manufacturing systems remain flexible and resilient in the face of dynamic environments, ensuring that operations remain efficient even as conditions evolve.

While these approaches offer significant benefits, integrating RL with DES poses unique challenges. Training AI engines requires a seamless pipeline between the AI engine and the DES software. However, DES environments and AI engines often operate on different platforms, use distinct programming languages, and handle varying data formats, necessitating considerable effort to ensure compatibility and smooth communication. Synchronising real-time data from the DES environment with the AI engine to accurately reflect dynamic manufacturing processes adds further complexity. Scaling up integration to support large-scale simulations while maintaining performance presents another significant challenge. Moreover, there are currently no low-code platforms available for implementing AI with DES models without specialised expertise. A major barrier to the combined use of simulation and RL is the differing backgrounds and tools used by developers. In particular, simulation model developers may lack the software tools knowledge and coding skills required for developing ML algorithms (Greasley, 2020).

To explore the potential of RL-DES integration in manufacturing, we reviewed relevant literature. Although research on this combination is currently limited, it is a growing area of interest. Guided by this review, we selected a specific use case to develop an in-house integration pipeline, aiming to find a practical approach to combining DES and RL. This work provides practical insights for developing RL algorithms trained with DES to support dynamic decision-making and process optimisation in manufacturing.

2 LITERATURE REVIEW IN REINFORCEMENT LEARNING COMBINED WITH DES IN MANUFACTURING SETTINGS

We reviewed the literature on the integration of RL with DES in manufacturing. A significant portion of the existing research has focused on applying RL to job shop scheduling and production flow problems. These models address the challenge of assigning jobs to resources based on dynamic priorities, availability, and processing times, which is a central issue in many manufacturing systems. For example, Choi et al. (2024) utilised RL to optimise buffer design and scheduling in mixed-model production lines, while Lang et al. (2020) explored real-time scheduling for flexible job shop systems, demonstrating RL's ability to handle complex decision-making in dynamic production environments. Similarly, Waschneck et al. (2018) applied RL to optimise global production scheduling, highlighting the integration of RL techniques with DES for improved scheduling performance.

In addition to job shop scheduling, RL has been widely employed for the control and dispatching of Automated Guided Vehicles (AGVs) in manufacturing systems. These systems often face challenges such as optimal routing, load balancing, and avoiding conflicts between vehicles. Sakr et al. (2023) demonstrated how RL could be applied to adaptive dispatching in semiconductor manufacturing, while Jaoua et al. (2024) proposed a digital twin-based RL framework for autonomous mobile robot dispatching, showing promising results in optimising AGV control in complex environments.

Another area of research is factory layout optimisation, where RL is used to determine the most efficient arrangement of machines and resources to enhance production flow. Choi et al., (2024) applied RL for optimising both production flow and factory layout, while Klar et al. (2024) integrated RL with simulation techniques to improve multi-objective factory layout planning. These studies underscore the versatility of RL in addressing various optimisation problems across different areas of manufacturing.

In terms of RL algorithms, Deep Q-Learning (DQN) has become a popular choice due to its effectiveness in handling complex decision-making problems in manufacturing systems. DQN has been widely used in job scheduling and resource allocation, where deep neural networks are employed to approximate the Q-function in large state spaces. For instance, Feldkamp et al. (2020) utilised deep RL for optimising modular production systems. Another noteworthy approach is Multi-Agent Reinforcement Learning (MARL), which has been applied to distributed manufacturing systems, such as AGV control and collaborative production scheduling. MARL enables multiple agents to interact and learn from each other, leading to improved overall system performance. Gankin et al. (2021) successfully applied multi-agent deep Q-learning to modular production control. Additionally, Proximal Policy Optimisation (PPO), a more recent RL algorithm, has gained attention for its stability and efficiency in continuous action spaces, particularly in dynamic production environments. Li et al. (2025) demonstrated the application of PPO in decentralised scheduling for distributed flowshops.

The DES environments used in these studies typically focus on modelling various manufacturing systems, such as job shops, flexible production lines, and AGV systems. Popular simulation platforms include Siemens Plant Simulation, which is often used in conjunction with RL to optimise real-time decision-making in production systems (Lang et al., 2020), and AnyLogic, which is a multi-method simulation software that integrates DES and RL for optimisation tasks (Choi et al., 2024). Many studies also utilise custom simulation platforms tailored to specific case studies, such as semiconductor production or automotive manufacturing, as seen in the work of Sakr et al. (2023).

The research landscape on DRL in manufacturing covers a range of applications, including scheduling optimisation, layout configuration, and energy efficiency. These studies collectively demonstrate the potential of integrating RL with simulation techniques, particularly DES, to address complex decision-making challenges in dynamic environments. However, despite promising results, real-world implementation of RL-based DES models still faces significant hurdles. One major limitation is deploying these models in real time, especially in large-scale, complex manufacturing systems where low latency and scalability are critical. Synchronising real-time data between DES and AI systems adds further complexity, while scaling integration for large simulations introduces performance constraints. Additionally, the lack of low-code platforms for AI-DES integration creates a barrier for simulation developers without machine learning expertise (Greasley, 2020).

Another key challenge is the limited transferability of RL models across different manufacturing environments. Most studies focus on specific industries or systems, raising concerns about their generalisability to other production settings. Furthermore, safety and risk management remain critical in RL applications involving AGVs and autonomous robots. Ensuring that RL models adhere to safety constraints and prevent risky behaviours is essential for their practical deployment.

Among the reviewed methods, DQN emerges as the most popular approach for optimising manufacturing operations, often employed due to its ability to learn effective policies with limited computational resources. PPO is also gaining traction, demonstrating superior performance in scenarios involving high-dimensional state spaces and continuous decision-making tasks. The focus on job shop scheduling across multiple studies indicates a consensus on its relevance and complexity within manufacturing, with RL techniques frequently outperforming heuristic and meta-heuristic methods. However, most of the existing literature emphasises single-agent frameworks, leaving multi-agent interactions and stochastic decision-making underexplored.

Finally, there is a growing interest in incorporating sustainability objectives into RL-based DES models, particularly in terms of optimising energy consumption and minimising waste (Eriksson et al., 2022). While this is still an emerging area of research, integrating sustainability into optimisation models is expected to become increasingly important as industries move toward more sustainable manufacturing practices.

In conclusion, while the integration of RL with DES in manufacturing has shown great promise, there are still several challenges that need to be addressed. Future research should focus on improving real-time implementation, enhancing model transferability, addressing data challenges, and incorporating sustainability considerations into optimisation models. These areas represent key opportunities for advancing the application of RL in manufacturing systems.

3 USE CASE

To investigate the integration of DES with RL, we selected a job shop scheduling problem—an inherently complex optimisation challenge that involves allocating multiple tasks to machines in a predefined sequence. The objective of our use case is to explore how RL algorithms can be leveraged to manage dynamic scheduling in the face of uncertainty, addressing some of the existing gaps identified in the literature. By focusing on a job shop scheduling problem within a DES environment, we aim to assess the performance of various RL techniques and their ability to optimise scheduling under changing conditions. This approach draws on the modular production scenarios explored by Gankin et al. (2021) and Mayer et al. (2021), expanding on their work to further understand how RL can improve real-time decision-making in manufacturing systems.

3.1 System Overview and Problem Description

The use case features a manufacturing system that employs Automated Guided Vehicles (AGVs) to transport materials between nine decoupled workstations, arranged in a 3x3 grid. This layout enables a re-entrant production flow, allowing AGVs to revisit specific stations multiple times per iteration. This re-entrant characteristic adds complexity, as not all stations perform every required operation in sequence. The system must intelligently manage AGV routing and scheduling to optimise production efficiency and minimise delays.

For this initial application, the system manufactures one product type. Each product is represented as a job j_i and enters the system on a workpiece carrier at the source. A job's production follows a process plan listing required operations o_{il} in the correct sequence to complete a product. The processing time for operation o_{il} at step l in the process plan is denoted as t_{il}. Workstations $S_{x,y}$ are located at positions x, y in the production grid and perform specific operations. Multiple workstations can perform the same operation, providing operation flexibility for jobs to choose between them. Each workstation processes one job at a time and does not include buffers. The system contains AGVs that move at a speed v_{AGV} to facilitate job transport between workstations.

The process plan specifies the usable workstations and their respective base operation times. The production flow proceeds through the following steps as shown in Table 1. For instance, Step 1 requires processing at either $S_{1,1}$, or $S_{2,1}$ with base times of 67 or 54 seconds, respectively. Step 2 is performed at $S_{3,1}$, $S_{3,2}, or\ S_{3,3}$ with base times of 120, 134 or 110 seconds and so on. These base times are then modified with a random variation of between -10 and 10 seconds, uniformly sampled at process time. This random variation means that the system evolves dynamically as the agent takes steps in the environment, forcing the agent to learn meaningful insights into the environment rather than develop a static strategy.

Table 1 *Process plan for the use case*

Step	Average Time (t_{il} in sec.)	Usable Stations ($S_{x,y}$)
1	67, 54	$S_{1,1}$, $S_{2,1}$
2	120, 134, 110	$S_{3,1}$, $S_{3,2}$, $S_{3,3}$
3	122, 110, 140	$S_{1,2}$, $S_{2,1}$, $S_{2,2}$
4	94, 85	$S_{1,2}$, $S_{1,3}$
5	154, 132, 148	$S_{2,3}$, $S_{3,2}$, $S_{3,3}$

3.2 DES Model in Siemens Plant Simulation

We developed this scenario in Siemens Plant Simulation software (Figure 1) due to its ability to model complex manufacturing systems, provide animated visualisation, and support online communication interfaces such as XML, MQTT, COM, and ActiveX. The primary objective in this case is to maximise throughput, defined as the number of completed units per time unit. Since throughput cannot directly train the RL agent, a reward function is designed to correlate with throughput and guide learning.

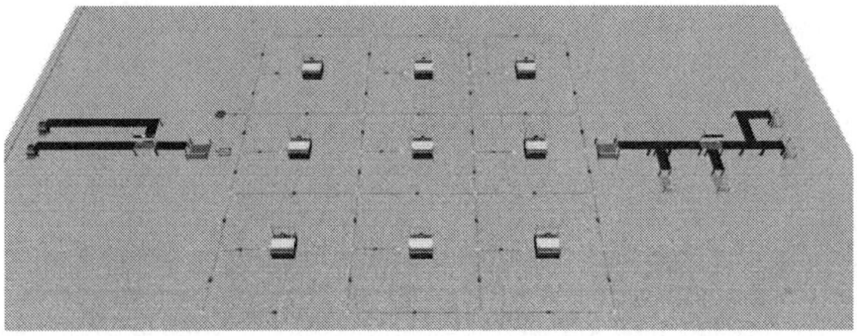

Figure 1 *Model in Siemens Plant Simulation Software*

3.3 RL and Communication Framework

For AI and machine learning development, we evaluated Python, MATLAB, and C++. While Siemens Plant Simulation includes a Neural Network block, its limited AI capabilities made it unsuitable. C++ lacked optimal AI library support, and MATLAB, despite its strengths in neural networks and RL, lacked flexibility and communication protocols. Python was ultimately chosen for its extensive AI libraries and customisation potential.

For system communication, the MQTT protocol was implemented as a lightweight messaging system ideal for IoT applications. Using a publish/subscribe model, it enables seamless data exchange between Plant Simulation and the AI environment via the Mosquitto broker (Eclipse Mosquitto, 2024). The AI and DES software act as MQTT clients, ensuring structured data flow.

3.4 Initial Application

The integration pipeline allows testing of various RL algorithms, starting with DQN and PPO. Initially, DQN was implemented as a Q-learning-based algorithm, first proposed by DeepMind (Mnih et al., 2015). Unlike the original DQN, which used convolutional layers for image-based inputs, our model employs fully connected layers with an array representation of the environment as the state input.

We then implemented PPO; a refinement of earlier policy-based algorithms proposed by OpenAI (Schulman et al., 2017). PPO was introduced to our system to address DQN's shortcomings, as DQN struggled to achieve the desired performance levels. Both algorithms share the same action, state, and reward spaces.

3.5 Action Space

The AI agent controls the AGV, selecting an action A whenever it becomes available or completes a task. Possible actions include moving to any available workstation, picking up a job from the source or another station, dropping off a job at the sink or another station, or waiting for a fixed period of 30 seconds. Given the 9-station layout with a source and sink, this results in 12 possible actions:
$A_{all} = \{A_{source}, A_{S_{1,1}}, \ldots, A_{S_{3,3}}, A_{sink}, A_{wait}\}$

3.6 State Space

The state S is encoded as a 19-element integer vector. The first 9 elements indicate whether each workstation is occupied or empty. The next 9 elements specify the remaining processing time at each station (in seconds). The final element represents the AGV status, detailing whether it is carrying a part and its processing step.
For example, if the AGV is carrying a fresh part while Station $S_{1,2}$ processes a part at step 3 with 37 seconds remaining, and Station $S_{2,1}$ holds a part at step 2 but has finished processing, the state vector would be:
S = [0, 3, 0, 0, 2, 0, 0, 0, 0, 0, 37, 0, 0, 0, 0, 0, 0, 0, 1]

3.7 Reward Design

Rewards are designed to encourage optimal behaviour by reinforcing productive actions and penalising inefficiencies. Positive rewards are given for picking up and placing parts at workstations, scaled by process step to promote workflow progression. Active processing at workstations is incentivised to ensure efficient station utilisation, while delivering a completed product to the sink yields a high reward to maximise throughput. Conversely, negative rewards are applied for moving to an unusable station, transporting an unfinished part to the sink, or waiting unnecessarily, discouraging unproductive actions.

3.8 Training Process

DQN employs a replay memory system for stable learning. Training follows a structured approach:

1. Initial experiences are collected using random actions until the replay memory is sufficiently filled.
2. The network is periodically trained using randomly sampled experiences.
3. An exploration strategy is used to balance exploration and exploitation. The probability of random actions starts high and decays over time, allowing the RL agent to learn an optimal scheduling policy.

This method enhances production efficiency while addressing the dynamic complexities of AGV-based job shop scheduling. However, as illustrated in Figure 2, DQN successfully optimises a simple case where each station has no processing time, but struggles when processing time is introduced (Figure 3).
PPO is an "on-policy" algorithm, meaning it updates based on recent interactions with the environment. It follows this loop:

1. Take actions in the environment according to the policy for a set number of steps.
2. Collect rewards and estimate policy performance.
3. Update the policy based on feedback.

Unlike DQN, PPO cannot leverage replay memory since past experiences come from outdated policies. While PPO's neural network architecture is similar to that of DQN, it generally achieves superior performance despite slower training, as it continuously refines policy updates. In our experiments, we set the episode length to 2,000 steps per rollout, which allows sufficient time for the environment to evolve given the randomness in station processing times. The results, shown in Figure 4, demonstrate that PPO consistently improves performance across training episodes.

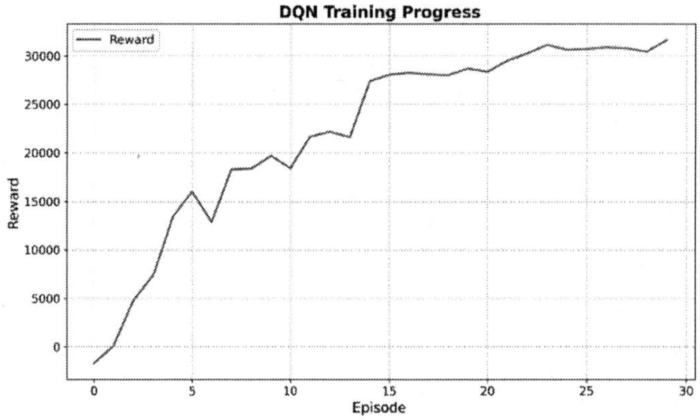

Figure 2 *Reward progression of the DQN agent in a simplified simulation with no processing time. The agent quickly learned to transfer parts sequentially between stations.*

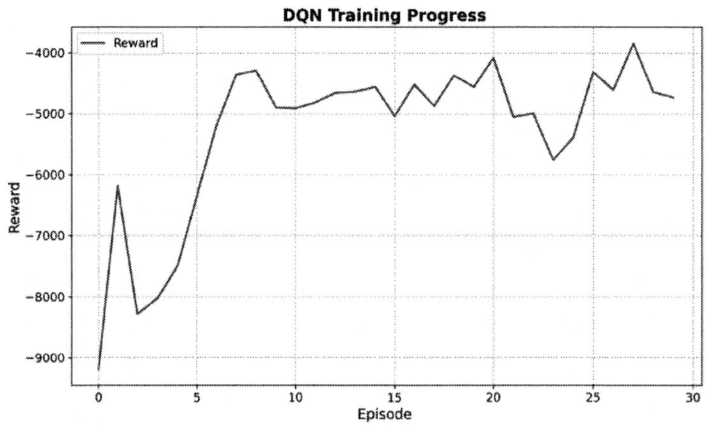

Figure 3 *Reward progression of the DQN agent in the simulation with processing time. The agent failed to adapt, resulting in poor performance and frequent negative rewards.*

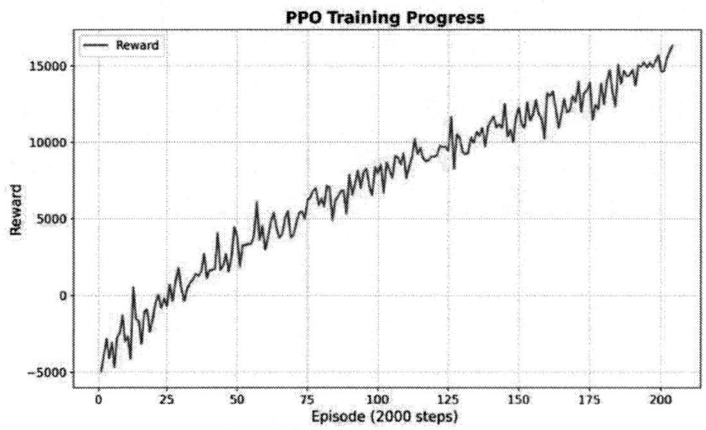

Figure 4 *Reward progression of the PPO agent throughout training, demonstrating steady improvement in policy performance.*

3.9 Preliminary Results

Our DQN implementation did not achieve the desired performance level. While it successfully optimised a simple case where each station had no processing time (Figure 2), it failed to generalise to scenarios requiring parts to undergo fixed processing times before moving to the next station (Figure 3). We attribute this poor performance to instability during training, which led the agent to frequently get "stuck" in loops of repeating actions that resulted in minimal or slightly negative rewards once exploration decreased. Due to these limitations, further development of DQN was discontinued in favour of PPO. However, with adjustments to the reward structure or simulation setup, we believe our DQN implementation could be improved.

In contrast, PPO significantly outperformed DQN, achieving near-human performance in our simulation, even with random variations in station processing times (Figure 4). The model achieved a throughput of approximately 100 completed parts per 2,000 steps. In comparison, human participants who manually solved the same problem using a GUI interface (which mirrored the MQTT-based agent interaction) managed around 120 parts per 2,000 steps. We believe further fine-tuning and hyperparameter optimisation could enable the PPO algorithm to match or exceed human-level performance.

4 CONCLUSIONS AND FUTURE WORK

This study explored the integration of DES with RL to enhance complex decision-making in manufacturing. By leveraging DES as a dynamic training environment, AI models can simulate real-world processes and generate synthetic data, mitigating challenges related to data scarcity and variability. This enables RL agents to adapt to changing production conditions and optimise decision-making in manufacturing systems.

Our findings demonstrate that RL techniques, particularly DQN and PPO, hold significant potential for improving manufacturing operations. DQN offers computational efficiency, making it well-suited for structured environments, while PPO performs effectively in complex, high-dimensional scenarios. Job shop scheduling remains a persistent challenge, where RL-based approaches consistently outperform traditional heuristic methods in dynamic scheduling and resource allocation.

For our use case, we developed a flexible RL-DES framework for AGV job shop scheduling within a re-entrant production flow. By integrating Siemens Plant Simulation with a Python-based AI environment through the MQTT protocol, we established a seamless communication pipeline. Our initial implementation of DQN and PPO provided promising results, laying the foundation for further enhancements.

Future work will focus on incorporating real-world complexities such as fluctuating demand, equipment failures, and maintenance constraints to assess RL performance under more realistic conditions. Additionally, we developed a debug tool that interacts with the DES model via MQTT, enabling human users to emulate AI signals, access AI-limited information, and compare their decision-making performance against RL algorithms. This comparative analysis will provide deeper insights into the effectiveness of AI-driven scheduling versus human expertise. These advancements will refine the RL-DES framework, bringing us closer to AI-driven decision-making in advanced manufacturing.

ACKNOWLEDGMENTS

Authors would like to acknowledge the UK High Value Manufacturing Catapult for providing the funding to develop the methodology used in this study.

REFERENCES

Chan, K. C., Rabaev, M., & Pratama, H. (2022). Generation of synthetic manufacturing datasets for machine learning using discrete-event simulation. *Production and Manufacturing Research*, *10*(1), 337–353. https://doi.org/10.1080/21693277.2022.2086642

Choi, H., Yu, S., Lee, D. H., Noh, S. Do, Ji, S., Kim, H., Yoon, H., Kwon, M., & Han, J. (2024). Optimization of the Factory Layout and Production Flow Using Production-Simulation-Based Reinforcement Learning. *Machines*, *12*(6). https://doi.org/10.3390/machines12060390

Choi, J., Park, J., Noh, S. Do, & Lee, J. Y. (2024). Optimization of buffer design for mixed-model sequential production line based on simulation and reinforcement learning. *Journal of Intelligent Manufacturing*. https://doi.org/10.1007/s10845-024-02525-w

Christiaens, S. (2023). The Data Dilemma: Four Common Barriers To AI Success. *Forbes*.

Del Gallo, M., Mazzuto, G., Ciarapica, F. E., & Bevilacqua, M. (2023). Artificial Intelligence to Solve Production Scheduling Problems in Real Industrial Settings: Systematic Literature Review. In *Electronics (Switzerland)* (Vol. 12, Issue 23). Multidisciplinary Digital Publishing Institute (MDPI). https://doi.org/10.3390/electronics12234732

Eriksson, K., Ramasamy, S., Zhang, X., Wang, Z., & Danielsson, F. (2022). Conceptual framework of scheduling applying discrete event simulation as an environment for deep reinforcement learning. *Procedia CIRP*, *107*, 955–960. https://doi.org/10.1016/j.procir.2022.05.091

European Commission. (2019). *Ethics guidelines for trustworthy AI.* https://ec.europa.eu/futurium/en/ethics-guidelines-trustworthy-ai/register-piloting-process-0

Feldkamp, N., Bergmann, S., & Strassburger, S. (2020). Simulation-Based Deep Reinforcement Learning For Modular Production Systems. *2020 Winter Simulation Conference (WSC)*, 1596–1607. https://doi.org/10.1109/WSC48552.2020.9384089

Fiona Zhao, Y., Xie, J., & Sun, L. (2024). On the data quality and imbalance in machine learning-based design and manufacturing—A systematic review. *Engineering*. https://doi.org/10.1016/j.eng.2024.04.024

Gankin, D., Mayer, S., Zinn, J., Vogel-Heuser, B., & Endisch, C. (2021). Modular Production Control with Multi-Agent Deep Q-Learning. *IEEE International Conference on Emerging Technologies and Factory Automation, ETFA, 2021-September*. https://doi.org/10.1109/ETFA45728.2021.9613177

Greasley, A. (2020). Architectures for combining discrete-event simulation and machine learning. *SIMULTECH 2020 - Proceedings of the 10th International Conference on Simulation and Modeling Methodologies, Technologies and Applications*, 47–58. https://doi.org/10.5220/0009767600470058

Jaoua, A., Masmoudi, S., & Negri, E. (2024). Digital twin-based reinforcement learning framework: application to autonomous mobile robot dispatching. *International Journal of Computer Integrated Manufacturing*. https://doi.org/10.1080/0951192X.2024.2314787

Klar, M., Schworm, P., Wu, X., Simon, P., Glatt, M., Ravani, B., & Aurich, J. C. (2024). Transferable multi-objective factory layout planning using simulation-based deep reinforcement learning. *Journal of Manufacturing Systems*, *74*, 487–511. https://doi.org/10.1016/j.jmsy.2024.04.007

Lang, S., Behrendt, F., Lanzerath, N., Reggelin, T., & Müller, M. (2020). Integration of Deep Reinforcement Learning and Discrete-Event Simulation for Real-Time Scheduling of a Flexible Job Shop Production. *2020 Winter Simulation Conference (WSC)*, 3057–3068. https://doi.org/10.1109/WSC48552.2020.9383997

Li, H., Gao, L., Fan, Q., Li, X., & Han, B. (2025). An end-to-end decentralised scheduling framework based on deep reinforcement learning for dynamic distributed heterogeneous flowshop scheduling. *International Journal of Production Research*. https://doi.org/10.1080/00207543.2024.2449240

Mayer, S., Classen, T., & Endisch, C. (2021). Modular production control using deep reinforcement learning: proximal policy optimization. *Journal of Intelligent Manufacturing*, *32*(8), 2335–2351. https://doi.org/10.1007/s10845-021-01778-z

Mnih, V., Kavukcuoglu, K., Silver, D., Rusu, A. A., Veness, J., Bellemare, M. G., Graves, A., Riedmiller, M., Fidjeland, A. K., Ostrovski, G., Petersen, S., Beattie, C., Sadik, A., Antonoglou, I., King, H., Kumaran, D., Wierstra, D., Legg, S., & Hassabis, D. (2015). Human-level control through deep reinforcement learning. *Nature*, *518*(7540), 529–533. https://doi.org/10.1038/nature14236

Roh, Y., Heo, G., & Whang, S. E. (2021). A Survey on Data Collection for Machine Learning: A Big Data - AI Integration Perspective. *IEEE Transactions on Knowledge and Data Engineering*, *33*(4), 1328–1347. https://doi.org/10.1109/TKDE.2019.2946162

Schulman, J., Wolski, F., Dhariwal, P., Radford, A., & Klimov, O. (2017). Proximal Policy Optimization Algorithms. *CoRR, abs/1707.06347*. http://arxiv.org/abs/1707.06347

Sakr, A. H., Aboelhassan, A., Yacout, S., & Bassetto, S. (2023). Simulation and deep reinforcement learning for adaptive dispatching in semiconductor manufacturing systems. *Journal of Intelligent Manufacturing, 34*(3), 1311–1324. https://doi.org/10.1007/s10845-021-01851-7

Waschneck, B., Reichstaller, A., Belzner, L., Altenmüller, T., Bauernhansl, T., Knapp, A., & Kyek, A. (2018). Optimization of global production scheduling with deep reinforcement learning. *Procedia CIRP, 72*, 1264–1269. https://doi.org/10.1016/j.procir.2018.03.212

AUTHOR BIOGRAPHY

CANSU KANDEMIR has 15 years of experience in the simulation and modelling of complex systems, specialising in Discrete Event Simulation. She is Technical Fellow for Manufacturing Intelligence at the Advanced Manufacturing Research Centre (AMRC), part of the University of Sheffield. Her research focuses on integrating Industry 4.0 technologies into modelling and simulation to enhance decision-making accuracy.

SCOTT HEROD received an MSc in Physics from the University of Nottingham in 2018 and is a Technical Lead for AI & Modelling at the Advanced Manufacturing and Research Centre's (AMRC) Design and Prototyping Group. He has 7 years of experience in machine learning, including reinforcement learning, machine vision, and knowledge management, as well as general software development including Virtual Reality applications and 3D visualisation software.

MATIN GHOJOGH received a MSc in Robotics and automation from the University of Sheffield in 2024. He has experience working in biomedical devices' R&D sector specializing in embedded systems design for 2 years. His interest in bionic limbs and Artificial organs lead to him joining the University of Sheffield seeking the knowledge of AI and robotics.

ALI NARAGHIPOUR holds an MSc in Robotics from the University of Sheffield. He has three years of experience in utilizing and development of AI based models for various sectors, specifically in the biomedical applications. Ali has explored various AI development sectors such as feature extraction, feature selection, signal processing, image processing, machine learning model development and reinforcement learning models. Ali specializes in leveraging cutting-edge techniques, such as AI, to drive innovation in the biomedical field, applying advanced methodologies to enhance diagnostics, analysis, and decision-making.

MARCO FRANCHINO received a MSc Mechanical Engineering from the *Polytechnic* University of Torino (Italy) in 2011. He is Lead Engineer for Manufacturing Intelligence at the Advanced Manufacturing Research Centre (AMRC), part of the University of Sheffield: Marco has wide R&D and industrial experience in Discrete Event Simulation, factory flow modelling, cost modelling, and cost prediction strategies focused on products, resources, and investments estimation. He is also an expert in trade studies to isolate the best/most balanced solution and decision-making techniques.

PAYAM SOULANTIANTORK is an academic in the department of Automatic Control and Systems Engineering at the University of Sheffield. He is an industrial automation and instrumentation expert with more than 6 years of industrial experience from 2007 to 2013. He has successfully developed and completed several industrial automation projects. His research interests are industrial automation, renewable energy real-time control and monitoring, programming and developing PLCs, supervisory, control and data acquisition (SCADA), Industry 4.0 and Cyber Physical Lab.

Proceedings of the Operational Research Society Simulation Workshop 2025 (SW25)
M. Luis, A. Harper, T. Monks, N. Mustafee, eds.
https://doi.org/10.36819/SW25.032

TOWARDS A DIGITAL TWIN FOR EMERGENCY RESPONSE: A HYBRID SIMULATION FOR MULTI-SECTORAL RESOURCE ALLOCATION

Dr. Otto Chen

Centre for Simulation, Analytics & Modelling;
Centre for Water Systems
University of Exeter, UK
c.chen2@exeter.ac.uk

Dr. Navonil Mustafee

Centre for Simulation, Analytics & Modelling
Business School
University of Exeter, UK
n.mustafee@exeter.ac.uk

Dr. Mehdi Khoury, Dr. Barry Evans,
Dr. Gareth Lewis, Dr. Qian Li,
Dr. Albert S. Chen, Dr. Slobodan Djordjevic

Centre for Water Systems
University of Exeter, UK

Dr. Lydia Vamvakeridou-Lyroudia
Dr. Dragan A. Savic
Centre for Water Systems,
University of Exeter, UK;
KWR Water Research Institute,
Nieuwegein, The Netherlands

ABSTRACT

Effective emergency response planning is vital for regional climate resilience, requiring coordination across multiple government sectors. Collective management of emergency resources enhances allocation efficiency at a regional scale, overcoming local constraints. However, prioritisation becomes challenging when resources are shared collectively. Evolving emergency events further complicate forecasting future demands, as shortages trigger the need for external support whilst increasing estimation uncertainty.

To address these challenges, we implemented an emergency response Digital Twin, integrating a Resource Allocation Model with short-term weather-related predictions and real-time updates. This paper focuses on the model's application within a hybrid simulation framework, tested in a flooding case study in Torbay, UK. The approach enables a holistic assessment of emergency response by leveraging collective resource advantages whilst considering cascading infrastructure failures. By improving resource distribution and resilience strategies, the model supports more effective decision-making for regional emergency preparedness.

Keywords: Emergency Response, Hybrid Simulation, Digital Twin, Climate Resilience, Flooding

List of Abbreviations

Abbreviation	Explanation
ABS	Agent-based Simulation
CI	Critical Infrastructure
DES	Discrete-event Simulation
DT	Digital Twin
ER	Emergency Response
OR/MS	Operation Research / Modelling & Simulation
RAM	Resource Allocation Model
RTS	Real-time Simulation
SD	System Dynamics

1 INTRODUCTION

Emergency response (ER) plays a critical role in regional climate resilience. Taking flooding emergency as an example, ER usually involves several actors from the first responders such as fire brigade, ambulance, police, local authority, and utility providers (e.g., power supply, telecom) to deliver required resources for safeguarding citizens. Resource requestors can be individuals or entities such as hospitals, schools, and train stations affected by floods. Requests for ER resources may also come from those maintaining Critical Infrastructures (CIs) like electrical substations and water pumping stations to ensure their steady operations during the crisis and avoid disruption to other services that are depending on them. As resources are limited, the emergency responders often face difficult decision-making situations during extreme events because of (a) pooling ER resources from multiple agencies and deploying them in a coordinated manner, and (b) prioritising ER resources allocation amongst the competing demand points. Those decisions are further challenged by the evolving nature of emergency events that may be ongoing.

This paper presents a decision-making tool for ER resource allocation that addresses the advantage of collective operation and resource sharing, seldom seen in practice due to the technical and operational challenges (Berariu et al., 2015, Fekete, 2019, Fekete, 2020). Such a tool should include a computational model (a computer simulation, for example) that suggests the optimal allocation of resources, in priority order, amongst the various demand points. The model should also take into account the cascading effects of the failure of CIs and their impact on several other services. Such optimal allocation could also consider additional resources that may be available from private sectors/regional agencies. Alternative journey planning for ER resources might also be employed using micro-simulation models of traffic to bypass roads prone to flooding and reduce delays (Fathianpour et al., 2023). The core computation model could be further extended through real-time data streams for increased situational awareness, enabling real-time experimentation (Harper et al., 2023). In modelling and simulation of Operation Research (OR/MS) literature, this is also referred to as real-time simulation (RTS) or a Digital Twin (DT). The difference in terminologies is based on the mix of historical and real-time data that are used for the parameterisation of the computational model (Mustafee et al., 2023a, Mustafee et al., 2023b).

This paper presents the Resource Allocation Model (RAM), which is a computational model and a decision-making support tool for ER, being applied to the EU ARSINOE project (https://cordis.europa.eu/project/id/101037424). The model is a hybrid simulation implemented in the software package AnyLogic (AnyLogic, 2023, Brailsford et al., 2019). The RAM is part of a wider work on the development of an ER Digital Twin (ER-DT) and its application to a flooding case study from Torbay, a tourism city prone to flooding in the Southwest of England, where it faces increasing climate challenges in ER resource adequacy and allocation.

2 A COLLECTIVE RESOURCE ALLOCATION STRATEGY FOR EMERGENCY RESPONSE

Cascading effects describe chain reactions in relation to the loss of service capacity amongst CIs, which are triggered by the failure of one or a sub-set of CIs; these are common occurrences in extreme weather events. For example, an electricity substation affected by flood may cascade the failure to a train station that is not directly inundated, thus affecting not only the former's but also the latter's service capacity. To enhance tain infrastructure resilience, effectively mitigating the cascading effects of such failures is crucial in a region. Resources for ER need to be properly dispatched with systemic consideration of the cascading effects.

However, although resource sharing amongst different agencies can potentially tackle inadequacies that may exist locally or at an agency level especially when encountering extreme (weather) situations, in reality, several challenges hinder emergency responders from applying the collective strategy. Agencies that own the resources are usually responsible for their own allocation and management. Without the collective operation, cascading effects can hardly be considered by individual agent's effort due to their systemic feature.

In collective operation, prioritising emergency response requested by affected CIs is a challenge, as resources shared would become competitive in the scenario. Furthermore, the priority order for tackling events with cascading impacts may differ significantly from the events without such knock-on effect, which increases the complexity of decision-making as to where the resources are to be sent. Therefore, relying on experts' personal experience and judgment by considering only the intuitive level, e.g., the importance of the individual CIs, is arguably not the best approach for the collective strategy. An enhanced approach for addressing the dynamics of resource allocation in collective context is necessary. This approach should consider the cascading effects of critical infrastructures (CIs) for holistic and regional interests. Forecasting the evolving weather impacts is also crucial. This is particularly advantageous in an era facing accelerating climate impacts.

These challenges raise key research questions: Can simulation effectively capture the dynamics of a collective emergency response strategy whilst considering cascading effects? This requires accurately representing system processes, logistics, and the behaviour of entities fundamental to emergency response (supply side), as well as critical infrastructure processes that demand emergency resources (demand side). Can the simulation approach proposed demonstrate the significance of addressing cascading effects in emergency response for climate resilience? Can it justify the benefits of the collective resource-sharing policy? Lastly, can the simulation developed identify the limitations of the tested policy's contribution?

3 MODELLING METHODOLOGY

Hybrid simulation developed using a combination of simulation techniques such as system dynamics (SD), discrete-event simulation (DES), and agent-based simulation (ABS), can better represent the evolving dynamics of a system under scrutiny (such as our multi-sectoral ER response) and engender greater insights (Brailsford et al., 2019, Mustafee et al., 2017, Mustafee et al., 2020). The RAM for the Torbay case study uses hybrid simulation that can be integrated into an ER-DT, where it serves as the core computational model for resource allocation element of the Torbay case, with several other models providing input to the RAM (refer to Section 5). The rationale for the use of DES, ABS and SD is presented next.

- **DES** is used for process modelling. The processes involved in the RAM are mainly the prioritisation of resources amongst competing demands from CIs, resource allocation and resource dispatch process, as well as modelling water level dynamics involved in ER (e.g., pumps involving pumping volume monitoring) and infrastructures (e.g., flood pumping process involving water level control).
- **ABS** simulates systems with complex interactions involving multiple agent types and numerous agent instances, leading to the emergence of the overall system state. In the RAM, ABS is applied to the logistics of resource dispatching, when and where (which CI?) to depart and return (the ABS state chart defines the logic). It also allows different types of agents/resources to conduct well-defined tasks; it determines when resources are to be released from a CI site, e.g., pumps being released from a CI site subject to water level (the resources are then available to a different site); engineers being released subject to shift timings.
- **SD** simulates complex feedback loops existing in a system and helps understand their dynamic behaviours through the evolution of simulated time. SD is used in the RAM to model the cascading effects amongst CIs. The priority of ER requests is calculated through SD.

Whilst ABS can also model processes like DES and can also model relationships for cascading effects like SD, applying ABS, DES, and SD as a hybrid simulation offers greater advantage for building the RAM. It reduces complexity, simplifies logic, and decreases computing time. Additionally, applying SD to model cascading effects is more intuitive, as SD naturally represents causal relationships, allowing modellers to clearly observe changes in cascading effects during the simulation. More importantly, applying hybrid simulation for the RAM leverages the strengths of ABS, DES, and SD, enabling each method to capture different dynamics where they excel, as addressing multiple dynamics is the main challenge in representing the ER resource allocation with evolving weather condition.

Figure 1 illustrates how the ER activities proceed in flooding situations when resources are requested by affected CIs. The figure presents the collective strategy in resource allocation, under the context of cascading effects. On the top of the figure are the critical infrastructures, which include not only those directly affected by floods, but also the interdependencies between them whereby, whilst not being inundated, are indirectly affected by the failure of other CIs. In the figure, the cascading effects as a result of these interdependencies are depicted using arrows; for example, the failure of infrastructure Type A will cascade to Types C, D and E. Here, Type A could be a power station supplying electricity to a hospital (C), school (D) and railway station (E). Thus, a hospital, school and rail station may be indirectly affected by a failed power substation that is inundated by flood.

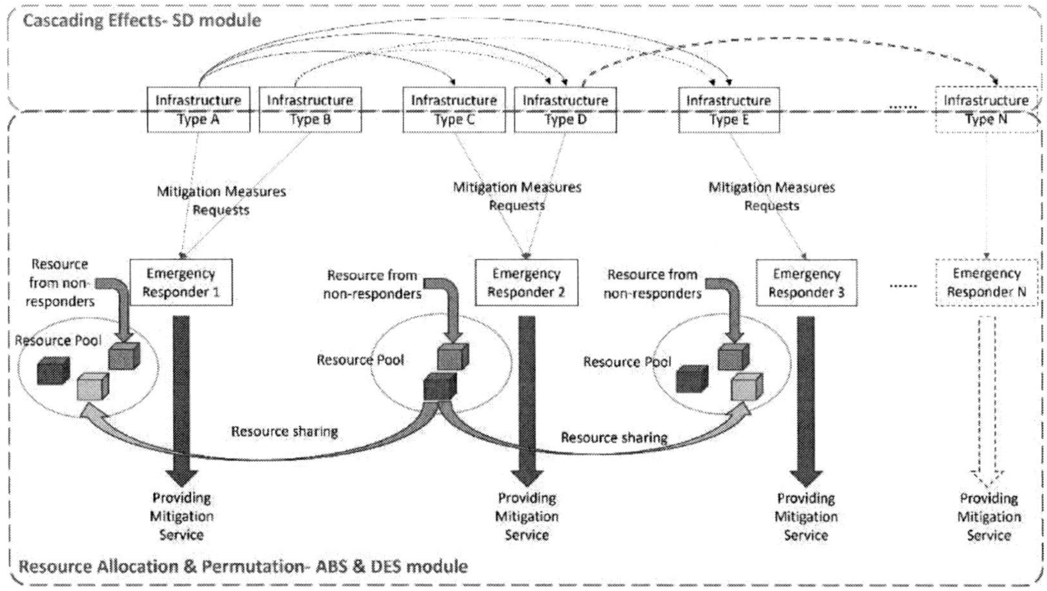

Figure 1 Schematic diagram of emergency response applying collective resource allocation and sharing.

The RAM uses the potential loss rate of service capacity (people served per day) as the KPI for assigning priorities towards competing ER requests. For instance, a flooded/failed power substation (CI Type A) serving 1,000 people can affect a hospital (CI Type C) located within its service area but is itself not flooded. The hospital may be serving a catchment of 600 people. This response request (which could take the form of a water pump and engineers being dispatched to site Type A) will generally have a higher priority than, say, another flooded power substation serving the same number of people (i.e., 1,000) but which does not have other CIs within its service area. As for resource sharing in the collective operation, it refers to sharing resources owned by individual responders, and resources supported by non-responders and external agents, e.g., private sectors like builders and local governments of other regions.

4 RESOURCE ALLOCATION MODEL (RAM)

Built with Anylogic (AnyLogic, 2023), the model applies a hybrid simulation approach that combines ABS, DES, and SD. The model provides priority ranking of resource allocation considering the cascading effects of affected CIs. Four primary agent types are implemented in the hybrid model (Figure 2). The *Resource Hub* agent is modelled at a global level, the *Infrastructure* and *Resource* agent at a local level, with the *Order* agent providing a conceptual link between the individual and the global levels. As this is a hybrid simulation, agent types include various combinations of ABS, DES, and SD modules, or they can be a standalone model.

- **Resource Hub agent** uses DES to implement the collective resource allocation strategy, encompassing multiple responders that own and offer their resources for ER. The current implementation of the RAM has only one command centre.
- **Infrastructure agent** models the CIs using ABS, DES and SD modules. The agent may have multiple sub-types, such as hospital, power sub-station, and train station. As shown in Figure 2, its

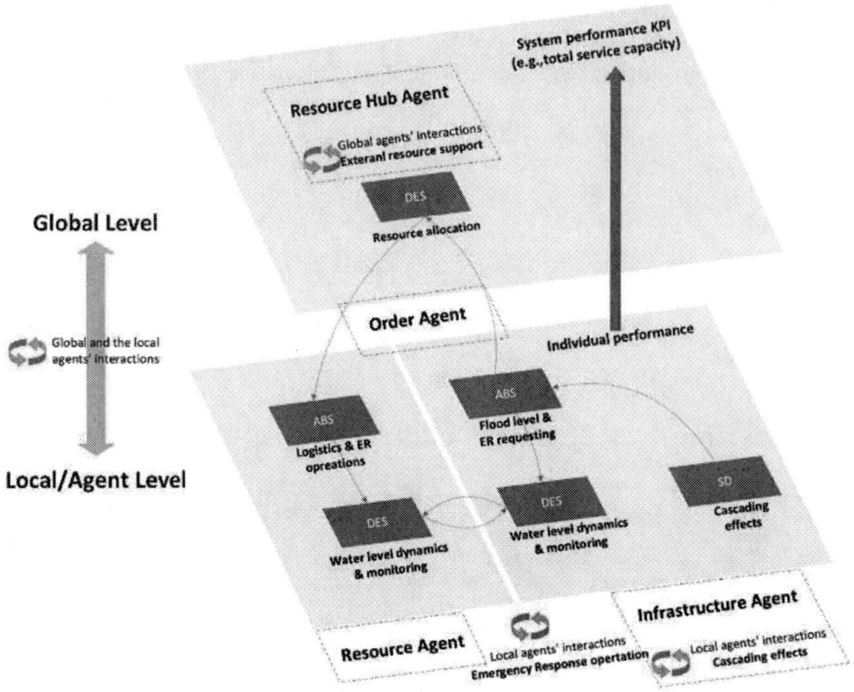

Figure 2 Conceptual model of the Resource Allocation Model (RAM).

ABS module requests ER according to the dynamics of water-related processes and flooding risks associated with CIs (these are modelled using a DES module with AnyLogic Fluid Library). For example, for a train station, a water-related process is the water level control in its underground space for the pumping process. Flooding of the space will disrupt train service, and a request for ER may be sent to the Resource Hub agent. The SD module of the infrastructure agent models the cascading effects and relations with other CIs, for calculating the loss of service capacity for priority ranking of ER resource allocation (implemented by the DES module of the *Resource Hub* agent). Figure 3 provides a screenshot of an instance of the *Infrastructure* agent.

- **Resource agent** represents ER resources that are allocated by the *Resource Hub* agent to the various instances of the *Infrastructure* agent based on demand and priority. The *Resource* agents have several sub-types, such as machines (e.g., generator, pump, digger), personnel (e.g., site manager), materials (e.g., sandbag), and vehicles (e.g., digger). A subset of *Resource* agent types may implement a DES module (using AnyLogic Fluid Library) that models water-related processes associated with a resource, e.g., water level monitoring for the pumping process of a pump agent. The agents perform well-defined tasks (as per their sub-types) and move through the system following the logic defined in the RAM start charts.
- **Order agents** are the instances of ER requested by instances of the *Infrastructure* agent. The order agents model the following: (a) interaction between the *Resource Hub* agent and instances of the *Resource agent*, and (b) interaction between the *Resource Hub* agent and instances of the *Infrastructure* agent.

5 SCENARIOS AND RESULTS

Four main scenarios are examined (Table 1), primarily to test whether the resource sharing (S) and the priority queuing (P) policies can contribute to infrastructure resilience (i.e., retaining better CI service capacity through better resource allocation policy). In the priority queuing

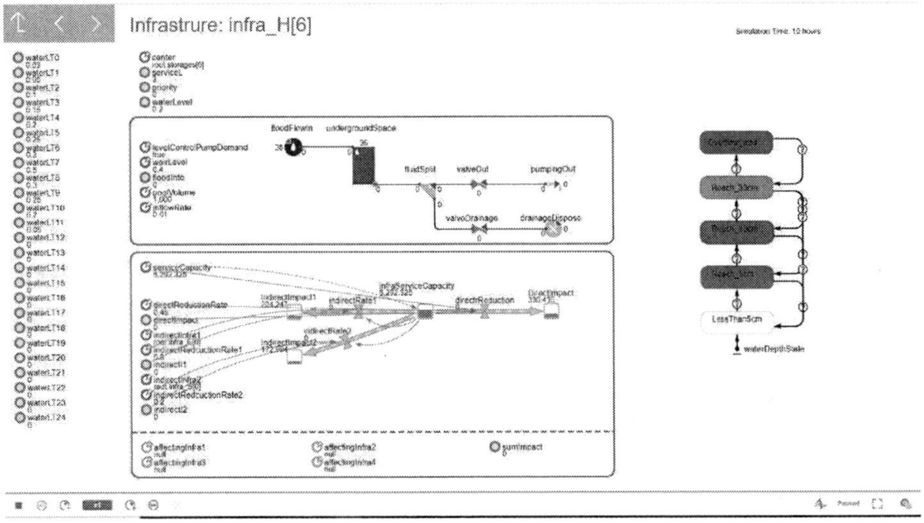

Figure 3 Infrastructure Agent with ABS, DES and SD components (screenshot from AnyLogic).

policy, in order to obtain better overall performance in retaining service capacity of CIs during flood events, the RAM allocates resources according to the priority of ER requests in a queue,rather than following the *'first come, first served'* principle. Additionally, three resource levels are defined, which explores how different resource levels affect the influence of the priority queuing policy.

Table 1 Scenarios for Experimentation.

Resource Level Grouping	Scenarios	Description
Default level x1	Baseline	**Baseline**: Scenario without resource sharing and priority queuing (implying *First Come, First Served*) **S**: Resourcing sharing scenario **P**: Priority queuing scenario **S&P**: Scenario with resource sharing and priority queuing
	S	
	P	
	S & P	
Default level x2	Baseline	
	S	
	P	
	S & P	
Default level x3	Baseline	
	S	
	P	
	S & P	

The results of scenario experimentation are shown in Figure 4. We first compare the three resource level groupings. Here we see that higher resource levels (i.e., default level X 2; default level X 3 – Table 1) lead to an increase in total service levels (total service capacity per day for 13 defined CIs in the model). However, the reason we tested different resource levels was that increasing the resource level would not always increase the service capacity. There would come a point where all the requests are completely satisfied through lower resource levels, with any additional increase unnecessary. The RAM experimentation can thus help identify the critical point. It can be seen from Figure 4 that the increase to resource level X 3 (meaning three times of the lowest amount of resource) did not contribute to service capacity compared to resource level X 2, particularly when the resource sharing (S) scenario or the resource sharing and priority queuing (S&P) scenario is adopted.

The results also verify that resource-sharing and priority-queuing policies can substantially benefit infrastructure resilience by retaining service capacity. In all three resource levels, the S, P, and S&P scenarios all perform better than the baseline scenario, however, with different extents of contribution. In the lowest resource level (default level X 1), adopting the sharing policy (S) can substantially benefit service capacity whilst adopting the priority queuing policy (P) alone cannot. This is because when ER resources are extremely limited, even queuing at the front position will not get the allocated resource quickly enough to realise the potential difference of capacity loss of two affected infrastructures. It is interesting to see when commonly adopting the S and P policy (S&P), the service capacity performs best amongst the four scenarios, implying the effect of sharing policy and the effect of priority policy work together to retain service capacity.

With resource level X 2, we can see that the S and P policies can both substantially contribute to service capacity alone. Although the S&P policy can also substantially benefit service capacity, it does not perform best as the way in resource level X 1; the S&P merely performs similarly to the S policy. The reason behind this is that the effect of the sharing policy alone is sufficient to supply not only the requests with earlier queued positions but also those with later queued positions. This means that even the latter queued requests can receive resources shortly after those with higher priority (i.e., a negligible time gap), so the additional effect of the priority policy does not occur.

In the highest resource level (X 3), we can see all four scenarios have similar performance, which means either the S policy or the P policy can no longer benefit the service capacity. It shows the circumstance that the resource availability is good enough to satisfy all the ER requests immediately, which implies there might be many resources that are idle and would never be used in the flood event.

The experimentation shows it is worth applying the S&P policy in the RAM, as there is a high possibility that the synergy of applying the S and P policies will occur, particularly in real-world situations where resources are inadequately available to meet ER demands.

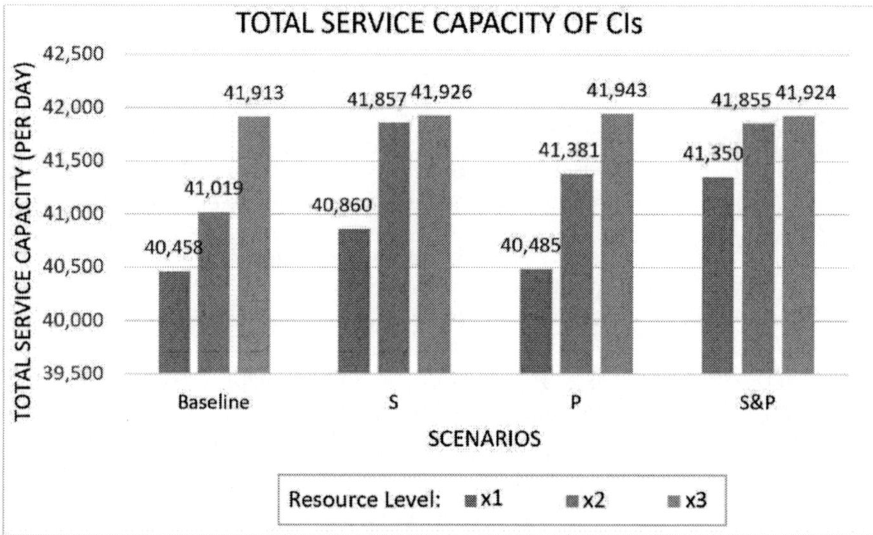

Figure 4 The results of scenario experimentation – RAM.

6 DESIGN OF AN ASPIRATIONAL DIGITAL TWIN FOR EMERGENCY RESPONSE

To facilitate the ongoing ER operation and to enable in-time assessment of decisions related to resource allocation (assessment of feedback from previous decision-making loops), an ER tool should ideally provide situational awareness by reporting the status of the ER in *real time*. In addition, an ER-DT could be further enhanced by including forecasts of weather conditions (e.g., rainfall), the evolving hazards (e.g., floods), and the relevant human activities affected (e.g., the prediction of traffic conditions affected by floods). All of those serve as an input to the RAM. However, modelling of weather and flood forecasts is outside the area of OR/MS, and requires the development of hybrid models that integrate knowledge constructs, methods, tools and techniques from disciplines such as water engineering and weather science (Tolk et al., 2021). Thus, an aspirational ER-DT will include not only an ABS-DES-SD hybrid simulation (Mustafee et al., 2017) for resource allocation (we refer to this as **Level-1**; Figure 5), but also integrate with modelling artefacts that forecast, e.g., weather, climate hazards, and models that predict damages to assets in real-time or near real-time. The latter artefacts contribute to the assessment of the priority of resource allocation by the OR/hybrid simulation model (**Level-2**). As a DT, the forecast models need to run efficiently along with the simulation of the ER resource allocation model, with multiple models working interactively and synchronously. Moreover, the sub-models which inform the OR model may need to be executed on different computers due to data access, model licence, or based on the availability of the required computational resource. To realise DTs that incorporate various computational models, including those from OR/MS, and execute in different simulated time-step orders, a distributed modelling approach could be considered. For example, this includes Parallel and Distributed Simulation (PADS) time synchronisation algorithms (Fujimoto, 1999) and standards like IEEE 1516 High Level Architecture (IEEE, 2010). These techniques ensure the synchronisation of simulation time and messages passed between the sub-models (**Level-3**)(Mustafee et al., 2023a). Figure 5 also includes an additional component for the visualisation of DT using online dashboards, which enable stakeholders to execute real-time experiments. The online dashboard could be a part of Levels 1-3.

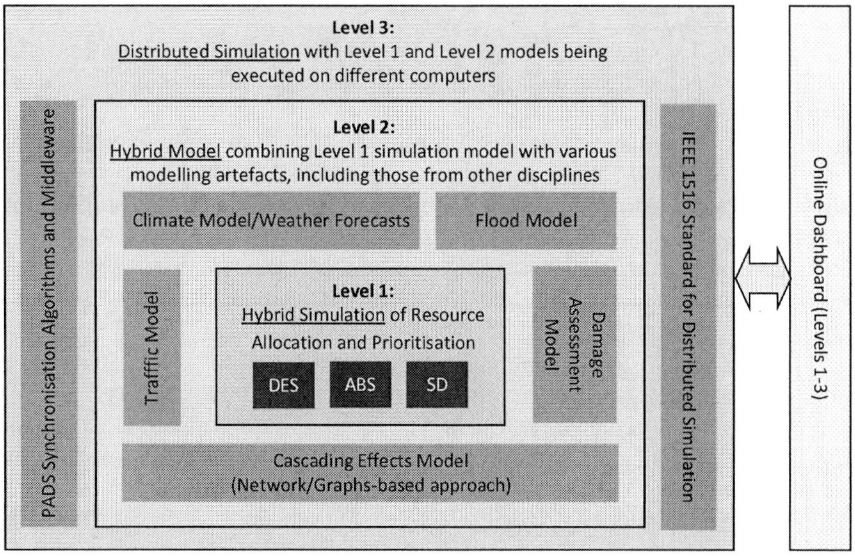

Figure 5: Design of an aspirational Digital Twin for Emergency Response, consisting of three levels. Level-1 is a hybrid simulation model; Level-2 is a hybrid model which relies on the hybrid simulation for resource allocation and inputs from several other models; Level-3 is the distributed execution of the Level-2 hybrid model using approaches from PADS. Finally, an online dashboard is shown, which can be a part of Levels 1-3.

The ER-DT for Torbay will implement some of the aforementioned aspirational design aspects, with the RAM being the core computational model for resource allocation (Level-1), taking input from a flood model (developed in CAFLOOD (Gibson et al., 2016, Guidolin et al., 2016)), a damage assessment model, a traffic model developed in SUMO (Krajzewicz et al., 2012), and aspects of a cascading failure model (Khoury et al., 2025), thereby realising Level-2 DT for emergency response. An online dashboard is also being implemented to visualise some of the elements of the ER-DT (Lewis et al., 2025).

7 CONCLUSIONS

The Resource Allocation Model (RAM) presented in the paper is being developed as a decision-making tool for the stakeholders of our EU ARSINOE case study. Its objective is to test strategies related to the collective allocation of ER resources, taking into account the cascading effects of the failure of CIs, which is a common occurrence during extreme weather events. The aspiration is that emergency responders will gain insight from the modelling work and devise strategies to effectively deploy limited resources that are available for ER. By adopting also the strategy of resource pooling at a regional scale, it will also contribute to enhancing regional climate resilience.

ACKNOWLEDGMENTS

The work presented in this paper is supported by the project ARSINOE: Climate-resilient regions through systemic solutions and innovations, funded by the European Union's Horizon H2020 innovation action programme under the agreement GA 101037424.

REFERENCES

AnyLogic. 2023. *AnyLogic Fluid Library* [Online]. Available: https://www.anylogic.com/features/libraries/fluid-library/ [Accessed].

Berariu, R., Fikar, C., Gronalt, M. & Hirsch, P. 2015. Understanding the impact of cascade effects of natural disasters on disaster relief operations. *International Journal of Disaster Risk Reduction,* 12, 350-356.

Brailsford, S. C., Eldabi, T., Kunc, M., Mustafee, N. & Osorio, A. F. 2019. Hybrid simulation modelling in operational research: A state-of-the-art review. *European Journal of Operational Research,* 278, 721-737.

Fathianpour, A., Evans, B., Jelodar, M. B. & Wilkinson, S. 2023. Tsunami evacuation modelling via micro-simulation model. *Progress in disaster science,* 17, 100277.

Fekete, A. 2019. Critical infrastructure and flood resilience: Cascading effects beyond water. *Wiley Interdisciplinary Reviews: Water,* 6, e1370.

Fekete, A. 2020. Critical infrastructure cascading effects. Disaster resilience assessment for floods affecting city of Cologne and Rhein - Erft - Kreis. *Journal of Flood Risk Management,* 13, e312600.

Fujimoto, R. M. Parallel and distributed simulation. Proceedings of the 31st conference on Winter simulation: Simulation---a bridge to the future-Volume 1, 1999. 122-131.

Gibson, M. J., Savic, D. A., Djordjevic, S., Chen, A. S., Fraser, S. & Watson, T. 2016. Accuracy and computational efficiency of 2D urban surface flood modelling based on cellular automata. *Procedia Engineering,* 154, 801-810.

Guidolin, M., Chen, A. S., Ghimire, B., Keedwell, E. C., Djordjević, S. & Savić, D. A. 2016. A weighted cellular automata 2D inundation model for rapid flood analysis. *Environmental Modelling & Software,* 84, 378-394.

Harper, A., Mustafee, N. & Pitt, M. 2023. Increasing situation awareness in healthcare through real-time simulation. *Journal of the Operational Research Society,* 74, 2339-2349.

IEEE 2010. IEEE 1516-2010 IEEE Standard for Modeling and Simulation (M&S) High Level Architecture (HLA) - Framework and Rules.: IEEE.

Khoury, M., Evans, B., Chatzistefanou, G., Vamvakeridou-Lyroudia, L., Chen, A., Mustafee, N., Savic, D., Pérez, N.C., Alcántara, J.R., & Santamarta, J. 2025. A Simulation Engine to Model the Cascading Failure of Critical Infrastructure Service. In: *Proceedings of the 2025 Simulation Workshops (SW25),* March 31-2 April, 2025, Exeter. UK Operations Research Society.

Krajzewicz, D., Erdmann, J., Behrisch, M. & Bieker, L. 2012. Recent development and applications of SUMO-Simulation of Urban MObility. *International journal on advances in systems and measurements,* 5.

Lewis, G., Khoury, M., Li, Q., Evans, B., Chen, A., Vamvakeridou-Lyroudia, L., Djordjevic, S., Savic, D., & Mustafee.N. 2025. Creating and Operating a Simulation-based Digital Twin Service for Hydrologic Flood. In: *Proceedings of the 2025 Simulation Workshops (SW25),* March 31-2 April, 2025, Exeter. UK Operations Research Society.

Mustafee, N., Brailsford, S., Djanatliev, A., Eldabi, T., Kunc, M. & Tolk, A. Purpose and benefits of hybrid simulation: contributing to the convergence of its definition. 2017 Winter Simulation Conference (WSC), 2017. IEEE, 1631-1645.

Mustafee, N., Harper, A. & Onggo, B. S. Hybrid modelling and simulation (M&S): Driving innovation in the theory and practice of M&S. 2020 winter simulation conference (wsc), 2020. IEEE, 3140-3151.

Mustafee, N., Harper, A. & Viana, J. Hybrid Models with Real-Time Data in Healthcare: A Focus on Data Synchronization and Experimentation. 2023 Winter Simulation Conference (WSC), 2023a. IEEE, 1148-1159.

Mustafee, N., Harper, A. & Viana, J. 2023b. Hybrid models with real-time data: Characterising real-time simulation and digital twins.

Tolk, A., Harper, A. & Mustafee, N. 2021. Hybrid models as transdisciplinary research enablers. *European Journal of Operational Research,* 291, 1075-1090.

AUTHOR BIOGRAPHIES

OTTO CHEN completed his PhD at the University of Bristol in 2019. He is currently a research fellow in the Centre for Water Systems, as well as Centre for Simulation, Analytics and Modelling of Business School, in the University of Exeter. Dr Chen has an extensive background and applications in hybrid simulation modelling and digital twins.

NAVONIL MUSTAFEE is Professor of Operations and Analytics at the University of Exeter Business School. He has research interests in simulation methodology, hybrid simulation and digital twins.

QIAN LI is Research Fellow at the University of Exeter. Her interests include hydraulic modelling, flood forecasting and early warning, climate change impact to critical infrastructure.

MEHDI KHOURY is a Senior Research Fellow at the University of Exeter, with experience in AI, serious gaming, network science, interest working with the water-food-energy ecosystems nexus, and has done work modelling the cascading failure for critical infrastructures.

BARRY EVANS is a Senior Research Fellow at the University of Christchurch. His research interests include hydraulic modelling, water-food-energy-ecosystems nexus, circular economy, evacuation modelling, geographical information systems, and remote sensing.

GARETH LEWIS is a Research Fellow in the Centre for Water Systems at the University of Exeter. His research is concerned with digital hydro informatics. He received an MBA from the Open University in 2007, an MSc in Data Science from University of Plymouth in 1993 and a BSc in Computer Science from University of Brighton in 1992.

LYDIA VAMVAKERIDOU-LYROUDIA is a Senior Research Fellow at the University of Exeter and director of Watershare at the KWR research institute. Her interests include optimisation techniques, multi-criteria decision making, and modelling techniques applied to water systems.

ALBERT CHEN is Professor at the University of Exeter. His interests include water resources, hydraulic modelling, urban drainage, flood forecasting and early warning, water-food-energy-ecosystems nexus, climate change impact to critical infrastructure.

SLOBODAN DJORDJEVIC is Professor in the Centre for Water Systems at the University of Exeter.

DRAGAN SAVIC (FREng, FICE, FCIWEM, FIWA, MASCE, CEng) is the UK's first Professor of Hydroinformatics at the University of Exeter, former CEO of KWR Water Research Institute, and is currently the Global Advisor on Digital Sciences at KWR.

Proceedings of the Operational Research Society Simulation Workshop 2025 (SW25)
M. Luis, A. Harper, T. Monks, N. Mustafee, eds.

https://doi.org/10.36819/SW25.033

CREATING AND OPERATING A SIMULATION-BASED DIGITAL TWIN SERVICE FOR HYDROLOGIC FLOOD

Mr Gareth Lewis
Dr. Mehdi Khoury
Dr. Qian Li
Dr. Barry Evans
Prof. Albert S. Chen
Prof. Slobodan Djordjevic

University of Exeter
Harrison Building, North Park Rd,
Exeter, EX4 4QF, UK
{g.lewis2, m.khoury, q.li6, b.evans, a.s.chen, s.djordjevic}@exeter.ac.uk

Dr. Lydia S. Vamvakeridou-Lyroudia
Prof. Dragan A. Savic

University of Exeter/
KWR Water Research Institute
Nieuwegein, The Netherlands
{lydia.vamvakeridou-lyroudia, d.savic}@kwrwater.nl

Prof Nav Mustafee

University of Exeter Business School
Building:One, Rennes Drive
Exeter, EX4 4ST, UK
N.Mustafee@exeter.ac.uk

ABSTRACT

Within the field of water engineering, digital twins represent an exciting new technology that offers opportunities within both simulation and visualisation to create applications that allow non-expert users (in water engineering) to visualise and hypothesise potential scenarios based on real-world situations allowing for both short-term tactical and longer-term strategic decision making and policy setting to be considered. However, digital twin implementation presents both developers and users with clear issues: what is and isn't a digital twin, what is the scope of their functionality to typical use cases and how can real-world data be used as inputs for simulation and to drive hypothetical what-if scenarios? This paper presents the design, implementation and operation of a flooding digital twin for the ARSINOE project based on flood, traffic and cascading failure modelling for the Torbay region of Devon. Simulation results are presented through a Mapbox-based website, and considerations are given to future development steps.

Keywords: Digital Twins, Water Engineering, Hydro informatics, Digital Water, DevOps, Visualisation, Decision-support, Policy-setting, Cascading Failure, Traffic Simulation.

1 INTRODUCTION

Over the last half-decade or so, water engineering academics have become increasingly fascinated with the potential of digital twins for operational decision making and policy setting activities. University of Exeter (UNEXE) has observed this through its involvement in multiple H2020 research projects (Fiware4water, Aqua3s, Waterverse, and LOTUS) that anecdotally show a staircase of involvement for hydro informatics.

Initially, water companies and local municipalities wanted to move from paper-based infrequent data collection (e.g. water companies collecting yearly metered data) to digital sensor collection. This collection of data naturally facilitates the use of dashboard technology to view (potentially) large amounts of geolocated time-series data alongside the existing role of model-based simulation and visualization, resulting in a desire to combine of real-world and simulated data sources to provide 'what-if' analysis on potential events and scenarios and to consider longer-term planning and potential impacts, particularly with respect to climate change and the desire for climate resilience. The use of real-time data in such computational models is frequently referred to as digital twins.

The paper draws on Exeter's experience in water engineering and digital water, along with current research on the development of digital twins for hydraulic floods as part of the EU-funded ARSINOE project. ARSINOE (https://arsinoe-project.eu/) is an H2020 project with the purpose to build an ecosystem for developing climate change adaptation solutions. For this project UNEXE has been working with Torbay Council (located in the South West of England) to develop a hydrodynamic digital twin of the Torbay region to support the Council with both short-term early warning and long-term planning around flooding events, including surface water run-off, highway flooding, sewer flooding, main river and ordinary watercourse flooding during intense rainfall events.

2 DIGITAL TWINS AND INFORMATION DASHBOARDS

From an academic-to-industry perspective, definitions of digital twins are not always helpful and can often come across as being overly proscriptive in terms of lifecycle and technology choices, e.g. IBM's definition (IBM, 2024) *'A digital twin is a virtual representation of an object or system designed to reflect a physical object accurately. It spans the object's lifecycle, is updated from real-time data and uses simulation, machine learning and reasoning to help make decisions'*. For the water engineering use cases that UNEXE tends to be involved with, digital twins are often (currently) purely concerned with day-to-day operations, i.e. collecting, displaying, and interpreting sensor data, so 'spanning the object lifecycle' is generally beyond our research-focused scope, i.e. determining what is possible rather than providing full-lifecycle solutions. Likewise, whilst water digital twins are updated from real-time, they don't necessarily employ machine learning or decision making, particularly in scenarios where users require more traditional visualization-only, or dashboard-type solutions.

For our work, we have developed a softer definition of dashboards and digital twins based on the model-view-controller (MVC) paradigm, which is a commonly used software design pattern, Figure 1. We have defined a dashboard to be a user-centric interaction primarily concerned with the visualization of data. From an MVC perspective, it is primarily concerned with the visualization (view) of data, with some consideration to how data is processed (controller) for visualization and a limited data set (model) that is being drawn from sensor and other data sources.

Conversely, our definition of a digital twin is primarily concerned with data processing through the development, simulation and evaluation of model (model & controller) and a limited visualization (view). The philosophy is that the digital twin does the 'heavy lifting' and the dashboard does the user interaction and visualisation.

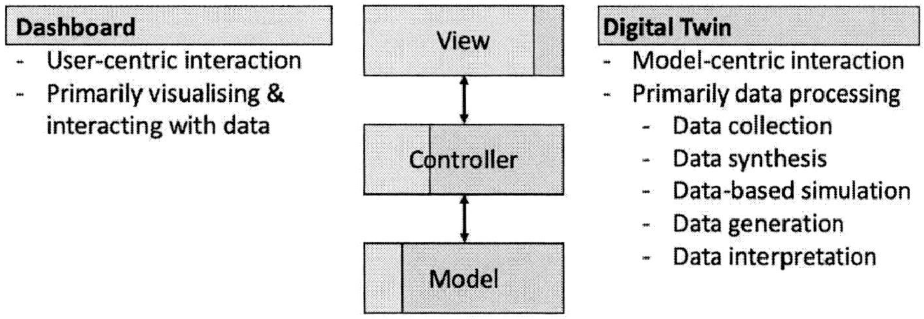

Figure 1 *Dashboard / digital twin demarcation based on the model-view-controller paradigm*

Again, anecdotally from our experiences with partners and end users on EU Horizon 2020 research projects, we have found that users generally want to talk about problems they are facing, aka Design Thinking 'pain points', rather than specific technology solutions. Towards this, the dashboard / digital twin model can be a useful framework for researchers to consider how user problems can be addressed in terms of the visualisations that users require, the data that is required to drive those visualisations and model / data processing that can be required to solve what-if / simulation -type issues.

3 THE ARSINOE DIGITAL TWIN

Our approach for data modelling and visualisation, Figure 2, uses a suite of simulation models sharing a common set of flood scenarios. The simulation models are CA Flood (based on Cellular Automata), Traffic Model (developed using SUMO traffic modelling application) and Cascading Failure Model (Khoury 2025), with two intermediary elements for depth data and epoch generation. The results of the modelling processes are visualised for web presentation, which is hosted through a web server, providing multiple levels of user access.

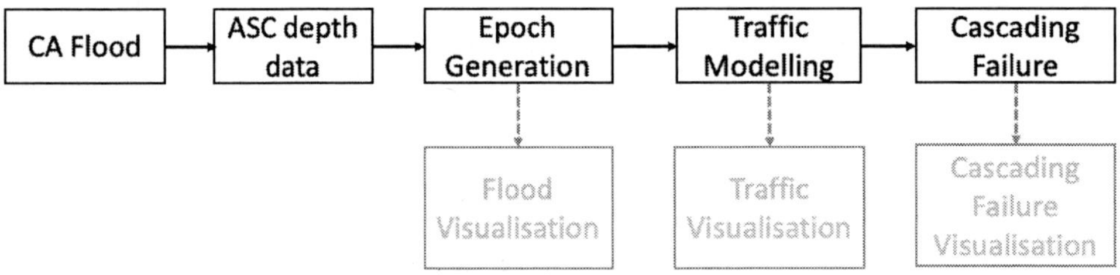

Figure 2 *The ARSINOE Digital Twin includes multiple simulation models, each developed using a different modelling methodology*

The simulation models that make up the ARSINOE digital twin are discussed in sub-section 2.1, followed by the description of the visualisation sub-systems (section 2.2), and finally the operation of the Digital Twin in section 2.3. The example application used is Torbay an eastly-facing bay in south-east Devon comprising of the towns of Brixham, Paignton and Torquay, and under the Torbay City Council, the partners of our project. Given their location, Figure 4, the bay area towns are susceptible to fluvial flooding, as well as costal over-topping, where strong onshore winds combine with high tides and/or spring tidal events to flood low-lying areas.

The three towns have distinct morphologies, Figure 3; Brixham is a 'traditional' fishing town, with a harbour nestled in a steep sided valley / estuary whilst Paignton is a quintessential Victorian seaside town, having a largely flat promenade on the seafront. Conversely, Torquay is a composite of these styles, with the harbour part of the town closely mapping to Brixham, whilst its Torre Abbey region is strikingly like Paignton's promenade, as a large and open low-lying area next to the sea.

Figure 3 *Brixham (top left), Paignton (top right), Torquay (lower left) and (lower right)*

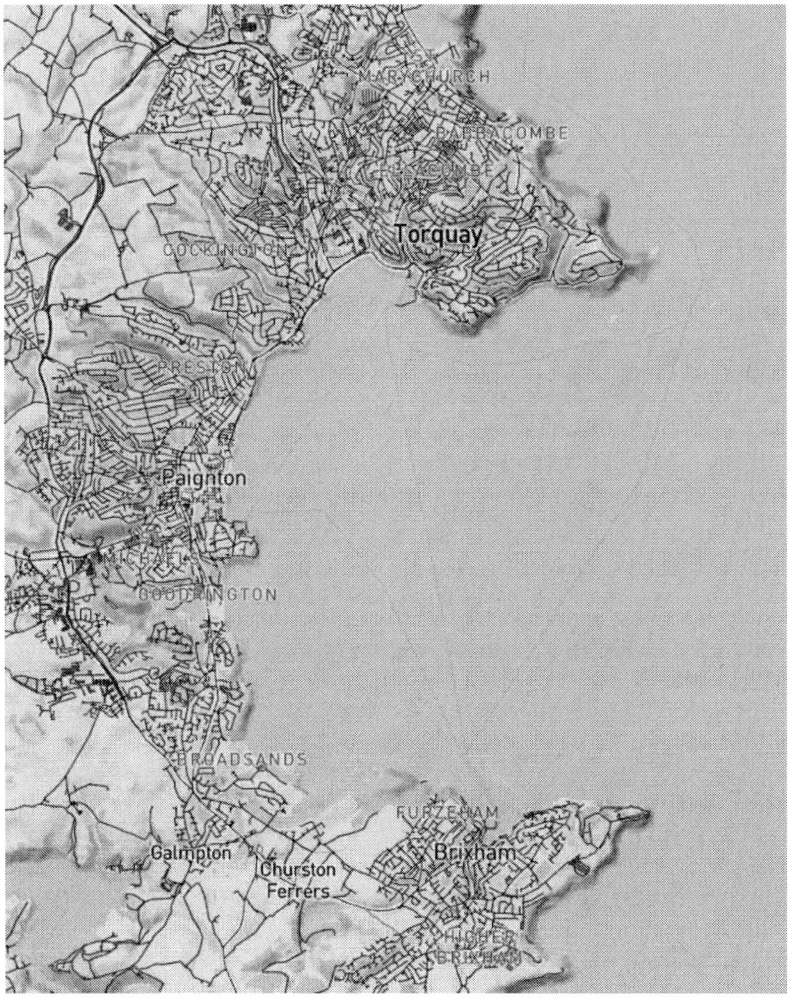

Figure 4 *Torbay region, showing Torquay, Paignton and Brixham towns*

3.1 Modelling process

3.1.1 CA Flood

CA Flood (Guidolin, et al., 2016) is a flood simulation application developed by UNEXE. It takes rainfall and ground conditions (elevation and land cover) to produce a time series of geolocated water depth information (stored as ASC files) shown in Figure 5.

CA Flood is agnostic concerning data sources, with Figure 5 detailing historic, current, forecast and synthetic rainfall as potential inputs. From a simulation perspective, this enables us to build flood models based on actual historic events, and current and forecast weather, whilst synthetic data provides the option of creating extreme scenarios that may consist of more intensive and/or longer rainfall events to stress short and long-term planning considerations.

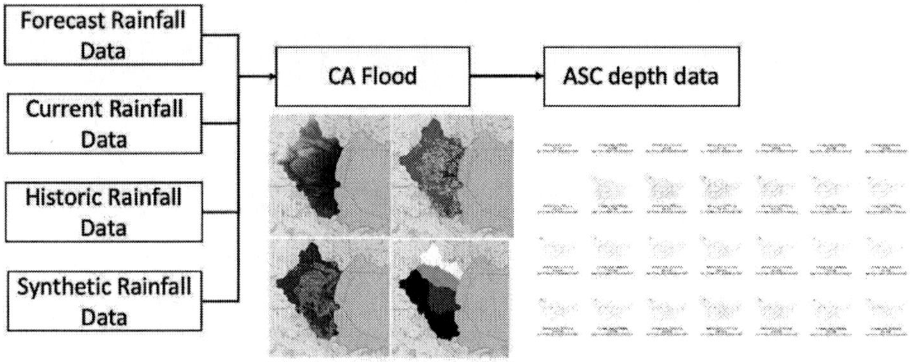

Figure 5 *CA Flood simulation process*

3.1.2 Epoch generation

CA Flood can produce time series data at any interval specified by users to describe the temporal dynamic behaviour of flooding events. For this project, we used a 15-minute time step to capture the temporal dynamics of fluvial flooding. However, for most of the interpretative simulation work using this data, 6hr epochs provided a better balance of data and response. To convert the input flood data into epochs, the worst / deepest depth was taken for each cell in the input ASC data.

3.1.3 Traffic Modelling

Our simulation model has two approaches, both using epoch-based water depth to determine impact on travel, with depths of <0.1m having no impact on travel, 0.1-0.3m having some impact on travel and >0.3m being impassable.

Our simple traversability approach iterates through each road segment in the road network using the location of the road as a look-up into the epoch-based depth data of the ASC file. The results are mapped to show the water impact on the traversability of the road segment, Figure 7.

Our 'risk' approach uses the SUMO traffic simulation application (eclipse, 2024) to conduct typical road journeys in the Torbay region, using the epoch water levels to determine the impact on the road network and the risk of using the road. The SUMO approach enables the 'importance' of roads to be determined alongside their traversability and allows the Council to allocate resources to critical road infrastructure.

This can be seen in Torbay where low-lying residential roads near the seaside are of low risk (given that they are largely just used for residential travel) whilst major arterial roads are more important, Figure 8.

3.1.4 Cascading Failure

Our approach to cascading failure is based on an interconnected network of critical infrastructure components drawn from diverse resources including power, water, telecommunications, schools, hospitals, care homes, and transport, such that components rely on the operation of other nodes in the network to function, e.g. a telecommunications mast will rely on a source of electricity provided by a local substation. To determine the impact of cascading failure, a two-step simulation process is undertaken.

Each critical infrastructure component is assessed for water-related damage, using its location in the epoch-based water depth and a 'depth to damage' lookup specific for each type of component. Then, for all components that are not disabled by water damage, their input components are assessed for damage, such that for a component to be operational, it must have access to working inputs.

Using this approach disables components that directly receive water damage, but also impact components that whilst not receiving direct water damage are receiving indirect operational damage due to components that they require being inoperable either from direct water damage or indirect non-operation, hence the 'cascading' failure.

3.2 Visualisation

Visualisation was realised through a Mapbox component and uses the visualisation artefacts created as part of the simulation process, Figure 2 . Mapbox was chosen as a visualisation package primarily as it provides a good level of performance, particularly with respect to the visualisation of large / complex GeoJSON files.

3.2.1 Visualising Flood Data

Flood data was visualised, Figure 6, as PNG data using Mapbox's raster image layer support, (Mapbox, 2024). The flood data was colourised using the traffic modelling breaks, such that depths of <0.1m were not drawn, 0.1m to 0.3m were visualised as light orange and >0.3m as dark orange. This had two benefits, firstly it was simple to see if the 'raw road impact' data aligned with the flood maps and secondly, by avoiding shades of blue, the flood impacts could easily be seen on the map and not confused with background /map water features (rivers and lakes).

Figure 6 *Paignton region showing fluvial flooding results from CA Flood simulation*

3.2.2 Visualising Traffic Data

Both approaches to traffic visualisation, described in section 3.1.3, used a GeoJSON model of Torbay's road network, with flood data colourised into the map on an epoch-by-epoch basis, and visualised through Mapbox's GeoJSON support (Mapbox, 2024). For simple network traversability, Figure 7, blue, yellow, and red were look-ups for the <0.1m, 0.1-0.3m and >0.3m depth ranges. Whilst for the flood risk simulation, Figure 8, roads were colourised from green (no risk) to yellow (some risk) to red (major risk).

A clear difference between the two visualisations is around the seaside area of Paignton (purple arrow), where the raw network shows many non-traversable roads (red), but the risk map details them as green (no risk). These are primarily residential roads and are, indeed, of little risk in flooding events – despite the inconvenience to local residence.

Likewise, the risk visualisation, Figure 8, results show a general low level of risk (green roads) but highlights risks occurring at major intersections (yellow junctions)

Figure 7 *Paignton Road network showing simple road traversability modelling*

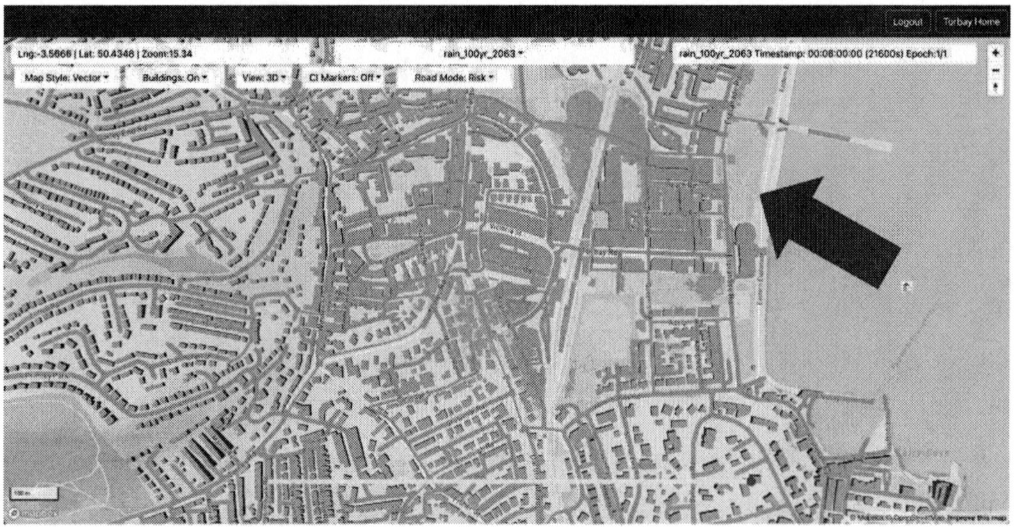

Figure 8 *Paignton Road network showing risk modelling*

3.2.3 Visualising Cascading Failure

The cascading failure visualisation, Figure 9, visualises the results of cascading failure simulation, section3.1.4. Each of the critical infrastructure components are visualised through a 'traffic light' of green (fully operational), yellow (having some impact) and red (unavailable). As expected, components in deep flood water tend to be unavailable, though there are instances where components well away from flooding are impacted. Most notable was the impact on schools (far away from flooding) that were impacted by a lack of bus and coach transport (due to the coach station being in the middle of a flood zone). The operation of the schools relies on students being able to get to and from the school, with local buses providing transport, their lack of operation greatly impacted the schools.

Figure 9 *Paignton showing critical infrastructure in response cascading failure simulation*

3.2.4 Side-by-Side Visualisations

Much of the simulation work done for the project has tended to be thematic, e.g. historic and forecast fluvial flooding events, historic and forecast overtopping events, permeable pavement strategies etc. Whilst these events can be viewed in isolation (sections 3.2.1, 3.2.2,3.2.3) we have used side-by-side visualisation to compare similar events together.

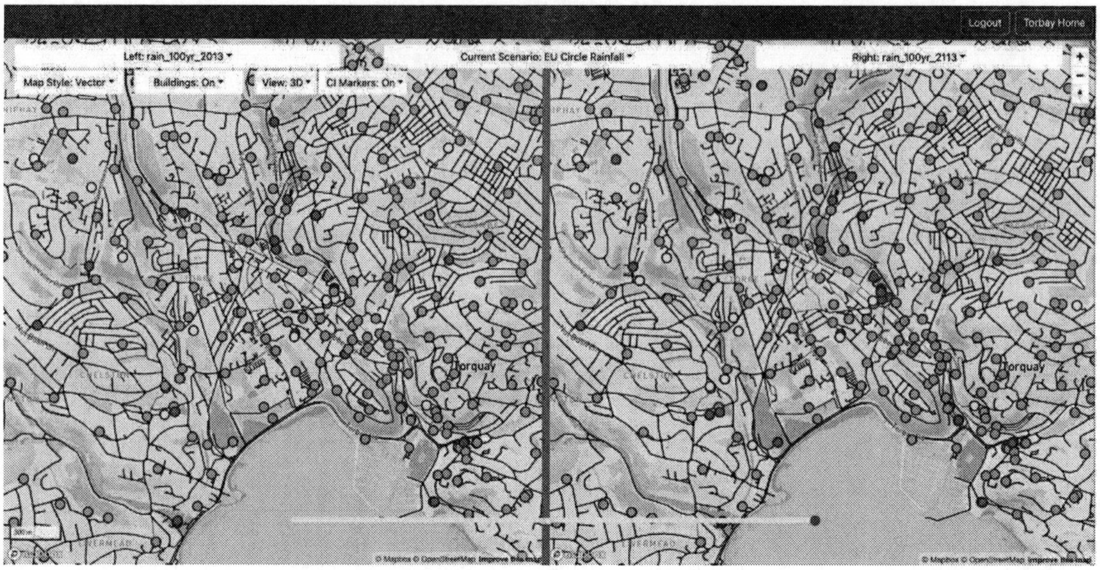

Figure 10 *Side-by-side flooding events in Torquay. 2013 (left) and 2113 – predicted (right)*

Figure 10 shows two simulated flood events 2013 (left) and a 2113 (right). User controls have been set such that both displays move in sync, i.e. the focus is shared, allowing users to compare the relative impact of different events on the same place. Whilst, to the casual observer, these events may look very similar, to flood experts, the nuances between the two simulations are highly revealing.

3.3 Operation

The ARSINOE Digital Twin modelling the Torbay service is realised as a web service using Django (Django, 2024) as a backend and an html-JavaScript-Mapbox client front end, Figure 11. The choice of Django was primarily that it was a Python-based web service framework that we were familiar with, although other web frameworks (Python or other language-based) would have been perfectly acceptable. However, Django also provides authentication and authorisation functionality (Django, 2024) as core components, removing the need to use external providers, e.g. KeyCloak, KeyLock etc. This enables us to limit simulation result data to authorised users only.

Currently, the digital twin aspect of the service runs as a standalone Python application that calls a Julia-based application to perform the cascading failure component and Python functions to perform all other simulation tasks.

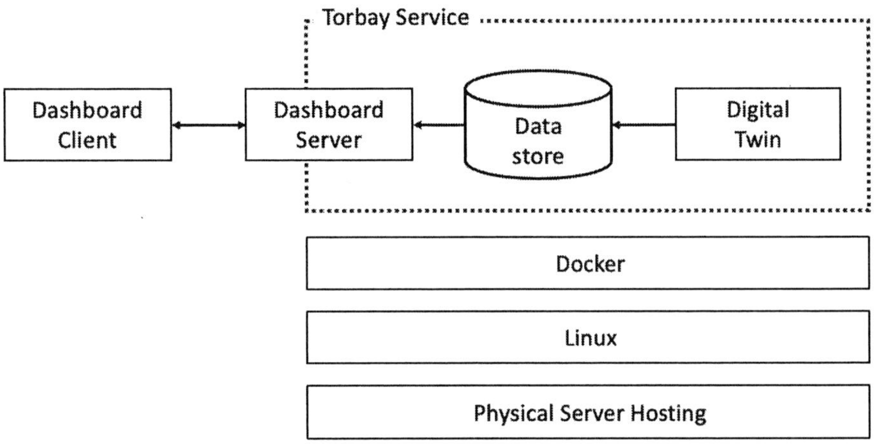

Figure 11 *The logical architecture of the ARSINOE Digital Twin; Torbay service (as a case study) is illustrated as a dotted box.*

The service is operated through Docker, being described as a set of interacting images in a single compose file. This enables a straightforward approach to testing and operation of the service and the use of environment files allows sensitive data (e.g. usernames, passwords, and API keys) to be kept away from the Docker images.

4 REFLECTING ON THE DEVELOPMENT OF THE DIGITAL TWIN

4.1 CA Flood-based Common Frames of Reference

Using CA Flood as source data for the traffic and cascading failure simulations has given researchers the confidence that although simulations are conducted in isolation, their results fit together, particularly with respect to visualisation.

The challenge with using CA Flood is that whilst simulation results can be highly detailed, the simulation process often takes a considerable time to run and there is a broadly exponential relationship between simulation size and execution time, Table 1.

Table 1 *CA Flood performance of 36hr rainfall event at 2m and 5m resolutions*

Resolution	Brixham 13km^2	Torquay 20km^2	Paignton 15km^2
2m	59 min	1hr 44min	2hr 13min
5m	4 min	5 min	4 min

4.2 Traffic Modelling

Using SUMO as a base for traffic risk modelling has provided us with a great deal of quality and functionality without the need to implement algorithms for traffic navigation and flow functionality from first principles. However, our current results only suggest very low levels of traffic risk and there is work to be undertaken to understand these results and validate that the simulation is providing the results expected from the inputs provided.

4.3 Cascading Failure

Developing a critical infrastructure-based approach to modelling cascading failure has enabled us to view both the direct impact of flooding on a component-by-component basis, rather than just viewing flood maps, but also the indirect impact of flooding through the cascading approach of failure. The core cascading failure engine is purely data driven and is currently being successfully applied to other case studies on the ARSINOE project.

4.4 Visualisation

Developing visualisation components for a browser-based Slippy Map has allowed us to present flood data in novel ways. The interactive nature of the visualisation allows data to be revealed on demand, such that layers of data and quantitative data can be revealed and hidden, the 3-dimensional visualisation of maps allows their natural elevation to reveal river channels and flood plains, and spatial controls allow the map to be moved, rotated and zoomed, to view the map from novel perspectives and sizes. The browser-based approach has also facilitated a dashboard application that has low barriers to use and can easily be shared by a wide range of users.

4.5 Docker

Using Docker as a development and operations (Devops) environment has enabled us to develop an overall service that is straightforward to install as a 24/7 service. However, to get to this position has been a challenge, given that Docker essentially brings Linux administration tasks and knowledge into traditional software development activities. A large part of this challenge has been moving away from pure Windows development to a more Linux-centric, or at least supportive, model of development.

4.6 Data Sources

Arguably, one of the biggest challenges of this simulation project has been the sourcing of suitable weather data. We have come to realise that both historic and forecast rainfall data have significant monetary value making it difficult to find free data. Currently, we are using free data from Weatherapi (WeatherAPI, 2024) that provides live (15minute) weather data and a 3-day forecast, both based on WGS84 locations with 2dp accuracy.

5 NEXT STEPS

5.1 Digital Twin Automation

On initial inspection, automating the digital twin process appears straightforward. The current digital twin exists as a Python application that calls SUMO and cascading failure processes to process CA Flood data into visualisable results. Dockerising this process and running it periodically will automate the process, though this does open obvious questions about response times, given the both the availability of forecast data from the Weatherapi service and the time taken to run CA Flood simulations.

Discussions will need to be undertaken with the Torbay pilot group to balance the quality of flood results against the time taken to generate the results. On another project, we are simulating flooding with forecast rainfall data. In this case we are working with an environment of 1km^2, but the data resolution is 30m (rather than Torbay's 1m) and the 3-day simulation takes around 1 minute to process. However, this is for a rural area and it's likely that moving to such a resolution will remove a lot of flood detail from the Torbay pilot.

5.2 Digital Twin Decision Making

As stated in the introduction, a key role for digital twins is the provision of 'what if' analysis. Currently, our work has been concerned with developing a simulation and visualisation pipeline that can facilitate this style of analysis. Initial discussions with stakeholders suggest that considering extreme weather events, in our case worse storms, can provide this. Therefore, consideration will be given to the creation of longer, harder and longer and harder weather events for the local region and their impact on the traffic network and static critical infrastructure.

5.3 Synthetic Data Generation For Simulation Validation

We have employed synthetic data generation in several 'real-world' data collection projects as synthetised data enables the creation of edge case data for situations where there is no real-world data to work from. With regards to digital twin decision making, there is a clear requirement to user synthetic data generation to capture the longer, harder, and longer and harder rainfall events. There is also a more implicit requirement to create worse flooding events to validate the operation of the SUMO-based traffic risk simulation work.

6 CONCLUSION

The work presented in this paper demonstrates a simulation-centric approach to creating a hydrologic flood modelling digital twin and associated web-based visualisation components that can provide limited and controlled access to a wide range of users. Like all software engineering projects, there is still plenty of development and refinement left in the project and it is likely that this will increase as our partners at Torbay Council engage with the application. However, our current approaches of CA Flood and Docker provide us with core technologies that will support our on-going activities.

ACKNOWLEDGEMENT

The ARSINOE project has received funding from the European Union's Horizon H2020 innovation action programme under grant agreement 101037424.

REFERENCES

ARSINOE Project. (2024). *ARSINOE Home Page*. Retrieved from https://arsinoe-project.eu/

Django. (2024). *Django Homepage*. Retrieved from https://www.djangoproject.com/

Django. (2024). *User authentication in Django*. Retrieved from https://docs.djangoproject.com/en/5.1/topics/auth/

eclipse. (2024). *SUMO Home Page*. Retrieved from https://eclipse.dev/sumo/

Guidolin, M., Chen, A. S., Ghimire, B., Keedwell, E. C., Djordjević, S., & Savić, D. A. (2016). A weighted cellular automata 2D inundation model for rapid flood analysis. *Environmental Modelling & Software*, 378-394.

IBM. (2024). *What is a digital twin*. Retrieved from https://www.ibm.com/topics/what-is-a-digital-twin

Mapbox. (2024). *Add a polygon to a map using a GeoJSON source*. Retrieved from https://docs.mapbox.com/mapbox-gl-js/example/geojson-polygon/

Mapbox. (2024). *Add a raster image to a map layer*. Retrieved from https://docs.mapbox.com/mapbox-gl-js/example/image-on-a-map/

University of Exeter. (2024). *CA Flood Homepage*. Retrieved from https://cafloodpro.com/

WeatherAPI. (2024). *WeatherAPI*. Retrieved from https://www.weatherapi.com/

AUTHOR BIOGRAPHIES

GARETH LEWIS is a research fellow in water systems at the University of Exeter. His research is concerned with digital hydro informatics. He received an MBA from the Open University in 2007, an MSc in Data Science from University of Plymouth in 1993 and a BSc in Computer Science from University of Brighton in 1992. https://experts.exeter.ac.uk/34895-gareth-lewis

MEHDI KHOURY is a senior research fellow in water systems at the University of Exeter. https://engineering.exeter.ac.uk/people/profile/index.php?username=mk483

QIAN LI is a research fellow in water systems at the University of Exeter. https://engineering.exeter.ac.uk/people/profile/index.php?username=ql310

BARRY EVANS was a senior research fellow in water systems at the University of Exeter. https://www.linkedin.com/in/barry-evans-183135205/

ALBERT CHEN is a professor in water systems at the University of Exeter. https://experts.exeter.ac.uk/48-albert-chen

LYDIA VAMVAKERIDOU-LYROUDIA is a senior research fellow at KWR. https://www.kwrwater.nl/en/experts-expertises/experts/lydia-vamvakeridou-lyroudia-phd-meng/

NAV MUSTAFEE is Professor of Analytics and Operations Management at the Centre for Simulation, Analytics and Modelling (CSAM) at Exeter. He is a Joint Editor-in-Chief of the Journal of Simulation. https://experts.exeter.ac.uk/22797-nav-mustafee

SLOBODAN DJORDJEVIC is a professor at the University of Exeter. https://experts.exeter.ac.uk/1421-slobodan-djordjevic.

DRAGAN SAVIC is a global advisor at KWR and professor at the University of Exeter. https://experts.exeter.ac.uk/1732-dragan-savic

Proceedings of the Operational Research Society Simulation Workshop 2025 (SW25)
M. Luis, A. Harper, T. Monks, N. Mustafee, eds.

https://doi.org/10.36819/SW25.034

ENHANCING RESILIENCE OF INTERDEPENDENT INFRASTRUCTURE NETWORKS THROUGH A CRITICALITY RANKING APPROACH

Georgios Alexandros Chazistefanou
Lydia Vamvakeridou-Lyroudia
Dragan Savic

2KWR Water Research Institute, Groningenhaven 7, 3433PE, Nieuwegein, the Netherlands
alex.chatzistefanou@kwrwater.nl,
lydia.vamvakeridou-lyroudia@kwrwater.nl,
dragan.savic@kwrwater.nl

Albert S. Chen
Slobodan Djordjevic
Lydia Vamvakeridou-Lyroudia
Dragan Savic

Centre for Water Systems, University of Exeter, EX4 4QJ, Exeter, United Kingdom

a.s.chen@exeter.ac.uk,
s.djordjevic@exeter.ac.uk

EXTENDED ABSTRACT

1 INTRODUCTION

Critical infrastructures are complex systems that support modern societies. These systems are often highly interdependent, making them prone to cascading failures that originate elsewhere in the system (Rinaldi et al., 2001). Additionally, the risks to these systems are increasing globally (Forzieri et al., 2018), which creates a need to enhance their resilience. However, since resilience enhancement measures are subject to resource constraints, prioritization approaches at an infrastructure asset level are necessary. This work proposes a modelling approach to rank infrastructure assets according to their criticality, capturing multiple criticality dimensions and multiple types of infrastructure interactions. The proposed methodology is general in nature and can be applied to enhance infrastructure resilience in urban and peri-urban regions.

2 METHODOLOGY

To develop the interdependent infrastructure criticality ranking framework, a multi-step procedure is adopted. Initially, infrastructure components that are exposed and vulnerable to each considered hazard are identified. Next, a simulation-based approach, where infrastructures are represented as a node-weighted directed multiplex network, is adopted, in order to estimate the impacts of the failure of each infrastructure component across multiple dimensions. Finally, these are combined to produce a composite index which serves to identify the most critical components of the interdependent infrastructure system.

3 APPLICATION TO THE TORBAY AREA & FINDINGS

A case study of flood hazard in a medium-sized urban region located in Torbay, UK was used to demonstrate the application of the proposed criticality ranking framework.The critical infrastructure systems that were considered consist of five interdependent networks (*electricity network*, *telecommunication network*, *water distribution network*, *gas distribution network*, and the *healthcare network*). It was found that assets belonging to the electricity and telecommunication networks were deemed the most critical from an impact-based perspective.

4 CONCLUSIONS

In the present work, a criticality ranking framework for assets in interdependent critical infrastructure networks is introduced. The framework is general in nature and can accommodate the consideration of various types of infrastructure interactions, various criticality dimensions and hazard types. The application of the proposed framework in Torbay demonstrates its feasibility in identifying important assets to prioritize resilience enhancement measures. Key limitations include the need for a significant amount of data for the application of the framework and the difficulties in validation of the results.

Keywords: Critical infrastructure, cascading effects, network science, multiplex networks

ACKNOWLEDGMENTS

The presented work here has received funding by the ongoing EU-funded project ARSINOE (GA 101037424, 2021-2025).

REFERENCES

Forzieri, G., Bianchi, A., Silva, F. B. e, Marin Herrera, M. A., Leblois, A., Lavalle, C., Aerts, J. C. J. H., & Feyen, L. (2018). Escalating impacts of climate extremes on critical infrastructures in Europe. *Global Environmental Change*, *48*, 97–107. https://doi.org/10.1016/j.gloenvcha.2017.11.007

Rinaldi, S. M., Peerenboom, J. P., & Kelly, T. K. (2001). Identifying, understanding, and analyzing critical infrastructure interdependencies. *IEEE Control Systems Magazine*, *21*(6), 11–25. IEEE Control Systems Magazine. https://doi.org/10.1109/37.969131

AUTHOR BIOGRAPHIES

GEORGIOS ALEXANDROS CHATZISTEFANOU is a PhD student in the Centre for Water Systems at the University of Exeter, funded by KWR Water Research Institute, where he is based. His background is in Civil Engineering, in which he obtained a diploma from Aristotle University of Thessaloniki first class. Prior to his current role, he was involved in the design of large-scale water infrastructure projects as a member of a consulting engineering firm.

ALBERT S. CHEN is a Personal Chair in Water and the Human Environment at the Centre for Water Systems (CWS), University of Exeter, with over 20 years of experience in Water research. He has participated in more than 40 international projects, and published over 90 peer-reviewed journal articles and 100 peer-reviewed conferences papers.

SLOBODAN DJORDJEVIC is a Professor of Hydraulic Engineering, the Deputy Head of Engineering and a Co-Director of the Centre for Water Systems, which he joined in 2002. At Exeter he served as the Director of Postgraduate Studies, Director of Education for Engineering, elected member of the University Senate, and most recently as the inaugural Associate Dean (International and Development) in the College of Engineering, Mathematics and Physical Sciences.

LYDIA VAMVAKERIDOU-LYROUDIA is the Programme Director of Watershare. She has an engineering background, with expertise and research interests focused mainly on computational modelling and hydroinformatics across a wide range of subjects. Before joining KWR Lydia was, since 2003, a Senior Research Fellow at the Centre for Water Systems, University of Exeter, UK, and still maintains a part-time position. Prior to that, she was a Lecturer at the Technical University of Athens (1990-2003).

DRAGAN SAVIC is a founder and former director of the Centre for Water Systems. He is the UK's first Professor of Hydroinformatics having held this post at the University of Exeter since 2001. He is a former CEO of KWR Water Research Institute, the Dutch drinking water companies' collective research organisation. Currently, he serves as the Global Advisor on Digital Sciences at KWR. Professor

Savic is a Chartered Civil and Water Engineer with over forty years of experience in research, teaching and consulting.

Proceedings of the Operational Research Society Simulation Workshop 2025 (SW25)
M. Luis, A. Harper, T. Monks and, N. Mustafee, eds.

https://doi.org/10.36819/SW25.035

STRATEGIC WORKFORCE MODELLING AND ANALYSIS AT NHS WALES: TOWARDS A STRATEGIC DIGITAL TWIN OF THE WELSH HEALTHCARE WORKFORCE

Dr Siôn Cave

Decision Analysis Services Ltd (DAS)

Grove House,
Lutyens Close,
Chineham Court,
Basingstoke,
Hampshire,
RG24 8AG, UK

SionCave@DAS-Ltd.co.uk

Ryan Cunningham

Health Education and Improvement Wales (HEIW)

Tŷ Dysgu
Cefn Coed
Nantgarw
CF15 7QQ

ryan.cunningham@wales.nhs.uk

ABSTRACT

Health Education and Improvement Wales (HEIW) is the strategic workforce body for NHS Wales. HEIW makes a valuable contribution to addressing strategic and specialist workforce issues, making Wales a great place to train and work for health and care staff and maximising the contribution of all professions and occupations through statutory functions. As part of HEIW's Workforce Strategy, Planning, and Intelligence function the HEIW Analytics team produces a range of workforce information and workforce modelling at a national and sub national level for NHS Wales. Workforce demand and supply modelling helps to support planning decisions that contribute to meeting patient needs and helps to investigate if current recruitment and retention will be sufficient to enable future demand to be met. HEIW have collaborated with Decision Analysis Services to develop a generic strategic workforce model to enable the rapid generation of national workforce demand and supply projections to support the strategic workforce planning. This is the first step towards developing a strategic digital twin of the Welsh healthcare workforce.

Keywords: Workforce planning, System dynamics, Digital Twin, National Health Service (NHS), Nursing, Wales

1 BACKGROUND

NHS Wales, established in 1948, is the publicly funded healthcare system for Wales and operates as a devolved entity under the Welsh Government. Its mission is to provide comprehensive, free healthcare to all Welsh residents, consistent with the broader goals of the National Health Service across the UK. NHS Wales emphasises localised community care and preventive services, reflecting Welsh policy priorities focused on integrating health and social care and improving public health outcomes (NHS Wales, 2024). Serving a population of over three million people (Welsh Government, 2024a), NHS Wales operates through seven Local Health Boards (LHBs) and three NHS Trusts (Welsh Government, 2020). These organisations oversee hospital care, general practice, community services, and specialised treatments, ensuring healthcare accessibility in both urban and rural areas across Wales.

NHS Wales faces challenges common to health systems globally, such as funding limitations, workforce shortages, and waiting times for specific services. As of June 2024 NHS Wales employed over 96 thousand medical, dental, nursing and midwifery staff including a large contingent of healthcare professionals, administrative support, and allied health workers (Welsh Government, 2024b). Health

Education and Improvement Wales (HEIW) is a special health authority within NHS Wales, dedicated to workforce planning, education, and training for healthcare professionals. Its mission is to enhance the skills and capabilities of healthcare staff to better serve the needs of the Welsh population. HEIW offers a range of training programs and continuing professional development opportunities for various healthcare professionals, including doctors, nurses, dentists, and pharmacists. Additionally, HEIW promotes research and innovation in healthcare education, aiming to improve both service delivery and patient outcomes. Collaborating closely with universities, health boards, and other stakeholders, HEIW ensures that Wales has a well-prepared and adaptable healthcare workforce to meet current and future demands (HEIW, 2024).

The HEIW Analytics team produces a range of workforce information and workforce modelling at a national and sub-national level for NHS Wales. Strategic workforce modelling has been identified as a critical component of the National Workforce Implementation Plan (Welsh Government, 2023). Building on the previous modelling work, HEIW has collaborated with Decision Analysis Services Ltd (DAS) to develop a generic workforce demand and supply simulation model to support strategic workforce planning. DAS has a long track record in developing strategic workforce models (DAS, 2024). This development work is the first stage in developing a strategic digital twin representing the Welsh healthcare workforces.

A digital twin is defined as a virtual model that mirrors the behaviour and performance of its physical counterpart through real-time data integration and simulation. There are three core components to a digital twin: (i) the virtual model, which enables the system to be represented and integrated with; (ii) the refresh rate, which provides information from the real system to update the model; and (iii) simulation capability, which allows for the testing and evaluation of alternative scenarios (such as future states, alternative configurations, etc.). Recent literature highlights the growing significance of digital twins in operational decision-making. Mustafee et al. (2023) distinguish digital twins from conventional simulation models by their ability to dynamically integrate real-time data, enabling updates and faster-than-real-time experimentation. This functionality enhances situational awareness and predictive capabilities, facilitating tasks like identifying bottlenecks in systems such as healthcare. Similarly, Onggo et al. (2018) describe the Symbiotic Simulation System (S3), a digital twin framework designed for Industry 4.0 applications, enabling real-time monitoring, optimisation, and control by connecting virtual and physical systems. Both studies underline critical challenges, such as data acquisition, model adaptation, and the development of robust integration frameworks, as pivotal to advancing the field

2 APPROACH – OVERVIEW OF STRATEGIC WORKFORCE MODELLING AND HEIW'S STRATEGIC WORKFORCE MODEL

2.1 The importance of strategic workforce modelling

Strategic workforce planning is often summarised as having the right people, with the right skills, in the right places at the right time (Taylor, 2005). This approach aims to align an organisation's workforce with its strategic goals and priorities. It involves assessing the future demands on the workforce in terms of the number of people needed, their skills, and the distribution of roles required to meet these demands. Strategic workforce planning also focuses on developing strategies to fulfil these future needs. Ideally, this planning process is continuous and closely integrated with the organisation's broader business planning activities. Workforce planning is about trying to achieve a balance – or at least reduce the imbalance – between workforce supply and workforce demand.

Strategic workforce planning is a complex process that requires a deep understanding of the broader system in which an organisation operates, including the internal and external forces that drive change and the potential future scenarios that may unfold. Key characteristics of a workforce system include the inherent delays in developing skilled workers (such as the time required for training) and the gradual decline of skills if not maintained. Other factors include loss rates from training pipelines and various career stages, as well as the workforce's appeal to new recruits. Additionally, workforce planning must account for intricate internal and external interactions that influence demand, such as the non-linear relationship between pay and attrition rates, and the interplay between workforce supply and demand. These dynamics make strategic workforce planning a nuanced and ongoing challenge.

2.2 HEIW Strategic Workforce Model.

HEIW's new Strategic Workforce Model (SWM) is designed to project the supply and demand of Welsh healthcare workforces over a span of up to 15 years, allowing for strategic simulation, comparison, and planning. Its purpose is to support senior leaders at HEIW in making informed decisions by providing insights into the range of possible outcomes and the uncertainties associated with them. The SWM enables testing of complex and multiple policy options—whether phased or concurrent—over time. It is important to note that a projection is not a forecast; it represents what might happen, not what will happen, with accuracy dependent on the quality of assumptions made. As the projection timeline extends further into the future, uncertainty naturally increases. Nonetheless, the model provides an evidence-based foundation for discussing workforce policy alternatives and assessing the potential impacts of various changes.

The model was developed based on 43 core requirements established through consultation with end users, such as modellers and policy analysts. A detailed technical specification outlined how these requirements would be met, and this plan, which included a project roadmap and assigned "owners" for each model component, was fully documented and approved before development began. The model was built using an agile, component-based approach, ensuring flexibility and continuous improvement, and includes thorough documentation and testing for each component.

Separate components (as illustrated below) were created for Preprocessing, the Simulation Engine and Results Analysis:

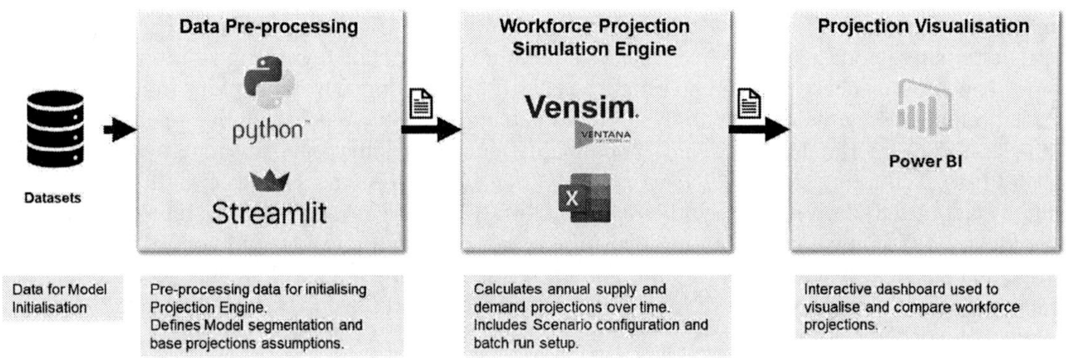

Figure 1 *Overview of the components of the Strategic Workforce Model architecture*

The simulation projection engine has been developed using the system dynamics (SD) modelling approach. SD is a modelling approach used to understand and simulate the behaviour of complex systems over time. It involves representing systems as interconnected feedback loops and stocks (accumulations) that change in response to various flows (rates of change). This approach is particularly valuable for exploring how different factors within a system interact with one another, including delays, feedback mechanisms, and non-linear relationships. System dynamics models have been widely used for developing strategic workforce models as they can provide insights into how a system might respond to policy changes, external forces, or internal adjustments. There are many examples of the use of SD for developing strategic workforce policy simulations, especially in the health and care sector (Cave & Willis, 2019).

System dynamics is well-suited for a strategic workforce model because workforce planning involves a range of interdependent factors that evolve over time, such as training pipelines, recruitment, retention rates, skill development, and workforce demand. Workforce systems are dynamic and influenced by feedback loops—such as the relationship between pay and retention or the lag between hiring and skill development—that can produce delayed or non-linear effects. By using system dynamics, a strategic workforce model can capture these complexities, allowing planners to test various scenarios and policy options over long-term time horizons. This helps in assessing the potential impact of different strategies, identifying potential bottlenecks, and anticipating unintended consequences, ultimately supporting more informed and robust decision-making.

The SWM model is currently focussed on the training pipeline on the supply side and main drivers of activity on the demand side. The SD model has been designed such that additional functionality can be easily added. The diagram below gives a sample stock and flow diagram for the supply side of the model:

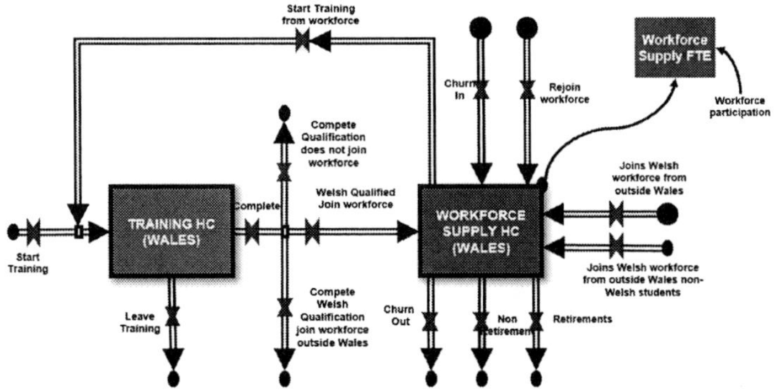

Figure 2 *Illustrative Stock and Flow diagram from the Strategic Workforce Model representing a generic training pipeline*

The SWM has been initially parameterised for the Welsh Nurse Workforce, covering 4 Fields, 10 Organisations, 12 Degree Programmes and 8 separate sources of demand. This required extensive stakeholder involvement through interviews and workshops at an organisation level for example to gain agreement of modelling methodology and to generate scenarios for analysis. The SWM has been designed to enable it to be rapidly reparametrized to facilitate the simulation of any of the core healthcare workforce groups.

3 IMPACT – STRATEGIC ANALYSIS OF THE WELSH NURSING WORKFORCE

The Nursing workforce is the largest and most diverse group of health professionals in Wales, and it faces significant challenges such as attrition, recruitment, retention, and changing skill mix. The generic demand and supply model has been parameterized for the nursing workforce using a range of data sources, such as population projections, workforce statistics, service activity, and university training data, to project the demand and supply of the nursing workforce over a 15 year time horizon.

The modelling seeks to evaluate potential future imbalances in the nursing workforce, determining whether an under or oversupply may occur. It also facilitates the creation of scenarios to better understand the impact and scale of implementing different policies and initiatives.

The strategic workforce model has been influential across NHS Wales through supporting senior leaders in the development of key policies actions outlined in the Strategic Nursing Workforce Plan. The modelling has provided a comprehensive and holistic view of the nursing workforce, enabling senior leaders to make sense of a complex environment and better understand multidimensional issues. Developing an evidence-based, data-driven model supports the process by quantifying and visualising current and future workforce needs and supply gaps, as well as evaluating the impact and feasibility of various strategies and interventions. By enabling senior leaders to explore various future scenarios and outcomes, and fostering stakeholder engagement and collaboration, data-driven actions and policies have been developed to better support the nursing workforce plan.

The demand and supply modelling project is still in its early stages and currently has limitations across various organisations, settings, and professions. The next phase of the project has begun, focusing on enhancing multiple areas to improve projections and support more robust and reliable decision-making. The nurse modelling has had a significant impact, and HEIW plans to update it throughout 2025. The modelling will be expanded to include projections for the midwifery workforce and smaller models will be developed to inform education commissioning and training for Allied Health Professionals and various medical specialties.

The diagram below provides some illustrative outputs from the model.

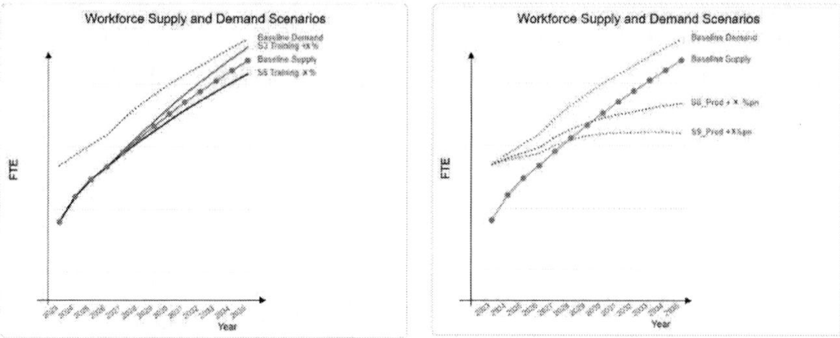

Figure 3 *Illustrative outputs from the SWM nursing analysis*

4 NEXT STEPS – ON THE ROAD TO CREATING A STRATEGIC DIGITAL TWIN OF THE WELSH HEALTHCARE WORKFORCE

Digital twins are virtual replicas of physical assets, processes, or systems that allow for real-time simulation and predictive analytics, benefiting industries from manufacturing to healthcare. Originally used to enhance operational efficiency, digital twins are evolving into strategic tools that support long-term planning and decision-making. Strategic digital twins integrate data-driven insights with broader business objectives, providing comprehensive, predictive capabilities that aid in strategic planning. The terms "simulation" and "digital twin" are sometimes used synonymously; however, we would agree with the body of thought that contends that they are different. Traditionally with simulation, you would need to set up input data representing history as well as the parameters for testing a scenario and repeat this process with more up-to-date data when reusing the model at a later date. A strategic digital twin is linked into a live data source and uses automated pre-processing to represent the real-world data in a format that the simulation can use. The strategic digital twin user will still set the scenario parameters for each run but is freed from the burden of updating and processing the historical data each time the model is used. This means that the strategic digital twin is likely to be used more frequently and become part of the routine monitoring and decision-making process, being used to enhance the routine monitoring dashboards.

The development of HEIW's Strategic Workforce Model is the first step to a strategic workforce digital twin of the Welsh healthcare workforce. This will enable HEIW to undertake rapid strategic analysis based on current workforce statistics and trends. This will streamline strategic analysis, enabling a rapid response to emerging workforce challenges and alternative scenarios and policies to be reviewed. By continuously updating the model input data, HEIW will be able to continuously forecast workforce needs, simulate the impact of different hiring and training strategies, and predict skills gaps before they impact health care delivery. Additionally, the real-time data and analytics provided by the digital twin will support continuous workforce management, enabling quick responses to unforeseen changes.

There are a number of initiatives being undertaken to make this ambition for a strategic digital twin of the Welsh healthcare workforce a reality. Key to an effective digital twin is the integration of the digital twin with real world data. The core datasets used by the SWM are being integrated and a data architecture is in development which will link directly to the simulation model. The SD based simulation engine is being continuously improved to allow more detailed analysis and the interface to the model is being updated to allow scenarios to be efficiently created, simulated, analysed and shared.

ACKNOWLEDGMENTS

The authors would like to acknowledge the efforts of Catherine Boreland, Josebha Santhini, Adebukonla Adenuga and Tiffany Lee from NHS Wales in the development of the Strategic Workforce Model.

REFERENCES

Cave, S., Willis, G. (2019). System Dynamics and Workforce Planning. In: Meyers, R. (eds) Encyclopedia of Complexity and Systems Science. Springer, Berlin, Heidelberg. https://doi.org/10.1007/978-3-642-27737-5_659-1

DAS (2024) FORESIGHT: THE VALUE OF STRATEGIC WORKFORCE PLANNING MODELS IN DELIVERING ENDURING SECTOR AND ORGANISATION CAPABILITY. https://www.das-ltd.co.uk/featured-content/2024/7/23/the-value-of-strategic-workforce-planning-models-in-delivering-enduring-sector-and-organisation-capability Accessed 10th November 2024.

HEIW (2024) About Us https://www.nhs.wales/about-us/ Accessed 10th November 2024

Mustafee, N., Harper, A. and Viana, J. (2023) HYBRID MODELS WITH REAL-TIME DATA: CHARACTERISING REAL-TIME SIMULATION AND DIGITAL TWINS, Proceedings of the Operational Research Society Simulation Workshop 2023 (SW23) C. Currie and L. Rhodes-Leader, eds. https://www.theorsociety.com/common/Uploaded%20files/Simulation-Workshop/SW23/doiorg1036819sw23031.pdf Accessed 22nd January 2025

NHS Wales (2024) About Us https://www.nhs.wales/about-us/ Accessed 10th November 2024

Onggo, Bhakti Stephan (2020) Symbiotic simulation system (S3) for Industry 4.0. In, Gunal, Murat (ed.) Simulation for Industry 4.0: Past, Present, and Future. (Springer Series in Advanced Manufacturing) 1 ed. Springer. Symbiotic simulation system (S3) for Industry 4.0 - ePrints Soton Accessed 22nd January 2025

Taylor S (2005) People resourcing, 3rd edn. Chartered Institute of Personnel and Development, London

Welsh Government (2020) Guidance - NHS Wales health boards and trusts. https://www.gov.wales/nhs-wales-health-boards-and-trusts Accessed 10th November 2024

Welsh Government (2023) National Workforce Implementation Plan: Addressing NHS Wales Workforce Challenges. https://www.gov.wales/sites/default/files/publications/2023-01/national-workforce-implementation-plan.pdf Accessed 10th November 2023.

Welsh Government (2024a) Mid-year population estimates (1991 onwards), by Welsh local authorities, English regions and UK countries, by single year of age and sex. https://statswales.gov.wales/Catalogue/Population-and-Migration/Population/Estimates/nationallevelpopulationestimates-by-year-age-ukcountry Accessed 10th November 2024

Welsh Government (2024b) Staff directly employed by the NHS: as at 30 June 2024. https://www.gov.wales/sites/default/files/pdf-versions/2024/10/3/1729067430/staff-directly-employed-nhs-30-june-2024.pdf Accessed 10th November 2024

AUTHOR BIOGRAPHIES

SIÔN CAVE is head of Decision Analysis Service's Analytics + Foresight Hub. The Hub is DAS' centre of excellence for data science, systems modelling and futures techniques. https://uk.linkedin.com/in/sioncave

RYAN CUNNINGHAM is the Head of Data & Analytics at Health Education and Improvement Wales (HEIW). HEIW is the strategic workforce body for NHS Wales.

Proceedings of the Operational Research Society Simulation Workshop 2025 (SW25)
M. Luis, A. Harper, T. Monks, N. Mustafee, eds.
https://doi.org/10.36819/SW25.037

LESSONS LEARNT FROM THE DESIGN AND DELIVERY OF A NATIONAL SYSTEM DYNAMICS TRAINING PROGRAMME TO THE NATIONAL HEALTH SERVICE IN ENGLAND

Dr Siôn Cave

Decision Analysis Services Ltd (DAS)
Grove House,
Lutyens Close,
Chineham Court,
Basingstoke,
Hampshire,
RG24 8AG, UK
SionCave@DAS-Ltd.co.uk

Vanessa Perez Perez

NHS England

Wellington House,
133-155 Waterloo Rd,
London,
SE1 8UG

v.perezperez@nhs.net

Dr Stephen Curram

Decision Analysis Services Ltd (DAS)
Grove House,
Lutyens Close,
Chineham Court,
Basingstoke,
Hampshire,
RG24 8AG, UK
StephenCurram@DAS-Ltd.co.uk

Emma Woodham

Decision Analysis Services Ltd (DAS)
Grove House,
Lutyens Close,
Chineham Court,
Basingstoke,
Hampshire,
RG24 8AG, UK
EmmaWoodham@DAS-Ltd.co.uk

ABSTRACT

This paper describes the design and delivery of a series of three training programs delivered to the National Health Service (NHS) in the England. The programs were delivered online between June 2022 and March 2024. The programs aimed to upskill NHS analysts in system dynamics and to demonstrate the potential contribution that system dynamics can make to the NHS demand and capacity planning challenge. The training covered all stages of the model development process, from scoping the analysis through to model testing. The training also described how stakeholders can be best involved during each of the stages of model development. Key to the training programs was the application of system dynamics to support "real-world" decisions that the participants were required to support. This paper includes an outline of the training methodology, examples of participant-developed models including associated benefits, and lessons learned from delivering the program. The described case studies include modelling urgent care provision, optimising blood donation, and supporting patients with respiratory conditions.

Keywords: System Dynamics (SD), Integrated Care Systems (ICS), Healthcare Modelling, Demand and Capacity Planning, Simulation training

1 INTRODUCTION

1.1 The English National Health Service

The National Health Service (NHS) in England is a publicly funded healthcare system and one of the four NHS systems across the United Kingdom. Primarily funded by the government through general taxation, along with a portion from National Insurance contributions, the NHS operates with the objective of providing healthcare services that are free at the point of use for the majority of UK residents. The NHS operates under the oversight of the Department of Health and Social Care and stands as the second-largest single-payer healthcare system worldwide, following the Brazilian Sistema Único de Saúde.

1.2 Strategic and Operational Context of Integrated Care Systems

In 2022, NHS England established Integrated Care Systems (ICSs) to foster collaboration among NHS organisations, local councils, and other frontline professionals to better meet the healthcare needs of local populations. ICSs face complex challenges in collaborative working, including differing organisational structures, priorities, and governance, as well as issues linked to returning to pre-pandemic operations and addressing long-standing health inequalities. Core functions of ICSs, such as capacity and demand modelling, aim to assess and address population health needs, prioritise interventions to improve health outcomes, and ensure the efficient use of available resources (The Kings Fund, 2023).

1.3 ICS Challenges and Modelling Needs

The landscape within ICSs is influenced by several key factors: changing health needs, limited capacity, required skillsets, resource constraints, financial pressures, and the need to integrate health and social care policies. ICSs require a safe space to test various scenarios to improve overall efficiency. Critical questions these systems face include strategies for reducing waiting lists, creating effective discharge pathways, identifying training needs for future healthcare demands, and assessing the impact of proactive engagement with specific population groups (The Kings Fund, 2023). Modelling these elements helps ICSs in making informed decisions on resource allocation and future capacity planning.

1.4 1.4. Simulation modelling approaches to healthcare

COVID-19 made the need for advanced modelling and simulation techniques in healthcare more evident. While there is a wide range of modelling and simulation approaches, each of them needs to be applied in the right context and at the right level.

The Health Services Research Network (2016) identified a suite of simulation methods including Discrete Event Simulation (DES), SD, Monte Carlo simulation, Agent-Based Simulation, and Behavioural Simulation which could be used to: 'test 'what-if' scenarios for service design, determine levels of uncertainty, provide visualisations and inform clear understanding and dialogue amongst stakeholders and develop forecasts/projections of future performance'.

DES and SD are both time-based representations of systems. Some of the decision criteria for selecting the approach have been explored by Brailsford et al. (2020). For instance, there are key differences in the way that the two approaches track items. DES tracks individual items around the system, e.g. individual patients. SD tracks how many items are in various parts of the system and how they flow between them.

2 APPROACH

2.1 Learning Objectives for System Dynamics Training

NHS England piloted System Dynamics as a promising tool to enhance demand and capacity planning capabilities. SD is a simulation-based approach used to understand and analyse complex systems over time. It involves creating models that represent the interactions between various components of a system, incorporating feedback loops, delays, and non-linear relationships. These models enable stakeholders to test scenarios, predict outcomes, and make informed decisions to improve system performance and address challenges. There is a long track record in the use of SD to represent strategic issues in health and social care (Cave and Willis,2020; Wolstenholme & Mckelvie, 2020).

A gap in internal SD capacity and capability was evident within ICSs and the health care system more generally, necessitating training to build these skills within NHS teams. This training programme, which was delivered between June 2022 and March 2024, aimed to demonstrate the potential of SD by designing pilots to introduce and explore this methodology in an NHS context. The specific learning objectives of the training included an introduction to SD concepts, skills for mapping and conceptualising systems, and training on the stages required to develop and validate SD models. Participants learned to use Stella Architect software for building and interpreting models and were also trained on strategies to secure buy-in from senior stakeholders.

2.2 Delivery Method and Training Structure

The pilot training programme was structured for small groups of around 10 participants per session, delivered entirely online in light of COVID-19 protocols. The participants were typically already involved in analytical activities and had a broad range of expertise and experience. Participant retention was very high indeed, with no dropouts from any of the training pilots.

Formal learning sessions were planned to be held bi-weekly, complemented by informal drop-in sessions to discuss ongoing progress. Training was delivered using a variety of approaches, including presentations, practical sessions, and group activities, focusing on problem-based learning and encouraging collaborative model-building. Resources and collaboration tools were used to create a community of practice, where participants could collectively develop their understanding and prototype models. Figure 1 below presents the modular structure of the training, illustrating the planned content for each module.

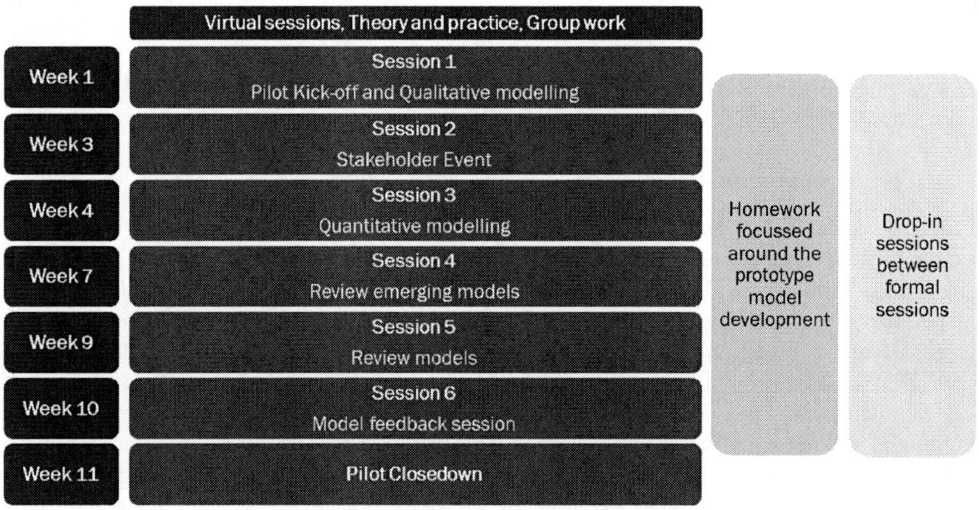

Figure 1 Modular structure of the training programme

The training modules considered the various stages of model development and review, from initial qualitative and quantitative modelling to model testing, validation, and closedown. Each pilot session covered crucial aspects of robust SD model development, including defining model specifications, constructing and documenting the model, and testing for validation and verification. Figure 2 below maps theses stages onto the specific modules (as per Figure 1) where they are covered:

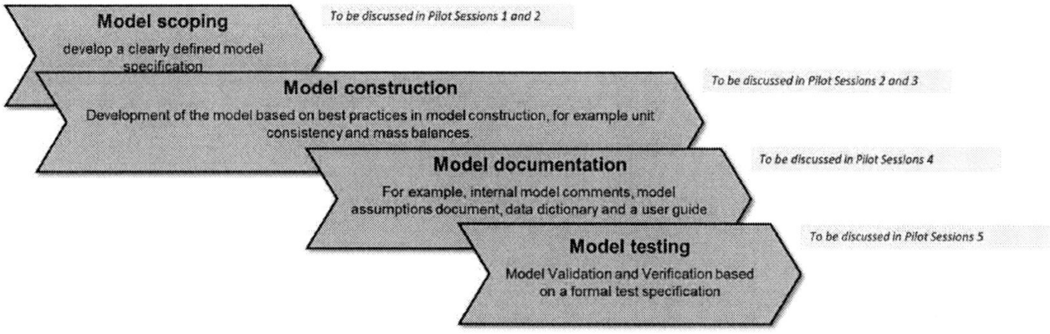

Figure 2 Key stages of the model development covered in the training programme

The training also included a comparison between SD and other simulation approaches (for example Discrete Event Simulation and Agent Based Model) to ensure the students knew when, and when not to apply SD.

3 DELIVERY

3.1 Pilot Delivery Timeline and Results

The three pilot programmes were successfully delivered across various English health and care sectors organisations, leading to the development of system dynamics models that addressed specific regional challenges.

Figure 3 below provides a timeline of the programme, including other sector wide training events.

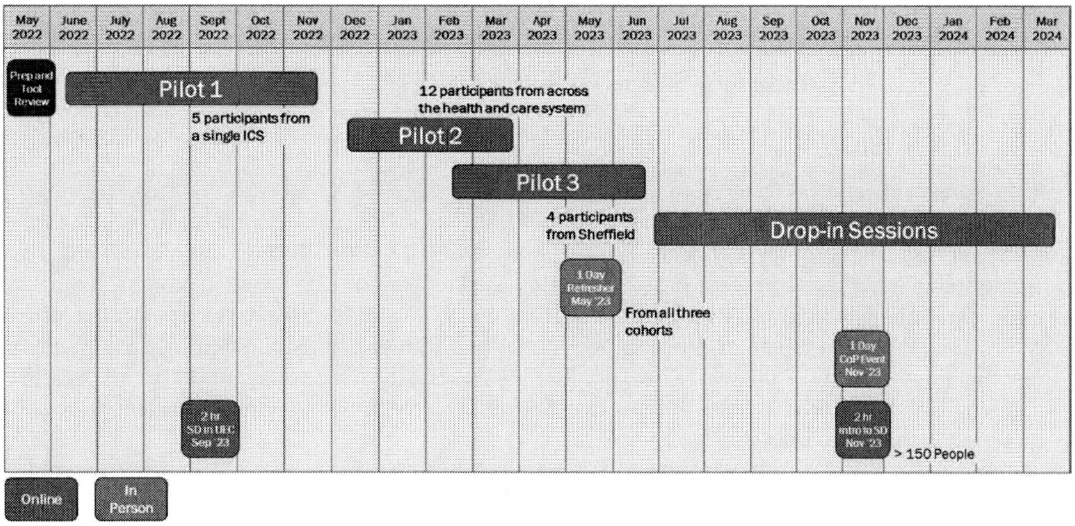

Figure 3 Training programme timeline

Figure 3 shows period over which the three pilots were run, along with the number of students taking part in each pilot. The Figure also illustrates the post pilot support provided which included drop-in sessions and a number of online and in person events. A large scale online event was also delivered to over 150 people from across the NHS which provided an overview of SD and details of the projects which had been delivered by the students.

3.2 Example projects

Fundamental to the pilots was the development of models supporting strategic issues the trainees were facing. A number of these modelling initiatives are described in table 1.

Organisation	Objective	Solution/Approach	Impact / Outcomes
Bristol, North Somerset, and South Gloucestershire (BNSSG) ICS	Address patient flow within Urgent and Emergency Care (UEC) services to reduce Emergency Department (ED) attendances and optimise triage processes.	Developed a model assessing the impact of workforce availability, patient triage, and community pharmacy services on UEC services.	Participants developed a shared quantitative model, presented key findings to decision-makers, and improved decision-making. Team, initially inexperienced in SD, received coaching on model scope and structure and created a shared model
NHS Blood and Transplant (NHSBT)	Optimise donor recruitment and blood collection to meet hospital demand and reduce health inequalities.	Developed a scenario-planning tool to test donor recruitment strategies and improve internal decision-making.	The model secured senior leadership support, promoted organisational change, and improved operational effectiveness.
Sheffield City Council and NHS Sheffield Integrated Care Board	Reduce pressure on secondary care by supporting COPD patients within community settings.	Group model-building process used to construct a system map, followed by quantification of core model components.	Insights into key variables interactions helped explore alternative methods, shifting focus to individual-level interventions and modelling.

Table 1 Example projects undertaken during the training programme

4 DISCUSSION

This paper reflects on the design, delivery, and outcomes of a national SD training programme developed for the NHS in England. The programme, driven by the need to improve demand and capacity planning, aimed to equip healthcare professionals with SD skills through online training sessions, supported by a series of problem-based pilots that used real-world healthcare examples. Key outcomes highlighted the practical benefits of SD modelling in various ICS contexts, as demonstrated by three pilot case studies on patient flow, blood donor recruitment, and community-based support for respiratory patients. Overall, this review emphasises that SD training, when tailored to real-world health challenges and delivered in a flexible, accessible format, can effectively enhance system-wide decision-making capabilities within the NHS.

Particular lessons learnt relevant to SD training delivery, particular in a health care context are described below

4.1 Lessons Learnt

4.1.1 Online Delivery Benefits and Challenges

The online format made the training accessible to participants across England, helping maintain high attendance rates and enabling flexible session planning around participants' schedules. However, the virtual nature of the sessions required careful planning to maintain engagement and ensure understanding. Online tools facilitated the rapid creation of a "community of practice" among participants, although feedback indicated a desire for occasional face-to-face interactions to enhance learning experiences.

4.1.2 Relevance of Realistic Examples

Utilising real-world healthcare examples helped contextualise the benefits of SD, making the training more impactful. Projects involving live cases with real implications saw greater participant engagement, although these required more time and resources for data acquisition and stakeholder involvement. Future training sessions may benefit from initially less complex models to allow participants to build foundational SD skills before tackling real-world challenges.

4.1.3 Specific Challenges for NHS Participants

The NHS-specific context introduced unique challenges, such as difficulty completing assignments between sessions due to winter pressures and limited availability of clinical staff for workshops, necessitating six weeks' notice. Clinical staff did not undertake the training, but the projects undertaken by the trainees required input from clinical staff, for example for mapping the system of interest or for exploring model assumptions. These constraints underscored the need for additional planning and flexibility in the training schedule to accommodate the operational demands of NHS staff.

4.1.4 Designing Training with Progressive Goals

Structured around realistic, achievable goals, the training approach fostered a sense of continuous progress among participants. Initial sessions did not require full access to the SD software, allowing participants to focus on conceptual understanding before advancing to software-based activities. Support for alternative approaches, as well as guidance on when SD may not be the ideal approach, provided a balanced perspective for participants, enhancing their decision-making capacity.

In conclusion, this paper describes an approach to upskilling NHS staff in SD, and the lessons learnt from delivering three training pilots. The pilots had a high retention rates and excellent participant feedback, and the trainees developed models that were applied to real strategic issues.

ACKNOWLEDGMENTS

With thanks to Janine Ibrahim, Bristol North Somerset and South Gloucestershire ; Emily Baldwin, NHS Blood and Transplant and Chris Gibbons and Andy Eames NHS Sheffield Clinical Commissioning Group and Sheffield City Council.

REFERENCES

Brailsford S, Churilov L, and Dangerfield B. et al (2020, updated in 2022) Discrete-Event Simulation and System Dynamics for Management Decision making. Wiley Charles

Cave S and Willis G. (2020). System Dynamics and Workforce Planning. In: Dangerfield, B. (eds) System Dynamics. Encyclopedia of Complexity and Systems Science Series. Springer, New York, NY. https://doi.org/10.1007/978-1-4939-8790-0_659

NHS (2020). NHS Long Term Plan. Published February 11,0202. https://www.longtermplan.nhs.uk/

The Health Services Research Network (HSRN) et al (2016). Change by design: systems modelling and simulation in healthcare. Tools for health service decision makers. Available at: <https://mashnet.info/wp-content/files/2016/09/Change-By-Design-Booklet.pdf> [Accessed 11 January 2023].

The Kings Fund (2023) Integrated care systems explained making sense of systems, places and neighbourhoods. The Kings Fund https://www.kingsfund.org.uk/publications/integrated-care-systems-explained. Published July 11, 2023.

Wolstenholme E and McKelvie D (2020) The Dynamics of Care: Understanding People Flows in Health and Social Care; Springer.

AUTHOR BIOGRAPHIES

SIÔN CAVE is head of Decision Analysis Service's Analytics + Foresight Hub. The Hub is DAS' centre of excellence for data science, systems modelling and futures techniques. https://uk.linkedin.com/in/sioncave

VANESSA PEREZ PEREZ received a master's degree in System Dynamics from University of Bergen in Norway in 2013. In the last 10 years, she has applied the System Dynamics modelling approach to demand and capacity modelling in healthcare and electricity sector in England and Colombia respectively. Her main contribution to the System Dynamics field has been raising the profile of advanced analytics and in particular, System Dynamics, in the healthcare sector in England.

STEPHEN CURRAM is a lead consultant within Decision Analysis Service's Analytics + Foresight Hub. He has many years' experience delivering System Dynamics studies as well as other modelling techniques. He was previously a lecturer in Operational Reasearch at Warwick Business School. https://www.linkedin.com/in/stephen-curram-21088564

EMMA WOODHAM She has been working as a consultant since graduating with a MMath(Hons) in Mathematics from University of St Andrews in 2011. Her specialisms include Systems Thinking, Data Analysis and simulation modelling. https://uk.linkedin.com/in/emma-woodham-26830a56

Proceedings of the Operational Research Society Simulation Workshop 2025 (SW25)
M. Luis, A. Harper, T. Monks, N. Mustafee, eds.

https://doi.org/10.36819/SW25.038

A CONCEPTUAL FRAMEWORK FOR PROMOTING SUSTAINABILITY IN SIMULATION OF HOSPITAL PHARMACY ASEPTIC UNITS

Fatemeh Alidoost
Navonil Mustafee
Alison Harper

Centre for Simulation, Analytics, & Modelling
University of Exeter, Business School
Exeter, United Kingdom
fa418@exeter.ac.uk
n.mustafee@exeter.ac.uk
a.l.harper@exeter.ac.uk

Thomas Monks

University of Exeter, Faculty of Health and Life Sciences
Exeter, United Kingdom

t.m.w.monks@exeter.ac.uk

Alice Harrison

Manchester University
NHS Foundation Trust
alice.harrison2@mft.nhs.uk

ABSTRACT

The healthcare sector contributes significantly to environmental impacts, mainly through consuming resources for patient care that generate waste and carbon footprint. For example, hospital pharmacy aseptic units, critical for preparing high-risk injectable medications, contribute to this impact through generating medicinal waste, personal protective equipment, and other disposables. Simulation modeling can help analyse and improve these processes by replicating ASU workflows. While conceptual modeling is recognised in simulation studies, few have applied sustainability perspectives to real-world healthcare settings. To address this, we developed a conceptual model (CM) framework with an NHS stakeholder to enhance sustainability performance in ASUs through minimising waste, improving operational efficiency, and alignment with the NHS net-zero carbon agenda. The Discrete-Event Simulation implemented using our CM will thus allow for the experimentation of sustainability strategies, such as batching and automation. The main research contribution of this work is to bridge the divide between operational efficiency and sustainability from the CM stage of the simulation study lifecycle, offering valuable insights for developing sustainable practices in real-world healthcare settings.

Keywords: Hospital Pharmacy, Conceptual Modelling, Simulation, Aseptic Units

1 INTRODUCTION

Sustainability refers to the ability to meet the needs of the present without compromising the ability of future generations, encompassing a balance of three key pillars: environmental, economic, and social sustainability (Marimuthu & Paulose, 2016). The healthcare sector's goal of promoting a healthy and sustainable society contrasts with the substantial environmental impacts and societal pressures caused by healthcare services, particularly hospitals, both through their operations and value chains (Karliner et al., 2019). Hospitals consume large quantities of energy, water, and other resources (Abdulsalam & Schneller, 2019), while also generating significant amounts of waste (Abd El-Salam, 2010; Ranjbari et al., 2022). Hospitals are shown to be responsible for 29% of the carbon footprint associated with health

services (Pichler et al., 2019). In this setting, medicines contribute to 25% of NHS's carbon footprint (NHS, 2022), highlighting the role of the hospital pharmacy department in combating NHS carbon emissions. These directly affect economic and environmental sustainability.
Hospitals are also characterised by challenging working conditions, including high workloads, job stress, and high levels of burnout (Hall et al., 2016), where this can directly affect the quality of care and service level (AlJaberi et al., 2017). Moreover, in several countries, the growing proportion of the ageing population is placing increasing pressure on health and care systems, representing challenges to maintain access to high-quality care while ensuring that it remains affordable and sustainable (Colombo et al., 2016); this aligns with social aspect of sustainability. The discussion in this section thus highlights the importance of addressing economic aspects of sustainability through improving processes and cost reduction attempts, environmental aspects of sustainability through decarbonisation, and social aspects of sustainability through enhancing resource utilisation and patient experience via more productive care services.

Aseptic Service Units (ASUs) in hospitals play a vital role in preparing high-risk injectable medications, such as chemotherapy and parenteral nutrition, under sterile conditions. The products within these units account for 3.1% of the total budget for NHS England; the demand for aseptically prepared injectables is expected to rise by 5% per annum (DHSC, 2020). Due to strict regulatory and safety requirements, ASUs consume significant resources, generate considerable waste, and have complex workflows. This makes ASUs ideal for applying economic, environmental and social sustainability goals. Discrete event simulation (DES) enables processes to be modelled at the individual level and facilitate exploring the potential interventions in the system without incurring costs and risks to an existing system to inform decision-making processes.

This study proposes a conceptual model for simulation of ASU of a hospital, developed with the objective of understanding sustainability and productivity-related performances of these units. The conceptual model is developed to test policies, ensuring improvements in both sustainability and productivity. The study critically evaluates opportunities for waste reduction and resource utilisation, offering a framework for decision-makers to assess the sustainable and operational impacts of potential interventions. The main contribution of this paper lies in bridging operational efficiency and sustainability, incorporating a framework to evaluate environmental, economic, and social impacts. Unlike previous conceptual models, this framework explicitly integrates sustainability metrics such as carbon emission minimisation, and staff utilisation, alongside traditional productivity measures. This study extends the literature on conceptual modelling (CM) with a focus on sustainability and to develop a conceptual model that fosters a shared understanding of sustainability-related challenges—particularly waste reduction—in ASUs, in collaboration with stakeholders.

2 BACKGROUND

The application of DES has been widely recognised in the context of healthcare due to its ability to model complex, dynamic systems with uncertainties (Philip et al., 2023; Zhang, 2018). Our short review of the literature shows DES has also been applied in hospital pharmacy settings to capture inefficiencies and examine the impact of scenarios including staffing level (Reynolds et al., 2011), inventory policies (Gebicki et al., 2014), and one-dose package medications (Furushima et al., 2018) in a risk-free (simulated) environment.

The majority of healthcare simulation studies conducted in the context of hospital pharmacy and allied services, have employed DES. Most of the studies have focused only on productivity-related objectives. For instance, Furushima et al. (2018) studied the impact of one dose package of medicines, aiming to support patient medicine adherence, on patient waiting times. Rupnik et al. (2019), in their DES model of logistics processes for sterilisation of reusable medical devices, tested additional surgical instrument and automated surgery scheduling strategies to improve material availability and reduce cost. More recently, Jebbor et al. (2023) designed a fully automated inventory replenishment system in hospitals and evaluated the proposed design through DES model of a virtual hospital. While these studies aimed to improve productivity-related performance, incorporating a sustainability perspective into DES models of hospital pharmacy could significantly expand the literature by introducing sustainability-related performance measures. Dewi et al. (2022) captured sustainability perspectives by providing a SD model to predict generated waste in dental care setting. This study captured environmental aspects, though capturing productivity performance while considering three pillars of sustainability remained unexplored.

Our review identified only one DES study for modelling ASUs. Alzouman (2017) developed a DES model to represent an aseptic unit of a hospital aiming to expand the production capacity, increasing the space utilisation and to identify some of the critical parameters in relation to system performance. While their study focused on staffing and production capacity for improving operational efficiency, it did not address sustainability aspects such as waste reduction or carbon footprint. Given the high waste levels associated with perishable medications, single-use personal protective equipment (PPE), and strict regulatory protocols in aseptic services, sustainability is crucial to reducing environmental impact while maintaining safety and compliance. This gap in the literature suggests a need for models that can simulate and test sustainability-driven interventions, such as batching and automation (refer to section 3.1.1 for further details), within aseptic units. Addressing these elements could help not only in optimising resource utilisation but also in supporting broader environmental goals in line with healthcare sustainability agendas.

Thus, the current study emphasises the importance of reducing waste within ASUs, particularly as these units generate significant amounts of medicinal and PPE waste. The reduction of medicinal waste not only cuts down on resource consumption (*contributing to economic sustainability and productivity*) but also decreases the carbon footprint associated with the disposal of hazardous materials (*contributing to environmental sustainability*). Additionally, improving the operational efficiency of ASUs through automation and batching has the potential to free up healthcare staff, allowing them to focus on more patient-centred tasks, ultimately improving the quality of care (*contributing to social sustainability and productivity*). Moreover, the risk of contamination for pharmacy staff have been reported by studies (Lancharro et al., 2016; Valero-García et al., 2021), highlighting the need for incorporating automation, for the entire or part of the medicine preparation process. This could not only contribute to reducing the risk of hazards for pharmacy staff and improving the *social aspects of sustainability*, but also, in combination with batching practices, has the potential to improve workflow by automating processes most prone to human errors.

3 CONCEPTUAL MODELLING

The simulation study life cycle proposed by Robinson (2014) outlined four key stages for a simulation study, namely conceptual modelling, computer modelling, experimentation, and real-world implementation. Conceptual modelling as an important stage of the simulation lifecycle (Kotiadis & Robinson, 2008), encompassing the process of abstracting a model from the problem aiming to overcome the complexity of simulation design, facilitate communication between modeller and problem owners, and assist in defining specifications of test designs (Derrick & Balci, 1997; Robinson, 2008a). In Balci's simulation lifecycle framework (Balci & Ormsby, 2007), the CM development follows a structured lifecycle, progressing through stages such as problem formulation, system investigation, high-level and low-level design, and integration. This structured approach enables the systematic development of simulation models, particularly for large-scale, complex systems, by establishing a foundation for verification, validation, and reuse across different applications.

CM frameworks in the literature have been proposed across a wide range of applications such as those designed to capture manufacturing and supply chain settings (Van Der Zee & Van Der Vorst, 2005; Van der Zee, 2006), healthcare (Kotiadis et al., 2014) and more generalisable CMs such as (Furian et al., 2015; Kotiadis & Robinson, 2008; Robinson, 2008a). Onggo (2009) presented a unified conceptual model representation using a case study of a hospital. Staff et al. (2023) proposed a CM framework of the perishable products in human milk banking, conceptualising the inventory management aspects for a simulation study. While the use of simulation is a well-recognised research stream in healthcare, few studies have provided detailed CM narratives for a real-world case study, in healthcare settings.

Incorporating sustainability objectives alongside conventional productivity metrics adds a new dimension to CM in healthcare simulation. This integration underscores the need for robust and adaptable CMs capable of addressing sustainability performance measures within the simulation. Fakhimi et al. (2017) emphasise the importance of balancing productivity with the Triple Bottom Line (TBL) of sustainability metrics, although there remains a gap in the literature regarding how CM frameworks can support sustainability-focused simulation in healthcare. Addressing this gap, in the current study, through a comprehensive CM narrative and framework can help bridge the divide between operational efficiency and sustainability, offering valuable insights for developing sustainable practices in real-world healthcare settings.

3.1 Conceptual Modelling for Simulation of Aseptic Unit

One role of the pharmacy department in hospitals is the preparation and supply of injectable medicines, for intravenous transmitted antibiotics, chemotherapy and monoclonal antibodies, as well as nutrition and cutting-edge medicines for cell therapy and clinical trials, within the ASUs. The aim is to provide sterile controlled environments for the production of high-risk injectable medicine in ready-to-administer (RtA) format. The review of aseptic units, conducted by NHS England and NHS Improvement in 2017/18 and 2018/19, highlighted deficiencies in sustainability aspects which resulted in proposals for the opportunity to improve patient care and deliver savings (DHSC, 2020). The recommendations include improvements in workload of nursing staff and increasing productivity through operational efficiency (via automation and shared services) as well as reduction of waste.

The need for waste reduction is further underscored by the Royal Pharmaceutical Society's sustainability policies, which emphasise minimising medicine waste to support environmental goals (RPharms, 2021). Moreover, the net zero NHS agenda calls for evidence to identify and understand the environmental impacts of the NHS services aiming to provide health and high quality care for all (NHS, 2022). Therefore, as illustrated in Figure 1, waste reduction contributes to reduce consumption and operational efficiency while reducing environmental impacts and economic burdens.

Waste generated by hospital ASUs significantly contributes to their carbon footprint. This includes medicinal waste due to limitations in medicine shelf-life and part-used vials, as well as products related to cleaning agents and PPEs (Harrison, 2024). Therefore, waste reduction presents an opportunity to lower the environmental impact of hospital pharmacies. This not only contributes to a reduction in carbon emissions and environmental sustainability but also promotes economic sustainability through potential cost savings from waste reduction and improving operational efficiency through enhancing resource utilisation.

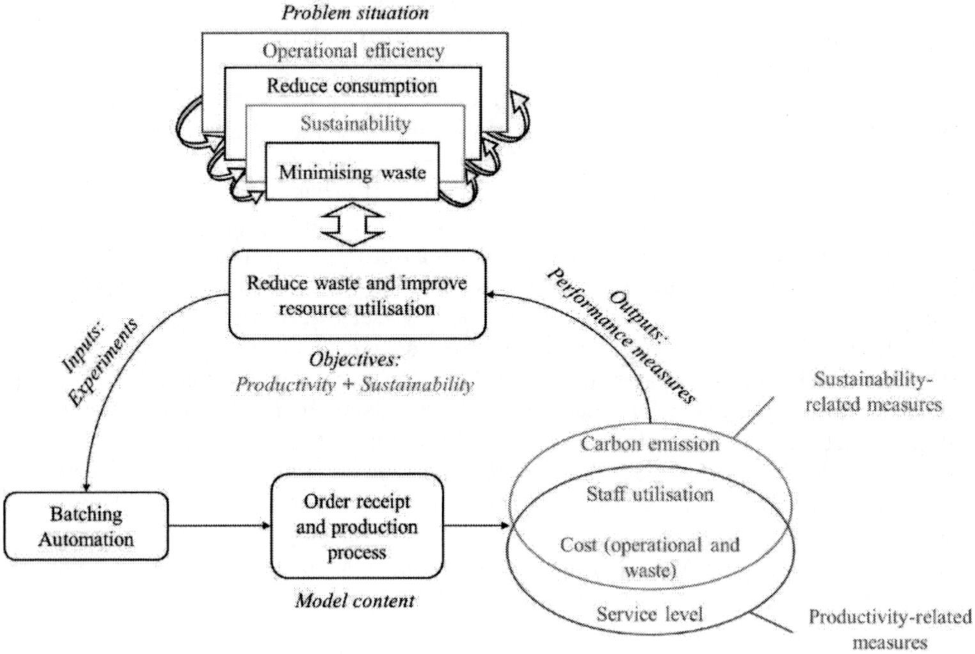

Figure 1 *An overview of ASU extended conceptual modelling framework for operational efficiency and sustainability*

Batching and automation are two strategies recommended in the literature which can contribute to both operational efficiencies and sustainability. Batching is the process of grouping medication preparations to maximise efficiency, reducing waste by minimising the number of medicine vials opened and the associated disposable materials used for each preparation (National Academies of Sciences & Medicine, 2021). A two year review of batching or vial sharing for the compounding medicines conducted by Smith (2015) showed that batching practice provide considerable cost savings. While the findings support economic sustainability of ASUs by reducing wastage costs, environmental and social sustainability - as well as productivity-related measures - are not investigated in the study. Batching promotes environmental sustainability by cutting down on the frequent disposal of medicinal by-products and single-use components—like syringes, vial caps, and other consumables—which would otherwise contribute to the carbon footprint. Furthermore, efficient batching can help streamline workflows, alleviating the time pressure and workload on staff, thus contributing to social sustainability by improving staff well-being and patient experience.

Automation, on the other hand, can transform operational processes within ASUs by minimising human error, enhancing accuracy, and increasing throughput (Geersing et al., 2020). In a study by Baan et al. (2022), an economic evaluation of vial sharing for expensive drugs using automation was assessed. This study highlighted the application of automation, as opposed to manual compounding, for preventing drug wastage, resulting in an economic advantage. However, there is still a lack of sustainability performance evaluation as well as resource utilisation in the literature. While the initial investment in automation can be substantial, it reduces the need for manual checks and repetitive tasks, freeing up skilled pharmacy staff to focus on patient-centred services rather than routine, labour-intensive activities. This can contribute to social sustainability by reducing burnout and enabling staff to allocate more time to quality care activities, while also promoting environmental sustainability by reducing waste for consumables. Thus, a cost-effectiveness evaluation of this with sustainability considerations would provide valuable insights to inform decisions about integrating automation for all or some of the steps in ASUs.

ASUs operate in a unique environment that combines the strict regulatory and quality control demands of both manufacturing and healthcare settings. From manufacturing, ASUs inherit complexities such as precision in process control and stringent requirements for product quality and safety. Simultaneously, the healthcare setting adds layers of complexity related to patient-centred care, the perishability and time-sensitivity of the healthcare products, and the high-stakes impact of service errors on patient health. Given this, this study integrates elements from frameworks proposed by Robinson (2008a) and Balci and Ormsby (2007), chosen for their adaptability across various systems.

Adapted from these studies and extending it to incorporate sustainability aspects, our CM consists of four main components, namely objectives including operational efficiency and sustainability, inputs (experiments), outputs (performance measures), and model content. Figure 1 illustrates the extended CM to capture sustainability related concepts for the ASU. The process begins with gaining an understanding of the problem situation through literature on ASU and informal interviews with domain experts, followed by establishing a set of modelling and general project objectives that incorporates both sustainability and productivity. These objectives shape the development of the CM, starting with defining the model's outputs, followed by determining the inputs, and then outlining the model's content, including its scope and level of detail, which will be further explained in sections 3.1.2, 3.1.3, and 3.1.4. The sequence of these steps is not a linear path, rather it is in an iterative and repeated process, as continuous revisions are required for the modelling process. The conceptual model was co-developed with the quality systems officer of an aseptic service (a co-author of this paper). Stakeholder engagement has played a critical role in defining system boundaries, identifying operational constraints, and the objectives. Interviews have informed design decisions, such as determining feasible batching policies, and waste management strategies. Considering the iterative nature of the CM and the ongoing exercise of the study, there might be refinement or more details for the future work.

3.1.1 Understanding the Problem Situation

The CM is derived based upon an understanding of the problem situation and the need to improve that problem. Most of the simulation studies, including the current study, are considered from collaborative discipline, and modellers engage with stakeholders, even if indirectly to define and develop solutions to problems (Monks et al., 2014). Furthermore, critical success factors for simulation studies are highly reliant on communication with stakeholders, and their involvement in the modelling process (Jahangirian et al., 2017). The modeller aims to foster a joint creation and acceptance of good quality solutions, as the outcome of the study is expected to inform stakeholders' (problem owners) decision making process, and thus, building trust starts from this step (Harper et al., 2021).

In this paper, to provide clarity in this regard, process mapping of the order receipt process and production of the aseptically prepared medicines have been conducted. The objective of the mapping activity was to trace the steps orders and products go through in aseptic unit to be prepared as per the prescription requirements while identifying the waste creation points within the unit. This process was informed using observation that was part of a separate study (Harrison, 2024) and informal semi-structure interviews with a domain expert (co-author of this study). The mapping went through several iterations to refine the processes included in the model, ensuring that inaccuracies were addressed and that the model aligned with the study's objectives. In the following a description of the ASU of a hospital pharmacy under study has been provided as well as the process mapped for the ASU.

The ASU under study operates through seven discrete steps across three main room types, namely support room, clean room, and central room, provides items encompassing multiple production processes. Products pass through during the process, while the receipt of the orders and release of the produced medicines are done in the central room. Before the ASU process begins, orders are already verified by a pharmacist prior to be sent electronically to the aseptic unit.

Figure 2 outlines the *order receipt process* and *production process* within the ASU. The physician prescribes patient doses required to be prepared in the ASU, and clinically verified prescriptions are sent to the AUS. The ASU staff then verify each prescription, determine the workload, and assess if multiple doses (batching) can be prepared. For patients on regimens that require the administration of the same drug and dose over several days, the ASU may prepare multiple doses (batches) simultaneously, where stability data and production method allow. After this, worksheets (containing information about the orders and preparation material required) are printed to be sent for production process.

As illustrated in Figure 2, the ASU *production process* starting point is where the orders are received. In the assembly area within the support room, an ASU operator organises all the required materials (e.g., drug vials, containers, needles, syringes) on a tray according to the worksheet. Another operator is responsible for verifying the assembled materials, including checking batch numbers and expiry dates. Throughout each stage of the process in different rooms, waste has been observed and categorised into two categories (according to Table 1), although misalignment with proper waste segregartion has been observed in this unit (Harrison, 2024). These categories are as follows:

- **Offensive waste;** including items such as disposable PPEs, packaging from starting materials and consumables, as well as cleaning agents.
- **Cytotoxic waste**, including sharps, empty or partially used starting materials (e.g., ampoules, vials), isolator gloves, and empty or full syringes. This cytotoxic waste is further segregated into small sharps bins and large cytotoxic bins within the clean room which we do not consider the further segregation for the current study.

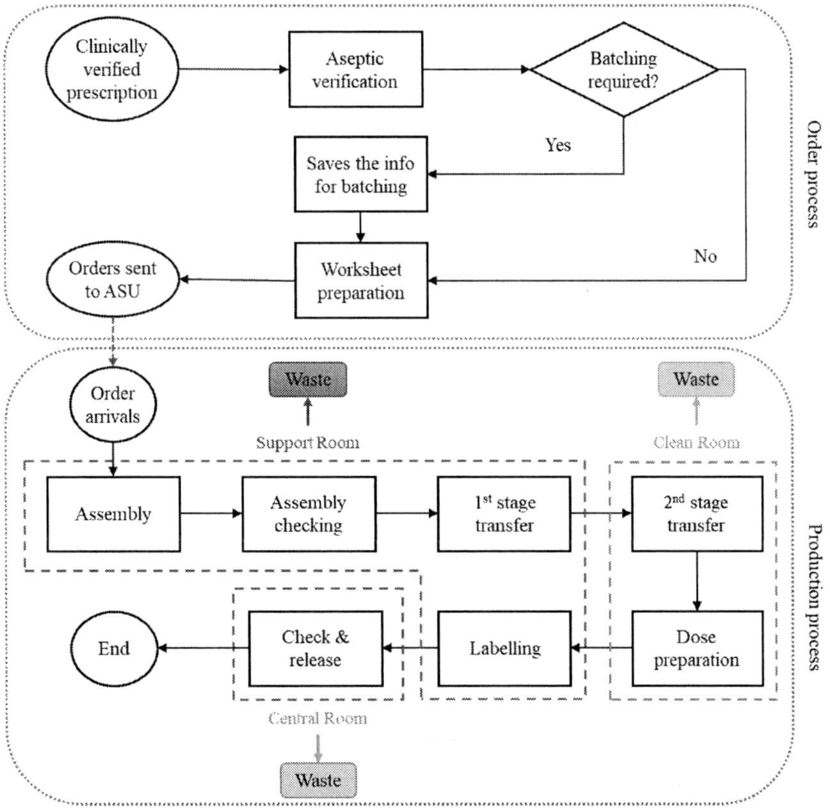

Figure 2 *Order process and production process within the ASU*

Table 1 *Waste streams identified in the aseptic processes, adapted from Harrison (2024)*

Processes	Main items of waste disposed	Type of waste	Reason for waste
Assembly & assembly checking	Packaging and PPEs	Offensive waste	Unwrapping materials
1st stage transfer	Cleaning agents	Offensive waste	Cleaning process Risk of hazards
2nd stage transfer	Cleaning agents	Offensive waste	Cleaning process PPEs
Dose preparation	Cleaning agents, components required to prepare the product (syringes, needles, spikes, etc.), partly used starting materials (e.g. vials)	Offensive waste Cytotoxic waste	Cleaning process Medicine requirements Errors in the process
Labelling	-	-	-
Check & release	Starting materials (empty packaging or part filled), filled syringes that require checking	Cytotoxic waste Offensive waste	Medicine requirements Risk of hazards

Accordingly, during the assembly and assembly checking processes, waste is generated due to starting material packages and PPEs consumed by staff. In the 1st stage of transfer, the assembled items are inspected and moved into the clean room through a rigorous two-step cleaning process to prevent contamination. This involves wiping all items with a sporicidal agent, spraying them with alcohol, and placing them in a transfer hatch for two minutes. These cleaning processes contribute to waste due to the disposal of cleaning wipes and chemical agents used for sterilisation. Once inside the clean room, materials undergo the 2nd stage transfer disinfection by a separate operator before manipulation within the main chamber of the pharmacy isolator to prepare the required doses. The preparation process itself often produces cytotoxic waste, especially when handling high-risk medications, as it involves the use of single-use isolator gloves for every production session, syringes, and other disposables that cannot be reused due to contamination risks. Moreover, cytotoxic waste is generated at this point if certain drugs, such as vials, are part-used.

Most preparation methods require an in-process check to ensure accuracy. Any errors at this stage lead to rework or discarding of the product, further increasing cytotoxic waste. Once the production is complete, the operator in the support room will label the final doses before sending out to the central room and the tray with finished product is placed into out hatch for transfer to the central room. Finally, a pharmacist inspects the product before it is released. At this point, empty packaging or partly used materials contributes to the cytotoxic and offensive waste generation.

3.1.2 Setting the Objectives

Modelling objectives specify how a simulation study is designed to support stakeholders in making informed decisions by evaluating different system configurations based on specified performance measures. According to Robinson (2008a), before narrowing down to specific *modelling objectives*, it is essential to first identify the overall *aims of the organisation* to understand how simulation can contribute effectively. In addition to these goals, *general project objectives* should also be outlined, including factors such as the project timescale, simulation run-time, visualisation requirements, ease-of-use, and potential for model reuse.

In this study, the main organisational aim is to minimise medicine waste within the ASU. Collaboration between the ASU team and our research team has identified several opportunities to reduce waste, with a focus on enhancing both sustainability and operational efficiency. Computer simulation offers a risk-free platform to test various interventions before actual implementation. This is particularly valuable given the high costs associated with the preparation of aseptic medicines as well as the waste generated in these units and their contribution to environmental impacts. Moreover, given the uncertainty of demand and the critical need to maintain a near 100% service level, there might be opportunities to address lead times within the system. By simulating potential improvements, the study aims not only to reduce waste but also to free up nursing staff for more personalised care and enhance the patient experience. For instance, batching medicine production have potential to reduce the amount of partially used vials which contributes to environmental sustainability. Moreover, while the process will be done for a batch of products in one go, there is potential to save staff time through one time cleaning procedure. Consequently, this research seeks to examine the impact of batching and automation strategies on both sustainability performance and operational efficiency within the ASU system. This is to evaluate cost and benefit associated with preparing medicines in batches and bringing automation process for medicine preparation process for all or batch orders. The general project objectives, as outlined in Table 2, have also been determined to guide this process.

Table 2 *Aims and objectives of the ASU study*

Organisational aim:
- To minimise waste in ASU including both offensive and cytotoxic waste

Modelling objectives:
- Productivity-related: efficiency for resource utilisation (both human resource and products used for aseptically prepared medicines)
- Sustainability-related:
    - Economic: reduction in cost of waste
    - Environmental: reduction carbon emissions from waste
    - Social: reduction in staff time

General project objectives:
- Time scale: by the end of 2025
- Flexibility: required for further development
- Simulation run speed: not a priority
- Visual display: a 2D visualisation would be useful for sharing the model with higher level stakeholders

- Ease of use: not a priority

3.1.3 Model Inputs and Outputs

After defining the objectives, the next step is to identify the model's inputs and outputs, which are referred to as the experimental factors (inputs) and responses (outputs). Responses represent the outcomes or results that stakeholders or the modeller intend to obtain from the model, rather than the interventions or modifications made to the system. These responses are directly aligned with the objectives previously established. The model tracks productivity performance and sustainability performance across three dimensions—environmental, social, and economic—using metrics derived from both literature and stakeholder input. Table 3 provides a summary of the model's inputs and outputs, which serve as the foundation for evaluating the system's performance.

Table 3 *Model inputs and outputs*

Model outputs (responses):
- Economic: waste doses
- Economic and environmental: waste volume
- Environmental: carbon emission
- Economic: cost associated with waste and resources
- Social and efficiency: resource (staff and medicines) utilisation and service level

Model inputs (experimental factors):
- Batching
- Automation
- Shared services (centralised operations) at Trust level (to be tested at the extended version of the model)
- ASU data and parameters including demand-related and cost-related data (refer to section 3.1.5)

3.1.4 Model Content (Study Scope and Level of Details)

Robinson's framework (2010) distinguishes between defining the model's scope and determining its level of detail. The scope sets the model's boundaries, while the level of detail specifies its depth. Defining the scope of a model involves identifying the entities, activities, queues, and resources that will be included.

Study scope: This study is focused on the operational side of the ASU, and any deficiencies associated with behavioural factors, including wasted resources due to prescription errors, or patients' non-adherence to the medications are out of the study's scope. Moreover, the *scope* of this modelling work includes products with or without batch production within the ASU. Moreover, only waste streams in production process, related to medicine and PPEs, categorised into offensive and cytotoxic waste (as discussed in section 3.1.1), is considered in the study's scope. Other waste streams such as domestic waste and cleaning agents has not been considered as they might have limited impact for experimental factors considered for the study.

Level of detail: Within the model boundaries, the components have been determined and categorised into four groups: Entities, Activities, Queues and Resources (Table 4), each of which are discussed in-turn.

Entities: The study focuses on medication units, vials, and PPE, as these items are common across different aseptically prepared medications. The important aspects to include for the products units will constitute arrival patterns, consumed quantities, and their attributes related to characteristics of waste and batching. Cleaning products are excluded due to their variability in their consumption and cost, thus, the respective waste from cleaning agents are further excluded.

Table 4 *Model components*

Component	ASU component	Detail	Inclusion
Entities	Product units	Quantity, attribute (with/ without batch), arrival pattern	Included
	Vials	Quantity: used, attribute (fully/ partly)	Included
	PPEs	Quantity: used	Included
	Cleaning products	-	Excluded
	Wasted vials	Quantity, volume, carbon footprint	Included
	Wasted PPEs	Quantity, volume, carbon footprint	Included
	Wasted cleaning agents	-	Excluded
Activities	Worksheet preparation	Cycle time, resources, routing	Included
	Assembly	*As for worksheet preparation*	Included
	Product preparation	*As for worksheet preparation*	Included
	Release	*As for worksheet preparation*	Included
	Administration	-	Excluded
Queues	Order process	Quantity, routing, priority rules	Included
	Production process	Quantity, routing, priority rules	Included
Resources	Human resources	Quantity	Included

Activities: order process (arrival of orders and the decisions for batching them) and production process are the key activities that the study aims to explore (refer to section 3.1.1). The study aims to assess how batching could affect the sustainability aspects, particularly contributing to reduce waste and improve operational performance (e.g. staff productivity). The timing of the processes is assumed to be stochastic. We have noticed that in preparation stage, the time may vary depending on the product type, with the mean time being used for these calculations. We have excluded indirect activities, such as those related to personnel rest times, answering phone calls, etc.

Queues: Regarding *queues* in the system, the prioritisation rules have been determined based on prescription time, and applicability of batching for the respective product.

Resources: Human resources required for the processes have been considered in different grades according to the ASU standards (Jones & Burns, 2021). According to the model components description so far, the model *assumptions and simplifications* have been determined as follows:

- The process times are considered stochastic, and the time associated with clean room processes will be presented as the mean.
- Waste generated from *processes* are included in the model, while waste associated with discontinued orders is outside the scope of this study.
- Waste associated with material packages are excluded, since they are unavoidable in the study scope.

3.1.5 Data Requirements

The data requirements element can be divided into three types according to Pidd (1997), *contextual data*, *data for model realisation*, and *data for model validation*. The contextual data are those required to develop an understanding of the problem situation, which has been discussed in section 3.1.1. The second type concerns data required to develop the computer model. This includes detailed data on process times, order arrival patterns (e.g. quantities, and frequency distributions), description of the product type (including bill of material for cost calculations) and the type of the waste (quantities, volumes (for carbon footprint calculations), carbon emissions), as well as scheduling and processing rules. These data will be provided within the case study setting for those related to quantities and volume and the use of publicly available reports for financial data and emission-related ones. Finally, the data required for model validation will be collected from historical data related to the ASU for a period of one month. However, the data regarding the waste is not normally collected as a routine process within the hospital, these will be collected during the site visit through observation and informal interviews with domain experts within the ASU.

4 DISCUSSION AND CONCLUSION

The healthcare sector's pursuit of sustainability is gaining momentum, with the agenda for net zero NHS and hospitals identified as major contributors to sustainability. Hospital pharmacy aseptic units (ASUs), responsible for preparing high-risk medications, are recognised as an area where sustainability interventions can have a profound impact.

This paper provides a conceptual model for a DES model to address the sustainability challenges. At the current phase, the conceptual model has been developed based on the modellers' perceptions on developing a DES model to capture the system's characteristics according to the modelling objectives. The validation of the proposed conceptual model will be in future steps when the computer model develops using a case study. Thus, there might be iterative processes between the conceptual model and the computer model and probable refinement and/or extension might be expected in the future work. Notably, as the relationship between the modeller and the stakeholder is likely to continue, this will contribute to building trust across the simulation lifecycle, resulting in a useful organisational tool for informed decision making (Harper et al., 2021). Moreover, refinements and/ or extensions to the model would be achievable considering both side's efforts for achieving a mutual understanding of the problem and model, from the very beginning of the study.

By modelling the flow of materials and processes within an ASU, the DES model will facilitate the identification of inefficiencies and waste generation points. The model also allows for the testing of various interventions, such as batching, automation, and centralised aseptic services, without disrupting actual hospital operations. This capability is crucial, as ASUs operate under strict guidelines and handle highly sensitive medications, where any disruption could have significant consequences on quality of patient care.

For future research, we intend to implement the model, as well as extending the model to evaluate automation and sharing services of the ASUs through simulating and interacting several ASUs under Trust levels. With the broad aim of improving sustainability, assessing the resiliency of the shared services will broaden the literature on the dynamics of sustainability and resilience practices within the healthcare system. The outcomes of this research have the potential to inform policy decisions and operational practices, driving significant improvements in the sustainability of healthcare services.

REFERENCE

Abd El-Salam, M. M. (2010). Hospital waste management in El-Beheira governorate, Egypt. *Journal of environmental management*, *91*(3), 618-629.

Abdulsalam, Y., & Schneller, E. (2019). Hospital supply expenses: an important ingredient in health services research. *Medical Care Research and Review*, *76*(2), 240-252.

AlJaberi, O. A., Hussain, M., & Drake, P. R. (2017). A framework for measuring sustainability in healthcare systems. *International Journal of Healthcare Management*.

Alzouman, O. (2017). *Production Line Enhancement of Aseptic Unit Using Discrete Event Simulation* Cardiff University].

Baan, S. D., Geersing, T. H., Crul, M., Franssen, E. J., & Klous, M. G. (2022). An economic evaluation of vial sharing of expensive drugs in automated compounding. *International journal of clinical pharmacy*, *44*(3), 673-679.

Balci, O., & Ormsby, W. F. (2007). Conceptual modelling for designing large-scale simulations. *Journal of Simulation*, *1*(3), 175-186.

Colombo, F., García-Goñi, M., & Schwierz, C. (2016). Addressing multimorbidity to improve healthcare and economic sustainability. *Journal of Comorbidity*, *6*(1), 21-27.

Derrick, E. J., & Balci, O. (1997). DOMINO: a multifaceted conceptual framework for visual simulation modeling. *INFOR: Information Systems and Operational Research*, *35*(2), 93-120.

Dewi, O., Sari, N. P., Raviola, R., Herniwanti, H., & Rany, N. (2022). Simulation Design of Dental Practice Medical Waste Management Using Dynamic System Model Approach. *Jurnal Penelitian Pendidikan IPA*, *8*(5), 2483-2492.

DHSC, D. o. H. S. C. (2020). *Transforming NHS Pharmacy Aseptic Services in England.* https://assets.publishing.service.gov.uk/media/5f9afdbdd3bf7f1e405d9a23/aseptic-pharmacy.pdf

Fakhimi, M., Stergioulas, L. K., & Mustafee, N. (2017). Modelling for sustainable development using the triple-bottom line: Methods, challenges and the need for hybrid M&S. 2017 Winter Simulation Conference (WSC),

Furian, N., O'Sullivan, M., Walker, C., Vössner, S., & Neubacher, D. (2015). A conceptual modeling framework for discrete event simulation using hierarchical control structures. *Simulation modelling practice and theory*, *56*, 82-96.

Furushima, D., Yamada, H., Kido, M., & Ohno, Y. (2018). The impact of one-dose package of medicines on patient waiting time in dispensing pharmacy: application of a discrete event simulation model. *Biological and Pharmaceutical Bulletin*, *41*(3), 409-418.

Gebicki, M., Mooney, E., Chen, S.-J., & Mazur, L. M. (2014). Evaluation of hospital medication inventory policies. *Health care management science*, *17*, 215-229.

Geersing, T., Klous, M., Franssen, E., van den Heuvel, J., & Crul, M. (2020). Robotic compounding versus manual compounding of chemotherapy: comparing dosing accuracy and precision. *European Journal of Pharmaceutical Sciences*, *155*, 105536.

Hall, L. H., Johnson, J., Watt, I., Tsipa, A., & O'Connor, D. B. (2016). Healthcare staff wellbeing, burnout, and patient safety: a systematic review. *PLOS ONE*, *11*(7), e0159015.

Harper, A., Mustafee, N., & Yearworth, M. (2021). Facets of trust in simulation studies. *European Journal of Operational Research*, *289*(1), 197-213.

Harrison, A. (2024). *An investigation of waste hierarchy strategies to reduce the environmental impact of hospital pharmacy aseptic service units* University of Manchester]. Manchester, United Kingdom.

Jahangirian, M., Taylor, S. J., Young, T., & Robinson, S. (2017). Key performance indicators for successful simulation projects. *Journal of the operational research society*, *68*(7), 747-765.

Jebbor, S., Chiheb, R., El Afia, A., & Gallab, M. (2023). Designing a fully automated and integrated inventory and replenishment system for hospitals. *International Journal of Systems Science: Operations & Logistics*, *10*(1), 1962429.

Jones, K., & Burns, A. (2021). Costs of health and social care 2021. *Personal Social Services Research Unit, University of Kent.*

Karliner, J., Slotterback, S., Boyd, R., Ashby, B., & Steele, K. (2019). Health care's climate footprint. *Health Care Without Harm and ARUP.*

Kotiadis, K., & Robinson, S. (2008). Conceptual modelling: knowledge acquisition and model abstraction. 2008 Winter Simulation Conference,

Kotiadis, K., Tako, A. A., & Vasilakis, C. (2014). A participative and facilitative conceptual modelling framework for discrete event simulation studies in healthcare. *Journal of the operational research society*, *65*, 197-213.

Lancharro, P. M., Iglesias, N. d. C.-A., González-Barcala, F.-J., & González, J. D. M. (2016). Evidence of exposure to cytostatic drugs in healthcare staff: a review of recent literature. *Farmacia Hospitalaria*, *40*(6), 604-621.

Marimuthu, M., & Paulose, H. (2016). Emergence of sustainability based approaches in healthcare: expanding research and practice. *Procedia-Social and Behavioral Sciences*, *224*, 554-561.

Monks, T., Robinson, S., & Kotiadis, K. (2014). Learning from discrete-event simulation: Exploring the high involvement hypothesis. *European Journal of Operational Research*, *235*(1), 195-205.

National Academies of Sciences, E., & Medicine. (2021). *Medications in single-dose vials: implications of discarded drugs.*

NHS. (2022). *Delivering a 'Net Zero' National Health Service.* https://www.england.nhs.uk/greenernhs/wp-content/uploads/sites/51/2022/07/B1728-delivering-a-net-zero-nhs-july-2022.pdf

Onggo, B. S. (2009). Towards a unified conceptual model representation: a case study in healthcare. *Journal of Simulation*, *3*(1), 40-49.

Philip, A. M., Prasannavenkatesan, S., & Mustafee, N. (2023). Simulation modelling of hospital outpatient department: a review of the literature and bibliometric analysis. *Simulation*, *99*(6), 573-597.

Pichler, P.-P., Jaccard, I. S., Weisz, U., & Weisz, H. (2019). International comparison of health care carbon footprints. *Environmental research letters*, *14*(6), 064004.

Pidd, M. (1997). Tools for thinking—Modelling in management science. *Journal of the operational research society*, *48*(11), 1150-1150.

Ranjbari, M., Esfandabadi, Z. S., Shevchenko, T., Chassagnon-Haned, N., Peng, W., Tabatabaei, M., & Aghbashlo, M. (2022). Mapping healthcare waste management research: Past evolution, current challenges, and future perspectives towards a circular economy transition. *Journal of hazardous materials*, *422*, 126724.

Reynolds, M., Vasilakis, C., McLeod, M., Barber, N., Mounsey, A., Newton, S., Jacklin, A., & Franklin, B. D. (2011). Using discrete event simulation to design a more efficient hospital pharmacy for outpatients. *Health care management science*, *14*, 223-236.

Robinson, S. (2008a). Conceptual modelling for simulation Part I: definition and requirements. *Journal of the operational research society*, *59*(3), 278-290.

Robinson, S. (2008b). Conceptual modelling for simulation Part II: a framework for conceptual modelling. *Journal of the operational research society*, *59*(3), 291-304.

Robinson, S. (2014). *Simulation: the practice of model development and use*. Bloomsbury Publishing.

RPharms. (2021). *Sustainability Policies*. https://www.rpharms.com/recognition/all-our-campaigns/policy-a-z/sustainability-policy/policies

Rupnik, B., Nardin, R., & Kramberger, T. (2019). Discrete event simulation of hospital sterilization logistics. *Tehnički vjesnik*, *26*(5), 1486-1491.

Smith, R. S. (2015). A 2-year retrospective review of vial sharing options for the compounding of cytotoxics. *European Journal of Hospital Pharmacy*, *22*(3), 161-164.

Staff, M., Mustafee, N., & Shenker, N. (2023). Conceptual Modeling for Perishable Inventory: A Case Study in Human Milk Banking. 2023 Winter Simulation Conference (WSC),

Valero-García, S., González-Haba, E., Gorgas-Torner, M. Q., Alonso-Herreros, J. M., Lletí, A. C. C., Poveda-Andrés, J. L., Calleja-Hernandez, M. Á., & Delgado-Sánchez, O. (2021). Monitoring contamination of hazardous drug compounding surfaces at hospital pharmacy departments. A consensus statement. Practice guidelines of the Spanish Society of Hospital Pharmacists (SEFH). *Farmacia Hospitalaria*, *45*(2), 96-107.

Van Der Zee, D.-J., & Van Der Vorst, J. G. (2005). A modeling framework for supply chain simulation: Opportunities for improved decision making. *Decision sciences*, *36*(1), 65-95.

Van der Zee, D. (2006). Modeling decision making and control in manufacturing simulation. *International Journal of Production Economics*, *100*(1), 155-167.

Zhang, X. (2018). Application of discrete event simulation in health care: a systematic review. *BMC health services research*, *18*, 1-11.

AUTHOR BIOGRAPHIES

FATEMEH ALIDOOST is a PhD candidate at Business School of University of Exeter, UK. She has been awarded MRes + PhD scholarship from the Business School (completed MRes with distinction and received dean's commendation for exceptional performance). Her research is focused on healthcare supply chain. Her email address is fa418@exeter.ac.uk.

NAVONIL MUSTAFEE is a Professor of Analytics and Operations Management at the University of Exeter Business School, UK. His research focuses on M&S methodologies and Hybrid Modelling and their application in healthcare, supply chain management, circular economy and resilience and adaptation due to climate change. He is a Joint Editor-in-Chief of the Journal of Simulation (UK OR Society journal). His email address is n.mustafee@exeter.ac.uk.

THOMAS MONKS is an Associate Professor of Health Data Science at University of Exeter Medical School. His research interests include open science for computer simulation, urgent and emergency care, and real-time discrete-event simulation. His email address is t.m.w.monks@exeter.ac.uk.

ALISON HARPER is a lecturer in operations and analytics at the Centre for Simulation, Analytics and modeling, University of Exeter. Her research interests include applied health and social care modeling and simulation, real-time simulation, and reusable modeling in healthcare. Her email address is a.l.harper@exeter.ac.uk.

ALICE HARRISON is a registered Clinical Scientist working in Pharmacy Aseptic Services at Manchester University NHS Foundation Trust. She has received an MSc in Clinical Pharmaceutical Science from the University of Manchester, as well as an integrated Master of Chemistry (MChem) from the University of Leicester. Her research focused on improving the sustainability of hospital pharmacy aseptic units. Her email address is alice.harrison2@mft.nhs.uk.

Proceedings of the Operational Research Society Simulation Workshop 2025 (SW25)
M. Luis, A. Harper, T. Monks, N. Mustafee, eds.

https://doi.org/10.36819/SW25.039

EVALUATING THE IMPACT OF STAFFING RECOMMENDATIONS IN MATERNITY UNITS IN FRANCE

Louis Niffoi

Laboratoire de Génie Industriel,
CentraleSupélec
3 rue Joliot Curie, 91190 Gif-sur Yvette, France
louis.niffoi@centralesupelec.fr

Oualid Jouini

Laboratoire de Génie Industriel,
CentraleSupélec
3 rue Joliot Curie, 91190 Gif-sur Yvette, France
oualid.jouini@centralesupelec.fr

Marija Jankovic

Laboratoire de Génie Industriel,
CentraleSupélec
3 rue Joliot Curie, 91190 Gif-sur Yvette, France
marija.jankovic@centralesupelec.fr

Pierre-François Ceccaldi

Service de Gynécologie-Obstétrique et
Médecine de la reproduction, Hôpital Foch
40 rue Worth, 92150 Suresnes, France
pf.ceccaldi-carp@hopital-foch.com

Guillaume Lamé

Laboratoire de Génie Industriel,
CentraleSupélec
3 rue Joliot Curie, 91190 Gif-sur Yvette, France
guillaume.lame@centralesupelec.fr

ABSTRACT

Sufficient midwifery staff is crucial for the quality of maternity care. However, the shortage of staff that France has been facing for several decades creates situations of understaffing. In order to determine the required number of midwives in a given department, several guidelines have been presented in the literature. Yet, we lack evidence on how these guidelines affect quality of care. The main objective of this study is to evaluate staffing guidelines provided by legal texts and the scientific literature. To do so, we observed a French public hospital maternity and built a discrete-event simulation model. The simulation model reproduces the structure, staffing schedules and patient characteristics of the maternity. We use the continuous support ratio as our main performance metric, since it has been shown to have a positive impact on patient outcomes. This ratio measures the amount of time that a midwife is able to provide direct support to labouring women under their care. Using our simulation model, we analyse the impact of different staffing recommendations on quality of care measured by the continuous support ratio. The results highlight the impact of availability and staffing levels on continuous support during labour. As expected, decreasing staffing levels lead to lower values of the continuous support ratio, but adding midwives has diminishing returns. The simulation approach can support trade-offs between ample slack in resources, which ensures that continuous support is always feasible, and tight staffing levels that lead to high workload.

Keywords: Discrete-event simulation, Staffing levels, Maternity units

1 INTRODUCTION AND LITERATURE REVIEW

Ensuring sufficient staffing is crucial for hospitals in general and for delivery units in particular. Evidence that lack of maternity staff has detrimental effects on mothers and babies is accumulating. In perinatal death enquiries in the UK, understaffing was cited as a contributing factor in up to 25% of cases of stillbirths (Bradley N Manktelow et al., 2016). In understaffed units, professionals must prioritise tasks, which can be at the expense of measuring vital signs, providing emotional support, administering medication, and responding to emergencies (Simpson and Lyndon, 2017). In reverse, higher staffing levels lead to more physically intact deliveries (Sandall et al., 2014). In a recent systematic review, higher midwifery staffing levels were associated with less epidurals, less perineal damage at birth, less postpartum haemorrhage, less maternal readmission, and less neonatal resuscitation (Turner et al., 2021). Recent observational studies show that having more midwives reduces readmission rates (Turner et al., 2024) and harmful incidents (Turner et al., 2024), and improves the mother's experience of care (Turner et al., 2022).

In contrast, we have ample evidence of the benefits of 'continuous support' in labour, i.e., the presence of someone with the labouring mother at all time. Continuous support reduces the duration of labour and caesarean section rate (Hodnett et al., ; Bohren et al., 2017). To ensure continuous support, some countries even enforce a 'one-to-one care' policy in labour, meaning that a woman in labour should always have a midwife by her side. This is the case in the UK: "Maternity services develop the capacity for every woman to have a designated midwife to provide care for them when in established labour for 100% of the time." (Department of Health, 2004). They can provide psychological and physical support, information (especially on the progress of labour), and help assess the mother's needs. In France, the number of midwives that should be present in a delivery unit is stated in a decree from 1998, where staffing ratios are derived from annual numbers of birth (*Décret no 98-900*, 1998). One-to-one care in labour is not mentioned in French regulations or guidelines.

If maternity was a programmed activity, it would be possible to hire the precise number of midwives per room to obtain the desired continuous support ratio. However, most delivery care is actually unscheduled: aside from scheduled caesarean sections and, to a lesser extent, induced labours, the initiation of labor cannot be scheduled. In this situation, where a delivery unit could be empty in the evening and full the next morning, how many midwives should the department employ? If there were many midwives looking for work, and no constraint on budgets, one could simply say: enough to ensure the desired support ratio at all times. Of course, the reality is different, and somehow stark: midwives are leaving maternity units in many countries, trainees drop out before graduating, and supply doesn't keep up with demand. Therefore, choices must be made, so that the limited midwifery workforce is distributed across departments adequately.

In France, we have two main guidelines to calculate how many midwives a maternity unit should employ. The first one is a 1998 decree that sets minimum levels of staff that maternity units should have for unscheduled delivery care (*Décret no 98-900*, 1998). Based on the annual number of deliveries at the hospital, the decree sets a number of midwives to employ. These figures are not optima, they're only legal minima.

The second guideline was produced by national scientific societies in 2020, following expert consultation (Sentilhes et al., 2020). The breakdown of institutions is different from the one used in the decree, but the logic remains similar: based on the annual number of births, a staffing level is recommended for unscheduled maternity care.

In the article, maternities are divided into eight categories, and staffing levels are given for each category. In the decree, there are two cases. For certain professions, such as care managers, their presence is conditional on a certain number of births per year. For others, there is a linear correspondence between the number of births and the staffing levels. For example, it is mandatory to have a midwife at all time for 1,000 births, then a full-time midwife for every additional 200 births.

We are not aware of any empirical evaluation of these French guidelines. Elsewhere, a slightly more elaborate staffing method exists in the UK, the Birth Rate Plus tool. Endorsed by the Royal College of Midwives, the tool uses historical data, but each delivery is weighted based on the mother and the baby's characteristics, to account for factors that justify additional support in labour, and on the duration of labour.

Evidence for the effectiveness of the Birth Rate Plus is weak (Griffiths et al., 2024). Despite its refinement compared to French guidelines, a simulation study showed that Birth Rate Plus recommendations breached the British standard of one-to-one care 37% of the time (Allen and Thornton, 2013). More generally, maternity staffing deserves more attention (Turner et al., 2021).

In this study, we explore the relationship between midwifery staffing levels and continuous support in labour, in a French delivery unit. We model the birthing area of a French maternity and simulate its operation, taking into account midwives' availability for labour care and considering different levels of midwifery staffing. We show the impact of staffing on continuous support, as the number of midwives is positively correlated with continuous support. Then, we highlight the importance of taking availability into account, demonstrating the need to measure midwives' availability in order to build a realistic model.

2 METHODOLOGY

We worked with Hôpital Foch, Suresnes, France. Around 3,500 babies are born in the maternity every year, providing a sufficiently large sample. We built a discrete-even simulation model of the delivery unit, excluding pre- and post-natal care.

To understand the patient's journey and model the service in the most realistic way, we spent time directly in the maternity service at Hôpital Foch. We observed the operation of the service during half a day, and informally asked questions to midwives. The goal of these visits was two-fold. First, we needed to understand the patients' requirements from their perspective to enhance our knowledge of the process. Second, seeing the facilities enabled us to qualify and quantify the architecture of the service.

We defined two pathways. The first is for pregnant women that are going to give birth. The second is for women who come for unscheduled appointments, e.g. because of reduced fetal movements, but then leave the department without giving birth. The first steps of the paths are the same–welcome desk, then they see the reception and guidance nurse (RGN)–, and they use the same monitoring rooms. More importantly, they use common resources, such as the RGN and the emergency midwife. The rooms as well are shared by the two types of patients.

2.1 Pathway and Resources

When a woman comes into the unit, she is welcomed by an agent, then transferred to the reception and guidance nurse (RGN) (Figure 1). After the examination by the RGN, the woman is seen by the emergency midwife and taken to the monitoring room, for fetal heartrate monitoring. There are three phases in this room. At the beginning, the midwife has to be here to setup the monitoring device, and she has to be here at the end as well. Inbetween, there is no need for the midwife to stay.

When the monitoring is over, the woman can either be admitted or leave the service. In the first case, there are once again two possibilities. If she has a scheduled caesarean, she gets changed and goes to the surgical block. When she exits the block, she spends a bit of time in the post-interventional surveillance room (PISR), then leaves the service. If she does not have a scheduled caesarean, she goes to a delivery room. At any time, she can join the caesarean path. If she does not, she gives birth in the delivery room. After this, she normally stays in the room for surveillance, then leaves the system.

We modelled three types of resources: the RGN, the emergency midwife, and the delivery midwives. Obstetricians can be involved in deliveries, e.g. if concerns are escalated that require a medical opinion, or for instrumental deliveries. However, our study focuses on midwifery staffing, so we did not include obstetricians in the model.

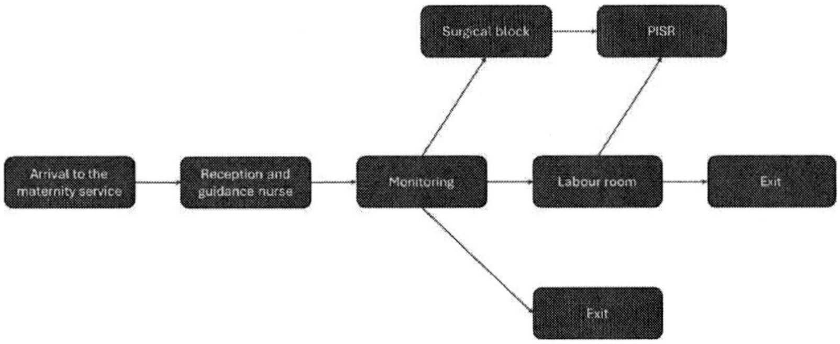

Figure 1 *Flowchart of the delivery suite*

The number of resources in the service is determined by internal policies, following French regulations. In this case, a single RGN and a single emergency midwife are present at all times. Delivery midwives work 12-hour shifts, from 8:00 am/pm to 8:00 am/pm. In practice, three midwives are present in birthing area at any time (a recent change from three during the day and two at night). This resource allocation constitutes our baseline scenario.

Rooms are also shared resources. The unit has three beds for monitoring, and nine delivery rooms. If all monitoring slots are taken, women wait; if all delivery rooms are taken, women are transferred to the post-interventional surveillance room (PISR). The room there is limited as well, only four places are available.

2.2 Model Parameters

2.2.1 Arrivals

We modelled two types of arrivals: women who will give birth, and women who won't (e.g., they came to check on reduced fetal movements). Arrivals were modelled using exponential laws, as they are considered unscheduled (although in reality this is not strictly the case, e.g. with inductions of labour).

We asked managers to provide information on how many patients were seen by the emergency midwife every day, and we used the annual number of births as well. Then, we were able to determine the daily number of arrivals in the two paths. We made the hypothesis that all days were similar, without weekday or seasonality effect. To model the arrivals distribution through the day, we asked once again the managers. It appears that two periods of the day are more busy than the rest from 8:00 a.m. to 10:00 a.m. and 6:00 p.m to 8:00 p.m. They correspond to patients that come to the hospital before going to work or after coming back from work. Concerning the rest of the time, managers agreed that daytime was busier than nighttime. A repartition was defined in accordance to these specificities, and was validated by the managers. Table 1 gives the precise distribution of the arrivals.

Table 1 *Distribution of patients arrivals throughout the day*

Hour	Attendance	Distribution for inter-arrival time between births (min)	Distribution for inter-arrival time between emergencies (min)
12:00 a.m. to 08:00 a.m.	Low	Exponential(210)	Exponential(79)
08:00 a.m. to 10:00 a.m.	High	Exponential(70)	Exponential(26.3)
10:00 a.m. to 6:00 p.m.	Medium	Exponential(140)	Exponential(42.6)
6:00 p.m. to 8:00 p.m.	High	Exponential(70)	Exponential(26.3)
8:00 p.m. to 12:00 a.m.	Medium	Exponential(140)	Exponential(42.6)

2.2.2 Routing

Routing probabilities are only needed at the end of the monitoring activity and during the labour activity. In practice, after monitoring, a woman can leave the system, have a scheduled caesarean, or go to the labour room. If she goes to the labour room, she can be transferred to surgical block at any time for an emergency caesarean. To determine the probability of each routing, we used information provided by the hospital.

2.2.3 Activity Durations

To determine the duration of each activity, we used experts' consultation. We interviewed three midwives and asked them for the duration of several steps in the process. We asked for the minimal duration, maximal duration, and the most probable value. Based on these interviews, we took the average of each value to build a triangular distribution. Table 2 synthetises the different activities and the associated distributions. The obtained values are estimates based on the midwives' knowledge of the system.

Table 2 *Distribution of activities' durations (min), based on experts' opinion*

Activity	Minimal value	Modal value	Maximal value
Reception and guidance nurse	10	15	25
Monitoring	40	60	80
Labour room	120	180	720
Surgical block	45	60	120

2.3 Output: Continuous Support

We considered the continuous support ratio defined at any time as:

$$Continuous\ support\ ratio = \frac{number\ of\ patients}{number\ of\ midwives}. \quad (1)$$

This ratio is inspired from the one-to-one care ratio (Allen and Thornton, 2013), but focuses on the ratio between midwives and patients, while the one-to-one care ratio gives the percentage of time where one-to-one is possible. It is possible to perform one-to-one care when the continuous support ratio is less or equal to one, which corresponds to a situation where there are as least as many midwives as mothers in the delivery unit. This ratio also provides further information, compared to the rate of one-to-one care. If the ratio is close to zero for a long time, there is a chance that the resource allocation is suboptimal because midwives are barely occupied. On the opposite, if the ratio takes great values such as three or more, this means that continuous support is impossible and the workload is high.

2.4 Model Validation

We implemented to model on the Simul8 discrete-event simulation software (Version: 30.0.0.4515). To ensure that the model aligned with reality, we observed the operation of the birthing area and took notes to model the patient's journey. We also collected information via informal discussions with midwives, in order to understand the steps where they intervene and their duration. Finally, we reviewed it with two of the department managers who agreed to take part in this process. Though they were not familiar with the software, the researcher detailed the whole process of admission and the different patients' paths, and the managers were asked to complete the list or correct it if needed. Following correspondence with them via email, the conceptual model was validated. Finally, midwives were asked to evaluate the coherence of the results regarding the main indicator (average time in system), and confirmed that this corresponds to the average time that patients spend in the birthing area.

We ran trial of runs with each run simulating 1 year. To determine the number of runs, the trial calculator of Simul8 was used. This tool gives the minimal number of runs required to satisfy a condition on the model's precision, regarding certain KPIs. We decided to choose a 5% precision on the model, as this value was used in literature (Baril et al., 2017). The main indicator of the model is the average time in the system, and Simul8's trial calculator suggested a minimum of 4 runs to obtain reliable results on this KPI. As the simulation ran quickly, we decided to conduct 10-run trials.

2.5 Experimentation

For each trial, two inputs varied: the number of delivery midwives and their availability. The main output was the support ratio, that was defined previously as the ratio between the number of patients and the number of midwives at all time in the service.

We assessed the impact of two parameters on the continuous support ratio: the number of midwives in the delivery unit, and their availability.

In all scenarios, we had one RGN and one emergency midwife, who were considered available 100% of the time. For delivery midwives, the current policy in Hôpital Foch is to have three midwives during day and night, and the previous one was to have three midwives during day and two during night. When modifying the number of midwives, we only tried two configurations: an equal number of midwives during day and night, or an additional midwife during day shifts compared to night shifts. We defined five possible configurations (Table 3).

Table 3 *Number of midwives in the different scenarios*

Scenario	Average number of midwives	Day shift	Night shift
1	2	2	2
2	2.5	3	2
3	3	3	3
4	3.5	4	3
5	4	4	4

The number of midwives is the main topic in this research, but having midwives who would be constantly busy with other tasks than supporting labouring women would be of little use. We needed to take into account the real availability for this key task, as accurate representation of resource availability can lead to huge differences in simulation results (Baril et al., 2017). Since we did not have figures on the distribution of midwives' working time between different tasks (direct care, documentation, administrative tasks…), we defined availability as an independent variable and tried different values.

We defined availability as the percentage of time where they are able to provide direct care to a patient, without being busy filling administrative forms or being called somewhere else. To obtain preliminary insights on the impact of competing tasks, we assessed five values for availability: 20%, 40%, 60%, 80% and 100%. Availability was defined stochastically (no predefined competing tasks), using Simul8's built-in 'availability' module.

3 RESULTS

3.1 Impact of the Number of Midwives

For a fixed availability, we varied the number of midwives in the birthing area from 2 (2 during day and night) to 4 (4 during day and night). The value 3.5 (respectively 2.5) represents the situation where there are 4 midwives (resp. 3) during day and 3 during night (resp 2). The results are presented in Figure 2.

The decree "périnatalité" (*Décret no 98-900*, 1998) gives legal minima to perform obstetrics, depending on the yearly number of births in the service. For Hôpital Foch (3500 births per year), it represents 13.5 full-time equivalent midwives. This corresponds to 2.8 midwives at all time in the service.

The second calculation method given in the literature (Sentilhes et al., 2020) also gives staffing recommendations depending on the number of births. These values are divided into categories. Between 3,000 and 4,500 births, it is recommended that 5.1 to 7.2 midwives are present in the service for unscheduled activity. For 3500 births, under the hypothesis that the relation between the number of births and midwives is affine, this corresponds to 5.8 midwives at all time.

Under the 100% availability hypothesis, there is an improvement of the support ratio when more midwives are added in the system. However, it has to be noted that the gap between 2.5 and 3 midwives is more important than the gaps between 3, 3.5 and 4 midwives. It seems that there is a point where adding midwives in the service is not as beneficial. This could create a suboptimal use of the resources, that would be more useful in another service. Moreover, this would decrease the cost/benefit ratio.

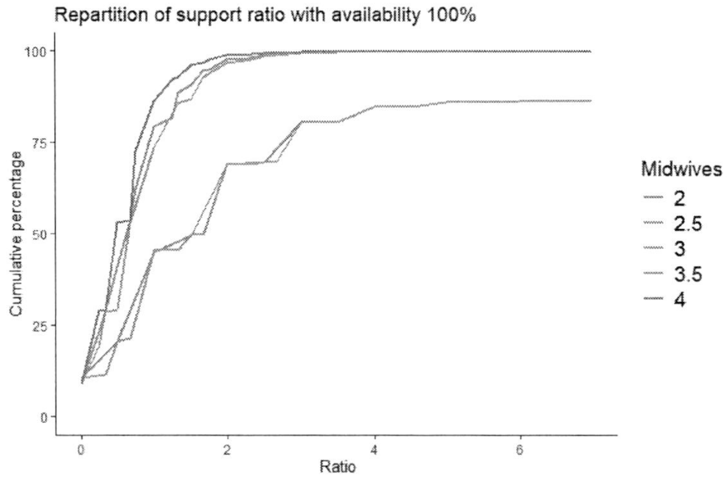

Figure 2 *Cumulative percentage of time spent by continuous support ratio, for different numbers of midwives in the unit, with 100% midwife availability*

This tendency also appears to be present for lower values of availability. Figure 3 shows the repartition of the support ratio for a 40% availability. Once again, the gain is maximal between 2.5 and 3 midwives. Independantly from midwives' availability, there is a point after which adding midwives becomes less and less beneficial (diminishing returns).

Another information provided by this figure is that the finite values of support ratio don't reach 100% of the total time. This means that there is a portion of time where this ratio is infinite, in other words there are no midwives available in the service to provide care to patients. In case the service has two midwives whose availability is 40%, this represents about 17% of the time. For the same availability but a total of four midwifes, it is only 9%.

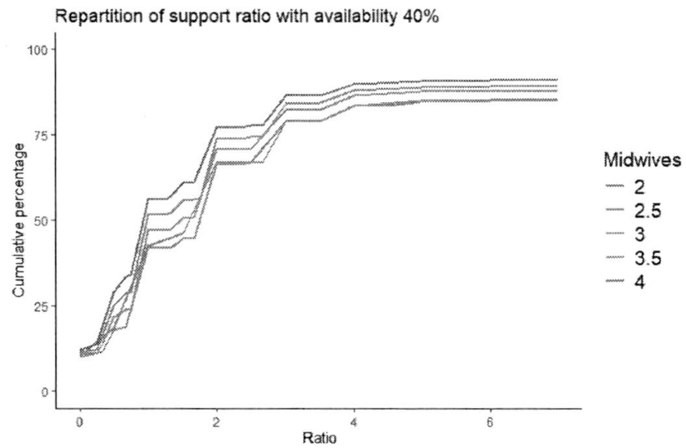

Figure 3 *Cumulative percentage of time spent by continuous support ratio, for different numbers of midwives in the unit, with 40% midwife availability*

3.2 Impact of Midwives' Availaibility

We are now interested in the impact of the availability of midwives, for a given staffing level. First, we focused on the current situation in Foch, with three midwives at all time, and another one with three midwives during night and four midwives during day. The first result shown by this graph is that availability has a strong impact on the support ratio. This is especially the case for low values of availability such as 20%, where the support ratio is infinite 31% of the time for a service with three midwives (0.05% for 100% availability).

It is noticeable that there is little difference in the lower values of the ratio between 40% and 60% availability. On the opposite, 20% appears to be extremely detrimental to the operation of the birthing unit. Although we don't know midwives actual availability, the literature suggests that around 15% of caregivers' time is spent on direct care with patient, and 15% is spent on indirect care (Leslie et al., 2021).

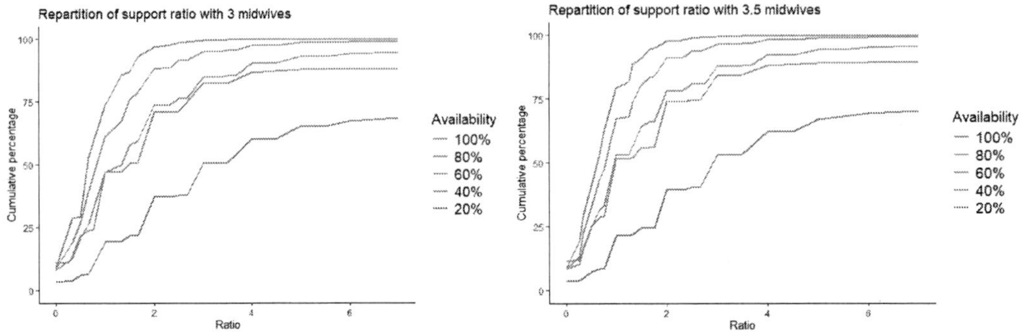

Figure 4 *Cumulative percentage of time spent by continuous support ratio, for different numbers of midwives in the unit, with 3 (left) and 3.5 (right) midwives, under different levels of midwife availability*

4 DISCUSSION

4.1 Summary

Using a simulation model and data based on experts' opinion, this study showed the consequences of different staffing policies on continuous support during childbirth. It also highlighted the importance of taking midwives' availability into account. Using different values of staffing and availability, we quantified the influence of staffing and midwives' tasks on the support ratio. As expected, continuous support and staffing are positively correlated, as are midwives' availability and continuous support. Our results align with a previous simulation study (Allen and Thornton, 2013). Even high levels of midwifery staff, under the hypothesis of full availability for direct care, cannot ensure one-to-one care.

The disparity between the results, depending on staff's availability, demonstrates the need for a precise modelling and quantification of midwives' tasks. It also calls into question the content of midwives' work, as time-studies in other healthcare professions show that direct care sometimes only occupies a fraction of working time, the rest being distributed between indirect care and administrative and other tasks. For example, Tipping et al. (2010) measured the repartition of hospitalists' time, concluding that only 17% of the time was spent on direct care, while the use of electronic medical record represents 34% of their time.

4.2 Strengths and Limitations

This study has several strengths. First, structural data based on a real French hospital were used, ensuring that the main steps in the patients' journey were respected. Then, the different distributions were determined using several experts' opinion. During the design phase, the whole model was validated as well by managers who work in this service, guaranteeing the adequation between the model and reality.

Our study also has limitations. First, we only focused on midwives. Even though midwives are central in the operation of a birthing unit, providing continuous support during labour may also be the role of nurses or nursing assistants. Their absence in the model lowers the number of people available to provide care, which has an incidence on the support ratio. Second, we used distributions obtained from interviews with experts. This gives less precision to the model than actual data from the hospital's databases, midwives being subjected to biases. It would be beneficial to obtain actual data, in order to fine-tune the distributions. Seasonal variability in the number of deliveries was not taken into account, despite being present in France (Régnier-Loilier and Rohrbasser, 2011). Finally, as previously mentioned, the exact activities of midwives are not well-known. We need to both qualify and quantify their work, to better understand of it affects the support ratio. In this study, we chose different values for midwives' availability, but further research could help understand the repartition and the duration of their tasks.

4.3 Future Work

In order to tackle some limitations of this study, we plan on developing further perspectives. Three main projects are planned so far.

The first plan is to have access to real data from the hospital. Using the databases of Hôpital Foch, we will be able to fine-tune the different distributions and arrivals. In particular, this will give a better understanding of the frequency and the repartition of arrivals throughout the day, and throughout the year. In addition, the duration of each step in the patient's path will be clarified.

To have a better representation of the situation in France, we plan on doing the same work in several hospitals, using their data to fit distributions.

Finally, in order to qualify and quantify midwives' activity, we will conduct a time-and-motion study in these three maternity units. This will give a more accurate view of the availibity of midwives, and the repartition of their tasks during the day.

REFERENCES

Allen, M., Thornton, S., 2013. Providing one-to-one care in labour. Analysis of "Birthrate Plus" labour ward staffing in real and simulated labour ward environments. BJOG Int. J. Obstet. Gynaecol. 120, 100–107. https://doi.org/10.1111/j.1471-0528.2012.03483.x

Baril, C., Gascon, V., Miller, J., Bounhol, C., 2017. The importance of considering resource's tasks when modeling healthcare services with discrete-event simulation: an approach using work sampling method. J. Simul. 11, 103–114. https://doi.org/10.1057/jos.2016.6

Bohren, M.A., Hofmeyr, G.J., Sakala, C., Fukuzawa, R.K., Cuthbert, A., 2017. Continuous support for women during childbirth. Cochrane Database Syst. Rev. 7, CD003766. https://doi.org/10.1002/14651858.CD003766.pub6

Bradley N Manktelow, Lucy K Smith, Sarah E Seaton, Pauline Hyman-Taylor, Jennifer J Kurinczuk, David J Field, Peter W Smith, Elizabeth S Draper, 2016. MBRRACE-UK Perinatal Mortality Surveillance Report UK Perinatal Deaths for Births from January to December 2014. MBRRACE-UK, Department of Health Sciences, University of Leicester.

Décret no 98-900, 1998.

Department of Health, 2004. Maternity Standard, National Service Framework for Children, Young People and Maternity Services.

Griffiths, P., Turner, L., Lown, J., Sanders, J., 2024. Evidence on the use of Birthrate Plus® to guide safe staffing in maternity services – A systematic scoping review. Women Birth 37, 317–324. https://doi.org/10.1016/j.wombi.2023.11.003

Hodnett, E.D., Gates, S., Hofmeyr, G.J., Sakala, C., 2012. Continuous support for women during childbirth. Cochrane Database Syst. Rev. https://doi.org/10.1002/14651858.CD003766.pub4

Leslie, H.H., Laos, D., Cárcamo, C., Pérez-Cuevas, R., García, P.J., 2021. Health care provider time in public primary care facilities in Lima, Peru: a cross-sectional time motion study. BMC Health Serv. Res. 21, 123. https://doi.org/10.1186/s12913-021-06117-9

Régnier-Loilier, A., Rohrbasser, J.-M., 2011. Y a-t-il une saison pour faire des enfants ?: Popul. Sociétés N° 474, 1–4. https://doi.org/10.3917/popsoc.474.0001

Sandall, J., Murrells, T., Dodwell, M., Gibson, R., Bewley, S., Coxon, K., Bick, D., Cookson, G., Warwick, C., Hamilton-Fairley, D., 2014. The efficient use of the maternity workforce and the implications for safety and quality in maternity care: a population-based, cross-sectional study. Health Serv. Deliv. Res. 2, 1–266. https://doi.org/10.3310/hsdr02380

Sentilhes, L., Galley-Raulin, F., Boithias, C., Sfez, M., Goffinet, F., Le Roux, S., Benhamou, D., Garnier, J.-M., Paysant, S., Bounan, S., Michel, C., Coudray, J., Rozé, J.-C., Elleboode, B.,

Ducloy-Bouthors, A.-S., 2020. Staffing needs for unscheduled activity in obstetrics and gynecology. Eur. J. Obstet. Gynecol. Reprod. Biol. 245, 19–25. https://doi.org/10.1016/j.ejogrb.2019.11.020

Simpson, K.R., Lyndon, A., 2017. Consequences of Delayed, Unfinished, or Missed Nursing Care during Labor and Birth. J. Perinat. Neonatal Nurs. 31, 32–40. https://doi.org/10.1097/JPN.0000000000000203

Tipping, M.D., Forth, V.E., O'Leary, K.J., Malkenson, D.M., Magill, D.B., Englert, K., Williams, M.V., 2010. Where did the day go?--a time-motion study of hospitalists. J. Hosp. Med. 5, 323–328. https://doi.org/10.1002/jhm.790

Turner, L., Ball, J., Culliford, D., Kitson-Reynolds, E., Griffiths, P., 2022. Exploring the relationship between women's experience of postnatal care and reported staffing measures: An observational study. PloS One 17, e0266638. https://doi.org/10.1371/journal.pone.0266638

Turner, L., Ball, J., Meredith, P., Kitson-Reynolds, E., Griffiths, P., 2024. The association between midwifery staffing and reported harmful incidents: a cross-sectional analysis of routinely collected data. BMC Health Serv. Res. 24, 391. https://doi.org/10.1186/s12913-024-10812-8

Turner, L., Griffiths, P., Kitson-Reynolds, E., 2021. Midwifery and nurse staffing of inpatient maternity services - A systematic scoping review of associations with outcomes and quality of care. Midwifery 103, 103118. https://doi.org/10.1016/j.midw.2021.103118

Turner, L.Y., Saville, C., Ball, J., Culliford, D., Dall'Ora, C., Jones, J., Kitson-Reynolds, E., Meredith, P., Griffiths, P., 2024. Inpatient midwifery staffing levels and postpartum readmissions: a retrospective multicentre longitudinal study. BMJ Open 14, e077710. https://doi.org/10.1136/bmjopen-2023-077710

AUTHOR BIOGRAPHIES

LOUIS NIFFOI is a PhD candidate at Laboratoire de Génie Industriel, CentraleSupélec, France.

OUALID JOUINI is a professor at Laboratoire de Génie Industriel, CentraleSupélec, France.

MARIJA JANKOVIC is a professor at Laboratoire de Génie Industriel, CentraleSupélec, France.

PIERRE-FRANÇOIS CECCALDI is a gynaecologist-obstetrician at Hôpital Foch, Suresnes, France.

GUILLAUME LAMÉ is a researcher at Laboratoire de Génie Industriel, CentraleSupélec, France.

Proceedings of the Operational Research Society Simulation Workshop 2025 (SW25)
M. Luis, A. Harper, T. Monks and N. Mustafee, eds.
https://doi.org/10.36819/SW25.040

SIMULATION MODELLING OF DELAYED DISCHARGE FROM HOSPITAL

Dr Ranga P. Abeysooriya

Centre for Operational Research,
Management Science
and Information Systems (CORMSIS)
University of Southampton
Southampton, SO17 1BJ, United Kingdom
r.p.abeysooriya@soton.ac.uk

Ms Nirmani Amarasinghe
Dr Laura Boyle

Mathematical Sciences Research Centre
Queen's University Belfast
Belfast, BT7 1NN, United Kingdom
namarasinghe01@qub.ac.uk
laura.boyle@qub.ac.uk

Prof Christine S.M. Currie
Dr Carlos Lamas-Fernandez

Centre for Operational Research,
Management Science
and Information Systems (CORMSIS)
University of Southampton
Southampton, SO17 1BJ, United Kingdom
christine.currie@soton.ac.uk
c.lamas-fernandez@soton.ac.uk

ABSTRACT

Delayed discharge happens when patients remain in hospital despite being medically fit for discharge. This situation negatively impacts patients for example through loss of mobility and independence, and creates operational difficulties for hospitals, such as reduced bed availability. This study presents a discrete event simulation model of the hospital discharge process in England's NHS, where patients are discharged to one of four pathways. The aim is to create a simulation model that tackles both capacity-related and non-capacity-related discharge delays and identifies the acceptance probability of difficult-to-place patients along with the estimations of their daily discharge capacities at four discharge pathways. The model captures the proportion of delayed patients who are considered to be difficult to place in onwards care and might be still delayed even when there is onward care capacity available. The simulation model is parameterised using published NHS England data. Two of the parameters were not known from the data and an optimisation approach is presented to estimate their value. We describe the model and computational experiments applied to five large NHS Foundation Trusts in the South East region of England. We fit the model both globally (for all five trusts) and locally (for each trust individually). The findings show that locally fitted parameters best match the data, revealing variations in patient placement challenges across trusts.

Keywords:

Discrete Event Simulation, Delayed discharge, Social care

1 INTRODUCTION

Delayed discharge from hospital happens when a patient is discharged after they are medically optimised[1]. This has a negative impact on patients, who face an increased risk of acquiring infections and may

[1] https://www.nuffieldtrust.org.uk/resource/delayed-discharges-from-hospital

experience declines in mobility and independence. Additionally, discharge delays reduce the availability of hospital beds, which can lead to longer ambulance handover times and delays in admitting patients from the emergency department[2]. This also creates a significant financial cost to the NHS.

Delayed discharge happens for a variety of reasons. Much of the delay is directly related to the available capacity in community care (for example 'awaiting availability of a bed in a residential or nursing home that is likely to be a permanent placement', 'awaiting availability of resource for assessment and start of care at home', and 'awaiting community equipment and adaptations to housing'). Some of the delays are not directly related to capacity, and might be attributed to other areas such as discharge processes or wellbeing concerns. In fact, in August 2024 the patients delayed over 14 days in England directly linked to a capacity problem amounted to only 35.4% . There are a number of reasons here, some might be linked to hospital processes, and some to patient circumstances (for example 'individual/family not in agreement with discharge plans' and 'homeless/no right of recourse to public funds/no place to discharge to') (NHS England 2024a).

The key contribution of this work is in developing a discrete event simulation model for both the delays that are directly related to capacity in community care, as well as the delays that are not directly related to capacity, for example lack of family agreement. This is achieved through identifying the proportion of patients in the population who are 'difficult to place' and estimating their daily probability of being processed for discharge. The study also makes novel use of NHS England published statistics on delayed discharge (NHS England 2024a). Two of the model parameters were not available from the data and a fitting procedure is developed to estimate them using the simulation. This paper is applied to the largest five hospitals of NHS Foundation Trusts in the South East region of England. Future work will consider the model applied to all NHS England hospitals.

Section 2 discusses the existing literature on modelling delayed discharge from hospital. Section 3 outlines the problem setting, the discrete event simulation model logic and introduces the algorithms for estimating unknown parameters. Section 4 introduces the data then details the parameterisation and implementionation of the simulation model. The results of fitting a single combination of parameters to all trusts (global fitting) and a combination of parameters for each trust (local fitting) are presented and discussed. The model with local fitting is applied to assess the impact of reducing discharge delays for difficult to place patients. Section 5 concludes and discusses future research directions.

2 LITERATURE REVIEW

The majority of delayed discharge simulation studies focus the impact of delayed discharge on downstream hospital units, without modelling the hospital link to community care. For example, (Qin et al. 2017) developed a discrete event simulation (DES) of an Australian hospital. The model was used to determine the impact of different hospital discharge strategies (such as allowing patients to be discharged at any time of the day) on the hospital's occupancy level. (Wong et al. 2010) used system dynamics to model a hospital in Canada, showing that smoothing out hospital discharges over the course of a week had a reduced bed requirements and emergency department length of stay. These studies did not model the link between hospital and community care, so the hospital discharge improvement strategies may not be feasible due to a lack of capacity in community care.

Focusing on the link between hospital and community care, Patrick et al. (2015) developed a DES of flow between hospital and community care in Canada. The model was formulated as an inventory management problem and incorporated patient preferences. Harper et al. (2021) modelled the process of hospital discharge to step-down community care, focusing on determining the optimal capacity of step-down care to minimise the cost of delayed discharge and under-utilised services. Onen-Dumlu et al. (2022) extended this model to determine appropriate capacity in three types of step-down intermediate community care in the UK NHS. All three studies represented capacity as the available number of beds or community care visits.

One limitation of these models is they assume a patient can be discharged from hospital if capacity is available in community care. Patients cannot always be discharged even if capacity is available, due to reasons such as disagreements with patients and families about the care placements and waits for equipment to be installed at home (NHS England 2024a). Boyle et al. (2023) developed a DES of delayed discharge that modelled the flow of patients from hospital to community care using a probability

[2]https://www.health.org.uk/publications/long-reads/why-are-delayed-discharges-from-hospital-increasing-seeing-the-bigger

of acceptance, rather than using a capacity. The study considered discharge to both intermediate and long-term NHS care, and modelled the concept of 'difficult to place' patients, who have a lower probability of being accepted to an onwards community care placement.

This paper builds on the previous research to consider the hospital discharge process as multi-faceted. Patients who are straightforward to place are modelled using the available capacity in community care, and a different process is introduced to model 'difficult to place' patients that does not directly depend on capacity. The study uses open source data published by NHS England to parameterise the model. A fitting procedure is introduced to estimate two parameters that are not available from the data.

3 METHODOLOGY

3.1 Problem description

The entry point of the model is the point at which hospital patients become medically fit for discharge (where we do not model the previous hospital stay). The exit point of the model is discharge to one of four pathways as described in the NHS England discharge to assess model (NHS England 2024b).

We consider that a proportion of delayed patients are 'difficult to place' in community care. They have a daily probability of being processed for discharge on any given day. If they are not accepted for discharge processing, they enter a delay state with a fixed duration of 1 day, until they can be considered for discharge processing again. Once patients are processed for discharge, they enter a queue for one of four pathways (NHS England 2024b):

- Pathway 0 – discharges home or to a usual place of residence with no new or additional health and/or social care needs;
- Pathway 1: discharges home or to a usual place of residence with new or additional health and/or social care needs;
- Pathway 2: discharges to a community bed-based setting which has dedicated recovery support. New or additional health and/or social care and support is required in the short-term to help the person recover in a community bed-based setting before they are ready to either live independently at home or receive longer-term or ongoing care and support;
- Pathway 3: discharges to a new residential or nursing home setting, for people who are considered likely to need long-term residential or nursing home care. Should be used only in exceptional circumstances.

Patients might still enter a virtual queue when there is capacity available if the are classed as difficult to place, this is the mechanism used to capture non-capacity related delays in our simulation. This means, that patients might also queue when they are discharged to Pathway 0 (which has no capacity issues), for example if there are issues in their discharge process.

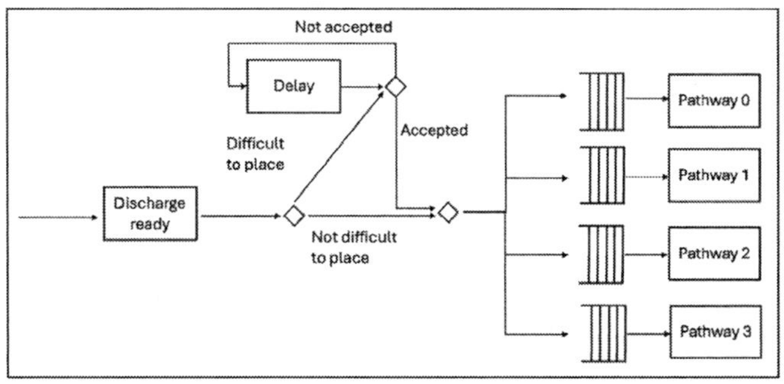

***Figure 1.** A conceptual model of the delayed discharge simulation.*

3.2 Simulation model

The simulation model was developed using the SimPy package in Python and follows the process in Figure 1, where the model entry point is the time at which patients are discharge ready and the exit points are departure to one of the four NHS England pathways (0-3).

Four resources are used to limit the capacity in each of pathways 0-3. If there are no spaces in the pathway, patients will join one of four queues for each of the pathways. Once a patient seizes a resource, they use it for 1 day before releasing it again, creating a daily availability of capacity in each of the discharge pathways. The resources have variable capacity, which changes daily. The range of daily capacity is estimated from the data, where the probability mass function of minimum and maximum capacity is derived from monthly discharge data on each pathway. While the maximum capacity is likely to represent a maximum (we assume that, for some months, some patients could not be discharged in a timely manner because of capacity issues), the minimum observed capacity is unlikely to have been a binding constraint (we assume that, for some months, the community had more capacity than the demand required by the hospital). To account for this, the simulation does not sample from the entire range, but only from values equal or higher to the c_0^{th} percentile. The parameter c_0 is fitted using the procedure of Section 3.3. It is assumed that there is no interaction between the pathways e.g. if a patient is queueing for Pathway 2 they cannot switch to Pathway 1. The delay state for difficult to place patients has a duration of 1 day and the capacity in this state is assumed to be unlimited.

Attributes are assigned to each patient and used for routing in the model. 'Difficult to place' is a binary attribute indicating whether a patient will experience difficulties in accessing care. The proportion of difficult to place patients is estimated from data. The 'pathway' attribute has four values, assigning patients to one of Pathway 0, Pathway 1, Pathway 2, or Pathway 3. The probability of belonging to pathways is estimated combining datasets which include discharge totals data with numbers of long-staying delayed patients for whom a pathway has been determined.

The 'probability of acceptance' parameter, which we denote by ρ, represents the daily probability of being processed for discharge on any given day. This is not recorded in data and is therefore unknown. We estimate the value of 'probability of acceptance' using the fitting process outlined in Section 3.3. For a given probability of acceptance, the length of delay attributed to this part of the simulation can be sampled by using a geometric distribution with a success probability equal to the probability of acceptance.

The key metric for the model is the empirical cumulative distribution function (ECDF) of delayed discharge time. Since the model entry point is the time when patients are discharge ready, all the time spent by patients in the model is delayed discharge time. The ECDF is characterised by seven points which we denote as the set D: patients with no delay, patients with delay up to 1, 3, 6, 13 and 20, and patients delayed 21 days or more. This is in line with the data nationally reported (NHS England 2024a).

3.3 Parameter fitting

The simulation model described in the previous section required estimating two parameters, the acceptance probability for difficult to place patients ρ, and the minimum percentile for sampling capacity c_0. This section presents a way of fitting the model output to the ECDF data available for each hospital, where the data available comprises the proportion of patients delayed w_{dh} for $d = 1, \ldots, D$ durations for each hospital $h, h = 1, \ldots, H$ in the dataset. We performed Algorithm 1 to find the ECDFs of the differences between each simulation run and the mean of the simulation output and Algorithm 2 to compare these with the data.

Line 7 in Algorithm 2 is used to break ties between parameters for which p'_{dh} is over one (ie. the real data deviates from the simulation mean more than any of the replications). In that case, we compared the deviation of the data to the median deviation observed during the simulation, and used the relative difference as a guide for the optimisation. We note that the value of $p_{dh} = 1 - p'_{dh}$ can be interpreted as the probability of simulation runs deviating from the simulation mean equally or more than the observed data, which is similar to a p value. When this value is below 0.05 we can conclude that only 5% of the simulation runs tested have deviated more from the simulation mean than the observed data, and hence the probability of the simulation being an accurate representation of the real data is low.

Algorithm 1: Pseudocode for setting up the simulated distributions for each comparator

---

for $h = 1$ **to** H **do**
  Simulate I replications from the simulation model
  for $d = 1$ **to** D **do**
    Find $\tilde{w}_{idh}$, the proportion of patients delayed for each replication $i = 1, \ldots, I$
    Calculate the mean proportion of patients delayed $\bar{w}_{dh}$
    Find the differences between the mean and the individual values for each replication, $\tilde{\delta}_{idh} = |\tilde{w}_{idh} - \bar{w}_{dh}|$
    Order the $\tilde{\delta}_{idh}$ in non-decreasing order
    Set the function $\tilde{F}_{dh}$ to be the ECDF of the δ_{idh}

Result: The set of $\tilde{F}_{dh}$ for $d = 1, \ldots, D; h = 1, \ldots, H$

Algorithm 2: Pseudocode for finding the overall model fit

Data: The set of $\tilde{F}_{dh}$ for $d = 1, \ldots, D; h = 1, \ldots, H$; observed proportion of patients delayed for each duration and each hospital, w_{dh}

for $h = 1$ **to** H **do**
  for $d = 1$ **to** D **do**
    Find the difference between the observed proportion and the mean proportion from the simulation model, $\delta_{dh} = |w_{dh} - \bar{w}_{dh}|$
    if $\tilde{F}_{dh}(\delta_{dh}) < 1$ **then**
      $p'_{dh} \leftarrow \tilde{F}_{dh}(\delta_{dh})$
    else
      $p'_{dh} \leftarrow 1 \frac{\delta_{dh}}{\tilde{F}_{dh}^{-1}(0.5)}$

Result: fit $\leftarrow \sum_{h=1}^{H} \sum_{d=1}^{D} p'_{dh}$

---

4 COMPUTATIONAL EXPERIMENTS

In this section we describe the implementation of the simulation model, and we parametrise it and fit the parameters ρ and c_0 for five hospitals. We further explore the fitted models to see how sensitive they are to the acceptance probability of difficult to place patients, ρ.

4.1 Data Analysis

We parameterise the model for the largest five hospitals of NHS Foundation Trusts in the South East region of England. They are University Hospital Southampton (RHM), University Hospitals Sussex (RYR), Frimley Health (RDU), East Kent Hospitals University (RVV) and Portsmouth Hospitals University (RHU). We denote this set by H. A list with their key statistics is shown in Table 1.

Table 1. *Key Statistics for hospitals in H*

Trust	Code	Beds[1]	Average Discharge ready per day						
			Mon	Tue	Wed	Thu	Fri	Sat	Sun
University Hospital Southampton	RHM	1087.5	148.56	158.81	169.94	159.90	184.85	108.74	79.75
University Hospitals Sussex	RYR	1756.2	261.94	311.15	312.65	306.00	330.23	205.53	161.19
Frimley Health	RDU	1331.2	115.25	164.69	161.12	160.90	171.53	94.85	75.58
East Kent Hospitals University	RVV	1105.6	91.12	119.40	110.73	122.96	121.74	80.91	60.19
Portsmouth Hospitals University	RHU	1104.7	132.33	145.98	143.50	141.50	152.45	84.40	60.40

[1]Average number of available general & acute beds.

Datasets are available for different time periods based on when data collection began; for our analysis, we used routinely collected data, made publicly available by the NHS and published between June 2023 and May 2024.

Arrivals: By utilizing NHS published statistics regarding the count of patients who no longer satisfy the criteria to reside and the number of patients who were or were not discharged on each day, we compute the average arrival rates for each day of the week. For every day, a random quantity of arrivals is generated through a Poisson distribution, which is based on that day's average arrival rate. This number presents count of patients entering for discharge and they are reported in Table 1.

Pathway capacity data: NHS England releases monthly data providing the total number of patients discharged each month according to their intended discharge destination, categorised by their intended discharge destination for pathways 0, 1, 2, and 3, which were used to estimate the available capacities per day at each pathway. We estimated daily discharge capacity from the data, and calculated a set of values ranging from the smallest to the largest daily capacity available for each pathway. We then constructed the ECDF for pathway i, denoted by C_i. The inverse of this function allowed us to sample capacity, ie. $C_i^{-1}(x)$, $x \in [0,1]$ provides a random sampling mechanism for daily capacity following the observed data. As described in Section 3.2 we assumed that while the maximum capacity is likely to represent an upper limit on capacity, the lower end of the distribution is not necessarily a constraint on actual capacity, but rather might be related to periods of time where demand was lower than capacity. To account for this fact, we used the parameter c_0, to limit the sampling to values larger to the c_0^{th} percentile. That is, we sampled using $C_i^{-1}(x)$, $x \in [c_0, 1]$. The value of parameter c_0 is estimated in Section 4.2.

Difficult-to-place proportions for pathways: The NHS provides monthly statistics regarding patients who have been hospitalised for more than 14 days and no longer satisfies residency requirements but remain undischarged, classified according to the reasons for their continued stay, which include pathway 1, 2, 3, and "other." Patients categorised as "other" includes pending discharge summaries, tests, medications, transportation, or may lack a discharge plan altogether. We assume that these patients can be assigned to pathways based on discharge rates. Consequently, the tally for each pathway includes both those awaiting discharge and those classified as "other." To determine the proportion of patients that are difficult to place for each pathway, we analysed the number of patients waiting for a pathway in relation to those who have been discharged plus those still waiting. We derived these proportions by taking the mean proportion of each pathway as denoted (see. Table 2), as the data exhibited minimal fluctuations over time.

Table 2. Pathways Statistics: Average Capacities, Proportions and Difficult to Place Proportions

Code	Capacities (per day)				Pathways Proportions				Difficult to Place Proportions			
	P0	P1	P2	P3	P0	P1	P2	P3	P0	P1	P2	P3
RHM	126.79	11.45	5.24	5.22	0.839	0.083	0.040	0.038	0.012	0.104	0.139	0.124
RHU	91.14	20.27	6.70	2.19	0.749	0.170	0.058	0.023	0.014	0.030	0.061	0.234
RYR	252.48	16.51	8.75	3.81	0.871	0.067	0.045	0.017	0.001	0.161	0.337	0.273
RDU	100.51	15.94	3.44	4.89	0.783	0.137	0.032	0.048	0.020	0.085	0.110	0.216
RVV	82.77	12.80	4.42	7.97	0.744	0.125	0.047	0.084	0.001	0.088	0.166	0.155

4.2 Fitting

We focused on fitting two parameters, namely, the probability of acceptance of difficult to place patients, ρ, and c_0. We performed a grid search, where a discrete sample of parameter combinations was evaluated using the fitness function returned by Algorithm 2.

The values tested are all combinations produced by choosing parameters as:

- $\rho \in \{\frac{1}{n}, n = 1, ..., 10\}$
- $c_0 = 0.0, 0.1, ..., 0.8$

For ρ, the value of n represents the mean value (in days) of extra delay that difficult to place patients will experience. For c_0, we considered equally spaced sampling between the full capacity range and starting at the 80th of the maximum capacity. For each parameter combination and each trust, we ran 25 replications of a simulated year. We performed two different fitting experiments. A global fitting where we select a single combination of parameters ρ and c_0 for all trusts (Global fitting) and a local fitting, where we fit a combination of parameters ρ^h and c_0^h for each trust $h \in H$. For the latter, Algorithms 1 and 2 are used in the same way, but the set H is restricted to the trust being evaluated.

Global fitting: The global fitting found the best parameters to be $\rho = 0.14$ and $c_0 = 0.3$. The results of the p_{dh} data are reported on Table 3.

Table 3. Probability of simulation runs deviating from the simulation mean equally or more than the observed data (p_{dh}), with globally fitted parameters $\rho = 0.14$ and $c_0 = 0.3$. The column headers represent the point being fitted, eg. ECDF_0 is the proportion of patients with no delay, ECDF_1 represents the proportion of patients delayed 1 day, etc.

	ECDF_0	ECDF_1	ECDF_1-3	ECDF_4-6	ECDF_7-13	ECDF_14-20
RHM	0.0	0.0	0.04	0.04	0.04	0.04
RYR	0.16	0.84	0.48	0.12	0.0	0.0
RDU	0.0	0.0	0.0	0.0	0.0	0.0
RVV	0.0	0.0	0.0	0.0	0.0	0.0
RHU	0.04	0.64	0.56	1.0	0.12	0.0

While for some of the trusts a few values of the observed data fell within the range observed in the deviation (eg. RYR, RHU), in general the simulation model is unable to accurately represent any of the trusts' delay profiles consistently. The approximation of the ECDF is shown in Figure 2. During the fitting process, the latest value of set D is not included in fitting calculations, since it is consistently 1. Note that these plots are not the true ECDF, but rather represent an interpolation of the ECDF values based on the estimations of the values from D. While in general the simulation model retrieves the shape of the ECDF, for two of the trusts (RDU, RVV) the fit is particularly poor, as indicated by the low p_{dh} values.

Local fitting: In this experiment, we fit ρ and c_0 independently for each hospital. While this increases considerably the number of parameters, it can help identify the particularities of each trust. For example, the local demographics might have an influence on the delay experienced by difficult to place patients, and the value of ρ. Equally, the local balance demand and offer of community care in the region impacts how accurate a representation of the capacity is the number of discharged patients in each pathway, regulated by c_0. The results of this fitting are presented in Table 4.

Table 4. *Best parameters and probability of simulation runs deviating from the simulation mean equally or more than the observed data, with parameters fitted locally. The column headers represent the point being fitted, eg. ECDF_0 is the proportion of patients with no delay, ECDF_1 represents the proportion of patients delayed 1 day, etc.*

	ρ	c_0	ECDF_0	ECDF_1	ECDF_1_3	ECDF_4-6	ECDF_7-13	ECDF_14-20
RHM	0.09	0.1	0.04	0.32	0.52	0.92	0.76	0.68
RYR	0.33	0.7	0.92	0.04	0.04	0.76	0.0	0.0
RDU	0.50	0.8	0.08	0.32	0.6	0.8	0.76	1.0
RVV	0.13	0.0	0.04	0.84	1.0	0.88	0.76	0.64
RHU	0.33	0.2	0.12	0.44	0.88	1.0	0.52	0.08

As expected, the simulation was more accurate across the board. In particular, for two trusts (RDU, RHU) all the p_{dh} values were over the 0.05 threshold, and for two further trusts (RHM, RVV) only one value was under the threshold. We also observe that the values of c_0 seem to fall in two groups, either on the lower or the upper end. A visualisation of the interpolated ECDF values for the observed vs simulated data is shown on Figure 2.

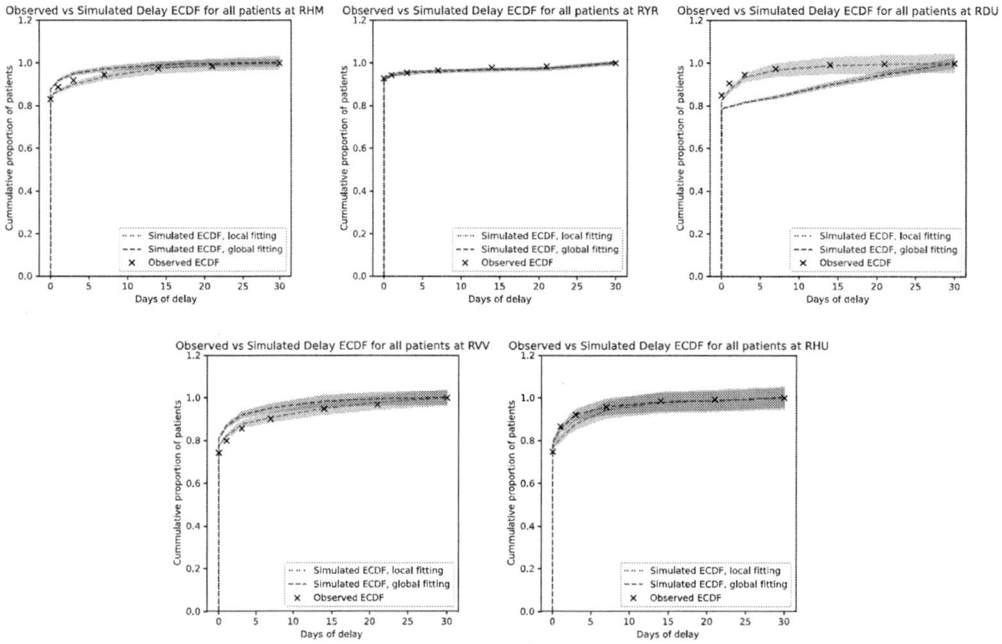

Figure 2. *Interpolated ECDF line for the values in D, both for simulation and observed data, when parameters are fitted locally.*

4.3 Varying acceptance probability

One action acute trusts might consider in order to reduce delays on discharge is to focus on difficult to place patients. Early planning or special discharge teams might be effective in achieving a higher rate of acceptance probability (ρ). To evaluate the potential of such interventions, we used the locally fitted models and conducted two runs, one with the locally fitted value of ρ_h, and one run assuming the perfect scenario where patients were always accepted ($\rho = 1$). For each experiment we conducted 25 simulation replications, and we report the ECDFs of delay, shown in Figure 3

As expected, the trusts that had a lower fitted ρ_h (RHM and RVV) showed the highest variation. Overall, the effect of ρ seemed to be limited, suggesting that most of the model variation on delay was produced by inadequate onward capacity.

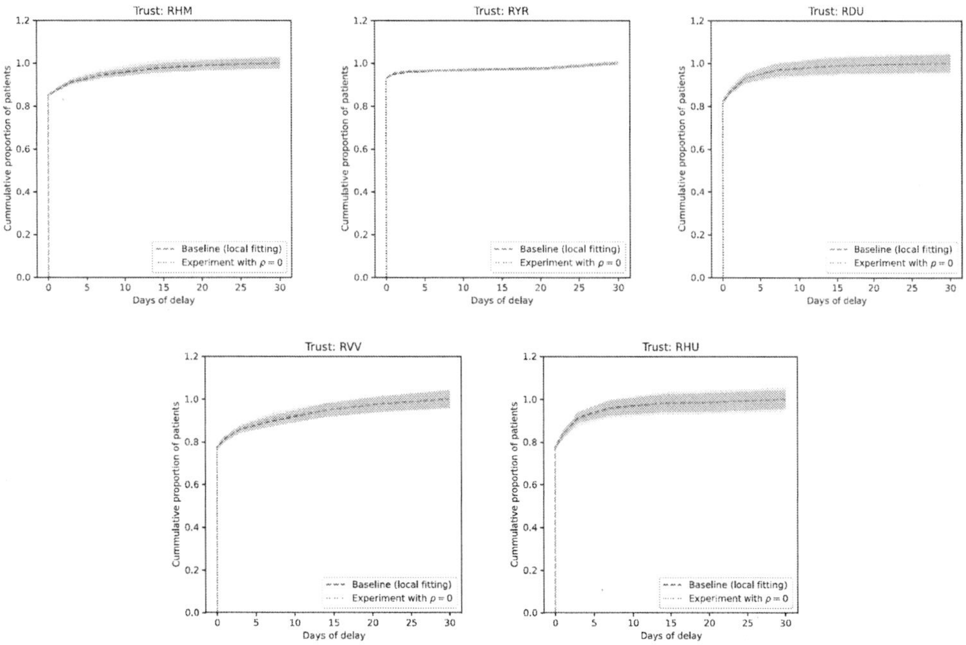

Figure 3. ECDF results when waiving the acceptance probability of difficult to place patients.

5 CONCLUSION

This paper presented a discrete event simulation model to investigate delayed hospital discharges based on the four pathways outlined in NHS England's discharge to assess framework. In our model, delay is caused by both downstream capacity constraints *and* non-capacity related difficulties in discharging patients. Another advantage of this approach is that it uses routinely published open-source NHS England data. We also presented an optimisation algorithm to estimate the value of unknown parameters from the simulation output.

The model was tested on data from the five largest hospitals within the South East England NHS Foundation Trusts. Parameter estimation for the unknown variables ρ and c_0 was conducted both globally (estimating a single value across all five hospitals) and locally (estimating independent values for each hospital). The experiment showed that locally fitted parameters provided the best match to the observed data, highlighting variations in the challenges of patient placement in downstream care across different trusts. The simulation model achieved a better fit to some trusts than others. This will be investigated further in future work. The best fitted simulation model was used to experiment with reducing discharge delays for difficult to place patients. Again, the results highlighted variations in the effect of this intervention across different trusts, despite being overall limited. Future work will explore fitting the model to a broader set of hospitals varying in size and location as well as validating the fitting in unseen data, therefore improving its generalisability and reducing the risk of overfitting. Adequately fitted models might be able to inform trusts on their local parameters compared to national averages, and help identify the bottlenecks contributing to delays in their area.

ACKNOWLEDGMENTS

This study was partly funded by the NIHR Applied Research Collaboration Wessex. The views expressed are those of the authors and not necessarily those of the NIHR or the Department of Health and Social Care.

References

Boyle, L. M., C. S. Currie, C. L. Fernandez, L. Nguyen, and C. Halpenny. 2023. "A discrete event simulation model of a hospital for prediction of the impact of delayed discharge". In *11th Simulation Workshop 2023*, 240–249. Operational Research Society.

Harper, A., M. Pitt, M. D. Prez, Z. Onen-Dumlu, C. Vasilakis, P. Forte, and R. Wood. 2021. "A Demand and Capacity Model For Home-Based Intermediate Care: Optimizing The'Step Down'Pathway". In *2021 Winter Simulation Conference*, edited by B. Kim, K. Feng, S. Masoud, Z. Zheng, C. Szabo, and M. Loper, 1–12. Arizona: Institute of Electrical and Electronics Engineers, Inc.

NHS England 2024a. "Discharge delays (Acute)". Available at https://www.england.nhs.uk/statistics/statistical-work-areas/discharge-delays-acute-data/. Accessed November 2024.

NHS England 2024b. "Implementation of a discharge to assess model". Available at https://www.england.nhs.uk/urgent-emergency-care/improving-hospital-discharge/case-studies/implementation-of-a-discharge-to-assess-model/. Accessed November 2024.

Onen-Dumlu, Z., A. L. Harper, P. G. Forte, A. L. Powell, M. Pitt, C. Vasilakis, and R. M. Wood. 2022. "Optimising the balance of acute and intermediate care capacity for the complex discharge pathway: computer modelling study during COVID-19 recovery in England". *PLOS ONE* 17 (6): 1–16.

Patrick, J., K. Nelson, and D. L. Dan. 2015. "A simulation model for capacity planning in community care". *Journal of Simulation* 9 (2): 111–120.

Qin, S., C. Thompson, T. Bogomolov, D. Ward, and P. Hakendorf. 2017. "Hospital occupancy and discharge strategies: A simulation-based study". *Internal Medicine Journal* 47 (8): 894–899.

Wong, H. J., R. C. Wu, M. Caesar, H. Abrams, and D. Morra. 2010. "Smoothing inpatient discharges decreases emergency department congestion: a system dynamics simulation model". *Emergency Medicine Journal* 27 (8): 593–598.

AUTHOR BIOGRAPHIES

RANGA ABEYSOORIYA is a Research Fellow at Southampton Business School. He completed his PhD in Operational Research from the Southampton Business School in 2017. Ranga also holds the position of Senior Lecturer in Industrial Engineering at the University of Moratuwa, Sri Lanka, with an interest in applying OR/MS in sectors such as healthcare, transportation, cutting & packing and manufacturing. His email address is R.P.Abeysooriya@soton.ac.uk.

NIRMANI AMARASINGHE is currently a PhD student in Mathematics at Queen's University Belfast. She completed her MSc in Operational Research at the University of Southampton. Her research interests include data exploration and analysis, with applications in operational research and management science. Her email address is namarasinghe01@qub.ac.uk.

LAURA BOYLE is an Lecturer in Data Analytics in the Mathematical Sciences Research Centre at Queen's University Belfast and an adjunct lecturer in the School of Computer and Mathematical Sciences at the University of Adelaide, Australia. Her research interests include simulation, data analytics, and operational research with applications in healthcare. Her email address is laura.boyle@qub.ac.uk and her website is https://pure.qub.ac.uk/en/persons/laura-boyle/.

CHRISTINE CURRIE is a Professor of Operational Research in Mathematical Sciences at the University of Southampton and a member of the Centre for Operational Research, Management Sciences and Information Systems (CORMSIS). She was Editor-in-Chief for the Journal of Simulation from 2015 - 2024. Her research interests include simulation optimization, digital twins, applications of simulation, and optimal pricing for transportation. Her email address is christine.currie@soton.ac.uk and her homepage is https://www.southampton.ac.uk/people/5wzzxf/professor-christine-currie.

CARLOS LAMAS-FERNANDEZ is an Associate Professor in Business Analytics/Management Science in Southampton Business School. In his research, Carlos is interested in using optimisation techniques in areas such as sports, health care, transportation and logistics. He has developed both heuristic and exact methods for cutting and packing, vehicle routing and facility location problems. His email address is C.Lamas-Fernandez@soton.ac.uk and his website is https://www.southampton.ac.uk/people/5xjdpm/doctor-carlos-lamas-fernandez

Proceedings of the Operational Research Society Simulation Workshop 2025 (SW25)
M. Luis, A. Harper, T. Monks, N. Mustafee, eds.

https://doi.org/10.36819/SW25.041

MODELLING LONG-TERM CHANGES IN POPULATION HEALTH STATE AND ASSOCIATED HEALTHCARE RESOURCE REQUIREMENTS

Dr Zehra Onen-Dumlu

University of Bath
School of Management
Bath, BA2 7AZ
United Kingdom
zod23@bath.ac.uk

Mr. Luke Shaw

NHS BNSSG ICB
100 Temple Street
Bristol, BS1 6AG
United Kingdom
luke.shaw4@nhs.net

Dr Richard Wood

NHS BNSSG ICB
100 Temple Street
Bristol, BS1 6AG
United Kingdom
richard.wood16@nhs.net

Prof. Christos Vasilakis

University of Bath
School of Management
Bath, BA2 7AZ
United Kingdom
c.vasilakis@bath.ac.uk

ABSTRACT

Longer-term healthcare planning is challenging given inherent uncertainties in future population demographics and health state, and wider unknowns regarding the economy, society and technology. The aim of this paper is to describe the development and early application of a mathematical model used to simulate the health state and associated healthcare resource consumption in a one-million resident population in and around Bristol (UK). The first stage of the modelling is to simulate population health over the next 20 years, according to five 'Core Segments' defined using the Cambridge Multimorbidity Score. This is done through a set of discrete-time difference equations, calibrated on patient-level data. The second stage is to apply to these projections the expected healthcare activity and cost information to derive totals per core segment. Baseline model results suggest 1.7% annual real-term cost growth, of which 0.9% is demographic and 0.8% is due to deteriorating population health.

Keywords: Population Health, Population Health Management, Decision Support Systems, Long-term Forecasting.

1 INTRODUCTION

Decisions around medium and long-term allocation of healthcare resources are fraught with challenges arising from the inherent uncertainties in population growth as well as developments in the economy, society and technology (Aarninkhof-Kamphuis et al, 2023). Against this background, health and care planners are frequently facing challenges on how to allocate healthcare resources effectively given limited budgets (Mitton et al, 2014; Seixas et al, 2021).

Mathematical and computer simulation models can help decision makers embrace these difficulties by providing indications of population growth and the likely long-term implications of different policies while accounting for their inherent uncertainty. Previous microsimulation models focus on specific types of diseases (e.g., Type 2 diabetes) or specific age groups (Lin et al, 2018; Kingston et al, 2018). More recently, the Health Foundation partnered with the University of Liverpool to develop a microsimulation model that projects patterns of illness until 2040 for a three-segment UK population aged 30 years and older (Watt et al, 2023).

The aim of this paper is to describe the development and early use of a modelling framework that estimates the possible extent of long-term health state changes and associated healthcare resource requirements in a regional population. In this research, we not only provide long-term population and resource projections but also develop simulation scenarios that flex the baseline (reference) scenario to consider various mitigations. These scenarios include improving health by reducing the probability of individuals developing chronic conditions and enhancing productive efficiency by reducing the cost required to meet specific health needs.

2 METHODS

The modelling framework we developed is based on two stages: the first derives 20-year population projections based on a set of discrete-time difference equations, and the second derives healthcare activity and related costs over the same time horizon. Application was to the Bristol, North Somerset and South Gloucestershire (BNSSG) healthcare system in South West England. Data is sourced from the System Wide Dataset, a patient-level linked dataset in BNSSG (BNSSG Healthier Together, 2024). The 20-year time horizon was set following consultation with decision makers, and represents a similar duration as to that used in the aforementioned Health Foundation study (Watt et al, 2023).

2.1 Stage One: Modelling Health State

Population projections are based on segmentation of the BNSSG adult (17+) population with respect to each individual's Cambridge Multimorbidity Score (CMS), which is calculated from the presence of 37 chronic conditions for each individual (Payne et al, 2020). This score is a transparent, simple measure of multimorbidity originally calibrated on data from United Kingdom general practitioner records and weighted on different clinical outcomes such as number of primary care consultations, emergency inpatient admissions and mortality. It is designed for use in system planning, policy making and allocating resources. The segmentation places individuals in to one of five 'Core Segments', according to their CMS at a particular time. For more detail of the Core Segmentation approach, including CMS thresholds and overall properties, see Wood et al (2023).

Individuals in the model are aged dynamically as time progresses, accounting, in an indirect manner, for the onset of comorbidities with advancing years. The model also includes temporal parameters relating to inflows (births – in our case, individuals turning 17 years of age, and immigration into BNSSG) and outflows (deaths and emigration from BNSSG), based on data from the Office for National Statistics (ONS). An illustration of the modelling framework is represented in Figure 1.

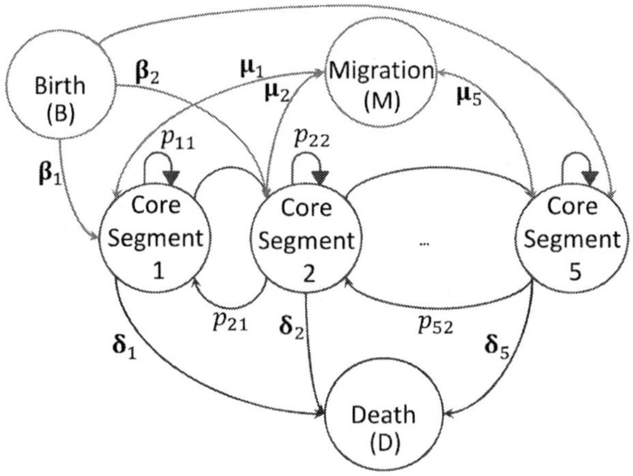

Figure 1 *The modelling framework at time t (notation can be found in Section 2.1.1)*

2.1.1 Notation, Formulation and Calibration

The model is essentially a set of discrete-time difference equations accounting for patient-level movements into and out of the five Core Segments (CS_i), representing the health state of the population, by means of birth (B), death (D), and in/out migration (M). The inner transition probability matrix is represented by P, where each entry $p_{ij}(t)$ corresponds to the probability of transition from Core Segment CS_i to CS_j within the t-th time period, where $t = 1, 2, \ldots, T$ and T is the modelling horizon.

These inner transition probabilities are estimated by observing individual state changes for each pair of time steps in the study as simple counts:

$$\hat{p}_{ij}(t) = \sum_{t=2}^{T} n_{ij}(t) / \sum_{z=1}^{m} \sum_{t=2}^{T} n_{iz}(t) \qquad (1)$$

where $n_{ij}(t)$ are the number of individuals in state j at time t, having been in state i at time $t-1$, and m is the number of core segments ($m = 5$ in this example), and $z = 1, 2, \ldots, m$. Estimated inner transition probabilities, derived over the previous 12-months for a rolling 18-month period from May 2022 to September 2023, are plotted in Figure 2. For use in the model, inner transition matrix values were given as the most recent annual values when there was evidence of a linear trend when applying linear regression to the data ($p<0.05$), or the mean value over the past 18 months if otherwise.

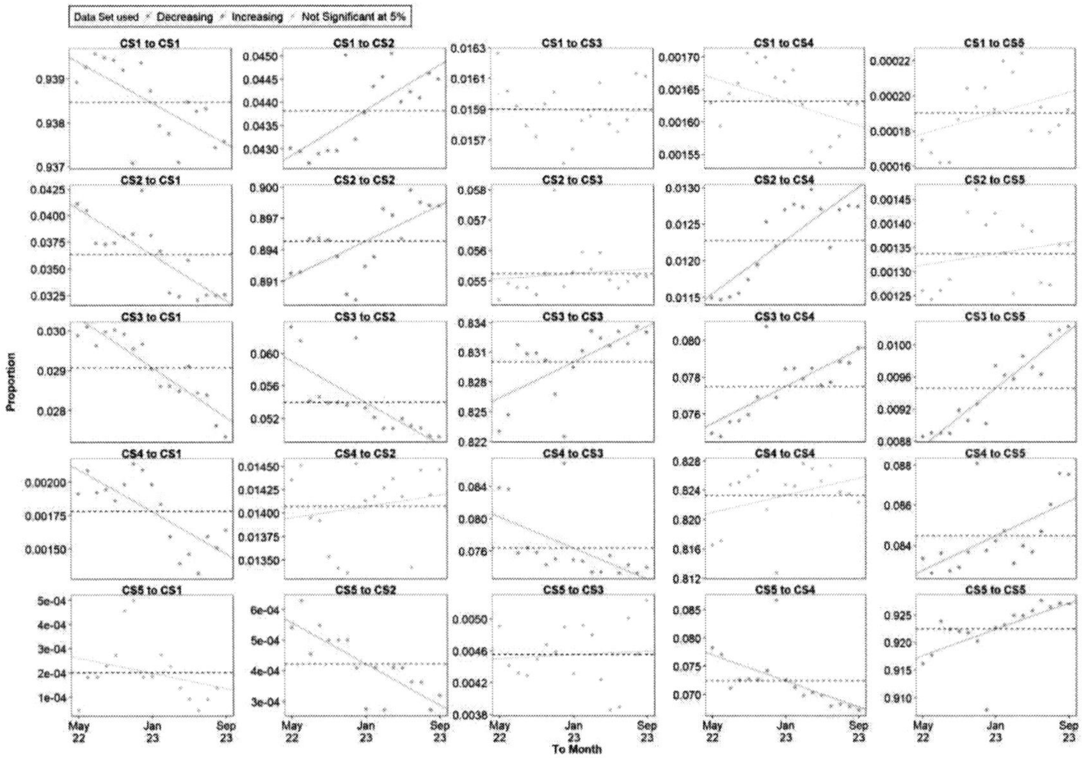

Figure 2 *Transition probabilities evolution between May 2022 and September 2023*

The following other input parameters were used:

- Initial population levels for the five Core Segments, using data as of September 2023.
- Time period, *T:* set to 20 years, i.e., covering the period from 2023 to 2043.
- Annual births, net migration, deaths projected each year, using ONS data (ONS, 2020).
- Proportion of births, net migration, and deaths that go into/out each Core Segment, as observed in the year ending Sep 2023.

See the Appendix for all input parameter values used in the modelling covered here.

The number of people in Core Segment j at time t can then be estimated through:

$$CS_j(t) = \sum_{i=1}^{5} p_{ij} CS_i(t-1) + M(t)\mu_j + B(t)\beta_j - D(t-1)\delta_j \quad (2)$$

where $B(t)$ represents the ONS projection of the number of adults turning 17 in year t, β_j the proportion of $B(t)$ that will enter CS_j, $M(t)$ the ONS projection of the net number migrating (i.e., immigration – emigration) in year t, and μ_j the proportion of $M(t)$ for core segment j, $D(t-1)$ the death ONS projection and δ_j the proportion of $D(t-1)$ that comes from CS_j.

2.1.2 Modelling Assumptions

In developing the modelling framework, certain assumptions and simplifications were made during the process. Here, we present a concise list of key assumptions that underpin our modelling framework (both baseline and scenario versions). It is important for users and stakeholders to be aware of these assumptions, as they form the basis upon which the model interprets and predicts outcomes. Assumptions are as follows:

- Discrete time step is one year.
- Transition probabilities p_{ij} between Core Segments are time-homogeneous.
- Parameters μ_i, β_i, δ_i are time-homogeneous.
- Births and in/out migration affect the Core Segment level populations immediately on the current year, and deaths affect values immediately in the next year.
- ONS population projections are evenly distributed within each 5-year age group as defined in the ONS data. Hence, the projection of the population turning 17 years old at year t equals 20% of projection of age cohort 15-19 at year t.
- Net migration projections are extracted from ONS data.
- Proportions of each Core Segment in *B(t)*, *M(t)* and *D(t)* equals the proportions at the current time (year 2023).
- Death rate from each Core Segment is calculated using total death ONS projections from ONS data and proportions for each Core Segment from local data at current time.

2.2 Stage Two: Modelling Health Resource Use and Costs

Typical healthcare activity and cost profiles are determined from recent local data, specifically the period from October 2022 to September 2023. Profiles are determined for each Core Segment and across a number of healthcare points of delivery (PODs), including Community contacts, Maternity contacts, Secondary Elective contacts, and Secondary Non-Elective contacts. The mean activity and cost values are used. Hence, for each Core Segment and each POD, there exists a value for mean activity consumption and mean cost, which is considered to be a typical activity and cost profile for a patient in that Core Segment. These profiles are uplifted by projected future numbers per Core Segment (Stage One output) in order to provide an estimate of total healthcare resource demands (Stage Two output). Carbon usage estimates are also projected alongside activity and costs using CO2 kg equivalent per activity values as sourced internally in BNSSG Integrated Care System sources, which in turn has been informed by estimates in the UK Treasury's Green Book (HM Treasury, 2022).

3 RESULTS

3.1 Baseline Projections

Simulated projections for the BNSSG population by health state are provided in Figure 3 (this is part of Stage One modelling output). This shows an estimated increase in the future size of all Core Segments with the exception of CS1 (the healthiest), which is estimated to reduce in size over the 20-year period.

With typical Core Segment level activity and cost profiles, the Stage One projections can be used to estimate total activity and cost requirements in future years by healthcare POD, as provided in Figure

4 for selected PODs (this is the Stage Two modelling output). This figure also includes lines representing projections if only using ONS population changes, and ONS population changes when adjusting for 5-year age-band and sex demographic changes. This supports what has been argued more widely – that future demands on healthcare services are greater than under demographic pressure alone – and point to the additional challenge of deteriorating population health (Kingston et al, 2018). According to our projections, this is particularly evident in areas such as Mental Health (not presented in Figure 4) and many Secondary Care settings such as Secondary Elective and Non-Elective. There are exceptions to this rule in places that appear intuitively reasonable (given population ageing), such as Maternity which is the only POD where the 'ONS Totals' forecast is higher than under the modelling.

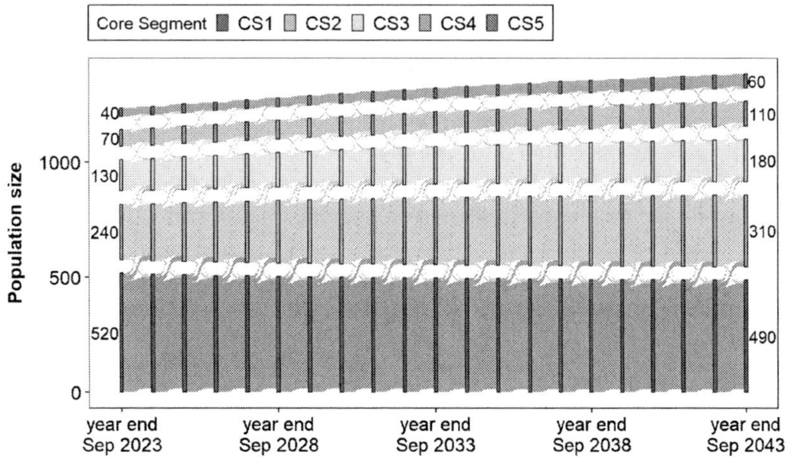

Figure 3 *Baseline model projections for Core Segment populations (in 1,000s), with the magnitude of between-segment flows indicated.*

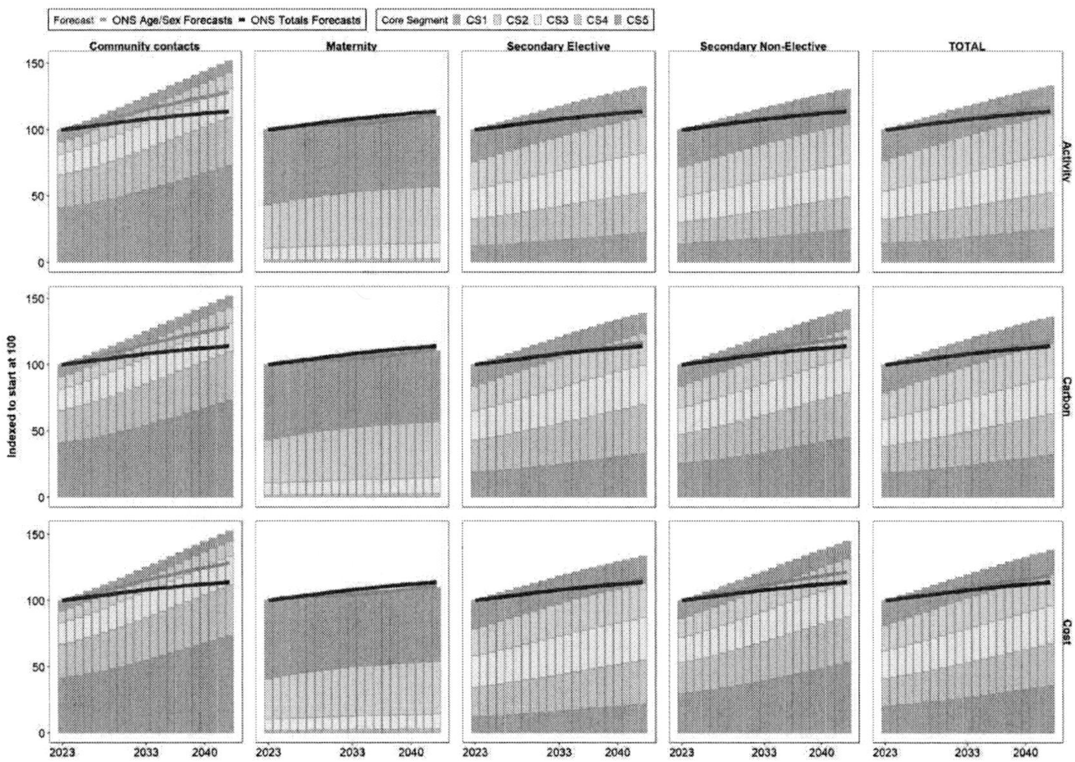

Figure 4 Baseline model projections for cost and activity for selected points of delivery.

3.2 Example 'Do Something' Scenarios

To illustrate the possible impact of interventions to the baseline projections, we consider the following two scenarios. First, we ask: how much of a decrease in the first-level upward transition probabilities (i.e., transitions only between adjacent Core Segments) would be required to reduce the 20-year cost growth to the 'ONS Totals' figures? To model this change we adjusted transition probability values (Stage One), representing initiatives to improve population health through essentially reducing the probability at which individuals transition to worse health states. Modelling results show that to achieve such an objective, a 30% reduction in upward transitions probabilities would likely be required, gradually phased in over the first five years (in equal increments).

Second, we ask: how much of a decrease in the cost per person per Core Segment would be required to reduce the 20-year cost growth to the 'ONS Totals' figures? This is a Stage Two intervention, as it represents an initiative to improve productive efficiency (meeting the same health need but with lower resources). Modelling results show that to achieve this objective, an 18% reduction to per-capita costs would be required (cf. per person average annual cost values in the Appendix table), gradually phased in over the first five years.

Figure 5 shows the other possible solutions and trade-offs to achieving different levels of 20-year cost growths. Specifically, on a strictly 'do nothing different' basis, we would have an average 1.72% annual cost growth over the coming 20 years, (observe the 1.72% label at centre of the graph corresponding to 0% on x-axis (representing productive efficiency) and y-axis (representing prevention effort). Any point along the black line achieves the same 1.72%, e.g., with population health deterioration characterised by a 20% increase in the CS upward transition probability (x-axis), we would have to reduce per-patient-costs-per-core-segment by 9.7% (i.e., 9.7% increase in 'productive efficiency') to achieve the same 1.72% cost growth. If population health deterioration was half as bad (10% increase in numbers going up CSs) and we had a 20% increase in costs required to meet the health needs equivalently to now, then we would need an average 4.13% annual compound cost growth averaged over the coming 20 years. The lighter purple line charts the position required to meet cost growths in accordance with demographic population changes (~1%), e.g., we could do this by the aforementioned 9.7% productive efficiency gain provided we also reduced the numbers going up CSs by about 8%. If we were funded to only meet population size growth (darker purple line), then we would need to extend prevention efforts to reduce CS upward transition probabilities by 10% instead of 8%.

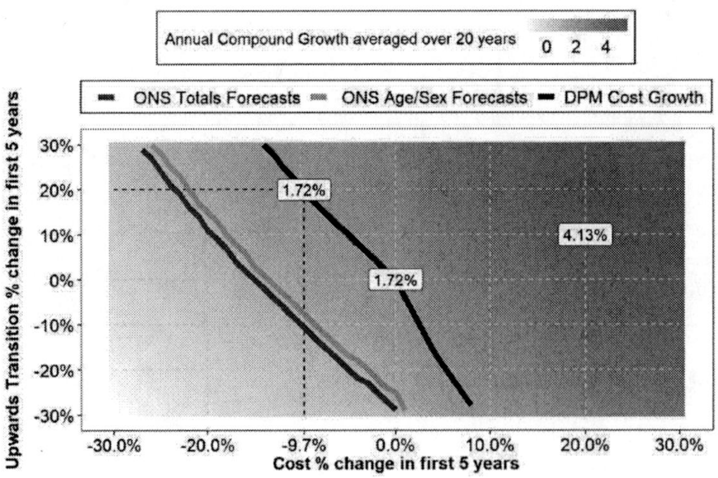

Figure 5 *Impact of % change over the next 5 years and its likely impact on annual growth over 20 years.*

4 DISCUSSION

Our modelling results provide insights into the changing demands on the National Health Service (NHS) to deliver the same quality service as is currently being provided. Indeed, one of the key assumptions in our model is that the balance between demand and capacity remains consistent over the entire time horizon. This implies that the patient needs are met in a similar manner throughout the period being studied, without significant fluctuations or disruptions in the care system's ability to provide services. By assuming a steady balance between demand and capacity, our model simplifies the projection process and focuses on understanding the dynamics within a stable framework. This assumption is crucial as it allows for a clearer interpretation of the model's outcomes, but it also means that any real-world variability in healthcare provision and patient needs are not captured in our projections. Stakeholders should consider this when applying the model's results to policy and decision-making contexts. This is useful but limited, as it is known that the NHS has been under immense system pressure and has been missing many key deliverables (DHSC, 2024). There are feedback loops and likely propagation of ill health that could result in sicker people who require more care sooner. Our model partially captures this effect through the increasing numbers of higher Core Segment population under the baseline output, however, this is based on constant transition probabilities and the propagation of ill health might be better represented by the scenarios under an increase in the y axis in Figure 5.

The main message of a population that is ageing and getting sicker is not new (Chang et al, 2020; British Medical Association, 2024), but our modelling attempts to quantify the effect and makes it applicable to health system decision makers using regional up-to-date health and population data. Our modelling results also show the impact of costs over time, with the sickest proportion of the population increasing proportionally by the most, at around 75% increase over 20 years.

The model is designed, as the Core Segments were, to run only for the 17+ population for BNSSG, not for children or health needs for those who live outside the region (and who may receive care in one of the health facilities of the collaborating health system). Our model is intrinsically tied to the ONS 2018 forecasts. Despite these limitations, it was developed in close collaboration with decision makers and has been used to inform financial forecasts, where proportional changes in POD expenditure is critical. The differences in the 5, 10, 20-year predictions at POD level have led to many discussions about how these results translate, and how the financial forecasts will be affected.

The capacity of capturing scenarios that improve population health and reduced financial pressures is an advantage of this model, as shown within the illustrative examples reported here. These point to the scale of changes required, despite the inevitable challenges on how to achieve either a 30% reduction in upwards transition probabilities, or an 18% in annual cost per person, or the combination of both.

Current work on extending the model presented here include increasing its fidelity by capturing additional critical population characteristics such as age as well as using a stochastic modelling approach to appreciate the inherent uncertainty in the system. How best to capture the likely impact of population level interventions such as reducing the burden of obesity or smoking cessation programmes remains underdeveloped. Future research includes options around assessing the generalisability of the model in different settings, especially in those where linked datasets are not readily available. Plans also include publishing the coded model in an open-source repository (such as GitHub) to aid with its potential adoption by different organisations.

APPENDIX

Table A-1 *Input parameter values used in the model*

<table>
<tr><th>Model Input</th><th>Value</th><th>Source</th></tr>
<tr><td>Initial Population</td><td><table><tr><td>CS1</td><td>410,656</td></tr><tr><td>CS2</td><td>191,668</td></tr><tr><td>CS3</td><td>106,895</td></tr><tr><td>CS4</td><td>56,925</td></tr><tr><td>CS5</td><td>28,002</td></tr></table></td><td>SWD</td></tr>
<tr><td>Inner Transition Matrix</td><td><table><tr><td></td><td>CS1</td><td>CS2</td><td>CS3</td><td>CS4</td><td>CS5</td></tr><tr><td>CS1</td><td>0.938</td><td>0.045</td><td>0.016</td><td>0.002</td><td>0.000</td></tr><tr><td>CS2</td><td>0.033</td><td>0.898</td><td>0.055</td><td>0.013</td><td>0.001</td></tr><tr><td>CS3</td><td>0.027</td><td>0.050</td><td>0.833</td><td>0.080</td><td>0.010</td></tr><tr><td>CS4</td><td>0.002</td><td>0.014</td><td>0.074</td><td>0.822</td><td>0.088</td></tr><tr><td>CS5</td><td>0.000</td><td>0.000</td><td>0.005</td><td>0.067</td><td>0.927</td></tr></table></td><td>SWD</td></tr>
<tr><td>Time Period</td><td>20 years</td><td>Decision makers</td></tr>
<tr><td>Annual births, net migration, deaths values</td><td><table><tr><td>Year</td><td>Births</td><td>Net Migration</td><td>Deaths</td></tr><tr><td>2024</td><td>11265</td><td>2890.581</td><td>8146.954</td></tr><tr><td>2025</td><td>11666</td><td>2798.444</td><td>8199.516</td></tr><tr><td>2026</td><td>11947</td><td>2681.534</td><td>8227.681</td></tr><tr><td>2027</td><td>12275</td><td>2599.427</td><td>8295.12</td></tr><tr><td>2028</td><td>12542</td><td>2615.07</td><td>8360.476</td></tr><tr><td>2029</td><td>12779</td><td>2599.277</td><td>8426.625</td></tr><tr><td>2030</td><td>12832</td><td>2531.316</td><td>8499.716</td></tr><tr><td>2031</td><td>12876</td><td>2498.084</td><td>8581.336</td></tr><tr><td>2032</td><td>12842</td><td>2502.875</td><td>8671.089</td></tr><tr><td>2033</td><td>12785</td><td>2516.646</td><td>8751.321</td></tr><tr><td>2034</td><td>12582</td><td>2394.422</td><td>8842.263</td></tr><tr><td>2035</td><td>12371</td><td>2282.226</td><td>8931.421</td></tr><tr><td>2036</td><td>12264</td><td>2229.16</td><td>9016.413</td></tr><tr><td>2037</td><td>12201</td><td>2218.158</td><td>9098.628</td></tr><tr><td>2038</td><td>12106</td><td>2138.67</td><td>9160.414</td></tr><tr><td>2039</td><td>12076</td><td>2032.762</td><td>9234.894</td></tr><tr><td>2040</td><td>12126</td><td>1863.384</td><td>9302.332</td></tr><tr><td>2041</td><td>12223</td><td>1774.691</td><td>9358.464</td></tr><tr><td>2042</td><td>12309</td><td>1705.832</td><td>9406.564</td></tr><tr><td>2043</td><td>12401</td><td>1610.552</td><td>9445.44</td></tr></table></td><td>ONS</td></tr>
<tr><td>Annual proportions of births, net migration and deaths</td><td><table><tr><td>Core Segment</td><td>Event</td><td>Proportion</td></tr><tr><td>CS1</td><td>Births</td><td>88.2%</td></tr><tr><td>CS1</td><td>Deaths</td><td>4.7%</td></tr></table></td><td>SWD</td></tr>
</table>

<table>
<tr>
<td></td>
<td>
<table>
<tr><td>CS1</td><td>Net Migration</td><td>61.6%</td></tr>
<tr><td>CS2</td><td>Births</td><td>10.0%</td></tr>
<tr><td>CS2</td><td>Deaths</td><td>7.3%</td></tr>
<tr><td>CS2</td><td>Net Migration</td><td>21.2%</td></tr>
<tr><td>CS3</td><td>Births</td><td>1.6%</td></tr>
<tr><td>CS3</td><td>Deaths</td><td>14.5%</td></tr>
<tr><td>CS3</td><td>Net Migration</td><td>10.2%</td></tr>
<tr><td>CS4</td><td>Births</td><td>0.2%</td></tr>
<tr><td>CS4</td><td>Deaths</td><td>25.0%</td></tr>
<tr><td>CS4</td><td>Net Migration</td><td>4.8%</td></tr>
<tr><td>CS5</td><td>Births</td><td>0.0%</td></tr>
<tr><td>CS5</td><td>Deaths</td><td>48.6%</td></tr>
<tr><td>CS5</td><td>Net Migration</td><td>2.3%</td></tr>
</table>
</td>
<td></td>
</tr>
<tr>
<td>Per person Average annual activity, Carbon emission and cost values</td>
<td>
<table>
<tr><th>Core Segment</th><th>POD</th><th>Activity</th><th>Cost</th><th>Carbon</th></tr>
<tr><td>CS1</td><td>Community contacts</td><td>0.155</td><td>15.9</td><td>3.57</td></tr>
<tr><td>CS2</td><td>Community contacts</td><td>0.324</td><td>35.9</td><td>7.45</td></tr>
<tr><td>CS3</td><td>Community contacts</td><td>1.01</td><td>120</td><td>23.3</td></tr>
<tr><td>CS4</td><td>Community contacts</td><td>2.9</td><td>353</td><td>66.8</td></tr>
<tr><td>CS5</td><td>Community contacts</td><td>9.99</td><td>1180</td><td>230</td></tr>
<tr><td>CS1</td><td>Maternity</td><td>0.031</td><td>50.7</td><td>3.92</td></tr>
<tr><td>CS2</td><td>Maternity</td><td>0.038</td><td>56.1</td><td>4.82</td></tr>
<tr><td>CS3</td><td>Maternity</td><td>0.018</td><td>28</td><td>2.31</td></tr>
<tr><td>CS4</td><td>Maternity</td><td>0.006</td><td>9.77</td><td>0.793</td></tr>
<tr><td>CS5</td><td>Maternity</td><td>0.001</td><td>1.87</td><td>0.151</td></tr>
<tr><td>CS1</td><td>Secondary Non-Elective</td><td>0.199</td><td>60.7</td><td>10.6</td></tr>
<tr><td>CS2</td><td>Secondary Non-Elective</td><td>0.334</td><td>133</td><td>23.1</td></tr>
<tr><td>CS3</td><td>Secondary Non-Elective</td><td>0.514</td><td>319</td><td>49.2</td></tr>
<tr><td>CS4</td><td>Secondary Non-Elective</td><td>0.81</td><td>733</td><td>105</td></tr>
<tr><td>CS5</td><td>Secondary Non-Elective</td><td>1.45</td><td>1930</td><td>246</td></tr>
<tr><td>CS1</td><td>Secondary Elective</td><td>0.89</td><td>121</td><td>29.3</td></tr>
<tr><td>CS2</td><td>Secondary Elective</td><td>1.67</td><td>240</td><td>69.6</td></tr>
<tr><td>CS3</td><td>Secondary Elective</td><td>3.13</td><td>503</td><td>149</td></tr>
<tr><td>CS4</td><td>Secondary Elective</td><td>5.33</td><td>873</td><td>310</td></tr>
<tr><td>CS5</td><td>Secondary Elective</td><td>6.81</td><td>1000</td><td>488</td></tr>
<tr><td>CS1</td><td>TOTAL</td><td>4.52</td><td>323</td><td>105</td></tr>
<tr><td>CS2</td><td>TOTAL</td><td>9.63</td><td>689</td><td>225</td></tr>
<tr><td>CS3</td><td>TOTAL</td><td>15.8</td><td>1370</td><td>368</td></tr>
<tr><td>CS4</td><td>TOTAL</td><td>25.2</td><td>2560</td><td>587</td></tr>
<tr><td>CS5</td><td>TOTAL</td><td>41</td><td>5050</td><td>955</td></tr>
</table>
</td>
<td>SWD</td>
</tr>
</table>

* SWD: System Wide Dataset; ONS: Office of National Statistics; CS: Core Segment

REFERENCES

Aarninkhof-Kamphuis, A., Voordijk, H., & Dewulf, G. (2023). Coping with uncertainties: challenges for decision makers in healthcare. Journal of Facilities Management. https://doi.org/10.1108/JFM-06-2022-0067.

BNSSG Healthier Together (2024). Population Health Management. https://bnssghealthiertogether.org.uk/staff-and-partners/knowledge-hub/population-health-management/. Accessed: 22/01/2025

British Medical Association (2024). The country is getting sicker, https://www.bma.org.uk/media/uvpd204n/bma-the-country-is-getting-sicker-september-2024.pdf. Accessed: 22/01/2025

Chang, E. S., Kannoth, S., Levy, S., Wang, S. Y., Lee, J. E., & Levy, B. R. (2020). Global reach of ageism on older persons' health: A systematic review. PLoS ONE, 15(1), e0220857. https://doi.org/10.1371/journal.pone.0220857.

DHSC (2024). Independent investigation of the NHS in England. https://www.gov.uk/government/publications/independent-investigation-of-the-nhs-in-england. Accessed: 22/01/2025

HM Treasury (2022) The Green Book: Central government guidance on appraisal and evaluation. London: HM Treasury. Available at: https://www.gov.uk/government/publications/the-green-book. Accessed: 22/01/2025

Kingston, A., Comas-Herrera, A., & Jagger, C. (2018). Forecasting the care needs of the older population in England over the next 20 years: estimates from the Population Ageing and Care Simulation (PACSim) modelling study. The Lancet Public Health, 3(9), e447-e455. https://doi.org/10.1016/S2468-2667(18)30118-X.

Lin, J., Thompson, T. J., Cheng, Y. J., Zhuo, X., Zhang, P., Gregg, E., & Rolka, D. B. (2018). Projection of the future diabetes burden in the United States through 2060. Population Health Metrics, 16, 1-9. https://doi.org/10.1186/s12963-018-0166-4.

Mitton, C., Dionne, F., & Donaldson, C. (2014). Managing healthcare budgets in times of austerity: the role of program budgeting and marginal analysis. Applied Health Economics and Health Policy, 12, 95-102. https://doi.org/10.1007/s40258-013-0074-5.

ONS (2020). Subnational population projections for England: 2018. https://www.ons.gov.uk/peoplepopulationandcommunity/populationandmigration/populationprojections/bulletins/subnationalpopulationprojectionsforengland/2018based. Accessed 22/01/2025.

Payne, R. A., Mendonca, S. C., Elliott, M. N., Saunders, C. L., Edwards, D. A., Marshall, M., & Roland, M. (2020). Development and validation of the Cambridge Multimorbidity Score. Cmaj, 192(5), E107-E114. https://doi.org/10.1503/cmaj.190757.

Seixas, B. V., Regier, D. A., Bryan, S., & Mitton, C. (2021). Describing practices of priority setting and resource allocation in publicly funded health care systems of high-income countries. BMC Health Services Research, 21, 1-15. https://doi.org/10.1186/s12913-021-06078-z.

Watt, T., Raymond, A., Rachet-Jacquet, L., Head, A., Kypridemos, C., Kelly, E., & Charlesworth, A. (2023). Health in 2040: projected patterns of illness in England. Health Foundation. https://doi.org/10.37829/HF-2023-RC03.

Wood, R. M., Budiman, T. A., Hassey, N., Onen Dumlu, Z., Vasilakis, C., Budd, F. J., ... & Kenward, C. (2023). Development and practical use of a risk-sensitive population segmentation model for healthcare service planning: application in England. International Journal of Healthcare Management, 1-10. https://doi.org/10.1080/20479700.2023.2232980.

AUTHOR BIOGRAPHIES

ZEHRA ONEN-DUMLU is a Lecturer (Assistant Professor) in the Information, Decisions and Operations (IDO) division at the University of Bath School of Management. Zehra's research focuses on healthcare operations management. She is interested in supporting decision making to improve healthcare operations and global health systems using analytical as well as empirical methods.

LUKE SHAW is a Data Scientist at NHS Bristol, North Somerset and South Gloucestershire Integrated Care Board. He is interested in using data for public good, in whatever form that may take.

RICHARD WOOD is Head of Modelling and Analytics at NHS Bristol, North Somerset and South Gloucestershire Integrated Care Board and is a Visiting Senior Research Fellow at University of Bath School of Management. His interests are at the interface of academic theory and practical application. His background is in applied mathematics and through his career he has worked in various fields including mathematical biology, quantitative risk assessment, and capital modelling.

CHRISTOS VASILAKIS FORS is Professor and Chair in the Information Decision and Operations (IDO) Division and Director, Bath Centre for Healthcare Innovation and Improvement (CHI^2) both at the University of Bath School of Management in the UK. He is currently Co-Director (Fellowships) of the LEAP Digital Health Hub.

Proceedings of the Operational Research Society Simulation Workshop 2025 (SW25)
M. Luis, A. Harper, T. Monks, N. Mustafee, eds.
https://doi.org/10.36819/SW25.042

DISCRETE EVENT SIMULATION TO UNDERSTAND AMBULANCE PERFORMANCE AND IMPROVEMENT STRATEGIES

Dr. Martina Fonseca

Sciensano
Rue Juliette Wytsman 14, 1050 Ixelles, Belgium
martina.fonseca@sciensano.be

Dr. Jonathan Pearson

NHS England
7 Wellington Pl, Leeds LS1 4AP, UK
jonathanpearson@nhs.net

ABSTRACT

Ambulance handover problems and deteriorating response times have been dominating the Urgent & Emergency Care space over the past years. The NHS England UEC recovery plan published in 2023 set out ambitions which include improved response times over the following two years.
Interventions are being considered nationally and by local systems to achieve these ambitions. This includes improving in-hospital patient flow, increasing the ambulance fleet, reducing unnecessary conveyances and increasing clinical assessment of calls. This work aims to help build a model that can represent the non-linear ambulance system and assess the effect of interventions on handover delays and response times. We use discrete event simulation to model the ambulance system. The model takes into account on-duty supply profiles, demand by category and models of care, job cycle time components and the emergency department status. We validate and provide sensitivity analysis for such a model.

Keywords: discrete event simulation, ambulance performance, non-elective patient flow

1 INTRODUCTION

Ambulance performance problems have been dominating the Urgent & Emergency Care (UEC) space (NHS England, 2023a). The recommended handover time – the time between an ambulance arriving at hospital site to clinical handover to the emergency department's care - is 15 minutes, with anything over 30 minutes being measured as a delay. During the Winter of 2021/2022 and 2022/2023, there were large handover delays (Figure 1), with a lot of people waiting a long time to be admitted into the emergency department (ED) (NHS England, 2023b). During the Winter of 2022/2023, on average 4,000 hours a day were lost nationally to such delays.
Similarly, response times – the time it takes from receiving a 999 call to a vehicle arriving at the patient's location – also deteriorated considerably since the Winter of 2021/2022 (NHS England, 2022).
Calls are triaged into four categories according to the condition of the patient:

- Category 1 for life-threatening calls or those needing immediate intervention and/or resuscitation;
- Category 2 for those considered to be an emergency or a serious condition needing rapid assessment, urgent intervention on-scene or urgent transport. This includes heart attacks, stroke, sepsis or major burns;
- Category 3 for urgent calls that are however not immediately life-threatening;
- Category 4 for less urgent calls.

Targets are in place for the mean and/or 90th percentile response time for these categories. For category 2, which can correspond to about two thirds of calls, the monthly target is for ambulance trusts to respond to those calls in 18 minutes on average and to respond to 90% of such calls in 40 minutes. However, since 2021 many of the targets have been missed on a continuous basis, including for category 2 (Figure 2).

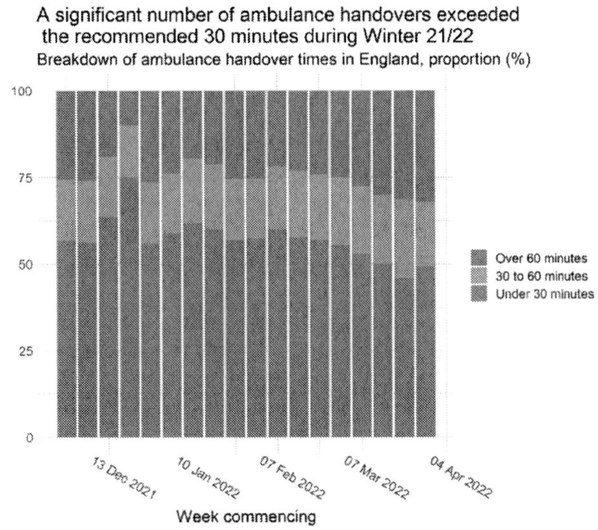

Figure 1 Breakdown of ambulance handover times in England. Source: daily ambulance collection (NHS England, 2022)

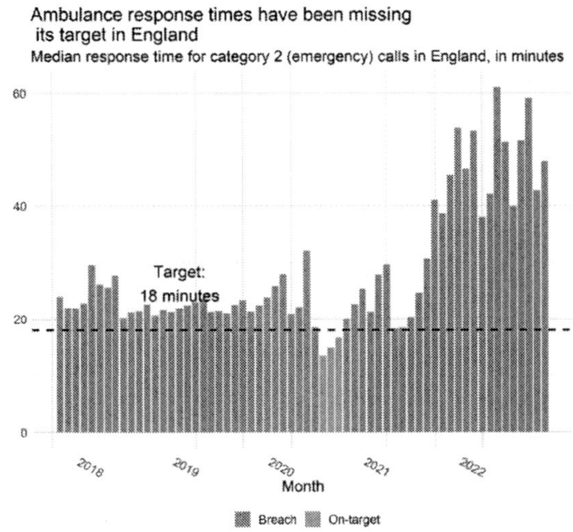

Figure 2 Average response time for category 2 calls in England. Source: AmbSYS (NHS England, 2023b)

The UEC recovery plan was published in January 2023 (NHS England, 2023a). Within it, it set out key ambitions which included improved response times and reduced handover delays. Interventions considered nationally and by local systems to achieve these ambitions include improving in-hospital patient flow, increasing the ambulance fleet, reducing unnecessary conveyances and increasing clinical assessment of calls. Given the non-linearity of the system and the influence of downstream settings such as ED, it can however be hard to make evidenced decisions about the best interventions.

This work aims to help estimate the impact that increasing the number of on-duty ambulance hours would have on handover delays and response times. As well as looking at changes in mean performance, we also wanted to look at the distribution (e.g. 90th percentile), and peaks. Therefore, we built a prototype discrete event simulation model for the ambulance setting to help understand the potential impacts of resourcing interventions and factors such as demand, ambulance job cycle time components, vehicle capacity on: ambulance occupancy; call response times; ambulance handover times.

METHODS

1.1 Conceptual model

When a call is made, availability to respond to it depends namely on the number of on-duty ambulance fleet, the on-duty workforce but also the instantaneous availability to be allocated to that incoming call. This in turn depends on when on-duty ambulances can be cleared from previous jobs (finish their job cycle time from allocation to clearance). Handover delays are leading to more ambulances queueing at the hospital site and an increase in ambulance job cycle time, which affects their availability for subsequent jobs. The relation between handover delays and response times is therefore non-linear. Characterising it can help understand the trade-offs and the effect of interventions.

Further, much of the ambulance performance improvements needed may not be in the sole direct gift of the ambulance service, as ability to handover depends on extrinsic factors like ED availability for clinical handover, which may in turn be affected by, successively: ED occupancy, bed availability in admitted patient care, inpatient discharge (to home, social care, ...). Though the model focusses on intrinsic factors and interventions to the ambulance system, it should ideally also capture – even if stylistically - when these are likely to have limited influence in the face of extrinsic drivers.

1.2 Discrete event simulation

As the dynamics to be modelled are flows and the queueing of entities (patients) for processes that require resource utilisation (ambulances), a system model is required. As we are interested in understanding the profiles' tails and not just the average and since we are expected to include individual effects in the model (e.g. reneging and queue prioritisation depending on individual characteristics) a Discrete Event Simulation (DES) is considered – quite commonly used in healthcare for such problems (Kotiadis et al, 2014). This approach models systems as networks of queues and activities, where state changes in the system occur at discrete points embedded in continuous time. The objects in the system are distinct individuals, each possessing characteristics that determine what happens to that individual, and the activity durations are sampled for each individual from probability distributions. This method has the advantage of intuitive and visual checks to the logic model, scenario (what-if) testing, granular modelling and the ability to assess performance in terms of distributions (including tail-end events) rather than just the mean. The restrictions of DES are mainly around the computational time for large footprints and the fact that a simplified model of the system will not intrinsically pick up dynamic behaviours. This means that absolute values should not be used for direct comparisons with reality but instead to inform a discussion of the underlying causalities and impacts of changes on the system.

We created our model using open-source programming language R and the Rsimmer library. The code is available via the project github repository (https://github.com/nhsengland/AmbModelOpen) and documentation via nhsengland.github.io/AmbModelOpen/.

1.3 Trajectory and characteristics

The pathway (Figure 3) that patients take through the system mostly depends on their initial attributes but routing can also depend on the system state at the time that a patient arrives at a branch in the trajectory.

For the 999 incident call generator, the 'arrival' rate of new incident calls is sampled from an exponential probability distribution with lambda set to 1/(mean arrival rate), where this rate is stratified by hour and weekday. The category of the call is then sampled from a user-supplied relative frequency distribution, which can vary by hour-day. Conditional on the category, the care model is sampled from a user-supplied relative frequency distribution ('hear-and-treat', 'see-and-treat', 'see-and-convey') as well as, for 'see-and-convey', an emergency department (ED) acuity level (1 – highest, 5 – lowest). If the care model is not 'hear-and-treat' (no transport), a request is made to the ambulance server for an ambulance (double-staffed vehicle - DSV) resource, with the priority set based on the category. The ambulance supply timeseries is user-provided The pertinent job cycle time components ('time from allocation to mobilise', 'time to scene', 'time at scene', 'time to ED site', 'time to clear') are then sampled from either empirical or lognormal time distributions. The 'time from call arrival to ambulance allocation' and 'time from arrival to ED site to ED handover' are emerging parameters rather than inputted ones, since they depend on the availability of resources (ambulance or ED). While the emergency department is not the core setting being modelled, it has a significant influence on ambulance handover. Here, to capture its influence, it is modelled stylistically as a server with a given capacity and server activity time (length of stay, LoS). Quite importantly, besides the 999 incident call generator, there is also a generator for ED walk-ins sampled from an exponential probability distribution, where the rate can be given stratified by hour, weekday and ED acuity. Priority of requests to this ED server will depend on the ED acuity. The LoS and walk-in demand are knoweable from existing data and hence expected to be user-provided, while the number of ED server resources n (simplified and stylistic compared to an actual ED setting which consists of various types of staff, rotas and bays) and level of absolute influence of ED acuity on prioritisation (not easily knowable) are meant to be calibrated until a realistic overall ambulance job cycle time is achieved.

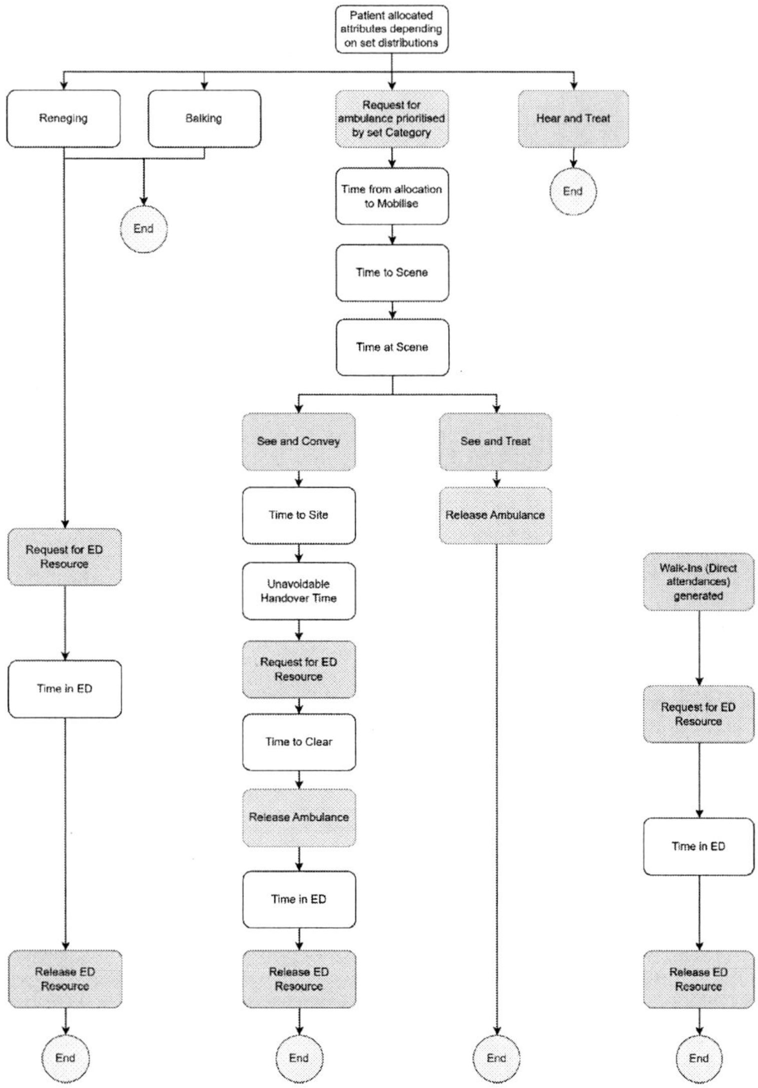

Figure 3 Reduced schematic of the patient trajectory

In terms of overall characteristics, the model can:

- Set ambulance demand over time, by category
- Set ED walk-in demand over time

- Set different care models
- Set ambulance supply over time
- Set ED resource supply (stylistic) over time
- Set a renege time (abandoning queue)
- Set balking criteria (not joining queue)
- Vary conveyance dynamically based on pressures
- Set more than one ambulance resource per incident
- Set a portion of supply as 'holdout' for higher priorities
- Escalate category three and four calls after long waits
- Simulate over 15 days for realistic levels of demand
- Monitor the utilisation; queues; key performance indicators (KPIs)
- Run the simulation up to 3-25 times with different seeds
- Run multiple scenarios / sensitivities in a loop and compile results

The model is not designed to:

- Escalate resources depending on time or simulation metrics (triggers)
- Vary behavior of ED prioritization based on pressures
- Reflect absolute relation between A&E performance and ambulance performance KPIs

1.4 Data

The model was created in such a way that its parametrisation could be achieved with parameters realistically available for population via known publications or aggregate statistics from restricted data collections accessible to key stakeholders.

The main data sources for these included the Daily Ambulance Collection (dAC) (NHS England, 2022) and Ambulance Quality Indicators (AmbSYS) (NHS England, 2023b) to inform on overall incident (call) demand; aggregate statistics from the Ambulance Data Set (ADS) (NHS Digital, 2024a) to inform on job cycle time empirical distributions to sample from (i.e. 'time from allocation to mobilise', 'time to scene', 'time at scene', 'time to ED site', 'time to clear') and incident (call) demand by hour-day and by category and care model; the NACC (National Ambulance Coordination Centre) report data to inform on vehicle supply; and aggregate statistics from the Emergency Care Dataset (ECDS) (NHS Digital, 2024b) to inform on competitive walk-in (direct ED) demand and on ED time in department (length of stay).

1.5 Analysis

1.5.1 Baseline scenario

For baseline scenario creation and model validation we used data from an NHS England ambulance trust during a two week period in the Winter of 2022/2023, to see how closely our model matched the real behaviour. Input data were obtained from the sources mentioned above. Dynamic escalations were not enabled for these baseline scenario runs or for the sensitivity analysis.

For the validation, we first looked at whether the simulated demand by hour-day resembled the user-input. Then, we were interested to check whether the relative pattern and direction of the mean and 90th percentile response time KPI by category emerged from the model and if the order of magnitude was sensible. We also looked at absolute levels, though matching this was not a primary aim. We also wanted to compare behaviour for a broader range of KPIs related to 'Time to Allocate', 'job cycle time (JCT)', 'mean response time', '90 %ile response time', 'ambulance arrivals', 'handover' and 'vehicle availability'. All these parameters have in common that they are emerging parameters from the model runs and behaviour, rather than resulting from straightforward model inputs, meaning that we can use them to assess the quality of the baseline scenario. The average JCT time was however used to calibrate parameters related to the ED, as explained previously. Validation information (i.e. not explicitly given as input to the model) was obtained from other data points from those same data sources (Table 2). Finally, we wanted to check visually the relationship between response time vs ambulance availability curve, since this should be expected to show the trade-off as a non-linear pattern with asymptotic behaviour towards each extreme.

1.5.2 Sensitivity

We show the behaviour for 6 KPIs as, in turn, 4 parameters are adjusted, keeping all others unchanged:
- X % improvement (reduction) in Average Time in Department (ALL attendances)-
- X% improvement (increase) in double staffed vehicle (DSV) Supply
- X %p shift from See and Convey to See and Treat (Cat3,4)
- X %p shift from See and Treat to Hear and Treat (Cat3,4)

The KPI's are:

- Mean category 2 response time - the mean time between receiving a call and arriving at the scene
- Mean time to allocate - the mean time between receiving a call and allocating a vehicle
- Mean job cycle time – the mean time a vehicle is on the job (from allocation to vehicle clearance)
- DSV availability – the ambulance double staffed vehicle (DSV) availability (%)
- A&E availability – the availability of the stylistic ED (%)
- Handover 30+ - the % of ambulances with a delay of 30+ minutes

2 RESULTS

2.1 Baseline scenario

The input to the modelling simulates reality as shown by the overall demand (black line) equating to the compound demand of the four categories (Figure 4). The supply (red line) of vehicles is shown to give an indication of the interplay between peaks of call demand and vehicle supply. Also note that given the typical vehicle job cycle times of over 2.5 hours, on average it also takes just about two and a half times as much supply as demand to maintain the current system.

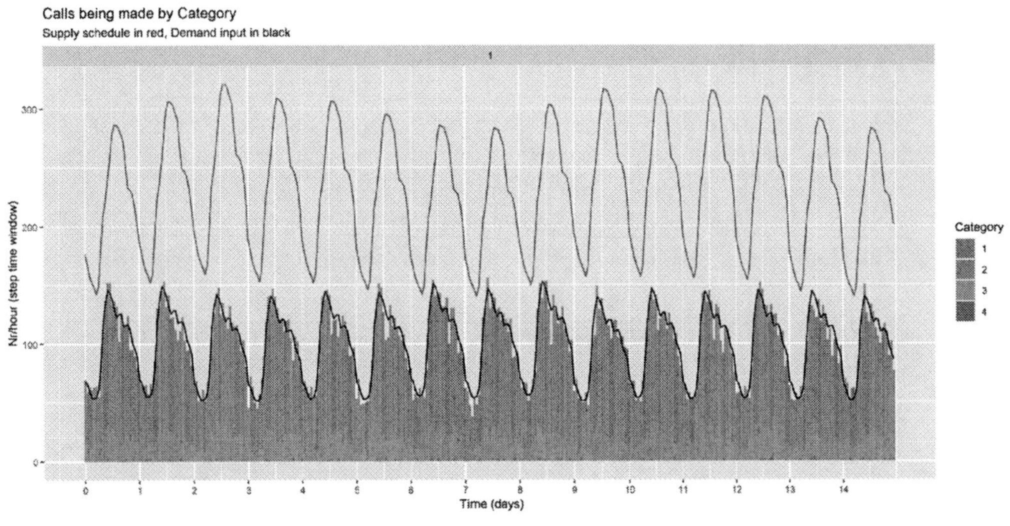

Figure 4 Average demand by hour of the simulation – face to face incidents. The colour coding relates to the category (1, 2, 3, 4). The black line shows the expected overall demand given inputs. The red line shows the vehicle on-duty profile (supply).

In Figure 5 the mean response time is shown to increase from category 1 to 2, 3, 4. The dashed line shows the empirical observed level for the respective month. The relation of response time among the categories is broadly preserved.

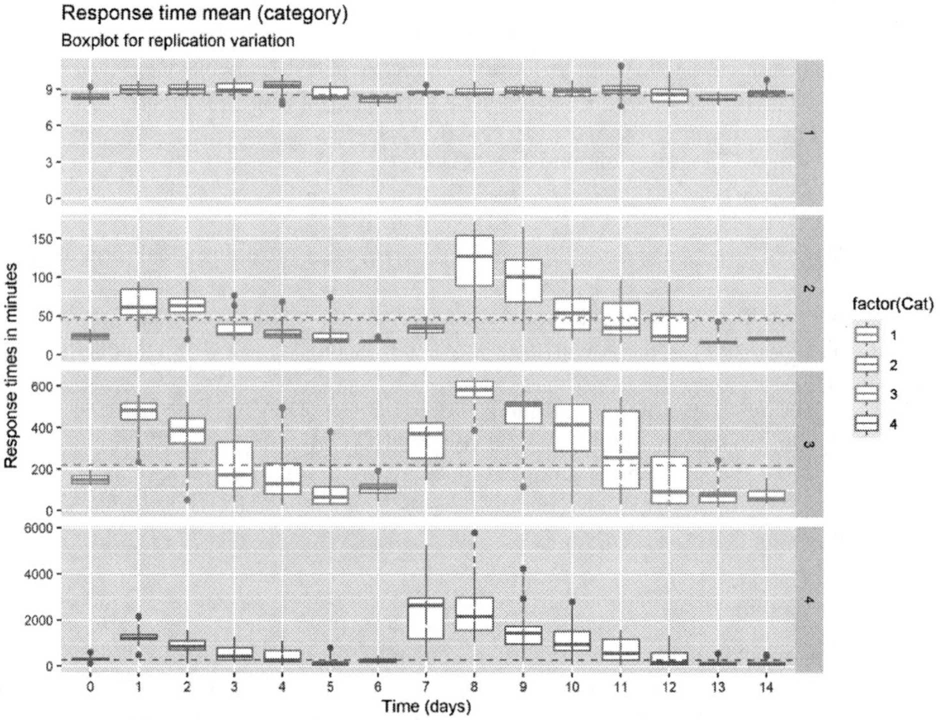

Figure 5 The daily mean response times obtained in the model run. Boxplots show variation across replications. Dashed lines shows observed monthly aggregate figure.

For the 90th percentile, we also observe an increase as expected from category 1 to 2, 3, 4, of reasonable magnitude (Table 1).

Table 1 90th percentile of response time by category. For 'simulation', this is the 90th percentile across the simulation time (2 weeks). Since we ran 10 replications (reps) we show the mean and 1.96 x standard error (SE) of the mean. The 'real-world' observed figure is also shown.

	Simulation - 10 replications		**Empirical**
Category	**Mean (of 10 reps)**	**1.96 x SE of mean**	**Observed**
1	17.1	0.5	14.88
2	117.8	30.3	110.02
3	558.0	41.0	585.7
4	2505.3	951.4	706.73

Table 2 shows the results for a broader range of key performance indicators (KPIs) related to 'Time to Allocate', 'JCT time', 'mean response time', '90%ile response time', 'ambulance arrivals', 'handover' and 'vehicle availability'.

The model overall showed good capability to replicate the behaviour of the real world scenario through its 'emerging parameters'. Quite notably good agreement was obtained for priority parameters of interest like category 2 mean and 90th centile response time, vehicle availability and average time to allocate a vehicle. The greatest deviations were found for category 4 calls, which can be considered expected due to their low volume (circa 1%) together with them being the lowest priority for allocation making them more susceptible to noise and more volatile under scenarios of pressure. Handover times were also overestimated, likely related to the fact that these are very dependent on the behaviour and performance in the emergency department and the effects of the competing nature of direct attendances. Although these are captured in the model, this was done so in a simplified stylistic way (with calibration in function of the average JCT time), which may prove too crude to properly capture all the intricacies.

Table 2 Results – baseline scenario. Comparison of KPIs between simulated and empirical (real-world).

Key performance indicator	Simulation	Empirical	Source for empirical
Average Time to Allocate – 'see and convey'	62 min	63 min	ADS
Average Time to Allocate – 'see and treat'	99 min	101 min	ADS
Average JCT time – 'see and convey'	204 min	199 min	ADS
Average JCT time – 'see and convey'	187 min	187 min	ADS
Cat1 mean response time	8.8 min	8.5 min	AmbSYS
Cat2 mean response time	48 min	47.9 min	AmbSYS
Cat3 mean response time	273 min	219.5 min	AmbSYS
Cat4 mean response time	917 min	261 min	AmbSYS
Cat1 90th %ile response time	17.1	14.9	AmbSYS
Cat2 90th %ile response time	117.8	110.0	AmbSYS
Cat3 90th %ile response time	558.0	585.7	AmbSYS
Cat4 90th %ile response time	2505.5	706.7	AmbSYS
Number of ambulances arriving at ED / day	1375	1373	dAC
Average (pre-) handover time	50 min	39 min	ADS
% handovers 30+ minutes	45%	35.3%	dAC
% handovers 30+ minutes	22.9%	17.0%	dAC
Vehicle availability	97.5%	98-99%	NACC

Finally, we performed visual inspection of the response time vs ambulance availability curve (Figure 6). We see the expected behaviour for the curve. In the central area ("shoulder"), the trade-off between both is marked. At a certain point, increasing levels of availability will not render improved response times (as other considerations like 'Time to Scene' become limiting). From a certain point of accentuated low availability, increasingly worsening response times are registered. The exact levels and point of trade-off for each local system will differ, but the overall behaviour is as described.

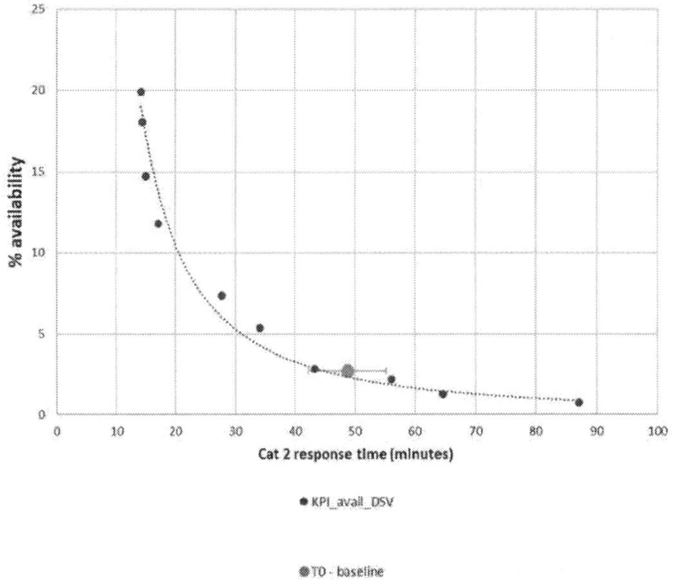

Figure 6 Non-linear relationship between double staffed vehicle availability and category 2 mean response time. Model-observed relationship when applying different levels of A&E strain. The 'baseline' is also shown.

2.2 Sensitivity

Scans are overlaid for compactness (Figure 7), though note that the sensitivity scan is not looking at comparable scenarios (levels of intervention), rather just looking at what happens when changing some of the main parameters impacting the model.

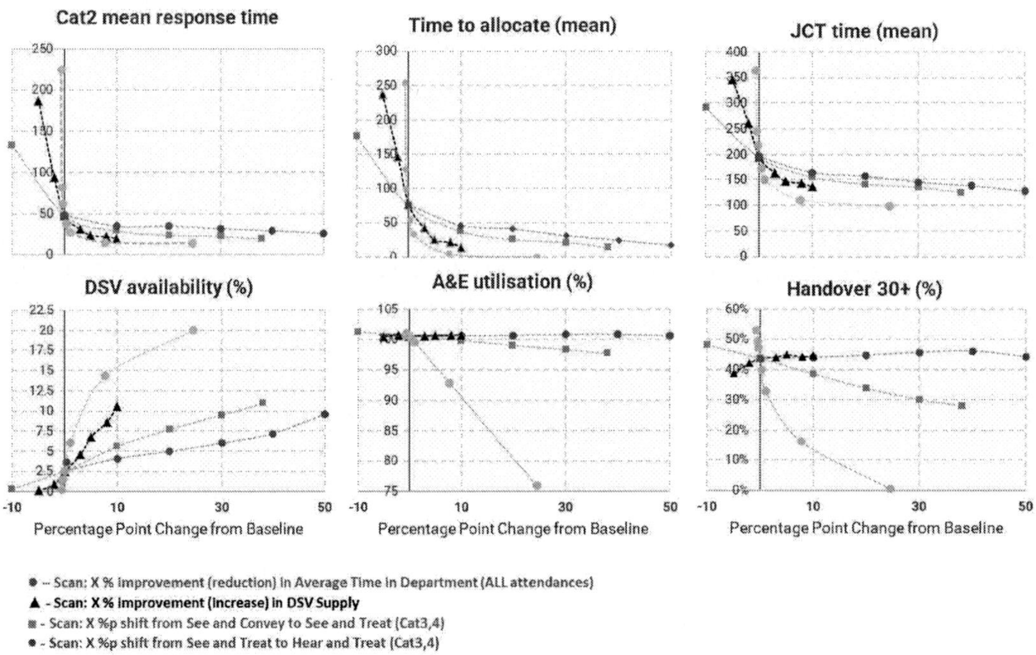

Figure 7 Sensitivity analysis. Changes to four parameters (scans). Impact shown against 6 KPIs

Overall, changes in conveyance or care model parameter are rather linear. Changes in A&E parameter are mostly non-linear / exponential.

Though not shown, we would also like to highlight that changes to the competitive nature of the admission process between ambulances and direct attendances, either via the overall volume of direct attendances or their relative prioritisation with respect to ambulance arrivals (at different acuity but also given a same acuity) has a significant impact in the model, via changes to the handover times.

There is a further common message between these and the 'A&E time in department' (LoS) parameter – downstream changes to the way the A&E department operates has an outsized effect (higher sensitivity) on KPIs, more than those on ambulance parameters. This implies, as suspected, that under a situation of considerable ED strain, solving ambulance performance solely via changes to aspects directly in the gift of the ambulance service is difficult and possible only to a certain extent. The likely best course of action is to increase downstream (ED) performance so that the overall flow can improve.

3 OPPORTUNITIES AND CHALLENGES

We built a model that can simulate the performance of the ambulance system. Good alignment was obtained between observed and model-generated KPIs. While not all absolute levels matched for emerging variables, overall relationships and trade-offs were as expected, which was the primary aim.

In terms of opportunities, the current model parametrisation means there is a range of possible levers to test *in-silico* for policy and delivery.

Illustrative questions that could be answered include 'what-if' questions on what happens to response times and vehicle availability when vehicle supply increases; supply schedule is changed; demand increases; demand by category varies; hear-and-treat rate is changed; rate of conveyance is changed; specific job cycle time component times decrease; "ED pressure" changes (via 'ED resource number, n' or 'time in department' parameters). Other questions could include considering:

- what type of change to one of the levels above delivers a given level of availability (or other KPI) improvement – i.e. goal-seek.
- under which (e.g. varying levels of ED pressure) conditions do the levers/interventions above provide diminishing returns or lower effectiveness;
- what happens to response times, availability and the use of escalations (compared to a 'no escalation' pressure scenario) when these dynamic escalations are allowed to occur: a) patients are allowed to balk or renege to a certain extent; b) conveyance rates are sensitive to pressure.

As for future improvements, on a technical level the sampling implementation of the model's non-stationary poisson process (NSPP) assumption could be improved. While for the the baseline scenario our model captures well the average number of arrivals (Figure 4), for different scenarios where for instance low arrival rates are followed by higher arrival rates a better NSPP sampling approach would be advised, namely by employing a thinning algorithm.

Conceptual gaps that could be addressed in future work include better dealing with second order dynamics related to escalations or behavioural phenomena (by patients or operators). The model is currently "too sensitive" compared to real-life, which likely relates to those second-order stabilising effects. While including feedback loops and dynamic escalations is relatively straightforward from a technical point of view – and implemented to some extent in the model (e.g. balking, reneging, adaptable conveyance at increased pressure) – parametrising such behavioural dynamics and escalations properly requires further qualitative and empirical research.

Further, we used a single stylistic resource-constrained ED server with a given 'length of stay' activity time, priority and (calibrated) number of server resources. This is sufficient to ensure that increased strain in ED translates into a relative increased strain in handover delays. However, for a better representation at an absolute level rather than just in relative terms of such handover KPIs - heavily reliant on ED performance and admission prioritisation decisions - another key improvement could involve coupling the current ambulance model to a well-calibrated ED module that better models ED performance and ED-specific dynamics related to the priority of direct attendances and ambulance attendances. Existing conceptual models could be leveraged (Mohiuddin et al, 2017; Squires et al 2024), adding them as a module to the existing ambulance one, within a wider open-source framework (Monks and Harper, 2023) that can best exploit the modularity and promote accessibility and knowledge exchange.

4 CONCLUSION

A solution has been built that can help policy stakeholders and local systems make evidence-based decisions when building effective recovery implementation plans for ambulance performance, under different operational contexts. Its open-source nature means it can be shared across systems for knowledge-sharing, functionality improvement and adapted case studies and that it can be coupled to ED models for further cross-setting analyses.

ACKNOWLEDGMENTS

The authors would like to thank the NHS England Urgent and Emergency Care (UEC) team for their guidance, expert advice and provision of aggregate statistics for proper model parametrisation.

REFERENCES

Kotiadis K, Tako AA, Vasilakis C (2014). A participative and facilitative conceptual modelling framework for discrete event simulation studies in healthcare. *J Oper Res Soc*;65:197–213.

Mohiuddin S, Busby J, Savović J, et al (2017). Patient flow within UK emergency departments: a systematic review of the use of computer simulation modelling methods. *BMJ Open*;7:e015007. doi:10.1136/bmjopen-2016-015007

Monks T, Harper A (2023). Improving the usability of open health service delivery simulation models using Python and web apps. *NIHR Open Res.* Dec 15;3:48. doi: 10.3310/nihropenres.13467.1. PMID: 37881450; PMCID: PMC10593330.

Squires H, Mason S, O'Keeffe C, et al (2024). What impact would reducing low-acuity attendance have on emergency department length of stay? A discrete event simulation modelling study. *Emergency Medicine Journal*; 41:27-33.

NHS Digital (2024a), Ambulance Data Set (ADS). Access: https://digital.nhs.uk/data-and-information/data-collections-and-data-sets/data-sets/ambulance-data-set

NHS Digital (2024b), Emergency Care Data Set (ECDS). Access: https://digital.nhs.uk/data-and-information/data-collections-and-data-sets/data-sets/emergency-care-data-set-ecds

NHS England (2023a). Delivery plan for recovering urgent and emergency care services. Access: https://www.england.nhs.uk/wp-content/uploads/2023/01/B2034-delivery-plan-for-recovering-urgent-and-emergency-care-services.pdf

NHS England (2023b), Ambulance Quality Indicators Data 2022-23. Access: https://www.england.nhs.uk/statistics/statistical-work-areas/ambulance-quality-indicators/ambulance-quality-indicators-data-2022-23/

NHS England (2022), Urgent and Emergency Care Daily Situation Reports 2021-22. Access: https://www.england.nhs.uk/statistics/statistical-work-areas/uec-sitrep/urgent-and-emergency-care-daily-situation-reports-2021-22/

AUTHOR BIOGRAPHIES

MARTINA FONSECA is chief data officer at Sciensano. She previously worked as an analyst and senior data scientist at NHS England and NHSX. She obtained her PhD in medical physics from University College London.

JONATHAN PEARSON is a lead data scientist at NHS England and previously NHSX. He obtained his PhD in nuclear fusion and plasma physics from the University of Dusseldorf.

Proceedings of the Operational Research Society Simulation Workshop 2025 (SW25)
M. Luis, A. Harper, T. Monks, N. Mustafee, eds
https://doi.org/10.36819/SW25.043

NAVIGATING HOSPITAL OPERATIONS THROUGH SIMULATION: A STUDY OF URBAN FLOODING DISASTERS AND PHYSICAL DAMAGE IMPACT

Sorour Farahi

University of Southampton
Southampton SO17 1BJ
s.s.farahi@soton.ac.uk

Steffen Bayer

University of Southampton
Southampton SO17 1BJ
s.c.bayer@soton.ac.uk

Sally Brailsford

University of Southampton
Southampton SO17 1BJ
s.c.brailsford@soton.co.uk

Stephan Onggo

University of Southampton
Southampton SO17 1BJ
b.s.s.onggo@soton.ac.uk

ABSTRACT

This paper presents a discrete-event simulation model of an entire hospital to investigate the impact of urban flooding disasters, specifically focusing on physical damage to the hospital building and its implications for patient care. A novel patient-centred health utility function is introduced to assess patient outcomes and inform patient prioritisation decisions. The model is used to simulate a two-wave disaster scenario: the initial wave represents physically injured patients due to the flooding, while the second wave captures patients with flood-related infections. Additionally, this paper experiments with strategies and policies to respond effectively to the disaster and enhance resilience. Preliminary results demonstrate the model's ability to evaluate hospital resilience and balance the needs of disaster victims and routine patients. This work is intended to lay the foundation for data-driven disaster preparedness and response planning.

Keywords: discrete-event simulation, simulation in healthcare, disaster management

1 INTRODUCTION

Urban flooding represents a serious and growing challenge, often resulting in widespread devastation, economic damages, and the loss of human lives (Halecki and Młyński, 2025). Among all natural disasters globally, floods occur with the highest frequency (Xie *et al.*, 2017) and are projected to increase over the coming decades due to global climate change and rapid urbanisation (Azadgar *et al.*, 2025). Given this context, the importance of modelling and simulating urban flooding disasters cannot be overstated, particularly in understanding their impacts on critical infrastructure such as healthcare facilities.

When urban flooding occurs, it can severely disrupt healthcare infrastructure due to physical damage. Urban flooding is a specific example of natural disasters that can cause such damage to hospitals. Maintaining operational capability becomes a significant challenge for healthcare units, which must continue their operations despite partial damage or destruction. Numerous studies have examined the resilience of hospital systems; however, this research specifically focuses on hospital resilience in the context of disasters that involve physical damage. Relevant studies on such disasters (Shahverdi, Tariverdi and Miller-Hooks, 2020; Mahmoud *et al.*, 2023; Carbonara, Pellegrino and De Luca, 2024) outline how these events can impact healthcare units in critical areas. This includes structural integrity, such as damage to the building framework; non-structural elements, such as damage to interior finishes and fixtures; lifeline support systems, which encompass power or water outages; and medical resources, including damage or failure of equipment and shortages of medical staff. In conducting a review of hospital studies related to disasters involving physical damage, the following gaps in the literature have been identified: notably, no individual study comprehensively covers all the consequences of physical damage on healthcare facilities, and current literature addresses only a narrow scope of damages and losses in their disruption scenarios. Additionally, while existing research has estimated system resilience, there is a lack of studies that design and evaluate specific response policies and improvement strategies beyond merely adding more resources.

The effects of urban flooding extend beyond immediate physical destruction; they also significantly impact the health of affected populations, as well as hospital buildings and operations. Research by Lane *et al.* (2013) and Paterson, Wright and Harris (2018) highlights various pathways through which urban flooding can lead to adverse health outcomes. Initial exposure to flood-related hazards can result in physical injuries and other health risks. Additionally, power outages can lead to severe conditions, such as carbon monoxide poisoning and heat- or cold-related illnesses (Dharmarathne *et al.*, 2024). Following such disasters, secondary hazards also emerge, including waterborne illnesses and respiratory infections due to prolonged exposure to contaminated environments (Mulder *et al.*, 2019; Jang *et al.*, 2024). This multifaceted impact underscores the necessity of understanding how urban flooding affects healthcare infrastructure and the populations it serves.

In addition to the physical and operational challenges posed by urban flooding, patient health outcomes are a critical aspect that warrants attention. The disruption of healthcare services during disaster events can compromise patient outcomes and overall health states. A review of the literature on whole hospital simulation models (Basaglia *et al.*, 2022; Miller-Hooks *et al.*, 2022; Ordu *et al.*, 2023) shows that the performance metrics commonly used are primarily limited to process-based outcomes, such as length of stay, waiting time, and resource utilisation, which focus mainly on the operational efficiency of hospitals. Mortality rate is the only health outcome-related metric typically considered in this literature. Incorporating a patient-centered Key Performance Indicator (KPI) that measures patients' health utility emphasises quality of care, as this KPI also takes health outcomes into account. It transcends conventional process-based KPIs, which are typically used to improve hospital operational efficiency. Additionally, the literature lacks sufficient attention to capturing the competition between routine and disaster patients over hospital resources during a disaster scenario. More importantly, in our context, the patient-centered KPI provides a basis for balancing the needs of disaster victims and routine patients.

Urban flooding disasters pose significant challenges for hospitals, causing physical damage to infrastructure, straining resources, and compromising patient outcomes. However, existing studies often overlook the multifaceted impact of disasters, including the absence of patient-centred KPI designed to assess patient health outcomes, and the need to balance the competing demands of disaster victims and routine patients. This research aims to address this gap by building a comprehensive Discrete-event Simulation (DES) model of an entire hospital under urban flooding disaster conditions. The model incorporates a novel patient-centred health utility function and simulates a realistic two-wave disaster scenario. This paper also designs response policies that can be used to experiment with the hospital simulation model during disaster scenarios and periods of hospital congestion. The ultimate goal is to provide managerial insights at the hospital level to prioritize patients, balance the needs of existing and disaster victims, and maintain quality of care during and after a major disaster.

The rest of this paper is organised as follows: Section 2 presents the simulation model of an entire hospital, including the design and framework of experiments, and proposes the patient-centered indicator. Section 3 presents the preliminary results. Finally, Section 4 concludes the study by summarising how the developed simulation model captures hospital operations and the impact of disasters, highlights the design of a health utility function, and discusses the next steps in completing this ongoing work.

2 HOSPITAL SIMULATION MODEL

2.1 Simulation Model Overview

A DES model of a hospital was developed using AnyLogic software. This model captures patient flows and resource dynamics across the entire hospital, including Accident & Emergency (A&E), outpatient, and inpatient care services. Inpatient care is further divided into surgical and medical wards. Figure A-1 illustrates a high-level flowchart of the patient flow process within the hospital. The hospital operates 24/7, every day of the week. Patients are assigned attributes such as Emergency Severity Index (ESI), age, gender, entry point, and exit point. Patient arrivals in the A&E are time-dependent, influenced by the specific hour of the day. Additionally, outpatient and inpatient arrivals vary according to the day of the week, reflecting the absence of elective patients on weekends. The model run length is set to 9 months with 10 replications. Furthermore, a warm-up period of 50 days is determined using Welch's method (Welch, 1981). The model is validated using face validity and extreme condition tests.

2.2 Experimentation Design

Two categories of experiments have been designed. The disaster scenarios reflect the real-world effects of urban flooding on the hospital and the population, while the response policies are strategies aimed at enhancing hospital resilience. In this study, we conduct three experiments as follows:

Experiment 1 (Baseline). This scenario represents the normal arrival patterns in hospital operations and usual rules policy under routine conditions, as explained earlier in 2.1.

Experiment 2 (Two-Wave Disaster Scenario and Usual Rules Policy). This scenario reflects the impact of immediate and secondary health implications of the disaster on the affected population. This scenario is designed based on insights from literature (Paterson, Wright and Harris, 2018), and real-world case studies (Mulder *et al.*, 2019; Musacchio *et al.*, 2021; Ziliotto, Chies and Ellwanger, 2024). The disaster strikes from day 150 and lasts for 10 days. The first wave of the disaster results in victims who are physically injured as a result of direct exposure to the flood and require surgery. In the second wave of the disaster, arriving patients have contracted respiratory infections and waterborne diseases and are admitted to the medical ward for treatment. This scenario also takes into account the specific demographic characteristics, such as the age profile of the disaster arrivals.

Experiment 3 (Two-Wave Disaster Scenario and Elective Cancellation Policy). One response policy to enhance hospital resilience during a disaster or surge in demand is the temporary cancellation of elective patient admissions (Nehme, Puchkova and Parlikad, 2022). This strategy involves suspending the inflow of planned outpatient and inpatient treatment cases, allowing the hospital to redirect its resources toward managing disaster arrivals and patients with emergency care needs. Implementing this policy scenario is a promising approach for addressing patient demand in the Two-Wave Disaster Scenario. By stopping elective admissions to both the inpatient and outpatient wards, the hospital can free up resources to better handle the high demand generated by the two disaster waves presented in this scenario. Therefore, reducing the influx of elective cases can help alleviate the expected congestion in the inpatient and outpatient wards.

2.3 Health Utility Function

Typically, models in the literature focus on process-based outcomes, such as length of stay, waiting times and resource utilisation, with mortality being the only health-related outcome considered. A major contribution of this model is that it incorporates health outcomes for all patients. To assess the patient outcomes, a health utility function is introduced in this paper, capable of evaluating patient health utilities at the population level within a hospital setting. The function assigns a utility score on a numerical scale from 0 to 1, where 1 represents perfect health and 0 indicates death, for each patient throughout their hospital stay. Based on findings from the literature (Needleman *et al.*, 2011; Kuntz and Sülz, 2013; Brazier *et al.*, 2017), several factors are considered in calculating health utility, including:

Base Utility. This reflects the patient's well-being upon arrival at the hospital and is dependent on gender and age.

Reason for Admission. This accounts for the temporary condition that has led to the patient's illness.

Utility on Admission. This is derived from the two factors mentioned above. Utility on Admission is calculated using the formula presented in Equation (1):

$$\textit{Utility on Admission} = \textit{Base Utility} * \textit{Reason for Admission} \qquad (1)$$

Curability. This factor assesses whether the patient has an acute or chronic condition, or if they have sustained an injury that results in permanent disability.

Effect of Delay. This reflects any delays the patient may experience in receiving treatment compared to the standard timeframe.

Effect of Treatment Quality. It reflects the adequacy of available resources and is quantified by the staff-to-patient ratio.

Final Utility. This measures the final health utility value for individual patients at discharge and is compared with Base Utility and Utility on Admission. Equation (2) outlines the formula proposed to calculate the health utility function:

$$\textit{Health Utility Function} = \textit{Base Utility} * \textit{Curability} * \textit{Effect of Delay} * \textit{Effect of Treatment Quality} \quad (2)$$

The health utility function is incorporated into the hospital simulation care paths, spanning from patient entry to discharge, and is used as an output KPI.

3 PRELIMINARY RESULTS

The simulation model was run for the three experiments outlined in 2.2. The patient-centred health utility function was used to assess the impact on patient outcomes across different patient categories.

Table 1 presents the average final utility scores for routine patients, including emergency admissions, direct referrals, and elective admissions. In Experiment 1, which represents the normal operations of the hospital, the average final utility score of 0.77 exceeds the utility on admission, which is 0.48. This indicates that most patients experienced an improvement in their health states compared to when they were admitted. The final utility score is below the base utility of 0.81, suggesting that while patients generally improved during their hospital stay, not every patient fully returns to their original health state.

However, under Experiment 2, the final utility drops to 0.48, 0.60, and 0.64 for emergency, direct referral, and elective patients, respectively. This decline in utility scores highlights the significant impact of the disaster on routine patient outcomes.

Table 1 Average Final Utility for Routine Patient across Different Experiments

			Emergency	**Direct Referral**	**Elective**
	Base Utility	Utility on Admission	Final Utility	Final Utility	Final Utility
Experiment 1	0.81	0.48	0.77	0.77	0.77
Experiment 2	0.81	0.48	0.48	0.60	0.64
Experiment 3	0.81	0.48	0.56	0.74	0.76

Experiment 3, designed to mitigate the impact of the disaster, shows improvements in final utility scores compared to the disaster scenario. While the utility scores remain lower than the baseline for emergency patients, the elective cancellation policy demonstrates its effectiveness in balancing the utility score of different routine patient groups during the disaster. The current model does not consider the impact of treatment delay due to the cancellation. This will be addressed in our future work.

Table 2 focuses on the disaster victims, categorised into first wave and second wave arrivals. Under Experiment 2, the final utility values for first wave and second wave disaster victims are 0.43 and 0.41, respectively. These low utility scores emphasise the severe impact of the disaster on the health outcomes of disaster victims.

Experiment 3 shows a notable increase in final utility scores for both first wave and second-wave disaster victims compared to Experiment 2. The final utility for both first wave and second-wave victims increases to 0.77. This suggests that the elective cancellation policy not only helps balance utility values among routine patient groups but also significantly improves outcomes for disaster victims by freeing up resources to address their immediate medical needs.

Table 2 Average Final Utility for Disaster Victims across Different Experiments

			First Wave Disaster Arrivals	Second Wave Disaster Arrivals
	Base Utility	Utility on Admission	Final Utility	Final Utility
Experiment 2	0.81	0.48	0.43	0.41
Experiment 3	0.81	0.48	0.77	0.77

4 DISCUSSION & CONCLUSION

This study developed an entire hospital simulation model that captures both hospital operations during disasters and the presence of scheduled patients. It also examines the impact of two waves of disaster, focusing on the initial and secondary health implications of urban flooding on the population. A distinctive aspect of this research is the creation of a health utility function, which serves as a patient-centric indicator for measuring health outcomes. This approach allows the system to be evaluated and improved not only through traditional process-based indicators but also via this patient-centred indicator that emphasises individual health utility. By integrating this health utility function into the simulation model, the study enables the tracking of each patient's health outcomes throughout their entire treatment journey within the hospital and enables the model to explore potential health-related trade-offs between disaster and routine patients under different response policies.

The preliminary findings from this paper demonstrate the potential of using utility measures to assess the impact of disasters and response policies on different patient groups. Although model parameters are currently being refined using literature and publicly available datasets to obtain more accurate values, the initial results show promising applications. The utility function enables hospital managers to prioritise patient groups based on their health needs and to allocate resources effectively to balance the utility across all patient categories. By comparing utility scores across scenarios, decision-makers can identify the patient groups most severely affected by the disaster and tailor response strategies accordingly.

The simulation model indicates capability for decision support in hospital disaster response. As this research is ongoing, future work should focus on expanding the range of disaster scenarios and response policies. Emphasis should be placed on scenario evaluation, specifically examining the impact of delayed treatment due to the cancellation as well as the impact of flooding on hospital infrastructure in addition to its effects on the population. Additionally, it is important to analyse results across diverse patient groups, such as different age demographics or ESI levels. Future efforts will also aim to provide insights regarding patient prioritisation plans for hospital managers.

ACKNOWLEDGMENTS

This research was funded by the UKRI ESRC South Coast Doctoral Training Partnership Grant Number ES/P000673/1.

APPENDIX

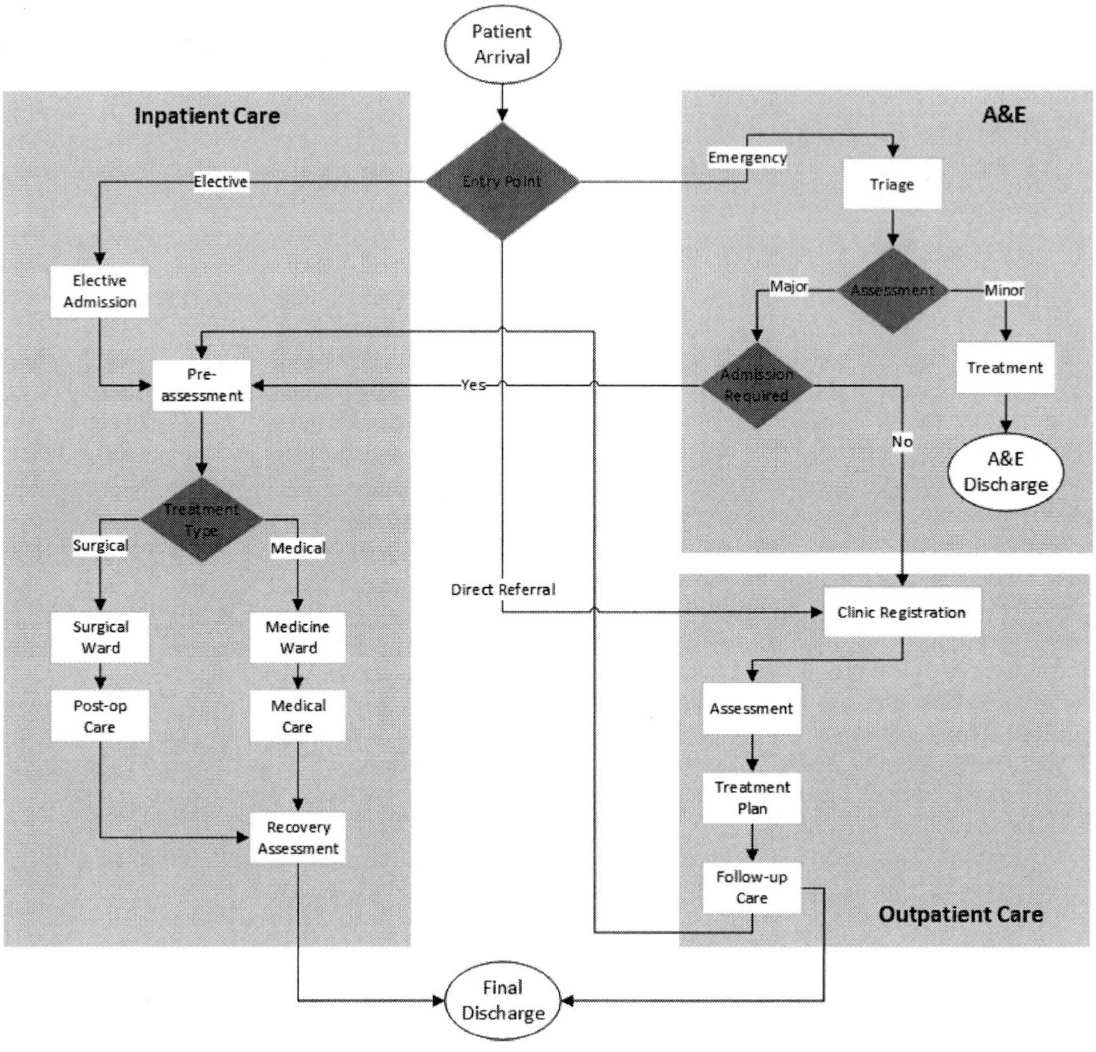

Figure A-1 High-level flowchart of the patient flow process within the hospital

REFERENCES

Azadgar, A. *et al.* (2025) 'Optimizing nature-based solutions for urban flood risk mitigation: A multi-objective genetic algorithm approach in Gdańsk, Poland', *Science of The Total Environment*, 963, p. 178303.

Basaglia, A. *et al.* (2022) 'A discrete-event simulation model of hospital patient flow following major earthquakes', *International Journal of Disaster Risk Reduction*, 71, p. 102825.

Brazier, J. *et al.* (2017) *Measuring and valuing health benefits for economic evaluation*. OXFORD university press.

Carbonara, N., Pellegrino, R. and De Luca, C. (2024) 'Resilience of hospitals in an age of disruptions: a systematic literature review on resources and capabilities', *Health Systems*, 13(3), pp. 192-228.

Dharmarathne, G. *et al.* (2024) 'Adapting Cities to the Surge: A Comprehensive Review of Climate-Induced Urban Flooding', *Results in Engineering*, p. 102123.

Halecki, W. and Młyński, D. (2025) 'Urban flood dilemmas: How European cities growth shapes flood risk and resilience strategies?', *Journal of Environmental Management*, 374, p. 124161.

Jang, M. *et al.* (2024) 'Changes in healthcare utilization after the 2022 Seoul metropolitan flood: Applying a generalized synthetic control approach', *GeoHealth*, 8(10), p. e2024GH001084.

Kuntz, L. and Sülz, S. (2013) 'Treatment speed and high load in the Emergency Department—does staff quality matter?', *Health care management science*, 16, pp. 366-376.
Lane, K. *et al.* (2013) 'Health effects of coastal storms and flooding in urban areas: a review and vulnerability assessment', *Journal of environmental and public health*, 2013.
Mahmoud, H. *et al.* (2023) 'The resilience of health care systems following major disruptive events: Current practice and a path forward', *Reliability Engineering & System Safety*, 235, p. 109264.
Miller-Hooks, E. *et al.* (2022) 'A flatter curve affords hospitals greater time to prepare for a pandemic surge', *Healthcare Analytics*, 2, p. 100076.
Mulder, A.C. *et al.* (2019) '"Sickenin'in the rain"–increased risk of gastrointestinal and respiratory infections after urban pluvial flooding in a population-based cross-sectional study in the Netherlands', *BMC infectious diseases*, 19, pp. 1-12.
Musacchio, A. *et al.* (2021) 'Planning for the health impacts of climate change: Flooding, private groundwater contamination and waterborne infection–A cross-sectional study of risk perception, experience and behaviours in the Republic of Ireland', *Environmental Research*, 194, p. 110707.
Needleman, J. *et al.* (2011) 'Nurse staffing and inpatient hospital mortality', *New England Journal of Medicine*, 364(11), pp. 1037-1045.
Nehme, R., Puchkova, A. and Parlikad, A. (2022) 'A predictive model for the post-pandemic delay in elective treatment', *Operations Research for Health Care*, 34, p. 100357.
Ordu, M. *et al.* (2023) 'A comprehensive and integrated hospital decision support system for efficient and effective healthcare services delivery using discrete event simulation', *Healthcare Analytics*, 4, p. 100248.
Paterson, D.L., Wright, H. and Harris, P.N. (2018) 'Health risks of flood disasters', *Clinical Infectious Diseases*, 67(9), pp. 1450-1454.
Shahverdi, B., Tariverdi, M. and Miller-Hooks, E. (2020) 'Assessing hospital system resilience to disaster events involving physical damage and Demand Surge', *Socio-Economic Planning Sciences*, 70, p. 100729.
Welch, P.D. (1981) 'On the problem of the initial transient in steady-state simulation', *IBM Watson Research Center*, 37.
Xie, J. *et al.* (2017) 'An integrated assessment of urban flooding mitigation strategies for robust decision making', *Environmental modelling & software*, 95, pp. 143-155.
Ziliotto, M., Chies, J.A.B. and Ellwanger, J.H. (2024) 'Extreme weather events and pathogen pollution fuel infectious diseases: the 2024 flood-related leptospirosis outbreak in Southern Brazil and other red lights', *Pollutants*, 4(3), pp. 424-433.

AUTHOR BIOGRAPHIES

SOROUR FARAHI is a PhD candidate at Southampton Business School, the University of Southampton, UK. She obtained a BSc in Industrial Management and a MSc in Operations Research from Persian Gulf University in Iran. Her research interests include simulation modelling applied in healthcare and disaster management. Her email address is s.s.farahi@soton.ac.uk.

STEFFEN BAYER is a Lecturer in Business Analytics within Southampton Business School at the University of Southampton. He is a member of the Centre for Operational Research, Management Sciences and Information Systems (CORMSIS). He is a member of the editorial board of Operations Research for Health Care and a past president of the UK Chapter of the International Systems Dynamics Society. Steffen's main research interest is the planning of health services. His past work includes studies on stroke care, renal care, human resource planning and home-based technology supported health delivery. He uses a variety of approaches in his research including qualitative research, system dynamics, agent-based modelling and discrete event simulation. His email address is S.C.Bayer@soton.ac.uk

SALLY BRAILSFORD is Professor of Management Science at the University of Southampton, UK. She received a BSc in Mathematics from the University of London, and MSc and PhD in Operational Research from the University of Southampton. She is a member of the Centre for Operational Research,

Management Sciences and Information Systems (CORMSIS). Her research interests include simulation modelling methodologies and the modelling of human behaviour in healthcare systems. Her email address is s.c.brailsford@soton.ac.uk.

STEPHAN ONGGO is a Professor of Business Analytics at Southampton Business School, the University of Southampton. He is a member of the Centre for Operational Research, Management Sciences and Information Systems (CORMSIS). His research interests lie in the areas of simulation modelling methodology (symbiotic simulation/digital twin, hybrid modelling, agent-based simulation, discrete-event simulation) with applications in supply chain, health care and disaster management. He is the associate editor for the Journal of Simulation and Flexible Services and Manufacturing Journal. His website is https://bsonggo.wordpress.com. His email address is b.s.s.onggo@soton.ac.uk.

Proceedings of the Operational Research Society Simulation Workshop 2025 (SW25)
M. Luis, A. Harper, T. Monks, N. Mustafee, eds.

https://doi.org/10.36819/SW25.044

DEVELOPING, VERIFYING AND VALIDATING A SIMULATION PLATFORM TO IMPROVE RESOURCE PLANNING FOR THE NSPCC HELPLINE

Mrs. Jess Cole

AtkinsRéalis
2 Chamberlain Square,
Birmingham, B3 3AX
Jess.Cole@atkinsrealis.com

Mr. Stephen Pollard

AtkinsRéalis
The Hub, 500 Park Avenue,
Bristol, BS32 4RZ
Stephen.Pollard@atkinsrealis.com

ABSTRACT

The National Society for the Prevention of Cruelty to Children (NSPCC) runs the Helpline call service, which is used by adults and professionals with concerns about a child. Helpline users can access it via different methods, including phone calls, emails and online webforms. The NSPCC requested a discrete event simulation of the Helpline, to improve its resource planning and explore 'what-if' scenarios of changing demand and resourcing.

This paper outlines the process of creating an integrated simulation platform, with a simple input interface and an output dashboard for the NSPCC to use in their operations. As the Helpline service is complex and interconnected, a detailed verification and validation methodology was undertaken, particularly to ensure the behaviours of resources represented actual operations. Following validation, the simulation platform was transitioned to Helpline staff, who were provided with training in its development and use.

The Helpline Simulation project was arranged in collaboration with the Operational Research Society's (ORS) Pro Bono team and was led by volunteers from AtkinsRéalis working in partnership with NSPCC staff.

Keywords: Discrete Event Simulation, Resource Planning, Verification and Validation, Simulation Platform

1 INTRODUCTION

The National Society for the Prevention of Cruelty to Children (NSPCC) is a UK charity which works to end child abuse and enable children to be safe and supported. It is a crucial communications channel, enabling the NSPCC to be there when children, young people and adults concerned about them are most in need. (https://www.nspcc.org.uk/about-us/ accessed 27 January 2025). A key service provided by the NSPCC is the Helpline call service, which is used by adults and professionals with concerns about a child. A separate Childline service provides support directly to children but was outside of the scope of this project.

The objective set by the NSPCC was to create a simulation platform which, based on expected resourcing and demand, could forecast an expected service level, including answer rates, number of emails and webforms answered, and any email backlogs at the end of the day. The project was requested by the NSPCC's Head of Data and AI, who has past experience with discrete event simulation and was therefore able to articulate clearly her hopes and expectations for the model. Once completed, the model was handed over to the NSPCC team, who intend to use the simulation platform to adjust its resource planning, in order to improve answer rates and to be resilient to variation in demand.

The project was a collaboration, with a team of volunteers from AtkinsRéalis working together with staff at the NSPCC. It was arranged in collaboration with the Operational Research Society's

(ORS) Pro Bono team and used a combination of corporate volunteering days sponsored by AtkinsRéalis and additional personal time volunteered by the team, for a total of approximately 8 weeks of total effort spread over a number of months. (https://www.theorsociety.com/ORS/ORS/Outreach/Pro-Bono/Pro-Bono-OR.aspx accessed 27 January 2025)

2 MODEL DESIGN AND BUILD

Due to the limited time available on this Pro Bono project a rapid prototyping approach was agreed. This was to ensure that an initial version of the Helpline simulation model was built to begin testing, and to deliver a serviceable simulation within a short timeframe. The Helpline processes, system and scope were captured in a process flow diagram, through a combination of interviews with NSPCC staff and review of NSPCC internal process documentation.

The model has two main processes, one handling phone calls and the other handling emails and webforms. At both levels, the initial assessment is performed by an advisor who will provide initial contact with the individual and triage the type of contact. Following this, if required, a practitioner will then provide further assessment which can lead to further action. There is also a system for call-backs if further contact is required following the initial phone call, email or webform. This is displayed in Figure 1.

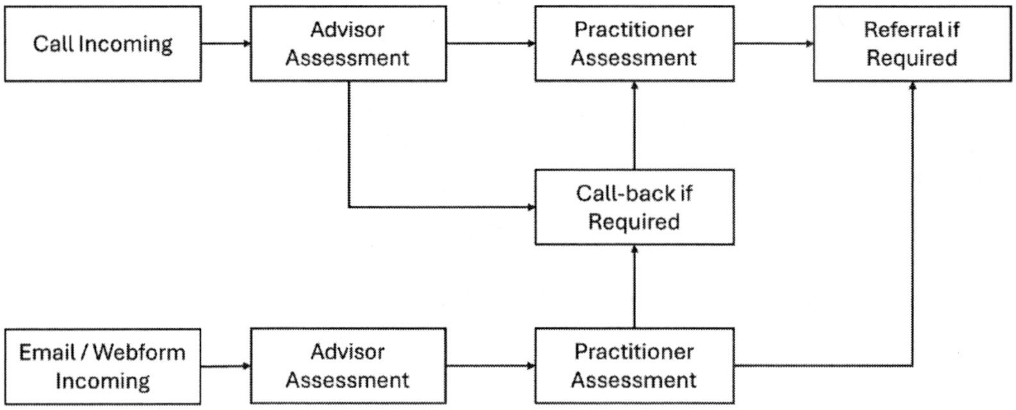

Figure 1 *Basic Helpline Process*

Operational data was analysed from the NSPCC's database to understand the characteristics of cases handled by the service. This included factors such as the quantities of calls, emails and webforms and their arrival rate profile, the probability of callers hanging up while waiting, the probabilities for each routing decision, and the timing distribution for each task. To respect data protection, and because the content of the calls was not pertinent to the project, no sensitive data was included in this analysis. This information was used to generate timing distributions for populating the discrete event simulation activities. The distributions primarily used an Erlang distribution due to the service-based nature of the activities or, where detailed data was not available, triangular distributions to provide simple three-point estimates. As cases can undertake different routes through the system depending upon, for example, if they require additional advice or referral, the data was also analysed to define initial probabilities for different routing options.

It was recognised that both timing distributions and routing probabilities could vary over time, and as the desired outcome for this work was an ongoing forecasting platform, it was important to develop the Helpline model in such a way that this information could be easily altered in the future.

Once this information was captured, an initial version of the model was built in Simul8. Simul8 was selected due to the Pro Bono team's experience with the software, and due to there being established routes available for charities to obtain a licence for the software. The model was constructed to run for one-week, inclusive Monday to Sunday, to align with the NSPCC's current system and to provide a week-look ahead using the latest demand forecast and expected resourcing level data from its system.

It also has the capability to run for multiple weeks into the future, using the end state from the previous week as the starting point for the next week and, similarly, using the demand forecast and expected resourcing level for future weeks as inputs.

While the process from the perspective of an individual case, a call, email or webform, was relatively simple, there is additional complexity due to the connections between different sections of the process and the prioritisation of different tasks performed by the same resource. Figure 2 shows the interactions and resource requirements of the different sections of the process.

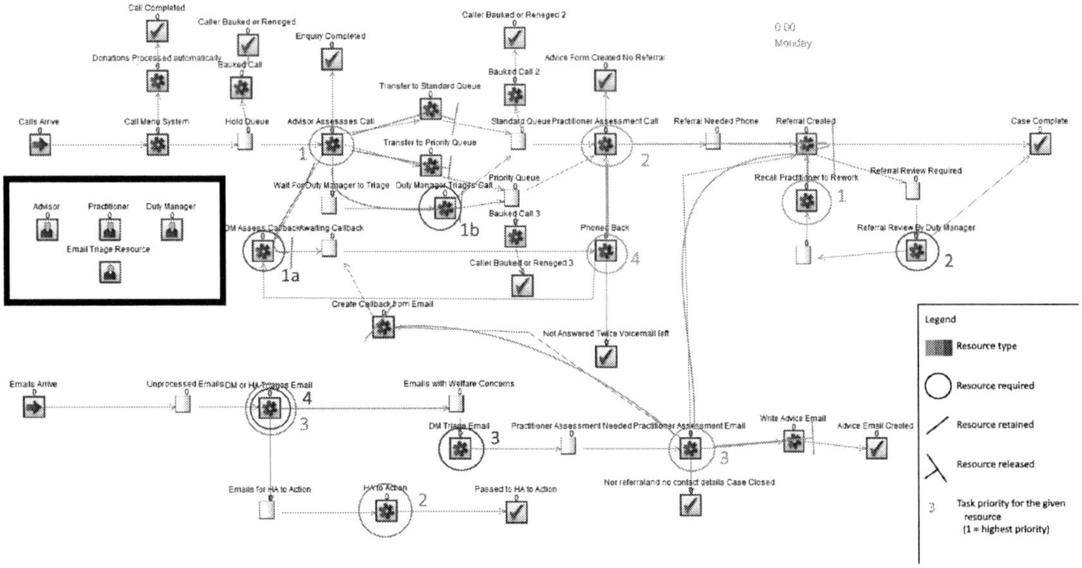

Figure 2 *Illustrated diagram indicating resource usage throughout a process*

This was created by capturing a screenshot from the Simul8 model and adding annotations in a graphical editing tool. This method of visually representing resource use and retention was helpful in discussing these concepts in a non-technical way and allowed several minor corrections to be identified and resolved. In the figure, orange highlighting indicates activities performed by advisors, green by practitioners and purple by duty managers, with priorities indicated using numbers from high to low.

As Helpline has different resource types, each with varying responsibilities and priorities, it was important to understand how each would respond when there are multiple competing demands within the system. Therefore, a prioritisation matrix was developed with the NSPCC to determine the assumed behaviours of Helpline operators when faced with multiple competing demands, including re-allocation of resources on email activities when a phone call was available. The prioritisation matrix shown in table 1 summarises the priorities agreed with the NSPCC. For duty managers, priority 1a and 1b are of equal importance, and the task waiting longest in either queue would be the next actioned.

Table 1 *Task Prioritisation Matrix*

Activity	**Advisor**	**Practitioner**	**Duty Manager**
Triages email	3		4
Action non-welfare email	2		
Triage email – welfare concern			3
Assess email		3	
Initial call assessment	1		
Call handling		2	
Callback assessment			1a
Call triage			1b
Call back		4	
Referral review			2
Referral rework		1	

3 MODEL VERIFICATION AND VALIDATION

Due to the interconnectedness of the model and different resourcing priorities, it was important to perform an extensive verification and validation review of both the contents and output of the Helpline model before it was handed over for active use by the NSPCC. Verification of the model, in this case determining the model structure accurately represented the Helpline's operations, was primarily achieved through review with the NSPCC. Validation of the model, determined through comparing modelled outcomes to actual outcomes, was performed against multiple weeks' worth of data to confirm the model was representative across a longer period of time.

3.1 Model Verification

To verify the different incoming streams, incoming emails, webforms, and phone streams, which each pass through a different set of triages and assessments by different resources, the team reviewed the individual journey of each type of case with the NSPCC team, to ensure that the model achieved the correct outcomes.

During the verification process, it became clear that there was a level of complexity within the call-backs' process that would be difficult to model exactly using a discrete event methodology. The identified issue was that the length of time between a callback request being created and it being actioned is often dependent on a number of factors, such as priority, staff availability and also preference of the user for a particular day or time of day to have the callback. Therefore, the model applied an agreed simplification to handle the rate at which call-backs occurred. This simplification applied a general distribution to capture the elapsed time between when the request is created and actioned. This then could be applied to any request and enable a range of possible outcomes that reflect the operations more closely.

Additionally, Helpline operators in training were not originally accounted for within the model structure. These operators may require additional review of their work by a more experienced operator or duty manager. In order to model this accurately, the model was updated to include an additional review decision point for a minority of cases assumed to be handled by operators in training. The percentage of cases assumed to be handled by operators in training could be modified in the future to represent the experience level of Helpline staff.

3.2 Model Validation

Once the model had been verified with NSPCC staff, the outputs of the model were measured against actual call answer rates achieved by the Helpline. This comparison was performed against three key criteria.

Firstly, the answer rates for both advisors and practitioners on an hour-by-hour, day-by-day and weekly basis. Secondly, emails and webforms answered by Helpline staff each day. Finally, the backlog of emails and callbacks at the end of each week. By performing validation exercises across each criterion individually and then collectively, the model inputs and logic could be updated to correctly represent the complex behaviour and patterns of practitioner assessments of calls and emails. This greatly improved the accuracy of the overall model, as practitioner call answer rates and emails answered in the model closely reflected actual performance.

Another challenging aspect of validating the model against actual performance was that of staff behaviour. One key part of this was staff break times and availability during operational hours. The NSPCC system programmed in anticipated break times for Helpline staff based on their shift pattern, which was used to determine in the model when staff would be available. However, during actual operations, staff would take breaks when demand was lower, leading to higher efficiency outcomes when compared to the model. Therefore, it was decided to remove the programmed break times from the shift pattern and instead use a generalised availability factor for each staff member. While this was a simplification, it enabled the fitting of this factor so that modelled outcomes matched actual operational performance.

4 TRANSITION INTO SERVICE USE

Following the verification and validation process, the model was transferred to the NSPCC for its testing and transition into active use by Helpline staff using their own Simul8 licence. As this model was not intended for purely single-use to provide an individual answer, but for ongoing operational use and development, it was important to ensure that it was straight-forward to both use and develop after the hand-over process was complete.

To support the use by NSPCC staff of the model, the team built an integrated platform to both vary the inputs into the simulation and analyse its outputs. The platform is formed from different parts which are displayed in Figure 3.

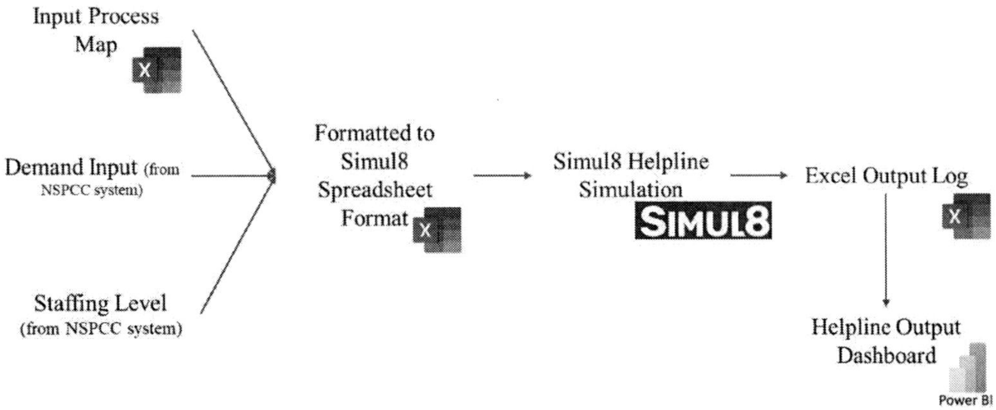

Figure 3 *Information Flow through Helpline Simulation Platform*

The simulation platform was designed so that a user of the model did not need to understand either the model itself or how to use the simulation software, but instead could interact with and update both timing distributions and percentages via the user interface. It provided a simple graphical interface within MS Excel, in the form of a process map, for altering both timing and probability information for the handling of cases. To keep the user interface simple, this only allows for updates to numeric parameters, and not to the fundamental structure of the process which instead would require direct edits to the Simul8 model structure. The workbook converted the input information into a format that could be interpreted by Simul8 for updating both timing and probability distributions. The model also received inputs from NSPCC's system to estimate demand and staffing level.

Additionally, the data from the model runs was output into a tabular format within MS Excel which could be analysed by Power BI. In order to do this, as Simul8 outputs multiple runs of the same scenario within a trial, to get a distribution of results, these results needed to be aggregated together. Therefore, the results were aggregated in Power BI to generate average, and upper and lower bands for the key model outputs that could then be visually displayed in the dashboard. This provided the NSPCC with a curated set of information which could then be easily displayed in graphical formats in a structure desired by Helpline staff and managers.

To support the ongoing development and upkeep of the Helpline model itself, the team also provided detailed documentation on the structure and development of the model, as well as training sessions in both Simul8 and the model logic to the NSPCC team. The training sessions were recorded and delivered alongside the documentation to provide a repository of knowledge for the simulation. Through this, it is intended that the NSPCC will be able to continue to use, operate and develop the Helpline simulation as a forecasting tool into the future.

5 CONCLUSION

The NSPCC received a simulation platform to forecast the expected service level of the Helpline based on an estimated weekly demand and staff level. The discrete event simulation of the Helpline was built using Simul8, in collaboration with NSPCC staff, to map out the process to be modelled and to analyse operational data to estimate inputs into the model.

The model, while relatively simple in its initial process, required a detailed verification and validation process to ensure that it accurately represented the operations of Helpline, and that its outputs corresponded with actual operations. After this process was completed, the Helpline simulation could be used to improve the NSPCC's resource planning and to explore 'what-if' scenarios of changing demand and resourcing.

In order to enable it to be more effectively used by NSPCC staff, a platform was constructed that allowed easy input and output of data into the Simul8 model using a combination of MS Excel and Power BI. To ensure ongoing support for the model, the team also provided documentation and training to NSPCC staff, so that they could continue to develop and utilise the model over the long-term for predictive forecasting of their operations.

ACKNOWLEDGMENTS

The authors of this paper would like to recognise their colleagues and fellow volunteers, Robert Stout, Ian Woodward and Neeraj Durgai for their time and contributions to this project. Thanks are also due to the Operational Research Society Pro Bono team for their support in setting up, organising and managing this opportunity. Additional thanks are also due to the NSPCC team, for their continuous support and active input into the modelling process and agreement to share this paper with the simulation conference.

AUTHOR BIOGRAPHIES

JESS COLE is a Senior Consultant at AtkinsRéalis, specialising in discrete event simulation and process improvement. She received her BSc Business and Management from Aston University in 2016 and worked at PwC prior to joining AtkinsRéalis. She has worked with clients in a variety of roles and industries, but focuses primarily on supporting clients to understand and improve their existing processes, or plan for future process change.

STEPHEN POLLARD is a Senior Consultant at AtkinsRéalis, specialising in operational research and simulation. He received a MSci (Hons) Physics from the University of Birmingham in 2017 and, following graduation, joined AtkinsRéalis. He has worked within a variety of different sectors, using operational research and simulation methodologies to forecast and optimise his clients' processes and systems.

Proceedings of the Operational Research Society Simulation Workshop 2025 (SW25)
M. Luis, A. Harper, T. Monks, N. Mustafee, eds.

https://doi.org/10.36819/SW25.045

MODELLING FOR SIMULATION MULTI-USE – TOWARDS A FRAMEWORK FOR COST-EFFECTIVENESS ANALYSES OF REPERFUSION TREATMENTS FOR ACUTE STROKE

Chi Nguyen

University Medical Centre Groningen
P.O. Box 30001, 9700 RB, Groningen
THE NETHERLANDS
p.nguyen@umcg.nl

Dr. Durk-Jouke van der Zee

University of Groningen
P.O. Box 800, 9700 AV, Groningen
THE NETHERLANDS
d.j.van.der.zee@rug.nl

Dr. Maarten M.H. Lahr,
Dr. Maarten Uyttenboogaart,
Prof. dr. Erik Buskens

University Medical Centre Groningen
P.O. Box 30001, 9700 RB, Groningen
THE NETHERLANDS
m.m.h.lahr@umcg.nl,
m.uyttenboogaart@umcg.nl,
e.buskens@umcg.nl

ABSTRACT

This paper considers the development of multi-use simulation models for cost-effectiveness studies of reperfusion treatments in acute ischemic stroke. The consistent and accurate multi-use models for cost-effectiveness studies for a specific health domain allow for cross-comparison and interpretation of findings. Furthermore, modelling efficiencies may benefit from exploiting system similarities. To explore requirements of multi-use models, a scoping review was performed to characterise simulation models for cost-effectiveness analysis of stroke reperfusion treatments. Findings were used to define a mixed model structure covering the treatment (acute phase) and long-term follow up, model qualities and a framework for model development. In doing so, changes to common modelling frameworks targeting single use models, addressing logistic analysis within a single time frame were considered. Although there would be clear benefits of multi-use models, these should be traded off against substantial efforts involved in their design and maintenance.

Keywords: Modelling frameworks, multi-use model, acute ischemic stroke, simulation model, cost-effectiveness

1 INTRODUCTION

The burden of stroke care presents a significant challenge to healthcare systems worldwide, requiring the critical need for new treatments and effective stroke organisation. In addition, the growing healthcare costs urge policymakers, health planners, and clinicians to consider both the costs and effectiveness of innovative strategies in stroke care for approval and reimbursement policies. Model-based approaches are an efficient and flexible means for performing cost-effectiveness studies. Generally, the common outcomes of cost-effectiveness studies are total costs, quality-adjusted life years (QALYs), and an incremental cost-effectiveness ratio (ICER). QALY is defined as a function of the length of life and the quality of life in the remaining years. An ICER is calculated as the incremental costs between two interventions divided by the incremental effectiveness, often QALYs, of two interventions.

A recent systematic review (Koca, 2024) showed the advancements of simulation methodologies in optimising acute stroke treatment services, paving the way for cost-effectiveness analyses that can inform healthcare decision-making. However, current simulation models are predominantly single-use and tailored to the specific needs of different research groups, often leading to inconsistencies in interpretation and quality assessment across studies. This fragmentation hinders our ability to draw comprehensive conclusions and implement effective policies.

Therefore, this paper focuses on two primary objectives:

1/ Explore modelling requirements on multi-use models for cost-effectiveness analysis of stroke reperfusion treatments.

2/ Using findings from 1, characterise the model structure, model qualities and needs for extensions of the current modelling framework to support the development of multi-use models.

2 STROKE ORGANISATION FOR REPERFUSION TREATMENTS

There are two types of reperfusion treatments for patients with acute ischemic stroke, including intravenous thrombolysis (IVT) and endovascular thrombectomy (EVT). IVT involves the administration of a clot-dissolving medication called tissue plasminogen activator. In EVT treatment, a blood clot is mechanically removed from an intracranial artery using an endovascular approach with aspiration catheters and/or stent retrievers. EVT is currently indicated for ischemic stroke patients with large vessel occlusion. The benefit of IVT and EVT is highly time-dependent, and time delays are associated with poor functional outcome. Essentially, time is brain – each minute counts (Widimsky et al, 2023).

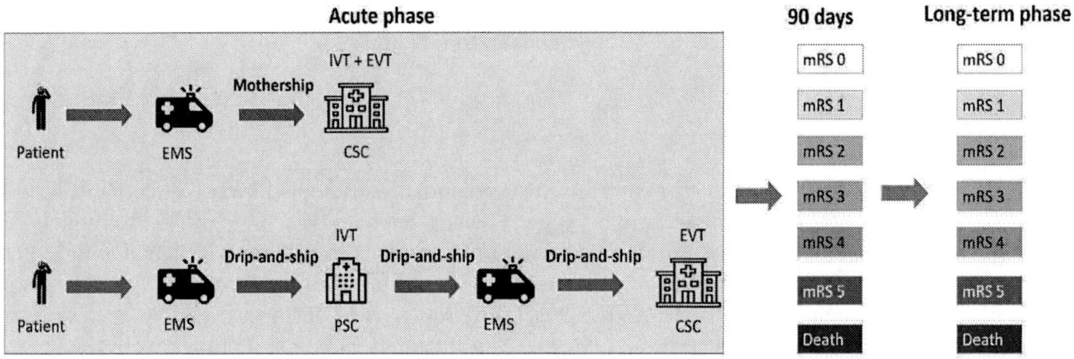

Figure 1 *Overview of stroke care pathway (both short-term and long-term phases)*
IVT: intravenous thrombolysis, EVT: endovascular thrombectomy, EMS: emergency medical service, PSC: primary stroke centre, CSC: comprehensive stroke centre, mRS: modified Rankin Scale

While IVT treatment is widely provided in primary stroke centres (PSCs) and comprehensive stroke centres (CSCs), EVT is only performed in CSCs (Figure 1). In the **mothership paradigm**, a suspected stroke patient is directly transferred to a CSC to receive IVT treatment and, in case of large vessel occlusion, EVT. In the **drip-and-ship paradigm**, a stroke patient is transferred to the nearest stroke centre (PSC) providing IVT and subsequently be transferred to a CSC to undergo EVT in case of large vessel occlusion. The type of treatment and time-to-treatment will affect the degree of disability of patients measured by modified Rankin Scale (mRS) with scores from 0 (no symptoms) to 6 (death) at 90 days, and mRS scores affect long-term healthcare of patients.

3 CHARACTERIZING SIMULATION-BASED STUDIES FOR COST-EFFECTIVENESS ANALYSES OF STROKE REPERFUSION TREATMENTS

3.1 Review set-up

We used a recent systematic review (Koca, 2024) to synthesise simulation models in optimisation of acute ischemic stroke treatment services. In addition, we performed a scoping review to summarise and provide recent evidence (from 2020 to 2024) on using simulation models in cost-effectiveness analyses of reperfusion treatments in stroke, adding another five studies. The literature search yielded 345 publications in PubMed. After removing 238 papers (abstract review) and 106 studies (full-text review) based on inclusion and exclusion criteria, five studies were included for the qualitative synthesis (Figure 1). Data extraction of included papers was conducted for model set-up according to CHEERS (Consolidated Health Economic Evaluation Reporting Standards 2022) (Husereau et al, 2022).

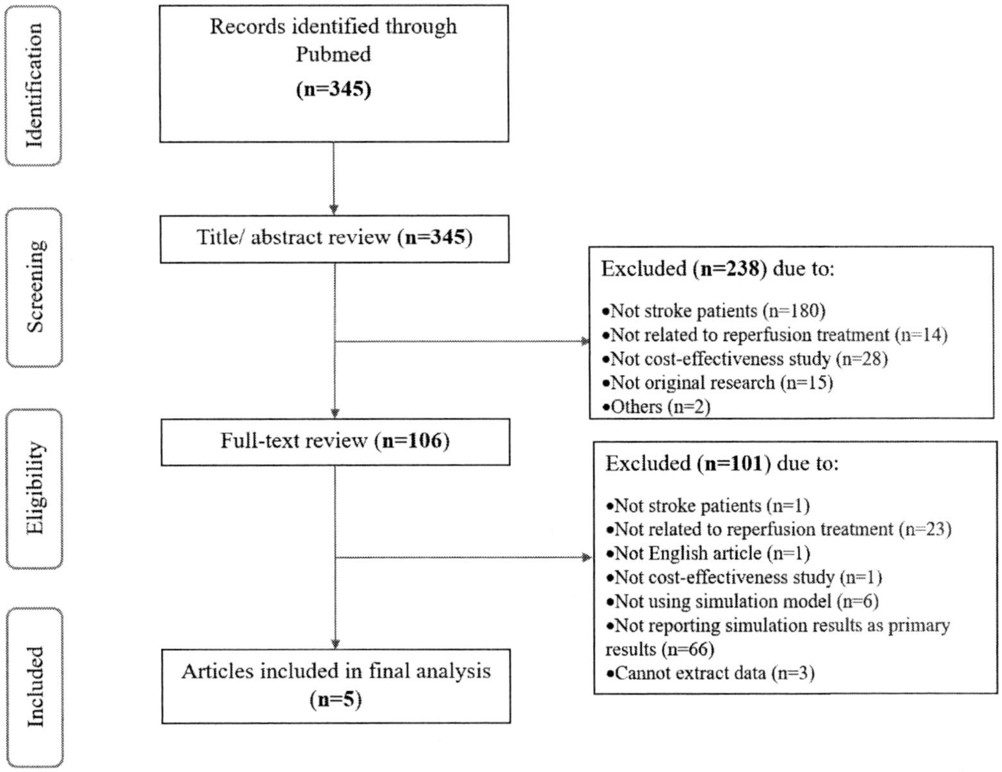

Figure 2 *Scoping review: flowchart of included studies*

3.2 Findings

The systematic review of (Koca et al, 2024) showed 27 studies using simulation models to optimise stroke services. Discrete Event Simulation (DES) emerged as the primary simulation modelling methodology in this systematic review (22/27 studies using DES), providing a robust tool for simulating stroke care services redesign. Model outputs encompassed enhancing thrombolysis utilisation, reducing treatment duration, and improving patient outcomes assessed through the mRS. Three studies reported costs and QALYs. The systematic review reveals potential applications of simulation models in cost-effectiveness analyses. It also highlights the role of simulation modelling in addressing a range of challenges encountered during the delivery of stroke care services, especially health service redesign for acute ischemic stroke treatment processes.

The descriptives of the five included studies from the scoping review are presented in Table 1. All cost-effectiveness studies considered stroke treatment in the short-term and long-term phases. In the short-term phase, four studies used a decision tree and one study used DES. In the long-term phase, four studies used Markov models with Monte Carlo simulation, and one study used DES. For each study, study set-up and modelling choices are shown according to the CHEERS guidelines.

Table 1 *Cost effectiveness analysis of stroke perfusion treatments – study set-up and modelling choices*

Study (year)	**(Gao et al, 2021)**	**(Zhu et al, 2023)**	**(van Voorst et al, 2024)**	**(Pinckaers et al, 2024)**	**(Nguyen et al, 2024)**
Country & setting	Australia, in CSC	USA, in stroke centre (acute module) and outside of stroke centre (chronic module)	Netherlands, in CSC	Netherlands, in CSC	Netherlands, in CSC
Population	AIS due to LVO & patients presenting after 4.5 h from symptom onset	AIS	AIS due to LVO & patients presenting after 6h from symptom onset	AIS due to LVO & patients presenting after 6h from symptom onset (until 24h)	AIS due to LVO & patients presenting directly in CSC
Interventions	EVT vs. best medical management	Current vs. 10 interventions (3 interventions related to reperfusion treatment: IVT, time to IVT, early IVT)	CT perfusion to select patients for EVT vs. providing EVT to all patients	EVT vs. best medical management	IVT+EVT vs. EVT alone
Type of model	Decision tree (short-term phase) and DES (long-term phase)	DES (short-term phase) and Monte Carlo simulation (long-term phase)	Decision tree (short-term phase) and Markov model with patient-level micro-simulations (long-term phase)	Monte Carlo simulation using decision tree (short-term phase) and Markov model (long-term phase)	Monte Carlo simulation using decision tree (short-term phase) and Markov model (long-term phase)
Model structure	The model was initiated from day 90 after stroke in one of seven health states (mRS0, mRS1, mRS 2, mRS3, mRS4, mRS5, and death). In the long-term, following each event, the patient could die or survive from such events, or die from other non-cardiovascular disease causes	The simulation model consists of an acute stroke module (DES) and a post-stroke chronic module (Monte Carlo). The Monte Carlo model simulates recurrent cardiovascular events and death. This module is characterised by seven mRS states (mRS0-mRS6). Individuals with a higher mRS are at a higher risk of stroke recurrence. After a recurrent stroke, patients may transition to an equal or higher mRS state.	The model consisted of a short-term 90-day model to simulate EVT patient selection strategies followed by a long-term yearly model and was used to simulate functional outcomes (mRS). In the long-term model, deterioration of mRS was simulated based on the probability of stroke recurrence and death inflated with patient specific hazard ratios.	A short-term decision tree was combined with a Markov model including 7 health states (mRS0-mRS6). Patients could improve in mRS, remain stable, deteriorate in mRS, or die) between 3-months and 1-year post-stroke. After 1 year, patients entered a Markov model with yearly cycles, in which patients could only remain in the same health state, deteriorate, or die	A decision tree was used in acute 90 days after stroke and medium phase (1 year) and Markov model was used in long-term phase (next 14 years). In the model, 5 health states were included: mRS 0-1, mRS2-3, mRS4, mRS5, and death. Patients could improve, remain stable, or deteriorate in their mRS score during the first 5 years but could only remain stable or deteriorate on their mRS score afterward

Table 1 *(continued) Cost effectiveness analysis of stroke perfusion treatments – study set-up and modelling choices*

Reason or reference for conceptual/ structure of model	The DES model was selected to avoid the use of fixed cycles lengths and improve the calculation efficiency	Acute stroke outcomes are predicted by both treatment status (receiving IVT or not) and onset-to-treatment time; DES is better suited to simulate empirical time distributions than Markov models	The model was based on previous research where validation of the proposed simulation model was accurate at 5years and at 10 years the majority of the simulated population had died	Not mentioned	The conceptual model was adopted and adjusted from previously published models.
Time horizon	25 years	Life time	5 years and 10 years	Life time	15 years
Discount	3% (costs and effectiveness)	3% (costs and effectiveness)	4% (costs), 1.5% (QALYs)	4% (costs), 1.5% (QALYs)	4% (costs), 1.5% (QALYs)
Data resources					
Effectiveness	International Stroke Perfusion Imaging Registry (INSPIRE) data	Published literature	Clinical Trials of EVT of Acute Ischemic Stroke in The Netherlands, registry data, and a local cohort.	Clinical trial	Published literature (Meta-analyses from clinical trials)
Costs	Published literature	Published literature	Published literature	Clinical trial	Published literature
Model validation	Validated outcomes from the simulation against long-term data for patients post stroke	Validated post-stroke all-cause mortality at 1, 5, 10 years in simulation against literature literature.	Not mentioned	Not mentioned	Used AdViSHE tool & validated mRS distributions between simulation and other follow-up clinical trials.
Software	TreeAge Pro	R, C++	Python software	R	TreeAge Pro
Data availability	Available following a reasonable request	Not mentioned	Available following a reasonable request	Available following a reasonable request	Available within the article and its appendix
Main outcomes	Total QALYs, total life years, total costs, ICER	Total QALYs, total life years, ICER, incremental net health benefit	Net monetary benefit, ICER	Total QALYs, total costs, ICER, incremental net monetary benefit	Total QALYs, total costs, ICER

AdViSHE: Assessment of the Validation Status of Health-Economic decision models tool, AIS: acute ischemic stroke, CSC: comprehensive stroke centre, DES: discrete event simulation, EVT: endovascular thrombectomy, IVT: intravenous thrombolysis, LVO: large vessel occlusion, QALY: quality-adjusted life year, ICER: incremental cost-effectiveness ratio, MI: myocardial infarction, mRS: modified Rankin Scale

4 MULTI-USE MODELS - MODEL STRUCTURE, QUALITIES AND MODELLING FRAMEWORK

4.1 Model structure – mixed model

Implementing a mixed model (a hybrid model) for cost-effectiveness analyses of reperfusion treatments in stroke provides a robust model structure for evaluating both short-term and long-term outcomes (Figure 2), matching requirements observed in recent studies (Section 3, Table 1, "model structure"). The model allows for estimating health outcomes and relevant costs according to different levels of model detail following type of model and modelling choices. This dual-phase approach not only captures the immediate benefits of acute stroke treatment but also highlights the importance of long-term recovery and resource allocation in managing stroke patients.

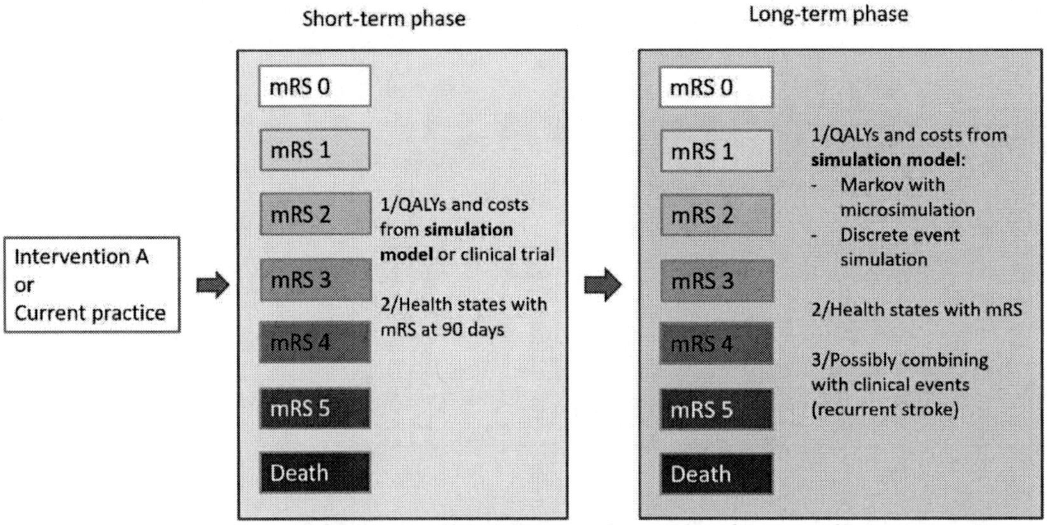

Figure 2 *Mixed model for cost-effectiveness analysis related to reperfusion treatments*

4.2 Multi-use models – users and requirements

A multi-use model in stroke research serves researchers, clinical physicians, and policymakers to enhance decision-making through the integration of various data sources and simulation models. In this paper, 'multi-use' refers to the ability of a model to be reused over time across various strategies, facilitating comparison of outcomes. In addition to the core qualities of validity, credibility, utility, and feasibility outlined by (Robinson, 2008), the following extensions offer a more nuanced view of the multi-use model's requirements:

Accepted by the field of interest (extension of credibility): For a multi-use model to be truly effective, it must gain acceptance among clinicians, researchers, and other stakeholders in the stroke community. This acceptance stems from the model's ability to reflect real-world conditions and its relevance to a specific group of patients. This acceptance can be fostered through collaborative development processes, engaging key opinion leaders, and incorporating feedback from practitioners who work directly with stroke patients.

Accuracy (extension of validity): While validity focuses on how well a model represents a specific case, model accuracy has to be extended by assessing the model's performance across a wider range of scenarios. This can be achieved through sensitivity analyses, which examine how variations in input parameters affect outcomes and improve decision-making.

Flexibility (extension of utility): Flexibility refers to the model's ability to adapt and be reused across different contexts and populations. This involves the ability to modify model components or parameters to suit various scenarios or research questions. Flexibility implies a strategic approach to reusing multi-use models, which can save time and resources.

Model life cycle costs (extension of feasibility): This involves evaluating the time, financial, and personnel investments needed to deploy and maintain the multi-use model.

4.3 Towards a modelling framework for simulation multi-use

The development of multi-use simulation models for cost-effectiveness analysis of stroke perfusion treatments sets specific requirements to modelling support vs. "common" single-use models for logistic analysis of operations systems. Next to the frequency of use, cost factors and cost analysis, the model type, i.e., a mixed model implies the need to adjust available modelling frameworks. Below, we show adjustments for the framework of Monks et al. (2017) supporting development of single-use models for analysing the acute stroke pathway assuming the possible treatment with IVT only. It is restricted to modelling the acute phase of stroke treatment. The framework supports the essential stages of understanding the problem situation, setting the modelling objectives, and determining model content (Table 2). Extending Monks' framework for multi-use and reuse models involves a structured approach that emphasises understanding all relevant populations, and implies a broader range of treatments and changes to stroke organisation. Therefore, the extension framework of Monks for the multi-use model includes: 1/ changing from homogeneous (single-use) to mixed model (multi-use), 2/ extension from short-term to dual-phase (short-term and long-term phases), 3/ various treatments (IVT, EVT), 4/ single-use model to multi-use model, 5/ changing from logistics analyses to cost-effectiveness analyses.

***Table 2** Model development for multi-use models – adjusting the framework (Monks et al. 2017)*

Framework of Monks et al.	**Extensions for multi-use model**	**Extensions for re-use model**
1. Understanding the problem situation		
• Determine study population: Decide subcategories of the stroke population the study might focus on.	✓ Determine all subcategories for reperfusion treatments (mothership patients, drip-and-ship patients, IVT patients, IVT and EVT patients). ✓ Include time horizon for analysis	✓ Choose from the range of all subcategories ✓ Choose time horizon based on age of population
• Assess current performance of the HASP (establish key figures such as IVT rate, time to treatment, etc) and interpret findings for setting the modelling objectives.	✓ Account for innovation: Diagnostics (CTP, CTA), new treatments (EVT), patient transfers, patient routing ✓ Extend performance measurement for EVT treatment and cost analysis	✓ Data sources for cost analysis (which costs should be included, how to estimate costs)
• Map the current process: Create a starting point for determining model content by building a process map that captures the status quo. (e.g. pre- and intra-hospital processes)	✓ Develop generic process map for representing the current process (in line with building blocks provided for specifying model content) ✓ Extend the process for short term (up to 90 days) and long term (time horizon) ✓ Identify cost drivers in short-term and long-term process	✓ Use process map to represent the current process ✓ Identify cost drivers within the processes
• Explore decision variables for use in experimentation: Process mapping and the assessment of HASP's current performance serve as a vehicle to elicit hypotheses about delays and barriers to treatment. Choice of decision variables may be linked to four areas: *1/ Pre-hospital logistics, 2/ Processes for identification of stroke patients in the ED, 3/ Communication between hospital departments, 4/ Work force scheduling*	✓ Add health innovations as possible decision variables: improved diagnostics and treatments ✓ Account for innovation: Diagnostics (CTP, CTA), new treatments (EVT), patient transfers (primary stroke centre, comprehensive stroke centre, emergency medical service), patient routing (pre-hospital triage) ✓ Identify costs when changing variables in experimentation	✓ Choose relevant innovations, variables related to the specific study ✓ Identify costs when changing variables in experimentation

Table 2 *(continued) Model development for multi-use models – adjusting the framework (Monks et al. 2017)*

• Choice of model (based on all problem situations in part 1/ table 2 and model structure in table 1)	✓ Mixed model ✓ The model (code, input parameters) should be provided as an open access online tool for re-use	✓ Mixed model (model types)
2. *Setting the modelling objectives*		
• Select response measures and target performance levels: Health outcome (primary level), logistic performance (secondary level), target levels	✓ Set up level of health outcomes and costs in short-term and long-term phases	
• Determine model outputs, see response measures and target performance levels; include activity durations to assess cause and effect.	✓ Short-term phase: % of mRS score, QALYs, costs of interventions, current practice ✓ Long-term phase: QALYs, costs of patients in long-term phase, ICER	✓ Choose outputs for short-term and long-term phases
• Determine model inputs that underlie experiments concerning alternative configurations of the HASP.	✓ Include model inputs for various interventions related to treatments ✓ Need for sensitivity analyses	✓ Choose/ adjust model inputs for different interventions
• Establish restrictions in solution finding: Consider budgets of care providers, physical space, and regulations etc., may restrict choice of configurations of the stroke pathway	✓ Develop all possible stroke care pathways in reperfusion treatments (IVT and EVT) for multi-use models	
3. ***Determining model content***		
• Establish model scope: Identify model boundaries, by either including or excluding a representation of elements of the HASP under study as model components. Choice of model components is facilitated by a library of most common components of a HASP.	✓ Add model components of short-term (innovation) and long-term phases.	
• Determine model detail, specifying attributes of model components. See Monks et al. (2017) for entity attributes that may be required across a broad range of objectives.	✓ Determine adjustable and fixed component attributes in model ✓ Determine level of mRS score (combination or 7 states), detail of costs along with interventions, transition probability in long-term phase	✓ Choose/adjust model component attributes
• Specify assumptions underlying model content: Facilitate the interpretation of the model and its workings by making assumptions on the HASP under study explicit.	✓ Effect of new intervention depends on new treatment and time to treatment (interaction with other interventions) in short-term phase ✓ Long-term outcomes depend on mRS at short-term phase (90-days after stroke)	
• Making appropriate model simplifications: Inappropriate model complexity increases modelling efforts and may obstruct interpretation of the model and results of the simulation experiments.	✓ Model simplifications should be discussed with stakeholders and users ✓ Model simplifications should be taken into account for multi-use	

CTA: Computed tomography angiography, CTP: Computed tomography perfusion, HASP: hyperacute stroke pathway, IVT: intravenous thrombolysis, EVT: endovascular thrombectomy, mRS: modified Rankin Scale, QALY: quality-adjusted life year, ICER: incremental cost-effectiveness ratio

5 DISCUSSION

By shifting towards multi-use simulation models, collaboration among researchers brings benefits for diverse health systems through standardising methodologies that can be adapted for different regional contexts. This approach allows for the pooling of data and insights, enhancing the robustness of cost-effectiveness analyses while reducing redundancy in model development. Incorporating extended qualities—acceptance, accuracy, flexibility, and feasibility—into the multi-use model framework can significantly enhance its relevance and application in stroke.

However, the transition from a single-use model to a multi-use model has challenges. Researchers must carefully consider the diverse health infrastructure standards and clinical practices across different regions. Addressing these variations while maintaining model integrity and relevance will require ongoing dialogue and collaboration among stakeholders, including researchers, clinicians, and policymakers.

5.1 Design of multi-use simulation models

While single-use models are typically rigid in structure, multi-use models may be more flexible, allowing for modifications to accommodate different stroke care systems, treatment protocols, and patient populations. Developing a multi-use model that is adaptable to various contexts can be complex, requiring careful consideration of stroke organisations and treatment protocols. Therefore, multi-use models require an initial investment in design but can be reused and adapted, reducing the overall effort for subsequent studies. In addition, design for the multi-use model with broad applicability may result in a loss of specificity for certain populations or treatment scenarios, potentially diluting the model's accuracy for specific studies.

5.2 Maintenance of multi-use simulation models

Maintenance of simulation models is crucial for ensuring their ongoing relevance and accuracy. This involves regularly updating the model to reflect new clinical evidence, new treatments, and data inputs. For multi-use models, ongoing maintenance and updates may be more demanding due to the need to accommodate diverse data inputs and stakeholder feedback.

- **Data updates:** Regularly incorporating new data from clinical trials, registries, and health surveys to ensure the model reflects current practices and outcomes.
- **User feedback:** Gathering insights from stakeholders who use the model to identify areas for improvement and functionality enhancements.
- **Standardisation of protocols:** Establishing standardised protocols for updating and maintaining the model to ensure consistency across different research groups.

5.3 Limitation

Our paper focused on reperfusion treatments for stroke in the acute phase. However, rehabilitation strategies play an important role in the stroke care pathway and future studies need to explore potential applications and extensions of simulation models in rehabilitation.

6 CONCLUSIONS

In conclusion, the integration of multi-use modelling approaches will be essential for advancing stroke care, ensuring health economic evaluation is both effective and accessible on a national scale and regional scale. In this paper, we explore current simulation models in cost-effectiveness analyses of reperfusion treatments in stroke and provide extensions for the framework of multi-use simulation models in cost-effectiveness studies. A mixed model is a promising candidate for multi-use models in cost-effectiveness studies. Design, maintenance, and adaptability need to be taken into account in the multi-use models to meet the diverse needs of various interventions with regional stroke care systems.

REFERENCES

Gao L, Bivard A, Parsons M, et al. (2021). "Real-World Cost-Effectiveness of Late Time Window Thrombectomy for Patients With Ischemic Stroke." Front Neurol **12**: 780894.

Husereau D, Michael A, Federico de Bekker-Grob, et al. (2022). "Consolidated Health Economic Evaluation Reporting Standards (CHEERS) 2022 Explanation and Elaboration: A Report of the ISPOR CHEERS II Good Practices Task Force." Value in Health **25**(1): 10-31.

Koca G, Kumar M, and Kamal N (2024). "A systematic review of computer simulation modelling methods in optimising acute ischemic stroke treatment services." IISE Transactions on Healthcare Systems Engineering **14**(3): 249-263.

Widimsky P, Snyder K, Sulzenko J, et al. (2023). "Acute ischemic stroke: recent advances in reperfusion treatment." European Heart Journal **14**: 1205-1215

Monks T, van der Zee DJ, Lahr MMH, et al. (2017). "A framework to accelerate simulation studies of hyperacute stroke systems." Operations Research for Health Care **15**: 57-67.

Nguyen CP, Lahr MMH, van der Zee DJ, et al. (2024). "Endovascular Thrombectomy Alone for Large Vessel Occlusion: A Cost-Effectiveness Evaluation Based on Meta-Analyses." Stroke **55**(10): 2482-2491.

Pinckaers FM, Evers SM, Olthuis SG, et al. (2024). "Cost-effectiveness of endovascular treatment after 6-24 h in ischaemic stroke patients with collateral flow on CT-angiography: A model-based economic evaluation of the MR CLEAN-LATE trial." Eur Stroke J **9**(2): 348-355.

Robinson S (2008). "Conceptual modelling for simulation Part II: a framework for conceptual modelling." Journal of the Operational Research Society **59**(3): 291-304.

van Voorst H, Hoving, JW,Koopman MS, et al. (2024). "Costs and health effects of CT perfusion-based selection for endovascular thrombectomy within 6 hours of stroke onset: a model-based health economic evaluation." J Neurol Neurosurg Psychiatry **95**(6): 515-527.

Zhu J, Kamel H, Gupta A, et al. (2023). "Prioritizing Quality Measures in Acute Stroke Care : A Cost-Effectiveness Analysis." Ann Intern Med **176**(5): 649-657.

AUTHOR BIOGRAPHIES

CHI NGUYEN is a postdoc at Department of Epidemiology, University Medical Centre Groningen, The Netherlands. Currently, she is working in health economics in stroke and atrial fibrillation. Her webpage is https://research.rug.nl/en/persons/chi-nguyen.

DURK-JOUKE VAN DER ZEE is associate professor of Operations at the Faculty of Economics and Business, University of Groningen, The Netherlands. His research interests include health care logistics, simulation methodology and applications. His webpage is http://www.rug.nl/staff/d.j.van.der.zee.

MAARTEN M. H. LAHR is a postdoctoral researcher at the HTA unit of the Department of Epidemiology, and member of the Healthy Ageing Team, University of Groningen, University Medical Centre Groningen, The Netherlands. His research interests include organisational models for acute stroke care and discrete-event simulation. His website is http://www.rug.nl/staff/m.m.h.lahr.

MAARTEN UYTTENBOOGAART is an interventional neurologist at the department of Neurology and Radiology, University Medical Centre Groningen. His research topics are clinical research on prognostic factors in and treatments for acute ischemic stroke, clinical research on neuroprotection in acute stroke and research on organisation and implementation of acute stroke care. His website is https://www.umcg.nl/-/m-uyttenboogaart.

ERIK BUSKENS is Professor of Population Health Management, University Medical Centre Groningen, and faculty of Economics and Business University of Groningen, The Netherlands. His research interests among others encompass the association and mutual dependencies between technological advances and the factual organisation of care to attain the desired health and possibly economic benefits. His webpage is https://www.rug.nl/staff/e.buskens.

Proceedings of the Operational Research Society Simulation Workshop 2025 (SW25)
M. Luis, A. Harper, T. Monks, N. Mustafee, eds.

https://doi.org/10.36819/SW25.046

OPERATIONAL VALIDATION USING SIMULATION MODELS DESIGNED AND CREATED WITH DIFFERENT PARADIGMS

Prof. Bożena Mielczarek

Wrocław Unoversity of Science and Technology
Wyb. Wyspiańskiego 27
50-370 Wrocław, Poland
bozena.mielczarek@pwr.edu.pl

ABSTRACT

Simulation is used to model social systems where it helps to study human behavior, technology diffusion, policy implications, demographic trends or overall impact of governmental decisions. Simulation models, in order to be a valuable decision support tool, should undergo extensive verification and validation (V&V) to confirm their reliability. Conducting V&V is always a major challenge, but it is especially difficult in the case of social simulations, which often reach far into the future and have limited access to empirical data. In this paper, we present the results of the operational validation (OV) stage for the simulation of the pension system. We conducted OV by comparing the performance of two models developed under the same assumptions but according to different paradigms: Monte Carlo and Discrete Event Simulation. As a result, the reliability of both models increased significantly. The proposed approach can facilitate the full V&V for social simulations.

Keywords: Operational Validation, Monte Carlo Simulation, Discrete Event Simulation, Social Systems, Retirement

1 INTRODUCTION

One of the more difficult challenges faced by a developer of a simulation model is to prove that the model adequately describes reality. The key concepts in simulation theory is therefore verification, validation, and reliability (Fishman & Kiviat, 1968). Model verification is the process of proving that the transformation of a model from one form to another occurs with sufficient accuracy. The verification process verifies that the conceptual model has been correctly translated into a computer program. Model validation, on the other hand, is the process of proving that the model, within the range of applications for which it was constructed, demonstrates satisfactory accuracy, consistent with the stated research objectives. The process of model validation attempts to verify that the simulation model correctly describes the real system. Thus, verification refers to the model's internal consistency, while validation refers to the relationship between the model and reality. If the simulation model and its results have been accepted by the users to whom the model is addressed, then the model can be considered reliable. Validation and verification (V&V) is defined as the process of proving that a simulation model correctly describes or approximates the real system in terms of those purposes for which it was developed. The purpose of the simulation model therefore determines the aspects that should be validated, as well as establishes the degree of detail of the validation analysis to be performed.

Conducting V&V is always a major challenge but it is especially demanding for social simulations, which are usually planned over a long time horizon. Verifying simulation population models, and closely related simulation pension models, faces the obstacle of lacking future data and the inherent uncertainty of existing forecasts (Jung et al., 2018). In recent decades, numerous scientific articles have addressed the V&V of simulation models (Law & Kelton, 2000; Sargent & Balci, 2017; Kleijnen, 1995; Hughes et al., 2006; Liu et al., 2012). Authors stress the impossibility of devising a single, universal strategy for conducting V&V due to the uniqueness of each simulation process, which by definition is strongly tied to the studied object. However, literature has proposed generalized guidelines for establishing methodological standards for V&V (Sargent, 2020). One of the dimensions included in these frameworks is, among others, operational validation, which aims is to ensure that simulation results are sufficiently accurate with research objectives.

To facilitate the validation process of social simulation models, we propose an approach to compare the results of two models built according to different simulation paradigms. Two pension models will serve as an example. The first model is a Monte Carlo (MC) simulation model (Mielczarek, 2022), while the second one (Mielczarek, 2023) is developed using discrete event simulation (DES). The remainder of this paper is organized as follows. Section 2 provides basic concepts relating to V&V of simulation models. Section 3 briefly discuses the idea and essence of simulation retirement models and covers the main assumptions of the defined contribution (DC) pension systems. Section 4 focuses on the simulation experiments that were conducted to validate the models. Finally Section 5 draws conclusions and summarizes the contribution of this research.

2 V&V OF SIMULATION MODELS

2.1 Main Methodological V&V Paradigms

The book of Naylor (1971) belongs to key publications addressing V&V of simulation models. It introduces a three-stage procedure for methodological validation. This multi-stage validation approach suggests that each methodological aspect is necessary for validating simulation experiments, yet none alone is sufficient to solve the validation problem. The rationalist approach assumes that a model or theory is a set of logical conclusions drawn from a series of synthetic judgments of the nature of indisputable truths "*that cannot be subjected to empirical verification or appeal to objective experience.*" Thus, the problem of validity is reduced to the search for a set of assumptions underlying the behavior of the system of interest. Empiricism, the second approach, is the extreme opposite of rationalism. Empiricism refuses to acknowledge those postulates and assumptions that cannot be verified independently. The last approach, positivist economics, claims that the validity of a model does not depend on the validity of the assumptions on which the model is based, but, on the contrary, on the model's ability to make predictions about the behavior of the variables contained in the model.

The three aforementioned approaches were used by Naylor to define three stages of model validity analysis. The first degree involves formulating a set of postulates about the hypotheses describing the behavior of the system (face validity), which should be accepted by those associated with the system under study (experts, managers, employees) and should not contradict the existing theory and the results of previous studies. The second stage involves quantitative and qualitative testing of assumptions using available statistical tests. The third step concerns testing the model's ability to make predictions about the behavior of the system under study. The aim is to check whether the results of the simulation process are comparable to the data that can be expected by subjecting the real system to observation. Historical data (so-called historical validation) from the real system and data obtained from simulation experiments are used for this purpose. It is also possible to simulate the operation of the system at some point in the near future and, after this period, compare the simulated data with the actual state.

The approach proposed by Naylor was developed later by other authors. Sargent (1983) proposed to relate V&V to the different stages of the model development process (Table 1). In his numerous works (Sargent, 2013; Sargent et al., 2016; Sargent, 2020) he discusses a graphical paradigm composed of several pillars: conceptual model validation refers to the theories and assumptions that underline the conceptual model; computerized model verification aims to test the computerized model and ensure its compatibility with the conceptual model; operational validation seeks to ensure that the results obtained through simulations have sufficient accuracy to meet the objectives of the studies; data validity determines whether the data used to build and test the model are adequate and correct.

A large collection of methods supports the discussed above methodological concepts and fits into these general paradigms. Balci (1997) was one of the first to describe a set of 77 techniques, which he classified into several perspectives. Since then, many new techniques have been developed in response to the possibilities created by simulation software environments and new emerging directions of simulation models applications.

Table 1 *V&V paradigm according to (Sargent, 1983)*

Philosophical approach	Description
Conceptual model validation	Theoretical assumptions
Computerized model verification	Computer program code
Operational validation	Results versus objectives
Data validity	Data correctness and adequacy

Traditional approaches can be successfully used to verify social simulations as well, but one must be aware of certain limitations when using them to test the quality and reliability of these models. The challenge may be to correctly define stakeholders and determine whose perspectives and requirements should guide validation. In the case of social systems, this is not as obvious as in the case of business processes. While expert knowledge can be valuable, it introduces a level of subjectivity that may limit the objectivity and reproducibility of the validation process. Many social phenomena lack sufficient historical data, which restricts the ability to perform robust quantitative analysis and validate models statistically. Establishing clear, objective metrics for validation can be difficult, as social simulations often aim to model qualitative and emergent behaviors rather than strictly quantifiable outcomes. Hofmann (2015) defines and discusses many limitations of applying empirical validation to social models and concludes that no formal framework can guarantee their validity.

2.2 Emerging Trends in Supporting V&V Methodologies

Simulation models are often loaded with very large data sets, which are either obtained from real objects or are speculative in nature. Data are also necessary to formulate hypotheses, help build the model, participate in the verification process, and are present at the stage of analyzing results, formulating conclusions, and presenting them to model users. Lynch et al. (2021) suggest that the basic set of tools used in the V&V process should include methods and techniques from the area of data analytics, including data wrangling, descriptive and sampling statistics, machine learning, and others.

The development of IT processes in companies creates the need for real-time analyses and short-term insights from available data. New challenges make it necessary for V&V of simulation models to be performed in shorter time and associated with increasingly complex data. This pressure makes it extremely important to select appropriate techniques, also considering the cost-benefit ratio of a simulation. Automation of V&V processes can be helpful here. Langenbach and Rabe (2023) propose automating V&V techniques, and distinguish four levels of automation. The authors assigned V&V techniques to automation levels based on their inputs. These automation levels were derived from existing automation levels to ensure that all relevant aspects of automation are covered.

Automation of V&V processes in social simulations can be however difficult for a number of reasons. One of them is the scarcity and quality of historical data. It can also be a challenge to integrate and analyze data from multiple sources (e.g., social media, surveys, public records), which can be technically complex and may lead to inconsistencies. The non-linear interactions and emergent behaviors inherent in social systems make it difficult to define rigid testing criteria. The privacy and sensitivity of source data is also extremely important. Collecting and using sensitive social data for validation can raise ethical concerns, especially if the datasets contain personal or personally identifiable information.

3 SIMULATION OF PENSION SYSTEMS

3.1 Simulation Methods in Social Systems

Simulation is widely used with the goal to make better and more informed decisions. In social sciences different simulation approaches help to study human behavior, technology diffusion, policy implications, demographic trends or overall impact of governmental decisions.

Simulation approaches differ significantly (Mielczarek, 2016). An MC model simulates a range of potential scenarios, each with an assigned probability of occurrence, and produces forecasts, usually in the form of relevant means, probabilities, and a dispersion of results around an expected value. System dynamics (SD) is a deterministic approach, particularly helpful when the goal of a study is to formalize a mental model of a complex phenomenon. Typically, SD models are not created to produce exact quantitative predictions, but are intended to explore multiple policy options and may enable a better understanding of the performance of large and complex systems. The DES model simulates processes over time and follows individual dynamic objects that interact with the system's resources. Individuals are described by attributes that may differ from person to person and can reflect risk factors such as age, sex, professional history, and previous career breaks. The routes of individuals and the times between activities are described by random values sampled from parametric and empirical distributions.

3.2 Assumptions of the Pension System Simulation Model

Pension systems in many European countries operate under a Defined Contribution (DC) scheme, which means that the amount of pension benefit is closely related to the amount of earnings during the entire period of employment and life expectancy parameter. The DC pension system is based on the concept, which assumes that savings accumulated throughout the entire period of paid work are recalculated at the time of retirement, taking into account the forecasted, average life expectancy (Eq. 1). In DC systems, an increase in life expectancy inherently results in a reduction of pension benefits. Moreover, the timing of retirement holds significance, as the longer an individual accrues pension contributions, the greater the accumulated capital, consequently shortening the expected duration of pension disbursements.

$$Pension_{k} = Accumulated\ Capital / Life\ expectancy_{k} \tag{1}$$

where k is the retirement age. In Poland the retirement age is 60 for women and 65 for men, but if a person decides to work longer, it is usually possible. Life expectancy is defined as the average number of months that people of a particular age could expect to live. It is determined jointly for men and women and published in (GUS, 2024).

The assumptions of the DC system (Figure 1) were reflected in two simulation models built independently using different approaches but based on the same empirical data.

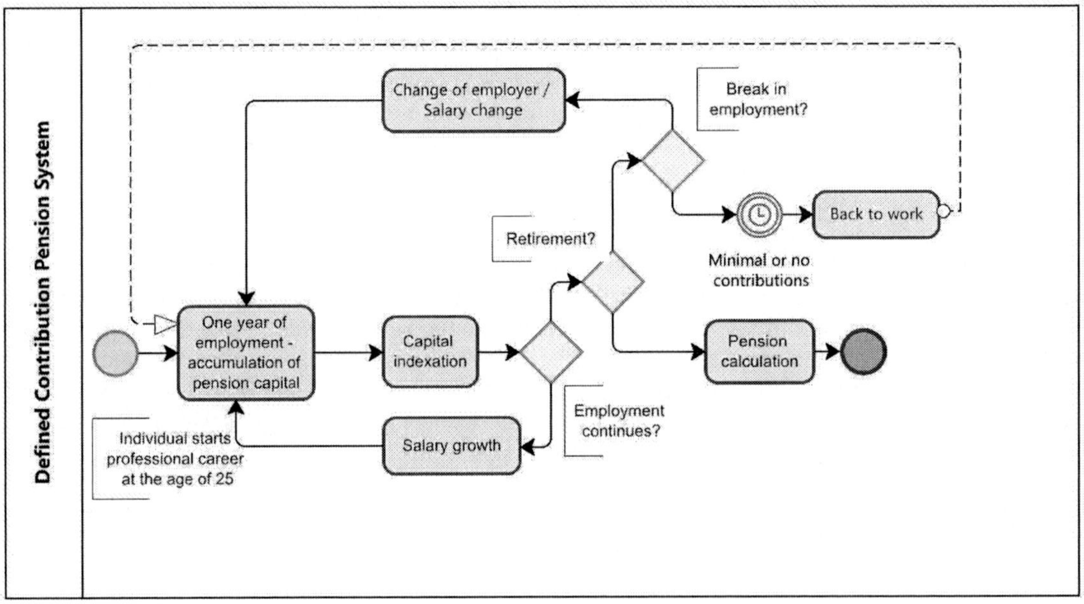

Figure 1 *Flowchart of the main simulation process applied in both simulation models*

The MC model is presented in the paper (Mielczarek, 2022), while a DES model is described in (Mielczarek, 2023). In both models, the logic process proceeds as shown in Figure 1 but the models were built according to fundamentally different simulation paradigms and various software environments were used. The main difference in the course of the simulation between these two models is that the DES model simulates the career paths of individuals, separately for men and women and for different occupational groups. The career paths are individualized and the values of the values of output measures are determined at the end of the simulation, first separately for each simulated individual, and only then averaged for the entire subgroup. The MC model simulates the averaged career path and, by performing several hundred repetitions, determines the values of the output measures for the entire subgroup. The MC model was developed in an Excel spreadsheet while the DES model uses Arena© simulation software.

An individual starts working at the age of 25. A contribution accumulated in the mandatory pension fund is deducted from her/his earnings. The employee's salary may change annually due to inflationary increases, but also due to job promotions. The size and frequency of these changes is generated from a random distribution adjusted on the basis of historical data, collected from national statistic databases. The capital accumulated in the pension account is indexed annually, and the amount of indexation varies and depends on the state of the economy in previous years. An employee may change the place of work, as well as interrupt the employment relationship. The length of interruptions is determined from a random distribution compiled from historical data published by (GUS, 2024). During an employment gap, an individual may still have contributions paid (such as during maternity leave), or there may be a pause in contributions (for example, when the person is unemployed and not receiving any benefits). When an employee decides to retire, the pension amount is calculated (see Eq.1) by dividing the accumulated and indexed pension capital by the average life expectancy.

3.3 Assumptions for Operational Validity

This article focuses on operational validity only. Sargent et al. (2016) described operational validity as the tool to determine whether the simulation's model output behavior has the accuracy required for the model's intended purpose. They propose that the model's accuracy should be tested under the set of experimental conditions. In the case of social systems, it is often not possible to compare the model's output directly with the system's actual behavior. In Poland, since the DC system was introduced in 1999, not enough time has yet passed to track the full 35 years (women) or 40 years (men) of pension capital accumulation. Therefore, the only way to validate the simulation model is to compare the results obtained within two different independent methodological paradigms, and using different simulation methods. In our case, this will be Monte Carlo and a Discrete Event Simulation.

Validation was conducted for historical data available for the years 2000-2022. The plan for operational validation is presented in Table 2. Three output measures were selected. These indicators are commonly used to assess how effectively the pension system provides retirement income that will replace earnings, the main source of income before retirement (OECD 2023).

- *First Pension*: the first pension that is paid to the retiree at the time of retirement;
- *Gross Replacement Rates (GRR)*: the ratio of the first pension to the last salary;
- *Probability of Target Replacement Rates (TRR):* probability of achieving the assumed replacement rate level, measured as a ratio of the first pension to the last salary, equal or less to 40%, 45%, 50%, and 70%. While GRRs measure income in retirement as a percentage of pre-retirement income, TRR is the portion of the pre-retirement income that will be replaced by the retirement income.

Each test was performed for retirement ages 60, 65, 67 in the variant for people earning the national average wage. Each time, 500 simulation replications were performed. The simulation begins when the person starts gainful employment at age 25 and ends when she reaches the assumed retirement age.

Table 2 *Plan for operational validation*

Test	Output Measure	Retirement Age
no 1	First Pension	60, 65 , 67
no 2	Gross Replacement Rate	60, 65 , 67
no 3	Probability of Target Replacement Rates 40%, 45%, 50%, 70%	60, 65, 67

4 OPERATIONAL VALIDATION

4.1 Test #1: First Pension

A Two-Sample Assuming Equal Variances test was conducted to verify whether the output values of the First Pension received at the moment of retirement for two simulation models are equal. The size in the two samples generated from two simulation models was identical at 500. Due to the high size of the two samples, it was assumed that a normal distribution would give a good approximation of the distribution of each of the means of the two samples.
μ_1: mean First Pension values from the population described by MC model
μ_2: mean First Pension values from population described by DES model
$\bar{x}_1$: sample average from 500 trials of model MC
$\bar{x}_2$: sample average from 500 trials of model DES
Alfa = 0.05
Null hypothesis H_0: $\mu_1 - \mu_2 = 0$
Alternative hypothesis H_2: $\mu_1 - \mu_2 \neq 0$

The results are shown in Tabel 3. By comparing the results we can conclude there is no significant difference in two means calculated based on the simulation output values sets from two simulation models. The difference in First Pension between MC and DES model is not significant. For all three experiments: *p–value* is always higher than 0.05 and *t(Stat)* < *t(Critical)*. The results do not determine that the model correctly represents reality. This only suggests that the two simulation models, despite their differences in design, produce similar average results in terms of the metric being tested.

Table 3 *Test #1. Comparison of mean values of the first pension from the MC and DES models*

	Retirement Age					
	60		65		67	
	MC	DES	MC	DES	MC	DES
Mean	7893	7934	14651	14694	18710	18706
Variance	1022954	927797	4044594	3505412	6859555	8349631
Observations	500	500	500	500	500	500
Pooled Variance	975375		3775003		7604593	
Hypoth. Mean Differ.	0		0		0	
df	998		998		998	
t Stat	**-0.65**		**-0.35**		**0.03**	
P(T<=t) two-tail	**0.26**		**0.36**		**0.49**	
t Critical two-tail	**1.65**		**1.65**		**1.65**	

4.2 Test #2: Gross Replacement Rate

A Two-Sample Assuming Equal Variances test was conducted to verify whether the output values of the GRRs, calculated at the moment of retirement for two simulation models, are equal. GRR illustrates the extent to which a retiree's financial situation changes compared to the period of professional and gainful activity. This is the ratio of the first pension to the last salary and represents the level of pension benefits relative to earnings when working.

As in the previous test, the size of the two samples was identical at 500. Due to the high size of both samples, it was assumed that a normal distribution would give a good approximation of the distribution of each of the averages from both samples.
μ_1: mean GRR values from the population described by MC model
μ_2: mean GRR values from population described by DES model
$\bar{x}_1$: sample average from 500 trials of model MC
$\bar{x}_2$: sample average from 500 trials of model DES
Alfa = 0.05
Null hypothesis H_0: $\mu_1 - \mu_2 = 0$
Alternative hypothesis H_2: $\mu_1 - \mu_2 \neq 0$

The results are presented in Table 4. By comparing the results we can conclude there is no significant difference in two means calculated based on the simulation output values from two simulation models. The difference in GRRs between MC and DES model is not significant. For all three experiments: *p–value* is always higher than 0.05 and *t(Stat < t(Critical)*. As for test #1, it is not legitimate to say that the two models correctly represent the phenomenon under study. However, given that the models have different structures, parameters, and the simulation process follows different paradigms, while their final outputs behave similarly on average, one can conclude that different modeling approaches capture the same underlying system dynamics effectively.

Graphical results comparing GRR values based on 500 trials are presented in Figures 2–4. The obtained values confirm the high comparability of the results of the two models.

Table 4 *Test #2. Comparison of mean values of the GRRs from the MC and DES models*

	Retirement age					
	60		65		67	
	MC	DES	MC	DES	MC	DES
Mean	0.45	0.44	0.64	0.63	0.74	0.72
Variance	0.00	0.00	0.01	0.01	0.01	0.01
Observations	500	500	500	500	500	500
Pooled Variance	0.00		0.01		0.01	
Hypoth. Mean Differ	0		0		0	
df	998		998		998	
t Stat	**1.09**		**1.70**		**1.87**	
P(T<=t) two-tail	**0.28**		**0.09**		**0.06**	
t Critical two-tail	**1.96**		**1.96**		**1.96**	

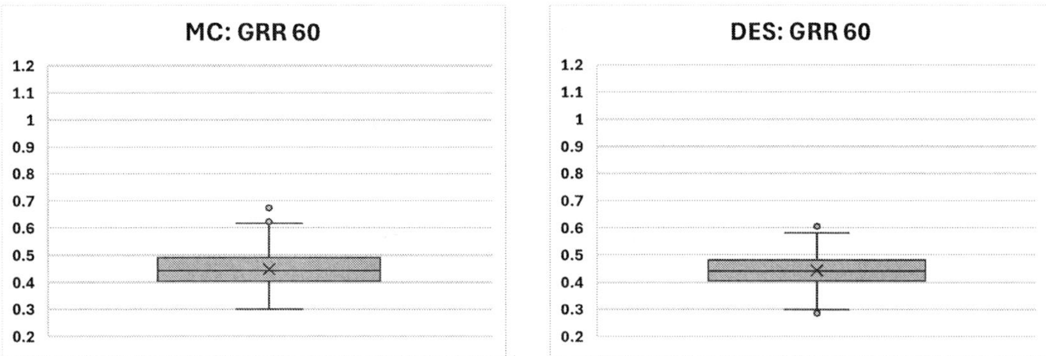

Figure 2: Box and Whisker plot for Gross Replacement Rates based on 500 trials from MC and DES model. Retirement age equals to 60

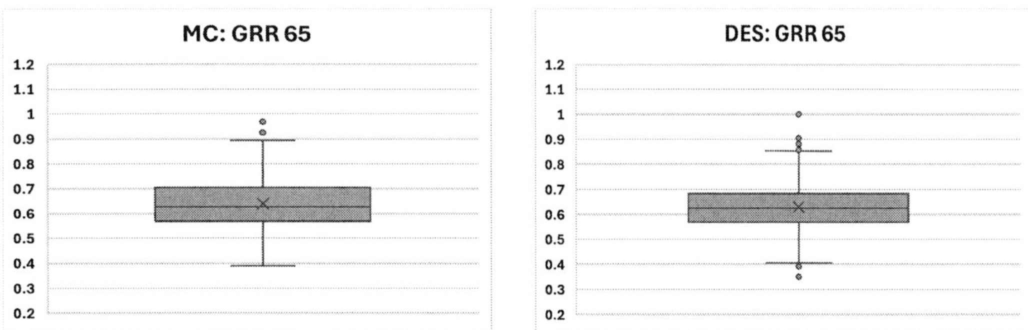

Figure 3 *Box and Whisker plot for Gross Replacement Rates based on 500 trials from MC and DES model. Retirement age equals to 65*

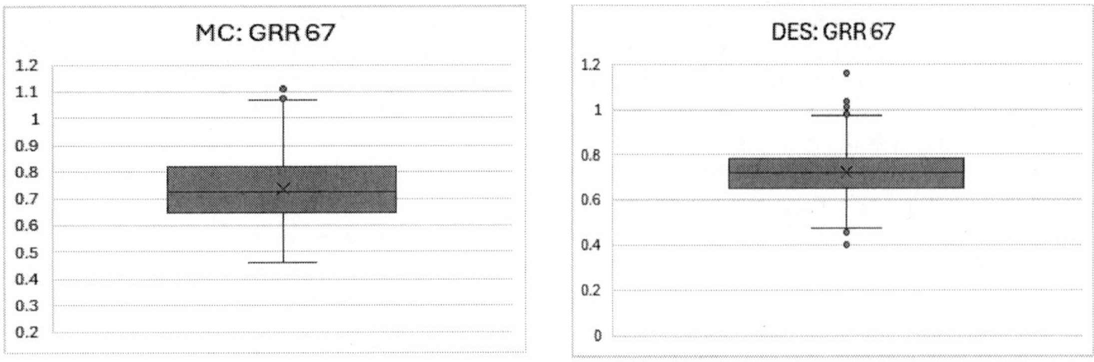

Figure 4 *Box and Whisker plot for Gross Replacement Rates based on 500 trials from MC and DES model. Retirement age equals to 67*

For each retirement age studied, i.e. 60 years (female), 65 years (male), 67 years (extended working life), the values of basic statistical parameters are very similar. What is noticeable, however, is the smaller height of the boxes for the results of the DES model, which indicates less variation in the obtained values in the model built according to the discrete event simulation paradigm. This is due to the way the randomness is modeled. In MC, each sampling is independent and therefore a significantly large number of replications must be performed to reduce the variance of the results. The DES model is based on a sequence of events over time. DES takes into account randomness only at times when an event occurs (defined as a change in the state of the system), but the overall course of the simulation is determined by dependencies and interactions between events. This leads to greater stability of results.

4.3 Test #3: Probability of Target Replacement Rate

The last test compares TRR values calculated for 40%, 45%, 50% and 70% levels and for retirement ages of 60, 65 and 67. The results are shown in Figure 5.

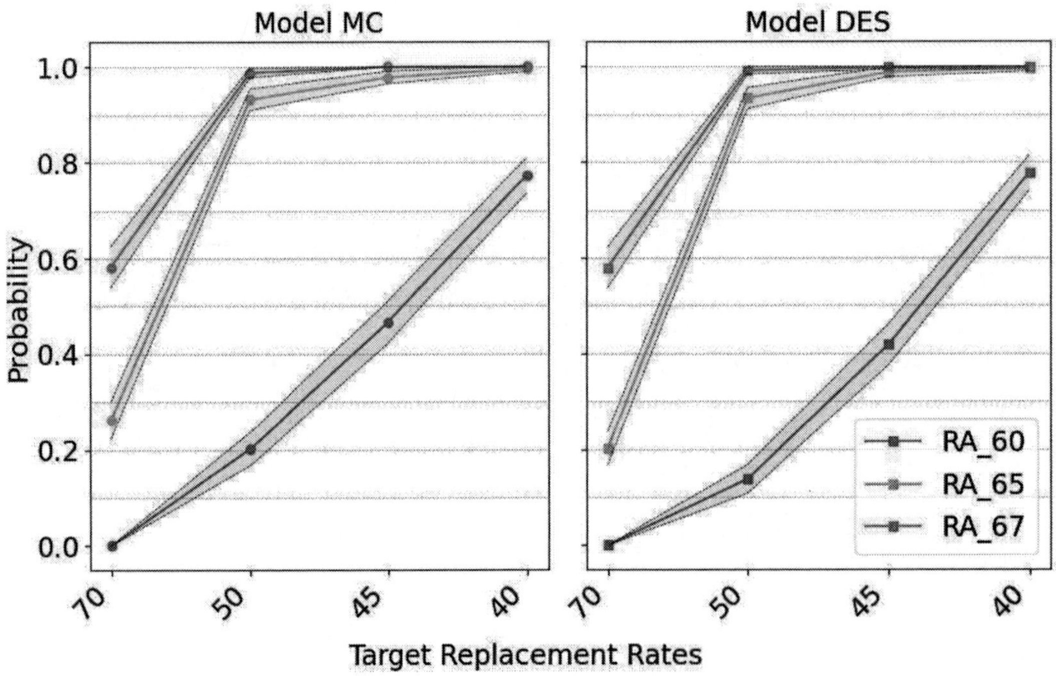

Figure 5 *Different TRR values obtained in both models for different retirement ages based on 500 trials from MC and DES model. The graph shows the probability of obtaining TRR values (bright, solid color line) along with confidence intervals (light color). RA stands for Retirement Age*

The goal of TRRs is to approximate the income that will be needed in retirement in order to maintain the previous (i.e. before the decision to retire) lifestyle. The TRR is usually higher for modest- and middle-income workers than for upper-middle and upper-income workers. The optimal TRR depends on individual spending needs, savings, and financial planning for retirement, but the most commonly indicated TRR level is 65%–75%.

We can observe small differences in the values obtained from the two models, but the characteristics of changes and interrelationships in the tested values are highly comparable. For the retirement age of 60, every increase in the level of TRR (from 40% to higher values) causes a significant decrease in the value of the TRR indicator. For higher retirement ages, changes between levels from 40% to 50% do not cause large changes in the TRR indicators.

5 CONCLUSIONS

The V&V of the model is an extremely important step in the simulation process. In order to verify the correctness of the model, it is necessary to check that the model behaves in a well-defined, predictable way. One of the key elements of V&V is operational validation, which is particularly difficult in the case of social systems that are characterized by the long observation horizons. Obtaining real-world data can prove difficult or even impossible. In such a case, to obtain a high degree of confidence, the model behavior should be explored as thoroughly as possible through comparison with other models.

In this paper, we proposed a comparison of models built using the same empirical input data, however developed under different simulation paradigms. This approach offers several key advantages. Different paradigms provide important insights into the interpretation of results, offering varied methods for analyzing system behavior. For instance, dicrete-event models focus on individual entities (discrete objects), while system dynamics models emphasize broader, aggregate trends. By combining these perspectives, one can achieve a more holistic understanding of system behavior.

Utilizing multiple paradigms allows for a more complete assessment of a model's precision and reliability, ensuring that different facets of the system are carefully explored and validated. Obtaining statistically indistinguishable results strengthens our confidence in both models. If both models, despite their distinct structures and assumptions, converge on similar results, it indicates the robustness of the conclusions. This enhances the overall credibility of the findings and provides stronger evidence for decision-making. Each paradigm has inherent strengths and weaknesses. Using models from different paradigms helps minimize the impact of biases or limitations that might arise if only one modeling technique were used. This leads to a more balanced evaluation of the system being studied. Different paradigms are suited to different types of problems. For example, discrete event simulation focuses at capturing operational flows, while Monte Carlo models can better simulate stochastic relationships. Using two models allows for greater flexibility in addressing the complexity of the system under study.

The results obtained confirmed the high agreement in output parameters of two models. Conducting extensive operational validation also provided us with an additional benefit. It was necessary to conduct many previously unplanned meticulous and detailed tests to ensure that the computer programming and implementation of the conceptual model were correct. As a result, the reliability of both models has increased significantly. The agreement between models reduces the risk that results are an artifact of the modeling technique or assumptions of one specific paradigm.

Although this approach alone is not enough to fully complete the V&V process, it can play a crucial role. In general, integrating models created from different paradigms results in a more thorough, dependable, and robust operational validation process, enhancing the accuracy of predictions and deepening system understanding.

REFERENCES

Balci O (1997) Verification, Validation And Accreditation Of Simulation Models. In: *Winter Simulation Conference Proceedings*, pp 135–141.

Fishman G S & Kiviat P J (1968) The statistics of discrete-event simulation. *Simulation*, **10** (4): 185–195.

GUS (2024) Główny Urząd Statystyczny (Statistics Poland). www.stat.gov.pl.

Hofmann M A (2016) Limits of Empirical Validation: a Review of Arguments with Respect to Social Simulation. In: *2015 Winter Simulation Conference (WSC)*, pp 4069–4080.

Hughes G R, Currie C S M & Corbett E L (2006) Modeling tuberculosis in areas of high HIV prevalence. In: Perrone L F, Wieland F P, Liu J, Lawson B G, Nicol D M, & Fujimoto R M (eds). *Proceedings of the 38th conference on Winter Simulation*. WSC '06. Piscataway, New Jersey: IEEE, Inc., pp 459–465.

Jung J, Bae J W, Lee C, Kang D & Paik E (2018) Objectivity based Self-Evolving Agent Model Validation for Social Issue Simulation. In: *2018 International Conference on Information and Communication Technology Convergence (ICTC)*, pp 1417–1419.

Kleijnen J P C (1995) Verification and validation of simulation models. *European Journal of Operational Research*, **82** (1): 145–162.

Langenbach K & Rabe M (2023) Approach for Classifying the Automatability of Verification and Validation Techniques. In: *2023 Winter Simulation Conference (WSC)*, pp 1665–1675.

Law A M & Kelton W D (2000) *Simulation modeling and analysis*. McGraw-Hill Higher Education: New York.

Liu J, Zhang W, Gao W & Yu Y (2012) Conceptual model for simulation and its verification & validation. In: *2012 IEEE International Conference on Computer Science and Automation Engineering (CSAE)*, pp 622–626.

Lynch C J, Gore R, Collins A J, Cotter T S, Grigoryan G. & Leathrum J F (2021) Increased Need for Data Analytics Education in Support of Verification and Validation. In: *2021 Winter Simulation Conference (WSC)*, pp 1–12.

Mielczarek B (2022) A Simulation Study of the Delayed Effect of Covid-19 Pandemic on Pensions and Welfare of the Elderly: Evidence from Poland BT - Computational Science – ICCS 2022. In: Groen D, de Mulatier C, Paszynski M, Krzhizhanovskaya V V, Dongarra J J, & Sloot P M A (eds.) Springer International Publishing: Cham, pp 326–340.

Mielczarek B (2016) Review of Modelling Approaches for Healthcare Simulation. *Operations Research & Decisions*, **26** (1): 55–72.

Mielczarek B (2023) Simulation Model to Forecast Gender Pension Wealth Gap in the Light of Demographic Changes. In: *2023 Winter Simulation Conference (WSC)*, pp 1387–1396.

Naylor T H (1971) *Computer Simulation Experiments with Models of Economic Systems*. John Wiley & Sons.

OECD (2023) *Pensions at a Glance 2023: OECD and G20 Indicators.* https://www.oecd.org/en/publications/pensions-at-a-glance-2023_678055dd-en.html

Sargent R G (1983) Validating simulation models. In: Roberts S, Banks J, & Schmeiser B (eds.) *Proceedings of the 1983 Winter Simulation Conference,* pp 33–337.

Sargent R G (2020) Verification And Validation Of Simulation Models: An Advanced Tutorial. In: *2020 Winter Simulation Conference (WSC)*, pp 16–29.

Sargent R G (2013) Verification and validation of simulation models. *Journal of Simulation*, **7** (1): 12–24.

Sargent R G & Balci O (2017) History of verification and validation of simulation models. In: *2017 Winter Simulation Conference (WSC),* pp 292–307.

Sargent R G, Goldsman D M & Yaacoub T (2016) A tutorial on the operational validation of simulation models. In: *2016 Winter Simulation Conference (WSC)*, pp163–177.

AUTHOR BIOGRAPHIES

BOŻENA MIELCZAREK is currently an Associate Professor in the Department of Operational Research and Business Intelligence, Wrocław University of Science and Technology (WUST), Poland. She received an MSc in Management Science, a PhD in Economics, and a D.Sc. in Economics from Wrocław University of Science and Technology. Her research interests include simulation modeling, hybrid simulation, social simulations, health-care research, logistics and transport simulation, and financial risk analysis. She is the director of the MBA executive program at WUST. Her e-mail address is: bozena.mielczarek@pwr.edu.pl

Proceedings of the Operational Research Society Simulation Workshop 2025 (SW25)
M. Luis, A. Harper, T. Monks, N. Mustafee, eds.

https://doi.org/10.36819/SW25.047

SUPPLY CHAIN DEVELOPMENT FOR CIRCULARITY IN AEROSPACE: AIRCRAFT SEAT CASE STUDY

Mr. Marco Franchino

AMRC, University of Sheffield
Western Bank, Sheffield S10 2TN
m.franchino@sheffield.ac.uk

Mr. Christopher Haynes

AMRC, University of Sheffield
Western Bank, Sheffield S10 2TN
c.haynes@sheffield.ac.uk

Dr. Cansu Kandemir

AMRC, University of Sheffield
Western Bank, Sheffield S10 2TN
c.kandemir@sheffield.ac.uk

ABSTRACT

This study addresses the challenge of waste reduction in the aerospace industry by focusing on the recyclability of aircraft interior materials, specifically aircraft seats. Currently, a significant portion of these materials end up in landfills. The research develops a Discrete Event Simulation (DES) model to visualise recycling practices for aircraft seats, assessing material types, volumes, and recyclability. By comparing current disposal methods with recycling opportunities, the model offers insights into the potential environmental and economic benefits of adopting circular economy principles. The findings suggest that supply chain decisions in the aerospace sector can significantly enhance sustainability by reducing carbon emissions and indicate a potential business case for recycling. The model serves as a very preliminary foundation and proof of concept for decision-making tools aimed at optimising material recovery for aircraft seat components, contributing to a more circular aerospace supply chain. Future work will aim to review this model with more accurate data and extend this approach to other components and industries, fostering cross-sector collaboration to promote sustainable development.

Keywords: Aerospace, Supply Chain, Circularity

1 INTRODUCTION

A growing awareness of environmental protection is prompting the aviation industry to develop aircraft that are lightweight and have a minimised environmental impact (Nagaraju et al., 2023). Airlines are striving to achieve carbon neutrality by 2050, in response to increasing governmental pressure to accelerate emissions reductions (Dixon et al., 2022).

Whilst in-flight emissions have historically received the most attention (www.sustainableaviation.co.uk/news/uk-aviation-industry-strengthens-commitment-to-achieving-net-zero-and-launches-first-interim-decarbonisation-targets/ accessed January 2025), there are other areas where aviation has the potential to reduce its carbon footprint. In particular, non-operational factors have a substantial impact, with tens of thousands of tonnes of material being consumed and disposed of as waste each year. The scale of the environmental impact is directly related to the mass of the cabin. The design phase of the product life cycle is critical because it is when the factors that determine its impact on the environment are largely set in place. Design is key to improving both operational and non-operational sustainability. In fact, studies estimate that over 80% of a product's environmental impact is set during its design (Delaney et al., 2022). Investigations have examined how cabins are designed today and identified a range of ways in which designs, and design approaches can be developed to deliver more sustainable products. Therefore, circularity practices like material recycling, for example, must be considered essential for reaching sustainability and carbon neutrality in the sector (Tsai et al., 2014).

Cabin interiors, which account for around 10% of an aircraft's empty weight and are replaced four to five times during the life of the airframe, represent a significant portion of an airliner's environmental footprint (IATA, 2018). However, the cabin is one of the most difficult parts of an aircraft to apply circular economy principles to, therefore accounting for a high proportion of the material from an aircraft that is sent to landfill or incinerated (Aerospace Technology Institute, 2022).

Many of the opportunities for increasing circularity require intra-sector and cross-sector partnerships that are currently underdeveloped to enable material and product flows at viable scales. Stringent certification requirements incentivise Original Equipment Manufacturers (OEMs) to rely on proven designs, technologies, and materials. This tends to suppress the introduction of novel, potentially greener technologies and encourage reliance on established designs and materials, many of which have negative sustainability characteristics. Also, as sustainability has not been a priority for the industry historically, there is a low level of understanding of the cabin's impact on the environment (except as a consequence of its weight). For a modern airliner, approximately 50% of all cabin products (by weight) are not currently being recycled, and even what is recycled is not necessarily repurposed within the aerospace sector (Aerospace Technology Institute, 2022). Each element of the cabin has its own technical and commercial challenges that contribute to this overall figure.

2 LITERATURE REVIEW

Discrete Event Simulation (DES) is a modelling technique whereby the simulation clock progresses from one event to the next chronologically. Events occur at separate points in time, and they are the only instances where the state of the system changes. DES typically models a complex system as an ordered sequence of events. Complicated sequences and hierarchical structures can be employed. Uncertainties associated with events can be included in models and their consequences in the system are analysed statistically. DES provides a risk-free environment to gain deeper insights and test decisions prior to making changes in the real-life manufacturing operations. Therefore, DES is a powerful tool for evaluating the impact of sustainability measures across various sectors, including aerospace. Researchers have applied DES to model and assess the environmental and operational effects of implementing sustainable practices as described by Moon (2016) in their extensive literature review.

Usually, deterministic methods like life cycle analysis (LCA) are used to analyse the environmental impact of a product's life cycle. A deterministic model allows the modeller to calculate a future event exactly, without the involvement of randomness. However, deterministic methods are unable to incorporate the dynamic aspects of a real-world system, especially during the manufacturing stages of a product. The use of static data and simplification results in average values that can impact the validity of the assessments (Reap et al., 2008).

In a DES-based simulation model that has been enhanced with LCA features, manufacturing process modules may be coupled to construct process chains. As a result, changes, especially those associated with operational time, can be tested beforehand and their effects on costs or emissions can be calculated. With the same logic, life cycle cost (LCC) analysis or any other form of economic evaluation can be applied to assess costs and investments (Blume, 2020). No commercial software fully integrates these aforementioned decision-making tools, especially LCA and DES. As a result, multiple researchers created their own solutions (Blume, 2020).

Prado and Villani (2010) analysed the applicability of modelling and simulation approaches in different phases of a product lifecycle, demonstrating how DES can be applied to improve sustainability in product development, overcoming the common issues with life cycle analysis (LCA), particularly the staticity of such methodology.

Widok et al. (2011) highlighted the integration of sustainability criteria into DES models, aiming to make the concept of sustainability more actionable. The authors discuss methodologies to incorporate environmental considerations into simulation models, enhancing decision-making processes.

An approach to combining a DES model with LCA methodology, with the goal of enabling a dynamic assessment of environmental issues in manufacturing systems, was given by Löfgren and Tillman (2011).

More recently, Rahn et al. (2022) demonstrated how an LCA can enhance DES by incorporating cradle-to-grave considerations specifically for aircrafts. Similarly, Franchino (2023) used DES to build a framework to test different scenarios in the aerospace manufacturing sector, evaluating key performance indicators to support sustainable decision-making. The framework developed allows for the comparison of alternative scenarios within a manufacturing environment, aiding the selection of more sustainable practices while keeping the business profitable.

Widening the picture to outside manufacturing environments, Mutingi et al. (2013) explored the complexities of simulating green supply chains, particularly focusing on reverse logistics, product recovery, reuse, and recycling. The study demonstrates how DES can be utilised to model and improve the sustainability of supply chain operations.

A lot of similar examples of how supply chains are empowered through DES were collected by Abideen and Binti Mohamad (2019) in their systematic review.

Recently, Chowdary and Rayside (2024) employed a DES modelling framework to demonstrate the viability of circular economy strategies in reducing plastic waste within an industrial setting, highlighting the role of simulation in developing sustainable recycling strategies.

These studies illustrate the versatility and effectiveness of DES in estimating the impact of sustainability measures across various sectors, within manufacturing environments and supply chains, providing valuable insights for researchers and practitioners aiming to implement sustainable practices. While the current body of research demonstrates the applicability of DES to sustainability in aerospace, significant gaps remain (Moon, 2016). The integration of stochastic variability in product condition (e.g., aircraft components wear and tear), for example, is underexplored due to the lack of reliable data because, as mentioned in the introduction, in-flight emissions have historically received the most attention, over non-operational factors. Few studies focus on the specific challenges of achieving circularity in heavily regulated sectors like aerospace, while being more prominent in sectors like automotive where sustainable practices have been adopted earlier than aerospace. An example is provided by Gianesello et al. (2017) that evaluated business models exploring the economic feasibility of recycling centres in the automotive supply chain.

In fact, the implementation of circular economy practices presents unique challenges in heavily regulated sectors, where these initiatives are traditionally less prevalent. A study by the International Civil Aviation Organization (ICAO) notes that, for the aviation sector, circular economy is still an emerging concept, and its application is not widespread resulting in scarce availability of reliable data (ICAO, 2019). In contrast, the automotive industry has made significant strides in adopting circular economy principles for decades (Aguilar Esteva et al. 2019).

Future research should address these gaps by combining advanced simulation techniques with emerging technologies to create robust, scalable solutions for circular supply chains in aerospace, taking inspiration by more established research and practices in different sectors like automotive.

3 METHODOLOGY

For our research we focused on a single element of the aircraft cabin: the aircraft seat. We developed a Discrete Event Simulation (DES) model in AnyLogic DES software to assess and compare scenarios to support decision-making processes. The model is based on several key inputs:

- Aircraft seat components: This includes material types (aluminium, foam, leather, fabric, and plastic), material costs, material quantities, and emissions associated with producing each material.
- Aerospace network: We focused on Western Europe as the geographical area of interest, considering aircraft fleets with varying seat compositions (e.g. number and types of seats) across different countries. The model also incorporates the regular overhauls required for seat components and orders from airlines for both new aircraft.

The costs of the materials used are summarised in Table 1, while the emissions data for material production are presented in Table 2.

Table 1 *Material costs*

Material	***Cost***
Foam	353 $/m³ *or* 3.92 $/kg
Leather	162 $/m² *or* 2,700 $/kg
Fabric	59.8 $/m² *or* 352.94 $/kg
Aluminium	4.4 $/kg
Plastic	2.5 $/kg

Table 2 *Emissions from material production*

Material	***Emissions (KgCO₂e per Kg)***
Foam	3.5
Leather	110.0
Fabric	26.2
Aluminium	5.0
Plastic	16.0

In the Baseline Scenario no recycled materials are considered. Seat manufacturers receive orders from the aircraft companies and supply new seat components accordingly. Material usage and associated costs are calculated over a five-year period. In contrast, the Recyclability Scenario introduces a hypothetical Seat Recycling Centre, located in the UK. We tested several variations of the Recyclability Scenario, adjusting parameters such as recycling rates, logistical efficiency, and processing capacity (see Table 3). Further to this, triangular distributions have been used to take into account the stochasticity of processing times within the recycling centre. After evaluating these variations, we decided to present the most balanced scenario in terms of cost-effectiveness and environmental impact. This balanced scenario offered the most practical and feasible results within the scope of our study.

The flowchart structure of the Baseline Scenario model with no recyclability is shown in Figure 1. Figure 2 shows the Baseline Scenario model flow. The Seat Manufacturer is connected to Aircraft Overhaulers and Airlines to provide the new seat components once orders are received. Likewise, Figure 3 shows the flowchart structure of the Recyclability Scenario model that includes the "recyclability route". Figure 4 shows this Recyclability Scenario model flow. Used seats from the Aircraft Overhaulers for every Airline are taken to the Seat Recycling Centre, materials are recycled at the material recycling centres and supplied to the Seat Manufacturer.

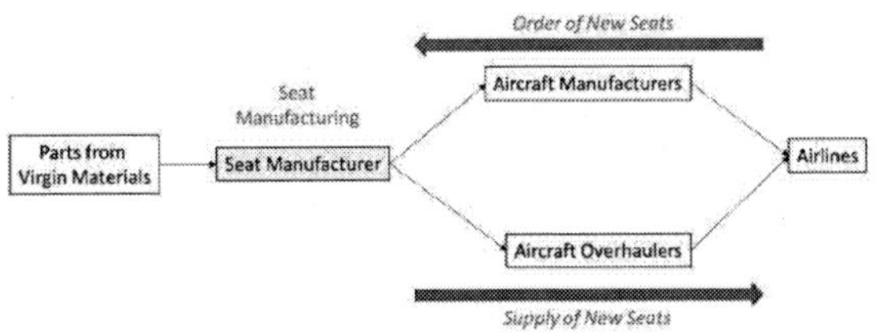

Figure 1 *Model Flowchart (Baseline Scenario)*

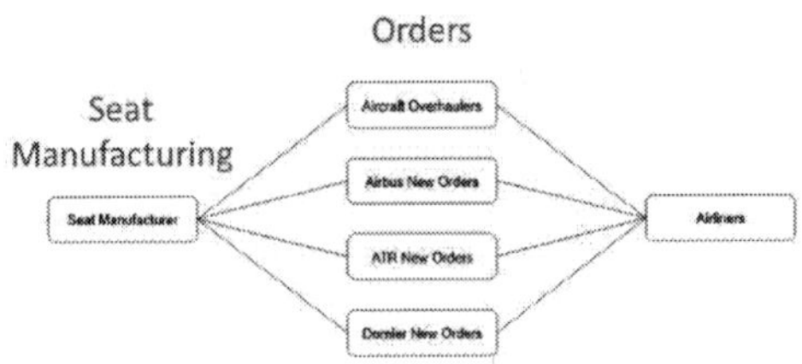

Figure 2 *Model Flow (Baseline Scenario)*

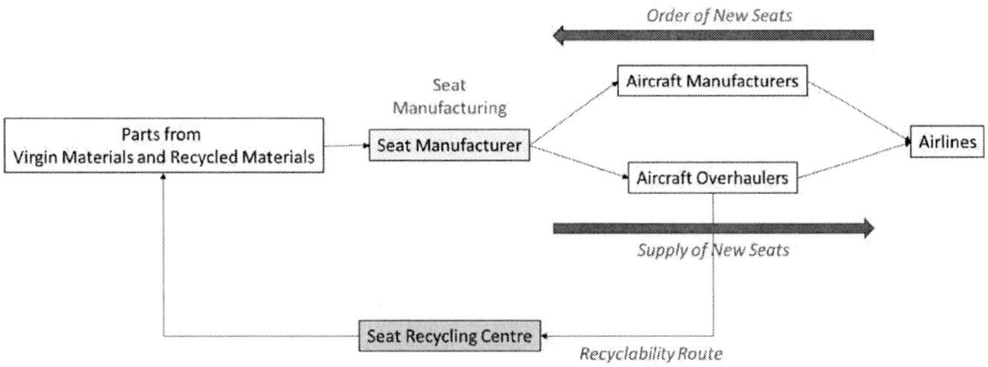

Figure 3: Model Flowchart
(Recyclability Scenario)

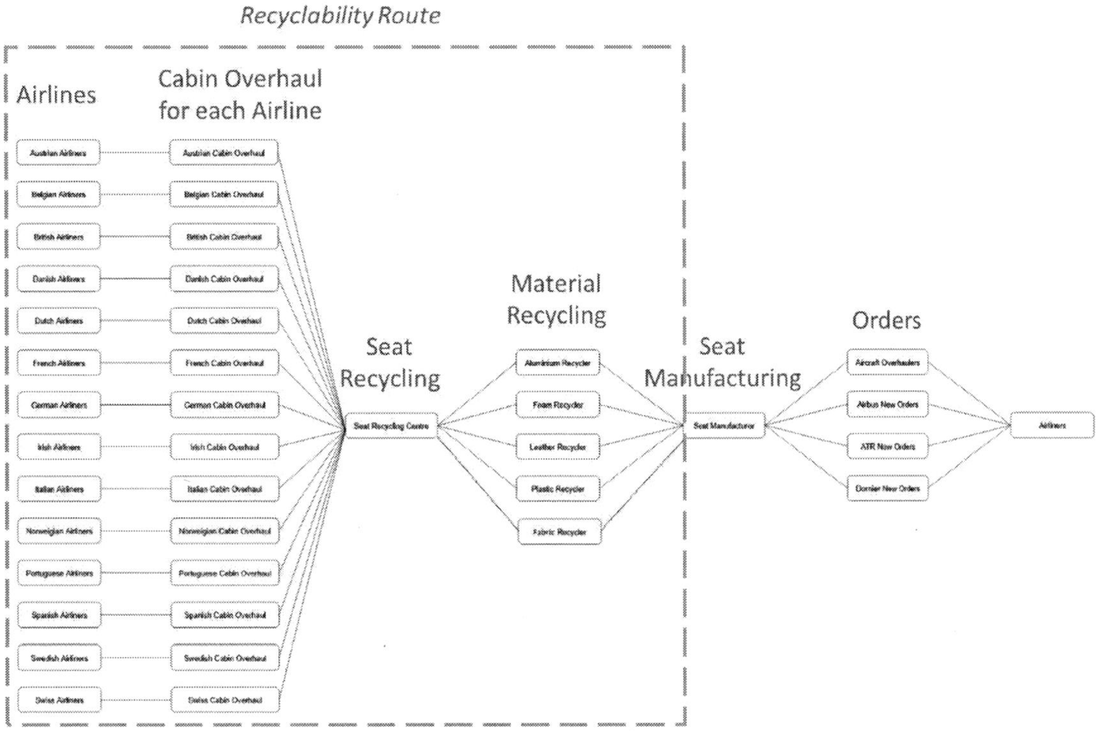

Figure 4 *Model Flow*
(Recyclability Scenario)

Table 3 *Recyclability Scenario parameters*

Recyclability Scenario Parameters
Materials recycling rates
Disassembly process time (e.g. number of processing lines, level of automation)
Material recycling process time (e.g. number of processing lines, level of automation)
Logistical efficiency, fixed and operational costs of vehicles (e.g. number of lorries, fixed and operational costs, loading logics)

Each country's aircraft fleet and corresponding seat configurations (number, type, and size with relative material composition) are incorporated into the model, with data sourced from online databases (https://www.planespotters.net/; https://seatguru.com/airlines/; https://seatmaps.com/airlines/ accessed October 2024). This includes the age of the aircraft, reflecting real-life conditions at the start of the model. An example (United Kingdom) is shown in Figure 5. The model starting point is August 2024.

Some airlines upgrade their cabin products every 5-7 years, while others may keep on-board products in operation for more years (IATA, 2019). In our model, aircraft seat overhauls are assumed to occur every five years, and aircraft are retired once they reach 30 years of age. The simulation model accounts for aircraft movements and the logistics of transporting seats to the Seat Recycling Centre. Airports with over 10 million annual passengers were chosen to serve as hubs for overhauls (https://airmundo.com/en/airports/ accessed October 2024). Once an aircraft is sent to the overhauler, the seats are removed, and new seats are placed in the aircraft before it is returned to service. As overhauls occur every 5 years, the model does not include the stochasticity in wear and tear of the seat and assumes that the seat degrades homogeneously, therefore the recycling process (i.e. material yield) is not affected by variability in the condition of the seat.

At the Seat Recycling Centre, the materials (leather, foam, plastic, fabric, and aluminium) are separated and processed. Once sufficient quantities are gathered, they are sent to specialised recycling centres. The parameters of the Seat Recycling Centre (e.g. number of lorries, level of automation, process cycle times) are customisable, for our calculation we tested configurations based on similar recycling centres active for different sectors (Gianesello et al., 2017). Recycled materials are then delivered back to seat manufacturers, reducing dependency on virgin raw materials. The percentage of recycled material incorporated into new seats, along with the resulting cost evaluation and emissions reductions, is calculated within the model. Seat manufacturers take orders from the aircraft overhaulers for new seats, and also from the aircraft manufacturers which are making new aircrafts to replace those being retired and given enough remaining capacity will make new aircraft to expand an airline's current fleets.

The simulation begins in August 2024, with a focus on optimising the recycling of aircraft seats across Western Europe. Material composition, costs, and emissions are key metrics used to evaluate the effectiveness of the proposed recycling framework.

The number of seats required in the modelling period equals to 251,361. Scenario comparison is shown in Table 4. The Recyclability Scenario shows the use of 70.11% recycled material with a minimum percentage of recycled material for foam (50.53%) and a maximum for leather/fabric (81.55%) being used. Emissions have been reduced in material production by 56.29%, from a minimum of 40.42% in foam to a maximum of 65.24% in leather/fabric.

The monetary values of recycled materials are reported in Table 5, these are obtained by multiplying the recycled quantities in weight (Recycled [tons] in Table 4) by the cost rates (Table 1). Values per Seat are obtained dividing the total values by the number of processed seats (251,361). A value of $415.60 per seat is generated by the recycling business. This figure can be used to assess the business's profitability; for instance, to remain profitable, the cost to acquire and process each seat must be less than $415.60.

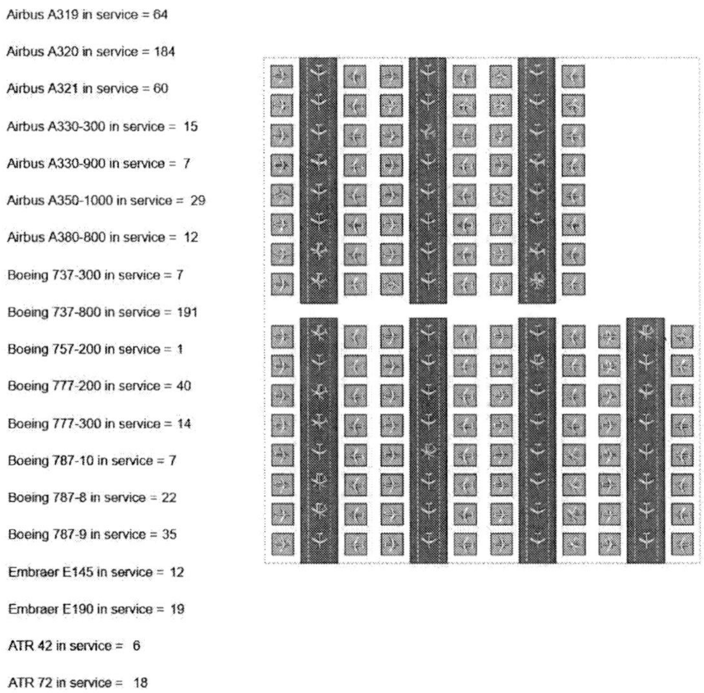

Figure 5 *Country Level aircraft fleet – UK example*

Table 4 *Scenario Comparison*

		Baseline Scenario			*Recyclability Scenario*				
Material	*Quantity needed [Tons]*	*Recycled [tons]*	*Recycled (%)*	*Emission s [tonCO$_2$e]*	*Recycled [tons]*	*Recycled (%)*	*Emission s [tonCO$_2$e]*	*Emission Reduction [tons]*	*Emission Reduction (%)*
Foam	1247	0	0	4363	630	50.53%	2636	1727	39.58%
Leather	35	0	0	3852	29	81.55%	3648	632	14.76%
Fabric	4	0	0	102	3	81.55%	131	524	80.00%
Aluminium	6262	0	0	31311	4687	74.85%	25011	6300	20.12%
Plastic	1881	0	0	30094	1262	67.09%	22170	7923	26.33%
Total	**9428**	**0**	**0**	**69721**	**6611**	**70.11%**	**30478**	**39243**	**56.29%**

Table 5 *Monetary value of the recyclability*

Material	*Total Value [$]*	*Value per Seat [$]*
Foam	$ 2,469,077	$ 9.82
Leather	$ 77,098,658	$ 306.72
Fabric	$ 1,119,802	$ 4.45
Aluminium	$ 20,623,765	$ 82.05
Plastic	$ 3,154,672	$ 12.55
Total	**$ 104,465,975**	**$ 415.60**

4 LIMITATIONS

It is important to note that our research utilised data provided by our research centre's aerospace partner companies. Where specific values were unavailable, reasonable assumptions were made based on reputable academic sources, databases and online data. While we acknowledge that deviations from real-world conditions may exist, the model is not intended to provide definitive answers. Instead, it aims to foster discussions and offer insights that can guide future efforts towards a more sustainable aviation industry.

The model assumes that aircraft seat overhauls occur every five years, which simplifies the representation of seat wear and tear. Stochasticity in the degradation of seats is not considered. As a result, variability in the condition of seats does not influence the recycling process or associated costs. This limitation could be addressed in future work; however, the lack of direct data on seat condition variability may affect the quality and reliability of such extensions.

Although the monetary value of recycled materials is outlined, the discussion of profitability lacks depth, as it was not the primary focus of our research. For instance, the costs associated with establishing and operating a Seat Recycling Centre (e.g. fixed and operational costs of vehicles) would require further validation. Future research could address these factors to provide a more comprehensive assessment of the economic viability of seat recycling within the aerospace sector.

5 FINDINGS

Within discussed limitations, our simulation model offers valuable insights and a preliminary foundation for making informed decisions toward more sustainable aircraft production and supply chain strategies. Key findings from the model include:

1. **Scenario Variations**: Multiple variations of the Recyclability Scenario were tested during the research, with the most balanced scenario presented. This scenario was chosen based on its environmental impact and cost-effectiveness, offering the most feasible and scalable solution within the scope of this study. Additional scenarios may be created and compared using different parameters.
2. **Carbon Emission Reduction**: Recycling materials substantially lowered carbon emissions from the manufacturing processes. The simulation highlights the environmental advantages of minimising virgin material use and optimising logistics for seat refurbishment and recycling.
3. **Geographical Implications**: The results suggest that establishing a centralised Seat Recycling Centre in regions like Western Europe (as simulated for the UK) can streamline the supply chain and increase the feasibility of circular practices within the aerospace industry.
4. **Cost Evaluation**: The monetary value of recycled material per seat serves as a reference point for assessing the recycling business's profitability. For profitability, the costs associated with

acquiring and processing each seat would need to remain below this figure. Additional cost parameters collected within the simulation can help assess such profitability.

5. **Scalability and Application**: While focused on aircraft seats, the model's framework is adaptable to other cabin components and potentially other industries. The findings reinforce the value of sector-wide collaboration in achieving a more circular economy within aerospace, especially as regulatory pressures and sustainability goals evolve. Evaluating scenarios with multiple recycling centres in optimised positions in the supply network will further help the economic and environmental analysis.

6 CONTRIBUTION

This research introduces a simulation model designed to evaluate material supply choices for aircraft seats, providing insights into cost and environmental impacts. The model aids decision-making by helping to prioritise recycling options for aircraft interiors. Although focused on aircraft seats, the methodology is adaptable to other components within the aerospace sector and beyond.

The ultimate goal is to extend the use of this model in real-world case studies, fostering collaboration across industries to promote sustainable practices and quantify benefits. Further industry engagement will be key to enhancing the practical application of this model in advancing circularity and environmental sustainability. Crucially, more accurate and more reliable data is required to ensure the precision and effectiveness of future applications and work.

ACKNOWLEDGMENTS

This research was funded by UK Catapult. Authors would like to acknowledge the High Value Manufacturing Catapult for providing the funding to develop the methodology used in this study. We also recognise the contributions of our aerospace partner companies, which provided valuable data that informed our research.

REFERENCES

Abideen A Z, Binti Mohamad F, (2019). Empowering Supply Chain through Discrete-Event and Agent-Based Simulation – A Systematic Review and Bibliometric Analysis, IEEE Access, vol. 8, pp. 123456-123470, 2020. doi: 10.1109/ACCESS.2020.1234567.

Aguilar Esteva LC, Kasliwal A, Kinzler MS, Kim HC, Keoleian, GA, et al. (2019). Circular economy framework for automobiles: Closing energy and material loops. Journal of Industrial Ecology, 25(4), 877-889.

Aerospace Technology Institute (ATI). (2022). Sustainable Cabin Design

Blume S A. (2020). Resource Efficiency in Manufacturing Value Chains. s.l. : International Publishing AG.

Chowdary BV, Rayside A. (2024). Sustainable recycling strategies to reduce plastic waste: application of circular economy principles and discrete event simulation modelling to beverage manufacturing industry. International Journal of Process Management and Benchmarking, 16(2), 139–163.

Delaney E, Liu W, Zhu Z, Xu Y, Dai JS. (2022). The investigation of environmental sustainability within product design: a critical review. Design Science. 2022;8:e15. doi:10.1017/dsj.2022.11

Dixon J, Bell K, Brush S. (2022). Which way to net zero? a comparative analysis of seven UK 2050 decarbonisation pathways, Renewable and Sustainable Energy Transition, Volume 2, 2022, 100016, ISSN 2667-095X, https://doi.org/10.1016/j.rset.2021.100016.

Franchino M. Framework for Sustainability in Aerospace: A Proof of Concept on Decision Making and Scenario Comparison. In: Kohl, H., Seliger, G., Dietrich, F. (eds). 2023. Manufacturing Driving Circular Economy. GCSM 2022. Lecture Notes in Mechanical Engineering. Springer, Cham. 2023. https://doi.org/10.1007/978-3-031-28839-5_74

Gianesello P, Ivanov D, Battini D. (2017). Closed-loop supply chain simulation with disruption considerations: a case-study on Tesla. International Journal of Inventory Research. 4. 257. 2017. 10.1504/IJIR.2017.090361.

IATA. (2018). "Best Industry Practices for Aircraft Decommissioning (BIPAD) 1st Edition," IATA, Montreal-Generva

IATA. (2019). "Best practices guide Cabin interior retrofits and entry into service program", February 2019

ICAO. (2019). ICAO Environment Report

Löfgren B, Tillman A. (2011). Simulation Supplemented with LCA. 17-18, 2011, Journal of Cleaner Production, Vol. 19, pp. 2015-2024.

Moon, Y. B. (2016). Simulation modelling for sustainability: a review of the literature. International Journal of Sustainable Engineering, 10(1), 2–19. https://doi.org/10.1080/19397038.2016.1220990
Mutingi M, Parasuram KV, Baiphisi D. (2013). Discrete-event simulation for green supply chain management: A conceptual framework. 7th International Conference on Intelligent Systems and Control (ISCO), Coimbatore, India, 2013, pp. 511-516. 2013. doi: 10.1109/ISCO.2013.6481208.
Nagaraju SB, Priya HC, Girijappa YGT, Puttegowda M. (2023). Lightweight and sustainable materials for aerospace applications, Lightweight and Sustainable Composite Materials, Woodhead Publishing, 2023, Pages 157-178, ISBN 9780323951890, https://doi.org/10.1016/B978-0-323-95189-0.00007-X.
Prado R P, Villani E. (2010). Discrete event simulation applied to aircraft development cycle. Brazilian Journal of Operations & Production Management, 7(2), 131-152. 2010.
Rahn, C, Schaller, F, Wenzel, S. (2022). "Using Discrete-Event Simulation for a Holistic Aircraft Life Cycle Assessment." Sustainability, 14(17), 10598. https://doi.org/10.3390/su141710598
Reap, J, Roman F, Duncan S, Bras B. (2008). A Survey of Unresolved Problems in Life Cycle Assessment. The International Journal of Life Cycle Assessment, Vol. 13, pp. 290-300.
Tsai WH, Chang YC, Lin SJ, Chen HC, Chu PY. (2014). A green approach to the weight reduction of aircraft cabins, Journal of Air Transport Management, Volume 40, 2014, Pages 65-77, ISSN 0969-6997, https://doi.org/10.1016/j.jairtraman.2014.06.004.
Widok A, Wohlgemuth, V, Page B. (2011). Combining sustainability criteria with discrete event simulation. 859-870. 2011. 10.1109/WSC.2011.6147812.

AUTHOR BIOGRAPHIES

MARCO FRANCHINO received a MSc Mechanical Engineering from the Polytechnic University of Torino (Italy) in 2011. He is the Lead Engineer for Manufacturing Intelligence at the Advanced Manufacturing Research Centre (AMRC), part of the University of Sheffield. Marco has wide R&D and industrial experience in Discrete Event Simulation, factory flow modelling, cost modelling, and cost prediction strategies focused on products, resources, and investments estimation. He is also an expert in trade studies to isolate the best/most balanced solution and decision-making techniques.

CHRISTOPHER HAYNES is a research engineer for Simulation & Modelling at the Advanced Manufacturing Research Centre (AMRC), part of the University of Sheffield. He has 5 years of experience in process modelling focused on manufacturing and supply chain in an industrial environment.

CANSU KANDEMIR has 15 years of experience in the simulation and modelling of complex systems, specialising in Discrete Event Simulation. She is the Technical Fellow for Manufacturing Intelligence at the Advanced Manufacturing Research Centre (AMRC), part of the University of Sheffield. She has contributed to research and development projects across the Automotive, Aerospace and Food sectors, optimising systems through various modelling techniques. Her research focuses on integrating Industry 4.0 technologies into modelling and simulation to enhance decision-making accuracy.

Proceedings of the Operational Research Society Simulation Workshop 2025 (SW25)
M. Luis, A. Harper, T. Monks, N. Mustafee, eds.
https://doi.org/10.36819/SW25.048

LOGISTICS NETWORK DESIGN FOR A SUSTAINABLE BLOOD SUPPLY CHAIN UNDER DISASTERS USING A SIMULATION APPROACH

Lama Soliman Khaled

Exeter Digital Enterprise Systems Laboratory
Department of Engineering
University of Exeter
Streatham Campus, Exeter, EX4 4QF, UK
l.soliman-khaled@exeter.ac.uk

Ahmad Attar

Exeter Digital Enterprise Systems Laboratory
Department of Engineering
University of Exeter
Streatham Campus, Exeter, EX4 4QF, UK
a.attar@exeter.ac.uk

Martino Luis

Exeter Digital Enterprise Systems Laboratory
Department of Engineering
University of Exeter
Streatham Campus, Exeter, EX4 4QF, UK
m.luis@exeter.ac.uk

Baris Yuce

Exeter Digital Enterprise Systems Laboratory
Department of Engineering
University of Exeter
Streatham Campus, Exeter, EX4 4QF, UK
b.yuce@exeter.ac.uk

ABSTRACT

Natural disasters, including earthquakes and floods, can cause substantial damage to public and private infrastructures, highlighting the necessity for resilient healthcare systems. Here, reliable distribution of blood products is vital as disruptions can severely impact patient care. However, blood supply chains (BSCs) face intricate challenges under disasters due to abrupt, drastic spikes in demand. Thus, identifying the optimal locations for the blood collection centres is essential to maintain a constant supply of these products to hospitals while minimising the overall cost of the chain. Meanwhile, carbon emissions of the BSC can also be a side concern for the decision-makers, especially in crowded and polluted cities. This study develops an agent-based simulation approach to configure the collection facilities and allocate them to demand points while considering mobile centres in addition to permanent ones. A real case is assessed, revealing cost-attractive scenarios that, if chosen, could cause a 25% increase in emissions.

Keywords: Blood Supply Chain, Disasters, Carbon Emissions, Agent-Based Simulation

1 INTRODUCTION

The impacts of natural disasters on healthcare systems have been observed recently better than ever before, especially after the COVID-19 outbreak and the Fukushima nuclear power plant explosion (Kundu et al., 2022). It has become evident that implementing a static healthcare supply system is not an effective approach; rather, it should be dynamic, responsive, and agile. While efficient emergency logistics could reduce this impact in the affected areas, the sudden and unpredictable nature of the disasters adds sizable challenges to planning and alertness efforts (Fahimnia et al., 2017). More specifically, such disasters tend to result in numerous injuries, necessitating immediate emergency blood supplies for the treatment of those affected, and making on-time deliveries in the blood supply chain (BSC) one of the most critical subjects under disaster scenarios. While delivery time efficiency and demand fulfilment are expected to be the main priorities for such healthcare supply chains, these activities can have environmental impacts, e.g., CO_2 emissions, that have widely been neglected.

It is also essential to acknowledge that although blood products must be accessible in hospitals and clinics for urgent treatments, they are inherently perishable. For example, the shelf lives for the whole blood, red blood cells (RBC), and platelets are 21, 42, and 5 days, respectively, and the longest life belongs to the blood plasma which can last up to 12 months (if kept at a controlled temperature).

Issues identified in the BSC include shortages, expired blood products, and the necessity to reduce supply chain costs. These issues are complex and demand significant time to resolve due to the multiple factors associated with them, such as the classification of blood as a perishable product, the fluctuations in the demand and supply, and the incurred costs and risks (Mansur et al. 2022). The difficulty of planning for the distribution of the right quantity of products for the next cycle, arises from the uncertainty and variability in the demand and supply conditions and the prediction inaccuracies, which may practically lead to either shortages or excess inventory. This has all led to the location-allocation modelling in BSC attracting attention. In general, location-allocation problems focus on determining the ideal geographic locations and the optimal allocation of the layers to succeeding and proceeding facilities to minimise the associated transportation costs (Attar et al., 2024b).

For modelling such a system, this paper applies an agent-based simulation (ABS) method using AnyLogic simulation software version 8.8.6 due to its flexibility in representing a range of agents, like donors, blood centres, collection sites, and hospitals, within the BSC. This approach makes it easy to add or adjust agents, allowing for a realistic look at how these entities interact and impact the overall system performance. In addition to that, ABS can demonstrate complex behaviour patterns and offer more valuable information about the real-life system. This study differentiates itself by incorporating the ABS to reduce both the total cost and CO_2 emissions, in contrast to existing literature that primarily focuses on inventory management and cost minimisation. The threefold hybrid view of ABS, cost, and sustainability in this paper enhances flexibility and offers a more detailed and dynamic representation of complex behaviours in the BSC.

Therefore, the main contributions of this paper are threefold: (i) introducing an agent-based simulation approach to determine the optimal locations for both temporary and permanent blood collection centres under disasters, (ii) incorporating the sustainability factors and CO_2 emissions in the BSC while ensuring cost-effective and timely operations, and (iii) demonstrating the effectiveness of the proposed concepts on a real case study. The structure of this paper is outlined as follows: a brief literature review is presented in Section 2. In Section 3, we define the studied problem and present the proposed simulation approach. A real-world case is investigated in Section 4 using the proposed approach. Finally, concluding remarks and directions for future research are provided in Section 5.

2 RELATED WORKS

In this section, we survey the available literature on blood supply chains under two different states: (i) Normal conditions, (ii) Disasters or Emergencies and (iii) Simulation Application in BSC.

2.1 Blood Supply Chain in Normal Condition

Arvan et al. (2015) is among the studies that considered the design of BSCs in normal conditions. considering transportation and blood processing times but excluding storage time. Their mixed-integer programming (MIP) model aimed to optimise blood bank location-allocation, minimising costs and reducing expired products. Zahiri et al. (2015) presented a mixed integer linear programming (MILP) model to make strategic and tactical decisions in the blood collection system in Iran to minimise the total costs. Multi-period planning horizons were considered in their study under uncertainty in the demand and quantity of donations. Zahiri and Pishvaee (2017) designed a mixed integer non-linear programming (MINLP) model for BSC networks under epistemic uncertainty to minimise the total cost, shortage, and unsatisfied demand. Blood group compatibility and perishability were also considered in their model, and the exact methods in GAMS optimisation software were used for solving the mathematical problem. Heidari-Fathian and Pasandideh (2018) designed a sustainable BSC network by suggesting an MIP to minimise the total cost and the total environmental impact of the optimal supply chain network design (SCND) while dealing with supply and demand uncertainty. To solve this mathematical model, they deployed the Lagrangian relaxation method.

Araújo et al. (2020) addressed BSC's tactical and operational decision planning by developing a two-stage, multi-period integer linear programming (ILP) approach under supply and demand uncertainty while considering the perishability of the products. They were the pioneers in deploying any of such studies in a case study in Portugal and aimed to minimise the total costs of shortage and waste in the system, simultaneously.

2.2 Blood Supply Chain in Disasters and Emergencies

The BSCND under disaster conditions or emergencies has long been an interesting concern in healthcare planning. Zahiri et al. (2014) addressed the location-allocation of mobile blood banks problem (fixed and temporary) in a multi-period decision horizon for emergencies. A stochastic MINLP model was developed to minimise the total cost of the system. The model integrates both tactical and strategic planning decisions to determine the optimal location of blood facilities and was solved the using exact solvers in GAMS software. Kohneh et al. (2016) developed a mathematical MIP model for the BSCND problem in disaster situations to minimise the total cost of the supply chain and maximize the coverage of donor groups. The study was implemented on a real case in Iran to determine the effectiveness of the model with demand uncertainty. Similar to many other studies in the BSC area, Kohneh et al. (2016) used exact solvers from GAMS as a solution method to solve the defined problem.

Fahimnia et al. (2017) designed a bi-objective, stochastic MIP model for the BSC to minimise the delivery time from blood facilities to hospitals during disasters while achieving the minimum total cost. The paper aimed to investigate the trade-off between BSC cost and delivery time using a hybrid of ε-constraint and Lagrangian relaxation methods. Cheraghi and Hosseini-Motlagh (2020) reviewed a disaster relief problem by considering how efficient the BSC is. MIP modelling was proposed for this scholastic problem where the model's objectives were to minimise the total cost and maximize the number of blood shortages at the demand points. GAMS was used to solve the problem when a disaster happens. Kamyabniya et al. (2018) examined robust Blood logistics planning for disaster relief by recommending an MIP model for the location-allocation problem to minimise the cost and shortage of platelets. The ε-constraint approach was used to solve the model where results showed the excess, as well as the shortage of platelets.

Ghasemi (2019) and Haghjoo et al. (2020) discussed the BSC location-allocation planning problem in disaster situations. The former proposed an MINLP model to minimise the total costs and considered demand uncertainty, while the latter designed a reliable MILP version to minimise demand uncertainty and facility disruption risks in the post-disaster period in Iran. Haghjoo et al. (2020) also applied two stochastic meta-heuristic algorithms, namely, the self-adaptive imperialist competitive algorithm and the invasive weed optimisation algorithm (IWO), to solve the problem. Khalilpourazari et al. (2020) proposed a mathematical model for the location-allocation problem in disaster conditions and three minimisation objectives: the total transportation time, cost, and unfulfilled demand. They used the Lexicographic weighted Tchebychff method to solve the problem and proposed a neural-learning process to learn from past experiences and to design an efficient blood supply chain under new challenges.

2.3 Simulation Application in Blood Supply Chain

Alfonso et al. (2013) developed a multi-period simulation model for analysing fixed blood collection sites and daily platelet production planning, later converted into a discrete event simulation model to evaluate blood collection scenarios. Duan and Liao (2014) used simulation-optimisation for red blood cells, incorporating shelf-life and blood group compatibility, employing Threshold and Tabu Search algorithms to minimise shortages and waste. Osorio et al. (2017) proposed a hybrid discrete event simulation and integer linear programming model for blood supply chain planning, tested in Colombia, which improved cost, shortages, and waste. Selvakumar et al. (2019) used discrete-event simulation to optimise a blood collection centre serving 152 hospitals in India, introducing the Pull system, which eliminated waste and improved service levels. The previous studies discussed primarily utilised discrete event simulation (DES) to model various aspects of the blood supply chain. In contrast, this study employs agent-based simulation (ABS) to capture individual donor behaviour and interactions, providing a more detailed representation.

Table 1 summarises the most related literature on the blood supply chain under normal conditions as well as disasters and emergency situations from different aspects including objectives, sustainability, and solution methods. As seen in this table, the combination of sustainability and disaster conditions was neglected in the past works. An extra contribution of the current study is its simulation-based modelling approach for this combination of assumptions, which is known to offer higher modelling flexibility and a more realistic representation of the studied complex system (Attar et al., 2016).

Table 1 Summary of related literature.

Research	**Objective (s)**						**Modelling Condition**		**Sustainability**	**Solution Methods**		
	Cost	Waste	Delivery time	Shortage	Coverage	Availability	Normal	Crisis		Exact	Heuristics	Scenario-Based
Alfonso et al. (2013)	☑			☑			☑				☑	☑
Arvan et al. (2015)	☑	☑					☑			☑		
Araújo et al. (2020)	☑	☑		☑			☑			☑		
Cheraghi and Hosseini-Motlagh (2020)	☑			☑				☑		☑		
Duan and Liao (2014)		☑					☑				☑	☑
Fahimnia et al. (2017)	☑		☑					☑		☑	☑	
Haghjoo et al. (2020)	☑							☑			☑	
Heidari-Fathian and Pasandideh (2018)	☑						☑		☑		☑	
Ghasemi (2019)	☑							☑		☑		
Khalilpourazari et al. (2020)	☑			☑				☑			☑	
Kamyabniya et al. (2018)	☑			☑				☑		☑		
Kohneh et al. (2016)	☑				☑			☑		☑		
Osorio et al. (2017)	☑			☑			☑				☑	☑
Selvakumar et al. (2019)		☑		☑		☑	☑					☑
Zahiri et al. (2014)	☑						☑			☑		
Zahiri et al. (2015)	☑						☑			☑		
Zahiri and Pishvaee (2017)	☑						☑			☑		
This paper	☑							☑	☑			☑

3 SIMULATION APPROACH

Simulation modelling in the context of the BSC involves utilising computer-based methods to replicate the movement of blood products across different stages of the supply chain. By using simulation models, it is possible to analyse how various factors (such as fluctuations in the demand and transportation delays) affect the overall performance of the BSC, ultimately resulting in timely and effective delivery of blood products to the patients in need. With the help of simulation, managers of the BSC can detect possible bottlenecks and formulate backup strategies to guarantee the availability of blood products in emergencies (Arani et al., 2020). To the best of our knowledge, only a few papers focused on the simulation of the BSC and have mainly deployed DES and mathematical programming. Figure 1 graphically shows the flow of blood products in the multiple layers of a BSC. The process begins from the donors who contribute their blood at designated collection facilities. In an emergency, these facilities are either temporary/mobile units or permanent collection centres. The collected blood is then transported to blood centres, where it goes through a series of laboratory tests to ensure safety and compatibility. Subsequent to the testing phase, the blood is preserved under specific conditions until called for in the BSC. Finally, blood units are distributed to demand nodes, including hospitals and clinics; where they are allocated to the patients and consumed for various medical procedures, such as surgeries, transfusions, and emergency care.

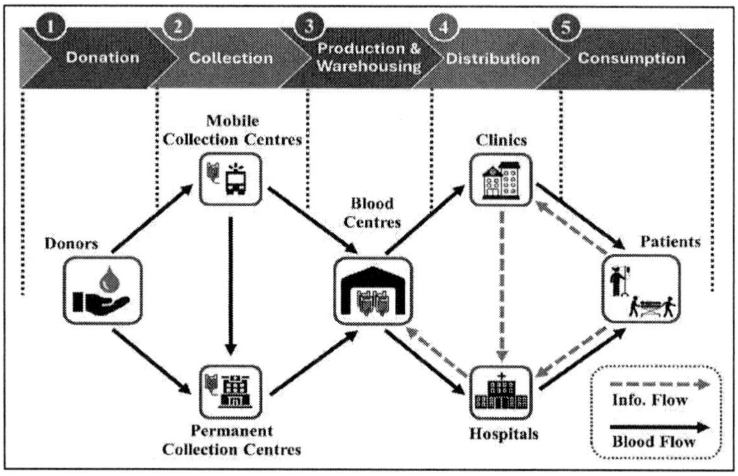

Figure 1 The material and information flow in the five layers of the studied Blood Supply Chain.

This study develops an ABS using AnyLogic simulation software which can effectively handle the individual decision-making entities of such networks and embrace social, non-monetary, and environmental aspects. Our simulation model in AnyLogic incorporates various agents to replicate all components of the system as demonstrated in Figure 1. This includes Donors, Mobile Collection Centres, Permanent Collection Centres, Blood Centres, and Hospitals/Clinics. These agents engage within the model to mimic the dynamics of the blood supply chain, encompassing the flow of blood products from collection and distribution to consumption.

The donor agents represent the individuals who can donate blood at either mobile collection centres or permanent ones. Several factors are taken into account when these agents make decisions, including proximity to collection centres and accessibility. The mobile collection centres and permanent collection centres act as flow aggregation points, with mobile centres being flexible in location, moving between different areas, while permanent centres remain fixed. The blood centres, on the other hand, serve as hubs for processing and distributing the collected blood to hospitals/clinics. Here, hospital (and clinic) agents represent the demand side of this chain, sending requests for specific blood types as needed. Figure 1 schematically demonstrates the logical flow of information in the demand side of this supply chain.

This model simulates interactions between agents as blood is donated, collected, processed, and distributed. Donors choose where to donate, and mobile centres decide their next step based on proximity to blood banks, either transferring blood to a permanent facility or delivering directly. Hospitals then receive the blood units to fulfil their requests. The request sent from each hospital/clinic is, by itself, a function of the incoming demand received from the patients (i.e., end consumers of the chain). In the following subsections, we describe some of the unique characteristics of the proposed simulation model including details of the donor groups, collection facilities, and the logic of the most important decisions made by the donor agents.

3.1 Permanent and Mobile Facilities

The map in Figure 2 shows the GIS locations of donor groups, permanent collection facilities, mobile blood collection facilities and regional blood centres based on their coordinate values (i.e., longitude and latitude) based on the dataset explored by Khalilpourazari et al. (2020). The referenced benchmark data is chosen due to its specifical emphasis on blood supply chain dynamics under disaster conditions which is the main focus of our study as well. In this dataset, there are 22 donor groups, and 9 permanent facilities spread in all districts of Tehran, the capital city of Iran. This provides a foundation for examining effective responses to sudden, high-demand scenarios, which makes the findings more applicable to real-life emergencies. A donation rate of 22.05 units per 1,000 people was used to estimate the blood supply for each district based on population data. Each donor group represents 1,000 individuals within one of Tehran's 22 municipal districts, simplifying the model by grouping donors based on geographical proximity. This approach aligns with prior studies such as Khalilpourazari et al. (2020).

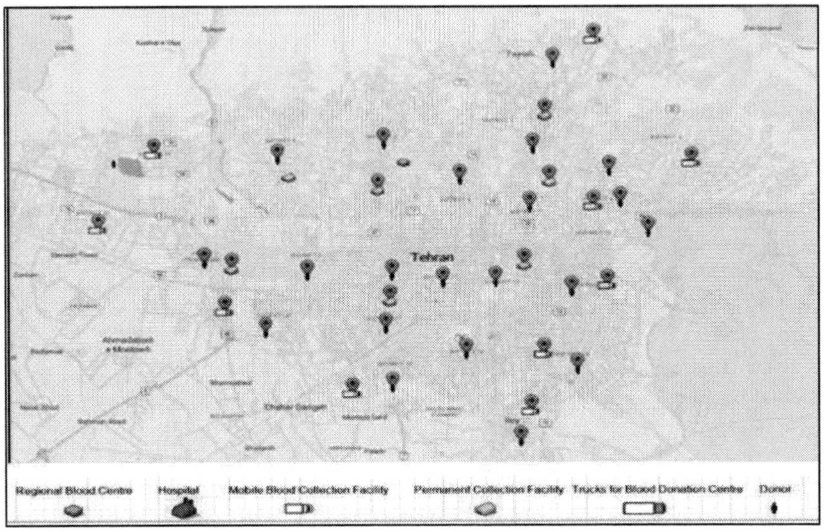

Figure 2 The GIS map of the affected region in Tehran using Anylogic simulation software.

In this case study, inspired by the optimal placements of the benchmark studies, the permanent blood donation centres are strategically located in districts 2, 3, 5, 6, 7, 9, 10, 11, and 12. This selection was made to maximise accessibility for donors across various areas. The mobile centres are then positioned in response to donor group needs and are located in areas that may not be as effectively serviced by permanent centres, ensuring comprehensive coverage during the donation campaign. The mobile centres preserve their location during the day. This is a realistic assumption from the existing blood collection norms in Tehran, which implies that while they can be moved to different locations on the subsequent days, their positions remain unchanged throughout the shift hours of each day. This approach allows for consistent planning and scheduling, and more importantly, ensuring that the donors know where to find the centres within the set timeframe.

3.2 Donors' Movement Logic

Donation methods include visits to mobile or permanent blood centres. Mobile facilities are flexible and economical but incur transport costs, while permanent centres provide stability at higher establishment costs. Therefore, in this paper, we seek to identify locations for permanent and temporary centres post-disaster, allocates donor groups to these facilities, and measures blood collection volumes over time. Figure 3 illustrates part of the proposed ABS model for a blood donation system that focuses on donor behaviour and their choice of donation locations. In this model, a blood donor agent begins the process in its first state of *DonorsGroup*, where it decides whether to seek a donation opportunity. If they decide to donate, the agent evaluates the available facilities through the *chooseDestination* decision point, which directs them to either a permanent or a temporary facility based on the shortest distance, i.e., to *ThePermanentBloodFacility* or *TheMobileBloodCollectionFacility* blocks, respectively. This model allows for the analysis of donor preferences and movement patterns, which can help optimise blood donation facility locations and resource allocation. A donor group corresponds to one of Tehran's 22 municipal districts, and each scenario includes at least 22 facilities. Donor groups may not visit some facilities in scenarios with more than 22 facilities. This outcome depends on the optimisation process, which assigns donors to facilities based on factors such as distance, capacity, and demand.

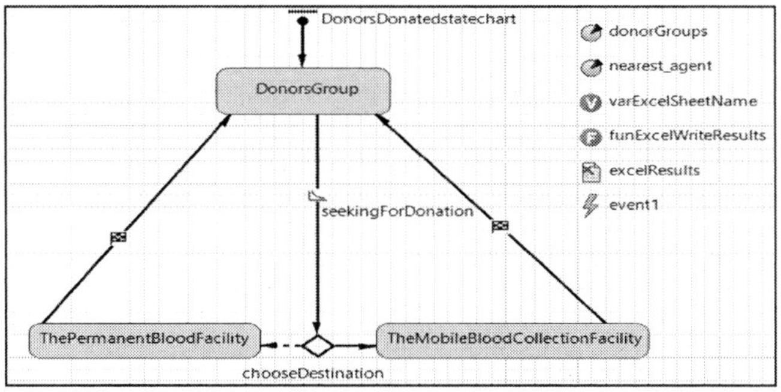

Figure 3 Flowchart of the movement logic of the donor agent in Anylogic simulation software.

4 SCENARIO DEFINITION AND DISCUSSION

In this study, we propose four scenarios with various collection centre configurations to assess the performance of the model. In addition to these scenarios, we also define a Base Model established based on the available benchmark studies, which consists of 9 permanent facilities and 22 mobile facilities across the 22 districts of the city. For all experiments, the simulation runs for a single day, representing the first period, to align with the benchmark data and reflect the urgency of blood supply following the earthquake disaster. Given this short timeframe, the constraint on the maximum number of times a person can donate blood in a year is not included, as it is not relevant in this context. The model takes into account the overall demand during the disaster period which comprises the normal, regular demand of the health centres and the new (temporary) demand added to the system due to the disaster. Based on our simulation experiments, the baseline scenario results in a total cost of $20,813.89 and a total emission of 43.33 kg. Table 2 shows the breakdown of the daily costs for each scenario, based on data provided by Khalilpourazari et al. (2020) The transportation costs differ between scenarios based on the number of mobile and permanent collection facilities. The total cost was calculated by combining various factors, including the holding cost, the fixed cost of establishing permanent blood collection centres, and the cost of operating mobile facilities from Table 2.

Table 2 The breakdown of costs involved in this experiment.

Type	Cost ($)
Cost of collecting blood from a donor (per Liter)	0.15
Holding cost (per Liter/day)	1.00
Fixed cost (per centre)	
Permanent blood collection centre	1518.23
Relocating mobile blood collection facilities	322.98
Transportation cost (per day)	
Base Model	28.26
Alternative Scenarios	
One	28.19
Two	28.19
Three	29.62
Four	28.26

The speed of the truck is considered to be 50 km/h and the blood per vehicle capacity is 100 units. The transportation cost of the scenarios was calculated by summing the distances that donor groups travelled to reach the collection centres. The cost per kilometre was determined using the vehicle's fuel consumption rate and the price of fuel reported by Montoya (2024). Finally, the total transportation cost was calculated by multiplying the total distance by the cost per kilometre, allowing for a straightforward comparison of costs across different scenarios. Despite the differences in the number of blood collection facilities in Scenarios One and Two (see Table 3), the transportation costs are both estimated to be \$39.15. This similarity in transportation costs can be attributed to the strategic decisions made in Scenario Two to optimise facility usage. Additional factors encompassed in our calculations are the costs associated with storing the collected blood, the total distance travelled for transporting the blood from the donors to the blood facilities, holding costs, and the overhead transportation expenses. The total emission, on the other hand, is calculated based on the fuel consumption and distances travelled by vehicles involved in blood collection. This comprehensive approach ensures that all important logistical and operational factors contributing to the blood supply chain are accounted for.

In Scenario One, we increase mobile facilities from the base model to 23 which raises the total cost slightly to \$21,136.80, while the emissions dropping to 43.22 kg. By analysing this scenario, we define Scenario Two which eliminates the excess mobile facilities that donors didn't use, leading to 9 permanent and 14 mobile facilities. This lowers the cost of the second scenario significantly in our experiments to \$18,229.98 and decreases the CO_2 emissions of the chain to 43.22 kg. Scenario Three includes 13 mobile facilities in the areas lacking permanent coverage, costing \$17,908.43 in total and reducing emissions to 54.42 kg. Scenario Four, with 7 permanent and 22 mobile facilities, offers the lowest cost at \$17,777.43 while maintaining the emission level consistent with the baseline at 43.33 kg.

Table 3 compares the arrangement of the permanent and mobile centres in these collection scenarios and summarises these corresponding results. In this table, we also report the standard deviation of 30 simulation runs, as well as the relative improvement (RI) of cost and emissions for each scenario compared to the baseline model. For more information on the calculation of RI, one may refer to the formulas presented by Attar et al. (2023a, 2023b, 2024a) for minimisation problems. Based on the reported results and analyses, we can conclude that Scenario Four is the most cost-efficient option while ensuring adequate coverage. This option, however, does not provide any improvements from the emissions side. Thus, if emission minimisation is given more importance, Scenario Two would be chosen for implementation which provides over 12% cost reduction while offering a slight decrease in the CO_2 levels of the supply chain.

Table 3 Number of facilities and the total cost of each Scenario.

Scenario	Facilities	Total Cost (Std. Dev.)	RI	CO_2 Emission	RI
Base Model	9 PF, 22 MF	\$ 20,813.89 (2.35)		43.33 kg	
Alternative Scenarios					
One	9 PF, 23 MF	\$ 21,136.80 (2.14)	−1.6 %	43.22 kg	**0.3 %**
Two	9 PF, 14 MF	\$ 18,229.98 (2.33)	12.4 %	43.22 kg	**0.3 %**
Three	9 PF, 13 MF	\$ 17,908.43 (2.83)	14.0 %	45.41 kg	−25.6 %
Four	7 PF, 22 MF	\$ 17,777.43 (1.93)	**14.6%**	43.33 kg	0.0 %

Furthermore, the results of our hybrid decision approach reveal that even with the attractive cost reduction expected from the third scenario, it could cause a severe jump (~25%) in the overall emissions of the system. These observations underscore the vitality of the proposed viewpoint for BSCs, in which the environmental implications of the decisions and the cost criterion are evaluated simultaneously.

5 CONCLUSION

This paper focuses on the location-allocation problem for blood collection facilities in the blood supply chain under disaster circumstances. Here, in addition to the fixed centres, we consider the realistic case of implementing mobile facilities to accelerate the collection of blood products. While seeking the minimisation of the total cost of the chain, we add the factor of sustainability by considering the associated carbon emissions. An agent-based simulation approach is developed for the system, and a baseline and four alternative scenarios were proposed to assess how different combinations of permanent and mobile blood collection facilities affect the total logistics costs and emission levels in this supply chain. Testing different configurations allows for identifying the most efficient setup that balances fixed costs, transportation expenses, and collection costs, ultimately determining the most cost-effective solution for the blood supply chain. For future research, the proposed approach can be enhanced by incorporating an efficient metaheuristic algorithm to achieve global optimal solutions. Another potential extension to this work is integrating network disruptions or blood compatibility. This would address potential risks and ensure proper blood type matching.

ACKNOWLEDGEMENTS

The first author would like to thank Funds for Women Graduates (FFWG) for their grant support. Also, this work received partial support from the UK-Indonesia Going Global Partnerships, funded by the British Council under grant reference A/05959/01/05/01.

REFERENCES

Alfonso E, Xie X, Augusto V, and Garraud O (2013). Modelling and simulation of blood collection systems: Improvement of human resources allocation for better cost-effectiveness and reduction of candidate donor abandonment. *Vox Sanguinis* 104(3): 225–233.

Arani M, Liu X and Abdolmaleki S (2020). Scenario-Based Simulation Approach for An Integrated Inventory Blood Supply Chain System. In: *Proceedings - Winter Simulation Conference*, 14 December 2020, pp. 1348–1359.

Araújo AM, Santos D, Marques I, and Barbosa-Povoa A (2020). Blood supply chain: a two-stage approach for tactical and operational planning. *OR Spectrum* 42(4): 1023–1053.

Arvan M, Tavakkoli-Moghaddam R and Abdollahi M (2015). Designing a bi-objective and multi-product supply chain network for the supply of blood. *Uncertain Supply Chain Management* 3(1): 57–68.

Attar A, Raissi S and Khalili-Damghani K (2016). Simulation–optimization approach for a continuous-review, base-stock inventory model with general compound demands, random lead times, and lost sales. *Simulation* 92(6): 547–564.

Attar A, Raissi S, Tohidi H, and Feizollahi MJ (2023). A Novel Perspective on Reliable System Design with Erlang Failures and Realistic Constraints for Incomplete Switching Mechanisms. *IEEE Access* 11: 51900–51914.

Attar A, Babaee M, Raissi S, and Nojavan M (2024). Airside Optimization Framework Covering Multiple Operations in Civil Airport Systems with a Variety of Aircraft: A Simulation-Based Digital Twin. *Systems* 12(10): 394.

Attar A, Irawan CA, Akbari AA, Zhong S, and Luis M (2024). Multi-disruption resilient hub location–allocation network design for less-than-truckload logistics. *Transportation Research Part A: Policy and Practice* 190: 104260.

Cheraghi S and Hosseini-Motlagh SM (2020). Responsive and reliable injured-oriented blood supply chain for disaster relief: a real case study. *Annals of Operations Research* 291(1–2): 129–167.

Duan Q and Liao TW (2014). Optimization of blood supply chain with shortened shelf lives and ABO compatibility. *International Journal of Production Economics* 153: 113–129.

Fahimnia B, Jabbarzadeh A, Ghavamifar A, and Bell M (2017). Supply chain design for efficient and effective blood supply in disasters. *International Journal of Production Economics* 183: 700–709.

Ghasemi S (2019). The Location Allocation Problem of after Disaster Blood Supply Chain. In: *Proceedings of 2019 15th Iran International Industrial Engineering Conference, IIIEC 2019*, 22 May 2019, pp. 127–131.

Haghjoo N, Tavakkoli-Moghaddam R, Shahmoradi-Moghadam H, and Rahimi Y (2020). Reliable blood supply chain network design with facility disruption: A real-world application. *Engineering Applications of Artificial Intelligence* 90: 103493.

Heidari-Fathian H and Pasandideh SHR (2018). Green-blood supply chain network design: Robust optimization, bounded objective function & Lagrangian relaxation. *Computers & Industrial Engineering* 122: 95–105.

Kamyabniya A, Lotfi MM, Naderpour M, and Yih Y (2018). Robust Platelet Logistics Planning in Disaster Relief Operations Under Uncertainty: a Coordinated Approach. *Information Systems Frontiers* 20(4): 759–782.

Khalilpourazari S, Soltanzadeh S, Weber GW, and Roy SK (2020). Designing an efficient blood supply chain network in crisis: neural learning, optimization and case study. *Annals of Operations Research* 289(1): 123–152.

Kohneh JN, Teymoury E and Pishvaee MS (2016). Blood products supply chain design considering disaster circumstances (Case study: earthquake disaster in Tehran). *Journal of Industrial and Systems Engineering* 9: 51–72.

Kundu T, Sheu JB and Kuo HT (2022). Emergency logistics management—Review and propositions for future research. *Transportation Research Part E: Logistics and Transportation Review* 164.

Mansur A, Vanany I and Arvitrida NI (2022). Horizontal collaboration in a decentralised system : Indonesian blood supply chain. *Supply Chain Forum: An International Journal* 00(00): 1–17.

Montoya, D. (2024) *Fuel efficiency in emergency: Understanding ambulance mileage.* ShunAuto. Available at: https://shunauto.com/article/how-many-miles-per-gallon-does-an-ambulance-get (Accessed: 14 October 2024).

Osorio AF, Brailsford SC, Smith HK, Forero-Matiz SP, and Camacho-Rodríguez BA (2017). Simulation-optimization model for production planning in the blood supply chain. *Health Care Management Science* 20(4): 548–564.

Selvakumar S, Shahabudeen P and Paul Robert T (2019). An Analysis of Re-configured Blood Transfusion Network of Urban India to Improve the Service Level: a Simulation Approach. *Journal of Medical Systems* 43(2).

Tzeng GH, Cheng HJ and Huang TD (2007). Multi-objective optimal planning for designing relief delivery systems. *Transportation Research Part E: Logistics and Transportation Review* 43(6): 673–686.

Zahiri B and Pishvaee MS (2017). Blood supply chain network design considering blood group compatibility under uncertainty. *International Journal of Production Research* 55(7): 2013–2033.

Zahiri B, Mousazadeh M and Bozorgi-Amiri A (2014). A Robust Stochastic Programming Approach for Blood Collection and Distribution Network Design. 3: 1–11.

Zahiri B, Torabi SA, Mousazadeh M, and Mansouri SA (2015). Blood collection management: Methodology and application. *Applied Mathematical Modelling* 39(23–24): 7680–7696.

AUTHOR BIOGRAPHIES

LAMA SOLIMAN KHALED is a Ph.D. candidate at the Department of Engineering at the University of Exeter. She joined the University of Exeter in 2019, as an MSc student in International Supply Chain Management. Prior to Exeter, she obtained her bachelor's and master's degrees from Heriot-Watt University in Edinburgh. Her research interests are supply chain management, simulation-optimisation methodologies, and sustainability.

AHMAD ATTAR received his M.Sc. and B.Sc. degrees as the top student in Industrial Engineering from IAU-STB in 2015 and 2011, respectively. He joined the University of Exeter, UK in 2022 as a Ph.D. student in Engineering, focusing on the simulation of resilient, sustainable, and cost-efficient supply chains. He has about a decade of experience in the industry and his main areas of research interest include simulation modelling, supply chain, reliability, airport management, and inventory modelling.

MARTINO LUIS is a Senior Lecturer at the Department of Engineering, University of Exeter, UK. He holds a Ph.D. in Operations Research from Kent Business School, University of Kent. His research interests are the applications of exact methods, (meta)-Heuristics optimisation, as well as simulation modelling in facility location problem, sustainable supply chain design network, inventory routing problems that focus on environment and sustainable operations.

BARIS YUCE is a Senior Lecturer at the Department of Engineering, University of Exeter, UK. He holds a Ph.D. in Engineering from Cardiff University. His research interests are supply chain Management, sustainable supply chain management, industry 4.0 applications, ontology applications, smart cities, smart buildings, renewable energy management, forecasting systems, deterministic and stochastic optimisation.

Proceedings of the Operational Research Society Simulation Workshop 2025 (SW25)
M. Luis, A. Harper, T. Monks, N. Mustafee, eds.

https://doi.org/10.36819/SW25.049

DOES CUSTOMER ORDER MATTER? EXPLORE THE DYNAMICS OF LOST-SALES REMANUFACTURING SYSTEM UNDER AR(1) DEMAND

Yan Lu

International Buisiness School (IBSS), Xi'an
Jiaotong-Liverpool University
Suzhou, China
Yan.Lu2302@student.xjtlu.edu.cn

Dr. Junyi Lin

International Buisiness School (IBSS), Xi'an
Jiaotong-Liverpool University
Suzhou, China
Junyi.Lin@xjtlu.edu.cn

ABSTRACT

This paper investigates the system dynamics of a hybrid manufacturing and remanufacturing system operating under the first-order autoregressive (AR(1)) demand and governed by lost-sales rules. Lost sales occur when customers, after encountering a stock-out, are unwilling to delay their purchases. This is particularly relevant in industries like groceries, clothing, and cell phones, where customers are more sensitive to stock-outs compared to backlog systems. Given the presence of autocorrelated AR(1) demand in these industries, the study focuses on how lost sales affect the system dynamics of a hybrid manufacturing-remanufacturing in a Closed-Loop Supply Chain (CLSC). The study finds that, under lost-sales conditions, the hybrid system performs better than a linear system in terms of reducing the bullwhip effect and inventory variance, when the autoregressive return parameter is lower—indicating weaker correlations between current and previous returns. Additionally, lost sales modify the influence of system structures on inventory variance under AR(1) demand. These insights provide key managerial implications for controlling bullwhip and inventory variance costs in products characterized by autoregressive demand patterns, particularly when facing lost-sales scenarios.

Keywords: Bullwhip effect, hybrid manufacturing and remanufacturing system, lost sales, AR(1) demand

1 INTRODUCTION

Closed-loop supply chains (CLSCs) can create profits by reclaiming products from customers and recovering their remaining added value. Additionally, they offer environmental advantages by preventing end-of-life products from ending up in landfills (Guide and Van Wassenhove, 2009). The estimated value of CLSCs in the European Union stands at €30 billion (European Remanufacturing Network, 2015). The European Commission aims to boost the value of the remanufacturing sector in Europe by €100 billion by 2030. In the United States, remanufacturing activities are contributing to over 180,000 full-time jobs (Dominguez et al., 2020).

This study explores the dynamic performance of a one-echelon CLSC, i.e. a hybrid manufacturing-remanufacturing system, focusing on the bullwhip effect and inventory variance under lost-sales situation. The hybrid manufacturing-remanufacturing system refers to a system where manufacturing and remanufacturing processes operate simultaneously to produce the same serviceable inventory for fulfilling orders (Lin et al., 2022). The bullwhip effect describes a situation where small fluctuations in consumer demand lead to large swings in production for suppliers further up the supply chain. This results in additional costs, such as frequent adjustments in machine operations, workforce hiring and layoffs, and maintaining excessive inventory levels (Goltsos et al., 2019). Understanding the dynamics of the hybrid systems and closed-loop supply chains (CLSCs) plays a critical role in improving their operational performance and enhancing economic visability.

In practice, inventory systems are generally divided into backlog systems and lost-sales systems (Disney et al., 2021). In backlog systems, customers are willing to wait for the product when it is out of stock, but this isn't the case in lost-sales systems. When purchasing items like groceries, clothing, or cell phones, customers may simply turn to other sellers, leading to opportunities for competitors. These situations are more sensitive to stock-outs than backlog systems (Disney et al., 2021). However, despite the practical importance of lost-sales scenarios, most current studies focus on backlog systems (e.g., Hosoda and Disney, 2018; Li et al., 2023; Lu et al., 2024). The insights derived from these hybrid systems are not applicable to system under constraints. Thus, there is a lack of understandings of the dynamics of a hybrid manufacturing-remanufacturing system under lost-sales constraints.

Motivated by academic gaps and practical observations, this paper aims to study the dynamics of a hybrid manufacturing-remanufacturing system governed by the constraint of lost sales and provide managerial insights to improve the system bahaviors under such constraint. Besides, we consider two kinds of customer demands, i.e. the stocastically independent and identically distributed (i.i.d.) and first-order autoregressive (AR(1)) demands. A wide range of industries, e.g., fashion and apparel industry (Koren and Shnaiderman, 2023), agricultural retail industry (Islam and Hoque, 2019), and food industry (Yang et al., 2017), have observed the i.i.d. demand. Furthermore, The demand auto-correlations, particularly AR(1) demand are common in industries including automobile, beverage, and fruit and vegetables industries (Box et al., 1994; Jin et al., 2015; Gaalman et al., 2022; Feng et al., 2024). Additionally, Ali et al. (2012) analyzed a weekly demand dataset over a two-year period for 1,798 stock keeping units from a European retailer and discovered that 30.3% of the demand processes follow an AR(1) model, which is a large percentile showing the extensive existence of AR(1) demands.

Motivated by above, we propose the following research questions:

1) How will the hybrid manufacturing and remanufacturing system perform under lost-sales situation?
2) How different the bullwhip behavior and inventory performance under i.i.d. and AR(1) demands in lost-sales situations?

By answering the research questions above, the study contributes valuable insights into the dynamics of supply chains governed by lost-sales scenarios, addressing an area often overlooked due to its complexity. The key contributions of the study are twofold: it explores the impact of the lost-sales situation on system dynamics performance and compares the behavior of lost-sales systems under i.i.d. and AR(1) demands with the hybrid systems without lost-sales constraints. By focusing on both i.i.d. demands and AR(1), the study will offer practical implications and suggestions into managing supply chains with lost-sales constraints, which are highly sensitive to stock-outs.

2 MODEL

2.1 Model

This study outlines a hybrid manufacturing and remanufacturing system that integrates both production of new products and the recovery of used products for remanufacturing. Based on the models from Lin et al. (2022) and Lu et al. (2024), the system features several key components: a portion of the products are returned after use and classified as recoverable inventory, with non-qualifying items discarded. A push policy directs all returned products into the remanufacturing line to meet new-product quality standards. The remanufacturing line has unlimited capacity, allowing flexible adjustments to meet demand within specific periods (Lin et al., 2022). In cases where remanufactured products are insufficient, the manufacturing line operates in parallel, sourcing raw materials just-in-time without capacity limits. There is also no capacity constraint for the manufacturing process. Returns are allowed between the manufacturers and raw material supplies, i.e., negative orders could happen in the system.

This model assumes a lost-sales scenario, meaning that if a product is out of stock, customers will not wait for restocking and will instead forgo their purchase. This behavior is typical in industries where immediate availability is crucial, such as daily groceries, clothing, and mobile phones (Disney et al., 2021). Under these conditions, inventory levels are strictly constrained; they cannot fall below zero. Consequently, the maximum amount that can be shipped to meet customer demand is limited by the available inventory at that time. In this setting, the actual fulfilled demand (shipment) is the lesser of the available stock or the incoming customer demand, which represents the desired shipment.

Table 1 *Notations of system variables, parameters and metrics*

	Notation of system variables		**Notation of system parameters**
d_t	Total market demand	L	Estimated lead times
$\hat{d}_t$	Forecasted market demand	τ_a	Exponential smoothing coefficient
c_t	Total completion rate	τ_c	First-order delay coefficient
$c_{m,t}$	Manufacturing completion rate	τ_p	Production delay
$c_{r,t}$	Remanufacturing completion rate	τ_m	Manufacturing production delay
i_t	Serviceable inventory	τ_r	Remanufacturing production delay
w_t	Work-in-process inventory	L_m	Manufacturing lead times
o_t	Total order rate	L_r	Remanufacturing lead times
r_t	Product return rate	α	Return yield rate
$o_{m,t}$	Manufacturing order rate	δ	Inventory proportional controller
$o_{r,t}$	Remanufacturing order rate	ϕ_d	Autoregressive demand parameter
$d_t^{i.i.d.}$	Manufacturing demand under i.i.d. demand pattern	ϕ_r	Autoregressive return parameter
$r_t^{i.i.d.}$	Product returns under i.i.d. demand patterns	O_m^{AR}	Manufacturing order under AR(1) demand
d_t^{AR}	Manufacturing demand under AR(1) demand pattern	r_t^{AR}	Product returns under AR(1) demand patterns
$\varepsilon_{r,t}$	i.i.d. and AR(1) returns with zero mean	$O_m^{i.i.d.}$	Manufacturing order under i.i.d. demand
S_t	Order-up-to level		**Notation of system metrics**
$\varepsilon_{d,t}$	i.i.d. and AR(1) demand with zero mean	BE	Bullwhip effect level
		IV	Inventory variance level

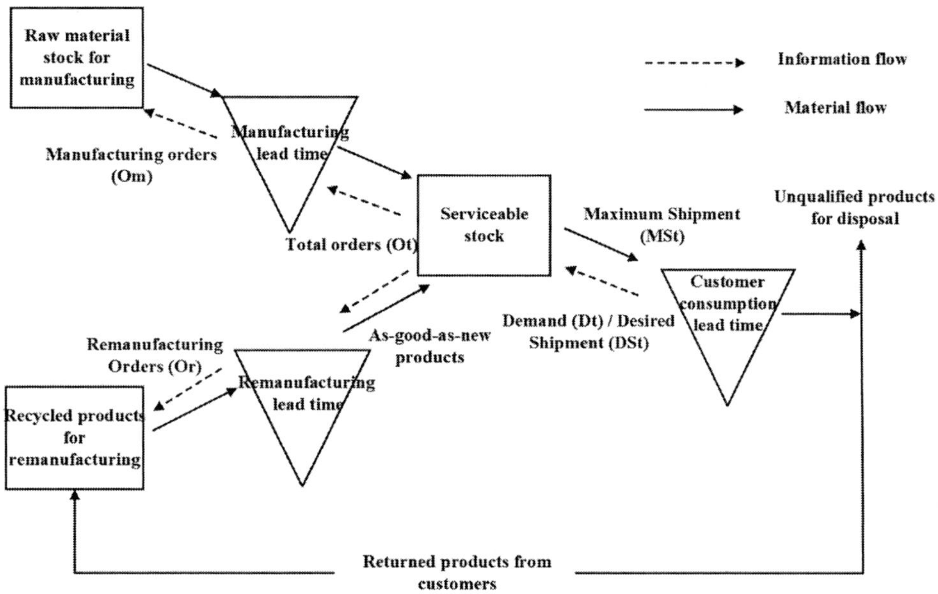

Figure 1 *Schematic of the model*

2.2 System Dynamics Model

This section examines the overall expression of demand and order placement. The general OUT policy, i.e., the modified (R,Q) policy, in a discrete time manner is adopted for inventory replenishment (Hosoda and Disney, 2018). It is assumed that customer demand, denoted as $d(t)$, in each time period t is fulfilled by two sources: newly manufactured products $c_{m,t}$ and remanufactured products $c_{r,t}$. The sequence of events related to placing orders is illustrated in Figure 2.

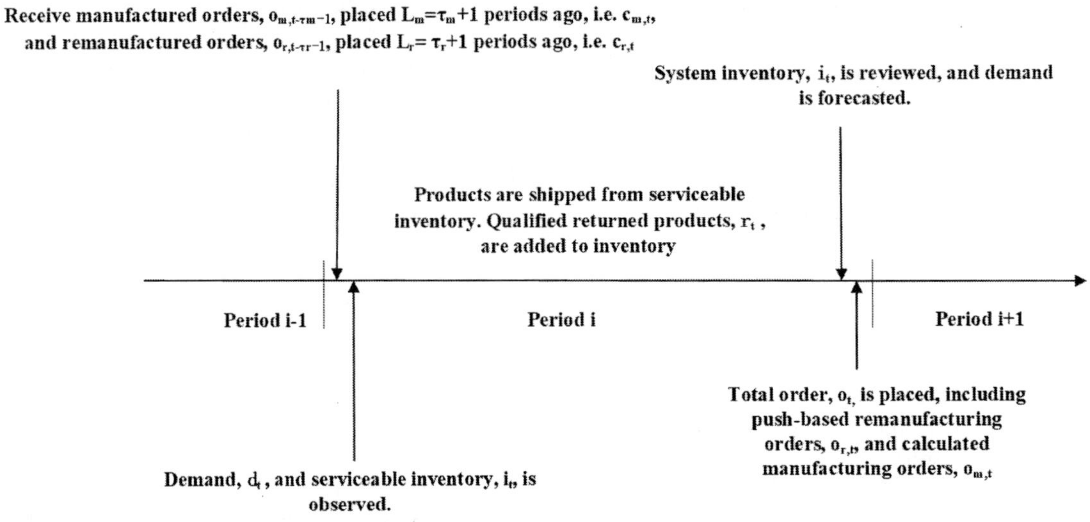

Figure 2 *Sequence of events*

- **Model 1 (with lost-sales constraint):**

In period t, market demand d_t is observed and fulfilled using system inventory i_t. Assuming perfect substitution between manufactured and remanufactured products, the inventory balance equation above applies. With lost sales constraint, the inventory is restricted to being non-negative:

$$i_t = [i_{t-1} + c_t - d_t]^+, \tag{1}$$

where $[\cdot]^+$=max$\{0, \cdot\}$ is the maximum operator. When $i_t = 0$, it means that either stock-outs have happened in t, or demand is exactly equal to the available inventory, i.e., $i_t = i_{t-1} + c_t$. The completion rate, c_t, is the sum of newly manufactured products $c_{m,t}$ and remanufactured products $c_{r,t}$, i.e., $c_t = c_{m,t} + c_{r,t}$. Also, the actual shipment, AS_t (which is also the satisfied demand) is the minimum of available inventory (at the start of t) and the demand:

$$AS_t = (i_{t-1} + c_t) \wedge d_t, \tag{2}$$

where $\wedge$ means taking the minimum of both sides.

- **Model 2 (without lost-sales constraint):**

The inventory is the cumulation of completed products substract shipments. Without lost sales, the shipments are equal to the customer demand, i.e., the system always ships whatever the customers want:

$$i_t = i_{t-1} + c_t - d_t \tag{3}$$

$$AS_t = d_t \tag{4}$$

Specifically, the OUT policy can be written as

$$o_t = S_t - (i_t + w_t)\,, \tag{5}$$

where w_t and i_t are work-in-process and on-hand inventory. S is the OUT level determined by estimated demand during lead time plus safety stock,

$$S_t = \hat{d}_t \cdot L + k \cdot \widehat{\sigma_L}\,, \tag{6}$$

where $\hat{d}_t$ is the forecast demand and $\hat{d}_t \cdot L$ refers to the forecast for market demand d_t during the estimated lead time. $\widehat{\sigma_L}$ is an estimation of the standard deviation of the demand, and k is a constant to meet a desired service level over L periods. For simplicity, k is set to 0, and L is increased by 1, i.e., $S_t = \hat{d}_t \cdot (L+1)$, which practically means that the safety stock is the extra inventory resulting from the increased L (Lin et al. 2022). The work-in-process inventory is then obtained:

$$w_t = \textstyle\sum_{t=0}^{t}(o_{t-1} - c_t)\,. \tag{7}$$

Equation (5) can be rearranged by substituting $S_t = \hat{d}_t \cdot (L+1)$:

$$o_t = \hat{d}_t + (\hat{d}_t - i_t) + [\hat{d}_t \cdot (L-1) - w_t]\,. \tag{8}$$

The POUT policy (Lu et al., 2024) is adopted by adding a proportional controller, $\frac{1}{\delta}$, $\forall\ \frac{1}{\delta} \in (0,1]$, to increase the flexibility of inventory error correction:

$$o_t = \hat{d}_t + \tfrac{1}{\delta}(\hat{d}_t - i_t) + \tfrac{1}{\delta}[(L-1)\hat{d}_t - w_t]\,. \tag{9}$$

The total orders o_t represent the combined quantity of manufacturing orders o_m and remanufacturing orders o_r, which were placed L_m and L_r periods ago. Here, L_m and L_r are positive integers ($L_m, L_r \in \mathbb{Z}^+$). $L_m(= \tau_m + 1)$ is the estimated manufacturing lead time, and $L_r(= \tau_r + 1)$ is the estimated remanufacturing lead time, with an additional unit added because orders are placed at the end of each replenishment period (Disney et al., 2021). To prevent long-term inventory drift, the following equations must hold between the estimated lead times (τ_p) and the manufacturing and remanufacturing lead times (Tang & Naim, 2004; Lin et al., 2022):

$$\tau_p = (1 - \alpha)\tau_m + \alpha\, \tau_r, \tag{10}$$

where α ($\forall\, a \in (0,1)$) is the average return yield. Products are returned to the manufacturer after a significant delay and sent to remanufacturing through a triage process. A first-order delay, with a smoothing factor τ_c , controls how remanufacturing units, rtrt, adjust to changes in collection volume, $\alpha \cdot d_t$, where α is the average return yield rate.

$$r_t = \beta \cdot \alpha \cdot d_t + (1 - \beta) \cdot r_{t-1}, \tag{11}$$

where $\beta = \frac{1}{1+\tau_c}$ (Lin et al., 2022).

This study models two kinds of demands, i.e. i.i.d. and AR(1) demand patterns. For i.i.d. demand, demands and returns are random numbers, $d_t \sim (\mu_d, \sigma_d^2)$,:

$$d_t^{i.i.d.} = \mu_d + \varepsilon_{d,t}, \forall \varepsilon_{d,t} \sim (0, \sigma_d^2), \tag{12}$$

$$r_t^{i.i.d.} = \mu_r + \beta \cdot \alpha \cdot d_t^{i.i.d.} + (1 - \beta) \cdot r_{t-1}^{i.i.d.} + \varepsilon_{r,t}, \forall\, \varepsilon_{r,t} \sim (0, \sigma_r^2), \tag{13}$$

where $\forall$ means "for every".

For products under AR(1) demand, demands and returns are in AR(1) process:

$$d_t^{AR} = \mu_d + \phi_d(d_{t-1}^{AR} - \mu_d) + \varepsilon_{d,t}, \varepsilon_{d,t} \sim (0, \sigma_d^2), \tag{14}$$

$$r_t^{AR} = \mu_r + \phi_r(r_{t-1}^{AR} - \mu_r) + \beta \cdot \alpha \cdot d_t^{AR} + (1 - \beta) \cdot r_{t-1}^{AR} + \varepsilon_{r,t}, \varepsilon_{r,t} \sim (0, \sigma_r^2), \tag{15}$$

Furthermore, we adopt both Exponential smoothing (ES) forecast method for demand. ES forecasting method is one of the most popular forecasting methods in practice and easy for firms to compute and understand (Lu et al., 2024).:

$$\hat{d}_t = \mu_m \cdot \hat{d}_{t-1} + (1 - \mu_m) \cdot d_t\,, \tag{16}$$

where $\mu_m = \frac{1}{1+\tau_a}$, is the average demand delay, and τ_a is the average age of the demand.

To analyze the bullwhip behavior in manufacturing orders ($o_{m,t}$), the variability ratio between demand (d_t) and both manufacturing and remanufacturing orders can be employed as a measure:

$$BE = \frac{var(order)}{var(demand)}. \tag{17}$$

Similarly, the variability ratio between serviceable inventory (i_t) and demand (d_t) is used as the measure of inventory variance:

$$IV = \frac{var(inventory)}{var(demand)}. \tag{18}$$

3 SIMULATION ANALYSIS

This section carries out simulation on Matlab[@] to explore the impact of lost-sales constraint on bullwhip and inventory variance. To understand such impact, we compare constrained lost-sales system with unconstrainted system and explore how demand processes (i.e., i.i.d. and AR(1) demands) and system structures ($\delta, \alpha, L, \tau_c$) impact the dynamic performance of the system under lost sales. Each simulation runs for 10,000 time steps, and we repeat the process 10 times for each set of parameter values to ensure accuracy. The recorded bullwhip effect and inventory variance values are the averages of all simulations. As a result, the total number of simulations is calculated as 10 times the number of parameter values and the number of parameters, resulting in 320 simulations for the i.i.d. demand in constrained/unconstrained system (10·4·8=320). Similarly, the total number of simulations for the AR(1) demand and returns in constrained/unconstrained system are 320.

Table 2 presents the baseline system parameters and the varying ranges used in the numerical study. Specifically, the lead times are set to $\tau_m = 8$, $\tau_r = 4$, and $\tau_c = 64$, reflecting real-world conditions where remanufacturing generally takes less time than manufacturing, and consumption has the longest lead time (Lin et al., 2022). An average return yield rate of 60% ($\alpha = 0.6$) is assumed, based on Yang et al. (2023). To offset the final value at a steady-state inventory level, τ_p is calculated as

$(1-\alpha)\tau_m + \alpha\, \tau_r$, giving $L = \tau_p + 1 = 6.6$ periods. The mean and variance for i.i.d. demans is 1 and 0.1 specifically. The autoregressive parameters for demand and returns, $\phi_d = 0.5$ and $\phi_r = 0.3$, are chosen to maintain system stability (Giri and Glock, 2022).

For varying settings, α ranges from 20% to 80% to analyze its effect on the hybrid manufacturing-remanufacturing system. The parameter $1/\delta$ varies between 0.125 and 1, with the latter representing an OUT model, to assess how different inventory adjustment speeds affect system dynamics. Additionally, τ_a ranges from 4 to 32, reflecting various levels of demand smoothing, and τ_c varies from 8 to 64 weeks, evaluating the impact of customer consumption lead times. The autoregressive parameters (ϕ_d, ϕ_r) range from -0.5 to 0.5 and -0.6 to 0.5, respectively, representing different levels of correlation in demand and returns. The simulation results are presented in Figures 3-9.

Table 2 *System parameter value settings for the numerical study*

System parameter	Baseline value (varying range)	References/justifications
τ_c	64 (8, 16, 32, 64)	Lin et al. (2022)
τ_m	8	Zhou et al. (2017); Lin et al. (2022)
τ_r	4	Zhou et al. (2017); Lin et al. (2022)
τ_a	16 (4, 8, 16, 32)	Lin et al. (2022); Lu et al. (2024)
α	0.6 (0,2, 0.4, 0.6, 0.8)	Zhou et al. (2017); Lu et al. (2024)
$1/\delta$	1 (0.125, 0.25, 0.5,1)	Tang and Naim (2004); Lin et al. (2022). The baseline setting is OUT policy by fully correcting inventory errors.
ϕ_d	0.5 (-0.5, -0.2, 0.3)	Hosoda and Disney (2018); Lu et al. (2024)
ϕ_r	0.3 (-0.6, -0.3, 0.5)	Hosoda and Disney (2018); Lu et al. (2024)
μ_d	1 (2, 5, 10)	The means of i.i.d. demand vary between 1 and 10.
σ_d^2	0.1 (0.2, 0.5, 1)	The variance of i.i.d. demand vary between 0.1 and 1.
L $(= \tau_p + 1)$	6.6 (8.2, 7.4, 5.8)	Fixed estimated lead times ranging between 5.8 and 8.2 are assumed to explore its impact on dynamic performance.

Overall, the hybrid system with a lost-sales constraint outperforms systems without this constraint in terms of reducing the system dynamics costs when demand is i.i.d. with a lower mean (Figs. 3-5 and 6). Under the baseline settings, bullwhip effect and inventory variance are reduced by 6.09% and 25.61%, respectively, by including a constraint of lost sales. This result also holds for AR(1) demand when the autoregressive parameter is low, indicating a weaker correlation between current and previous period returns (Figs. 3-5 and 8-9). The lost-sales constraint contributes to reductions of 1.50% for bullwhip and 10.04% for inventory variance under the baseline settings. However, for i.i.d. demand with a higher mean, or when the autoregressive parameter is higher in AR(1) demand, unconstrained inventory systems perform better than constrained lost-sales systems, as the bullwhip effect and inventory variance increase under lost-sales settings (Figs. 6 and 9).

This conclusion also applies to AR(1) demand when the autoregressive return parameter is lower, meaning a weaker correlation between current and prior returns (Figs. 3-5 and 8-9). However, when i.i.d. demand has a higher mean or the autoregressive return parameter is larger, indicating a stronger correlation between current and previous returns in AR(1) demand, unconstrained inventory systems perform better than lost-sales constraints, as the bullwhip effect and inventory variance increase in the lost-sales context (Figs. 6 and 9).

Fig. 3 shows that a higher return yield rate reduces the bullwhip effect and inventory variance under i.i.d. demand in both unconstrained and lost-sales systems. While this trend also holds for the impact of return yield rate on the bullwhip effect and inventory variance in unconstrained systems with AR(1) demand, there is a notable difference in lost-sales settings: the return yield rate unexpectedly increases inventory variance under AR(1) demand. This contrasting effect of return yield rate on bullwhip effect and inventory variance in AR(1) demand is unique to the lost-sales scenario (Fig. 3.2).

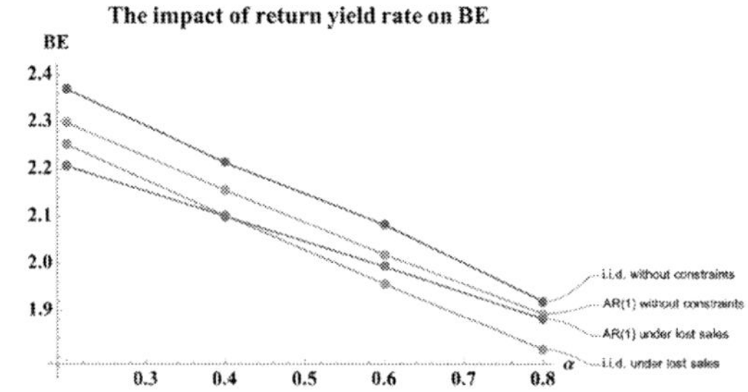

Figure 3.1 *The impact of α on bullwhip effect*

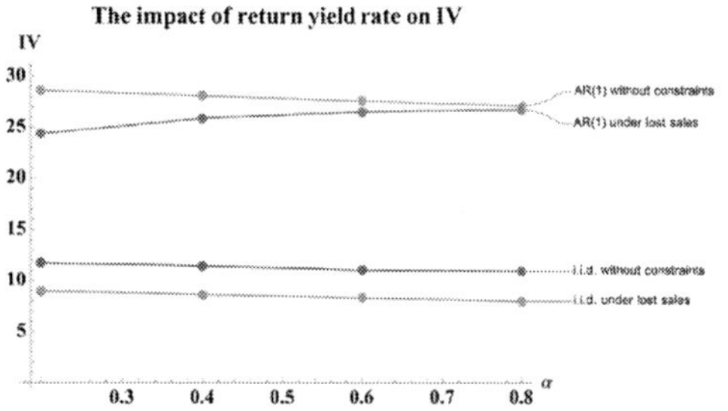

Figure 3.2 *The impact of α on inventory variance*

Figure 3 *The impact of return yield rate on bullwhip effect and inventory variance*

Figure 4 illustrates a trade-off between the proportional controller and the bullwhip effect/inventory variance for both i.i.d. and AR(1) demands. Increasing the proportional controller intensifies the bullwhip effect for both demand types in unconstrained and lost-sales scenarios. Under AR(1) demand, inventory variance consistently declines as the proportional controller increases in both settings. However, for i.i.d. demand, the effect on inventory variance differs: in an unconstrained system, increasing the proportional controller reduces inventory variance, while in a lost-sales setting, it follows a U-shaped pattern. This variation is attributed to the presence of lost sales.

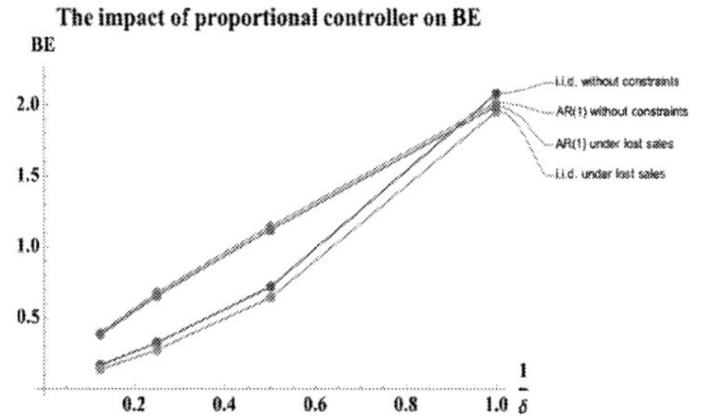

Figure 4.1 *The impact of* $1/\delta$ *on bullwhip effect*

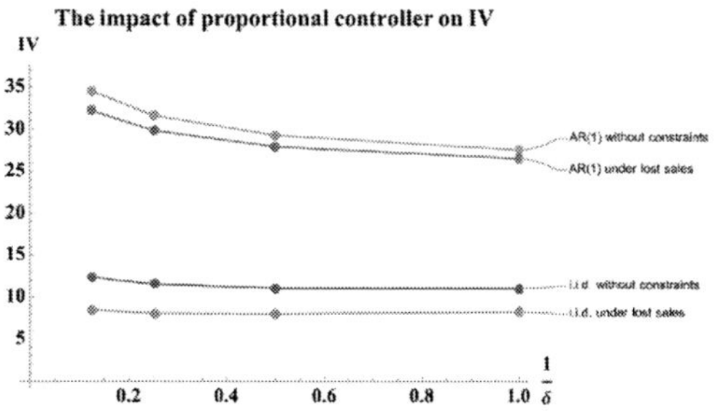

Figuge 4.2 *The impact of* $1/\delta$ *on inventory variance*

Figure 4 *The impact of proportional controller on bullwhip effect and inventory variance*

Figure 5 shows a trade-off involving customer consumption lead time for both i.i.d. and AR(1) demands in unconstrained and constrained lost-sales scenarios. Customer consumption lead time increases the bullwhip effect and exhibits an inverse U-shaped impact on inventory variability under both demand types. Since the effect of customer consumption lead time on bullwhip and inventory variability is similar in systems with/without lost-sales constraints, we can conclude that lost sales do not modify its impact on these metrics.

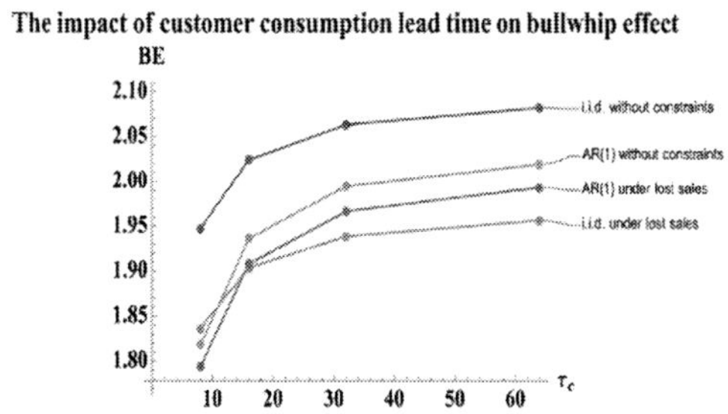

Figure 5.1 *The impact of* τ_c *on bullwhip effect*

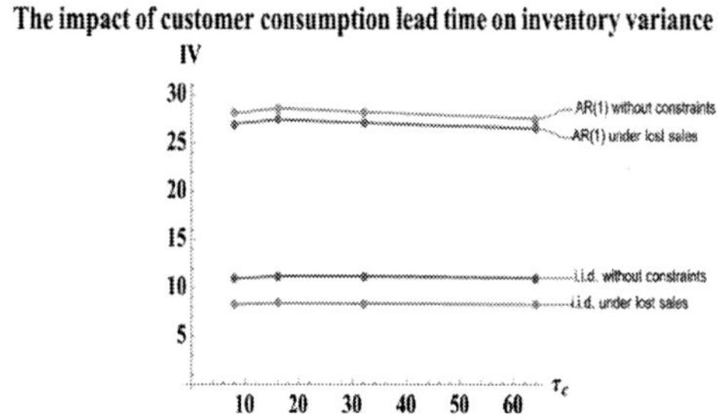

Figure 5.2 *The impact of* τ_c *on inventory variance*

Figure 5 *The impact of customer consumption lead time on bullwhip effect and inventory variance*

Figures 6 and 7 indicate that in systems without lost-sales constraints, the mean and variance of i.i.d. demand have no impact on bullwhip or inventory variability. However, in lost-sales scenarios, the dynamics change: the bullwhip effect intensifies with a higher demand mean and lessens with increased demand variance. Likewise, inventory variability increases with the demand mean and decreases with demand variance. These contrasting effects arise due to the unique conditions in lost-sales settings.

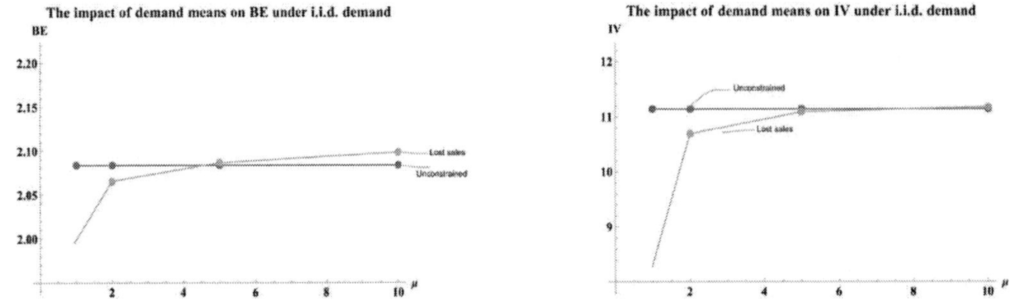

Figure 6.1 *The impact of* μ *on bullwhip effect* **Figure 6.2** *The impact of* μ *on inventory variance*

Figure 6 *The impact of demand means on bullwhip and inventory variance*

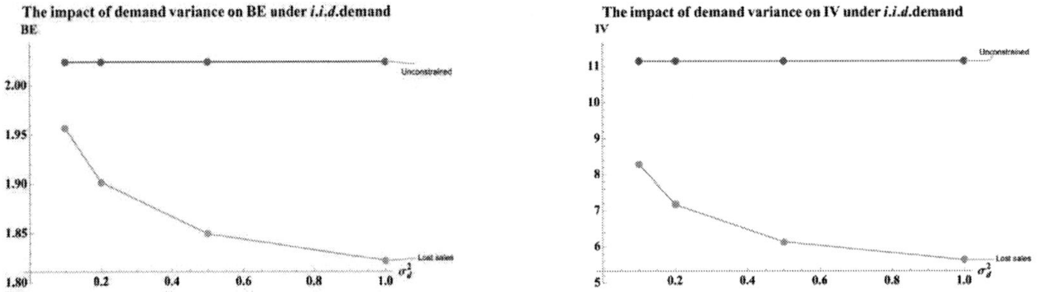

Figure 7.1 *The impact of* σ^2 *on bullwhip effect* **Figure 7.2** *The impact of* σ^2 *on inventory variance*

Figure 7 *The impact of demand variance on bullwhip and inventory variance*

Figure 8 reveals that in lost-sales systems, the autoregressive demand process has an inverse U-shaped effect on the bullwhip effect and a positive impact on inventory variance. The impact of the autoregressive returns parameter differs significantly between unconstrained and constrained systems. In the hybrid systems without constraints, the parameter shows a U-shaped relationship with the bullwhip effect and an inverse U-shaped effect on inventory variance. In contrast, under lost sales, both the bullwhip effect and inventory variance consistently increase with a higher autoregressive returns parameter. Notably, contrary to findings in most studies on hybrid systems under lost sales, which suggest that constraints improve bullwhip and inventory variance (e.g., Disney et al., 2021; Wang et al., 2023), when the autoregressive returns parameter reaches about 0.4 in baseline settings, unconstrained systems exhibit greater bullwhip and inventory variance than lost-sales systems (Figure 9).

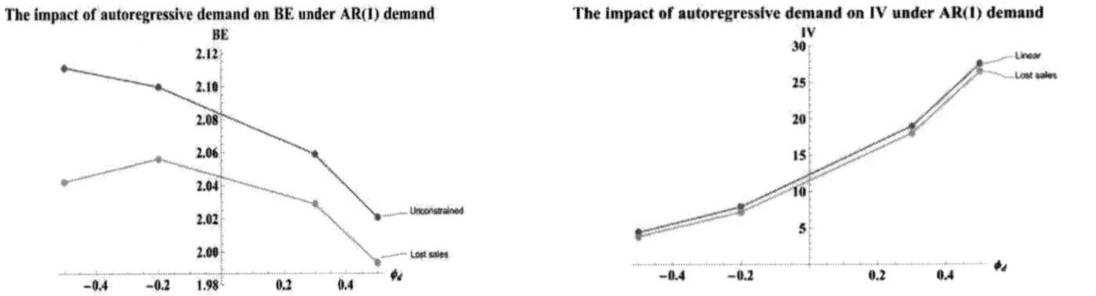

Figure 8.1 *The impact of* ϕ_d *on bullwhip effect* **Figure. 8.2** *The impact of* ϕ_d *on inventory variance*

Figure 8 *The impact of autoregressive demand on bullwhip and inventory variance*

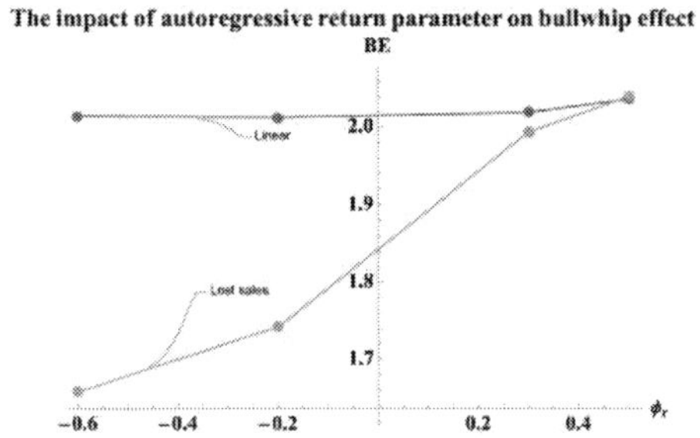

Figure 9.1 *The impact of ϕ_r on bullwhip effect*

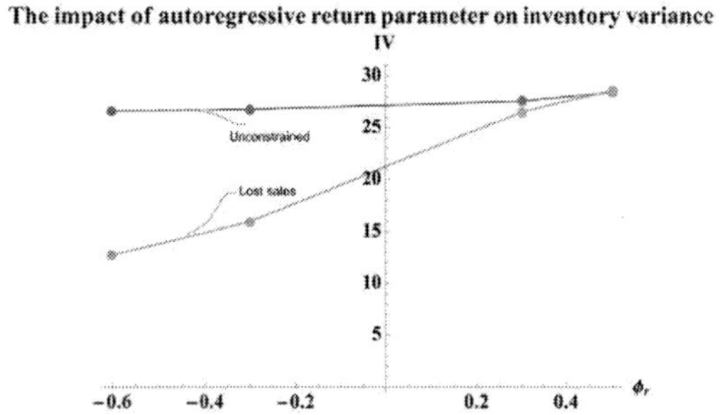

Figure 9.2 *The impact of ϕ_r on inventory variance*

Figure 9 *The impact of autoregressive returns on bullwhip and inventory variance*

4 DISCUSSION AND CONCLUSION

This section outlines the key managerial insights drawn from this paper's findings. Overall, lost-sales systems tend to outperform unconstrained systems when the mean demand of i.i.d. demand is lower or when there is a weaker correlation between current and previous returns under AR(1) demand. When demand is higher, or the AR(1) returns parameter increases, unconstrained systems is more effective. Therefore, in industries with a weak correlation with past-period returns, lost-sales systems offer better control over inventory variance and bullwhip effects. Supply chain managers can select either lost-sales or unconstrained systems based on product demand characteristics. For products with lower average demand or weaker correlations, lost-sales systems offer optimizing production and replenishment.

Second, the lost-sales setting alters the impacts of the return yield rate and proportional controller on inventory variance, with a trade-off between bullwhip effect and inventory variance. While a higher return yield rate reduces the bullwhip effect, it increases inventory variance. Managers should weigh these impacts and aim to find an optimal return yield rate that balances bullwhip reduction with manageable inventory variance. Different products may require different strategies; for high-return items, such as electronics, higher return yield rates may help reduce the bullwhip effect, while low-margin items may benefit more from keeping inventory variance lower with a reduced return yield rate.

Additionally, the proportional controller increases the bullwhip effect but has a U-shaped impact on inventory variance under AR(1) demand in lost-sales settings. This U-shaped relationship suggests an optimal level of proportional control where inventory variance is minimized. Managers should aim to balance the proportional controller to avoid excessive fluctuations in inventory, potentially using a weighted approach to manage system costs associated with bullwhip effects and inventory variances.

Under lost-sales constraint, the customer consumption lead time also affects bullwhip and inventory variance under AR(1) demand: customer consumption lead time increases the bullwhip effect while having an inverse U-shaped effect on inventory variance. If minimizing bullwhip costs is the priority, managers should target a shorter customer consumption lead time. For managing inventory variance, an intermediate lead time may be more effective for a hybrid system.

Finally, a trade-off is observed in the impact of autoregressive demand on bullwhip effect and inventory variance. If controlling bullwhip costs is essential, managers should avoid intermediate autoregressive demand parameters. However, if inventory variance is a primary concern, a weaker autocorrelation in products with AR(1) demand should be encouraged. Additionally, because a higher autoregressive returns parameter increases bullwhip and inventory variance, managers should aim to reduce the autocorrelation of returned products to control overall system dynamics costs.

REFERENCES

Ali, M.M., Boylan, J.E. and Syntetos, A.A., 2012. Forecast errors and inventory performance under forecast information sharing. *International Journal of Forecasting*, *28*(4), pp.830-841.=

Box, G.E.P., Jenkins, G.M. and Reinsel, G.C., 1994. Time Series Analysis, Forecasting and Control, 3rd Edn (Englewood Clips, NJ, Prentice-Hall).

Disney, S.M., Ponte, B. and Wang, X., 2021. Exploring the nonlinear dynamics of the lost-sales order-up-to policy. *International Journal of Production Research*, *59*(19), pp.5809-5830.

Dominguez, R., Cannella, S., Ponte, B. and Framinan, J.M., 2020. On the dynamics of closed-loop supply chains under remanufacturing lead time variability. *Omega*, *97*, p.102106.

European remanufacturing network. (2015). European remanufacturing network. ERN. Retrieved March 24, 2023, from https://www.remanufacturing.eu/

Feng, Y., Che, A. and Tian, N., 2024. Robust inventory routing problem under uncertain demand and risk-averse criterion. *Omega*, *127*, p.103082.

Gaalman, G., Disney, S.M. and Wang, X., 2022. When bullwhip increases in the lead time: An eigenvalue analysis of ARMA demand. *International Journal of Production Economics*, *250*, p.108623.

Giri, B.C. and Glock, C.H., 2022. The bullwhip effect in a manufacturing/remanufacturing supply chain under a price-induced non-standard ARMA (1, 1) demand process. *European Journal of Operational Research*, *301*(2), pp.458-472.

Goltsos, T.E., Ponte, B., Wang, S., Liu, Y., Naim, M.M. and Syntetos, A.A., 2019. The boomerang returns? Accounting for the impact of uncertainties on the dynamics of remanufacturing systems. *International Journal of Production Research*, *57*(23), pp.7361-7394.

Hosoda, T. and Disney, S.M., 2018. A unified theory of the dynamics of closed-loop supply chains. *European Journal of Operational Research*, *269*(1), pp.313-326.

Islam, S.S. and Hoque, M.A., 2019. An optimal policy for three-tier supply chain for processing an agricultural product with a stochastic demand. *International Journal of Services and Operations Management*, *33*(3), pp.287-310.

Jin, Y.H., Williams, B.D., Tokar, T. and Waller, M.A., 2015. Forecasting with temporally aggregated demand signals in a retail supply chain. *Journal of Business Logistics*, *36*(2), pp.199-211.

Koren, M. and Shnaiderman, M., 2023. Forecasting in the fashion industry: a model for minimising supply-chain costs. *International Journal of Fashion Design, Technology and Education*, *16*(3), pp.308-318.

Li, Q., Gaalman, G. and Disney, S.M., 2023. On the equivalence of the proportional and damped trend order-up-to policies: An eigenvalue analysis. *International Journal of Production Economics*, *265*, p.109005.

Lin, J., Zhou, L., Spiegler, V.L., Naim, M.M. and Syntetos, A., 2022. Push or Pull? The impact of ordering policy choice on the dynamics of a hybrid closed-loop supply chain. *European Journal of Operational Research*, *300*(1), pp.282-295.

Lu, Y., Lin, J., Huang, S. and Chen, J., 2024. On the bullwhip behaviour of a hybrid manufacturing and remanufacturing system under autocorrelated demand and returns. *Omega*, p.103209.

Parisio, A. and Jones, C.N., 2015. A two-stage stochastic programming approach to employee scheduling in retail outlets with uncertain demand. *Omega*, *53*, pp.97-103.

Tang, O. and Naim*, M.M., 2004. The impact of information transparency on the dynamic behaviour of a hybrid manufacturing/remanufacturing system. *International Journal of Production Research*, *42*(19), pp.4135-4152.

Wang, X., Disney, S.M. and Ponte, B., 2023. On the stationary stochastic response of an order-constrained inventory system. *European Journal of Operational Research*, *304*(2), pp.543-557.

Yang, S., Xiao, Y. and Kuo, Y.H., 2017. The supply chain design for perishable food with stochastic demand. *Sustainability*, *9*(7), p.1195.

Zhou, L., Naim, M.M. and Disney, S.M., 2017. The impact of product returns and remanufacturing uncertainties on the dynamic performance of a multi-echelon closed-loop supply chain. *International Journal of Production Economics*, *183*, pp.487-502.

AUTHOR BIOGRAPHIES

JUNYI LIN is an Associate Professor in Operations Management at XJTLU. His research focuses on dynamical modelling and design of supply chain systems to overcome real-world system dynamics issues such as bullwhip effect. He reguarly publishes research works in various international journals, such as EJOR, IISE, IJPE, Omega, IJPR, and TRE.

YAN LU is a PhD student at Xi'an Jiaotong-Liverpool University. Her research interests are in taming the system dynamics behavior of closed-loop supply chain. Her recent work is published in OMEGA-the International Journal of Management Science.

Proceedings of the Operational Research Society Simulation Workshop 2025 (SW25)
M. Luis, A. Harper, T. Monks and, N. Mustafee, eds.

THE PRACTICE OF M&S RESEARCH FROM A COUNTRY-SPECIFIC PERSPECTIVE AND THE CHALLENGES AND OPPORTUNITIES FOR INTERNATIONAL COLLABORATIONS

Navonil Mustafee

University of Exeter
Exeter EX4 4PY, UK
n.mustafee@exeter.ac.uk

Anastasia Anagnostou

Brunel University of London
Uxbridge UB8 3PH, UK
anastasia.anagnostou@brunel.ac.uk

Masoud Fakhimi

University of Surrey
Guildford GU2 7XH, UK
masoud.fakhimi@surrey.ac.uk

John Fowler

Arizona State University
Tempe, AZ 85281, USA
john.fowler@asu.edu

Varun Ramamohan

Indian Institute of Technology Delhi
New Delhi 110016, India
varunr@mech.iitd.ac.in

Oliver Rose

University Bundeswehr Munich
85579 Neubiberg, Germany
oliver.rose@unibw.de

Mehdi Souier

University of Tlemcen
Tlemcen 13000, Algeria
mehdi.souier@univ-tlemcen.dz

Mamadou Kaba Traore

University of Bordeaux
33400 Talence, France
mamadou-kaba.traore@u-bordeaux.fr

Jayendran Venkateswaran

Indian Institute of Technology Mumbai
Mumbai 400076, India
jayendran@iitb.ac.in

1 ABSTRACT

International collaborations are a fundamental cornerstone of research. Modelling and Simulation (M&S) has benefited from such collaborations among researchers and practitioners from different countries. Yet, challenges remain impeding the development of multi-country engagement in scholarly work, limiting the current state of disciplinary advancement in our field.

The closing plenary panel for Simulation Workshop 2025 (SW25) brings academics (with industry experience, including grants with industry) from Algeria, France, Germany, India, the US and the UK, who reflect on their experiences pursuing international research collaborations, impediments and how they are trying to overcome them, advice for future generations they are training, the opportunities and the rewards of persistence!

The panel will broaden our understanding of the *"practice of M&S research"* from a country-specific perspective, including resourcing for cutting-edge research, funding landscape, working with industry, research networking, representation in scholarly societies and Editorial Boards, teaching and PhD supervision, and development of early career researchers as future leaders in our field.

POSTER ABSTRACTS

AUTOMATED TEXTILE PROCESSING TO ENABLE CIRCULAR TEXTILE MATERIALS, EXPLORATION OF CONFIGURATION REQUIREMENTS OF AN AUTOMATED TEXTILE SORTING AND PRE-PROCESSING FACILITY (ATSP)

Michael-Manuel Mendoza-Bollam, Matthew Watts, Jack Bowen, Stephen Murphy, Jacqui Snow and Terie Purse
The Manufacturing Technology Centre, The University of Exeter
The Automatic-Sorting for Circular Textiles Innovate UK research programme consortium aims to support the transition to circularity of the UK used textiles industry. It aims to catalyse the development of an Automated Textile Sorting and Pre-Processing facility (ATSP). To support this goal, the Manufacturing Technology Centre, collaborating with Circle8 Textile Ecosystems analysed the key factors that would impact production throughput of an ATSP system by using Discrete Event Simulation. It was found that: (1) The generic ATSP's production throughput is constrained by its machine cleaning protocol, where total annual throughput decreases as cleaning cycle time increases. (2) Average output bale purity increases for all types of output bales as sorting accuracy increases. (3) Average output bale purity is higher for garment types that are searched for in later sorting machine cycles. Behaviours (2) and (3) are believed to be linked to sorting machine accuracy, sorting protocol and sorting cycle sequencing.

THE DYNAMICS OF SCALE-UP CREATION IN ENTREPRENEURIAL ECOSYSTEMS

Vahid Hajiebrahimi Farashah, Susan Howick and Bernd Wurth
University of Strathclyde, University of Glasgow
Entrepreneurial Ecosystems (EEs) play a pivotal role in fostering entrepreneurship, driving economic growth, and creating social value for regions. However, a significant challenge within EEs is that many startups fail to grow into scaleups, which are high-growth companies that significantly contribute to economic and ecosystem development. This challenge constrains the ecosystems' overall growth and their benefits to the regions. This study explores the dynamics of scaleup creation within EEs, identifying key barriers such as a lack of talented human capital and insufficient high-scale investment. Given the complex, multi-stakeholder nature of EEs and their numerous interdependencies, there is a need for tools that can effectively capture and analyse these dynamics. Leveraging System Dynamics (SD) modeling including Causal Loop Diagrams (CLDs), this research conceptualises the mechanisms driving scaleup creation and their broader implications for ecosystem performance. The findings offer a systemic perspective for researchers, highlighting the interdependencies between related factors and providing insights to enhance the growth of EEs.

EVALUATING PRODUCTION EFFICIENCY IN AN ALGERIAN PLASTIC PACKAGING COMPANY USING ARENA SIMULATION

Sara Fatima Zohra Megaiz, Fouad Maliki, Mehdi Souier and Mohammed Dahane
University of Tlemcen, University of Lorraine
Simulation is increasingly recognized as a powerful tool for optimizing production systems in Algeria's plastic packaging sector, which faces growing demand and the need to improve efficiency while minimizing costs. This study uses Arena simulation software to model the production processes of an

Algerian packaging company. Two scenarios one accounting for machine breakdowns and another without failures were tested to evaluate performance metrics like cycle time, throughput, and work-in-progress inventory. The analysis revealed that the Cutting and Sewing machine is a critical bottleneck, limiting throughput. Based on the simulation findings, the company invested in a new machine, boosting production by 26% and significantly reducing cycle time. The study highlights the importance of integrating predictive maintenance and failure scenarios for enhanced reliability and efficiency. These outcomes demonstrate the value of simulation for data-driven decision-making, enabling sustainable growth and competitiveness in manufacturing.

DEVELOPMENT OF A VIRTUAL FARM FOR EVALUATING CLIMATE CHANGE ADAPTATION STRATEGIES IN SALMON AQUACULTURE

Suleiman Yakubu and Lynne Falconer
University of Stirling

Climate change is impacting the aquaculture industry, affecting seafood production and creating new challenges for companies worldwide. Rising sea temperatures, storms and other climate stressors are all affecting the growth, health and survivability of farmed fish. The industry must adapt, but responsible climate action requires better understanding of the complex factors that influence fish production.

Most assessments focus on simplified cause and effect relationships, but farmed fish are subject to a range of dynamic environmental conditions as well as additional production and operational procedures that also influence production. To address this complex challenge, we present a virtual farm model for salmon aquaculture that we have developed using system dynamics. The model is designed to simulate the farm environment and the fish response, allowing users to explore the effect of different climate and operational-related scenarios on salmon growth and farm production. This model is being extended into a decision support tool.

A FREE AND OPEN-SOURCE CROSS-LIBRARY ANIMATED VISUALISATION PACKAGE FOR DISCRETE EVENT SIMULATIONS

Samantha Rosser and Daniel Chalk
University of Exeter

Many popular programs for Discrete Event Simulation (DES) allow users to create engaging animated visualisations of pathways. However, the cost of this software can be prohibitive, and sharing and reuse of models can be difficult. In contrast, the Python programming language excels at allowing users to create models that can be shared, reused and adapted, but the visualization capabilities are more limited. To address this, we have developed a free Python package, vidigi, which allows the creation of animated visualisations from models created using the SimPy and Ciw libraries. The animations can be incorporated into web applications and will update when users change simulation parameters. An animation of an emergency department has been used to help staff across the NHS understand the potential of DES, and there are plans to use the package in NHS projects relating to bed occupancy, stroke pathways, elective flow, and air ambulance provision.

A SIMULATION-BASED APPROACH TO IMPROVE EMERGENCY DEPARTMENT EFFICIENCY AND MEET NHS TARGETS

Thamer Almohaya, James Batchelor and Edilson Arruda
University of Southampton

Emergency Departments (EDs) in the UK face significant challenges in achieving the National Health Service (NHS) target of treating 76% of patients within four hours. This study employs Discrete Event Simulation (DES) to address operational inefficiencies and identify practical solutions that bridge the gap between current realities and performance goals. Using real-world data from Southampton University Hospital, the DES model evaluates three key interventions: (1) introducing an additional triage nurse and room to enhance front-end efficiency; (2) increasing nursing and healthcare assistant staffing to improve patient flow; and (3) reducing laboratory turnaround time (TAT) by 20% to alleviate diagnostic delays. The analysis identifies cost-effective strategies that reduce delays, optimise resource utilisation, and enhance patient throughput. The study highlights the critical role of DES in aligning resource management with performance goals, offering actionable insights for quality improvement in dynamic and resource-constrained healthcare environments. These findings support scalable, evidence-based interventions for ED efficiency and patient outcomes.

SYSTEM DYNAMICS MODELLING OF CONTAINER SHIPPING SYSTEM UNDER DISRUPTIONS - THE IMPACT OF THE 2024 POLYCRISIS: RED SEA ATTACKS, PANAMA DROUGHT AND U.S. TARIFFS ON EAST ASIA – NORTH AMERICA TRADE ROUTE

Hongdan Chen, Haobin Li and Lavanya Meherishi
National University of Singapore, University of Exeter

In 2024, the container shipping system faced disruptions from the Red Sea crisis, Panama Canal delays, and U.S. tariff hikes, exposing vulnerabilities in global logistics. This complex system is governed by dynamic, non-linear interactions that often lead to counterintuitive outcomes, complicating cause-effect analysis and response prediction. During disruptions, stakeholders act independently as a feedback from the system change, driving the system toward new equilibria. However, the interconnected nature of these interactions presents significant challenges for understanding system responses and planning interventions. To address these issues, this study employs system dynamics modeling to capture causal relationships, feedback loops, and adaptive behaviors. The model simulates disruption scenarios to identify intervention points and develop strategies for enhancing resilience and mitigating future disruptions in global shipping networks.

MULTI-FIDELITY MODELLING AND OPTIMISATION FOR LONG-TERM PUBLIC SECTOR CAPACITY PLANNING

Graham Burgess, Luke Rhodes-Leader, Rob Shone, David Worthington and Dashi Singham
Lancaster University, Naval Postgraduate School

In long-term capacity planning, public sector organisations must meet the public need over time with tight financial budgets. Examples of such problems arise in housing, healthcare and prisons. The overall aim of this research Is to investigate an integer-ordered, multi-fidelity simulation optimisation approach to long-term public sector capacity planning problems. To this end, we study a problem in housing. Here, decision makers must split their resources between emergency shelter and permanent social housing to alleviate homelessness. We present three models of multi fidelity for the homeless care system in California, USA. These are a fluid model, an M_t/M/h_t queueing model and a discrete-event simulation model. We then propose and solve a deterministic optimisation problem based on the fluid model. Using policy-based shape constraints, we minimise unsheltered homelessness while planning for long-term relief to the system via permanent housing. Finally, we discuss ongoing work on integer-ordered, multi-fidelity simulation optimisation.

DYNAMIC LEGO-BUILDING: A BUILDING-BLOCK APPROACH ENABLING MODULARITY IN SYSTEM DYNAMICS

Lucas Meneguim, Daniel Guzzo and Daniela Pigosso
Technical University of Denmark

Simulation modeling enhances decision-making by enabling ex-ante exploration of "what-if" scenarios. However, adoption is hindered by the time, resources, and expertise needed to develop models. Additionally, knowledge on reusing model structures remains fragmented and informally retained by practitioners. This study proposes a building-block-based modeling approach (BBMA) to improve the reuse and customization of system dynamics models. It aims to advance BBMA adoption by (i) reviewing literature on reusable model components to identify design requirements, (ii) demonstrating BBMA through an inductive case study in shared mobility, and (iii) evaluating results against design requirements. By promoting modular, scalable, and reusable modeling, this research encourages the system dynamics community to streamline model development and foster knowledge transfer.

MODELLING STRATEGIC INTERACTIONS BETWEEN REGIONAL AND NATIONAL WAITING LISTS TO IMPROVE PATIENT OUTCOMES

Euan Barlow
University of Strathclyde

The waiting list for inpatient and daycase orthopaedic surgery more than doubled following the COVID pandemic. In Scotland, this issue receives much media attention, and the government and health service are under pressure to resolve this issue and improve patient outcomes.
A mathematical modelling approach combined predictive models of future waiting list additions and removals, with a discrete event simulation of patient pathways. The model has been populated with data from all Scottish NHS boards, and estimates the potential impact of different levels of additional system capacity. The model response is investigated under various scenarios of future waiting list activity.
This work is a collaboration between academics, and clinical practitioners and managers. The work has been presented at national orthopaedic planning meetings, has potential to shape the national response to the waiting list challenges for orthopaedics, and also to be translated for other procedures.

A SUPPLY CHAIN FRAMEWORK FOR EXTENDED BLOOD TYPE MATCHING IN SICKLE CELL PATIENTS

Folarin B. Oyebolu, Nicholas Gleadall and William J. Astle
University of Cambridge

Blood transfusions are life-saving treatment for individuals with sickle cell disorder (SCD), but current manual blood allocation methods use limited red cell blood type information, increasing the risk of immunological incompatibility. Our work aims to exploit extended blood type information measured by a new genetic test, introduced by the National Health Service in England, to enable more comprehensive blood typing. We previously presented a centralised blood supply chain model with which we demonstrated an up to 98% reduction in alloimmunisation risk to SCD patients compared to current guidelines. Building on this, we extended the model to account for the hierarchical structure of the supply chain, transport between stock holding units (SHUs), and lead times. Simulation experiments across scenarios revealed a reduction in alloimmunisation risk of at least 88% with unrestricted transport of blood units and 75% with transportation penalties. These findings highlight trade-offs between transportation costs and patient safety, offering insights for optimising blood allocation policies to improve care for SCD patients.

SIMULATION-BASED OPTIMISATION OF OFFSHORE WIND INSTALLATION SUPPLY CHAIN UNDER UNCERTAINTY

Ahmad Attar, Martino Luis and Shuya Zhong
University of Exeter, University of Bath

As a result of the market's rising demand, decision-makers in the wind energy industry are dealing with various difficulties with their supply chains and logistics. The building and management of offshore wind farms, situated far in the sea, bring even more sophisticated challenges — during both the installation and maintenance phases. Many of the previous studies ignored the inherent uncertainties in the system in favour of deterministic parameters to make their models tractable. The goal of the current research is to investigate an integrated framework for the offshore wind farm supply chain that optimises all necessary offshore activities during the installation phase while accounting for a variety of realistic uncertainties, notably weather conditions and operating time. Since the system under study is naturally complicated, advanced methods of modelling from the field of operations research, such as mathematical programming and computer simulation, are applied in this study.

SIMULATING AMBULANCE SERVICES IN COMPLEX ENVIRONMENTS

Mark Tuson, Geraint Palmer, Vincent Knight, Paul Harper, Sarie Brice, Leanne Smith and Daniel Gartner
Cardiff University, Welsh Ambulance Service Trust

Ambulance services have a duty of care to the population and to maximise patient outcomes following a medical emergency. The ambulance location-allocation problem has been widely studied, but the focus has predominantly been on minimising response times or maximising coverage, not explicitly considering patient outcomes.

We propose a metaheuristic algorithm designed to maximise patient outcomes within a heterogeneous population, and with a mixed fleet of vehicles by finding better fleet allocations.

To test the real-world impact of these solutions we developed a discrete event model for ambulance services with heterogeneous vehicles, a feature of our simulation is the ability to incorporate the impact of varying congestion rates across the different regions represented in the model.

Our approach is informed by, and tested on, real-world data from Jakarta, Indonesia. Using the simulations, decision makers were better able to understand ambulance fleet capacity needs and allocations, and their impact on patient outcomes.

CLINICAL PATHWAY MODELLING OF A TRAUMA & ORTHOPAEDICS DEPARTMENT

Matthew Howells, Paul Harper, Daniel Gartner, Geraint Palmer and Antonio Riccioli
Cardiff University, Cardiff and Vale University Health Board

COVID-19 disruptions have exacerbated elective care backlogs globally, with Orthopaedics among the most affected specialties. Orthopaedics faces dual pressures from these backlogs and an ageing population, necessitating efficient solutions. This research, in collaboration with Cardiff and Vale University Health Board's Trauma & Orthopaedics (T&O) department, models clinical pathways (CPs) to address these challenges.

Using the ALERGIA algorithm in Python, we learn probabilistic automata to generalise CPs provided by the T&O department. The algorithm incorporates potential CPs absent from the dataset while filtering statistically insignificant pathways, enhancing the robustness and relevance of the approach. Additionally, we introduce a novel use of the learned automata to parametrise a discrete-event simulation (DES) of the orthopaedic surgical pathway, enabling staff to make informed decisions on demand and capacity planning. The DES model is planned to be paired with system dynamics model to model population health, and it's effect on the department.

TRANSFORMING THE PRODUCTION SPEED MANAGEMENT SYSTEM INTO A SIMPLE ONLINE DIGITAL TWIN: A DES-BASED TUNING APPROACH

Ahmad Attar, Rongxu Liu, Tzu-Chun Lin, Martino Luis, Shuya Zhong and Voicu Ion Sucala
University of Exeter, University of Bath

The production speed management system (PSMS) is one of the main built-in components of smart, continuous manufacturing lines. These systems generally analyse a restricted scope of input data to mitigate alterations in the production line. The decisions made in these systems also tend to be excessively conservative, focusing on local modifications to the production process. These all constitute a primary disadvantage for such management systems. This research investigates the application of discrete event simulation (DES) to fine-tune the internal algorithms and decision-making processes of PSMS in a food and beverage production line. The objective is to provide the PSMS with a comprehensive view and promote its decisions to a system level. By applying this approach, the built-in PSMS acts as an online digital twin, resulting in a significant improvement in the overall productivity of the line.

OPTIMISING CARDIOLOGY SERVICES: FORECASTING AND SIMULATION FOR STRATEGIC PLANNING
Elizabeth Williams and Mark Tuson
Cardiff University
Cardiovascular diseases remain the leading global cause of death, necessitating efficient healthcare resource planning. This research, conducted with Cardiff and Vale University Health Board, addresses the growing demand for cardiology services, focusing on optimising catheterisation laboratory (cath lab) capacity. Using time-series forecasting, historical patient data was analysed to project future resource needs, distinguishing between elective and unscheduled cases. A discrete event simulation (DES) model was developed to simulate patient flow, cath lab utilisation, and bed occupancy, incorporating real-world parameters such as procedure durations and staff availability. This approach enables scenario exploration to improve scheduling, reduce waiting times, and achieve operational targets. Results have directly influenced strategic planning, highlighting the need for expanded cath lab resources. Insights from the DES model are forming the foundation of a business case for additional infrastructure investment, ensuring sustainable service delivery. This study demonstrates how combining forecasting and simulation can drive data-driven decision-making, enhancing cardiology care and patient outcomes.

A HYBRID SIMULATION APPROACH FOR ADVANCING SAFETY IN CONNECTED AUTOMATED VEHICLES
Traecy Elezi, Anastasia Anagnostou and Fotios Spyridonis
Brunel University of London
Traffic safety remains a significant challenge, even as autonomous vehicles promise transformative improvements in reducing accidents and enhancing road safety. However, with autonomous vehicles still in the early stages of development, ensuring safety in dynamic and complex traffic environments remains a critical concern. The Artificial Potential Field (APF) approach offers a promising solution by simulating how vehicles adjust their motion, speed, and interactions with surrounding vehicles to maintain safety. This study aims to simulate traffic conditions using various safety field models implemented within a multi-agent framework. The objective is to evaluate the suitability of APF models for real-time safety applications over extended periods and under diverse traffic scenarios and through a hybrid-simulation approach to pinpoint advantages and drawbacks against existing risk assessment methodologies.

AFRICAN FEDERATION OF OPERATIONAL RESEARCH SOCIETIES: AN OPPORTUNITY TO BUILD BRIDGES TO OPERATIONS RESEARCH AND SIMULATION DEVELOPMENT IN AFRICA
Mehdi Souier and Safa Bhar Layeb
University of Tlemcen, University of Tunis El Manar Tunis

The IEEE AFROS 2024 is the third International Conference of the African Federation of Operational Research Societies (https://afros2024.com/) for Operational Research and Management Science (OR/MS). It was held from November 3 to 5, 2024, in Tlemcen city in Algeria, It was organized by the Manufacturing Engineering Laboratory of Tlemcen university (MELT) and the Tunisian Decision Aid Society (TDAS) and the Higher School of Applied Sciences of Tlemcen in a hybrid format, offering both onsite and online participation opportunities.
AFROS 24 focused on various contributions to support AFROS's goals. In particular, it aimed to advance knowledge, stimulate interest, promote education, and encourage the application of OR in Africa, while also fostering greater information exchange among African OR teams and communities. This paper describes this event activities, topics and the conference publication proceedings and special issues.

AUTHOR INDEX